TACTICS and TECHNIQUES
in PSYCHOANALYTIC THERAPY
VOL. II.: COUNTERTRANSFERENCE

TACTICS
and
TECHNIQUES
in
PSYCHOANALYTIC
THERAPY

VOL. II:
COUNTERTRANSFERENCE

edited by

Peter L. Giovacchini, M.D.

in collaboration with
Alfred Flarsheim, M.D.
and
L. Bryce Boyer, M.D.

Jason Aronson, Inc.

CONTENTS

Contributors

Bruno Bettelheim, Ph.D.
Stella M. Rowley Distinguished Service Professor Emeritus, The University of Chicago, Chicago, Ill.

Sidney J. Blatt, Ph.D.
Professor of Psychology, Yale University, New Haven, Conn.

L. Bryce Boyer, M.D.
Chairman, Continuing Colloquium: "Psychoanalytic Methods and Questions in Anthropological Fieldwork," American Psychoanalytic Association; Co-Chairman, Research Committee, San Francisco Psychoanalytic Society, San Francisco, Calif.; Member, International and Mexican Psychoanalytic Associations.

Bertram J. Cohler, Ph.D.
Associate Professor, Departments of Behavioral Sciences and Education, The University of Chicago, Chicago, Ill.

Stanley W. Conrad, M.D.
Clinical Associate Professor of Psychiatry, University of Miami School of Medicine; Former Editor, The *Bulletin of the Philadelphia Association for Psychoanalysis*; Member, American Psychoanalytic Association.

Alfred Flarsheim, M.D.
Clinical Assistant Professor of Psychiatry, University of Illinois College of Medicine, Chicago, Ill.; Consultant Psychiatrist, The Sonia Shankman Orthogenic School, The University of Chicago, Chicago, Ill.; Professor of Psychiatry, Garret Theological School, Evanston, Ill.

Peter L. Giovacchini, M.D.
Clinical Professor, Department of Psychiatry, University of Illinois College of Medicine; Editor, *Tactics and Techniques in Psychoanalytic Theory*; Co-Editor, *Adolescent Psychiatry: Annals of the American Society for Adolescent Psychiatry;* Editorial Board, *International Journal of Psychoanalytic Psychotherapy;* Clinical Associate, Chicago Institute for Psychoanalysis, Chicago, Ill.

Betty Joseph
Member, The British Psychoanalytical Society.

Robert J. Langs, M.D.
Clinical Assistant Professor of Psychiatry, Division of Psychoanalytic Education, State University of New York, Downstate Medical Center, Brooklyn, N.Y.; Visiting Staff Psychiatrist, Hillside Division, Long Island Jewish-Hillside Medical Center; Editor-in-Chief, *International Journal of Psychoanalytic Psychotherapy*.

Peter A. Martin, M.D.

Clinical Professor of Psychiatry, University of Michigan and Wayne State University Colleges of Medicine; Lecturer, Michigan Psychoanalytic Institute.

Arnold H. Modell, M.D.

Training and Supervisory Psychoanalyst, Boston Psychoanalytic Institute; Assistant Clinical Professor of Psychiatry, Harvard Medical School; Associate Visiting Psychiatrist, Beth Israel Hospital, Boston, Mass.

Daniel Offer, M.D.

Associate Director, Psychosomatic and Psychiatric Institute, Michael Reese Hospital; Professor of Psychiatry, The University of Chicago, Chicago, Ill.; Member, Chicago Psychoanalytic Society.

Herbert A. Rosenfeld, M.D., F.R.C. Psych.

Member, British Psychoanalytic Society.

David Roth, M.D.

Attending Staff, Institute for Psychiatric and Psychosomatic Research and Training, Michael Reese Hospital, Chicago, Ill.; Institute for Psychoanalysis, Chicago, Ill.

Harold F. Searles, M.D.

Clinical Professor of Psychiatry, Georgetown University School of Medicine, Washington, D.C.; Supervising and Training Analyst, Washington Psychoanalytic Institute; Washington Psychoanalytic Society (President, 1969-71); Consultant in Psychiatry, National Institute of Mental Health, Bethesda, Md.

Richard F. Sterba, M.D.

Member of the American and International Psychoanalytic Associations; Clinical Professor of Psychiatry, Emeritus, Wayne State University, Department of Medicine, Detroit, Mich.

Robert J. Stoller, M.D.

Professor of Psychiatry, University of California, Los Angeles, Calif.; Member, the Los Angeles Psychoanalytic Society and Institute.

Vamik D. Volkan, M.D.

Professor of Psychiatry, University of Virginia Medical School, Charlottesville, Va.; Director, Psychiatric Inpatient Services, University of Virginia Medical Center, Charlottesville, Va.; Faculty Member, The Washington Psychoanalytic Institute, Washington, D.C.; Secretary, The Virginia Psychoanalytic Study Group.

Preface

This is the second volume of what had originally been planned as a single volume. My requests for articles for the first volume resulted in an unexpected abundance of papers. To have published all of them would have resulted in a book that would tax the reader's arm muscles. Consequently, I was persuaded by my publisher and colleagues to edit another volume.

Once again I asked for papers, since the surplus from the first volume would not have been sufficient to publish as a book. The response, as had occurred previously, was gratifying. My colleagues and friends apparently are either loquacious people or they have many ideas stored within their minds that are striving for expression.

Here, too, one can detect a very definite pattern. In contrast to the first volume, very few papers emphasize that psychoanalysis can be conducted in cases where it had been considered contraindicated. In this volume, most of the papers assume that it is a suitable process for patients suffering from characterological disorders and some psychoses. The focus is on various aspects of the psychoanalytic process regardless of the type of psychopathology.

Most of the authors, nevertheless, chose to discuss patients suffering from severe psychopathology. I suspect that this was the outcome of two factors. First, I believe it is a reflection of the quality of contemporary psychoanalytic practice. Many persons seeking professional help suffer from characterological problems and fewer are being turned away by analysts. The manifestations of emotional disturbance undoubtedly have changed throughout the years, but it is doubtful that there are basic differences in psychopathology. Thus, it seems reasonable to assume that some psychoanalysts believe that the treatment of such patients can be rewarding and gratifying. In my opinion, the second factor refers to the author's belief that the various aspects of the psychoanalytic process are easier to discern during the treatment of more disturbed patients than the so-called classical psychoneuroses.

No one would deny that these patients are difficult to treat psychoanalytically. But then, what patient isn't? Every psychoanalysis has its share of difficulties which do not seem to be directly related to diagnosis. Many of the authors of this volume concentrate on these difficulties.

I knew that the analysts I would invite to submit papers would write about their treatment experiences since they are all devoted clinicians. However, I was truly amazed at the number of papers I received that focused upon or related primarily to countertransference problems. Apparently, there has been a shift from looking exclusively at the patient to focusing upon the interaction between patient and analyst, bringing the analyst's participation to the fore. Psychoanalysis, rather than being the esoteric ritual that some have asserted, has become a highly interpersonal affair. These papers emphasize that analysis is not concerned with simply dissecting various layers of the patient's personality as they are reflected in transference projections. Besides exploring what is going on within the patient's mind, the psychoanalyst is also concerned with what is occurring within himself. The psychoanalyst's respect for the patient's inner life is conveyed by his willingness to explore his own mind when it is therapeutically feasible or required.

Generally, countertransference has received increasing attention by psychoanalysts. Rather than being considered a sign of instability in the analyst and therefore a therapeutic obstacle to be overcome as soon as possible, such reactions are considered by analysts as being potentially useful for analytic resolution, and with some patients, an indispensable ally. For the latter reasons, clinicians are now fairly frank in discussing their feelings about patients with colleagues instead of suppressing their reactions because they believe it is wrong to feel anything personal about a patient. This book reflects the continually growing preoccupation with countertransference, a deserved and rewarding interest.

Many of these articles do not stress the need for changes in psychoanalytic technique. However, one senses a more relaxed atmosphere than that described in analyses reported years ago. As stated, austerity seems to have vanished and frank revelations of previously withheld feelings by the analyst occur more often in the cases reported here. Nevertheless, other facets of the analytic interaction, such as restricting one's activity to clarification of the transference relationship rather than managerial manipulation or education, seem to be more strictly adhered to.

There are fundamental analytic principles, important basic principles that are the essence of analysis. Still, the flavor of the clinical experiences described in various articles does not indicate that the analyst has to adopt a rigid posture. Quite the contrary, analytic technique seems to be characterized by a looseness that is hard to describe outside the context of an actual analysis.

I believe it is reassuring to everyone and particularly to the young analyst to believe that there are no clear-cut criteria as to what is correct or incorrect conduct during analytic treatment. There is a range of reactions that the analyst might have, some that might even be considered nonanalytic, that allow the analytic process to continue unfolding. This does not mean that there are no rules; indeed, there are many and there are, as stated, basic principles that cannot be transgressed. However, these allow considerable latitude for the analyst, and his style and personality need not be hampered as long as he devotes himself to certain fundamentals.

If one were to abstract the most frequently recurring themes in these pages, usually covertly expressed, three interrelated ones seem to emerge. The analyst's orientation stresses respect for the patient's autonomy, a firm adherence to intrapsychic determinism, and honesty. In my opinion, these are the fundamental tenets of psychoanalysis which can be conveyed in a variety of ways consistent with the analyst's personality.

Although it may seem self-evident that the combination of such attitudes would represent the essence of psychoanalysis, extended discussions of how they interact as part of the analytic process are rare. Autonomy has been too often swallowed up by the imposition of the analyst's ideals upon the patient. Psychic determinism has frequently been displaced onto an emphasis on the environment and social interactions (see Chap.1). Honesty has become a catchword, something about which one can blindly proselytize without examining in which particular context it best fits.

Honesty can be singled out here because it is a much more general attitude than the other two themes. It is basic to every psychoanalytic interaction but why it should be requires explanation. Honesty should not just be accepted as a virtue without further exploration. It, too, has to be examined from a psychoanalytic perspective.

The candor and willingness to examine one's reactions is an honest activity. Indeed, to be otherwise would be self-deception, and if the analyst has to indulge in self-deception, how can he possibly help the patient overcome inner forces that cause him to deceive himself? Some of these papers demonstrate that the honest revelation of a countertransference attitude sometimes breaks up a therapeutic impasse and leads to a greater respect by the patient for intrapsychic processes. Thus, honesty promotes and encourages the intrapsychic viewpoint and psychic determinism.

Honesty has further technical implications. I am referring to the motive behind making an interpretation. Winnicott once stated that the reason he made interpretations was to let the patient know he was still alive and to demonstrate that he could make mistakes, that is, he was not omnipotent. In spite of the witty and comic nature of this statement, it has profound and serious implications.

Note that Winnicott said nothing about trying to change the patient's behavior by interpretation. He is merely emphasizing the limitations of the analytic setting and perhaps correcting the patient's distortions. This hopefully will lead the patient to further his understanding about his transference projections and thereby to further psychic integration.

The use of interpretation to effect change is also a subject that requires elaboration and once again honesty comes to the fore. The analyst may find some aspect of the patient's behavior objectionable. Instead of examining what is, in essence, a countertransference reaction or directly forbidding the patient to continue his unacceptable behavior, the analyst may give him an interpretation. The purpose of the interpretation is, in effect, a command. The analyst uses "professionalism" to make the patient stop doing something he cannot tolerate. The function of interpretation has been perverted; instead of increasing understanding, it is used as a moral imperative. Many analyses simply consist of discovering the manifestations of psychopathology and then forbidding them. The interpretation is presumably in the patient's best interest, but, in actuality, it is clearly an intrusion upon his autonomy. It is also deceptive because basically it is designed to maintain the analyst's comfort and has very little to do with the patient's needs. Some of the analysts in this book, if they cannot tolerate some manifestations of the patient's psychopathology, believe it is better to tell him directly or refer him elsewhere rather than to disguise their intolerance by an interpretation. It is more honest to tell the patient that he must make some adaptation to the analyst's needs. This change of behavior has nothing to do with the analytic task except insofar as it allows the analyst to create a comfortable setting wherein analysis can proceed.

These are subtle but fundamental attitudes which are indispensable to the maintenance of the analytic setting. Analysis has lost its peremptory qualities if one believes that the articles in this book are typical of the analyst's orientation. I do not believe they are yet, but many students find it easy to identify with the models presented here. Of course, universal agreement has not and will not be reached. The authors of this volume often disagree with each other.

I wish to thank my students for having challenged psychoanalytic tenets and causing me to reformulate tenaciously held principles. My patients have also helped me to examine various facets of the psychoanalytic process and to acknowledge that certain cherished dictums, in effect, represented prejudices that were not really analytic fundamentals. I also wish to thank innumerable colleagues all over the world for lively and challenging discussions which have had profound effects upon me, often without my being aware of their influence or source. Finally, I wish to thank the University of Illinois College of Medicine and Miss Mabel Glisan, in particular, for the extensive secretarial assistance that is required to produce such a lengthy volume.

Introduction

The Psychoanalytic Orientation

Peter L. Giovacchini, M.D.

This book is about psychoanalysis and is written by psychoanalysts. It emphasizes a particular way of looking at life, and in a more specialized sense defines a unique treatment approach. Clinicians, of course, direct their main interest to the therapeutic aspects of psychoanalysis. However, such an orientation also manifests itself in other ways; the effects of psychoanalysis extend beyond the narrow confines of the consultation room.

In spite of the various books written on psychoanalytic technique, and there have not been many, a volume appearing at this particular time can have special significance. In view of society's present annihilation of the individual by its trend toward anonymity and exaltation of the group, the articles in this book raise a voice that is at cross currents to the contemporary trend. True, it is a highly technical book, but one which deals with issues and presents viewpoints that have been devalued in much of contemporary psychiatric literature and replaced by orientations that are touted as being more universally meaningful.

Viewing society in terms of a movement that obliterates individuality may seem to be an unwarranted generalization. Granted, contemporary society is not homogeneous and also what might be true today could be different from yesterday or tomorrow. There are groups and subgroups with apparently different standards and values which may be isolated from one another and develop in separate directions. Factions may attempt to impose themselves upon the whole of society. The pressure to conform has led to rebellion and all traditional mores have at one time or another been challenged. In this respect one can think in terms of a counterculture.

Still, after closely examining the counterculture, one notes that its values are also stereotyped and in spite of flamboyant attempts to capture an autonomous stance, persons in such groups have also lost the essence of individuality. Freud and many others before him repeatedly stated that any group has a leveling effect. No matter what the purpose of the group, the individual member becomes submerged by the group's identity, which is not necessarily congruent with his, and the collective intellect tends to be below the individu-

al's capacity. Although Freud recognized that some groups have noble purposes and unselfish achievements, creativity can flourish only when a person
is working as an individual. Today's society, as varied as it may be, tends to
rob a person of his autonomy; this is true even of many movements which are
aimed at restoring it.

These circumstances are reflected in our clinical experience, and the patients seen today by psychotherapists and psychoanalysts present problems
centering around a nonexistent or uncertain identity. Our patients stand in
marked contrast to those that were described by the early analysts. They saw
clear-cut clinical pictures with circumscribed symptoms rather than the diffuse and sometimes vague dissatisfactions that so many of our patients present. As some of the chapters here indicate, one is not stating that today's
patients are fundamentally different from those seen by Freud and his co-
workers. Even though Freud spoke of classical psychoneuroses and most of
the patients described in this book can be considered examples of characterological disorders, one is not particularly struck by fundamental differences
in psychopathology. Rather, the authors emphaszie that the manifestations of
psychopathology are different, not psychopathology itself.

The fact that the surrounding culture contributes to the *manifestations* of
emotional disorder is well-known. Freud's classical hysterics seem to have
been the product of an ostensibly sexually repressive mid-Victorian milieu
and such cases are rarities in the United States. In other countries, however,
for example, India, where in the upper classes, something similar to a Victo-
rian morality exists, patients suffering from somatic conversions are fairly
frequent. Similarly, among certain strata of our society, one occasionally
encounters such patients—usually in relatively uncomplicated groups, that is,
insofar as roles are well-defined and the accepted and nonaccepted is concretely established. These groups may, of course, have many complicated
features.

Generally, such concrete orientations are lacking in the current American
scene; instead, one is faced with double-bind messages and a contradictory
morality. The ensuing dilemma affects everyone, not just youth; the older
generation, although somewhat better established than the younger, is far
from secure in its beliefs and consequently, its identity. Thus, the problems
the clinician faces are characterological in nature, and not the comparatively
simple id-ego conflicts Freud so diligently described. Society has imposed
many tasks upon the individual that necessitate unique types of adaptation.
Previously, one belonged in a circumscribed niche with a fairly well-structured
identity. He knew his tasks and he knew how to deal with them. Today things
are different and this may constitute a stress which taxes a person's adaptational
capacities. The latter is reflected in his symptomatology.

Does a shift in the manifestations of psychopathology necessitate a different approach, or perhaps a different conceptual orientation in order to deal successfully with such patients? Many believe it does and focus their attention upon adjustment to community standards. The authors of this book, as demonstrated by the types of patients they chose to describe, apparently believe otherwise.

Before discussing some of the factors involved in an adherence to the psychoanalytic position, I wish to dwell briefly upon some current therapeutic approaches which represent shifts away from psychoanalysis; they also represent shifts from the individual to the group. The latter may in some way be related to the unique stresses that characterize contemporary society. It is well known that when a mass is exposed to a common danger, it will form a structured group. The libidinal ties to the leader and between individual members of the group protect against commonly perceived dangers. This, of course, occurs at the expense of autonomy and necessitates certain restrictions and curtailments of behavior and expression.

The group mind, rather than the individual mind, seems to determine many current psychotherapies. Therapeutic approaches often focus upon behavioral control and the elimination of aberrant behavior—aberrant as defined by the group or society. Such control is achieved by environmental manipulation without any consideration of what is going on within the patient's mind. Rather, a system, sometimes a very complex and ingenious one, of reward and punishment is used in order to coerce the patient into changing for what ostensibly is in his best interest. From Pavlov to operant conditioning.

This is an extremely interesting situation. Society has somehow evolved from where a person felt relatively secure in a predetermined niche to one where the individual feels submerged in a morass of contradictory standards, deceit and chaotic instability, a setting where he does not know who he is or the purpose of his existence. Whereas once, one felt secure, even if constricted and unsatisfied in his identity, now one is terrified by a lack of identity—truly an existential crisis. More and more, we are confronted with patients who feel themselves drowning in a sea of anonymity. Is it not startling, although perhaps understandable, to note a parallel development in psychotherapy or any therapy designed to deal with emotional problems? Treatment has moved from what one may call the interior, the intrapsychic, to the exterior, the needs of society which are met by conformity. Behavioral control, that is, the elimination of behavior which threatens the status quo, maintains general harmony but the needs of the individual are completely ignored.

Lest the reader conclude that the assertion that the individual's needs are completely ignored is an extreme position, a viewpoint which I, too, once held, all he has to do is attend a psychiatric hospital or ward staff meeting or to read nurses' and doctors' notes. If he were to accuse the ward personnel of using coercive tactics without any consideration for the patient's individual psychopathology, the response might be violent denial *or it might not*. In many instances, the staff will frankly state that to deal with the intrapsychic is tantamount to pampering the patient, a patient who is considered in dire need of controls. I am acquainted with a ward where the staff boasts of the ''Brownie Points'' system for acceptable behavior. To tailor one's therapeutic stance to the patient's illness is unthinkable.

Hospitals often refuse to accept patients who do not meet their standards of behavior. Length of hospitalization is frequently predetermined. In other words, one has to be sick in a fashion that is acceptable to the hospital, and the duration of the illness must be limited from the onset. This is a highly moralistic viewpoint which centers upon judgments of a person's behavior. Behavior is not viewed as a symptomatic expression of psychopathology and the adaptive nature of symptoms is completely ignored. Such situations strike some of us as so ridiculous that at times we miss the tragedy inherent in them.

However, other therapies have evolved, which on fleeting inspection appear to be countertherapies to behavioral controls in much the same fashion as a counterculture has been erected against the Establishment. In fact, these therapies are the therapies of the counterculture. Instead of focusing upon behavior, treatment is aimed at enhancing communication, the experiencing of feeling and the establishing of roles and transactions in order to grasp the relevant and meaningful. In these therapies, one has to get in touch with the deeper recesses of the self, but at the same time show concern for and do something about all the injustices and irrelevancies of a degenerate society. Doing something may range from encounter to withdrawal by a return to the land, an abnegation of our savage civilization. Finding oneself through a myriad of meaningful experiences, by encounter, emoting and enhancement of sensitivity, supposedly leads to one's true core and a life characterized by honesty and relevance. These therapies are usually conducted in groups and are frequently accompanied by considerable howling and screaming.

Although therapies designed to control behavior and those whose aim is to increase sensitivity and understanding, such as encounter group therapy, seem to be antithetical to one another, there are, nevertheless, many similarities when one proceeds beyond phenomenology. Although the latter therapies may, in some instances, emphasize freedom, one is still expected to behave in what some observers would call a stereotyped, routine fashion. Certainly, a person's behavior may be flamboyant and appear idiosyncratic and individualistic but then everybody else is also behaving idiosyncratically and individualistically and their patterns are uniformly the same. One *has* to be happy or sad, angry or loving; one *has* to be autonomous and relevant. To dictate autonomy is the ultimate dictatorship, since the distinction between autonomy and conformity disappears and once again one is left with a robot—perhaps one who can scream—but, nevertheless, a person who has only a group identity which he mistakenly assumes is his own. The difference between the Establishment and the counterculture is determined more by clothes and hair styles than by minds with basically different orientations.

In the midst of all these societal changes and evolving therapies, one sometimes hears that psychoanalysis is dead. Critics emphasize that psychoanalysis was the product of a mind that belonged to a stable, restrictive, prejudiced mid-Victorian culture. Today we seek liberation and psychoanalysis does not belong in the same company that strives for enlightenment and meaningfulness. The fact that psychoanalysis was, to a large measure, shunned and even reviled by the conservative leaders of the culture in which it was founded seems to be forgotten. In this decade, by contrast, its autocratic, ritualistic, and repressive features are stressed rather than the false accusation made in Freud's time, that psychoanalysis encourages sexual license. Psychoanalysis has received many blows; it has, at times, masochistically submitted to deprecations. It has been attacked because it was believed it would lead to a society that is in superficial ways similar to what we actually have today. And now, that very society shuns it because it is too much like the Establishment it is reputedly renouncing. This is a case of damned if you do and damned if you don't. Perhaps it would be best to resign ourselves to its demise and see what develops.

The authors in this volume, among others, do not think one can be complacent about psychoanalysis. In fact, they proceed as if there were no controversy; they simply assume that it is an effective therapeutic method and then go on to discuss in massive detail the innumerable factors that are involved in psychoanalytic treatment. Many of the chapters are devoted to the difficulties that one might experience in treating the patient psychoanalytically, so many difficulties that one might be inclined to believe that criticisms of psychoanalysis could be rationalizations for those who feel inadequate to deal with its intricacies. Many of the chapters discuss the intricacies of psychoanalysis in a calm, nonjudgmental fashion and demonstrate over and over again how experience and instruction can help one overcome difficulties. As stated in the preface, the recognition and the understanding of the role of countertransference for therapeutic technique represent fundamental advances.

Some analysts would assert that the treatment of patients suffering from severe characterological psychopathology and the stirring up of intense countertransference feelings cannot be considered in terms of classical analysis. At best, one is using a psychoanalytically oriented psychotherapy (whatever that may mean) and the therapist has modified his technique to meet the needs of very sick patients. At worst, he has manipulated treatment to the extent that it no longer can be considered analysis. These alleged deviations sometimes satisfy those practitioners who feel that analysis has to be transformed into something nonanalytic in order for it to remain relevant. Here again, we have a schism between classical psychoanalysis and contemporary society in which we often hear demands that therapy be modified in order to be meaningful in the current setting. This usually refers to teaching the patient how to live in an enlightened but homogeneous frame of reference.

Even what appears obvious, such as the good inherent in the striving for justice, peace, equal opportunity, the affirmation of oneself as a human being with feeling and sensitivities, in my mind, is deceptive. From a general viewpoint, any movement, no matter what it stands for, to some extent threatens one's autonomy. A group is still a group and to some extent stifles individuality. As stated, Freud and others believed that intellectual achievements of a group are below that of an individual. Although team research may yield valuable data, I believe that truly creative work has to be done by an individual in isolation.

In any case, the blurring of one's individual identity when he becomes a member of a group cannot be denied. It may be minimal and it may be necessary for group formation, but for our purposes, it has to be acknowledged.

Classical psychoanalysis, in contrast, was constructed on the fundamental assumption that nothing is important for treatment except the individual, and that which characterizes the person as an individual, his mind. The psychoanalytic setting is so constructed that the reality of the surrounding culture does not exist as such; references to reality can be regarded as reflections of various mental operations of the analysand. I realize that many contemporary analysts will not accept this position. Still, it is fundamental to the work of many of the contributors to this book, and they assert further that insofar as one accepts a separate reality apart from that in the patient's mind, one is moving in the direction of managerial manipulation and away from analysis. True, management may sometimes be needed in order to enable the patient to survive between sessions. Still, to repeat, in classical analysis, one has the patient's mind and an ego that reflects the patient's mental operations, a metaphorical way of describing transference; all other influences are incorporated in this context and the analyst acts as a servant to a process, a process which is from time to time helped along by pointing out obstacles that prevent the patient from understanding what is going on within himself.

Within psychoanalysis, the concept of treatment as a spontaneously unfolding process has in some quarters been forgotten, and this has had a significant influence on technique. The therapist reflects society's concern, and indeed he might, since he is a product of his times, and has insisted on the prerogative to be seen as a real person. The latter refers to the analyst as a person in the external world with feelings and attitudes of his own; in other words, as a separate human being rather than simply a reflection of the patient's transference projections. This is the therapist's nonanalytic aspect, which many have recommended should be introduced into the treatment.

Many clinicians, including analysts, become confused when considering their roles as analyst and nonanalyst within the therapeutic setting. The current culture would be more inclined to accept the nonanalyst role since to be seen as a real person is quite in accord with its aims. Some analysts believe that one has to be more than an analyst in order to practice psychoanalysis, and there are some viewpoints in this book that would support such a thesis. Thus, one can sense some of the sources of our confusion. If one considers that the current classical analytic position is one where the analyst is more than a reflection of the patient's transference feelings, then classical analysis would be compatible with some of the elements of our culture, more precisely, some of the elements of our counterculture. However, if today's position is seen as a modification of the classical position, then it can be admitted that the counterculture is antianalytically oriented.

In some ways, this book highlights a paradox. Rather than deviating from the original classic position that was so well described, but perhaps not so often practiced by Freud, many of the analysts here seem to be rediscovering such a position in the treatment of severely disturbed patients. Thus, not only is the counterculture antianalytic but many analysts who knowingly or unwittingly have accepted many of its standards are also antianalytic, if analysis is considered as Freud originally described it. The authors of this volume have not deviated from analysis. On occasion they have been accused of deviating *because they have not deviated*.

These are very complicated issues. Insofar as there are so many factors involved one cannot expect universal agreement.

To be a real person often signifies the analyst's concern that the analysand do what the analyst and society, perhaps the most liberal segments of society, consider best for him. The doctor has to be meaningful and concerned about the patient's fate. I and many of my colleagues believe that an analyst can be a sensitive, concerned person and still remain an analyst in the traditional sense. He is concerned about the patient developing autonomy and capacity to make his own decisions about his fate. The analyst does not wish to impose his own or society's standards upon his patients.

Practically every institution has been affected by vast, sweeping, and inconsistent cultural changes. As mentioned, psychoanalysis has not remained immune; it has not been a staunch, impregnable bastion, aloof and unshakeable. On the contrary, it has undergone many changes and these have led to schisms within various psychoanalytic organizations, so that now we have splinter groups. But even in the most orthodox circles, one hears what essentially amounts to the dictum that the analyst must engage in some other activity which goes beyond analysis. This, of course, means something better than analysis, and it is at this point that analysis becomes an alloy, not of copper and gold, as Freud once said, but of society's relentless although troubled striving for anonymous equalization. Analysis will no longer be an exclusive, ecclesiastical cult; it is no longer lofty and esoteric but often one wonders whether it is still analysis.

Not that analysis has to be a secret cult in order to be analysis, even if at the beginning Freud made it into something like one, presumably to protect himself from the rejection he suffered from the world about him. This book repeatedly demonstrates that one can discuss analytic experiences with perfect frankness and candor, without defensiveness or reactive superiority and arrogance. Among other things, several authors demonstrate that one does not have to resort to extremes when dealing with any aspect of psychoanalysis, theory or technique, nor does one have to conform to society's need for "relevance," coercion or indulgence. Neither does one have to completely isolate oneself, condemning all dissenters as emotionally inadequate or resistive or Philistines. It is possible to achieve a democratic approach to psychoanalysis without modifying it to the point of nonexistence and to retain a classical position without pretentiousness or arrogance.

If one were to equate classical with conservative, then many of the authors of this volume would be considered reactionary. *This is not so.* Some have been considered quite modern in their perspective but they have not seen the need to extend themselves beyond the analytic role. They have retained the classical position but they have divested it of its priestly robes and have applied it to patients suffering from problems which in some way seem to be precipitated by cultural stresses. In no way, however, has the intrapsychic receded into the background; on the contrary, it has received increased emphasis. Here is another interesting situation. Insofar as society's role in precipitating emotional crises and existential dilemmas has been increasingly recognized, these analysts work even more exclusively within the frame of reference of the operations of the patient's mind rather than focusing upon interpersonal relationships. The culture's contribution is acknowledged in terms of its traumatic effects upon psychic structure. It is dealt with, however, from an intrapsychic frame of reference.

In essence, many of the authors in this book are rediscovering the classical position for psychoanalysis. Their enthusiasm is apparent and they have followed the fundamental tenets of the psychoanalytic process into areas that previously received very little attention. The respect for the intrapsychic is highlighted by some of the authors' attention to what is going on within their own minds relative to the patient. Hence, the increased interest in countertransference becomes understandable. This is not new, but such a *focus* can be considered an innovation. It demonstrates that the classical position is not a fossilized, archaic remnant of the past. It is truly exciting and represents a radical departure from current norms and promises hope for the achievement of autonomy and a solid identity. Although other therapies would claim that they are rebellious insofar as they also strive for autonomy, psychoanalysis, or rather *the rediscovery of psychoanalysis, is a voice in the wilderness calling for the return to the individual—indeed, making him the center of the universe rather than simply a replaceable part of a larger unit such as society or the family.* The psychoanalytic approach, by focusing upon the intra-psychic, demonstrates its respect for the patient as a person with subtle mental operations worthy of understanding. To repeat, psychoanalysis is at cross-currents with the trend toward anonymity and conformity, which I believe characterizes both the Establishment and the various types of counterculture. *From this viewpoint, it is the only truly rebellious movement that exists today.*

However, we are not concerned about being rebellious. We are more concerned in working within a field we truly enjoy, and recognize that such work is best performed if one can be honest with one's self and one's colleagues. In this book, countertransference problems and errors are candidly discussed. This has led not only to better psychoanalysis and the capacity to treat a larger group of patients than once was thought possible, but has divested psychoanalysis of its mystical aura, making the classical position a liberal scientific position which fulfills many needs both for the patient and the therapist.

Part 1

THE PSYCHOANALYTIC PROCESS: GENERAL CONSIDERATIONS AND COUNTERTRANSFERENCE FACTORS

INTRODUCTION

Peter L. Giovacchini, M.D.

The papers in this section focus upon one or another aspect of the therapeutic process. As expected, there is some overlapping of ideas, but each author presents us with a fresh perspective. I believe this is related to the enthusiasm they feel about having acquired and communicated what to them are valuable insights after many years of conducting analyses. They believe that they have been able to organize numerous clinical experiences and can extract certain general principles which may be applicable to the analyses of many patients.

As stressed in the preface, most authors chose to discuss patients suffering from severe psychopathology. This, in itself, is striking but perhaps can be explained by the need to understand the patients we currently see as well as the ensuing need to extend the application of the psychoanalytic method. These factors were extensively discussed in a previous similar volume (*Tactics and Techniques in Psychoanalytic Treatment*, Vol. I, Aronson, New York, 1972). What I found to be truly astonishing was the preponderant focus upon countertransference issues that characterizes many of the following articles.

True, I asked psychoanalysts with whom I feel considerable affinity to contribute to this volume. But I did not tell them what to write about. Such a request would have been both presumptuous and impossible with such independent thinkers. Thus, I was amazed when I received so many articles whose chief focus was upon countertransference, either directly or indirectly.

This is an indication of the psychoanalyst's increased security as it is reflected in his candor and willingness, indeed his eagerness, to reveal how and why patients may disturb him. He sees no reason for being condemned because he uncovers his feelings toward patients; rather, he wishes to utilize his reactions for therapeutic advantage and to extend his understanding of the treatment process.

Other articles in this section deal with special technical maneuvers or particular difficulties one encounters in the treatment of some patients. Here, too, as in the recognition of countertransference stemming from the analyst's needs, the patient is not blamed for difficulties and complications. Instead, these authors seek understanding and technical innovations which will permit the analytic process to continue to unfold.

The atmosphere conveyed in this section seems to be almost antithetical to that which might have existed during the early days of psychoanalysis when the discussion of technical factors was the central theme. Richard F. Sterba, in the introduction to his paper, gives us some of the flavor of the setting in which treatment issues were then discussed. I believe what he describes is in marked contrast to the ease and frankness of discussion one would expect among the authors of this section. Sterba, himself one of the original pioneers, wrote his introduction and submitted his paper, which is a reprint, because he has a modern, active mind. Not that his colleagues were not creative and sensitive people; of course, we all owe them a tremendous debt because they established the fundamental foundations of psychoanalysis. Still, as is often the case with pioneers, they have to cling to certain tenets in a rigid fashion in order to consolidate their identity, the precarious and insecure identity of a young science that has experienced, if not an entirely hostile, certainly a dubious acceptance.

Sterba, along with many of the other contributors, introduces the personal element as an intrinsic aspect of the psychoanalytic process. Apparently such an orientation met with a cool or, perhaps more accurately, a heated reception by the circle of analysts surrounding Freud. Today, one might dispute the specific factors Sterba describes, and some of the chapters stress a different orientation. Still, Sterba's approach is strikingly modern and his article, which may have originally been published prematurely, certainly deserves a revival insofar as it is perfectly in context with what we may refer to as the countertransference orientation.

Some of the articles introduce a note of caution. Many an innovative focus, especially one which might have been resisted, may finally be embraced with tremendous enthusiasm and highly valued. There is a danger that the initial enthusiasm may be escalated to an idealized fervor and the new orientation achieve an exalted position. Since some segments of modern society exalt sensitivity to other person's feelings and full awareness of one's own, the countertransference focus may become a sustenance for megalomanic needs. I believe that in our eagerness for clarification, some of us may have carried our convictions beyond the observable data, but this should lead to no harm as long as such ideas are communicated and explored by friendly and equally curious colleagues. Eventually, there will be some leveling and although then one is dealing with less dramatic and inclusive concepts, their significance and place among the many elements that constitute the analytic process will become firmly established.

Chapter I

Various Aspects of the Analytic Process

Peter L. Giovacchini, M.D.

TRANSFERENCE AND PSYCHOPATHOLOGY

To refer to Freud's conclusion that patients suffering from what he classified as narcissistic psychoneuroses do not form transferences almost amounts to belaboring the point. Many investigators, Boyer (1961); Byschowski (1952); Giovacchini (1972); Kernberg (1972); Khan (1960); Modell (1963); Searles (1963); and Winnicott (1955); to mention a few, have reported intense transference reactions in patients suffering from severe psychopathology. I refer to this point, however, because Freud made it the basis for his opinion that such cases cannot be treated psychoanalytically.

Freud (1914) conceptualized transferences as a repetition of infantile orientations toward the analyst. In order to achieve this, the patient has to convert ego-libido into object-libido, an increase in one leading to a decrease in the other. Schizophrenic patients and patients suffering from characterological defects would, according to Freud, be so narcissistically fixated that they could not cathect external objects, and therefore, not form transferences.

Today one is not particularly concerned about the question of the occurrence or nonoccurrence of transference. However, I believe at this point some questions regarding the transference neurosis are relevant. Freud defined the transference neuroses, a nosologic entity, as psychoneurotic conditions capable of having ties with external objects and forming a transference neurosis. He makes the following definitional statement about the transference neurosis:

> ". . . we regularly succeed in giving all the symptoms of the illness a new
> transference meaning and in replacing its ordinary neurosis by a 'transference-
> neurosis' of which he can be cured by the therapeutic work. The transference
> thus creates an intermediate region between illness and real life through which
> the transition from the one to the other is made. The new condition has taken
> over *all the features of the illness,* but it represents an artificial illness which is
> at every point accessible to our intervention" (italics mine) (Freud, 1914).

Freud did not state that the transference neurosis referred exclusively to an oedipal conflict. Rather, he emphasized that the transference neurosis encompasses the patient's total psychopathology, including defensive primitive regressions. True, when Freud formulated the various psychoneuroses he made the Oedipus complex the central conflictual core, but when dealing with the transference neurosis specifically he included other more primitive psychic elements, and he did not specifically mention the oedipal level of psychosexual development in this quote.

The concept of the transference neurosis becomes even more important when it is considered the essential element that makes analytic treatment possible. Granted that seriously ill patients may make transference projections, they do not, according to some analysts, form a transference neurosis, and therefore are not analyzable. They may form narcissistic transferences, but these cannot be resolved, at least not in the same orderly, and to some extent, predictable sequence as occurs in the resolution of the transference neurosis. Anthony has made some pertinent comments relative to this point. (See Giovacchini, 1973.)

Thus, we are faced with two technical questions. If what we are calling a narcissistic transference, the characteristic transference of patients suffering from narcissistic fixations, is fundamentally different from the transference neurosis, can it nevertheless be used for analytic purposes? If so, then, we can ask the further question as to what constitutes a narcissistic resolution in contrast to the resolution of the transference neurosis.

As already discussed, it is debatable whether the transference neurosis is, in fact, such an oedipal, psychosexual, circumscribed entity as some have asserted. It is also debatable whether the implicit assumption that we know a good deal about the resolution of the transference neurosis is valid. Freud (1914A) spoke of repetition, lifting of repression, and working through, but do we really know what working through means? Freud states:

> ". . . giving the resistance a name cannot result in its immediate cessation. One must allow the patient time to become more conversant with this resistance with which he has now become acquainted, to *work through* it, to overcome it, by continuing, in defiance of it, the analytic work according to the fundamental rules of the analysis. Only when the resistance is at its height can the analyst, working in common with his patient, discover the repressed instinctual impulses which are feeding the resistance; and it is this kind of experience which convinces the patient of the existence and power of such impulses. The doctor has nothing else to do than to wait and let things take their course, a course which cannot be avoided nor always hastened" (italics Freud's).

This is a masterful description of complicated psychic processes but it is not completely satisfying. Freud would have been the first to admit that closure has not been achieved and when dealing with the intricacies of subtle analytic interactions, final pronouncements are unlikely.

The treatment of patients suffering from characterological defects teaches us that in some instances transferences can be used for therapeutic gain. In turn, one learns about character structure, psychopathological vicissitudes, and the therapeutic process itself. One can think in terms, perhaps overly simplified, of the establishment and resolution of the narcissistic transference and study the specific vicissitudes involved in such a resolution.

Before discussing technical factors, however, one has to explore further the various elements that cause us to label some transferences as narcissistic transference and others as nonnarcissistic.

Narcissistic and Nonnarcissistic Transference

Rather than thinking of two exclusive, clinically delineated entities, some analysts find it more useful to view transference, as any other psychic element, in terms of an hierarchal continuum with varying degrees of psychic differentiation and organization. All transferences involve infantile primary process factors, but the contribution of infantile elements varies in different transference reactions. Still, if one views the psychic apparatus as containing all of its antecedents, differing, of course, in their functional propensities, any transference will have some elements of early developmental stages. Consequently, every transference would have a narcissistic element. Its effect on behavior and adaptation may be minimal, but, insofar as analytic therapy involves regression, early developmental stages acquire increased significance during the analytic interaction.

Freud described transference from several viewpoints. At first (Breuer and Freud, 1895) he described it phenomenologically. The patient had certain feelings toward the analyst, in Breuer's case, primarily sexual, which have no realistic justification. Next, Freud (1900) wrote about the transference of unconscious cathexis to preconscious cathexis. In the Dora case (Freud, 1904) he refers to the therapeutic implications of transference and of how failure to recognize it could lead to treatment failure.

These ideas were formulated prior to Freud's group of papers which were primarily centered upon technical considerations. He had not as yet restricted the concept of transference to certain specific types of neuroses. Although Freud considered both Breuer's case of Anna O. and his own of Dora to be hysterics, there has been considerable speculation as to whether they were, in fact, patients suffering from rather severe characterological problems. (See Deutsch, 1960; Lindon, 1968; Reichard, 1956.) If these speculations are correct, it would seem as if Freud were dealing with transference in cases that had, at least, some similarity to what he later classified as narcissistic neuroses.

Freud's first comprehensive clinical formulations emphasize the resistive aspects of transference. He (Freud, 1912) describes the pursuit of a pathogenic complex from its conscious derivatives to its unconscious sources. As one pursues such associations the analyst finally reaches a point where he is touching upon a hidden conflict. According to Freud, it is at this point that transference emerges as a resistance. This formulation concentrates upon the defensive aspects of transference, and today might be considered a description of a defense transference. It does not, however, restrict itself to any specific neurosis, although whatever the psychopathology, the ego has to have a sufficient degree of organization to support such a sophisticated defense as repression.

Freud felt that although transference is an obstacle, and he was referring specifically to negative or erotic transference (Freud, 1914, 1914B), analytic treatment is not possible without its resolution. He (Freud, 1912), did not believe that hidden monsters could be destroyed in effigy. He also stressed the value of the positive transference and saw it as a vehicle for cure.

Negative transference, on the other hand, led to therapeutic complications. He acknowledged that all feelings are a mixture of both positive and negative feelings, that is, they are ambivalent, and neurotics are more ambivalent than normal persons. Apparently the patient is decreasingly analyzable according to the propensity he has for negative transference. Thus, Freud concluded that the paranoid patient is not analyzable because of the intensity of his negative feelings which would be experienced as negative transference in a therapeutic relationship. Freud (1912) summarizes these ideas in the following statements:

"Thus the solution of the puzzle is that transference to the doctor is suitable for resistance to the treatment only insofar as it is a negative transference or a positive transference of repressed, erotic impulses. If we 'remove' the transference by making it conscious we are detaching only those two components of the emotional act from the person of the doctor; the other component, which is admissible to consciousness and unobjectionable, persists and is a vehicle of success in psychoanalysis exactly as it is in other forms of treatment."

Later in the same paper Freud stresses:

"Ambivalence in the emotional trends of neurotics is the best explanation of their ability to enlist their transferences in the service of resistance. Where the capacity for transference has become essentially limited to a negative one, as is the case with paranoics, there ceases to be any possibility of influence or cure."

Finally, Freud states:

"It cannot be disputed that controlling the phenomena of transference presents the psychoanalyst with the greatest difficulties. But it should not be forgotten that it is precisely they that do us the inestimable service of making the patient's hidden and forgotten erotic impulses immediate and manifest. For, when all is said and done, it is impossible to destroy anyone *in absentia* or *in effigy*." (italics Freud)

In these statements, Freud revealed that the paranoid patient is capable of transference, even though it is only a negative transference. The paranoid patient is classified under the rubric of the narcissistic neurosis. Nevertheless, negative transference is still transference; therefore, Freud's assertions that the narcissistic neuroses do not form transferences now have to be modified. From this discussion, it would seem clear that Freud concluded that some patients suffering from narcissistic neuroses restrict their transferences to negative transferences and this factor makes them analytically untreatable. The latter is due to the fact that the negative transference is one of the chief vehicles for resistance, the other being the erotic transference, which causes the patient to attempt to sabotage the analysis by falling in love with the analyst and reducing him to the status of lover (Freud, 1914).

I believe that Freud's view about negative transferences is extremely important, because it gives us a theoretical basis for considering analyzing cases suffering from characterological disorders. It tells us that such patients are capable of an emotional involvement with the analyst. The assertion that a hostile involvement cannot be used for therapeutic gain is contradicted by clinical experience.

Although one may feel reluctant to accept the Kleinian technique of interpretation, which strikes some analysts as being overly active, imaginative and not supported by the patient's material, her group has repeatedly demonstrated that the negative transference is a valuable and indispensable therapeutic tool. The psychic processes underlying such interactions are very complex but the projection of destructive introjects into the analyst is a central theme (Klein, 1930, 1946, 1952).

The original formulations regarding transferences as being only resistance have been considerably expanded, Freud, himself, being the main contributor of such extensions. Basically the patient projects infantile feelings onto the analyst, a process which occurs spontaneously if the analyst remains nonintrusive.

The analyst creates a setting which is conducive to regression. By allowing the patient to feel free to verbalize whatever he wishes, by not passing judgment, by remaining calm and accepting feelings and attitudes the patient fears and is often guilty and ashamed of, moral restraints are diminished and the patient feels sufficient security and acceptance so that he can regress. The regressed state is characterized by corresponding infantile orientations and feelings and it is within this framework that the patient relates to the therapist.

The distinction, then, between a positive and negative transference would have to be understood in terms of the level of regression. (See section on Therapeutic Regression.) Freud (1915) clearly pointed out that hate is a much more primitive emotion than love. Therefore, transference feelings of hatred would presumably emanate from earlier developmental stages than those of transference love. However, as Freud (1914) also stressed, eroticized feelings also stem from primitive developmental levels, but this conclusion was not explored further in terms of specific stages.

The distinction between narcissistic and nonnarcissistic transference has to be considered in a similar fashion, that is, in the context of their developmental antecedents as they are recapitulated, in some measure, in various regressed states during analysis. Essentially, the former would stem from a narcissistic phase and the latter could presumably emanate from any later psychosexual stage, not just the oedipal phase. The question of the capacity for object relations is relevant here, and one might again raise Freud's objection concerning narcissistic states since, if transference is an object relationship with the therapist and narcissism precludes object libido, then how can one have transference? Let us return to this question later.

For the moment, I wish to discuss pregenital transference and the types of object relationships involved. In the obsessive-compulsive neurosis, Freud (1909) postulated a relative fixation on the anal-sadistic stage of psychosexual development. The patient has succeeded in reaching an oedipal position, one which is weakly established and because of earlier sadistic elements is disturbed by conflict and guilt. Freud (1896) described the early traumas of the obsessional and the hysteric which are responsible for their respective points of fixation, but in any case, regardless of the actual or fantasied existence of such traumas, the onset of the neurosis is accompanied by a regression from the oedipal position. In the obsessive-compulsive neurosis, the patient regresses to the anal-sadistic phase, a pregenital stage.

During treatment, the obsessional patient relates to the analyst from such an anal, pregenital orientation, one which is mobilized as a defense against underlying oedipal strivings. In an overly simplified fashion, the analytic process consists in analyzing the pregenital defense transference in order to unearth and resolve the oedipal conflict.

I have never been able to find in any of Freud's writings a distinction between the initial transference as a defense and the transference that is formed when the underlying oedipal conflict is unearthed. As mentioned earlier, he states that the whole neurosis was replaced by the transference neurosis and this would have to include adaptive and defensive superstructures as well as the basic conflictual situation. In this connection, Freud (1916) states:

> ". . . the whole of his illness's new production is concentrated upon a single point—his relation to the doctor. Thus the transference may be compared to the cambium layer in a tree between the wood and the bark, from which a new formation of tissue and the increase in the girth of the trunk derive. When the transference has risen to significance, work upon the patients' memories retreat

far into the background. Therefore, it is not correct to say that we are no longer concerned with the patient's earlier illness, but with a newly created and transformed neurosis which has taken the former' place. We have followed this new edition of the old disorder from its start, we have observed its origin in growth, and we are especially well able to find our way about in it, since as its object, we are situated at its very center.''

To recapitulate, this discussion has distinguished between positive and negative transferences, pregenital, and oedipal transference. Certain types of transferences are resistances to therapy and others are the vehicles of cure. What caused Freud to exclude narcissistic developmental stages from other pregenital stages which are capable of forming transferences is that narcissism is conceptualized as a developmental stage where object relations are not yet possible.

A narcissistically fixated patient, however, is not completely fixated; there are varying degrees of development to his psyche, even though his inner core is primarily narcissistic. This is obvious, because one could not exist, except perhaps in a state of extreme catatonic withdrawal, without some object involvement. In analysis, a patient may, to some extent, recapitulate any early developmental stage during the transference regression but never exactly reproduce it. Later acquisitions are not entirely lost; the patient usually can still talk, understand complex ideas, remain continent, and perform most of his adult functions, functions which are way beyond the capacity of the neonate. Even in the most regressed states during analysis, there is still some object involvement although it is a primitive type of part-object involvement.

Again, it is useful to view the object relationship qualities of transference from the viewpoint of an hierarchal continuum. Insofar as any transference is a recapitulation of an infantile state, the types of object relationships typical of such states would be similarly infantile. From this viewpoint, the regression of narcissistically fixated patients would be characterized by primitive object relationships, which are fragmented ones, but in which contact with another person is still possible.

This viewpoint emphasized that *absolute* distinctions between narcissistic and nonnarcissistic transferences are no longer necessary. Rather, one is dealing with varying degrees of primitive and more sophisticated adaptations and object relationships. Every transference, even those of highly structured psychoneurotics, has a narcissistic element and the converse would also be true—that no matter how primitive the patient's psychic organization may be, there is still some oedipal element present. True, the narcissistic element may be negligible and the oedipal element so weak that it has very little significance; still, these are quantitative rather than qualitative differences.

The contribution of different levels of the psyche is evident in clinical material. Even in the best organized psychoneurosis, pregenital elements can be clearly discerned in material which seems to be basically oedipal. This is especially vivid in the obsessional neurosis and Freud (1909) masterfully described the interplay of sexual and sadistic currents in his classical case of the "Rat Man." However, in hysterics, too, patients who supposedly have more firmly reached the highest levels of psychic organization, one is struck by the amount of pregenital elements in the oedipal configuration. Surprisingly, one often finds oral elements, that is, more primitive pregenital elements than those usually found in the obsessional neuroses. On the surface, this appears puzzling because one would expect a relatively pure presentation, so to speak, of the Oedipus complex and less involvement with the more primitive levels of the personality in patients whose emotional development has advanced to fairly mature phases. This contradiction, however, is only apparent and due to a simplistic concept of emotional development which assumes that there is a unidirectional progression from the primitive to the sophisticated and that the persistence of early developmental stages are detrimental to later ego integration. I will return to this issue later.

Conversely, very disturbed patients often bring forth oedipal material in a much clearer fashion than patients classified as transference neuroses. Schizophrenic patients frequently produce oedipal material in an open, undisguised fashion. It is often directly and crudely expressed. The latter gives it its psychotic character, but in terms of content, incestuous feelings and preoccupation with castration are in the foreground. In fact, in extreme instances, the oedipal material, or at least one aspect of it, is acted out. Self-castration in schizophrenics has been reported fairly frequently.

The frank expression of the Oedipus complex as well as the frank expression of any psychic elements that are usually in a state of repression is characteristic of patients suffering from severe psychopathology. If such behavior occurs in the external world, it is labeled "acting-out." When these feelings are directed toward the analyst, we have what is called "psychotic transference." However, what is being experienced still belongs, to a large measure, to higher levels of psychic organization even though the lack of sophisticated defenses and its concrete and crude expression reveal its primitive qualities. This situation once again emphasizes that transference has to be viewed from another perspective other than a series of sequentially ordered psychosexual stages of development and impulses appropriate to these phases being directed toward the analyst. The admixture of these stages, as just discussed, necessitates another viewpoint, if we are to assess the meaning of these phenomena in terms of treatability. Furthermore, the process of resolution of transference, of working through, also requires elucidation which can best be considered an extension of these concepts.

Dynamic and Developmental Aspects of Transference

It is now germane to examine further Freud's (1912) first comprehensive description of the mechanisms and dynamics of transference. He viewed the developing psyche as evolving characteristic styles based both upon constitutional factors and experiences with the outer world which remain with one throughout life. This leads to the production of what the translators of the Standard Edition called stereotyped plates, or what might also be referred to as templates. These templates receive reinforcement or as Freud states: "are constantly reprinted afresh" by external circumstances and objects. They are not, however, permanently fixed and are susceptible to change. This would imply that therapy can lead to fundamental character alterations.

Freud conceptualized such stereotyped plates in terms of libidinal impulses, postulating that only a portion of such impulses achieve full psychic development. This portion is directed toward reality, is consciously experienced and becomes incorporated as part of one's character. The other larger portion becomes fixated at some earlier developmental stage. It can be further elaborated in fantasy or remain completely repressed in the unconscious.

Uncompleted development can be compared with an uncompleted task. Zeigarnik (1927) demonstrated by carefully controlling variables that interrupted uncompleted tasks are retained in memory better than completed tasks. They are taken up again later with enthusiasm and persistence. Zeigarnik discussed this phenomenon in terms of motivation. Frustration, due to failure or interruption, does not necessarily lead to abandonment of the goal. On the contrary, Zeigarnik demonstrated that the incompleteness of a task increases the motivation to achieve a resolution.

Lagache (1953) links this type of motivation to repetition. Uncompleted actions are subjected to the compulsion to repeat (Freud, 1920) in order to achieve mastery. Lagache believes that a fundamental feature of the readiness for transference is this repetitive tendency.

Zeigarnik's results are interesting and although one should be cautious in transposing the findings of a circumscribed although carefully executed experiment to such complex phenomena as human interactions, his conclusions are, nevertheless, suggestive in at least two interrelated respects.

First, they can be considered in terms of the therapeutic process in general. If one views psychopathology, as one is more prone to do nowadays, as a developmental arrest, then one can think in terms of a drive (I am using the term "drive" loosely) toward higher levels of integration. *The incompleted task of development creates a specific tension within the psyche, apart from that due to intrapsychic conflict or adaptive failure, which can ultimately be manifested as a motivation for analysis.* I believe there are considerable data that make such an hypothesis plausible, data which would indicate that some patients suffering from ego defects are quite suitable for analysis. (See next section on Therapeutic Regression.) In the past, I thought of the analytic process in terms of releasing an inhibited developmental drive. (See Giovacchini, 1965.) These speculations about interrupted tasks can also be included within the context of arrested development. Autonomy is not achieved. The patient is aware that something fundamental is missing and often shows eagerness for analysis.

The second implication of Zeigarnik's findings refers to the readiness for transference in a similar fashion as the readiness for analysis. In a sense, bringing transference into the discussion specifically is a subcategory of the discussion of readiness for analysis. Since needs and even affects have not been able to achieve ultimate differentiation and attain a certain degree of autonomy, they are more prone to be brought to the surface so the task of development can be completed. Being brought to the surface means being exposed relative to an external object, and since these are arrested needs and feelings—that is, archaic ones—this type of object relationship would be classified as transference. Of course, readiness for analysis generally and readiness for transference specifically is determined by a variety of factors, including external factors, such as the cultural milieu and the life situation. Still, from an intrapsychic developmental viewpoint, the fixation just discussed may make significant contributions to a propitious attitude toward analysis, rather than the reverse, which has so frequently been stressed. Apparently, Freud (1914) was making a similar point when he stated:

> "If someone's need for love is not entirely satisfied by reality, he is bound to approach every new person whom he meets with libidinal anticipatory ideas; and it is highly probable that both portions of his libido, the portion that is capable of becoming conscious, as well as the unconscious have a share in forming this attitude."

Freud, in the above passage, is describing transference phenomena in general, that is, how a person reacts with preset infantile attitudes when frustrated. Next, he explains how this transference specifically directs itself toward the analyst. He states:

> "Thus it is a perfectly normal and intelligible thing that the libidinal cathexis of someone who is partly unsatisfied should be directed as well to the figure of a doctor."

Unsatisfied libidinal cathexis is usually associated with primitive psychic mechanisms. Freud's next comment is:

> "It follows from an earlier hypothesis that the cathexis will have recourse to prototypes, will attach itself to one of the stereotype plates which is present in

the subject; or, to put the position another way, the cathexis will introduce the doctor into one of the psychical 'series' which the patient has already formed.''

Here the emphasis is on the introjection of the analyst rather than the projection of what Freud, borrowing the term from Jung, next refers to as an imago. Still, in the previous passage, Freud is discussing feelings, which are part of a template, being directed toward the analyst. Although not specifically stated, the directing of a template toward the analyst may involve the mechanism of projection.

Freud (1894, 1896) was the first to view systematically emotional disturbance in terms of conflict and defense. He considered certain defenses as being somewhat typical of particular psychosexual orientations. Projection was conceptualized as a primitive defense mechanism characteristic of the paranoid patient and indicative of an early ego organization.

Clinicians recognized that the human condition makes use of all defense mechanisms at some time or other. It is the predominant use of a cluster of defenses which distinguishes one personality organization from another. In transference, however, all patients make use of projection as an elemental psychic mechanism, no matter what constitutes the content of transference. Thus, the transference phenomenon makes use of primitive psychic mechanisms, regardless of the psychosexual level which is being handled in analysis.

Again, this narrows the distinction between narcissistic and nonnarcissistic transference. The essence of transference in psychoanalysis is the projection of infantile, or relatively infantile elements into the mental representation of therapist. Thus, the basic mechanism of all transference is primitive; its content may involve different levels of ego integration.

Transference has received considerable attention in the recent literature. Calef (1971) reviews the concept of transference neurosis in terms of its relationship to the infantile neurosis and the presenting neurosis. He studies the infantile element in the transference neurosis and wonders whether the latter concept is a useful one, clinically speaking, or whether it is an abstraction that has little clinical validity. Harley (1971) makes a quantitative distinction between transference in general and transference neurosis, the latter referring to a greater degree of cathexis of the analyst. The contribution of primitive aspects of the personality to the formation of various types of transference has to be considered further and clinical observation amply illustrates that the projection of primitive elements can indeed be massive.

Loewald (1971) believes that although the transference neurosis involves all levels of the personality it is not simply a repeat performance or a continuation of the old illness. He feels that it is "indeed a creature of the analytic situation.''

Insofar as there is little reference to the content of what is projected in the transference in these particular recent papers it becomes germane to inquire further and to determine how the content involves object relations in general and the relationship with the therapist in particular. Perhaps, one can again develop a continuum which will involve narcissistic phases of development more directly than has already been discussed.

When considering higher levels of organization, one deals with fairly sophisticated feelings such as sexual impulses. At these better integrated levels the psyche is able to distinguish between its various parts. Impulses and needs are differentiated and perceived in a distinct fashion. The gratifying external object is also viewed as a separate entity and its satisfying mode is seen as one particular aspect, a functional aspect of the person rather than comprising one's total response to the external object and completely defining the essence of the object relation.

The progressively hierarchical elaboration of needs has to be brought into focus in order to understand the subtle aspects of transference, aspects which I believe will make the dichotomy of narcissistic and nonnarcissistic transference and its therapeutic implications unnecessary. To proceed, let us examine certain ideas regarding primitive stages of development of impulses in contrast to what has just been stated about sophisticated, well-structured needs. This discussion will not deal with instinctual theory in general, something one might expect when dealing with the evolution of needs, but will restrict itself to the discussion of impulses as they are involved in transference projections of early developmental elements.

There have been many hypotheses about early developmental stages, instinctual impulses, and object relationships. Fairbairn (1941) believes that libido is object-seeking rather than being primarily motivated to seek satisfaction. He focuses upon primitive ego states where the object remains undifferentiated. Winnicott and Khan (1953) criticize Fairbairn's concepts in the following manner:

> "Fairbairn does start off with an infant that is a whole human being, one experiencing the relationship to the breast as a separate object, an object that he has experienced and about which he has complicated ideas. It is this way of working that makes the author theorize categorically that 'libido is object-seeking,' etc. But, the author as we shall see later, finds it very difficult consistently to maintain this view by which the infant is always a separate entity, seeking objects from within his own entity existence."

It seems as if the essence of Winnicott's critique is that libido being object-seeking presupposes a level of psychic organization that could not be present at the earliest stages of psychic development.

Fairbairn (1952), defining identification, states:

> "I employ the term 'primary identification' here to signify the cathexis of an object which has not yet been differentiated (or has been only partly differen-

tiated) from himself by the cathecting subject. This process differs, of course, from the process ordinarily described as 'identification' viz., an emotionally determined tendency to treat a differentiated (or partially differentiated) object as if it were not differentiated when it is cathected. The latter process should properly be described as 'secondary identification'.''

Winnicott wishes to preserve consistency between various levels of organization and emphasizes that in order to relate to an object there has to be sufficient structure. He replies to Fairbairn's statement:

"Now if the object is not differentiated, it cannot operate as an object. What Fairbairn is referring to, then is an infant with needs but no 'mechanism' by which to implement them, an infant with needs not seeking an object, but seeking de-tension, libido-seeking satisfaction, instinct tension seeking a return to a state of rest or unexcitement; which brings us back to Freud.''

If libido were, indeed primarily object-seeking then one might expect that the tendency to form transference is also primary. However, with progressive structuralization the basis of the object relationship would become increasingly sophisticated and transcend instinctual needs. Still, it may not be necessary to retain such dichotomies as object-seeking and gratification of needs.

The neonate is not sufficiently differentiated either emotionally or neurologically to have complex feelings. At best, one can state that he reacts with some discomfort when he experiences an inner need. *The object and the gratifying function it performs are not separated.* The object, whether internal or external, is at first, perceived only in terms of its functional capacity. So, if one states that libido is object-seeking, at such primitive developmental stages, it does not make much difference since the object is recognized only in terms of gratifying needs and reinstituting equilibrium, as Winnicott stated. It does not have to be perceived as separate; it may be perceived as part of the self. All of these hypotheses are relevant to the theme of transference since it is these early orientations that are recapitulated in the transference of patients suffering from severe character pathology.

Such transferences are considered primitive, and Modell (1963) has stated that the analyst is treated as if he were a transitional object. I believe that Winnicott's (1953) idea of the transitional object should be discussed now. I wish to fit it in the hierarchy I am developing and to try to understand this concept which has, in my mind, been frequently misunderstood.

During early stages of psychic development, Winnicott conceptualized a phase where the ego reacts to the world as if it were both part of himself and separated at the same time. Winnicott states this poetically by emphasizing that the child and his mother never raise the question of such a distinction. The illusion is maintained that the child controls and creates the world, a world that will satisfy needs perfectly when demanded. The creation of an object that is both inside and outside is referred to as primary psychic creativity. According to Winnicott, the child's ego acquires the ability to create an object because of optimal maternal care, which means that the mother's existence for a period of time is dependent upon her exclusive devotion to her infant, referred to as primary maternal preoccupation (Winnicott, 1952, 1956, 1961). It is this self-created object that Winnicott (1953) calls the transitional object and it is representative of a phase of development where outside and inside are not distinguished because the mother helps maintain the illusion that such a distinction does not exist. Furthermore, the mother supports the creation and maintenance of the transitional object by her primary maternal preoccupation. She, in actuality, corresponds exactly to what the child has created, and he can reinforce the establishment of the self-created object which is similar to the mother as a breast part-object. One might say that the mother supports the self-created introject by being congruent with it in much the same fashion as the presence of the external object reinforces the maintenance of the mental representation of that object. (See Beres, 1957.)

The concept of the transitional object is not simply that of a progression from an objectless phase to part-objects and then to whole objects, nor is it merely a transition point in the differentiation of me and not-me. It is all of these things, to be sure but it is much more. In essence, Winnicott is emphasizing "space" between delusion and reality, between omnipotent control and relating to an object in a fashion that transcends needs. (See Winnicott, 1952, 1960, 1967.) Here we have an interesting admixture of structure, function and psychic development in the context of object relations.

Let me amplify this conclusion about an admixture of structure, function and ego integration. I find it useful to think of Winnicott's transitional object and transitional phenomenon as a registration, so to speak, of a state of integration brought about by a successful mothering experience. *The achievement of integration can easily be experienced as autonomous, as is true of any experience which one has made truly one's own. The ultimate effect is a state of satisfaction and the expansion of one's capacities to find sources of gratification.*

In effect, the transitional object represents the internalization of the mothering function, although according to Winnicott, the child believes he has created it himself. In any case, the internalization of a function also becomes a structural acquisition; that is, it leads to ego integration and ego expansion. This is generally true, but especially during formative stages of development. Thus, the transitional object can be thought of as an object, that is, structure, or as a function, that is, an ego modality. Consequently, distinctions between structure and function, object and need are not sharply delineated during early developmental phases. Needs direct the psyche toward objects either internal or external, and even when one has achieved relative autonomy, the ego's self-reliance may still be based upon the maintenance of a self-created transitional object.

The contributions of early developmental phases to later transference phenomena can now be discussed in terms of the content of the projection. The latter is the main reason for the review of these ideas.

As can be inferred from the above discussion, precise distinctions between structure and function are later developmental acquisitions. In early phases, needs, methods of gratification, and parts of the self are not distinguished from each other. Inside and outside, ministrations from others or self-created gratifications characteristic of auto-erotic activities are all equivalent. Thus, the projections of transferences based upon such primitive states would not contain well-structured feelings and wishes, since the latter have not yet differentiated.

During analysis, one notes that such patients are projecting parts of the self into the analyst, sometimes completely fusing with him and giving him omnipotent control. Freud's (1912) formulations of feelings being directed toward the analyst, and the converse, the analyst being incorporated around a template, are germane to an understanding of these neonatal stages. Introjective-projective mechanisms are dominant; the boundary between the inner and outer world is imperfectly formed. Thus, the narcissistic transference may be qualitatively distinguished from nonnarcissistic transferences by the content of the projections.

Still, even with the most highly structured patients, the transference also includes a projection of parts of the self, as well as instinctual impulses. For example, the analyst often becomes a representative of the patient's superego. Even though the superego is a relatively later acquisition than such primitive registrations as the transitional object, it is still a structural aspect of the psyche.

To summarize these ideas briefly, narcissistic transference, the transference of early developmental phases, involves the projection of parts of the self rather than discrete feelings and wishes. However, during primitive narcissistic phases the gratifying object and the gratifying function are not distinguished. Functional modalities and internal and external objects are equated. The latter logically follows because internal and external are not yet or are only imperfectly separated. Furthermore, internal objects are also poorly differentiated, so as Winnicott reminds us, a poorly differentiated object is not an object at all, but a part of the self. Thus, the projection of a part of the self is equivalent to the projection of a feeling or wish, or of an internal object or introject, or as Freud (1912) stated, the projection of an imago.

The Narcissistic Transference and the Analytic Process

If the difference between narcissistic and nonnarcissistic transferences are differences of degree of operative infantile elements, as has just been stressed, perhaps the same may be said about the analytic interaction of patients experiencing such transferences. In any case, I would now like to turn to some clinical material to illustrate specific constellations of transference projections which I believe are typical of a certain class of patients suffering from characterological defects.

A middle-aged and somewhat successful commercial artist had had many analysts throughout the course of his life. Some had him lie on the couch, and others made him sit up because they felt he was "too sick" for analysis. The patient preferred the couch but he never changed therapists because he was dissatisfied with them. He moved on to another therapist for one of two reasons: his work, which consisted of commissions in different cities and countries, forced him to be itinerant. Consequently, he had to find a new therapist with each move. The other reason he changed therapists was because they could not stand him and would reject him outright, or refer him elsewhere. When he finally came to me, he was assured of a position which would keep him in the city permanently.

His first appearance was striking from many viewpoints. He was an odd-looking person, and although styles are now quite liberal and tolerate a considerable amount of flamboyance, he still managed to look queer. I still cannot say exactly what it was about his appearance that struck me. There was a peculiar, incongruous quality to the way the various parts of his clothing fitted each other. He was not particularly mod or hip; but the discrepancy between his corduroy pants, knit shirt and velvet tie seemed enormous. The colors also clashed in a memorable fashion.

There was also an incongruous quality to the way his body carried his clothes. He was obese and flabby and although his clothes were neat and fit him well, folds of fat seemed to be draped into the pleats of his shirt. Generally, his appearance seemed awkward and clumsy. He was not an attractive person.

Perhaps his most disconcerting feature was the distinctly offensive odor he emitted. The patient that followed him compared it to the sweaty smell of a locker room after a team has returned from a vigorous game. I found it decidedly unpleasant.

My immediate reaction, however, was not entirely negative. The patient seemed to be making a considerable effort to be obnoxious; so much so, that I was, to some extent, intrigued. I found that I was able to adjust to almost everything he presented to me, but I wondered how long I would be able to stand the smell. I decided, however, not to make any comment about it at the moment and simply to wait and see what developed.

The reason he sought analysis never emerged clearly. Apparently, he did not really know; he just knew that he could not exist without a daily visit to an analyst's office. I could sense an urgent and poignant appeal, but he would have looked ridiculous if he tried to bring such sentiments to the surface. He referred to himself as a hippopotamus and I must say that such imagery seemed appropriate.

I will refer briefly to his past to emphasize the background of his narcissistic fixations. His father was a pretentious failure and probably an alcoholic. He had constantly berated the patient during childhood and even now he took great pleasure in pointing out to his son that he was a worthless, mediocre person who would never achieve success as an artist or be able to get married and have a family. The patient was a loner and had never married or had any particularly close relationships with anyone. His father constantly pointed out how superior *he* was, how successful he had been as a scholar and athlete and in the world of business. Actually, these were grandiose self-evaluations that bordered on the delusional, according to the patient. From a vocational viewpoint, the patient had apparently achieved considerably more than his father.

His mother, on the other hand, was described as an extremely confident woman. She was a talented painter, and an accomplished musician, as well as a beauty, with considerable poise and charm. Whatever task she undertook, she was able to master and carry through to perfection.

As the patient described further reactions toward his mother throughout the course of analysis, I formed the impression that this woman had very little feeling for people. She emerged as a cold, insulated person who used people, rather than relate to them. The family lived at a very high financial level, not because of the father's income, but because of the mother's considerable inherited wealth, and they had various servants and maids. As far as the patient could recall, the children were raised almost exclusively by governesses. The mother's participation in their care was kept at an absolute minimum. Furthermore, because of the mother's somewhat tyrannical attitude and coldness, none of these governesses stayed for any prolonged period of time. Consequently, the children were exposed to a series of indifferent and sometimes cruel maids.

The patient recalled that his father blustered at everyone except his wife; he was manifestly afraid of her. The best he could do was use some inept sarcasm against her. She responded with contemptuous indifference. The patient amplified the description of the parents' relationship by emphasizing that his mother treated his father as if he were a "piece of trash," that he did not exist as a human being.

The above is, in essence, his description of the atmosphere surrounding his early years. He has a sister four years older, toward whom he felt some fondness and who apparently had a schizophrenic breakdown during early adolescence. She has never recovered and continues to live in an institution. Otherwise, he characterized his life as dull and colorless. He felt unhappy, but as was true for all of his feelings, he could not feel with any degree of intensity. Most of the time he felt dead and empty and generally futile.

In school he was capable of doing well and attracting the attention of his teachers. However, as soon as they praised and encouraged him, he would withdraw and alienate himself. He would also do poorly in his work, just managing to get by. Consequently, his academic life was characterized by quick, short-lived successes followed by mediocre performance. He continued this pattern in his later vocational life.

He viewed himself as a contemptuous, cantankerous unlikable eccentric, and he went to considerable trouble to present himself in such a fashion. No one liked him; he lived alone with virtually no friends. On occasion he would have a relationship with a woman but these were also short-lived and usually died because of lack of emotional involvement and indifference.

His demeanor struck me as pathetic and yet there was something about him that was likable in spite of the lugubrious picture he painted.

. I also found his attitude about analysis quite interesting. Although he presented himself as dull and stupid, he displayed remarkable sophistication about psychoanalysis. Directly and indirectly, the patient indicated that he understood the subtle aspects of the analytic process. In fact, there were times when I felt inclined to take notes, not for clinical recording, but for didactic reasons, as a learning experience for me.

His faith in analysis was also striking, especially in view of the fact that most of his therapists never even considered using analysis with him. He went into considerable detail to describe exactly what had occurred with several therapists, carefully emphasizing what he considered to be their shortcomings and how they were technically wrong in their approach. He was not bitter, simply sad. He did not believe I would make the same mistakes such as, for instance, managerial intrusion about his way of living, but he doubted that I would be able to tolerate his presence, not from a technical viewpoint, but because my personal feelings would supersede my clinical orientation.

My feelings varied. I recognized that I was dealing with a very disturbed, emotionally scarred person who on the surface was most unappealing. However, he was intriguing and showed an extraordinary amount of knowledge about psychoanalysis. This was not simply an intellectual grasp; he seemed to be extremely sensitive about the nuances of the psychoanalytic process, and although he viewed his therapeutic experiences as disastrous—as he viewed his entire life—he still retained a tremendous faith in analysis, certainly more than his therapists, as he described them. I might have joined them since I could easily feel my ambivalence, but I was, to some extent, able to identify with his analytic attitude. He sensed my response and for a while our relationship became very friendly, although not in an overt sense. But the consultation room was infused with an aura of acceptance, mutual understanding, and hopefulness.

The ensuing transference stood out in sharp contrast to the almost evangelical atmosphere of our beginning contact, but the conviction of having been forewarned sustained me. First, he showed me how helpless he was. He told me of innumerable instances where he behaved as a perfect fool. Detail after detail was spun out with monotonous fastidiousness to demonstrate his superb talent for self-defeating and humiliating behavior. Since he seemed to make tremendous efforts to put himself in shameful situations, no one felt any sympathy toward him or offered to extricate him from the dilemmas he created. He succeeded in irritating everybody and I could feel similar annoyance. In fact, he had such a maddening quality that, at times, I felt like shaking some sense into him. However, I would then recall that the patient had hinted that I might have some such reaction so my curiosity was able to submerge my negative reactions, which I was able to clarify as a mixture of impatience and a wish to get rid of him. He described himself as a "perfect jerk"; silently, I was inclined to agree with him and yet I knew that I was, at the same time, dealing with an intriguing and complex person who had something within him that was both fascinating and worthwhile.

In my office, he not only described but also demonstrated some aspects of his silly behavior. It took the form of being extremely dependent and demanding, but his attempts were fruitless. The questions he asked were basically questions without answers or of such a nature that he knew that I would not or could not answer. For example, he would ask me many personal questions, even wanting to know about the minute details of my sexual life, although he was sophisticated enough to know that there was no chance whatsoever of a response. In a similar self-defeating fashion, he would demand to know how he should conduct himself in certain situations, wanting me to explain many things to him, even what he meant by a certain statement. He demanded that I guide his conduct and even asked me to dictate what he should *feel* on specific occasions. In other words, he was trying to lure me into doing what he had criticized his former therapists for doing, that is, to take over complete control of his life. He also seemed to want to construct a relationship where he could fend me off and attack me if I were to give into his demands.

At times, I found his demands amusing because they were so flamboyant that I did not feel any compunction to become involved. On the other hand, I sensed that beneath his "ridiculousness" he was, in fact, making a poignant appeal, one that he had to mask by facetiousness and silliness, since to face his overwhelming needs and what he considered to be the inevitability of frustration would have been unbearably painful.

The patient did not expect me to respond. He tolerated analytic silence extremely well. In fact, he expected it and would have been surprised if I had responded. He also expected that I would make fun of him or be sarcastic, but deep down within himself he did not actually believe I would react in such a fashion. However, he firmly believed that eventually I would not want to have anything further to do with him and would ask him to leave, as had many of his former therapists.

His futile demands were not too difficult to tolerate. His odor, which had been so pervasive during the first interview, had disappeared entirely for the time being. Slowly, he gave up asking for advice and knowledge and began attacking analysis because it was "fraudulent and inept." The content of his attack was devastating and cruel, but his affect was not; instead, he still continued playing the fool.

At times, he spoke in such a low voice that he was inaudible. Often his words were so garbled that he would be virtually unintelligible. Most frequently, however, his associations consisted mainly of crude, predominantly anal obscenities. The latter were either directed toward me or spread all over, not being attached to any particular person.

To illustrate the extremes he would go to in order to appear foolish or provocative, he once brought in a lengthy magazine article on woman's liberation and spent the entire session reading it to me.

Interspersed with such activities were what might be considered grandiose, hypomanic moments when he would lecture to me about the principles of psychoanalysis. Now he did not impress me as being astute and sensitive, as he had at the beginning of treatment. He also reviled me for being a bad analyst, or more precisely, not as good an analyst as he was, since he had the power of extrasensory perception and could by intuition penetrate deeply into another person's mind. He also had an uncanny ability to predict the future, usually catastrophic events such as earthquakes and airplane crashes.

After having soared for some time in a hypomanic swirl, he returned to obscenities. I was momentarily taken by surprise at the end of a session when he suddenly turned toward me and shouted: "How long are you going to put up with this garbage and shit?"

I did not feel, however, that he really wanted me to stop him. I realized that he had provoked many former analysts by such behavior and I did not know which had been more offensive to them, his "strewing of garbage" or his megalomanic pretensions. I do not believe that I felt uncomfortable with such material.

Gradually, the patient's attacks and demanding questions changed their form and caused me states of momentary extreme discomfort. He began questioning my reasons for everything I did. For example, he would want to know why I wore a particular suit of a specific color. He commented every time I moved in my chair. If I coughed, he would want to know why I was being defensive, what it was in his material that caused me to react. He called attention to every aspect of my behavior, making me feel constrained and at times immobile.

Since this patient, I have noted similar patterns in patients suffering from characterological problems. This patient became especially irksome when he demanded to know *why* I made an interpretation rather than paying any attention to its content. When I pointed out how he ignored what I said, he would return to his old habit of reviling me or once again continue with his crude, fecal obscenities.

I realized finally that my discomfort was due to the fact that I felt emotionally paralyzed. I also concluded that this was a countertransference reaction in the sense that I was reacting to the patient's projections. He had a need to control me and I was reacting to this need.

Patients suffering from ego defects often fear loss of control through being overwhelmed by chaotic feelings or being assaulted by a cruel and intrusive outer world. Parallel to this fear is the equally disturbing feeling that they are complete automatons, subjugated and controlled by outside forces. They feel themselves helpless and vulnerable, without autonomy or a separate identity.

Since treating this patient, I have noted a similar trend to render me immobile in many patients who have characterological problems. As I have stated, I reacted at first with discomfort and found him difficult and trying. I was, at the time, particularly puzzled because I believed I had been comfortable when he was "strewing me with garbage" and hurling fecal obscenities at me, and now he was only firing questions. Once I understood that I felt my freedom and autonomy to be hampered, I relaxed and did not let his "prosecuting attorney" type of questions interfere with my usual way of doing things. I stopped being on my guard and did not react to his criticisms. Instead, I regarded them as unavoidable projections.

I will return to the subject of the analyst's countertransference reactions to feeling intruded upon by the patient. (See section on Technical Considerations and Countertransference Problems.) For the present, I wish to explain why in some instances the patient's behavior is no longer threatening, once understood, as I believe occurred in my patient, and in other cases, the problem continues, even though the analyst is very well able to comprehend how the patient is displaying an essential aspect of his psychopathology. Briefly, if the patient confines his attempts to constrain the analyst or to make him give up his role as analyst to verbal associations and does not really expect him to respond to his demands, the analyst can resolve his discomfort by converting it into analytic curiosity. If, on the other hand, the patient intrudes upon the analytic setting by insisting upon the analyst's participation in the content of his material, then the situation may become unmanageable. For instance, some patients demand that the analyst intercede for them in a real life situation in a way that would be completely disruptive to analysis. One patient demanded that I persuade his angry homosexual partner to resume relations with him. (See section on Technical Considerations and Countertransference Problems for more detailed examples.) This patient, however, would have been disappointed if I had responded directly. He was, in a way, testing me to see if I could survive both his worthless, hateful inner self, "garbage," and his counterphobic assault which was designed to protect him from the fundamental fear of being overwhelmed and submerged by me.

Patients whose self-representations are poorly integrated and who feel vulnerable, unloved and rejected suffer from painfully low self-esteem. They are full of self-hatred and feel assaulted (one patient called it "crushed") by hostile, constricting introjects.

My patient described himself as being full of "stinking, putrefying pus" and as long as such putrescence was festering inside of him, it would continue undermining any steps he might take to improve his own life. He saw his self-representation as being poorly delineated, since he often could not distinguish where his person ended and the external world began. He also felt that there were infiltrating forces inside of him that were eating away and controlling what might perhaps be the healthy aspects of his personality. Consequently, as the analysis demonstrated, he had to project the hateful, dangerous aspects of the self along with their controlling infiltrating qualities into me.

The reference to "stinking, putrefying pus" acquired special interest because, while the patient was spewing forth invectives and obscenities with the greatest intensity, he once again began emitting an offensive odor. Although, as I have explained, I had little difficulty in tolerating his verbal attacks, the stench again became unbearable. I finally confronted him with the disruptive quality of is odor, both for myself and other patients, and he took remedial measures.

Since then, I have had several other patients who emitted offensive body odors and in each instance it was a manifestation of a depreciated self-image which the patient was trying to bring to the surface for reasons similar to the ones formulated here. I also found that some patients attempt to hide what they consider objectionable parts of the self with strong perfume. Here, however, they also reveal the "foul" part of the personality because the perfume calls attention to odors, and to some people is as objectionable as what they seek to cover up.

One may question the technical correctness, from an analytic viewpoint, of prohibiting the patient from an olfactory revelation of a part of the self. In this instance, technical consideration receded into the background since I and my other patients could not stand the smell. Perhaps another analyst with a higher threshold might have been able to work in such a context without imposing prohibitions. (This topic will also be elaborated upon in the technical section). For the moment, I may summarize the situation by emphasizing that since the patient's odor bothered me, it had succeeded in penetrating into the world of my reality perceptions, and I could no longer deal with it as an aspect of the patient's projection of fantasies of his inner world. The effects of his odor went beyond the confines of our analytic session and extended into those of other patients.

Still, I was quite aware of how necessary it was for this hateful material to surround and be projected into me. By surviving this projection and the coercion inherent in its content, I was able to "detoxify" it. (This subject also demands expansion and will be elaborated in the next section on Therapeutic Regression.) Now, I wish to emphasize that some new understanding was achieved which, I believe, is extremely important for our understanding of the development of many narcissistic transferences and their course during therapy and which applies to many cases suffering from characterological problems with immense disturbances of the self-representation.

The patient's material took a gradual turn and instead of heaping excrement on me he began talking, peculiarly enough, in a sentimental fashion about the composition of such excrement. He was haunted by the melody of a fraternity song where one of the chief refrains was "a diamond in the dung." He felt that hidden in all these vile feces was something of value.

He had an especially memorable dream where he was giving me a huge oil painting which was not only absolutely worthless, but a travesty of art. I had once defensively commented to him—when I was reacting adversely to his efforts at coercing me—that he was indulging in a travesty of free association. In any case, this painting was absolutely worthless and in the dream I was accepting the fact of its lack of worth. At this point, he felt anxious and awakened. We both felt puzzled about his anxiety since from a superficial viewpoint it seemed as if I were simply accepting his giving me unacceptable parts of himself, in this instance a combination of his artistic self and the general worthlessness he felt. These were psychic elements he had to get rid of by projection, and in the dream it seemed that all I was doing was making myself available for his projections. Rather than creating anxiety this should have been comforting and allowed restful sleep to continue as occurs with successful wish-fulfillment dreams. Instead, this dream had the disruptive effect of a nightmare.

Although I said nothing I found it peculiar and interesting that he selected a painting to depict worthlessness and "putrescent" feelings. He had in the past been able to select all types of objects to represent such negative feelings. All of these objects were cleverly picked and represented appropriate metaphors. Art was carefully excluded from his associations since this was the one area where he felt he had some talent. The artistic aspects of his self-representation seemed to be the only qualities he valued about himself.

The patient's association emphasized that it was my acceptance of the worthlessness of his painting that specifically bothered him.

Now, I must digress from the patient's associations and report some vague feelings of uneasiness that had been developing within me for several months prior to this dream. I knew that the feelings of worthlessness he had projected into me would ultimately be to his advantage. Still, there were hints in his material that indicated that in my allowing such a projection simply by not interfering with its spontaneous development, I was also depriving him of something essential. Often there was considerable wit to his abrasive material. Frequently it seemed to have an organization that might even be considered artistic; it was not always gross. Even though he was trying very hard to degrade me, I did not feel degraded. This may, in part, have been due to the analytic setting, but, paradoxically, not only did I not feel degraded but, at times, I felt enhanced. This was not due to any new insights since I had none, but, on occasion, without having any reason for doing so that I was aware of, I reacted as if something pleasant had happened to me. This was particularly puzzling since it vacillated with the uneasiness I also described.

The patient's associations to his dream made me recall these feelings. He continued his associations and concluded that the picture in the dream contained a valuable masterpiece underneath the poor surface painting. This thought was connected to his anxiety and he reported that he was afraid that I either would get rid of the painting as garbage since I would be unaware of its true worth, or if I decided to explore further by trying to erase the covering painting, I would unwittingly destroy the underlying masterpiece.

These associations enabled me to explain the dilemma—a transient but, to me, important dilemma that I had been experiencing. Although the psychic processes underlying the resolution of the transference projection are complicated and have to be understood in the context of regression (see section on Technical Considerations and Countertransference Problems), I was reacting on the basis of metaphorically seeing myself as a garbage disposal unit who feared destroying something valuable that may have been projected along with the garbage. My feeling of enhancement, I believe, was related to responding to the valued aspect of the self, a rudimentary, if you will, embryonic core that was put into my psyche. I am well aware of the concrete way I am expressing myself, but the patient and I were thinking in such terms. These metaphors can be reduced to such psychic processes as fusion with corresponding introjective and projective mechanisms which will be discussed in the sections that are to follow.

The patient began to report intense feelings of inferiority, and he attributed to me all of the abilities which he valued and longed for himself. On several occasions he did something successful, and then became frightened that he would spoil his abilities by putting them into practice. He felt that they were safer when seen as my abilities. He believed he could succeed only if I were to accompany him everywhere. Next, he became able to let himself succeed by thinking that he was imitating me, and that his abilities were really mine. This was striking because it even applied to particular artistic knowledge and skills about which I know nothing.

His feeling was that I, and not he, could protect the valued knowledge and skills from the "garbage" that he also projected into me, and therefore his talents were safe only if he thought of them as residing in me and thought of himself as borrowing them imitatively. When he did this he felt an enhancement of his self-esteem similar to that which I had felt when he began project-ing valued parts of himself into me.

Resolution of the transference in this case and in other cases of severe character disorder depends upon the synthesis of the valued and the destruc-tive aspects of the self, and their integration into the total ego. This is experi-enced subjectively as painful acknowledgement that neither the patient nor the analyst are omnipotently perfect. But this is mitigated by the recognition that neither of us is omnipotently destructive either. This is a long and slow process, and the patient I have described has made some progress in this direction although this progress has been uneven and there have also been periods of painful regression.

Since then, I have been able to recall other cases where the transferences have taken a similar course. A scientist in his middle twenties had many paranoid symptoms. At times, he would decompensate to the point where he would become completely delusional and require hospitalization. As is true with some paranoid patients, he would also have periods of astute rationality and display considerable charm. My experience with patients similar to this one led me to conclude that they often have a considerable amount of what might be called a relaxed psychic organization in spite of their stubborn rejection of reality in order to cling to their delusions.

During treatment this patient had a delusional episode which he acted out. He heard voices instructing him to put a plan into effect that would end all wars. At the same time, the Mafia felt this would cut into their profits so they had made arrangements to kill him. He tried to contact the F.B.I., several senators and finally the president of the university which employed him. He sought all of these persons for both protection and to augment his plan to save the world. After a short period of hospitalization which did not necessitate missing a single analytic session he reintegrated and from that point on con-tinued to be eminently rational for a long time.

For reasons which are not relevant for my purpose of discussing certain features of the narcissistic, in this instance psychotic transference, the patient, after one more year of treatment had another psychotic episode, but this one was confined to the transference and kept in the treatment rather than being acted out in the external world. He became extremely agitated because he knew the Mafia (with a name such as mine, this organization often shows up in patients' fantasies or delusions) was paying me $50,000 a year to literally pick his brains, that is, to take them away from him and rob him of his power. I chuckled—I could not help myself—and wondered aloud why the Mafia had to pay such a large sum of money to do something I was obliged to do for nothing—rather, that his fee had already included such a service. At first, the patient was bewildered; obviously my reply was most unexpected. Then he burst out laughing and jocularly shouted that I really enjoyed picking his brains.

The patient understood that I was making myself available for his projections. My experience has taught me that these so-called sick patients understand the psychoanalytic viewpoint very quickly. The session now took a serious turn and he began talking about his delusion which by his very examination had now been transformed into a fantasy. He saw himself projecting hatred, a hatred based upon a need for perfection and one which caused him to be devastatingly self-critical and to hate himself for constantly falling short of his omnipotent ideal. He was either a Titan or nothing. He also recognized that such strivings only interfered with realizing his potential; therefore, he attributed his self-hatred to me. When he was dominated by his delusions, he believed that I hated him, wanted to destroy him and considered him despicable and worthless. Still, I wanted to pick his brains, indicating that with all his violence and destruction, there was something I valued, that is, the brains I wanted to pick. He realized that his fantasies (his brains) were of value in the analysis and he gradually adopted a similar viewpoint toward aspects of his earlier life that he had previously feared so much that he had to project them.

The patient discussed and elaborated the content of his delusion, specifically picking his brains, for many months. He repeatedly referred to his mother who apparently did not allow him to be an individual in his own right. From what I gathered, she could relate to him only as an appendage of herself. She died in a state hospital when he was four years old. The point the patient was emphasizing was that he had to carefully protect any integration he achieved from his mother's assault and that she felt destroyed by her son's psychic structuralization, a structuralization which would apparently impede her ability to project hated parts of herself into him. The patient now revealed it was this *rudimentary organized self* that he had projected into me. Picking his brains also had a positive connotation; I was picking them in order to preserve them. Nesting in his cosmic destructiveness was an embryo—a potential for development that had to be protected. Although I might be his persecutor, I was still entrusted with a vulnerable, valuable structured part of the self. He referred to me as a Swiss bank or safety deposit vault.

He revealed that his paranoid projections served him in many ways. Not only was he projecting hatred, self-hatred and unacceptable parts of himself into the outer world, but he was also projecting a rudimentary organized self in order to preserve it from a devastatingly destructive maternal introject.

This need was enacted in what was initially a transference psychosis. However, once the patient understood that he not only needed a persecutor, he also realized that the persecutor was not just a persecutor, but someone who was being entrusted with a structured part of the self. In relation to this latter projection, the destructive persecutor still resided within himself in the form of the raging maternal introject.

This is another example of the transference of a patient suffering from severe character pathology. When the patient decompensated, he was no different from any paranoid schizophrenic, at least in terms of his surface behavior. When it was possible to study the content of his transference projections, one could recognize various positive adaptive components as well as his need to get rid of self-depreciatory attitudes. Imbricated within these attitudes was a rudimentary, organized self which was vulnerable to an assaultive maternal introject that would not permit individualization. In fact, his need for omnipotent projection was in part an attempt to protect this delicate structure from an all-powerful, vindictive mother.

Another patient, a lawyer in his mid-thirties, was in some respects similar to the commercial artist. After eight months of treatment he developed a paranoid transference, that is, he felt I was the cause of all his difficulties. Still, he was not particularly bitter and it was quite apparent that he valued his sessions. He was never late nor had he ever missed an appointment. His dependence became more manifest when it was necessary for me to cancel sessions, as occurred during vacations. Nevertheless, he raved and ranted and blamed the treatment for all his difficulties.

Finally, the patient decided to terminate treatment, reasoning that if seeing me caused him problems, all he had to do was to stop seeing me. It was remarkable, however, that it took nearly a year before he reached this seemingly obvious conclusion. He had been offered an extremely lucrative position in a distant city. In spite of the paranoid content of his associations, his departure from treatment was friendly and warm.

I had heard nothing about him for several years when a colleague told me that the patient had returned to Chicago, presumably for a short visit, and while here he had a psychotic breakdown. The reasons for his decompensation were related to seeing his mother once again, but they are not relevant here.

His psychosis, however, was very interesting. He felt that everything of value had been wrested away from him. My colleague had learned that after the patient stopped treatment for several years he had a delusion that he was carrying me on his shoulder, sometimes the right shoulder, and other times the left, in the shape of a bird. This bird would from time to time hurl imprecations at him, but the patient also acknowledged that there was some comfort in his presence.

For some reason, which was never well understood, the bird flew away. The patient first experienced overwhelming panic and then developed delusions that his "insides were running," that there were creatures crawling through his body with the power of tiny atom bombs, periodically exploding and leaving hollow empty gaps within him. Ultimately he would be reduced to a "festering void." He had viewed the bird, in spite of its obscene and derogatory language, as a protector. He also compared it to an eagle possessing strength and, as he put it, organized and efficient.

For an equally unknown reason, the bird returned, and the patient completely reintegrated. My colleague was able to ascertain that not only did this bird serve as a repository for all the self-destructive hatred he felt within him, but it embodied all that was good as well. The patient's initial complaint emphasized that he had lost the only valuable thing he had ever possessed. He had learned to trust this bird and he felt that beneath its unkempt and ugly exterior (the bird seemed to have some characteristics of a raven) was a strong, solid scaffold, an emotional structure capable of many achievements.

These three patients had what might be considered classical examples of narcissistic transferences. They were severely disturbed persons who could decompensate into a disruptive psychosis. Consequently, it is not surprising that their transference projections would be consonant with their primitive orientations. They projected hateful and hating parts of the self onto the analyst. But within all this hatred was a part of the self that had the potential to achieve good things for the patient. Resolution of the transference depended upon synthesis of the hated and the valuable parts of the self that were projected into the analyst, and reinternalization of the now more manageable product of the synthesis.

Thus, the analytic process protects these valued parts of the self. Narcissistically fixated patients also fear that whatever good they possess will be devoured by hateful, destructive introjects. The transference results in a projection of both bad and good into the analyst. The patient, because of the security and reliability provided by analysis, has faith in the analyst's ability to keep bad and good introjects separate, a faith he does not have in himself.

Freud described the sublimatory process as consisting of a desexualization of sexual impulses by having such impulses pass through the subject's ego before being once more directed to external objects (Freud, 1914B). Similarly, in the narcissistic transference, the patient projects his rudimentary organized self into the analyst. When he once more incorporates it as his own, there has been a realignment of various parts of the self that permit further development.

I believe the latter is a special feature of narcissistic transferences that has received very little emphasis and a feature that may cause us to view such patients and their projections somewhat more optimistically in terms of potential for growth and treatability.

THERAPEUTIC REGRESSION

Since the type of treatment being considered here is analytic, no distinctions are being made between therapeutic and analytic regressions. I acknowledge that regression in other types of psychotherapy may take an entirely different course from that which will be described.

The essence of the analytic process is the formation of transference as the patient allows himself to regress. The analysis provides a setting in which the patient can regress in comparative safety. How this is accomplished is in itself a fascinating subject, one which has been referred to in general terms, such as the constant reliability of the setting (Winnicott, 1947, 1954), its intrinsic supportive elements (Boyer and Giovacchini, 1967), and other elements emphasizing the secure atmosphere that analysis creates apart from the structuralizing potential of interpretation. As stated, this subject deserves much further discussion (see section on Therapeutic Considerations and Countertransference Problems), but for the moment, I wish to explore further the consequences of the analytic setting, that is, the therapeutic regression.

The same question can be raised concerning regression as was raised about transference in general, that is, are there essentially different types of regression—one, so to speak, characteristic of patients with fairly intact egos such as those attributed to the transference neuroses and another type of regression characteristic of patients suffering from severe psychopathology such as character disorders, which include the psychoses. Is there a fundamental, qualitative difference between the regression of patients suffering from different types of psychopathology?

One can argue against making such qualitative distinctions if one accepts that transferences, narcissistic and nonnarcissistic, are essentially similar in nature. Then the ego state that corresponds to the transference projection, a regressed ego state, can be distinguished from other regressed states only in quantitative terms.

Here I wish to explore some elements which I believe are common to all regressed ego states, but which are more clearly discernible in patients suffering from relatively severe psychopathology. Furthermore, it may be these characteristics of regression that are the most germane in determining therapeutic outcome as well as the capacity to utilize the analytic interaction.

Most patients present themselves with some degree of unity and cohesion. The more disturbed patient achieves only a precarious and defensive unity, a superstructure which hovers over the rest of his personality in an awkward and unharmonious fashion, Winnicott's (1960) false self. Thus, one would expect that the less disturbed patient not only has greater cohesion and unity but one that is more representative of his true self. In either situation, there will be some defensive element to, at least, the patient's superficial organization.

This organization, a pseudo-organization which involves superficial layers of the personality in severely disturbed patients, is lost once regression begins. True, in some instances, the patient may not feel secure enough to relax his tight controls; he may even accentuate them, and then one is faced with what has been called a defense transference. I believe this situation has to take into account the analyst's countertransference as a causative and aggravating factor (see section on Therapeutic Considerations and Countertransference) but, for the moment, I wish to pursue the course of regression as it occurs when relatively unobstructed.

Regression and Fragmentation

Regression leads to fragmentation of the ego and this can have its effects both within the analysis and the outside world. Such splitting of the ego can often be dramatically manifested by its effects on the identity sense.

For example, the lawyer patient to whom I have referred, described himself as a person with low self-esteem who sometimes did not know whether he was "fish or fowl." In general, however, he saw himself as occupying a particular role in society both professionally and socially, but within these spheres he felt he was operating at a very low level.

Shortly after beginning treatment, he began to pursue many activities frenetically. He developed an intense interest in art and music, he began to read books on anthropology, enrolled in an adult evening course, and took tennis, golf and judo lessons. He also became involved in perfecting his dancing.

I learned about these pursuits in a piecemeal fashion. In fact, his associations during the initial weeks of therapy were practically incomprehensible. He never stayed on a subject; he seemed to be jumping all over in a rambling, incoherent, disconnected fashion. I had a view of a disjointed person whose parts were not integrated or synchronized with each other. He even walked in an awkward, uncoordinated, clumsy fashion, in spite of the athletic programs he had undertaken.

One day he mentioned the décor of his apartment and then, as usual, moved on to another subject. Approximately one week later, he again described his apartment but quite differently from what I believed I had previously heard. Then, several days later, he again talked of where he lived and this time I was certain that he was describing either a different apartment or one that had been completely redecorated in an astonishingly short period of time. My curiosity forced me to ask him about the rapidly changing panorama of his dwelling.

I was surprised to learn that he was talking about different apartments. He was renting new apartments but never relinquishing the old ones. Each one had a particular motif which he would use for a specific purpose. One was the "scholar" apartment, a place where he kept his books and which he used primarily as a study and library. Then he had an apartment where he gave dinner parties, his "host" apartment. He had a special place whose use was limited to seducing girls. He even had an apartment that was primarily devoted to living in, that is, he slept there and used it for no other particular purpose. All in all, in a period of six weeks he had accumulated ten apartments. Naturally, without his mother's wealth, he would not have been able to support this expensive type of dissociation.

He was able to continue functioning at work. He also had a "professional or vocational" apartment, since he could fit his job into one of the many compartments he had constructed for himself. On my couch, after the initial stage of disconnectedness, he enacted different roles. Again, there was no continuity nor could I predict which part he would assume during any particular session.

In contrast to the low esteem he displayed during the beginning of treatment and the blurred pictures he had of what might be called a general self, he now thought of himself as a very distinct person. He also viewed himself in a somewhat exalted fashion; there was both a hypomanic and slightly omnipotent flavor to his feelings about himself. However, he could only deal with a very segmented facet of his personality and seemed to work very hard to restrict himself to a narrow frame of reference.

It slowly dawned on me that these roles served at least two purposes. Generally, they served to compensate for his basically diffuse and poorly organized ego with its amorphous and loosely structured self-representation. Still, as far as I could determine, he had not used such defenses in recent times. Later, I learned that as a very young child he would vigorously assume certain fantasied roles and because of his commitment to the part he played, alarmed his playmates but never his mother. After analysis began, he could use these roles in another way, that is, protectively and defensively against the fear of being swallowed in the regressive process that had been set in motion.

This patient's striking and bizarre behavior, I believe, illustrates an important feature that is characteristic of regression in the treatment of all patients, but which is especially manifest in patients suffering from character disorders. This patient revived defenses that he frequently used during early childhood, defenses that were designed to maintain his identity even though it was a fragmented identity. *Insofar as one is dealing with ego defects, that is, structural pathology, changes in the ego and its subsystems are more prominent during regression than is instinctual regression.* Thus, regression brings into focus certain types of infantile adaptations which are currently manifest, although they may be used in a covert fashion so that they are not easily discernible in the patient's daily life or in his initial presentation to the therapist.

The above discussion is a restatement of the familiar concept that regression recapitulates infantile states of organization, Freud's (1900) formulation of formal regression. Here, I am attempting to identify what Freud would have called the topographical element more precisely. *The study of patients suffering from character disorders illustrates that therapeutic regression is characterized by further fragmentation of the self-representation.*

Whatever unity the patient may have achieved is, to some extent, disrupted by the regressive process. Splitting mechanisms operate in the regression of such patients, as they do in all regressed states. Since moving backwards, so to speak, along the developmental path always involves some loss of coherent organization, some separation of unified elements and various degrees of splitting must occur in the regressions of all analytic patients.

The regression of the patients discussed here illustrates that splitting is more than just a manifestation of a disintegrating process; it also has an adaptive component, even though such adaptations were more appropriate to the early traumatic environment than to the present. The early environment continues to exist within the psyche in the form of threatening introjects. I believe that this is a significant feature of analytic regression. *The regressive process involves a loss of integration but in spite of its disintegrative features, the elements of the regression are still adaptive and serve the patient in a definitive fashion.* Perhaps the adaptive effect of regression is responsible for its being bearable and manageable.

Patients demonstrate that their adaptations are pathological insofar as they restrict their capacities to adapt to the present external world and consequently, do not work as they should. At this point, it becomes germane to comment about how the concept of defense and adaptation are being used here and how these concepts are important to further our understanding of analytic regression.

Regression, Defense, and Adaptation

Defense has been traditionally described in terms of intrapsychic conflicts (Freud, 1894, 1896). Freud enumerated various defense mechanisms that were principally designed to maintain the repression of unacceptable instinctual impulses consisting of erotic or hostile feelings. These familiar concepts have proven useful to our understanding and therapy of psychoneurotic patients.

Freud's traditional concept of defense cannot be extensively applied for the understanding of the narcissistic neuroses. These patients do not have discrete symptoms attributable to intrapsychic conflict. As stated, their pathology is mainly structural and their difficulties consist primarily in coping with the outer world. Of course, every patient has some structural pathology and some element of intrapsychic conflict, but, as Freud, (1924, 1924a) emphasized, patients classified as narcissistic neuroses have problems that are mainly related to difficulties between the ego and the outer world. Their adaptations are often bizarre, and they cannot master problems of reality either because they misperceive reality or because their level of integration is low and, therefore, they do not have the executive apparatus which would enable them to deal with complex situations.

These patients develop techniques to compensate for their adaptive failure. One could consider these techniques defensive, although if we do, we extend the concept of defense beyond a psychic mechanism that maintains repression of unacceptable impulses. These techniques are unique to each individual and, as mentioned, brought to the fore during analytic regression.

Also as stated, these characterological defenses, as they may aptly be termed, were constructed and used extensively to cope with the traumatic infantile environment. In order to orient oneself during the therapeutic regression in a fashion that is consonant with such archaic defenses one has to construct an ambience that will be in resonance with them. By transference projection, the patient attempts to create a setting that will support his regressed ego state.

The patient constructs the analytic ambiance (transference) in terms of his familiar infantile reality. The patient, however, has also constructed the outer world on the basis of his needs and adaptations, and the regressed state in therapy recapitulates this reconstruction.

First, one must expand upon what is meant by the statement that the patient constructs his reality according to his needs and adaptive techniques. Then the relevance of such a construction to analytic regression has to be understood further.

The child is raised in a specific environment which widens as he develops, but which retains certain distinctive features. Whatever the traumatic or non-traumatic features of this environment, the child learns to adjust by using techniques that can be considered either pathological or nonpathological. The latter judgment often depends upon how useful and efficient these techniques are in dealing with an external world that is generally shared.

In any case, everyone has his *private reality* based upon early infantile experiences. The less in tune this private reality is with the reality that most people acknowledge, the more relevant it is to what we call psychopathology. The disparity between one's private reality and objective reality determines how maladjusted one is and how needful one feels, and often leads to seeking psychotherapy.

As long as a patient can remain in his private world, usually by finding a supportive segment in the general reality, he may be able to use restrictive and restricted defensive techniques. For example, persons whose early life has been dominated by assault and violence may find the life of an army combatant one in which they can thrive. Their need to express violence and maintain paranoid vigilance could find suitable expression and usefulness during combat. Adjustment problems become manifest during peace, so these patients have to continue waging their private wars.

Once the regressive process is well under way, the analytic atmosphere often becomes taut. The reasons for this permit us to understand how the construction of a private reality is relevant to analytic regression. The patient creates an arena where a perpetual contest seems to be raging. The analyst feels attacked, not necessarily in a direct fashion such as being judged stupid, incompetent or worthless. These usually are obvious projections of the way the patient views himself, as emphasized in some of the clinical examples cited earlier. Frequently, however, the patient creates an atmosphere where everything seems heavy and tense without any coherently directed demands, complaints or deprecations.

Such situations can be understood as specific forms of projections which are characteristic of basic psychopathology. In other words, the patient puts something objectionable from within himself into the analyst, as has frequently been discussed. However, one often discovers that in addition to projecting, *the patient has created a psychoanalytic ambiance that is an approximate reproduction of the infantile traumatic environment*. This is an environment that he has learned to cope with.

Is this type of regression to be distinguished from what occurs in patients who have been diagnosed as suffering from lesser degrees of psychopathology? True, in the psychoneurotic patient, one is usually dealing with the transference of infantile feelings, discrete impulses, and the general setting maintains a fairly even mood. It is not, as a rule, a heavy or oppressive ambiance. On the other hand, by virtue of the fact that the patient has achieved a fair degree of psychic integration, one can infer that his early environment was not particularly traumatic. During his regression he also produces his early environment, but insofar as it was not significantly disturbing, it is not noticeable and not usually different from the general analytic atmosphere. This viewpoint emphasizes that differences in therapeutic regressions are differences in degree and not in kind.

The regressed state just described may in some instances be uncomfortable, and possibly stormy, but it still represents an equilibrium. As stated, the patient creates an environment, albeit traumatic, but one which is familiar to him and, because of a variey of characterological defenses, he can maintain some degree of psychic organization. This state, however, changes as the analysis progresses and the regression deepens.

Further Regressive Disorganization

Increasing disorganization from the above state of relative equilibrium occurs in varying degrees, in my opinion, in all analytic patients. However, in some instances, perhaps where there is considerable psychic integration to begin with, it may not be noticeable, prolonged or intense.

I believe I can best describe the state of regressed disorganization by briefly presenting a clinical example.

The patient, a middel-aged business man, sought analysis for a variety of reasons, but mainly because he felt he did not fit in the current scene. He had a fairly structured life; his work determined his routine and his life style seemed to be well established. Nevertheless, he was aware of inner emptiness and, although married and a father, he did not derive satisfaction from any relationship.

He had been extremely successful and had amassed a small fortune. He attributed his success to his overwhelming drive and capacity to plunge forward, not to succeed necessarily, but to keep himself constantly in a state of frenzied action. He needed a battleground. Relaxation was something unknown to him, and when he contemplated slowing down his tempo, he felt frightened and confused.

The reason for seeking treatment was a recent coronary and his physician's insistence that he lead a calmer life. It was interesting that the patient did not believe he was afraid of dying; he was, however, terrified of the idea of living a quiet, peaceful life. Now, because of his cardiac condition, he might not be capable of continuing at his old pace.

For our purpose, the significant factor in his analysis was his attempt to create a struggle with me similar to the battles he used to wage with his competitors. The situation in the consultation room differed from the one he had described in the external world. I had received the impression that he was unusually astute, clever and maneuverable in his business relationships, and, indeed, his witty and comprehensive descriptions confirmed this impression as did the success and reputation he had achieved. With me, however, he was coarse, clumsy, and obvious. He even seemed stupid, and rather than giving the impression of a masterful, well-coordinated opponent, he appeared as he described in a fantasy, as a punch-drunk boxer who had tremendous physical strength and was impervious, even oblivious, to the blows that were heaped upon him. He had no skill or finesse.

He could not hurt anymore and he could survive. This was what he felt about the analysis. If he could not fend me off, he could, at least, block my blows, but this state of numbness would not lead to progress. Very early in the analysis, after about two months, he whined and complained that he was not getting anywhere, but he still felt the need to defend himself against me. He viewed the analytic process as basically assaultive. There were some similarities in his relationship with me and his relationships in the business world, but in the analysis, he was petulant, obtuse, sometimes vulgar and obscene; in other words, he had regressed.

The patient was raised in extreme poverty during the Depression. His father was a laborer who was unable to provide for his very large family; they received most of their meagre sustenance from Welfare. He recalled his early childhood in a very tough slum area and compared his life in the home with that outside. They were both rough environments where one was being constantly abused or attacked. His attitude had to be one of vigilance and preparedness. In spite of the exigencies of such a setting, he, nevertheless, got along quite well. In fact, he found his own gang and because he was strong and enterprising, was able to achieve a position of prestige and leadership.

The situation he created in the analysis was similar, in my mind, to the childhood environment he had described. He presented himself as a "tough guy," crude, obscene, and belligerent. This was in sharp contrast to the cultured, well-mannered, although aggressive person he also was.

I found that, in addition to being cast in a role of a person who both abandoned and exploited him (clearly a replica of his mother), I was being made a representative of the oppressive jungle of the ghetto in which he spent his childhood. He had managed to pervade the analytic atmosphere with such a dead-end feeling that I felt both intrigue and tension, and when I was most immersed in his world, I shared his despair.

The latter point requires explanation. I felt despair when I was unaware of how I was involved. Gradually, I began to realize that, in some way, he was making me into an antagonist. He was viewing me as someone who would attack him, someone toward whom he would have to be vigilant and defensive. He attempted in many ways to provoke me into attacking him; specifically, he tried to get me to argue with him. He was very skillful in raising questions and focusing upon topics that would easily draw one into a debate.

In spite of his skill in bringing up intriguing and provocative issues, I felt no desire whatsoever to be drawn into an argument. This surprised me because it is contrary to my natural inclination.

Although the patient was demanding and belligerent and insisted on arguing with me, it was, nevertheless, easy to remain in an analytic frame of reference. I surmised that he did not really basically care whether I reacted or not. My presence and surroundings were sufficient, and it gradually dawned upon me that in his mind he had converted me and my office into a shabby and dangerous slum. I reacted to this but instead of being provoked by him, I felt a heavy sense of oppression and sorrow.

Once I realized the reason I felt the way I did, that is, the meaning of the impact that the situation had upon me, I was able to obtain relief by making interpretations. I emphasized that he had created a situation in analysis where he felt he could survive, not comfortably, since no one could under such circumstances, but still survive because it was a familiar situation—one where, in a sense, he had been trained to deal with the exigencies of his particular world. This was related to many of the character defenses that he was now exhibiting before me.

At first, the patient reacted in a characteristic fashion and defended himself against what he had construed as an assaultive interpretation. He denied everything I said and considered all my explanations worthless. He spent many hours, as I might have anticipated, logically dissecting my interpretations in order to disprove them.

He pursued a ruthless demolition course, but again I felt no need to fight back. In fact, the more he argued, the more secure I felt about the accuracy of my observations. Gradually, the patient started to contradict his own arguments; he presented arguments and counterarguments. However, his counterarguments, which supported my interpretations became more and more convincing and his refutations increasingly weaker. Without any reinforcement from me, he finally accepted what I had said.

He became increasingly agitated during his unsuccessful attempt to refute me. He found himself particularly paralyzed with waves of anxiety and became completely incapacitated in his daily life. He had to stop working and stayed in bed all day. He did, however, keep his daily appointments with me.

He felt weak, helpless, and vulnerable. What dismayed him most was his inability to carry on routine activities; such pedestrian tasks as washing, shaving, and dressing became inordinately burdensome. If he were an adolescent, I would not have hesitated to classify him as an identity diffusion syndrome, such as Erikson (1959) has described.

Disturbances in the identity sense manifest themselves in many ways. As he stated, he was "losing his grip." He no longer knew what the purpose of his existence was. He saw his present business preoccupation as meaningless. Everything he had once valued was now empty and shallow. He did not know where he fit and in a deeper sense he did not know who he was. He was clearly describing an existential crisis.

At one point, he begged me to hospitalize him, because, as he described, he now had no anchor and was floating away in an inchoate void. He had lost interest in everything—family, friends and work, but instead of apathy and indifference he felt terror.

In spite of his panic, I did not believe that he really wanted to be hospitalized. He gave sufficient hints warning me not to give in to his helplessness. In fact, although on the surface he seemed to be falling apart, emotionally speaking there was still a quality about him that caused me to feel relatively unperturbed about his condition. There was evidence of psychic strength and integration amidst the prevailing chaos.

It became apparent that withdrawal from his usual routine also meant that he was giving up some of his defensive adaptations. He had virtually given up all of his business activities, but once the intense phase of anxiety passed, one could detect some satisfaction and a sense of accomplishment in that he no longer felt compelled to maintain the exhaustive pace that characterized his life prior to this deep analytic regression.

His anxiety gradually subsided and he felt that something within him was "emerging." It was as if he were shedding a tight, constricting "skin" and something inside could now develop.

There are, of course, many technically relevant details about this patient that could be profitably discussed, but here I wish to focus upon the course of his regression, a course which I feel is somewhat characteristic of patients in general and those suffering from ego defects in particular. To recapitulate, after settling down in treatment, the patient attempted to create an atmosphere that in many ways resembled his traumatic infantile past. He then regressed further, presumably to a state where his identity was not yet formed. At first, he experienced this situation in a painful, terrifying fashion. He lost his sense of existence and found himself, relatively speaking, without an identity. He was, at the same time, without his usual defenses. He was not able to use his usual adaptive techniques. (See Alexander, 1956, and Winnicott, 1954.)

Even though he seemed to have lost some of his defenses, the world he lived in had also changed. Insofar as he no longer projected his previous inner struggle into it, he did not need to defend himself against it, or at least, against that part of it he had constructed. I sensed with him, as I have with other patients, that to have reacted to his helplessness by trying to rescue him, something which he invited me to do from time to time, would have led to the construction of an environment similar to the one surrounding him when he was attempting to make basic identifications. This, as far as I could reconstruct, was a hostile, depriving environment, but one that would try to take care of him. The attempt, however, was fruitless and the environment was totally inept. In the analysis, he was asking me similarly to try and to *fail* to rescue him. I could clearly feel that any maneuver on my part to do something about his panic was doomed to failure as had happened in childhood and would lead to even greater helplessness and despair, perhaps suicide. *Any direct response on my part could lead to nothing but the recapitulation of early environmental failure.*

The Infantile Environment and The Analytic Ambience

Since the analytic environment was different from the childhood environment, by not being assaultive and threatening it did not support the patient's defenses. If he had, however, succeeded in getting me to respond to his helplessness, then he would have found himself in a situation similar to that of infancy. Again, the regression produced an ambiance corresponding to infantile stages of development; more precisely, he attempted to reproduce such an ambience.

It was fairly easy not to become part of his private reality and not to react aggressively to his provocativeness, or to attempt to rescue him when he expressed helplessness. I believe this was due to the fact that he really did not want me to respond at that particular level. Even when he was extremely anxious and demanding, I still had the feeling that part of him was telling me not to react directly to the content of his demands.

I have noted this same combination of near panic and calm reflection during deep regressions not only in this patient but also in other patients suffering from characterological psychopathology. I have also noted that the more I have succeeded in not representing the incompetent infantile environment, even though the patient may see me as incompetent, the less anxiety the patient experiences, and his capacity for self-observation correspondingly increases.

The question of the analyst's incompetence requires further discussion. Even though the analyst does not respond directly to the content of the patient's associations—and therefore does not become a representative of the depriving past—the patient may still view him as inadequate to meet his needs and generally incompetent. Paradoxically, this often occurs in a setting where the analyst is treated with respect and it is obvious that the patient's confidence in the analysis is well established.

I believe two factors are involved in this seeming paradox. One involves the patient's projections and the other is related to certain developmental changes that are occurring within the patient during the course of treatment.

Regarding the patient's projections, I have found it convenient to consider the transference regression of patients suffering from ego defects as consisting of: 1) the projection of instinctual impulses and introjects, as well as parts of the self, and 2) the construction of an *ambience* which reproduces elements of the infantile past. I believe all transferences involve both components, but in patients suffering from characterological problems, the reconstruction of the childhood environment is easily discernible. In any case, my patient, when seeing me as incompetent, was projecting specific disappointing and therefore disruptive introjects into me as well as certain unacceptable parts of the self-representation. This, in terms of treatment, had a liberating effect. The patient felt relieved because he was able to rid himself of these oppressive aspects of his personality. Quite clearly, he needed to see me in a depreciated fashion and this gave him comfort and stability in spite of his suffering because of the lack of coherence of experience during regression. He could both project, and at the same time, was able to preserve me as an analyst. *The latter was facilitated by my not becoming a part of the environment he was attempting to construct.*

At first, it may be confusing to distinguish between the projection of a feeling and a part of the self and viewing the analytic situation as if it were an aspect of the traumatic past. The distinction becomes most evident if the analyst behaves in a fashion that is consonant with the patient's infantile needs or defenses. Then, the patient often reacts in the same way he once did by feeling hopeless disappointment, since the analyst has become part of the patient's reconstructed environment.

To put the situation more succinctly, *it is the analyst's response that permits the patient to continue projecting introjects, rather than successfully constructing the disappointing environment that is consistent with such a deep regression. If the analyst consistently functions as an analyst, that is, non-judgmentally observing and not anxiously responding, the patient will continue projecting, but will not be able to fixedly reproduce his world. He can maintain such a world only when the analyst is willing to participate in it.*

Thus, it becomes understandable that the patient can hate the analyst because he does not fulfill his infantile demands, and, at the same time, respect him because he allows the patient to project specific aspects of the self and does not support his need to reconstruct the early environment. The patient is able to obtain relief from some of the disruptive pressures and constrictions these archaic primitive elements produce. The analyst, by not becoming submerged in the inchoate morass of the inept past, continues being available for the patient's projections.

I wish to discuss these processes further. To respond directly to the content of the patient's associations may reinforce the introject that has been projected into the analyst. The analyst's response may take the form of a defense against the role that the patient has attributed to him. This is still regarded as a confirmation by the patient, because he recognizes such defensive attempts. The analyst confirms the patient's projections, whether he assumes the role attributed to him or reacts against it, and the assumption of this role *paradoxically makes it difficult for the patient to continue projecting.*

Instead of simply projecting onto the analyst, the patient places him in the center of his private world and reacts to him with his usual psychopathologically constructed adaptations. This reaction to confirmation of the patient's projections may constitute a massive projection of basic orientations, but I prefer to call this phenomenon *externalization* (Giovacchini, 1967). It differs from projection, a more discrete phenomenon, since it is not limited to just a segment of the patient's psyche. The patient continues to react in his usual psychopathologically constricted fashion, now concentrated in the analysis. The environment which has become a reflection of his total personality is brought into the analysis. This does not lead to any relief of internal pressures or the release of one's developmental potential as does an analytically accepted projection. I have noted that when the patient is projecting discrete parts of his psyche rather than externalizing, he experiences a feeling of freedom and spontaneity in spite of the anxiety he might be otherwise feeling.

Deeper Regressed States

Alexander (1956) conceptualized two types of regression, one referring to an ego state that reproduced the stage of fixation, the phase wherein the principal trauma occurred. The other referred to an ego state characteristic of a developmental stage that preceded the trauma.

Although such clear-cut phases of fixation and specific traumas are not easily discernible in the patients discussed here, I believe that Alexander's distinctions are relevant. True, in patients suffering from characterological disorders, trauma is pervasive and one can think, as discussed, of a generally traumatic environment (Khan, 1964). However, one can also conceptualize specific periods in the patient's life when the effects of early object relations were maximal and where defenses against threatening external objects consisted of such primitive mechanisms as withdrawal, splitting, and introjective-projective defenses. One can also conceptualize stages prior to the introjection of disruptive external objects.

When the patient regresses to an amorphous ego state where the self-representation is unformed, there is also a lack of structure of disrupting, constricting introjects. Since this regressed state is reminiscent of the infantile epoch when these introjects were first introjected, they are more tenuously established within the psyche than they were before the regression occurred. Consequently, the psyche can get rid of them, so to speak, relatively easily by projection. Although the ego is somewhat formless during such a regressed state, it is, nevertheless, burdened by the projection of such inner constrictive forces.

Although stormy, this particular regressed state has enormous therapeutic potential. Frequently, patients during this stage of treatment have described themselves as "emerging." A schizoid patient described himself as emerging from a cocoon. Others have related numerous birth fantasies and dreams. One can often discern a core of structure amidst all the chaos and confusion, a core that is waiting to be released and continue a course of progression that has become stifled because of the lack of a holding environment as Winnicott (1952) described.

I am once again referring to an organized rudimentary self which has been submerged by hateful introjects and self-hatred. The regressed state, in a sense, goes back before the period when such psychic organizations were firmly established and therefore permits their projection. Thus, the rudimentary organized self has an opportunity to develop further. To some extent, it, too, is projected and the analyst functions as a caretaker (see previous section) as well as an "incinerator" to rid the patient of objectionable parts of the self.

During regressed states, patients also resort to adaptations that are appropriate to the particular traumatic environment they are recapitulating. Actually, they have been adapting to the current world in a similar fashion. The regressed state demonstrates the appropriateness of such techniques when they were acquired and they are more easily discernible since they are more intense during such periods of analysis. The patient, by accentuating such psychopathological, distorted adaptations, not only makes it possible to gain considerable insight about an important phase of development, but creates the opportunity to demonstrate to himself their inappropriateness. This is facilitated by the release of his rudimentary organized self.

AFFECTIVE STATES AND ANALYTIC RESOLUTION

Exploring the deep regressions accompanying transferences of patients suffering from severe psychopathology causes one to question how much can be gained therapeutically in allowing patients to suffer from such painful affective states. In view of their stormy and apparently disruptive aspects, some therapists might feel that the ensuing disorganization will be detrimental, indeed even dangerous, to treatment and definitely not in the patient's best interest. Consequently, some form of treatment other than analysis might be recommended or some manuever might be suggested in order to avoid such disturbing affects, to make the patient more comfortable and presumably more amenable to therapy. Perhaps the patient should be hospitalized or put on a regime of drugs which will re-establish sufficient emotional equilibrium so that he can become involved in a therapeutic relationship without being too frightened.

In some instances, the patient may be so completely disorganized that analytic therapy, for the moment, is out of the question; the main problem is custodial. Ths quality of the patient's disorganization, nevertheless, has to be considered further in order to determine how one should relate to it. Should one attempt to do away with it, that is try to re-establish equilibrium, or should one's therapeutic attitudes focus on areas other than the patient's behavior? Are the patient's symptoms purely disruptive or do they have adaptive significance which has to be understood and which may lead to insights that could result in ego integration?

Undoubtedly, in extreme cases, the patient's behavior may be a manifestation of disruptive and disintegrating inner forces. Still, one cannot consider psychic disintegration and integration in absolute terms. What may be disintegration from one particular developmental level or ego state could be a defensive adaptation preventing further psychic dissolution when considered on the basis of a lower level. Although stormy and apparently disruptive, the patient's orientation may be a symptomatic expression designed to protect him from complete emotional collapse. The question as to whether therapy should seek to do away with such behavior has to be considered from this viewpoint.

For example, a middle-aged man was hospitalized by his relatives because of increasing agitation and auditory hallucinations. He heard voices which usually hurled imprecations at him. He also had visions of seeing biblical figures, such as Christ and various patriarchs from the Old Testament. The hospital embarked upon a routine designed to reestablish reality testing and treated him with heavy doses of thorazine and insulin shock. In two weeks he calmed down and was completely free of hallucinations. One week later he was discharged.

From the viewpoint of manifest behavior the patient was once again well. The hospital considered him to be markedly improved and believed their therapeutic regime was quite successful. However, although he was no longer experiencing anxiety, the patient felt miserable. He did not return to his job.

He felt that life was completely meaningless and would gladly have committed suicide if it were "worth the effort."

He was extremely bitter and critical about the hospital but he was unable to determine why he felt so hostile. With this frame of mind he sought analysis. Although life in general was hopeless, he still had faith in analysis and he felt extreme resentment toward his brother who had been responsible for his hospitalization rather than directing him toward analytic therapy.

The patient, in spite of his resentment, had manipulated others into taking care of him. It became clear during the analysis that he wanted the outside world to control him and hospitalization was a means to achieve such control. However, he did not anticipate that the hospital would take over such absolute control, that is, "forbidding" him to have symptoms. He needed his hallucinations and without them found life too burdensome. His voices and visions sustained him. During the first week of analysis he confessed that his purpose in seeking treatment was to regain the "ability" to once more hallucinate.

This was an interesting attitude because, in essence, the patient was telling me that he was not yet ready to give up his symptoms, symptoms that had been prematurely taken away from him. He longed for them because in spite of their bizarreness they served him in some fashion, and even though he suffered from considerable anxiety, his present emotional state, although less flamboyant, was even more painful.

Although I could not compare his present orientation with his previous one, I sensed that his current existence was artificial. He did not seem to be himself. He seemed to be going through the motions of living, or rather existing, because he had given up everything that was part of his past life—work, friends, hobbies, and many artistic and intellectual interests. He acted as if he were a mechanical man, a robot devoid of any feelings except emptiness. To me, he seemed completely out of character, although as stated, I had no standard of comparison.

One might consider such an orientation representative of a state of extreme apathetic withdrawal which is fairly characteristic of many schizoid patients. However, I was puzzled and was unable to think only in terms of defensive reactions.

The patient covertly convinced me that his present feelings and his psychic orientation were atypical. He had constructed a defensive superstructure that was not synchronous with the rest of his personality. He seemed to be a perfect example of what Winnicott (1960) described as a false self, a precarious and tenuous integration.

His defenses were what we might call schizoid insofar as he withdrew from all human contact and avoided situations which required involvement. This massive withdrawal and the underlying emptiness which became so evident during the course of his analysis seemed, in a sense, to be out of character. He perceived himself as a blank person without affect, without any resources to cope with an overwhelmingly complicated and threatening external world. Previously, the patient had many character defenses which finally achieved psychotic proportions. However, regardless of the severity of the psychopathology, he always had intense, perhaps overly intense feelings and never felt empty and blank. He experienced his identity in a very definite, if at times megalomanic fashion. As he described his past, one could feel with him his nostalgia for those turbulent but colorful times. Although he felt inner disruption, he still felt something, and this to him was better than feeling nothing.

I have known patients who entered treatment describing what Federn (1952) called apathetic terror. These are essentially patients who view themselves as non-entities and are practically devoid of feelings. They may defend themselves with as-if types of defenses or they may go through life as though they lived in a vacuum.

This patient indicated that his basic character structure was fundamentally different from those patients suffering from amorphous and blank self-representations (see Giovacchini, 1972). His orientation seemed to have been basically paranoid, but one which was capable of considerable feeling.

He believed that the hospital had robbed him of his feelings. Previously he had been able to position various aspects of the self somewhere in the external world. Affects and anger could be balanced with the rest of his personality by being alternately projected and introjected. Thorazine somehow interfered with his ability to do this. Metaphorically, it seemed that tranquilizers simply absorbed all affects, that is, drained off both internal disruptive feelings as well as devoured his projections. Consequently, he was reduced to an empty shell. The patient described such a drug-induced state as one of depletion and presented the hopeless picture of being permanently impaired. This attitude proved to have defensive features and gradually he regained affects and the *capacity to be paranoid*. However, it seemed correct to believe that the drugs did, indeed, interfere with his ability to produce affects and this depleted state continued for some time.

Although affects in such patients can be disruptive, to some extent the patient values them. They are still part of the self and the inability to generate a feeling, even one which distorts reality when it is projected, may on the surface produce a symptomfree picture, but one which leads to a quiet but devastating misery.

The value of the affective state is also highlighted from a therapeutic viewpoint. To feel depleted and without adaptive techniques makes it difficult for the patient to relive the primitive regressions previously discussed, which could lead to freedom from constrictive introjects and release his inherent developmental potential. Insofar as he is no longer able to cathect and project, or more precisely, drugs have interfered with such capacities, *he has lost the opportunity of cathecting disruptive introjects and to make transference projections. The latter allows the patient to position various parts of his self as he had previously done with his symptoms,* and eventually, because some stability has been reached in an extremely regressed state, he can achieve states of higher integration.

The elements of the therapeutic process relevant to these principles will be discussed elsewhere (see next section, and Giovacchini, 1965). An essential therapeutic ingredient, however, stands out in an obvious fashion in all analytic interactions. The patient must have the opportunity to live out during treatment his typical characterological modalities and to maintain some degree of balance, an adaptation based upon such psychopathological mechanisms. This patient emphasized that once he was no longer able to feel and to project, the ensuing state was considerably more painful and produced a therapeutic impasse because the paradox of being symptomfree made parts of the self unavailable for transference projections.

As previously mentioned, the projection of parts of the self refers not only to hate-ridden introjects; there is also an organized inner core capable of development that is entrusted to the analyst by the transference projection. In an affectively depleted state induced by tranquilizers, this rudimentary organized self is also depleted and the patient's potential for emotional growth is correspondingly diminished.

This attitude about the negative therapeutic effect of drugs, I realize, can be and has been challenged. Some psychiatrists would not think in terms of affect depletion, but simply in terms of taming desruptive affects and presumably, in some instances, increased control to make the patient therapeutically amenable. Still, it is not tamed or controlled affects that give the patient the opportunity to deal with the primitive and chaotic within himself. Tamed affects are not particularly helpful in reproducing the regressed transference such patients have to experience in order to attain higher levels of ego integration. So whether one thinks in terms of depletion of affect or affect management, the distinction is quantitative and the patient still has lost the capacity to become immersed in primitive adaptations which both reveal his basic psychopathology and make is possible for him to cope with it.

When one's orientation is nonanalytic and the patient's behavior is so out of contact with reality that he is completely inaccessible, and perhaps even dangerously violent, some type of restraining influence may be necessary. However, when one gives drugs to achieve control, their influence in determining future structuralization has to be examined. Frequently, one hears that the patient has to be given controls he does not have, that he has to learn to set limits and not to let his instincts run rampant. Granted, this may have to be done, but it is my impression that it is usually done so the world around him can stand him and it is questionable whether such controls are going to be helpful from the viewpoint of analytic structuralization. Of course, there are many other viewpoints beside the analytic one, but that is the one that is of concern here.

In regard to the current focus upon behavioral control, the question of managing the patient's behavior deserves emphasis. Not only is control of behavior considered desirable, but, in some cirlces it is considered vital for later therapeutic achievement *in the analytic sense*. This is the point that is being challenged here. Control may be necessary for many reasons, but control through drugs, as just described, may make the patient more amenable to superficially accepting the therapeutic setting but incapable of dealing with parts of the self which have in one way or another been wrested from him and which are essential for analytic interaction.

TECHNICAL CONSIDERATIONS AND SOME COUNTERTRANSFERENCE PROBLEMS

Various elements of the analytic process are highlighted in patients suffering from characterological disturbances. I do not wish to belabor the point further regarding the amenability of such patients to psychoanalysis, but I will again refer to patients who suffer from severe psychopathology and have an interesting positive attitude regarding analysis.

These patients seem to have a fundamental knowledge of the analytic process, even though they may never have had any prior experience with analysis, or have read anything technical about it. Still, in spite of their positive attitude, there may be some very difficult moments during treatment and specific countertransference problems may be stimulated.

For example, a woman in her early thirties consulted me after having seen several other psychiatrists. She specifically sought me out because she had heard that I did not reject patients for analysis because they were "too sick." Not that she considered herself too sick, but she felt that someone with such an attitude might be more inclined to accept her as an analytic patient.

She started her first session, as did my artist patient, (see section on Transference and Psychopathology), by telling me that most analysts, for some unexplainable reason, have a resistance to doing analysis and then she substantiated her opinion by giving examples of her experience with prominent local analysts. Here too, I must emphasize that none of the events she recounted were viewed with rancor or anger. She was not bitter about these relationships, simply sad. In spite of being rejected so often by psychoanalysts, she still had not lost faith in psychoanalysis.

So much for her attitude, which as one one can see was more Catholic than the Pope. She could be quite specific about psychoanalysis and go beyond merely enunciating her faith. She was able to point out particular errors that could completely disrupt the analytic setting, errors which therapists had made but which were accepted by them as an intrinsic aspect of the analytic process. Only rarely did she rebuke or attempt to correct them.

The patient was well aware of her manipulative abilities and how she could seduce men into giving in to her wishes. She felt, however, that an analysis should not be designed to gratify infantile needs in spite of her subtlety and skill in articulating such needs. She emphasized that the analyst should confine himself to analyzing and not get involved with the content of her associations.

For example, she spoke of her first analyst as a warm and attractive person. She had found him personable and sympathetic and was glad to begin treatment with him. These positive feelings, however, in a vague, undefined way disturbed her. The first several months of analysis with him went well. She continued feeling "good" about the treatment and believed that she presented herself in a charming fashion, as indeed she was quite capable of doing, as I subsequently learned. Gradually, she became aware of the fact that he would engage her in many conversations that had very little, if anything, to do with the workings of her mind. Instead, they referred to current events and opinions about various philosophical and artistic themes.

At this point, I wish to stress that it must have been very easy to get drawn into such conversations because she was basically an extremely interesting person with very attractive ideas. Had I not been forewarned, it is quite possible that I may also have abandoned the analytic position. I am certain I did anyway at times.

To return to her first therapeutic experience, the patient finally confronted her therapist with his involvement with her. She did this gently and apparently it was not received as a rebuke. He replied that he was merely trying to be her friend. She thought to herself that she had friends, what she really needed was an analyst. Still, she continued seeing him for a year. She did not want to hurt his feelings. She also convinced him that she had improved sufficiently that now treatment, successful treatment, could be terminated. They left each other on friendly terms.

She immediately sought another analyst, but this time she used a different tack. Instead of making her charming side foremost, she emphasized all of her infantile qualities. This analyst, nevertheless, found her appealing and "made jokes" about her childish orientation and adaptations. According to the patient, he refused to take her seriously, at least to the degree where he would consider analyzing her. Again, she left in an ostensibly amicable fashion, although, in fact, she resented both experiences. Her third analyst began analyzing her and things seemed to be progressing in an acceptable fashion. The patient has an unusual talent for changing her voice, making it compatible with particular childhood periods. She could act as if she were a provactive child or a demanding, needy little girl. Or she could become a witch. In other words, as I also observed many times, she could reveal her ego state by the tone of her voice. Her third analyst, according to the patient, did not feel inclined to accept the diagnostic advantages of such vocal mimicry. Instead, during one of her more babyish ramblings, he sternly asked, "Is that the way a grown-up woman should talk?" This time she keenly felt her anger and retorted, "What do you know about how a grown-up woman *should* talk?" She then left his office and never returned.

As stated, this patient apparently had embraced certain fundamental analytic principles and seemed to have a propensity to encounter situations where these principles were violated. One wonders why, if the patient had so much faith in analysis and seemingly wanted so very much to be analyzed, she had such difficulties in finding someone to analyze her? I wish to point out, however, that in spite of her intense motivation for analysis, and she was, indeed, sincerely motivated, her analysis was a long and difficult one. It was, nevertheless, truly rewarding for both of us.

Her former therapists probably sensed the underlying severe character disturbance and were reluctant to get analytically involved. The patient's sensitivities, however, were, according to her, transgressed, and it was this transgression that defined the therapist's nonanalytic response. Examining the latter will reveal basic analytic principles that the patient was able to grasp keenly. *Perhaps the nature of her psychopathology contributed to her adeptness at understanding fundamental psychoanalytic tenets.*

What was the patient referring to when she talked about transgressions? I believe it can be summarized in the following three ways: 1) The therapist should not get involved with the content of her associations, 2) he should not make any moral judgments about her behavior, and 3) he must let her experience her psychopathology through disturbed affective states rather than attempt to make her feel well. These are fairly explicit and straightforward technical prerequisites for any analysis, but, apparently the patient's basic character, perhaps her helplessness or her subtle provocativeness, caused therapists to lose sight of them. Later, I will comment further on this point because after several years of treatment, I could see more clearly how she threatened my analytic identity by producing some paradoxes, which I now believe are fairly typical of this group of patients.

Sensitivity to Transgressions and Character Structure

For the moment, I wish to concentrate upon how her psychopathology made her especially sensitive to psychoanalytic transgressions, that is, to nonanalytic approaches. As stated I feel this is typical of a paticular group of patients who have similar characterological constellations which are based upon narcissistic disturbances. I have seen several patients who seem to have the unusual ability to embrace the essence of psychoanalysis.

These patients can be described as being extremely sensitive to any kind of intrusion. Their childhoods were experienced as intrusive. Their mothers or guardians had a tremendous emotional investment in them and were also apparently unstable narcissistic persons who constantly "impinged," to use Winnicott's (1950) apt expression, on their children. Consequently, as patients, they demand an absolutely nonintrusive therapist, although, as will be discussed later, the situation is not quite that simple.

These patients' self-representations are so tenuously structured that the outside world, as did their infantile world, threatens their autonomy. Their defensive adjustment is designed to preserve whatever remnants of autonomy they have, and this makes them especially sensitive to nonanalytic approaches which are frequently intentionally directive and managerial. Under these circumstances, the patient often feels submerged (Giovacchini, 1964). They feel that others are imposing elements of themselves into them rather then understanding how their mind works in order to release them from the forces that constrict their autonomy.

For example, a middle-aged professional man even resented an interpretation. He felt that what I told him was *my* impression of the situation and, therefore, when I conveyed what *I* felt to be an important insight, I was really imposing parts of myself into him since my conception was formed according to specific attributes of my psyche.

In order to preserve himself, he had to angrily attack my presumptuousness in having any opinion about him. Or by the use of irresolute logic, he would microscopically dissect what I told him, ultimately reducing it to an absurd error. He did not believe I was stupid, simply presumptuous.

After one such demoliton of an interpretation, I sadly commented that it seemed that all I could do was make wrong interpretations. Remaining consistent, he went on to indicate I was wrong again; he was not aware of the inherent contradiction in his reply. I was surprised, although I should not have been. This was an interesting paradox, one among others that such patients create.

The passing of moral judgments is especially odious to such patients because, once again, their autonomy is being questioned, this time in terms of their choice of value systems. There are many factors involved here. The patient finds it necessary to fight against fusion in order to preserve individuality. To accept another person's morality or to have one's value system approved or disapproved is tantamount to being engulfed by the other person.

The professional man to whom I have just referred always had to be right by having me always wrong. If I were right, then he would be wrong. Not only would one submerge the other, but the patient, in order to feel worthy, had to support himself by having someone inferior around him so he could sustain his superiority. He had to have someone to trample upon, a reversal of the original symbiotic relationship to his mother. There are many methods such patients employ to handle their original symbiotic relationship or to prevent its formation in a therapeutic relationship. Still, their main purpose is to preserve a tenuous identity.

The goal of analysis is to foster autonomy and the analytic setting is so constructed to facilitate the achievement of an integrated identity sense. *Thus, the aims of analysis coincide with these patients' needs.* The nonanalytic approach threatens them since anything designed to manage their lives or pass judgments, even by subtly introducing the therapist's value system, makes them feel worthless—or more to the point, nonexistent. Contrary to what has been commonly accepted, these patients would appear to be admirably suited for analysis, much more so than the classical psychoneurotic who presumably feels more secure in his identity. Certainly, these patients, in analysis, are quite intolerant of any deviations from analysis, even though in some instances, as the woman patient who had consulted several therapists illustrated, they may masochistically put up with them. Other better integrated patients are able to tolerate nonanalytic diversions during the course of analysis, since they feel sufficiently stable that they do not experience such diversions as encroachments.

I wish to emphasize that I am not generalizing that all patients suffering from characterological defects and identity problems have this particular affinity for analysis. Other patients may behave quite differently, often clinging to the therapist and demanding salvation, or they may be so concretely oriented that a psychoanalytic approach seems almost ludicrous. Nevertheless, patients such as I have described are not scarce and it is interesting that some psychoanalysts are reluctant to treat them analytically, in spite of their faith and eagerness, even desperation, to get involved in analysis.

Complications and Paradoxes

I have alluded to the paradoxes these patients produce, paradoxes which I believe excite countertransference reactions that are detrimental to analysis, or that create the illusion that these patients are psychoanalytically untreatable. I also believe that many experienced psychoanalysts can consciously sense that they will be presented with such paradoxes sometimes during the course of treatment and this causes them to reject these patients as analysands. Perhaps one is now confronted with another paradox, that is, the skillful, sensitive analyst is more likely to make an error in judgment regarding treatability because he is better able to unconsciously predict the course of treatment.

I will illustrate what I believe to be a characteristic paradox such patients create. This paradox refers to the patient's insistence that we let him experience affects during the session. I have referred to the value of an affective experience in the previous section; here, I am referring to the patient's complaint that the analyst blocks the production of affects, even though he is not aware of having done so.

The clinical situation I intend describing has its counterpart in daily life. If let us say, a friend is upset, perhaps because of the death of a loved one, our instinctive reaction is to cheer him up or to distract him by diverting his attention to other areas. For example, if a man "breaks down," that is, compulsively sobs or cries, our natural inclination is to comfort him with the intention of changing his ego state. In everyday life, as in therapy, we could be doing him a disservice. This situation was highlighted during analysis when a patient accused me of not letting him experience anger. I am now referring to one of the paradoxes I have alluded to. The patient complained that my polite and rational disposition made it difficult for him to sustain anger during his session. He did not exactly expect me to respond or to provoke him, but he did not want me to dispel his rage. The atmosphere I created was not conducive to the support of an angry affect. As stressed, the patient related this to my personality. But more was involved beside me. He gradually revealed that the psychoanalytic process itself made it difficult to maintain an irrational affect.

Psychoanalysis attempts to make the irrational rational. In so doing, it strips the irrational of its feeling. This may perhaps lead to insight formation and as such is valuable. However, it also deprives the patient of fully experiencing an affect to its ultimate resolution. Both the presence of the analyst and his interpretative activity interfere with this process. *To some extent, every interpretation is premature* since one cannot determine how long the patient has to experience an affective state in order to achieve resolution.

When I pointed out to the patient that he felt angry toward me because he had projected certain psychic elements into me and was reacting on the basis of certain thwarted intrapsychically derived demands, he understood what I said and saw the logic behind it. Still, he could not rid himself of the feeling that my motivation for making such an interpretation was because I could not tolerate his angry feelings. He also believed that there was a defensive self-justifying element to my explanation.

One might ask the obvious—why not remain silent since, in a sense, the patient seems to be demanding that the analyst allow him simply to bare his feelings without dispelling them by interpretation? Many analysts have deliberately remained silent for these same reasons, and often it has worked out well. This patient, however, would interpret my lack of response as being due to feeling angry but he would feel it was justified by external circumstances rather than feel impelled to examine its intrapsychic source.

No response seemed appropriate. Interpretative activity designed to promote analytic integration, in itself, became an obstacle to progress. To me, this consituted a paradox. I felt paralyzed and deprived of my analytic autonomy.

I wish to return later to the discussion of the feeling of helpless impotence which I believe many analysts experience in similar circumstances. Before entering into such a discussion, I would like to refer to another similar disturbing situation.

Another patient, who had been abandoned by his parents shortly after birth and had lived in a series of institutions, felt it was necessary to recapture what might be referred to as his primal loneliness. In essence, he needed to regress to a very early phase of development where he could really feel his hopelessness and isolation. If he could face these painful feelings in their full intensity, he could possibly transcend them and emerge as a whole person.

He felt fragmented and believed that whatever present relationships he had, were either fraudulent, or tenuous and shallow. By once again being truly alone and surviving such a state he could start anew; that is, move forward without having to form defensive object relations. Here, again, is an example of a patient whose associations can be directly transcribed into a psychoanalytic theory of treatment.

This need to experience an affective state which, in some way although not exactly, was related to an early childhood phase of development, led to an analytic impasse. He needed to experience this loneliness in the transference context, yet my very presence made it impossible for him to experience such a state fully. It intruded on his loneliness, and the poignant sadness he should have felt was replaced by frustration and resentment. I would not leave him alone so he could be abandoned. In a sense he felt attacked, but this was an entirely different situation, because being attacked meant that his existence was acknowledged even though with hostility. Before being able to bring other people into his world, he had to feel completely alone. Afterwards he could let others enter in a meaningful fashion. I was pushing my way in before he was ready to receive me. This, again, is a paradoxical situation. Analysis should create a setting where such primitive states can be re-experienced in the transference regression; still, it is the setting itself which interferes with achieving them.

This patient and the middle-aged woman I discussed earlier presented themselves in a fashion that seemed favorable to analysis. To repeat, they had faith in analysis and were eager to get involved in such a relationship. Still, several therapists refused to attempt analysis and in spite of the patient's enthusiasm, I also felt reluctant to begin such a relationship. They did, indeed, prove to be difficult analysands, although they were also quite rewarding because they patiently taught me analytic principles. The reason they proved to be hard to treat, however, was because of the paradoxes I have just described. *They were, in a sense, demanding that I adopt an analytic role which would obliterate my existence as a person.*

I believe my initial reluctance to treat these patients may have stemmed from an unconscious recognition that they would demand that I conduct myself in an unattainable psychoanalytic fashion.

I am reminded of a similar reluctance to get analytically involved, presented in a paper by Gitelson (1952).

Gitelson believed that if a patient dreamed, especially in the first dream, of the analyst as he is, that is, in an undisguised fashion, then the patient should be referred elsewhere. This did not take the patient's psychopathology into account. Rather, he concluded that perhaps there was something about the appearance and personality, or style of the analyst that was too similar to some significant person in the patient's life. Consequently, the patient would develop an intense transference which might be incapable of resolution. Certainly, this is an interesting idea.

A colleague presented a patient at a seminar where we discussed cases considered especially difficult to treat or which had complications develop during the course of analysis. We called this a "special problems" seminar and Dr. Gitelson was our chairman. It so happened that the patient that was being discussed had been referred to the presenter by Dr. Gitelson. He made the referral because the patient dreamed about him in an undisguised fashion.

It was interesting to note in the subsequent treatment that whenever the patient referred to Dr. Gitelson, she never indicated that he represented a reality figure. On the contrary, she often split the transference, assigning certain roles to her analyst, and other roles to Dr. Gitelson. These roles often changed, the analyst sometimes being the bad object and Dr. Gitelson being idealized, or the reverse. The patient was quite capable of dealing with these feelings as transference phenomena and everyone in the seminar was convinced that Dr. Gitelson would have been eminently suited to analyze her.

Still, Dr. Gitelson's reluctance to start analysis deserved further exploration. It became apparent during the course of discussion that his conscious reasons for refusing to analyze this patient were rationalizations, perhaps correct in some instances, but they did not seem to apply wholly to this patient. We concluded that Dr. Gitelson's arguments about becoming too much of a real person to the patient represented a reaction formation, although as with all reaction formations, that which is being defended against also emerges. We also believed that in a particular sense he was correct.

The analyst brought this case to the seminar because he felt frustrated. No matter what he did or did not do, it would prove to be wrong from the patient's viewpoint. This situation was somewhat different from my experience with the patient who assailed all of my interpretations and proved them, in his own mind, to be wrong. In this instance, the analyst felt disturbed when the patient convinced him that she was going to commit suicide.

Much of her analysis consisted in bringing feelings of self-hatred and inadequacy to the surface. She fluctuated between reviling herself or vehemently blaming others for the helplessness that enveloped her. This tormented self-representation emerged after the analyst had apparently made inroads upon superficially hysterical defenses. When she first saw Dr. Gitelson, she presented herself as a manipulative and seductive woman. Only later did her helpless vulnerability come to the surface.

The patient's early life, still a current theme, was characterized by people becoming intensely involved with her and then abandoning her. Her mother, apparently, was psychotic and later (when the patient was going through puberty) died in a psychiatric institution. She recalled how her mother would become intensely involved with her, "swoop all over her" and then teasingly withdraw.

Currently, one could see this pattern working in many relationships, a pattern that was manipulated and provoked by the patient. With both men and women, even children, she would become involved in a friendly fashion mainly based upon her desire to be sympathetic and helpful. A first, there would be reciprocation, but then the relationship would become so intense that either the patient or the other person or both, would become tremendously frightened and the involvement would suddenly be terminated. The patient's behavior often resembled that of the mother's sudden withdrawal but just as often she would be precipituously abandoned. It became apparent that these involvements toward and away from relationships were based upon the need for and fear of fusion, but this formulation need not be elaborated here.

Within the analysis, as might be expected, she repeated this constellation. On the surface this appeared to be a desirable analytic sequence, that is, the spontaneous unfolding of the transference. It was precisely at the point where the transference projections had reached a peak that the treatment seemed to flounder.

The patient understood that this basic early traumatic situation had to be re-experienced in the transference context. However, she also felt that the final outcome would be suicide. She insisted that the analyst rescue her from being engulfed by her hateful and disruptive self. She was also convinced that she had to experience abandonment in order to achieve resolution. Analytic rescuing, however, did not include abandonment, and because of fusion with an omnipotent being she would not feel her helplessness. Consequently, she would never face or resolve the pain of abandonment.

To repeat, the transference situation was different from her traumatic past in at least one important respect; whereas an intensive relationship with her mother inevitably led to abandonment, her relationship with the analyst, in contrast, precluded being abandoned. The patient had attributed megalomanic, omnipotent qualities to him. The situation with her mother was based upon other types of projections.

It is, of course, not surprising that tranference projections are not exact replicas of the infantile traumatic situation. Throughout the course of development the patient's introjections undergo constant revisions, and primary process elements derived from *later* stages of development and experiences are attached to some of the initial introjects. For example, the mother's initial responses to the patient were probably directed at administering to her biological needs. The patient was tortured by the *tantalizing* aspects of the relationship. Later, she felt abandoned which, in turn, made her feel helpless, vulnerable, and hated. This response, which was incorporated into the self-representation, was her predominant orientation during the crucial periods of her analysis. Whereas with her mother she required love and nurture to sustain her so that maturation and development could occur in a continuous fashion, the analyst was needed defensively against painful feelings which developed *later*. Her need for the analyst resembled her need for her mother insofar as she helplessly reached out and sought an intense relationship, but it differed in that she was seeking omnipotent rescuing from consuming self-hatred, in itself a *consequence* of inconstant and destructive mothering.

The patient was aware of her magical expectations and could verbalize them directly. Seeing herself as a hateful person and attempting to defend herself against inner assault by turning toward some omnipotent being in order to make herself good must include feelings and attitudes that are the outcome of later stages of development. The neonate is not capable of such complicated feelings and defensive reactions. Thus, in this regard the tranference situation differs from the original traumatic one. I believe that, to some extent, all transference relationships differ in some similar respects from the disruptive past.

In any case, the therapist was intimidated. If he allowed omnipotent fusion to continue, by not analyzing it or by accepting the role assigned to him, treatment would bog down. If, in contrast, he did not respond to the content of the patient's associations, the therapist was coerced into believing that the patient would kill herself. This dilemma caused him to seek the advice of colleagues.

Dr. Gitelson's ostensible reason for refusing to take the patient in therapy had been his belief that the analysis of the transference would become unmanageable because he was too similar to some significant person in the patient's life. Consequently, the patient could not experience transference as transference; instead, she would consider her feelings as belonging to the current reality.

What seemed apparent now was that Dr. Gitelson had correctly understood the dream, but he had not realized that the patient was dreaming about her *need* to cast him as a real figure in her past life.

To try to rescue her would be directly responding to her needs and therefore being a real part of her life. This, as emphasized, interfered with experiencing and working through her feeling of abandonment. Not to deal directly with her helplessness and self-hatred, that is, remaining in an observational frame of reference rather than being a participant—in other words, maintaining an analytic perspective—could result in a dead patient.

Thus, the patient required the analyst to function in two different roles simultaneously in order for her to survive and to be analyzed. This was an impossible situation and may have been what Dr. Gitelson was responding to. The dilemma Dr. Gitelson felt was more likely in response to an intrinsic aspect of this patient's psychopathology than because of any actual similarity with some significant person of the patient's childhood.

The necessary assumption of various roles by the analyst is not an uncommon occurrence in the treatment of many patients. The need for megalomanic rescuing is also fairly common in patients suffering from severe characterological problems. I believe my colleague's patient differed quantitatively from other patients suffering from ego defects in that she was able to convince him that she would, in fact, kill herself if he did not minister to her primitive needs to be rescued. Whether he fostered this by unwittingly making an implicit promise that rescuing would be forthcoming or whether this patient's disturbance was such that her survival was, indeed, tenuous regardless of the analyst's behavior cannot now be decided. In any case, the crucial point here in contrast to other patients is that my colleague's patient demanded, or rather her psychopathology required that the analyst *actually* assume two different roles simultaneously, whereas other patients are content with their fantasies about viewing the analyst from different perspectives.

My patients, I believe, demonstrated similar phenomena creating the same basic dilemma. When one of them had to experience loneliness, the same types of demands were being made of me. I was supposed to be there and not be there at the same time, clearly an impossible feat. I was also being asked to be analyst and nonanalyst simultaneously. Not being there meant letting her experience the full impact of loneliness and sadness as others in her past life had done; being there meant being the observing analyst but by doing so, I would be interfering with the generation of the affective state that I would be observing and analyzing.

I have presented this case, not simply to give another example of a paradox, but also because I wish to emphasize that our judgments about treatability, when incorrect, can be attributed to certain common countertransference difficulties. However, in this instance, one can think in terms other than individual countertransference idiosyncrasies and bring to the fore certain technical difficulties which would cause a majority of analysts to react adversely, especially if they had not recognized these difficulties. Dr. Gitelson was a very skillful, experienced analyst who was highly intuitive and not at all reluctant to conduct a self-examination. As he reflected on some of his initial reactions to this patient, he admitted that there was something about her that made him feel that he did not want to analyze her. He was extremely adept at making judgments concerning analyzability; his predictions were usually borne out. Here, however, he was willing to agree with the group that he might have had some prescience about future difficulties that he simply did not want to deal with. Note that no one felt that this patient could not be analyzed. We also definitely felt that Dr. Gitelson could have analyzed her *if he had wanted to. The unconscious anticipation of future difficulties, such as those I have called paradoxes, make analysts reluctant to analyze some patients but it does not make patients unanalyzable.*

To some extent, paradoxes exist in all prospective analytic patients. The analyst as a transference figure is an indispensable factor of the psychoanalytic process. The analyst as analyst, however, cannot help but intrude, even though he keeps his presence down to a minimum. Nevertheless, in psychoanalysis, as is true for experimental approaches too, the observer in some way affects the data of observation. All patients require the presence of the analyst as a transference figure, but at the same time, his presence interferes with the spontaneous and full generation of primitive affective states.

Reluctance to Analyze

Reluctance to analyze patients is often manifested by the construction of rigid criteria to determine analyzability. On hearing some of these criteria, I have sometimes wondered whether a patient who could meet these standards would feel any need for analysis. The reactions other analysts had to the patients I have described, I believe, are examples of reluctance to analyze, supported by formulas about treatability.

I recall how my colleagues and I, as students, flocked to institutes in order to learn the secrets of this esoteric method of treatment. Although we were taught strict criteria to determine who is analyzable and who is not, we were not particularly adept at using them. My first control patient was a delusionally paranoid patient and an active homosexual. No one seemed to believe that analysis was contraindicated, although the full extent of his symptoms had not been discovered at the beginning of treatment. Still, I recall case after case presented at our beginning clinical seminars that turned out to have what we called a schizoid core. It is noteworthy that during these initial sessions with such patients no one felt reluctant to analyze them. I gained the definite impression that, although we clung to Freud's criteria about analyzability and demanded what we considered good ego strength, we nevertheless unhesitatingly accepted many cases that ultimately revealed severe character pathology. We tended to gloss over such formulations and instead emphasized the patient's strengths and hysterical features.

As the years have passed, I have noticed that my colleagues have developed a reluctance to treat patients analytically in contrast to what might be called an eagerness when they first started practicing psychoanalysis. Of course, one can question this observation and state that this may be true of my particular group and that it is unfair to generalize. Still, the number of analysts in the United States is not that large and I have noted similar attitudes among many colleagues in different parts of the country and even the world. Colleagues in England, where the attitude about analyzability is considerably more liberal than here, have told me that as they grow older they feel less inclined to get analytically involved with some kinds of patients.

One could claim that as the clinician gets older and gains more experience, he does not have the same pressing need of the younger man to establish a practice. After all, he has been successful and can now afford to choose patients about whom he has some special interest or toward whom he has some affinity based upon personal preference. Such would not indicate anything about a developed reluctance to analyze.

Undoubtedly such factors are operating, but I believe that this is only a partial explanation and that something else is involved.

An experience with the Chicago Psychoanalytic Society strengthens this viewpoint. As Chairman of the Program Committee arranging for Regional meetings, I sent questionnaires to the membership in order to determine what types of workshops they would prefer. The most popular workshop was one dealing with the topic, "Psychoanalysis and the Community." Several members wrote that the trend was away from the one-to-one relationship and was moving in the direction of the group. One psychoanalyst went so far as to state that psychoanalysis as a treatment modality was "dead." These perhaps are extreme views, but they could be considered reflections of a trend.

It seems plausible to assume that the more experienced analyst has greater sensitivity about how the patient will react to the analytic process. Perhaps unconsciously he can sense that at some stage of analysis, the patient will present him with a paradox similar to those described and which, to repeat, occur in varying degrees in all analytic patients. Thus, as discussed and to be discussed further (see pages 100 and 117), the older analyst, having experienced many such trying situations, *develops resistance to analysis as he gains more experience.*

Countertransference Reactions: General Considerations

Countertransference reactions to these difficult analytic situations have certain uniform qualities. Countertransference is determined both by idiosyncratic qualities of the personality of each individual analyst and by factors that are common to most analysts. These may be the outcome of certain characterological features which may regularly be found in persons who have chosen to be psychoanalysts. To be sure, this does not mean that analysts may not have many other character traits that allow wide variations of personalities. Nevertheless, it is the common denominators that are of special interest.

The type of patient I am discussing creates a particular dilemma for most analysts. If he tries to function as an analyst by making transference interpretations, the patient may react as one of my patients did, by objecting that I am trying to intrude my preconceived notions, or at least ideas that contain part of myself, into him. Not to function as an analyst, whatever form that may take, produces guilt. So whatever the analyst does, he is wrong; he has to pay a price for it. *He feels paralyzed.*

This is a crucial situation whenever it arises, and with the more regressed patient, it is more crucial. In some instances, the better integrated patient is able to experience important affective states and tolerate the analyst's presence. However, with patients suffering from severe psychopathology, affects are intense and painful and their sensitivity to external influences is so great that they find them totally disruptive. This latter situation has to be recognized and somehow dealt with in order that analysis may continue.

At first, one feels at a loss as to how to deal with such a situation, since anything one does is intrinsically wrong; however, recognizing the basis for such a bind helps make the atmosphere somewhat less taut. *The problem changes from knowing how to deal with the patient to discovering how to deal with oneself.* The analyst has to rediscover how he can once again achieve relaxation and regain analytic calm.

Instead of interpreting how the patient is relating to the analyst, I find it helpful to tell the patient how I am reacting to him. In essence, I confess to the patient how perplexed I feel and describe the dilemma I am facing. If my feelings are not particularly strong as is the usual situation with better integrated patients, I find that the discussion of my countertransference attitude is not necessary and I can proceed with the analysis. With severely disturbed patients such a revelation is received with sympathetic understanding. Even when the patient has felt spiteful and triumphant, there is still a soft quality to his response that indicates acceptance and, at times, even concern for my dilemma.

The atmosphere during such periods of analysis is often tense and seems to be full of strife. The patient has projected his primitive and exposed self into the analyst and has, in many instances, fused with him. His complaints about the intrusive analyst frequently represent his fear of being engulfed by this fusion and having his possibly minimal autonomy obliterated in a destructive fashion. He is, at the same time, concerned about destroying the analyst. If the analyst can survive the fusion and not respond directly to the content of the patient's projections or the helplessness which is, in fact, a part of himself, considerable analytic progress has been made. The analysis has passed through a crucial and decisive phase.

At this point the fusion aspects of the transference are the most intense and the course of the analysis will vary according to the traumatic aspects of the patient's early symbiotic phase of development. The analyst's countertransference response may serve as an important indicator of the specific qualities of the early symbiotic interaction and facilitate the understanding of the patient's developmental vicissitudes. Modell (1975) has described how the analyst often reacts with boredom to the closed-off, narcissistic patient. Flarsheim (1975) discusses his murderous reactions to a patient which later were understood to be recapitulations of the early relationship with the mother. In a similar vein, I (Giovacchini, 1972) have described how a countertransference response was provoked by the patient's projections and this interaction was a replica of the patient's crucial childhood relationship with his parents.

To use one's affective responses as a diagnostic indicator, so to speak, regarding the course of treatment may seem to be a somewhat hazardous procedure. This may be particularly precarious, especially when one is dealing with helpless patients as Adler (1972) has described, or suicidal patients as has been discussed by Boyer (1972). Searles (1973, 1975) focuses upon extremely intense reactions he has experienced that may cause one to wonder whether the disruption the analyst feels may make him unable to continue in the objective fashion analysis requires. Still, I believe that it has been the experience of most analysts who work with very disturbed patients to feel intensely and to view such feelings as an intrinsic and indispensable aspect of the therapeutic process.

Winnicott (1947) believes that the generation of hate in countertransference is an achievement for the patient. If the patient can experience an affect such as hatred, and if he can provoke others to hate him, he is creating a situation where love can also exist. To hate someone means that his existence is acknowledged. Winnicott (1956, 1971) also emphasizes that the patient is constructing a situation where he can fight against his environment in order to establish autonomy. These ideas can be extended in many different directions. Here I wish to focus upon the technical question as to whether one can depend upon the analyst's feelings to determine therapeutic stance. Can one rely on something so personal and often irrational as an emotional response, a response which is often painful and disruptive?

Two factors may help us determine whether a disruptive affect can be analytically useful. The first refers to that portion of the analyst's response that has been directly generated by the patient's projections. This does not mean that personal elements do not contribute to his response but the fact that the patient acted as an initial stimulus produces a situation where idiosyncratic elements promote understanding rather than distortions. True, for a while, the conflictful elements of the therapist's personality whose cathexis is precipitated by the patient's projections may dominate the picture and his therapeutic vision may be blurred. However, the experienced analyst will eventually question himself and wonder how and why he feels disturbed. Actually, *the more experienced analyst has integrated the concept of psychic determinism as a characterological modality.* He will pause to examine his feelings and seek their origins. He will look within himself and locate the intrapsychic sources of his reactions. He will also seek the precipitating factors and will discover them in the patient.

The second factor that makes countertransference responses useful rather than chaotic refers to the analyst's overall reactions to his feelings, and his discovery that they have been stimulated by the patient's projections. If the analyst reacts to such transference-countertransference situations with interest rather than anxiety or anger and does not react to the patient's projections in a condemnatory, accusatory manner, then the experience can lead to ego integration for both analyst and patient. This requires a capacity for dissociation; *the analyst may feel anxious or angry but his attitude about his fear and anger is nonanxious and benevolent.* He is reacting and at the same time is analytically interested in his reactions.

Perhaps such a pronouncement appears unctuous and self-evident. Nevertheless, I feel it is justified to emphasize the therapist's attitudes because the patients that are being focused upon are especially adept at creating strife and controversy. Without realizing it, the analyst finds himself arguing with the patient or making interpretations in an accusatory fashion.

The controversial atmosphere these patients create is difficult to describe. Still, it is familiar to most analysts and one can also detect it even in a clinical seminar during certain case presentations. I recall one particular episode where a colleague was reporting the patient's material and he interrupted himself frequently to express how tedious her complaints about her husband were. He emphasized that for years he had been hearing the same old thing. When several members of the group pointed out the symptomatic and defensive meaning of such complaints, he fully agreed and went on reporting his material in a calmer manner. During the next seminar, he began his discussion with indignation and exasperation. His opening words were, "She is doing it again, nagging about her husband, the same old thing." Even though we all believed that our colleague's orientation was not in the best analytic tradition, we, nevertheless, could feel with him and share some of his exasperation.

Unwittingly the analyst will reply in a critical or argumentative fashion to certain associations. The colleague just discussed was presenting monotonous, repetitive material and it was irritating, not just because of its irrationality, but because it was resistive to interpretation and never changed. *Whatever countertransference difficulties one has towards such patients will be augmented by the controversial atmosphere the patient has created but which the analyst has supported.*

If, on the other hand, it is "natural" to respond with exasperation as happened in our seminar, how can one overcome an attitude which leads to an impasse? The analyst has to examine his reactions to the patient in terms of the patient's character structure, but to gain understanding of the total picture rather than to blame someone else for his feelings.

Countertransference and Analytic Ambience

Once again, it is useful to consider the transference regression in terms of two components, the projection of feelings and parts of the self, and the creation of an ambience which recreates the early traumatizing environment. The controversial atmosphere which the patient is creating and in which the analyst may be participating is a replica of the infantile past. An analyst may not find it too difficult not to get involved in the content of the patient's infantile wishes or even to be a receptacle for hated introjects. Under these circumstances, he can maintain an overall perspective and not mix his analyzing self with what has been projected into him. It can be considerably more difficult, however, not to become part of the ambience the patient has created.

These different components of transference can be stated as differences between content and form. The latter is more elusive and easily overlooked. Before one knows it the patient has been able to spin an atmosphere around himself, and the analyst finds such an atmosphere unwittingly surrounding him. More specifically the analyst, as happened with my colleague, finds himself responding more to the tone, the formal qualities, of what the patient says rather than the content. If one pauses to examine content, more often than not it is fairly innocuous. Our colleague was responding more to the nagging and repetitive quality of what he heard rather than concentrating on what his patient was actually saying.

Why one becomes more easily involved with the ambience the patient creates rather than with the patient's projections is, undoubtedly, dependent upon many factors. The analyst's individual orientation is more likely to come to the fore under such circumstances. Some analysts may be more sensitive to certain issues rather than others, such as nagging. Here then, one is dealing with idiosyncratic countertransference responses, although there are particular qualities that all of us, more or less, uniformly react to. Generally, however, what these patients create is not usually so flamboyantly repulsive or obvious.

There are other factors that tend to get the analyst involved which may contain only minimal countertransference elements. The analyst may get caught in a trap he could not have anticipated. The possibility of having been able to prevent such a situation seems remote in some instances.

For example, a schizoid young man in his twenties had been in analysis with me for two years. He had been able to attach himself to a young lady who took a platonic interest in him. This suited him well since his basic orientation was homosexual and he was terrified of heterosexual involvement. He was able to form a relatively comfortable dependent relationship with this girl and they became roommates.

After being together for several months, his friend started staying out all night once or twice a week and then her absences became more frequent. He spoke of all this with considerable anger. I could understand why and how he would react to rejection.

After she was gone every night for approximately a week, he confronted her with her absences and what he feared was confirmed. She had attached herself to someone else, another girl, and was having a homosexual affair. The patient was furious and when telling me about it, he was sobbing and feeling anxious to the point of panic. He bitterly resented that she found others more important than him, that others were more influential and meaningful to her.

In view of his almost nonexistent self-esteem and narcissistic vulnerability his intense reactions were understandable. He blamed himself for being repulsive and alienating everyone that he attempted to get close to. He mercilessly berated himself. He writhed on the couch, tore his hair, and was truly miserable. In order to ease his pain somewhat, I commented that although our main interest was in understanding his self-condemnatory needs, he was nevertheless being unfair by blaming himself entirely for his unpleasant situation. His girl friend, apparently, had serious problems of her own and I tried to reassure him that irrational sources within her had something to do with her having chosen to leave him for a homosexual partner. To my surprise, I learned that the patient was expecting such a response and rather than feeling reassured by what I had said he felt even greater hopelessness and rage, both at himself and at me.

My rationale was simple. I only wanted to ease the extreme emotional upheaval he was experiencing, so that analysis could proceed. He had not only torn his hair but he had beaten his head against the wall, to the extent that I was feeling uncomfortable in watching him hurt himself. For my own comfort, I felt impelled to calm him. What I had not realized was that much of his behavior was designed to provoke me to react as I did. This became apparent later in the analysis. At the moment, after the initial wave of rage passed, he felt inconsolably depressed and misunderstood.

His associations emphasized that I was only interested in his roommate's problems and not at all in his. I was trying to excuse her behavior but had no concern whatsoever for his feelings. This, he noted, was a familiar pattern, one he had to endure throughout his life.

He described his home situation, one where he never felt understood nor was anyone at all interested in understanding him. His father, a prominent leader in the business community and various political organizations, conserved the majority of his attention for himself. The mother was described as remote. Whatever concern and feeling they expressed was directed to his two brothers. The patient is a middle child, and the parents were, even though minimally, involved with his siblings. The oldest brother was considered unusually gifted and the mother used him for her narcissistic enhancement. The father had groomed him to follow in his footsteps and today his brother is in a very high-echelon administrative position with a wealthy and prestigious company. The younger brother, in contrast, had always been a troublesome child. He suffered from encopresis during most of his childhood, refused for long periods of time to go to school and was at the time of my patient's treatment a serious drug problem. He commanded the parents' concern; they had brought him to see innumerable psychiatrists and for a while he was placed in a residential treatment center. With the parents' limited concern flowing toward the younger and older brothers, nothing was left over for my patient.

My attempts at consolation completely misfired. I had unwittingly been drawn into a situation that was a replica of his family constellation. I say unwittingly because I knew nothing about these particular aspects of his background. They only came to the surface later in the analysis, and indeed, the patient went to considerable lengths to conceal them from me. It was certainly not my intention to neglect and demean him by referring to his roommate's neurosis. On the contrary, my interest had been to restore his self-esteem.

Furthermore, I do not believe any particular countertransference attitudes were involved in my response. Perhaps my discomfort at the patient's hurting himself and some of my dismay about the intensity of his suffering may stem from certain inner sensitivities. Still, this type of sensitivity is not unusual, whatever its genetic sources, and the colleagues who have heard this material were able to empathize with my feelings and response.

To summarize briefly, this is an example of a situation where I was made to fit into an ambience the patient created. However, unlike other situations, I do not believe this was based on any of the analyst's particular sensitivities or vulnerabilities, that is, potentially disruptive countertranference reactions. True, all of the analyst's reactions have their unconscious component, what we might define as a countertransference element, but some responses have more of this component, one which contains more or less conflictual elements, and others are based primarily upon reality elements. I believe that, in this example, my response was based principally upon a current reality situation. Therefore, some patients are especially adept at drawing the analyst into their traumatic environment and reliving it in the consultation room. Such a situation can cause serious complications for the analytic relationship and, in extreme cases, may make analysis unmanageable.

From a technical viewpoint, I cannot formulate any specific technique other than analysis for dealing with such situations. In the latter instance, I weathered the storm of the patient's agony and imprecations. Gradually, I was able to see what had happened, and we discussed the situation. This helped considerably and he finally managed to understand how he had cast me in a particular role, a role into which he had manipulated me. He understood that my puzzlement and ignorance about what was going on was ultimately the most helpful therapeutic factor. It enabled the patient to look within himself and to understand the intensity of his reactions rather than to continue blaming the external world or one aspect of the external world, me. The analyst's awareness of his confusion and ignorance can preclude his setting up defenses designed to justify himself or to attain assurance that he really knows what is happening. The analyst's lack of defensiveness may create a situation favorable to analysis rather than reinforce the patient's irrational convictions, which are strengthened when they are directly denied or when the analyst tries to interpret them because he wishes to demonstrate to the patient that his intentions are well motivated. Worse still is the situation where the analyst really believes his interpretations are made in the patient's best interest rather than that they are rationalizations for his need to escape from a dilemma which makes him feel uncomfortable and helpless.

These disruptive situations can be considered from another viewpoint. They have up to this point been described as complications of treatment which lead to an impasse. This often happens, but here again the analyst's orientation is crucial. *One can also view them as phases of analysis that have to emerge in order to deal with certain fundamental transferences that are inevitable in view of the patient's psychopathology.* Often we are confronted with a series of crucial periods which recapitulate the traumatic effects of the infantile environment. The vicissitudes of the early nurturing relationship are relived during treatment. If the patient's childhood was punctuated by a sequence of crises, these have to emerge in the treatment. Thus, the impasses of early development become impasses in treatment. These are, however, impasses that are intrinsic to the patient's psychopathology and become impasses in treatment only when the analyst reacts adversely.

In view of the timelessness of the unconscious, one cannot predict the duration of such a situation nor how long it has to be experienced. Any expectations the therapist may have concerning length of time will be experienced by the patient as the analyst's impatience. Frequently patients will view such impatience as an intrusion, as has been discussed, and similar to the impatience directed toward them during their formative years.

As children, many patients suffering from characterological defects have felt extreme helplessness in view of the unattainable, narcissistically derived expectations of their parents. Often an analytic impasse represents a moratorium to ward off their demands of others so that they can discover their own expectations of themselves. *In order to consolidate an autonomous identity, patients may have to project their rage and helplessness into the analyst. They may use various techniques to achieve such a countertransference state.*

Projection of Helplessness

Perhaps it may not always be necessary that the analyst react by actually feeling what is projected into him, but he often does. In many instances when the therapist is not consciously aware of responding to the patient in terms of what has been projected into him, he may still be reacting in a defensive fashion. This may take many forms, including denial, reaction formation and professionalism, as has been discussed.

Frequently, less experienced analysts are not as defensive as more seasoned veterans, at least in terms of admitting their feelings of helplessness. True, the young analyst may not be aware that he is reflecting the patient's feelings; on the contrary, he may believe that he is not responding at all to the patient and that his feelings simply represent his true state of ineptness. This situation is analogous to the one where the patient cannot understand that his feelings toward the analyst are the outcome of transference. He believes they are real. Similarly, the inexperienced analyst who really does feel inadequate also believes his feelings are representative of the true state of affairs, rather than countertransference. In both instances, the patient's transference and the analyst's countertransference, there is usually some validity to the assertion that a reality factor is operating.

The question, nevertheless, can be raised as to why the analyst has to react at all and does not simply continue viewing the patient from an analytic perspective. Patients, after all, project all types of feelings and parts of the self into the analyst. This is transference and the process takes place within the patient's psyche. He really does not put elements of his psyche into the analyst; he merely feels he does. Still, often enough the analyst responds as if something has actually been put inside of him. He acts as a container, a "contenido," as our Latin American colleagues would say.

A further question can be raised as to whether analysts who react in a fashion consonant to the patient's projections are doing so because something intensely personal within themselves has been stimulated. This is always a possibility and as analysts we have to be constantly sensitive about the irrational within ourselves. Still, helpless feelings are so frequently encountered in the analysis of many patients, that if idiosyncratic elements are involved, they are sufficiently common to therapists that this transference-countertransference situation deserves further scrutiny.

A final question can be raised concerning the patient. Patients suffering from helpless and vulnerable self-representations, patients whose feelings of inadequacy are overwhelming, are in the experience of many analysts the rule rather than the exception. As the years go by the treatment of such patients has become a fairly routine activity and although there are often stormy moments due to the deep regression experienced by patients, analysts are sufficiently familiar with such phenomena that they are able to deal with them with relative equanimity. However, from time to time, one encounters a patient who creates difficulties beyond the ordinary. Consequently, one wonders if these patients behave in a subtle but destructive fashion and because of certain characterological peculiarities or special defensive adaptations, they are especially adept at undermining the therapist's equilibrium. This may be self-defeating in that the patient is defeating the treatment. The analyst feels that something disruptive is occurring within himself and he may then seek the advice of colleagues. It is this type of situation that is frequently discussed in seminars and workshops, one which is often referred to as a therapeutic stalemate or impasse.

I believe that such patients have special methods of relating that are more likely to provoke disruptive types of helplessness. I am distinguishing these countertransference reactions from those that I have just discussed, when the patient created an impasse by presenting the analyst with paradoxical situations. What I am about to describe is in no way paradoxical but it renders the analyst just as therapeutically impotent.

The Psychoanalytic Impasse and the Analyst's Values

For example, a colleague told me about a patient who made him feel tremendously anxious. He could not understand his feelings since basically he liked the patient, a bright, enterprising and inventive man in his early thirties. Nevertheless, the patient had created a situation which made the analyst feel helpless. He did not know what to do—specifically how to make interpretations. He admitted that he could not understand what was going on; consequently, he looked forward with dread to each session and felt angry at the patient. However, the analyst was not quite certain whether his anxiety and helplessness produced his anger or whether his anger overwhelmed him to the point that he was no longer able to function as an analyst. My colleague even considered the third possibility, that is, that his anger and helplessness arose from two different sources.

I was particularly struck by the fact that he brought up the third possibility since as analysts we are very familiar with the other two. My colleague wondered also why it occurred to him, and this became the starting point of our investigation. I introduced the possibility that he was reacting to the content of the patient's projections, an obvious assumption but one which had not occurred to my colleague because of the intensity of his feelings. He immediately saw his helplessness as being a counterpart of the patient's helplessness. Still, why the rage? And why should he feel the helplessness so intensely that he could no longer function?

I was reminded of other situations where such impasses have occurred, but rather than experiencing helplessness, the analyst felt very angry at the patient without being particularly aware as to why he should feel this way, since these were not instances of flagrant acting-out or obnoxious behavior. On the contrary, these patients were usually mild-mannered and compliant, and talked freely.

There are many reasons why analysts feel anger toward their patients. Here I wish to refer to one in particular, one which I believe applied to my colleague and one which is frequently encountered in the treatment of patients suffering from severe character pathology.

The patients that came to my mind as I was discussing my colleague's dilemma were characterized by two striking features: (1) They ascribed the causes of their difficulties to the external world, and (2) they expounded an ideology to which they attributed magic rescuing powers. One might now ask why these situations are in any way unusual. Are not these features fairly frequently encountered in patients suffering from characterological psychopathology, especially patients with an inclination toward a paranoid orientation? I have learned that the root of many countertransference difficulties with such patients was often found in the ideologies these patients selected. (See Giovacchini, 1972a.)

My colleague's patient exploited people in petty and trivial fashions. He seldom paid his bills and was otherwise completely unreliable in financial matters. He would take women out to dinner and manage not to have enough money to pay the check. He was extremely parsimonious and would read newspapers others had discarded on a bus or train in order to avoid spending money. My colleague, in contrast, always took care of money matters scrupulously and honestly. He also was an extremely generous person who more often than not picked up the check at restaurants when dining with friends and colleagues.

His patient had been dwelling upon his monetary manipulations to the exclusion of anything else. Unconsciously, my colleague was responding with rage and discomfort.

In another instance, one of my patients had expounded the virtues of various schools of psychotherapy other than analysis. He was subtly attacking analysis by comparing it unfavorably with the schools he was concentrating upon. Both these patients had basically paranoid cores and often produced bizarre material, bordering on the delusional, but it was not their obvious craziness that was disturbing. *They were attacking our value systems*.

In both instances, the therapist reacted to the content of the patient's projections and the patient was succeeding in undermining the therapist's analytic security. The analyst became impatient and felt that he was faced with an analytic impasse. He was faced with an impasse, however, because he felt uncomfortable and angry. *He also felt that the patient was trying to impose something upon him which he could not accept, something which threatened his autonomy*. Viewed retrospectively, this was a situation which recalled the infantile traumatic environment. Thus, *the patient defended himself against the assault on his embryonic identity by producing a similar dilemma within the analyst*. Why does the patient so often succeed? Is it due to some particular idiosyncratic quality in the analyst? Or does this situation permit generalizations? One can discuss both points of view.

First, one has to consider the form of the patient's material. Both my colleague's patient and mine presented their viewpoints in a logical, rational fashion. My colleague's patient was extolling his own viewpoint as a reasonable way of life, and if saving money were an ultimate aim, he was an eminent success. My patient's arguments were also presented in a concise, logical fashion.

In spite of the fact that we understood that our patients' exaltations of their viewpoints were the result of defensive needs against feelings of helpless vulnerability and fears of being assaulted and overwhelmed, we, nevertheless, felt threatened. The fact that the patients were displaying problems of delusional proportions was *obscured by a seemingly rational superstructure*. It was this rationality that disturbed us. We found ourselves debating with our patients, using persuasion and argument rather than considering the patients' intrapsychic motivations. With obvious craziness, as stated, we would have been more comfortable. Thus, the psychoanalytic impasse is due to a combination of factors which result in a specific interaction between patient and analyst, one which includes the patient's psychopathology and the analyst's self-representation and ego ideal. *This is an impasse, but not necessarily a therapeutic obstacle. It becomes an obstacle only if the therapist makes it into one.*

The fact that the analyst feels uncomfortable is not the problem. It becomes a problem only when the analyst demands, or even simply expects, the patient to change in a fashion so that he will no longer feel disturbed. In other words, an impasse arises when the analyst, in order to regain calm, somehow insists upon the patient changing the *manifestations of his psychopathology*.

The question can be raised whether it is inevitable that the analyst feel disturbed. Because of particular characterological adaptations, it may be necessary for the patient to attempt to provoke certain reactions in the therapist, but should the patient be allowed to succeed? If one were familiar with such situations and could anticipate them, perhaps it would be possible to simply analyze them without feeling personal upheaval.

Some authors (Winnicott, 1947) do not believe this is possible. The argument usually given is that in order to be able to evaluate the situation, one has to have an emotional response first, which acts as a spur, so to speak, which then leads to comprehension. Such a countertransference response becomes a diagnostic vehicle.

In the analytic situation, the therapist has to be sensitive to his personal reactions, disruptive or otherwise. Naturally, he should understand his personality make-up as clearly as possible. Consequently, adverse reactions which lead to such impasses are scrutinized in terms of blind spots.

Blind spots in the analyst, however, are as inevitable as are the manifestations of the patient's psychopathology and with proper analytic scrutiny can be utilized for therapeutic advantage. Still, once the analyst has had an experience, or several experiences, similar to those just described here, he has learned something about his own specific sensitivities. When one becomes more familiar with such problems, countertransference reactions become milder.

The necessity for a diagnostic countertransference can be compared to the generation of anxiety. Anxiety as a signal stimulates various responses within the ego's executive system which is designed to master a problem situation. In some instances, one may be so familiar with the problem that anxiety is not felt. One reacts automatically, perhaps reflexively. (See Schur, 1958.)

With patients, something similar may occur. The therapist, because he is so familiar with the particular patients who need to disrupt him, can assess the transference situation without necessarily getting emotionally involved. He may not have to feel disrupted in order to locate the patient's need to disrupt.

However, the patient can be subtle and the analytic relationship, at best, is difficult. This discussion raises the question as to whether it is absolutely necessary for the analyst to experience adverse feelings in the countertransference. Perhaps not absolutely necessary, but this is an abstraction about a hypothetically ideal analyst. Being human includes having failings. Possibly without such failings there would be no treatment of patients who have so often been used by persons who have to deny their own failings.

THE THERAPEUTIC PROCESS

The countertransference situation just discussed occurs during states of deep regression, states which recapitulate essential elements of an infantile traumatic situation. Experience demonstrates that if such regression can be maintained without intense disruption so that analysis continues, higher states of ego integration can be achieved. One can even think in terms of resolution, although in contrast to what we have been taught about resolution of oedipal wishes in the classical psychoneuroses, here one is dealing with the structuring of missing or defective parts of the self.

Whether analysis can provide the patient with psychic structure he has never had is a frequently debated question. If because of infantile privation (see Winnicott, 1956, 1971) the ego does not acquire adaptive techniques, can they be learned later in life while one is being analyzed? Some analysts and learning theorists believe that unless a child is provided with helpful experiences at a particular time, his ability to achieve a specific skill will be considerably diminished. Langer (1948) describes a chattering period somewhere during the first year of life as an optimal period for learning language. Later in life the acquisition of language skills becomes increasingly difficult and in some instances impossible. Some analysts compare patients in characterological defects to patients with organic defects due to poor nutrition, metabolic problems, or congenital disorders. If one is born with only one leg, no treatment will be able to get him to grow a new one.

The psyche, however, is considerably more resilient than the soma. As a result of analytic treatment, patients acquire abilities they never had before—adaptations which are the outcome of psychic structuralization and indicative of higher states of ego integration. If one continues to think of analysis as a method primarily based upon the acquisition of insight rather than education, then the analytic process has to be understood in terms of its structure-forming potential.

In the framework of severe psychopathology one can study the analytic process from three different but interrrelated perspectives: (1) projection of constricting introjects; (2) resolution of the symbiotic fusion, and (3) introjection of parts of the analytic interaction.

Projection of Constricting Introjects

The transference regression recapitulates although it does not exactly duplicate early developmental stages. As discussed in the section on regression, the patient projects hostile, disruptive introjects into the analyst. To some measure, this frees him. Being partially rid of such introjects by giving them to the therapist for the moment permits the patient to take in experiences that were previously unavailable to him. Here, one is referring to a positive aspect of regression, an aspect that is often overlooked because it is frequently obscured by the patient's rage and attacks upon the analyst. The atmosphere, on the surface, may be so tense that it is very difficult to see anything good in it or potentially constructive.

For example, a middle-aged woman in her early forties would scream at me because I was not taking care of her properly. I was selfish and preferred others to her. I hated her and wished her dead. She stressed that I did not care whether she thrived or perished.

Clearly, this was a reflection of her early relationship with her mother, a woman who was described as being preoccupied with the patient's only sibling, a younger sister. The mother was also a weak, ineffectual alcoholic who had a masochistic relationship with a cruel, tyrannical husband. The patient has succeeded in viewing me as one who turned away from her; in the transference context, she was able to express her rage, something she had not been able to do previously.

The patient's behavior during analysis showed considerable deterioration. Her outbursts of anger kept increasing in frequency and intensity and she seemed to be losing all elements of self-control. It seemed as if the analysis had reduced the patient to a state of utter degradation and misery.

Imagine my surprise when a colleague, a personal friend of the patient, complimented me on how well she was doing. Apparently, she had become assertive and self-confident and was able to participate in all types of activities that had once frightened her. She had been unable to give dinner parties, because she felt she did not know how. She had felt incapable of learning anything new and now she had enrolled in several adult courses and discussion groups and was doing very well. She was also selfish, arbitrary, and overbearing and could become petulant and angry if she did not get her own way. This, too, was in marked contrast to her usual timid and withdrawn demeanor.

Her behavior outside of the analysis seemed to be a mixture of mature and immature behavior, but it was certainly considerably more mature than what I saw. The patient was able to leave the immature part of herself, or at least a good portion of it, with me.

As the analysis continued it became more apparent that she was able to use the mechanism of ego-splitting. The hateful, condemning parts of herself, her inhibiting and devouring introjects were projected into me. When she left me, she was able to leave these disruptive forces behind and she could relate to the outside world with considerably greater freedom. This increased her self-esteem and gave the general impression of a patient who had made considerable analytic progress.

On the other hand, the ego state that the regression had reached, an ego state prior to a stable registration of hostile introjects, was an archaic one. The patient was relieved of primitive constricting introjects which had impeded emotional development and she could now express needs and seek adaptive techniques which once had been unavailable to her. Therefore, the needs she expressed in the analysis were consonant with the regressed state, while her behavior in the external world, although distinctly different now, still contained many immature elements. However, even the immature elements were different from previous ones. Before treatment she used a variety of primitive defenses, mainly masochistic submission and schizoid withdrawal, similar to that of her mother. Now, she seemed to have shed this superstructure and was able to bring forth elements of her infantile personality that had, as far as we know, never emerged.

The patient was now capable of utilizing some beneficial experiences in the outer world. She could integrate them because of a fluid ego state which was no longer hampered by constrictive introjects. Still, she approached external objects in a voracious, all-consuming fashion which was to be expected since this was a primitive ego state. What seemed to be enthusiasm, eagerness to learn, and becoming involved was experienced by some of her acquaintances as frightening. They tended to withdraw.

The situation with this patient was similar to the clinical illustrations in the section on regression. Here, however, I am not emphasizing the emergence of an identity sense in particular, although this is important, but instead, am referring to the patient's greater capacity, because of regression, to benefit from objects in the external world. I am also emphasizing how the analytic situation is used for this purpose and how the ego's splitting facilitates this process. Furthermore, I wish to call attention to how the patient's relationships in the outer world and those in the analysis gradually merged and achieved greater unity.

The turbulent atmosphere this patient created within the analysis gradually become calmer as she developed the capacity to use splitting mechanisms *within* the analytic session itself and view me in different ways, rather than seeing me as a repository for only evil. She would revile and attack me, as she had done for many months, but would then abruptly switch her associations to accounts of the constructive aspects of her daily life and see that I somehow fitted within this context. As she gained reassurance that she had needs which could be gratified, her peremptory and sometimes impetuous demands became modulated. She compared herself to a rough, crude savage, suddenly thrust into a highly complex, civilized society. In her fantasy, regardless of his gaucheness, the savage is kindly received and patiently taught the customary means of gratification. While she was being analyzed others were able to teach her how to make proper requests regarding almost everything, such as table manners and the various amenities of daily life. Slowly, the savage ceased to be a savage.

This, in effect, was a description of a series of ego states she was experiencing. Being rid of constrictive introjects, for the moment, by projecting them into the analyst, permitted her to seek gratifying experiences. But first, she pushed herself forward, one might say, in a crude, awkward perhaps "savage" fashion. However, the increase in self-esteem and the reassurance she achieved when the external world demonstrated that her needs could be met led to the acquisition of higher states of ego organization. *Needs now became desires.* Her sensory range expanded. She could experience pleasurable feelings, a capacity which was not permitted to develop during childhood.

Freedom from constricting introjects made it possible to incorporate potentially helpful experiences from the external world. Although the patient's ego state, at first, was regressed and primitive, there was still an increase in reality-testing as this function was less impaired and distorted by harmful internal psychic elements insofar as the latter were partially decathected because of the transference projection. She shed her savage qualities and in a positive feedback sequence was able to tame the primitive within herself.

Frequently, during the treatment of patients similar to the woman just described, the analyst despairs. He may be aware of the massive projections that are occurring in the transference but the patient's ravings and rantings may be so venomous that the therapist may lose hope that anything good will come out of them. What is being lost sight of is that the upheaval that both analyst and patient are experiencing is, in itself, an important aspect of a potentially integrative experience. The analyst may be the last to perceive the manifestations of the patient's characterological advances.

It is not really important whether the analyst is aware of the patient's improvement. The patient's awareness, however, is crucial, because if he can experience himself more fully, he will be able to direct himself toward experiences that will enhance his autonomy. Analysts who treat such patients may have to forego the gratification of directly seeing them develop emotionally, or at least, there may be long periods of time when the only course in treatment seems to be downhill.

Complications occur when the therapist attempts to *cure* the patient, which may mean trying to introduce order into the surrounding chaos. Interpretation, on the other hand, may facilitate dissociation in a positive sense. Demonstrating to the patient that he is reliving infantile reactions which he had never been able to express previously in his current life allows the patient to continue feeling turbulent infantile rage and disappointment, and, at the same time, become increasingly aware of the adaptive value of his reactions. As the split widens within the patient there is considerable easing of tension in the analyst.

Symbiotic Fusion and Autonomy

These psychic states are characterized by a lack of discrimination between the self and external objects. In order to form an introject, the ego has to be able to perceive an external object if the representation of that object is to be retained as part of one's psychic apparatus. Here it is important to recognize that patients who have regressed to such early developmental levels are functioning with psychic processes characteristic of fusion states, that is, of the symbiotic phase. The resolution of the symbiotic fusion is an important aspect of a process which may enable the patient to overcome his difficulties and to pursue further his previously interrupted emotional development.

The mechanisms involved in the passage through the symbiotic phase as it occurs during the unfolding of the transference are perhaps the most important elements in the therapy of patients suffering from characterological psychopathology. Depth of regression as a separate topic has already been discussed (see section on Therapeutic Regression). Regression to primitive levels may be essential to the analysis of all patients, but with better-integrated patients, as mentioned, the regression may not be so intensely experienced or dominate the therapeutic relationship. However, insofar as analysis involves acquisition of new psychic structures or higher levels of structuralization the symbiotic phase has some relevance to the analytic interaction.

The ego states previously described, where the analyst has become a repository of hostile introjects, is very close to a fusion state. The patient's rage and protestations separate him from the hatred and the hated objects which were once part of himself. He is now able to place objects back in the external world—objects with which he was once fused. In the process of projecting, he is also releasing the rage attached to such objects, a rage which was acquired after fusion had already been initiated. These patients experience many feelings during treatment beside rage; often they attribute magical wisdom to the analyst and they may feel extremely comfortable, even blissful.

Before proceeding, I once again wish to emphasize that I do not believe that analytic treatment proceeds in a well-ordered, predetermined sequence. This is never true and it is especially untrue of patients suffering from characterological problems. I am simply emphasizing that there are fairly typical ways of viewing the transference regressions of analytic patients and it is possible to understand phenomena in treatment that phenomenologically appear confusing and, at times, chaotic. The disorganization that dominates many analyses can be understood in an organized fashion. Sequences will vary but certain interactions occurring within a constant setting will have a somewhat predictable course. However, it may be understandable only retrospectively rather than predictable.

Clinical experience demonstrates that the projection of hostile introjects into the therapist also represents a fusion state as well as being on the edge of one, as has been described.

The patient is projecting parts of his self-representation which have incorporated the hateful qualities that have been attached to his introjects. He is, in a sense, securing relief by ridding himself of aspects of the self that cause him the most misery. Attributing to the analyst qualities that belong to his identity sense occurs in the setting of symbiotic fusion. The patient is maintaining separateness in regard to his hostile introjects which are now placed outside of himself. (This was discussed in the section on the Narcissistic Transference and the Psychoanalytic Process.) Additional clinical examples, I believe, are relevant here.

The first example is derived from direct observation behind a one-way mirror. We were observing a mother and her eight-month-old male child. The infant was busily occupied playing with a wide variety of toys while his mother was sitting unobtrusively in the middle of the room. The child crawled from toy to toy, playing with some and finding others too difficult. He became visibly frustrated with some of the more complicated toys and would resolve some of his frustration by simply throwing them away. He might, however, return to them. In the meantime, the mother kept sitting impassively and her son never turned to her for help. In fact, he totally ignored her. It seemed as if she were not there; he never acknowledged her presence, preferring to continue on his own, and finally rejecting what he could not master.

At a prearranged time, the mother got up slowly and quietly walked out of the room. The infant continued as if he were totally oblivious of her until she was completely through the door. At this point, he abruptly stopped playing and had a vicious temper tantrum. He kicked, screamed, and beat his fists on the floor. He was a pathetic sight and seemed to be falling apart completely. His behavior gave the impression of a mixture of rage and despair.

In the midst of his disruption a female member of the observation team approached him with the aim of cuddling and pacifying him. She tried picking him up but he violently resisted her efforts. The more she tried to appease him the more vigorously he fought her. He was absolutely inconsolable. Being unable to soothe him, she left. His mother entered once again. The child immediately stopped crying, instantaneously became calm and continued playing as he had been before. This occurred without any ostensible awareness of his mother's presence.

These data are the result of direct observation and one cannot make exact formulations about mental processes from behavior alone. However, what occurred is suggestive. The infant acted independently in his mother's presence, and then suffered what one might call a separation panic following her departure. A stranger only made him react with greater anxiety and violence. The mother's return reestablished his previous equilibrium and permitted him to continue behaving as if he needed no one. The child seemed to be able to *maintain autonomy within a symbiotic context.*

In analysis one frequently encounters transference situations where the patient is behaving in a fashion similar to this infant. The patient may ignore the analyst's presence, pay no attention to his interpretations and minimize his importance in innumerable ways. Therefore, it is striking that when the analyst informs him he will be gone for some time, as on a vacation, the patient may have intense reactions which seem surprising in view of his usual indifference. In many such instances, these are examples of autonomy within a symbiotic context: the patient can maintain his autonomy only in a dependent setting.

Course of Symbiotic Fusion During Analysis

Autonomy within a symbiotic context is designed to maintain defensive equilibrium. The achievement of separation from the analyst can be a crucial determinant of analytic progress. Once such patients can experience symbiosis, and acknowledge their involvement, they begin to emerge from the fusion and achieve individuation. There are different sequences as to how this may occur. The following vignette demonstrates a particular sequence.

A 28-year-old graduate student spent most of the beginning months of his analysis trying to impress me with his brilliance and erudition. Some of his associations were provocative in that he was able to concentrate upon areas I valued (see previous section). Occasionally, I would debate with him.

Gradually the atmosphere changed. He began praising me and instead of seeking situations in his daily life where he might criticize me, he sought persons who were more inclined to view me positively. This was a phase of idealization and he did what he could to maintain an ideal image of me.

The transference was characterized by omnipotent fusion. He attributed magical powers to me and expected omnipotent salvation. The fusion was comfortable, sometimes blissful. Ours was a good and wise relationship and the rest of the world contained all the trivial irrationalities of mankind. Although the feelings involved in this fusion were derived from primitive infantile expectations, our relationship was, on the surface, reasonable and friendly and did not seem megalomanic or based upon a paranoid orientation to the outer world.

This type of transference is not unusual in patients suffering from characterological problems with basically psychotic constellations. The inevitable frustration has been frequently described. (See Giovacchini, 1965.) Here I wish to emphasize how the vicissitudes of this transference state can be understood in terms of acquiring further ego structure. This will eventually lead us to a discussion of the resolution of the symbiotic tranference. Before one can discuss this topic, however, one has to explore further how various psychic elements are distributed between patient and analyst.

This patient's characterological defenses, I believe, are characteristic of many patients who are seen in analytic practice. Often, one encounters persons who present an arrogant, prepossessing exterior, demeaning others to aggrandize themselves. On the surface they present a picture of narcissistic invulnerability, a reaction-formation to their underlying vulnerability. Several such cases have already been described. Although defensive manifestations may vary, for we frequently see patients whose basic inadequacies are plainly showing, the core of the personality, which, to some extent, must remain hidden, is vulnerable and overwhelmed by hatred and self-hatred. The superstructure erected by the ego is designed to protect from such a disruptive self-representation.

Klein (1946) and Fairbairn (1952) emphasized how the bad object is internalized so that it may be controlled. If the ego fails to maintain such control it is overwhelmed and this might be experienced as panic, a state that Jones (1929) refers to as *aphanisis* (this concept is, however, somewhat more complicated) or as rage, which is familiar to clinicians as a consequence of narcissistic injury. Feeling that one can no longer control his behavior or affects is a state where one's fundamental and sustaining narcissism is disrupted. The patient also experiences narcissistic vulnerability because the parts of the self that can no longer be submerged are hateful and unacceptable and cannot be reconciled with the ego ideal.

Morse (1972) discusses these issues and criticizes Winnicott's concepts of the true and the false self because he believes that Winnicott attributes the false self to the ego and the true self to the id. From this, he concludes that the true self is kept incommunicado from the external world, whereas the false self maintains object contact. This is an extremely complicated subject which cannot be viewed in such a simplified fashion. The relevant point here is that whereas Klein and Fairbairn think in terms of a controlled, internalized "bad object," Winnicott, according to Morse, has an opposite concept in that the true self, which would be equivalent to a good object or a good self-object, is kept submerged by a defensive superstructure.

The term "self" means that one is not dealing with a structural concept such as an id locale. Winnicott was referring to various aspects of the ego, a multifaceted structure. The true self is turned toward instinct-powered aspects of the psyche and on external objects linked with spontaneous expression, whereas the false self is turned toward objects in the outer world that must be controlled. The true self would be the essence of one's aliveness but that does not make it equivalent to instinct.

Klein's (1952) concepts are relevant insofar as one is dealing with primitive defensive adaptations designed to maintain some organization in a psyche where there is a lack of integration, unity and harmony, where self and object representations threaten each other and lead to fundamental splits. Such dissociations become manifest during psychoanalytic treatment.

The split may be directly manifest, as in patients where the hated self is located in the split-off portion of the psyche or projected into external objects or the ambience the patient has constructed (see section on Therapeutic Regression). The bad aspects of the self are controlled in various fashions, depending upon the patient's past experiences and the defensive adaptations derived from such experiences. My patient was able to control unacceptable parts of the self by keeping them submerged by a grandiose superstructure, one method among many and one which did not require any particular degree of psychic dissociation.

During treatment the patient reinforced his defensive adaptations in two ways, both involving fusion. First, he maintained his equilibrium by projecting the devalued self into me. This increased his grandiosity because he was able to rid himself of his inadequacy. He had someone toward whom he could feel condescendingly superior. His second method of strengthening his defensive position occurred later in therapy when he projected his grandiosity into me and then fused with this positive projection. Here one has a common megalomanic transference fusion, a phenomenon that has been familiar to clinicians for many years, and one which also involves the further projection of the bad self into the environment or external objects. To recapitulate, the patient first projected his vulnerability and hateful self into me. Then it seemed that he extended this projection from me to the external world, creating a setting which made it possible to effect a grandiose fusion.

Conceptualizing these events as fusion states can be justified both theoretically and clinically. Insofar as we are dealing with self-representations, their projections would constitute fusion states. It does not matter whether the projected elements are representative of a developmentally arrested and malformed self or an overcompensatory, megalomanic ego state that dominates the identity sense. *The analyst is perceived as some aspect of the patient's identity and regardless of whether it is a positive or negative aspect, this type of tranference involves megalomanic fusion.*

Clinically, this is borne out by periods of analysis where the patient feels "at one" with the analyst. He may be silent, and since he feels that he and the analyst are joined, the analyst knows what is going on inside of him. Words are not needed and would disturb unity by indicating there are two people, speaker and listener (see Flarsheim, 1973). Some patients often call themselves by the analyst's name, or vice versa, indicating a blending of identities. As occurred with my patient, these stages of analysis can be very comfortable, even blissful for patients, but it is still a defensive tranference state which is maintained by a basic paranoid orientation.

The reproduction of early omnipotence within the symbiotic transference is often unstable. The patient may find that he cannot obtain the sustenance he needs, that is, he cannot maintain himself with the delusion of magical salvation. Fusion with an omnipotent analyst is simply not enough to permit him to keep his vulnerable and hateful self in that part of his mind which represents the external world and objects. The megalomanic transference fusion becomes even more difficult to preserve if the analyst does not foster or reinforce it. Its breakdown may take various forms.

I will only briefly mention the disruptive sequelae of the dissolution of the megalomanic transference fusion, which has to be emphatically distinguished from resolution of omnipotent symbiosis, since this subject has been focussed upon in considerable detail in the psychoanalytic literature (see Boyer and Giovacchini, 1967, and Giovacchini, 1972). The patient is likely to experience disintegrative feelings because he is disappointed in the analyst who has usually implicitly promised magical rescuing. The analyst has helped secure the projection of the hateful self, and by his omnipotent goodness, to elevate the patient to an exalted state, clearly an omnipotent reaction-formation against his inner core of helpless vulnerability. However, this collusion between analyst and patient, which can be referred to as a *mutual delusion*, often flounders because the patient cannot derive what he needs from what is essentially an hallucinatory wish-fulfillment. Because of such disappointment the patient's rage and frustration may reach suicidal proportions at worst, or the discontinuation of treatment at best. The patient's anger is considerably less if the analyst did not reinforce the projection of omnipotence; he is still frustrated and may regress even further. This regression may take several forms which can lead to the resolution of the symbiotic transference.

After experiencing bitter disappointment and regressing to a state of almost total helplessness, my patient began good-naturedly to accept the inevitable, that is, he gradually became aware that I could not create an omnipotent, exalted person. He began to view our relationship on a more realistic basis and became more tolerant of our imperfections. His period of acute frustration was short-lived and considerably ameliorated by interpretation of the defensive meaning of his need to idealize me. He then became collaborative and felt obligated to help me overcome my inadequacies so I could achieve sufficient skills that would enable me to help him.

I believe the sequence this patient illustrated is more common than is generally recognized. Searles (1975) thoroughly discusses such reactions and presents abundant clinical material. He stresses that patients have a need to cure the analyst; finally, patients reach a stage in treatment where their main focus is on helping the analyst overcome personal inhibitions and inadequacies. Searles does not explain this situation as Klein (1930) would have, that is, as making reparations for destructive feelings. He does not see his patients' motivations stemming from a need to restore the objects that they have damaged in their fantasies. Instead, Searles believes that everyone goes through a phase where he has to be a psychotherapist and the execution or even awareness of this need has become interfered with by disruptive object relations which, in turn, are responsible for his psychopathology.

I do not believe I can go as far as Searles has done although his thesis is intriguing and deserves consideration. Nevertheless, I have witnessed repeated instances where patients have adopted what might be called a maternal, guiding attitude toward me. This could be a consequence of symbiotic fusion, but one which differs considerably from the megalomanic, idealized fusion just described. The patient has fused what he considers to be the damaged part of himself with the object representation he retains of me. Then he attempts reparation, as Klein describes.

My patient incorporated various aspects of me and then endowed the introject with unacceptable aspects of his self-representation. This was followed by a prolonged period of treatment (two years) during which he tried to construct a less objectionable representation of me and of himself since he had effected a fusion.

In this case, as in those reported by Searles, the constructive elements of analysis seemed to begin with his manifest need to care for me. Freud (1915) might have been referring to a similar phenomenon when he described the sequence required for sublimation. As discussed in a previous section (The

Narcissistic Transference and the Analytic Process), he stated that a sexual instinct first has to be detached from the external object and then turned back toward the ego. Object cathexis thus becomes narcissistic cathexis. Then, while in the ego it undergoes desexualization and finally it is returned to the external object in a sublimated, that is, a desexualized, form. Here, too, the patient forms an introject of the analyst based upon the projections of the damaged aspects of his self-representation. This constitutes a fusion, one which does not necessitate a view of the analyst as an external object. By being able to retain the analyst within his ego, the patient has somehow created a situation which permits him to work over the damaged analyst and to heal him. He finally can return the analyst to the external world, an adequate and valued analyst to whom he can relate in a healthy, competent fashion. The sequence of a return from the external world to the ego and then back to the external world is exactly the same as Freud's concept of sublimation, a mechanism which Freud considered integrative and progressive in terms of psychic development rather than psychopathologically defensive. The positioning of the analyst in this nonomnipotent fusion seems to stimulate the patient's healing potential which in a symbiotic state is a self-healing potential.

Not all patients become the analyst's mentor, nor do all patients follow this same sequence from an idealized fusion to one where the patient can relatively comfortably use the analyst as a repository of his vulnerable self. Indeed, quite the opposite process was described earlier when I referred to the analyst as being the repository of the patient's organized self (see section on The Narcissistic Transference and the Analytic Process). However, in that instance the same processes were still involved, only it was the analyst's ego that the introjects had to pass through and then become functionally significant in promoting ego integration. But it was a healthy part of the patient's ego that was projected and in other periods of treatment the bad analyst was also introjected and worked over in the fashion just described.

Two other reactions related to those described often followed the megalomanic fusion, according to the experience of many analysts. The first is a common situation where the patient remains helpless and the analyst is given complete healing powers. This relationship sounds identical to the idealized fusion, except now the analyst is not particularly idealized. He is held in high esteem because he has survived the patient's destructiveness. The aura is not one of omnipotence, as previously described, nor does the patient expect to achieve perfection. Although there are many primary process elements attached to this relationship, the difference between this state and the idealized fusion is primarily quantitative. *It is also recapitulation of an early developmental phase where the patient was totally dependent but the more sophisticated concept of omnipotence had not yet developed.*

The second sequel to the idealized symbiosis is one where the analyst is converted into the hated part of the patient's self-representation. This is an overtly paranoid situation; the patient requires someone to persecute him or needs another person toward whom he can feel condescendingly superior. In spite of a generally hostile orientation, the patient, nevertheless, indicates his need for treatment and can separate his feelings and the task of analysis. In other words, both patient and analyst can maintain an observational perspective provided that the analyst recognizes the adaptive value of being maligned and does not try to interfere with the patient's projections. The patient feels a sense of freedom from oppressive forces within him since he has been able to compartmentalize them within the mental representation of the analyst. This permits certain integrative forces to become operative. Their mechanisms will be discussed after considering various developmental factors.

Developmental Phases and Psychic Organization

Freud (1900, 1911) formulated a stage of omnipotent wish fulfillment as an early developmental phase. The regression of many disturbed patients apparently recapitulates such a phase. The patients just described, in contrast, experience, at times, what seems to be total dependence without any particular omnipotent tinge.

One gains the impression from the therapy of such patients that this type of dependent transference closely recapitulates a developmental phase that does not include omnipotence. The dependent transference creates a situation that can lead to further ego structure and integration whereas the idealized symbiosis which includes omnipotence does not seem to have a therapeutic potential. As stated, the latter, if it persists, leads to fixation.

Viewing such clinical material causes one to question whether a stage of omnipotence should be considered part of the ordinary developmental sequence. *I believe it is more useful to postulate a phase of total dependence without omnipotence and to consider stages of omnipotence as either pathological variants or defensive adaptations.* To feel omnipotent requires the capacity for the formation of structured affect and cognition, both of which would be beyond what the neonate can achieve. Later, during the course of emotional development, one can become aware of how inadequate, in the most general sense, maternal care was and how disruptive the stage of total dependence has been. Omnipotent orientations to combat this underlying disorganization and vulnerability can be constructed only when the child at least recognizes there is an external world that has to be controlled, an impinging reality that cannot be integrated with inner impulses and needs. Thus, although trauma leaves its mark during neonatal stages of dependence, omnipotent defenses are not structured until much later. An omnipotent stage of dependence, as such, does not exist but is formed later as a superstructure, so to speak, to an early dependent phase which has not been successfully traversed. Megalomania can be considered a defensive distortion caused by an ego defect due to improper maternal care when the infant was totally dependent.

Improper maternal care can have many forms from physical assault to complete neglect. The quality of mothering will determine character structure and psychopathology. This is another subject. Here I am simply referring to a developmental situation where the infant has, to some extent, been damaged very early, and depending upon the degree of trauma, his subsequent development will be affected and particular characterological defenses will be constructed. Among them is one which is characterized by megalomania.

From one point of view, to be megalomanic represents an achievement. It leads to adaptation and cohesion. There are many patients who have not developed this capacity and they often reveal their chaotic, structureless inner core, sometimes to the extent that they are totally inept and cannot survive without custodial care. The patients discussed here have, at least, characterological defenses which maintain them. On the other hand, such defenses block further development.

A transference characterized by regression to a megalomanic phase is, in essence, a defense transference. This type of regression often occurs early in the treatment of patients suffering from severe characterological problems and it may persist throughout most of the analysis. Then, the analytic task is almost wholly concerned with working through such an orientation. There are, of course, many variations to the manifestations of the megalomanic transference which depend upon the individual's background and specific traumas. Briefly, one encounters a spectrum ranging from blissful fusion to paranoid depreciation of external objects, sometimes including the analyst, in order to maintain an omnipotent core. One need not discuss phenomenology further here.

The common denominator I wish to stress is that the patient is trying through his megalomania to defend himself against the consequences of inadequate mothering he has suffered during infancy. Even though the experiences the patient had with his mother occurred so early that they are not even capable of being given verbal expression, they had profound effects upon the developing psyche which led to pathological distortions of psychic functioning. Developmental patterns are disturbed and the construction of a cohesively integrated ego is impeded. The core of the ego, that is, the self-representation which I have discussed as being the essence of the identity sense, does not achieve autonomous status. In Winnicott's (1953) terms the transitional object is not formed; inner establishment of gratifying experiences does not occur. From the viewpoint of later developmental phases, one can state that the lack of registration of experiences which reestablish homeostasis leads to faulty maternal introjects.

Gratification has many meanings and, as Spitz (1965) has convincingly demonstrated, to be gratified is not solely determined by ministering to nutritional needs. To lack the memory of gratifying experiences has profound effects upon one's sense of worth and general security. The panic associated with not knowing whether one will be cared for and the chaos that results from the relentless impinging of inner impulses is crippling to the security demanded for the establishment of self-esteem and a firm identity-sense.

One can understand why such patients persistently bring the frustration of their early life into treatment and seldom leave them. The struggle to affirm themselves by seeking reassurance that they will be cared for, that is by trying to prove that they are *capable of being gratified* dominates the treatment and it is responsible for its often monotonous and repetitive qualities. However, as they relive their traumatic experiences, the ensuing panic, or the paranoid, omnipotent defenses designed to protect them from such inchoate terror, make the analysis stormy; this may be trying for the therapist but it breaks up any monotonous sequence that he may have allowed himself to settle into.

Can the analyst make up for what essentially was a frustration of dependent needs at a neonatal stage of development? The question has been frequently discussed and opinions are divided. Bettelheim (1966) believes that the effects of early mishandling can, to a large measure, be undone by responding to the child's needs. He believes that one can provide the product or action directly or symbolically (Sechehaye, 1947). Winnicott (1956, 1973) basically agrees with this position and discusses how he may hold a patient's head or function in some fashion that goes beyond interpretation in order to supply something that was missing in the patient's early life. Both are referring mainly to children,but many analysts would agree that the same principles apply to adults. I have argued the opposite viewpoint, indicating that mother's milk, so to speak, is gratifying only at a specific time, and to attempt to supply it afterwards, that is, when there has been considerable maturation and emotional development, even though faulty, cannot make up for the initial deprivation. Now, I believe that the question has to be stated differently and more succinctly in order to understand the relevance of the gratifying therapist to the analytic process.

Often, patients suffering from characterological problems punctuate treatment with periods of denial of dependence, alternating or even occurring with periods of clinging dependency. Whatever the sequence, if a therapist remains nonintrusive and does not *intentionally* attempt to render gratification in response to the patient's demands or to deal directly with his omnipotent defenses, the analysis eventually reaches a phase where the patient becomes truly aware of his bewilderment regarding his expectations and fear of disappointment. Sometimes his dilemma is expressed directly or it may be enveloped in clouds of anger which obscure but are still sufficiently transparent so that one can perceive the helpless, frightened infantile core they contain.

The therapist's presence, the fact that he has led the patient to this position, and they have both survived the regression, constitutes an experience of *primal gratification* for the patient. This does not just refer to the analyst's physical presence, that he has to simply be there and then everything will work out well. True, he has to be there, but he has to be there in such a fashion that the patient need never lose himself. The patient must be able to carry the introject of the analyst with him wherever he goes and the analyst must make his presence constantly available in the consultation room. During this stage of analysis, there is no absent mother except insofar as the patient determines that absence. The patient must feel toward the analyst as children react to mothers who are capable of relating to them in terms of primary maternal preoccupation, as Winnicott (1956) described, that is, as if nothing else existed for the mother except her child who is the center of her universe.

The analyst must have particularly strong feelings toward the patient at this stage of analysis, perhaps much stronger than at other phases, and must be content to recognize that feelings toward patients vary during different periods of treatment. This does not mean, however, that the analyst makes special efforts to make his presence felt. On the contrary, that would be intrusive and detrimental to ultimate analytic resolution.

The analyst's nonintrusive devotion to the patient is manifested by his willingness to allow the patient to experience his fundamental helplessness in his presence. This is both supportive and gratifying. By acknowledging the patient's helplessness through interpretation, which may or may not consist of verbalization, the analyst is conveying to him that he recognizes that he has needs which have never been met and which now cannot be directly responded to. However, the *need to have someone understand* what is going on within him, particularly that he has not been able to form a stable inner representation of a nurturing source, enables the patient to more solidly incorporate the source of understanding.

No particular technical innovations are recommended. The analyst uses his usual tools of interpreting within the transference context and continues creating a setting where the patient can face the intrapsychic sources of his reactions. When treatment goes well, the patient often goes through a phase where he fuses with the analyst, carries the analyst with him and often gains spontaneous insights.

This does not exactly constitute the gratification of previously unmet infantile needs but the need to be unambivalently understood is an upward extension of such needs. The *analytic introject* represents a higher structural state than the regressed one that is being experienced in the transference. Successful treatment of patients suffering from severe character disorders depends upon whether they are able to traverse this gap.

Inherent in any living organism is a tendency (some would call it a drive) to achieve a certain level of structure. Regarding humans, one refers to a maturational potential and timetable. Throughout the years I have been conducting psychoanalyses, I have become increasingly convinced that the analytic process directs itself toward releasing a similar psychic developmental potential that has been stifled by early trauma. The mind is a subtle and marvelously complex system. Among its most wondrous characteristics is its orientation toward achieving higher levels of organization, an innate quality which becomes gratifyingly apparent after arduous analytic work and the attainment of terrifying levels of regression. In analysis a tendency toward structuralization reaches its apogee within the gap created between a part of the patient's mind that experiences primal frustrations and helplessness and one that has incorporated a benevolent, understanding analyst.

I have repeatedly referred to how the patient defensively protects a part of himself which can be called the rudimentary organized self. It is this embryonic core of organization that is prevented from developing further because of constrictive psychopathology. These developmental forces, to a large measure, become liberated when the patient is experiencing primal frustration in the presence of both an observing external and omnipresent introjected analyst.

Insofar as the patient experiences some gratification during treatment this leads to the development of the rudimentary organized self to a point where the patient *can structure needs that are capable of being gratified.*

As stated, the analyst cannot gratify archaic needs but in the current transference setting the patient is not really experiencing the impact of neonatal frustrations. His physical maturation has made his needs more complex; he is not reliving a need for mother's milk because, as stated, it would not be adequate. *He is, however, reliving the feelings of disruptive frustrations that overwhelm him and the overpowering loneliness of abandonment.* Not to have his needs met at such early stages did not permit him to develop to the level where he could be acknowledged and feel like a person. *He could not construct a cohesive self because what he felt was not responded to—that is, not recognized—and if there were no one around to respond to him—which means devoted to him—then there could be no external reinforcement of his potential to achieve a stable sense of being.*

Later in life and during analysis, the essence of the patient's frustration does not reside in infantile unmet needs. Rather, it is related to the *lack of acknowledgment of the self that was signified by unmet needs,* and it is this lack rather than the needs themselves that leads to crippling frustration. *It is the failure of the rudimentary organized self to flourish that causes the agonizing anguish that is at the core of most of the psychopathology that confronts us.*

From this viewpoint, the question of whether the analyst supplies a corrective experience by gratifying infantile wishes is no longer relevant. True, the analyst gratifies, but on a different plane than simply satisfying discrete impulses. His interpretative, understanding presence supplies something that is essentially the antithesis of maternal abandonment, something that is vital for the resumption of interrupted development.

Freud believed the essence of the analytic process was making the unconscious conscious, and this somehow led to overcoming conflicting forces. When dealing with patients suffering from characterological problems *the need to be understood is equated with survival*, and consequently, the analyst's observational frame of reference assumes more vital importance than even Freud described.

In spite of stormy moments and repetitive monotony, analysis is a fascinating process. To see a person attain higher states of ego organization, to free himself from constricting inner forces, and to discard ineffective and disruptive characterological modalities is an exhilarating experience.

Many things happen in analysis which are still shrouded in mystery. This adds to its fascination. How the analyst's interpretative activity and unambivalent devotion to understanding how the patient's mind works leads to psychic structuralization is far from a closed issue. Related to this question is the not too rarely encountered situation where the patient's analysis progresses, regardless of, or rather in spite of, what we do. The facilitation of the unfolding of an inherent developmental drive is a subject that requires continuous exploration. In this section I have touched upon some aspects of it, but of course, one has to travel a very long distance before achieving closure. The complexity of the psyche and its psychoanalytic exploration represents man's exploration of his private universe, perhaps one no less vast than the cosmos.

References

Adler, G., "Helplessness in the Helpless." *British Journ. of Med. Psychol.*, 45, No. 4:315-326 (1972).

Alexander, F. (1956), "Two Forms of Regression and Their Therapeutic Implications" in *The Scope of Psychoanalysis,* pp. 290-305. New York: Basic Books, 1961.

Beres, D., "Communication and the Creative Process." *Journ. of the Amer. Psychoanal. Assoc.* V:408-423 (1957).

Bettelheim, B., *The Empty Fortress*. New York: Free Press, 1966.

Boyer, L. B., "Provisional Evaluation of Psychoanalysis with Few Parameters Employed in the Treatment of Schizophrenia." *Internat. Journ. of Psychoanal.*, 42:389-403 (1961).

Boyer, L. B., "A Suicidal Patient." *Internat. Journ. of Psychoanal. Psychotherapy*, 1:7-31 (1972).

Boyer, L. B., and Giovacchini, P. L., *Psychoanalytic Treatment of Characterological and Schizophrenic Disorders*. New York: Jason Aronson, Inc., 1967.

Breuer, J., and Freud, S. (1895), *Studies on Hysteria. Stand. Edit.*, 2. London: Hogarth Press, 1955.

Bychowski, G., *Psychotherapy of Psychosis*. New York: Grune and Stratton, 1952.

Calef, V., "On the Current Concept of the Transference Neurosis." Introduction, *Journ. of the Amer. Psychoanal. Assoc.*, 19:22-26 (1971).

Deutsch, F., *The Mysterious Leap from the Mind to the Body*. New York: International Universities Press, 1960.

Erikson, E. H., "Identity and the Life Cycle." *Psychol. Issues* I. (1959).

Fairbairn, W. R. D., "A Revised Psychopathology of the Psychoses and Psychoneuroses." *Internat. Journ. of Psychoanal.*, 22:250-279 (1941).

Fairbairn, W. R. D., *Psychoanalytic Studies of the Personality*. London: Tavistock Publications Ltd., 1952.

Federn, P., *Ego Psychology and the Psychosis*. New York: Basic Books, 1952.

Flarsheim, A., "Therapist's Collusion with the Patient's Wish for Suicide." *This volume*, 1974.

Freud, S. (1894), "The Neuro-Psychoses of Defense." *Standard Edit.*, 3:45-61. London: Hogarth Press, 1962.

Freud, S. (1900), *The Interpretation of Dreams. Standard Edit.*, 4 and 5. London: Hogarth Press, 1953.

Freud, S. (1904), "Fragment of an Analysis of a Case of Hysteria." *Stand. Edit.*, 7:3-125. London: Hogarth Press.

Freud, S. (1909), "Notes Upon a Case of Obsessional Neurosis." *Stand. Edit.*, 10:151-249. London: Hogarth Press, 1948.

Freud, S. (1911), "Psychoanalytic Notes on an Autobiographical Account of a Case of Paranoia (Dementia Paranoides)." *Stand. Edit.*, 12:1-82. London: Hogarth Press, 1958.

Freud, S. (1912), *The Dynamics of Transference. ibid:* 97-109.

Freud, S. (1914), "Observations on Transference Love: Further Recommendations on the Technique of Psychoanalysis, III." *ibid:* 157-172.

Freud, S. (1914a), "Remembering, Repeating and Working-Through: Further Recommendations on the Technique of Psychoanalysis II." *ibid.*:145-157.

Freud, S. (1914B), *On Narcissism: An Introduction. Stand. Edit.*, 14:67-102. London: Hogarth Press, 1957.

Freud, S. (1915), *Instincts and Their Vicissitudes. ibid.*:103-140.

Freud, S. (1916), *Introductory Lectures on Psychoanalysis. Stand. Edit.*, 16, Chapt. 27. London: Hogarth Press, 1963.

Freud, S. (1924), *Neurosis and Psychosis. Stand. Edit.* 19:149-157. London: Hogarth Press, 1961.

Freud, S. (1924a), "The Loss of Reality in Neurosis and Psychosis." *ibid.*:183-191.

Giovacchini, P. "The Submerged Ego." *Internat. Journ. of Psychoanal.*, 43:371-380 (1964).

Giovacchini, P., "Transference, Incorporation and Synthesis." *Internat. Journ. of Psychoanal.*, 46:287-296 (1965).

Giovacchini, P., "Frustration and Externalization." *The Psychoanal. Quart.*, 36:571-583 (1967).

Giovacchini, P., "The Blank Self" in *Tactics and Techniques in Psychoanalytic*

Treatment; edited by P. Giovacchini. 364-380, New York: Jason Aronson, Inc., 1972.

Giovacchini, P., "The Treatment of Characterological Disorders." *ibid.*: 236-253.

Giovacchini, P., "Countertransference Problems." *Internat. Journ. of Psychoanal. Psychotherapy*, 1:112-127 (1972A)

Giovacchini, P., "Character Disorders: With Special Reference to the Borderline State." *Internat. Journ. of Psychoanal. Psychotherapy*, 2:7-37 (1973).

Gitelson, M., "The Emotional Position of the Analyst in the Psychoanalytic Situation." *Internat. Journ. of Psychoanal.*, 33:1-11 (1952).

Harley, M., "The Current Status of Transference Neurosis in Children." *Journ. of the Amer. Psychoanal. Assoc.*, 19:26-41 (1971).

Jones, E. (1929), "Fear, Guilt, and Hate" in *Papers on Psychoanalysis,* 304-320. Boston: Beacon Press, 1961.

Kernberg, O., "Treatment of Borderline Patients" in *Tactics and Techniques in Psychoanalytic Treatment.* 254-291, P. Giovacchini, ed. New York: Jason Aronson, Inc., 1972.

Khan, M. M. R., "Clinical Aspects of the Schizoid Personality: Affects and Technique." *Internat. Journ. of Psycho-Anal.*, 41:430-437 (1960).

Khan, M. M. R., "Ego Distortion, Cumulative Trauma, and the Role of Reconstruction in the Analytic Situation." *Internat. Journ. of Psychoanal.*, 45:272-277 (1964).

Klein, M., "The Psychotherapy of the Psychoses." *Brit. Journ. of Med. Psychol.*, 10:242-244 (1930).

Klein, M., "Notes on Some Schizoid Mechanisms." *Internat. Journ. of Psychoanal.*, 27:99-110 (1946).

Klein, M., *Developments in Psychoanalysis.* London: Hogarth Press, 1952.

Lagache, D., "Some Aspects of Transference." *Internat. Journ. of Psychoanal.*, 34:1-10 (1953).

Langer, S. (1948), *Philosophy in a New Key.* New York: Mentor Books, 1956.

Lindon, J., "On Regression: A Workshop." *Psychoanal. Forum,* 2:293-316 (1968).

Loewald, H., "The Transference Neurosis: Comments on the Concept and the Phenomenon." *Journ. of the Amer. Psychoanal. Assoc.,* 19:54-67 (1971).

Modell, A., "Primitive Object Relationships and the Predisposition to Schizophrenia." *Internat. Journ. of Psychoanal.,* 44:82-293 (1963).

Modell, A., "Affects and Therapeutic Alliance in Narcissistic Disorders." *This volume,* 1975.

Morse, S., "Structure and Reconstruction." *Internat. Journ. of Psychoanal.,* 53:487-500 (1972).

Reichard, S., "A Reexamination of 'Studies in Hysteria." *Psychoanal. Quart.,* 25:155-177 (1956).

Schur, M., "The Ego and the Id in Anxiety." *Psychoanal. Study of the Child.* 13:190-220 (1958).

Searles, H., "Transference Psychosis in the Psychotherapy of Chronic Schizophrenia." *Internat. Journ. of Psychoanal.,* 44:249-291 (1963).

Searles, H., "The Patient as Therapist to His Analyst." *This volume.* 1975.

Sechehaye, M. (1947), *Symbolic Realization.* New York: International Universities Press, 1951.

Spitz, R., *The First Year of Life*. New York: International Universities Press, 1965.

Winnicott, D. W. (1947), "Hate in the Countertransference." *Collected Papers, Through Pediatrics to Psychoanalysis*. 194-203. New York: Basic Books, 1958.

Winnicott, D. W. (1950), "Aggression in Relation to Emotional Development." *ibid.*: 194-203.

Winnicott, D. W. (1952), "Psychosis and Child Care." *ibid.*: 219-228.

Winnicott, D. W. (1953), "Transitional Objects and Transitional Phenomena. *ibid.*: 229-242.

Winnicott, D. W. (1954), "Metapsychological and Clinical Aspects of Regression Within the Psychoanalytical Setup." *ibid.*: 278-294.

Winnicott, D. W. (1955), "Clinical Varieties of Transference," in *Collected Papers:* 295-300. New York: Basic Books, 1958.

Winnicott., D. W. (1956), "The Antisocial Tendency." *ibid.*: 306-316.

Winnicott, D. W. (1956a), "Primary Maternal Preoccupation." *ibid.*:300-306.

Winnicott, D. W. (1960), "Ego Distortion in Terms of True and False Self." *The Maturational Process and the Facilitating Environment*. 140-152, London: Hogarth Press, 1965.

Winnicott, D. W. (1967), "The Location of Cultural Experience." *Playing and Reality*. 95-103, London: Tavistock Publications Ltd., 1971.

Winnicott, D. W. (1971), "Delinquency as a Sign of Hope." In *Adolescent Psychiatry:* 2, Feinstein, S., Giovacchini, P., and Miller, A. eds., 363-372, New York: Basic Books, 1971.

Winnicott, D. W., "Fragment of an Analysis" in *Tactics and Techniques in Psychoanalytic Treatment*. 455-694, P. Giovacchini, ed., New York: Jason Aronson, Inc., 1973.

Winnicott, D. W., and Khan, M. M. R., Review of "Psychoanalytic Studies of the Personality" by W. R. D. Fairbairn. *Internat. Journ. of Psychoanal., 34*:329-333 (1953).

Zeigarnik, B., "Das Behalten Erledigter und Unerledigter Handlungen." *Psychol.-Forsch., 9*:1-85 (1927).

Chapter II

The Patient as Therapist to His Analyst

Harold F. Searles, M.D.

INTRODUCTION

This paper is devoted to the hypothesis that innate among man's most powerful strivings toward his fellow men, beginning in the earliest years and even earliest months of life, is an essentially psychotherapeutic striving. The tiny percentage of human beings who devote their professional careers to the practice of psychoanalysis or psychotherapy are only giving explicit expression to a therapeutic devotion which all human beings share. As for the appreciably larger percentage of human beings who become patients in psychoanalysis or psychotherapy, I am suggesting here not merely that the patient wants to give therapy to, as well as receive therapy from, his doctor; my hypothesis has to do with something far more fundamental than that. I am hypothesizing that the patient *is ill because, and to the degree that,* his own psychotherapeutic strivings have been subjected to such vicissitudes that they have been rendered inordinately intense, frustrated of fulfillment or even acknowledgement, admixed therefore with unduly intense components of hate, envy, and competitiveness; and subjected, therefore, to repression. In transference terms, the patient's illness expresses his unconscious attempt to cure the doctor.

When I suggest that the patient is ill because of the developmental vicissitudes of this particular striving, from among the various emotional strivings which comprise the human affective equipment, I am putting the matter, of course, too simply. It is well-known that any neurotic or psychotic symptom is determined by a multiplicity of causes. I wish here to highlight a theme—a determinant of neurosis and psychosis—which would be erased by too many qualifications; therefore, I do, indeed, assert that *I know of no other determin-*

A shorter version of this paper, entitled ''The Patient as Therapist to His Therapist,'' was presented at a colloquium of the Postdoctoral Program of the Department of Psychology, New York University, New York City, Sept. 29, 1972, and also to the combined annual meeting of the Washington Psychiatric Society and the Washington Psychoanalytic Society, Washington, D.C., Nov. 10, 1972.

ant of psychological illness which compares, in etiologic importance, with this one.

There is admittedly, at a glance, a jarring note of contrivance, of artificiality, about suggesting that a human infant can be viewed as an intended psychotherapist. It is more congenial to think in terms of human beings' love, or nascent capacities to develop love, for one another and of their desire to help the other to fulfill his or her human, psychological potentialities. I am endeavoring, of course, to be more specific and explicit than that, and above all I am focusing upon the situation of psychoanalytic therapy, wishing to highlight both the irony and the technical importance of the (to my mind) fact that the more ill a patient is, the more does his successful treatment require that he become, and be implicitly acknowledged as having become, a therapist to his officially designated therapist, the analyst.

Parenthetically, throughout this paper henceforth I shall use the terms "therapist" and "analyst" interchangeably—a dubious procedure in a paper about this particular subject but necessary, in my opinion, to facilitate the exposition. I do not forget that the analyst, unlike the patient, has equipped himself with psychoanalytic training, and I shall touch later upon some of the difference this makes as regards their respective abilities to utilize effectively their mutually powerful, basically human, therapeutic strivings. At this juncture I wish to mention, as regards the special case of the patient who is himself a psychoanalyst or is acquiring psychoanalytic training, that I have done or am doing by now a considerable number of training analyses, and have found that, for the purposes of this paper, the therapeutic strivings at work in each of these patients, powerful as they are, are no more so than I have found in my nontraining analysands.

Later I shall briefly discuss the relatively scanty existing literature about this subject. At the moment, it is fair to say that psychoanalytic literature is written with the assumption that the analyst is healthy and therefore does not need psychological help from the patient, who is ill and is therefore in need of psychological help from, and unable to give such help to, the analyst. My own training analysis was a highly classical one and I emerged from it markedly less ill than I had been at the beginning; but it is a source of lasting pain to me that the analyst, like each of my parents long before, maintained a high degree of unacknowledgment of my genuine desire to be helpful to him.

In doing psychoanalytic therapy and in supervision of such work on the part of colleagues, I have found over and over that stalemates in treatment, when explored sufficiently, involve the analyst's receiving currently a kind of therapeutic support from the patient of which both patient and analyst have been unconscious. Thus ironically and, in the instances when this *status quo* does not become resolved, one can say indeed tragically, in those very instances wherein the analyst is endeavoring most anguishedly and unsuccessully to help the patient to resolve the tenacious symptom, or the tenaciously neurotic or psychotic *modus vivendi,* at an unconscious level the analyst is most tenaciously clinging to this very mode of relatedness as being one in which he, the analyst, is receiving therapy from the patient, without the conscious knowledge of either of them.

This paper is allied with, and based upon, many of my previous writings Searles, 1965, 1971, 1973). In my first published paper (Searles, 1951) and n many subsequent ones, I have tried to highlight the analyst's unconscious gratifications in a treatment-resistant mode of patient-analyst relatedness which he is making every effort, consciously, to help the patient resolve. A till earlier, never published, paper (Searles, 1949) suggested that there is an element of reality in all the patient's distorted transference-perceptions of the analyst, in keeping with Freud's (1922) statement regarding projection that we do not project "into the sky, so to speak, where there is nothing of the sort already." One of my papers (Searles, 1972a), concerning my work over nearly twenty years with an awesomely psychotic woman, had as its main theme the highlighting of the reality-components (each of which had long remained unconscious to me) in her highly distorted, psychotic transference reactions.

One might think—erroneously, I believe—of the whole subject of this paper as being understandable in terms of the patient's fulfilling, in any one current situation under study, some neurotic or psychotic need on the part of the analyst. This view is erroneous for at least two reasons: (1) It does not credit the patient with potential therapeutic initiative, at a predominantly unconscious, if not conscious, level—the initiative being the active striving, to function or continue functioning as therapist to the analyst. (2) It does not take into account the dimension of months and years of time. Patients manifest, over the course of months and years of treatment, an interest, a genuine caring, as to whether the analyst himself haas been growing and thriving during and as a result of their therapeutic ministrations to him.

In 1961 I reported (Searles, 1961a) my experience in analytic work regarding the reality-relatedness between patient and analyst as differentiated from the transference-relatedness, "the evolving reality relatedness . . . pursues its own course, related to and paralleling, but not fully embraced by, the evolving transference relatedness over the years of the two persons' work together." (p. 378 in Searles, 1965). In another paper in 1961 I reported Searles, 1961b) that "It has been my impression . . . that the evolution of the reality-relatedness proceeds always a bit ahead of, and makes possible, the progressive evolution and resolution of the transference, although to be sure the latter, in so far as it frees psychological energy and makes it available for reality-relatedness, helps greatly to consolidate the ground just taken over by the advancing reality-relatedness." (p. 557 in Searles, 1965). In the present paper I hypothesize a large step further: the evolution of the transference from, say, the patient's transference-reaction to the analyst as being a harshly dominating father to perceiving the analyst as a much gentler but threateningly devouring mother-figure. Such involves a crucial element of the patient's success *in reality* as a therapist who has been attempting to help the analyst to modify the latter's *real* harsh-father identifications.

As in all my previous writings, I cannot hope to "prove" anything here; psychoanalytic work is too intuitive, too much dependent upon data which cannot be articulated in spoken, and even less in written words for that to be possible. But, as before, I hope that this paper, which emerges from my psychoanalytic experience, will prove sufficiently evocative, for colleagues, from their own psychoanalytic experiences, to acquire the subjectively convincing "proof" for them also. If my hypothesis is indeed valid as I obviously am convinced it is, then nothing less than a metamorphosis in our concepts of the nature of the curative process in psychoanalysis flows from it.

Space here allows me to include only a very few of the clinical experiences, from my work with neurotic and psychotic patients, typical of those which have caused me to formulate this hypothesis. The hypothesis is of particular significance for psychotic patients, for psychosis involves the patient's not having achieved, in infancy and childhood, the firm establishment of an individual human self, and in my view this tragedy is explicable primarily by the particularly severe vicissitudes with which his very early therapeutic strivings were met, beginning in late infancy and early childhood, prior to the time when he would normally have become able to achieve, and within his family setting would have been helped to achieve, individual selfhood. Instead, life consisted basically in his postponement, as it were, of his individuation, in the service of his functioning symbiotically as therapist to one or another of his family members, or to all collectively in a family symbiosis. For him now as a chronological adult in psychoanalytic treatment, the crucial issue is whether he and the analyst can function in such a manner that (1) a transference symbiosis can develop, a symbiosis which will at first be highly distorted or pathological, as contrasted to that epitomized by the healthy-mother and healthy-infant symbiosis; (2) the nuclei of reality in this pathologic symbiosis can become sufficiently evident to both patient and analyst that this symbiosis can gradually evolve into what I call a therapeutic symbiosis (Searles, 1959a, 1965, 1973), which is essentially a mutually growth-enhancing symbiosis like that of normal infancy; and (3) the mutual gratifications as well as further growth-frustrating aspects of this mode of relatedness can be dealt with, by both participants, such that a healthier individuation can occur, this time, for both of them.

In the course of phases (1) and (2) one encounters transference data, as have come to see clearly only in recent years, which bring to light the pa tient's heretofore-unconscious, lifelong, guilt at having failed in his therapeutic effort, begun very early in life, to enable his ego-fragmented mother to become a whole and fulfilled mother to him. In my experience of recent years, it is only insofar as he can succeed in his comparable striving in the treatment, this time toward the therapist, that the patient can become sufficiently free from such guilt, and sufficiently sure of his symbiotic worth, so that he can now become more deeply a full human individual. Individuation has become free of its connotation of a murderous dismembering, or lethal abandonment of the mother for whom the patient has not only been made to feel responsible, but whom the patient has genuinely loved and wanted to somehow make whole and fulfilled.

Clinical Examples: Patient's Therapeutic Attempt to Enable Analyst to Become Free from Some Neurotic Symptom or Character Trait in the Latter

1. Mrs. A., a twenty-eight-year-old woman, clearly had had a strong parental relationship with the youngest of her three siblings, a brother five years younger than herself, and it was early evident to me that there was much repressed grief in her concerning the loss of this relationship which had been a most important area of her childhood and that of the brother. During the first three years of analysis she scarcely mentioned him from one year to the next, and then only most disparagingly and in passing, indicating that she thought of herself as having simply treated him in a disdainful, bullying manner.

But in the fourth year of the analysis, as her memories of their relationship began to emerge from repression, she recalled that the last several times she had fought with Eddie, when she was sixteen or seventeen years of age, he had won. "I guess that's why I stopped bringing them [i.e., their fist-fights] about. Actually, as I recall, I was quite pleased that he could beat me up. I guess that gave me some respect for him. I always thought he was a little drip; so after I found he could beat me up, I stopped . . ." She said all this in a tone that made clear that she had had a very loving motive toward him in all this—a motive of helping him to become a man. I conveyed to her my impression of her tone, and suggested that she had been so motivated; but her dismissing response made clear that she was not yet able to accept anything like so loving an image of herself.

Later on in the session she said, in another context, "My [eldest] sister says I was horrible to Eddie; so I guess I was." It seemed clear to me, although not yet interpretable, that she was afraid, at an unconscious level, lest she kill her sister, were she—the patient—to come to see how cruel was the self-image which her sister had fostered in her in relation to their brother. She spoke in this session of how "cruel," in retrospect, had been her sister's pitying attitude toward Eddie as being a weakling, and her fostering in the patient a similar view of him. There were strong clues, partly accepted by her, that I was currently equivalent to Eddie in the transference relationship.

Later on in the session she said, again in reference to Eddie, that "After we stopped fighting, we stopped having anything to do with one another. We never acknowledge one another's existence. We never talk; we never phone; we never write." It was apparent, although not yet timely to interpret to her, that after having helped Eddie to become a masterful male toward her, she and he had to shun one another partly because of the sexual temptation with which their relationship was now imbued.

This brief example is typical of those in my experience, both in terms of indicating how deeply repressed have been the patient's therapeutic strivings toward the other family member(s), and in terms of the clarification of the transference relationship.

2. Miss B., a long-hospitalized woman forty years of age, devoted a considerable part of her time recurrently, over years of her treatment, reacting to me as being her ambivalence-ridden, indecisive and therefore unfirm father. It was clear that her own needs included a need for me to become a stronger, more firmly limit-setting father toward her; but it was equally clear that she was trying persistently to help me resolve the genuine flaw in myself which formed the nucleus of reality upon which her transference was based. Through outrageously and persistently obstreperous behavior, which involved both blatant sexual provocativeness as well as physical onslaughts of various kinds, she eventually succeeded in fostering in me a degree of decisiveness and firmness, expressed in masterful limit-setting, which I had not achieved before with anyone, either patients or other persons in my life. I worked for thirteen years with this woman, the most deeply ill patient I have ever treated, and over-all, I helped her much less than I wish it had been within my power to do. Still, I did help her considerably; I learned much from her; and one of the most certain things I learned was that one of the important determinants of her illness had been a self-sacrificing effort to enable her father to become a man.

3. Mrs. C., a thirty-two-year-old attorney, had been beaten severely on occasion by her father when she was a child and he was a relatively young and physically vigorous man. In the later years of her upbringing, with the advent of adolescence and the father's aging and depression, his beatings had ceased. He was old and incapacitated with arthritis at the time she began analysis with me. As year after year went by in the analysis, years during which her loving and erotic, as well as murderously rageful feelings toward me as a father figure remained largely under repression, she became increasingly discouraged. At a conscious level, her discouragement had to do with the tenacity of the symptoms, for the relief of which she had sought analysis initially—namely, certain obsessive-compulsive rituals and a moderate but persistent

alcoholism, both of which interfered appreciably with her professional work. Both these symptoms were expressions, in part, of her unconscious defiance toward me, as I represented her demanding, domineering father. At an unconscious level, however, her discouragement was related also to her inability to galvanize me into being the vigorous and virile young father who had beaten her, despite year after year of contemptuously defiant, acting-out behavior and various forms of verbal incitement. Her provocativeness clearly was not only expressive of an unconscious yearning for the erotic fulfillment which her father's beatings had provided her but it also was an effort to rejuvenate me, who was perceived as an aging, impotent, helpless father in the transference. Meanwhile, during that phase of analytic work, her grief about his aged and chronically ill condition was discernible directly only in brief glimpses.

4. After several years of analysis, Mr. D., a thirty-four-year-old man, said, in reference to his resistance to analysis, "I feel as though I won't participate—as though I sit down and refuse to take part . . ." I commented, "You say you feel as though you sit down and refuse to take part—*I'm* the one who's sitting down here." He agreed immediately, "Yeah—I've had the idea from time to time that you are depressed—and that I've got to do something to bring you out of yourself—to get you to blow up or—get you to lash out, or . . . [a few minutes later, without any further intervention from me]—When I think of my mother seated, she's always behind something—[clearly an allusion to my being seated behind the couch]—behind her sewing machine, or behind her cookbooks, looking up recipes . . ."

In a later session, he confided that he had long desired to be able to experience, and convey to me, a fantasy so vivid "that you would be able to say, 'Boy, that's a marvelous fantasy!' " It was clear that he was giving expression to his long-familiar exasperation with himself for his relative inability to experience, and convey to me, anything but highly reality-bound associational material. But, at an apparently less conscious level, he was alluding also to my own characterologic inability to express undisguised, unambivalent enthusiasm for the contribution the other person has made, or is making. Thus, here again, was a glimpse of his therapeutic striving on behalf of his depressed mother, personified by me in the transference.

Upon hearing his statement, I was struck immediately by the fact of my adult life long inability to express such enthusiasm—an inability which I had never acknowledged openly in my work with him, and an inability which I manage, most of the time, to keep largely secret from myself. I well know that it was not entirely, nor not even primarily, due to any lack on his part of ability to experience and report fantasies, that I was unable to say, "Boy, that's a marvelous fantasy!", for no matter how abundantly suitable an occasion he might provide me for saying this, I am unable to say it. The inability emerged now, at this phase in the analysis after considerable growth in him (in this regard as well as in other ways). Although his therapeutic help had not proved sufficient to enable me appreciably to resolve my problem, he had helped me confront it much more clearly than I characteristically do—and that surely must be a help toward its eventual resolution.

I have dwelt at some length upon this brief clinical vignette because it comprises a typical example of how the analyst's psychopathology can remain masked—by introjective processes within the patient and projective processes within the analyst, and, by the same token, of how subtle is the patient's therapeutic striving—largely unconscious.

One might believe that this therapeutic striving of the patient is newly developed in the analysis; but my experience consistently has indicated quite otherwise—namely, that it has significant transference connections to his earlier life experience, and that it was indeed at work in him, though at an unconscious level, at the beginning of analytic work. When it emerges most clearly in the course of analysis, the transference connections between the analyst and earlier figures in the patient's life, toward whom this therapeutic striving has been devoted, are convincingly tangible.

5. Mrs. E., a forty five-year-old woman, was sneezing, blowing her nose, and clearing her throat frequently in one of her analytic sessions. For years she had suffered from multiple allergies, and frequently had sinusitis with postnasal discharge, as she evidently did now. I felt, as I had felt during earlier years of her analysis regarding her allergic symptoms, that her physical discomfort was being used unconsciously by her in a neurotically hostile manner. In the course of this session she commented, while clearing her throat for the nth time, that she had many times to make an heroic effort to keep from vomiting here. I was familiar with such comments from her (as well as from occasional other patients) earlier in the analysis, and she seemed, as usual, quite unconscious of any sadistic gratification in making me feel recurrently threatened lest she suddenly vomit copiously all over my couch, carpet, and God knows what else in my office.

There emerged during this session data indirectly indicating that the theme of whether she were able to *feel* was unconsciously at work. Once, for example, she commented, in reference to pain in her sinuses exacerbated by her violent sneezes, that she evidently is able to feel, all right. Upon hearing this I felt like mentioning to her tartly that she was functioning, however, in a way which made *me* feel very *un*feeling toward *her;* I felt convinced that she was projecting upon me her own subjective callousness and indifference to human suffering. I more than once felt like telling her that I found myself feeling that she could sneeze her goddam head off, for all I cared. I was reacting to her enormous, but still largely unconscious, demandingness— demands for sympathy, admiration, and so on; any list would be endless—and to her also largely unconscious hostility and threats. The implicit threat that she vomit was only one among a constellation of threats being conveyed to me. She gave me reason to feel intimidated. I feared her long-familiar capacity for character-assassinating me among her many social acquaintances, some of whom knew me personally. Thus, on more than one count I felt unfree to use, as shared investigative data, my "unfeeling" reaction that she could "sneeze her goddam head off," for all I cared.

Driving home at the end of the day I realized, with great relief, that my being "unfeeling" is *one* among the gamut of emotional responses available to me in my work with patients, and that this reaction can be as useful, for mutually exploratory analytic work, as any others among the many emotional reactions (jealousy, anger, tender feelings, sexual feelings, and so on) which I long ago had become accustomed to using in my psychoanalytic work as data for the patient's analysis. The relief which accompanied this realization was tremendous, for until then I had found reason to fear, for several decades at crucial junctures in my personal and professional life, that I "really am" unable to feel, to care. That is, I had feared that this unfeeling one, subjectively not human, was the only real me—the only way, deep down in my core, that I really am.

In earlier years of this woman's analysis I had become aware of important ways in which work with her was proving of unusual therapeutic value to me (as well as of considerable such value, certainly, to her), and had found much evidence of powerful, and by no means entirely unconscious, therapeutic strivings on her part toward me. During the ensuing few days after this realization which I had experienced while driving home, I felt certain that it, like a number of analogous ones earlier in our work, had been predominantly a result of her therapeutic strivings—in this instance largely unconscious, so it appeared—on my behalf. My feeling in those few days was one of deep gratitude toward her. No one could possibly have helped me, so I felt, with anything more personally significant to me than this; this is where I had most been needing someone's help.

I am mindful of the transference aspects of the material of the session which I have mentioned though a discussion here is beyond the scope of this paper. I at no time lost sight of the fact that I was personifying for her a number of figures from her past, notably her mother, whom she tended to experience as being indifferent to her suffering. As I mentioned earlier, this paper is intended not to focus upon transference phenomena *per se,* but rather upon those real increments of the analyst's personality-functioning which serve, for the patient, as the nuclei of external reality and evoke his transference reactions.

Clinical Examples of Patient's Therapeutic Striving to Enable the Mother to Become Truly a Mother

The healthy infant-mother symbiosis, which normally provides the foundation for later individuation, under tragic circumstances fosters the child's becoming not a truly human individual. He becomes what one might call a symbiotic therapist, whose own ego-wholeness is sacrificed throughout life in a truly selfless devotion, to complementing the ego-incompleteness of the mothering person, and of subsequent persons in his life who, in his unconscious, have the emotional meaning of similarly incomplete mothers. Their ego-functioning is dependent upon his being sustainingly a part of them. Such "negative" emotions as hatred and guilt, cited often in the literature concerning early ego development and the family dynamics of schizophrenia, are indeed a significant part of this etiological picture; but it is, I suggest, more than anything the patient's nascent capacity for love and for the development of mature human responsibility, which impels him to perpetuate this mode of relatedness.

Whereas the foregoing clinical examples, predominantly from neurotic patients, attempted to illustrate the patient's therapeutic effort to help the analyst resolve some neurotic symptom or character trait, in the following examples from patients who were suffering from some degree of schizoid or schizophrenic illness, the patient's therapeutic striving is referable more to a preindividuation, than postindividuation, developmental era. The patient's therapeutic striving is to function as mother to his biological mother (the latter's ego development in regard to her own mothering effort, being fixated at, or having regressed to, an infantile level) so as to enable her to become sufficiently integrated and mature that she will become able to function truly as a mother to the patient. This striving of the child is both "selfish" and "altruistic." The two aims are, at this level of primitive child-mother functioning, not as yet differentiated.

In a recent discussion of autism, I suggested (Searles, 1973) that for the analyst to help the autistic patient become able to participate in a therapeutic symbiosis (that is, a symbiosis similar in nature to a healthy infant-mother symbiosis), the analyst must first have become able to immerse himself in the patient's autistic world. This then fosters the patient's identifying with the analyst who can so immerse himself in the other's world: the patient, partly through such identification, becomes increasingly able to immerse himself in the analyst's more usual "own" world, and the rapid flux and interchangeability of a therapeutically symbiotic kind of relatedness flows from this. Khan (1963, 1964) has described the necessity for the analyst to come to function as the maternally protective shield (in my term, world) for such a patient, and I suggested that *the analyst must first accept the patient as comprising his (the analyst's) maternally protective shield* (functionally= "outer world," much as the womb is the outer world for the fetus).

Mrs. F., a thirty-year-old schizoid woman, early in the third year of her analysis mentioned that her parents were visiting her and her marital family at present. Mrs. F. had learned that her mother, in her distant home city, had

ɔeen spending her time watching television or going to movie matinees. Mrs.
Ӻ. said that her mother had been finding life boring and commented that her
mother watched television and went to movies rather than getting a part-time
ob as a saleslady or secretary, or joining some women's social organizations.

"Somehow that seems to me such a waste; yet it's what she did so
much of when I was a child," Mrs. F. reminisced, in a tone of regret
and longing, ". . . movies and occasional romantic novels; I guess
those were her only real interests . . .''

This was a glimpse, of which I came to see convincingly many—
although, regrettably, I never found it feasible to interpret them to Mrs.
F. as such—of her feeling of having failed to enable her mother to fulfill
herself as a mother to her. The Oedipal-rivalry component in these data
is also, of course, obvious.

In the preceding day's session she had mentioned having learned
from her mother that the latter had given to the church library all the
books which the daughter had acquired and treasured during childhood
and adolescence, and thrown away all her daughter's stored clothing. "I
had the feeling of being disposed of as deceased," she commented. The
mother was showing her usual selfish-child concern with feeling inhos-
pitably and inconsiderately treated by her husband and various of his
relatives; and the patient added, in a tone more of genuine regret and
sadness than blame, that on her own occasional trips with her husband
and children to her parental home, "She (her mother) has *yet* to prepare
a nice supper for us."

A few sessions earlier, there had occurred, as there had a great many
times before, a predominantly silent session. But this one was different
in quality. Before, the silences had been extremely tense ones which
had often involved my having exasperated, frantic feelings of the sort
which, I surmise, were largely at work in her emotionally rootless,
discontented mother. During this particular session, she indicated that
she was feeling unusually calm and relaxed, and asked whether I
reacted differently when she is feeling so. Indeed I did, though I did not
tell her so; I felt calm and relaxed, and experienced her as a source of
nonverbal strength and solidity. In the course of this session she commented, "I can imagine my father holding me on his lap and cuddling
me; but I can't imagine my mother." I had much misgiving, after that
hour, about not having told her—confirmed for her—how I was feeling;
I had never felt so with her before. Always before, her silences had been
unpleasurable to me in one way or another.

In retrospect, I feel that I had withheld from her, unwisely and
hatefully, a vitally needed confirmation of her at least partially success-

ful mothering of me. Probably wisely, she discontinued our analytic work not many months thereafter.

Her having said, ". . . but I can't imagine my mother" is a testimony of the crucial significance, in one's therapeutic striving, of one's ability—or in this instance, inability—to achieve a fantasy of the other person's functioning in the striven-for manner, the manner fulfilling both for the other person and oneself. In my work with hospitalized schizophrenic patients, and in what I have heard from colleagues of their work with similar patients, the therapists' experiencing of nighttime dreams and daytime fantasies of the patient in which the latter—who in daily life is still very ill—is perceived as functioning as a healthy person, are crucial criteria of successful treatment.

With Mrs. G., a thirty-four-year-old woman whose psychodynamics are in some ways very similar to Mrs. F's, and whose analysis proceeds with strikingly little change year after year, I am becoming gradually much more receptive to her maternal effort to enable me to function as mother to her. Her effort is, as in all such instances, a highly ambivalent one, with strong rivalrous components (on negative-oedipal but also infantile-omnipotence grounds) to demonstrate that the mother is incapable of functioning as mother. However, the issue is proving to be more amenable to analysis than it was with Mrs. F. The resolution of particularly stalemated phases of the work involves my realizing, for example, how genuinely gratifying it is to me to go on being one of the fruits borne by the fruit tree which is one of her early-mothering images of herself. My often-exasperated efforts to encourage and insist upon her functioning more productively and spontaneously, as most neurotic analysands usually do, run aground upon the fact of my having (formerly unconscious) stakes in her continuing to maintain her usual early-mother orientation in the transference, as in her daily life.

Mr. H., 42 years of age, was suffering from ambulatory schizophrenia when he began analysis 15 months ago, but has improved to the point that his ego-dysfunctioning has been of no more than borderline schizophrenic severity for some months now. Previously filled with hatred to a degree potentially dangerous to himself as well as to others he has now become capable of relatively sustained, predominantly loving relations with his wife and children, as well as in the analytic setting; and he is manifesting a steadily strengthening kinship with his fellow human beings—although, in all these regards, such development ments still encounter considerable disavowal on his part by persistent hostility and rejectingness.

His upbringing, like that of his older brother with whom there prevails a powerful and largely unconscious symbiosis, had been left largely to servants, and an abundance of evidence, from the beginning of the analytic work, indicated that their mother had been strikingly deficient in motherliness. Mr. H. was convinced that not only his nursemaids, but his mother as well, "despised" both himself and his brother; and he soon manifested, in our analytic work, a conviction that I, likewise, equivalent to such a mother or nursemaid, despised him.

The particular point I wish to make for this paper is that when, in a recent session, the patient said, "Mother didn't want anything to do with us," although this was said in an offhand attempt at glossing-over manner, there came through in it a feeling of deep, pervasive, and subjectively ineradicable shame. Moreover and most significantly, the shame had in it a perceptible quality that this was shame not so much that he and his brother had proved unworthy of the mother's caring for them but, much more meaningfully, that the two brothers had failed shamefully in their long-sustained effort to enable the mother to become, and to know the fulfillment of being, truly a mother. Space does not allow me to include the corollary data—abundant but significant mainly in its nuances of feeling which cannot be conveyed fully and convincingly in a written report such as this—which reassure me that his analogous effort in the transference situation is proving, this time, much more successful.

Miss J., a forty-two-year-old spinster who had become schizophrenic in the course of decades of living largely as a recluse in the service of her widowed and eccentric mother, became during the first year of her stay at Chestnut Lodge so emaciated, mute, and motionless that I, like the others concerned with her care, feared that she would die. The psychoanalytic contribution to the favorable change in this state of affairs consisted essentially, I believe, in my coming to function, over a period of some months, very much as a comfortably silent and unmoving inanimate object during our sessions. This seemed to provide her with a context in which she could become alive again. In retrospect, I now see that in order for me to have become able so to function, I had to become immersed, in a relatively unanxious, contented, self-gratifying way, in her seemingly inanimate world.

Over the ensuing months and, in fact, for many years, we had many stormy sessions, sessions in which she often reacted to me as being crazy, confused, and disorganized, meanwhile acting out, herself, a great deal of such psychopathology. During one phase of about two years in length, in about the fifth and sixth years of her treatment, the therapeutic sessions all took place in her room, and were therapeutically symbiotic in quality to the greatest degree that I have ever experienced with any of my patients; this, I feel sure, is related to the fact of her having had a better outcome than any others among my chronically schizophrenic patients thus far have achieved. During those two years I experienced her as winning a gentle victory over me: my earlier fury, contempt, and other "negative" feelings toward her for her inability (seemingly, her refusal) to come to my office for the sessions, gradually gave way to an atmosphere of the utmost shared contentment, in which I was receptive to and appreciative of her good mothering of me, and she, likewise, basked and throve in this symbiotic atmosphere. There were abundant indications of symbiotic processes at work during this time. Meanwhile her social worker told me one day in astonishment that she had had a dream the previous night of Miss J., in which Miss J. was a mother happily nursing her baby. Several others among the personnel members told me how amazed they were at the favorable changes they were seeing in Miss J.

One of the tenacious forms of resistance in Miss J.'s treatment has been her idealization of her upbringing. After many years of treatment, despite her having long ago become healthier than her family had ever known her to be, being relatively well-established in outpatient living, and functioning much of the time during the sessions more in a normal-neurotic fashion than a borderline schizophenic fashion, she is still almost totally unable to remember and report any but conventionally "nice" memories and feelings about her parents and other family members. Meanwhile, there has been no lack of negative-transference phenomena, in which she has reacted to me as being essentially a crazy mother whose craziness is known only to Miss J. herself.

Her first reported memory of her mother which I heard as realistic, rather than her usual saccharine, idealized images, occurred after some three or four years of analysis. The content of the memory was mundane enough; but I thought it highly significant that it was reported during a session (in her room, as usual in that era) when the female patient who occupied the adjoining room, and who for weeks had frequently stormed in loud and overwhelming rage, was raging even more loudly than I had ever heard her. Whether Miss J. will ever be able to integrate her past experience of the mother's comparable behavior into a more realistic image of her mother, now long dead, I do not know. A "nervous breakdown," in the phrase of her siblings, which had incapacitated the mother for many months following the father's death, and had required the patient to leave high school and begin taking care of her, has never been remembered or acknowledged in any way by Miss J. as having occurred, despite many years of analysis.

Her move to outpatient living was very slow in coming about, and it gradually became clear that one of the many sources of her unconscious resistance to this move was her equating it, unconsciously, with a mother's abandoning of her little child. For example, my notes following a session early in the fifth year include this paragraph:

"She spoke with great disapproval of how mothers in effect abandon their children, as she sees in her trips into Rockville [the small city in which the sanitarium is located] where, she said, she sees mothers leave their children at loose ends, playing near the streets and so on, while they (the mothers) do their shopping. This I have heard a number of times before. But I was greatly interested when she said, this time, that she herself does not have a child, but that if she had one, she wouldn't want to 'keep running back' to the child. She would want it so well taken care of that she wouldn't 'have to keep running back.' This happens to be exactly the same terminology she has used [for years] in expressing her objection to moving out—namely, that such a move would be pointless because she 'would have to keep running back to the hospital.' I now realize that for her to move out of the hospital is unconsciously equivalent to a mother's abandoning her child (the child being me and, no doubt, various other persons in the hospital). [I would now add that the child was, much more largely, the sanitarium or 'hospital' as a whole]. I recall her saying recently that as a person gets older they become like a child, and agreeing with my comment, in response, that one may feel like a mother to one's own mother."

As her years in the sanitarium went on, she had a series of roommates in the various double rooms in which she lived. A number of these persons were highly psychotic and openly disturbed, and at least a few of them sufficiently homicidal that I was impressed with her ability to live with them in an increasingly firm, assertive, and forthright manner. Although I have not the slightest doubt that her poorly integrated, infuriating qualities stimulated many of the upsets of her various roommates, her conscious therapeutic concern for them seemd to me unmistakably genuine; and whereas a full four years elapsed, in one of the sanitarium cottages where she lived, before she ever set foot in the living room (lest, upon doing so, she immediately be held totally responsible for all that transpired there), she came to do so freely, and to participate in a generally much-appreciated and constructive way in the weekly or biweekly unit meetings of patients and staff.

The last roommate she had, for about a year before moving to an apartment of her own in Washington, was a highly psychotic woman whose verbal and physical behavior was often highly disorganized. Miss J. would state that Edna was, once again, "in a whirl." In one of her analytic sessions with me during that year, she asked me whether she could go to New York City on the following Sunday to visit her female cousin and miss her Monday hour. I said that it was all right with me; for reasons I shall not detail here, I did not respond in an analytic-investigative manner as I would with a neurotic patient. She then said something about not being sure she could do it—i.e., make the trip to New York City alone. "I feel so little in New York. . . . I guess I always think of New York as a big city in a whirl. . . ."

The idea struck me that she projected onto New York City her own still largely repressed confusion, and tended to feel responsible—a responsibility overwhelmingly awesome to me as I sensed it—for what she perceived as the gigantic confusion of the big city. Her psychosis had first become overt, many years before, shortly following a visit to this cousin, and I felt that here I was being given a brief glimpse into the nature of her psychotic experience then. Later on, in looking over my notes, I realized that New York City was unconsciously equivalent to her overwhelmingly confused mother for whom the patient felt totally responsible.

About two years later, she was describing her weekly visit to her current social worker at Chestnut Lodge, a woman toward whom Miss J. has a mother-transference which involves, amidst clearly ambivalent feelings, a great deal of admiration, fondness of a sisterly sort, and maternal caring for the social worker. She said, "Recently she's been so busy, her office looks like a whirl!", making an illustrative whirling gesture with her arm as she said this.

Mrs. Joan Douglas (a pseudonym, of course), whose history and course thus far in psychotherapy I detailed in a recent paper (Searles, 1972a) and therefore shall touch upon only briefly here, was chronically and severely psychotic at the time when I began working with her, nearly twenty years ago. I have seen her four hours per week since then. For various reasons, carefully and recurrently considered, tranquilizing drugs have not been used in her treatment. For the past seven and one half years I have taped (with her knowledge) all the sessions, have earmarked and filed all these tapes, and have spent dozens of hours in careful playbacks of selected ones, in my attempt to better understand the processes, destructive as well as constructive, at work within and between us.

From the outset her ego-fragmentation was enormous and her delusions were innumerable and ever-changing. She was long convinced, for example, that there were 48,000 Chestnut Lodges among which she was constantly being shifted; that there was literally a chain on her heart and machinery in her abdomen; that her head, as well as mine and other persons', was repeatedly being replaced by other heads. She often experienced both herself and me, bodily and *in toto,* as being replaced by a succession of other persons during the psychotherapy hours. She was so vigorously and tenaciously opposed to psychiatry that for several years she refused steadfastly to come to my office at Chestnut Lodge, and had been there only some three or four times during the first 10½ years, after which she finally began coming with some regularity. During the past nine years, since I left Chestnut Lodge, she has been coming by taxicab to my office, some ten miles from the Lodge, and for the most recent several of those years, has been sufficiently reality-oriented and collaborative, despite continued severe psychosis, as to no longer need a nurse or aide to accompany her.

As regards her history, she apparently suffered from a significant degree of schizophrenia in childhood. Her mother, in the words of her eldest brother, had "loved to dominate" the girl, had beaten her brutally on occasion up into the teens, and generally had had an intensely ambivalent and therefore highly unpredictable relationship with her. As an example of the mother's unpredictable moods, which included both manic and depressive episodes, the brother described how she would return from Mass in a beatific mood, and within moments would be furiously throwing a kitchen pot at one or another of the children.

Although the patient had been able to complete high school with a brilliant academic record, to become accomplished in various athletics, and to marry and bear four children, she gradually had become overtly psychotic at the age of 33, within about a year following the death, from natural causes, of her mother. She had been overtly psychotic for about four years when I became her therapist. I was to learn that her relationship with her emotionally remote father had contributed importantly, also, to the foundation of her awesomely severe psychosis; but that relationship is less clearly relevant to the theme of this paper.

For many years her real identity was anathema to her to such a degree that, when one addressed her by her own name, one was met by a degree of unrelatedness from her which was often intolerable to me. She experienced a succession of personal identities, many of them nonhuman, and frequently changing *in toto* in the midst of a session, just as she usually perceived me as multiple at any one moment, as changing unpredictably, and frequently as being nonhuman. All these delusional experiences, while appreciably lessened in severity, are still present to a formidable degree.

In one session after some half dozen years of work, she explained to me, "You see, my mother was my mind," and this was said in such a tone as poignantly to convey the implication, "—and when I lost her, I lost my mind." It was painfully clear during the hour to what an awesome extent she indeed had lost her mind, as measured by the incredible depth of her confusion, quite unreproducible here. For years she had been performing various crazy actions, and had come to reveal more and more clearly that, in doing so, she was following obediently the directions which she heard coming from "that woman in my head," evidently an introject, no matter how greatly distorted by the patient's own anxiety and hostility, of the crazy mother of her childhood.

In one of the more amusing of our sessions in that era—sessions which much more often were far, indeed, from being amusing—she suddenly reported to me, "That woman in my head just said, 'Don't have anything to do with that frump out there'." She confirmed my amused assumption that "that frump" referred to me. At another point in the hour when I suggested, as had long been my custom, "Let's see what comes to your mind next," she protested vigorously, "You keep asking me what's in my *mind! She's* in my mind; but *she* has nothing to do with *me*!" She went on to make it evident that she felt that I utterly ignored her whenever I would endeavor to encourage her to express what she was experiencing. Usually we think of the person's mind as the locus and core of the self; but she emphasized that this was not true for her. It is now evident in retrospect that when I had been trying to help her explore and articulate what was in her mind, she had been reacting as though my effort had been to crush her emerging autonomy—to castrate her individuality (she had accused me on innumerable occasions of doing all sorts of physical violence to her), by making her introjected mother-image totally and permanently dominate her ego-functioning.

By the tenth year I had long since become impressed, in my work with all my schizophrenic patients, with the power and depth of the positive feelings between the to-become-schizophrenic child and his mother. My notes made following one of the sessions with her include the following:

"She was incredibly confused, as usual, throughout this hour. That is, she was no more confused than usual; but the degree of her confusion, present for several years now, I still find quite incredible. The bulk of it has to do with a tremendous confusion about identity.

"I bluntly mentioned to her, midway through the hour, that I found something like 90% of what she told me to be gibberish, or words to that effect. My saying this was no doubt related to the significant things she said at the end of the hour, and I feel that my increasing bluntness is a useful part of the work. In this regard I recall that about six weeks ago I told her bluntly, 'You're a silly woman who is spending her life here in this looney bin, talking nonsense, while your life goes down the drain.'

"Despite her great confusion she managed to bring out, in a confused and indirect and displaced kind of way, the fact that her mother had run her life in an utterly singlehanded and autocratic fashion up until Joan 'went into St. Thomas' Hospital', which I assume was at the age of eight when [as I had long known] she had had her mastoidectomy [the first of a series of surgical operations]. She went on to make clear that thereafter the doctors had taken over the management of her life, and that they had done a highly inefficient job. She had been speaking of her mother in the same admiring, loyal spirit as she has shown rather consistently in her references to her mother for several weeks now, while speaking in the same spirit of her older and only sister, Ellen. I then said, 'So perhaps, when you went into St. Thomas' Hospital and the doctors took over the management of your life, you couldn't help feeling guilty, couldn't help feeling that you were being disloyal to your mother, simply because these doctors were running your life now, instead of she.' Joan clearly and explicitly agreed.

"At the end of the hour as I went downstairs, she called after me loudly and defiantly, 'The doctors here haven't done a *goddam thing* for me: I'm *still* a blithering idiot!' I heard this as an expression of her loyalty to her mother, and of her determination not to let me and the others on the staff here be useful to her, because this would be tantamount to disloyalty to her mother.

"Also in the course of this hour, I was struck once again with how terribly confused a person the mother must have been; I felt that Joan's confusion is largely based upon introjection of this confused mother. When she was describing things that the mother used to say, I said, 'I suppose it would be hard for you to think that she may ever have been susceptible to being confused,' and Joan flatly disclaimed any such possibility. This is an indication of how Joan is struggling to maintain a picture of her mother as a very strong person [an effort to ward off unconscious disillusionment, guilt and grief in relation to the mother]."

Some three weeks later, I came to her session feeling fatigued and sick with hay fever and an external auditory canal infection. Therefore, I was relatively free from my compulsive, competitive, driving, coercive countertransference orientation, to which she is attuned and which she provokes. She, I am sure, partially in response to my changed feeling-state, was comfortably settled in her chair, and spoke unanxiously of feeling "set." She said, yawning comfortably, "I'm certainly a woman and I'm never going to be a men." For all the years, her confusion about her sexual identity, as well as mine, had been enormous; a man was, to her, still multiple, as I was usually a multiple transference figure to her—hence her saying "a men."

Later in the same hour she told me of a time when "my mother . . . was having a nervous breakdown . . ." This was, for me, a landmark dénouement. She described vividly her mother's having talked vehemently about " 'When you were in Spain. . . ,' where the girl had never been, and something about " 'saving England','" and much other material on a par with the patient's own delusions. Joan went on, saying "I told her, 'You can't bear to have all those thoughts in your mind!' ", in a tone of earnest and urgent solicitude. I suggested, "You wanted to relieve her of some of the burden of them." She promptly confirmed this, nodding and saying, "I was *trying* to." It was evident that she had been precisely as nonplussed, helpless and concerned as I had felt with her.

By this time, I had become aware of a number of instances in which her somatically experienced suffering was based on her perceiving various persons about her, for example, staff members and fellow patients in the cottage, or townspeople seen during her escorted trips into town, as suffering various forms of physical anguish, and her unconsciously taking those percepts into her own body image, in an attempt to heal them within herself. Despite the obvious defense which this represented against her largely unconscious sadism and murderous hostility toward these persons, it had become clear that her loving solicitude and therapeutic concern had an element of indubitable sincerity and genuineness.

Some three years later, during my supervision at another hospital of the psychotherapy of a borderline-schizophrenic young man, I was reminded of Joan when the patient said that he wanted to "sever the bonds of sickness to Mother. The way I'm bowing my head now is the way she does. It's like I have the struggles of a child still inside me." I regarded the image of the child, struggling within him, as being comprised not only of elements of his own childhood self, but also of elements of the child in mother, struggling against sickness, elements which he had taken, partly with a therapeutic motive, into his self-image. One of the striking aspects of this paper is the recurrent theme of how extremely immature are the areas of the parent's ego which are involved in these types of symbiotic fusion with the child, and how early in life the patient is called upon to try to function as a parent and therapist to the parent. Joan's inability to differentiate actual adults from actual children was extreme. One of her tenacious delusions was that children are "arrested adults." For several years she recurrently called our sessions, derisively, her "baby-sitting" with me, and in more recent years she has made it clear that a major source of contention between herself and her mother, beginning in early childhood, was her insistence that *she* was the mother, and that her mother was the child or baby. Joan shows, to this day, a cynical-child quality that I have recognized as a defense against dependent needs in persons who had to function prematurely as parent to their parents, and who had very little childhood of their own. Joan once told me, "I grew up at the age of eight."

In the seventeenth year of our work, her consciously lovingly concerned and unconsciously murderously competitive efforts to bring surcease to various mother-figures was evident in a session, most of which is too delusionally distorted, too bewildering, to warrant reproducing here. It was beginning to dawn on me that she felt overwhelmed by my intended therapeutic devotion to her, devotion which presumably contained more murderous competitiveness than I could yet integrate (although I had long been familiar with sustained urges to murder her). Identifying with the aggressor, she spent most of the sessions in being preoccupied with how to rescue her delusionally distorted, gigantic but victimized mother. She incessantly felt unappreciated, unsuccessful and worst of all unacknowledged, in her endless striving to be of use, of help, to her mother.

She was looking tearful throughout most of this session. A very slowly developing capacity to grieve, bit by bit, was one of the major aspects of her therapeutic progress, and stood in marked contrast to the paranoid grandiosity which formerly had shielded her against feelings of loss; but the increments of healthy grief were accompanied by such intense affects of depression that I felt threatened by the possibility of her suicide. She looked earnest and very serious during this session.

At the beginning of the session she refused, as usual, to accept the name Joan, identifying herself as Barbara (one of innumerable names she applies to herself). Midway along the session, speaking of multiple, highly delusionally distorted, fragments of her image of her mother, she said, "I gave them to you [that is, literally put them into me, a familiar delusion], and you didn't help them. *I* couldn't; they hated *me*." She went on (and this clearly now had reference to her roommate, a highly psychotic young woman who was often placed into cold, wet-sheet packs), "I didn't want to make her *more* tense. . . . A couple of times I had to put them in straitjackets. . . . The way Mrs. Schultz [the name of her long-deceased mother; her mother transference to her roommate—her misidentification of her roommate as being literally her mother—had been evident before] talks about her life, it's always been terrible; she's always been the rubber outside the hemisphere, and rubber's always been hard to cure [a glimpse, here, of her irrepressible, usually caustic and mocking, wit] . . . . I spoke to Dr. Mitchell [the name of the former ward administrator many years before, whom she recurrently referred to as still being present] about them; *he* didn't make them any better."

I felt certain she was talking about her current young roommate when she said (in the excerpts below, my comments are in brackets):

". . . And that kid was in the room yesterday, and she wanted to behave well, I guess, and I started to talk to it [her hostility was often expressed in her experiencing others, including me in the sessions, as being nonhuman, and even inanimate], and somethin' grabbed it, 'cause it looked like *that* [she affected a shocked facial expression] at me—like a real baby. [Kid—'Kid'—ya mean the kid (realizing only now that she was speaking of her young roommate; one often had no way of knowing whether she were describing interactions with hallucinatory figures).] Yeah; the one who's knifed me to death. [Looked at ya very wide-eyed] I have *never*—uh—*felt* as *much antagonism,* and *hate,* and *loathing*—and I *grabbed it* by the shoulders, you know, and I said, 'Now your *mother* wants me to help her fix your head! And *she* doesn't have a license. *I* have a license.' I tried to reason with her, and at the end of that he [N.B. *I gave* me such a *sock;* he practically knocked my *head* off my *shoulders*! Now whaddya make of that?—and *no conversation, ever.* [From—the Kid?] Um (as a confirmation). A real baby . . . and [speaking now of some other delusionally distored mother-figures] I gave them you as a doctor; but *you* didn't make them any better. You made them terrible—[Well, in a way that was a relief, wasn't it?] No. [You'd been trying *so* hard to help them. It would have been distressing if *I* had been *able* to, and *you* had *not*.] *Oh, no,* because I had to rely on *other* people to *help* them. they *really hate me;* they did *not like* me. [Spite of *all* your efforts, huh?] Yeah; I was just trying to make them feel more comfortable, less aggressive, and I couldn't understand why each person that went in there [That is, went, as a miniature, literally and bodily into the body of the person he or she was endeavoring to cure] had to make them *worse*. . . ."

Later in the session she said, "The mother is at Chestnut Lodge, of course. . . The mother doesn't want to be alone. . . . The women at the Lodge need a doctor. . . ." [This was one of the innumerable sessions during which I believed it was important to be careful about interpreting lest I say something that would lead to her suicide; her shockingly intense, murderous hostility tended to be directed, suicidally, against herself, now that her predominantly paranoid murderousness had shifted gradually into depression. Previously my concern had been, not that she kill me but, during particularly stormy and enraging sessions, that I kill her.]

Seventeen months later (the nineteenth year of our work) during a particular session, she clearly expressed her therapeutic strivings.

When I motioned her into my office from the waiting room, as usual I did not address her by name. For the first ten minutes she was silent, as was not infrequent. She seldom looked at me. Her demeanor was one of helplessness, troubled feelings, bewilderment, vulnerability, and uncertainty as to whether she could trust me. She seemed to be listening to hallucinatory voices rather than thinking—many times before she had flatly stated that she had no mind, and was a radio through which people in the walls expressed themselves. A few times she nodded obediently, apparently in response to hallucinatory voices.

Then, she talked, and I felt she was giving me a tremendous working over by saying many caustically depreciatory things in a highly delusional way. I had long since realized that everything she said, no matter how delusional, consciously or unconsciously alluded to something in the immediate situation. She repeatedly implied, "If the shoe fits, wear it." I was often aware, through feelings of guilt, inadequacy and self-condemnation, that the shoe fit all too well. Because her accusations were so indirect, I felt unable to retaliate with sufficient savagery to feel free.

Nonetheless this session proved to be more collaborative than many. She seemed largely unconscious of how much she was doing to make me feel discouraged and depressed; but she expressed the feeling that I did not need her in any way, even to feel entertained by her, an important revelation. Despite the accusing, reproachful, condemnatory, competitive, mocking, and beseeching working-over that she was giving me, she was still entertaining, by virtue of her caustic wit and the fabulously creative imagination which possessed her more than was possessed by her.

The collaborative yield of the session was evident in various ways. She made many realistic references to Chestnut Lodge—which, for her, was un-usually good contact with reality. Parenthetically, during the past few years she has become aware that there is only one Chestnut Lodge where, she now realizes, she has lived for years. Forty-two minutes along in a two-hour session, she accusingly and reproachfully said: ". . . you hold onto me and push me away all at the same time . . .", a highly perceptive and succinct statement of reality, as I knew also from playbacks of tapes from earlier sessions. This was also a transference reaction; I represented her mother, who had simultaneously held her close while pushing her away. Some minutes later she protested: "You keep talking to me like my mother!"

Fifteen minutes later she despondently said, ". . . My mother . . . she doesn't seem to need me for nothin' . . .", and six minutes later, was saying of someone else she had invoked, "I amuse *her*." She felt reproachful toward me, as a mother, since if she *is* able to amuse this other person, she fails in her therapeutic attempt to amuse *me* (that is, another mother).

She also made several realistic new comments about her ex-husband, of whom she had not spoken for many months. Later, she said, "I would *like* to engage a psychiatrist . . . .", which was perhaps the greatest degree of verbal acceptance of psychiatry I had ever heard from her, apart from the marital connotation of the word *engage*.

I wish to highlight her efforts to entertain me (as the personification of her depressed mother).

Throughout nineteen years of treatment, confusion had been her predominant symptom, confusion defended against by innumerable and ever changing delusions. Only after some dozen years of my endeavoring primarily to rescue her from a life filled with manifold anguish, realistic as well as psychotic in nature, and permeated by this confusion, did I gradually come, bit by hard-won bit, to experience a kind of esthetic appreciation, at first highly guilt-laden and furtive, of her confusion. Her confusion had, from another viewpoint, a truly breathtaking creativity, far more fascinating, wondrous and, of course, alive than, for example, a beautiful and intricate Persian rug. With this gradual change in my orientation, which required some few years to become really well-established, I became also more receptive to, and appreciative of, her tremendous wit and her indomitable sense of humor. Of both her wit and her humor I had been well aware from the beginning.

Earlier, I had been so desperately concerned to help her that I had been largely unaware of how basically concerned she was in trying to be helpful and alleviating to me, if only by entertaining me with schizophrenic confusion which, for many years, was all she had to give me to relieve my depression. My depression was to a degree real but tremendously intensified, in her perceptions of me, by her depressed-mother-transference. Its reality was accentuated by much that she said and did, I believe largely unconsciously, which would be enough to greatly depress any psychotherapist.

In the next session, two days later, she said, "The human race is in a shambles," and she was able to recall realistic memories of her childhood, in which her mother had made repeated trips to Italy, evidently in line with her operatic ambitions, while leaving Joan and her siblings in the care of a succession of maids. She remembered not a succession but a chaotic myriad of vague parent-figures. The feeling tone of the session, significantly for this paper, was mutually enjoyable. I had learned that she throve in sessions in which, no matter how much reason for despair, we both were able genuinely to enjoy.

Two sessions and five days later, before inviting her in for the session, I confided briefly to my tape recorder my anxiety that she was invading my life so thoroughly that I would go crazy; the preceding session with her had been more disturbing to me than usual. But this session, a two-hour one as has been the case once each week for years, proved to be relatively collaborative and therapeutically fruitful. I was slowly becoming more appreciative of the healthy ingredients of her delusional thinking. For example, she expressed a delusion that she had been an architect in New York City and had designed many buildings there. Instead of my responding, as I usually had, to the arrogant grandiosity of her tone, I asked her what buildings she had designed, and I was impressed when she named a half dozen well-known buildings; this was, for her, a rare nugget of reality relatedness.

Later in the session I had occasion to suggest to her that maybe, while she was here in the office, she missed her current Chestnut Lodge roommate, to which she replied, seriously and thoughtfully, "Maybe so," a rare acknowledgement from her. For years I had noted that the form and content of the sessions were enormously influenced by her unconscious separation feelings toward the cab driver or the nurse or aide who had accompanied her to the session, or her unconscious feelings about having briefly left various sections of Chestnut Lodge.

Also in this session the role of her terror of her projected envy was becoming clearer in her saying, for example, ". . . this head [gesturing toward her head]—of course, it's not a head; it's just a piece of paper— . . ." In earlier years I had been sufficiently preoccupied with my own feelings of envy of her, for many well-founded reasons, and was so burdened with guilt about it, that I had failed to understand that her never experiencing her head as being her own head was because she feared her mother's envy. Her mother, in various ways, had lost her head in legendary outbursts of volcanic fury. Joan's therapeutic effort was aimed at protecting her mother from the realization of the mother's own state of deprivation.

Three weeks later, she was tearful, sad, feeling burdened and intruded upon. There were indications that her identity was dominated by identification with memories of her mother, who was more disorganized than usual during a certain period of Joan's childhood. At that time the mother gave birth to twins, only one of whom, a male, had lived, whereas the other, a female, died shortly following delivery. During a session she made references to "the baby," a concept which encompassed both the dead baby girl and the live baby boy, and I had reason to know that she, as a child, had not only been invaded by the psychotic introject of the grief-crazed mother, but had striven thereby to rescue the mother by taking into herself the mother's burden of tragedy and psychotic reaction to tragedy.

Three weeks later she stated with conviction, as she frequently had before, that she is dead, this time explaining that she had died the night before in order that her mother not be killed. She stated that her Daddy had killed her over and over. Innumerable times in previous years she had accused me, when she perceived me as a remote and murderously omnipotent father in the transference, of murdering her. She was experiencing herself and her only living sister as being in effect, artificially conglomerated Siamese twins: she showed me one hand, saying, "That's me," and the other "is Mrs. Bradley" (her sister's married name). Never before had she conveyed so tangibly how important to her, how much a part of her, the sister is, the only one among all her numerous relatives who has found it endurable to keep on visiting Joan during the past ten years. She visits for a few days once or twice each year.

In the next session, two days later, I privately thought, as she walked into my office from the waiting room, that she looked like hell. She was wearing no lipstick; she was looking pale and old; her hair was unkempt; there was a button off the top of her familiar and unbecomingly tentlike Navy blue jumper; she was wearing sneakers rather than the reasonably attractive leather shoes she often wore, and no stockings. I thought, with a familiar dull hopelessness, of the setting in which she had lived her daily life for many years, amidst other chronically schizophrenic patients, and with a highly psychotic roommate—a setting where, despite the best efforts on the part of the administrative, nursing, aide and other staff members, the alleviating of such chronic self-neglect seemed hopeless. Throughout the whole hour her demeanor was one of tearfulness, vulnerability, and hurt; meanwhile, in her verbal communications, she was being her usual, extremely formidable self, giving me the usual tremendous working over throughout nearly the whole session.

Nonetheless, during the course of the session her communications provided realistic new glimpses of her parents' marriage, and valuable evidence that her tenacious self-neglect was part of an effort to evoke in me her mother who, as I knew, had striven incessantly and coercively to care for her clothing. It was apparent that she was trying to evoke this mother in me not only because she needed that mother, but as a way of resuscitating the mother who had been dead for 23 years.

She spoke, too, of "Ma" as being a "tempestuous woman," and indeed she had been. "He brawls," she went on; the mother indeed had had a strongly phallic quality, and had often run the home in a brawling manner. "I had a daughter," she later said, as indeed she has—a daughter as loathsome to her as is her own real identity, for between her and this daughter her conflicts with her own mother had raged, during Joan's daughter's childhood, to such a degree that years ago the two reached a point of denial of one another's existence. She later said, "I honestly don't know where my mother is"—a strikingly realistic statement, for her, and still later referred to ". . . that Mrs. Schultz [her mother] who was a good friend of mine [a memorable expression of positive feeling for her mother]," and went on to say that "I lived for centuries as an element" (in earlier years of our work she frequently had identified herself as being a boundless element—light, electricity, and so on—or as being filled with radioactive material), and stated, with a tone of partial accomplishment, that she has now become an animal, but is not yet a human being.

A prominent aspect of this session was my proving able not to be trapped into pursuing the bits of realistic reporting. I learned this was not only one of her ways of sadistically tantalizing me, but also one of her efforts to mobilize me as her mother, in a manner unconsciously intended to be therapeutic for this mother overwhelmed by depression and apathy. She was trying coercively to put her together—to put together the fragments of her healthy ego-functioning, out of the welter of psychotic material.

Five days later she was looking tearful and pensive. I felt that she was reacting primarily to the fact that Thanksgiving, with all its nostalgic connotations, was only two days off; only after the session did it occur to me that her sadness probably had more to do with the fact that Thanksgiving meant, also, the missing of our usual two-hour Thursday session. During this session it was evident that she was grieving particularly for the relationship with her daughter—new material, indeed—and she spoke repeatedly and realistically of her sister, also. Part of her delusional experience during this session was experiencing us as being in a gigantic statue. Someone was able to see out from the eyes of the statue and was reporting that no Coast Guard ship was approaching. She conveyed vividly the bleakness and remoteness of the scene, viewed from the eyes of the statue.

She asked of her mother, "Is she dead?" in full seriousness and as though this were the first time any such intimation had come to her, although many times and for many years I had told her, at times gently and at times with scornfully impatient harshness and bluntness, that her mother had died many years ago. "There's a lot of water behind the eyes of the statue, she said movingly.

She remarked later, "People who have murdered may pretend to be crazy," which clearly referred to us. Many times in past years she had accused me of having murdered her mother, and still feared, at an unconscious level, that if her mother were indeed dead, then she must have killed her—either in murderous rage or, more likely, through neglect.

Nine days later, as I was returning from the men's room in the middle of a two-hour session, I had thought that I had been having my psychosis vicariously in a controlled way through her over the years, with myself remaining safely apart from it, and that the hundreds of tapes of our sessions represented my psychosis. Half an hour later in the session she said, while wiping her face with her palms and pushing against her cheeks in a pathetic way, "I don't know how to run my expression . . . ." There was transitory, powerful, submerged anger detectible in her facial expression on occasion; but she was pathetically not in contact with it. A few minutes later she spoke of a "machine supposed to represent the mind of God." Since the early months of our work she had described, on occasion, either herself or me as being, quite concretely and literally, a machine.

Fourteen days later, I began feeling overwhelmed for a few seconds, with accompanying feelings of panic, when I realized that the things she was saying and feeling were based upon lampoons or satires, some conscious and many unconscious, of various real aspects of myself. Her outpourings felt like an avalanche. She still did not know the enormous impact her delusional thinking had upon me, as well as upon other persons in her daily life.

It was evident in this session that I was still emotionally unprepared to occupy the transference role she desperately needed me to occupy a gigantic but psychotically fragmented mother.

Five days later, in a session two days before Christmas, she looked very sad, unhappy, and tearful. She emphasized, as she had before, that people cannot have any emotional relatedness with one another unless they are members of the same parental family; her compulsive family loyalty had been one of the most powerful sources of her resistance. In this session, for the first time, she revealed that she had given her four children, with whom she had severed all ties many years before, to her mother. She wanted to provide her mother with fulfillment, at last, as a mother; it had long been evident that she had not found fulfillment in mothering Joan.

During this session her rapidly changing perceptions of myself and her were even more delusionally distorted than usual. For example she saw the eyes of many different persons fleetingly in my eyes. I experienced a submerged and disturbing agitation of an unusual degree. As far as I could discern, this was related to the intensity of ths reality-unrelatedness between us. Only after the session did it occur to me that she had been more resistive, hostile, rejecting, and emotionally unrelated toward me than usual because of an increased need for closeness at the Christmas holiday. Such closeness was permissible, according to her superego standards, only with members of her family. Many years before I had seen her and her sister rush warmly into one another's arms during one of her sister's visits, in a manner which was expressive of genuine familial love, and in retrospect I could see that during this session, Joan had to vigorously defend herself against the expression of such feelings toward me at Christmas time.

A week later I found her to be more psychologically *here* in the session, more tangibly related to me, than she had been in a very long time—perhaps ever. Further, and significantly for the theme of this chapter, she emphasized that she had found that both her mother and father (each clearly related to me in the immediate transference situation) had regarded her as worthless and as contributing nothing worthwhile to either of them.

Three weeks later, I learned from the nurse in charge of her unit that Joan had been crying upon returning to Chestnut Lodge from her session with me on that day and had been talking, at the same time, of her mother's death—for the first time since this nurse had known Joan. Two sessions later, she spoke realistically of her mother's hatred of her: "But I can't get over why she hates me so much . . . . because my mother doesn't like me . . . ."

Five days later she said, gesturing toward her head, "I think I usta run in and out of myself," which I understood as meaning "in and out of fantasy." For many years I had been trying to help her differentiate between fantasy and reality, and this was a welcome indication of progress in that direction. She referred to herself at another point in the session as being an "earthquake"; I mention this as a sample of her persisting and incredible degree of identity distortion.

Regarding her going into and out of fantasy, I had much evidence, from both her psychotherapy as well as from the historical data provided by one of her siblings, that her mother also had gone into and out of fantasy a great deal. Four months later, the patient said, "My mother feels she can't survive unless she's playing a part." It was evident that Joan's childhood participation in her mother's fantasies, a result not only of the mother's domination of her but also of the patient's effort to help her mother survive, had been one of the main sources of Joan's chronically fantasy-ridden, schizophrenic mode of existence.

Four days later, I had just returned from a professional trip, a trip which I felt had been nothing less than triumphant for me in my part-career as an authority on the psychotherapy of schizophrenic patients. In my session with Joan on this day, I found myself feeling, as usual, completely inept and fully deserving of her delusionally expressed but demolishingly effective scorn toward me. It became increasingly clear that I had needed her to confirm, recurrently over the years, the lowest areas of my self-esteem—to reassure me that I am indeed worthless, as I privately feel oftentimes. To be sure, I could see transference connections between myself and her head-in-the-clouds mother who needed recurrently to be deflated down to earth, as well as between myself and her remote, intellectual father who had tenaciously ignored the interpersonal work at hand that desperately needed getting done; but there has been this significantly real core in her transference perceptions of me. In more recent times, as for various reasons my hunger for vilification has lessened somewhat, I gradually have become better able to weather her insults and hold her to our realistic collaborative task.

A week later, in the early part of the session, she suddenly, unexpectedly and very movingly became unusually tearful, protesting, "You keep looking at me so much, when there is someone in your right eye who needs your attention!" It seemed clear that she felt undeserving of my interest. A half hour later she spoke about an overzealous doctor, clearly a reference to me. As long as she felt therapeutically ineffective toward me as a transference figure, it only augmented her feelings of guilt and worthlessness whenever she did get a glimpse of me as genuinely wanting to be helpful to her.

Still later in the session she stated that her mother is not dead, and that she herself is dead, having been murdered. This I heard as typical of her unconscious guilt about her mother's death, but also of a genuinely loving devotion to her mother and a readiness, therefore, to sacrifice her own life in order that the mother might live. Repeatedly in the session she perceived "that man from Tunis" in my left eye—the origin of this perception, like that of most of her perceptions, I had no way of knowing ("Tunis" = two-ness?)—and Al Capone in my right eye, and she repeatedly and forcefully accused me of multiple murders and other evil deeds. At one point I felt a rageful urge to beat the craziness out of her, and I sensed this urge as similar to those which had impelled her mother to repeatedly and brutally beat her daughter. One of the currents at work in this surely complex interaction was, I remain convinced on the basis of much corollary data, Joan's therapeutic struggle to resuscitate her dead (= depressed) mother, as personified by me.

Three weeks later she said to me, in the midst of the session. "You're the man from Pakistan." I had been confronted with such communications from her innumerable times before and this, like so many of the others, was said to me very decisively and directly. The new aspect of this instance is that I immediately asked, "Is this what the voices just told you?" and she agreed. I gained a deeper appreciation of the havoc wrought upon her sense of personal identity by her being assailed by such unexpected, forceful, and unequivocally emphatic hallucinatory voices, and realized, more clearly than before, that her incessant verbal barrage against my sense of personal identity was a reflection of what was happening to her during the session.

By contrast, material also emerged highlighting various gratifications which resulted from having no mind of her own—notably a freedom from feeling responsible for what would otherwise be her own thoughts. I had been familiar, from previous sessions, with her experiencing herself as a radio through which people in the walls, for example, were communicating. On some of the occasions when she has said such things—which of course tend totally to nullify my efforts with her—I have reminded her, ironically, that of course she realizes that I, too, am just a radio.

Eight days later, in an unusually collaborative and useful session she said, "You don't seem to realize you've interviewed nine hundred quaduary trillion people in this chair," gesturing toward her chair. This seemed only somewhat of an exaggeration of her stream of successive ego-identity fragments over the years. She was also able to say later ". . . but I got it all mixed up, I guess, in my mind . . ." which was a rare acknowledgement of her confusion.

Eleven days later, a major theme which ran through a session was her reproach toward me and others as being callous and brutal with extremely vulnerable, delicate structures. For example, she pointed out that the people at Chestnut Lodge are living inside a baby. As usual with her delusional thinking, she referred to this as though it were entirely obvious. She stays in her room most of the time, and remains very quiet so as not to damage the baby. Parenthetically, for years the ward staff have been concerned about her massive self-isolation. This building, too, she continued, is the inside of a baby. She was very harsh with me, as so often before, for being so unfeeling; there were innumerable allusions to my being callous and brutal as well as inept. A second and interrelated main theme emerged in the session with equal clarity: she was desperately in need of maternal assistance from me (as well as from others in her daily life), but manifested a fiercely destructive competitiveness with anyone's endeavor to provide such assistance. Early in the session there were unusually clear depictions of her childhood rivalry with her mother; they were involved in a chronic and unresolved power-struggle about who was the mother and who was the child. The prize was omnipotence, as well as the more conventional oedipal goals; and, for the patient, there was the motive of recurrently rescuing the mother from depression by provoking her with outrageously insolent and arrogant behavior.

A month later, during a session where as usual she seemed largely unaware of her castrative rivalry toward me and of the impact this was having upon me, she was able to say, "My mother has always been disgusted with me," a highly accurate statement of an important aspect of her childhood. She had told me that during childhood she suffered from vomiting, and that her mother's fury at her recurrent vomiting had often provoked the mother to beat her. The vomiting served, I believe, to bring the mother back to earth, so to speak, from her fantasyland.

Fifteen minutes later in this same session she concluded one of her usual bewilderingly delusional, dreamlike narratives with, ". . .—so that's where we are now." I realized that this meant that she is fixated at a particular point in an ongoing fantasy. Her intrapsychic life was now becoming sufficiently coherent that I could sense that currently her days were dominated by developing, continuing fantasies. Half an hour later in this two-hour session, she spoke of ". . . mother's . . . sublime . . . ethereal" qualities, so reminiscent of her brother's description of the mother returning from Mass in a beatific mood. Thus, I had a glimpse of how she identified with mother in her fantasy-dominated mode of living. Twenty minutes later, she said thoughtfully and simply, "Mrs. Schultz raised her children," a comment full of tremendous implications of grief and guilt, for she, by contrast, had abandoned her four young children to be raised by others. But here, too, emerged hints (similar to those I reported from an earlier session) that she had done so partly, if not primarily, to thus provide maternal fulfillment to other mother figures.

It occured to me immediately following a session three weeks later that she cannot assume her real identity as long as I cannot be transformed into a gigantic mother. A month later I wrote the following note, after a session: "The main value of this session is that it is dawning upon me increasingly how *many*—I *now* surmise *all*—of her responses are founded predominantly upon identifications with me as she perceives me. It is dawning upon me how amazingly much she needs for me to *be* her *world,* in the transference relationship, for her to become well, and it seems to be exclusively interpretations of *this* that prove to be useful interpretations."

Perhaps the main reason why this has been so difficult for me to experience fully is that it has required my acknowledgment of her tremendous importance to me. Because of the particular symbiotic relationship she had with her mother, she became equivalent, in countertransference terms, to my own early, symbiotic mother. I am convinced, not only from my work with Joan and other schizophrenic patients, but also from supervisory experiences with many therapists who were treating such patients, that *the more readily accessible to himself are the therapist's own symbiotic-dependent feelings, the better he is equipped to help the patient to become conscious of similar feelings, so that the patient need no longer act out symbiotic yearnings through the schizophrenic postponement of individuation.*

Within the first five minutes of a session one month later she stated that her head was that of a fellow patient in her cottage whom I knew was chronically schizophrenic. She described in detail that the head contained a man in a bizarre position which was causing him much physical suffering. It was apparent that this distortion of her body image, typical of innumerable ones of which I had heard before but expressed more clearly than most, was based in part upon her primitive attempt to bring her fellow patient's suffering in for me, hopefully, to cure. As usual I felt mocked for my ineptitude as a therapist, but impressed once again with how thoroughly her existence depended upon her attempts to cure all her fellow patients as well as mankind in general, as an omnipotent therapist.

Her sister visited her a month later for two or three days, for the first time in some eight months. In her usual interview with me toward the end of her stay, she emphasized how impressive Joan's progress had been, although she did not disregard the persistent manifestations of her tenacious psychosis. In my interview with the patient a bit later during the sister's visit, I was both amused and impressed that Joan was equally oriented toward evaluating how much progress her patient, namely her sister, had made in the several months' interim since the previous visit. She detailed and caricatured, with consummate perception and mimicry, certain of the sister's lifelong compulsively driving characteristics, so much like some of mine, and expressed genuine distress that the sister was still incapable of sharing Joan's current orientation of taking life as it comes. Two days later it was apparent that her having taken "the Mrs. Bradleys" (her sister's married name; she perceived her sister, as usual, as being multiple figures rather than one person) into her own body image, protectively and restoratively, had been done not only out of loving feelings toward her sister, but also as a defense against projected murderousness and contempt toward her. Toward the end of this same month, she said of herself, "We're virtually the whole human race," in a tone both grandiose and burdened as well as simply human. I heard this as an expression of simple and profound truth on the part of one who had achieved, after a long and tragic struggle, kinship with fellow human beings, but had yet to come to terms with the psychotic conflict between her omnipotence-based murderousness toward her fellow human beings, and her at least equally intense loving and therapeutic concern for them.

DISCUSSION

1. *Goals and Techniques Involved in the Patient's Therapeutic Strivings:*   One of the patient's strivings is to help the other person (in the treatment situation, the analyst) to fulfill his human potentialities. The patient strives to help the analyst to share those modes of interpersonal relatedness which are relatively anxiety-free for the patient, and anxiety-laden for the analyst; a simple example is the nonobsessive patient's teasing the analyst, in a way that is basically intended to be a helpful "come off it" about the latter's obsessive fussing with the ventilation, lighting, or what-not of the office. Another way of putting it is that the patient endeavors to help the analyst to share in the patient's relatively nonneurotic areas of ego functioning. He is endeavoring to contribute to the analyst's emotional growth, integration, and maturation.

Particularly in the instances of more severely ill—schizoid or schizophrenic—patients, such goals are relatively undifferentiated from the goal of the patient's endeavoring to provide himself with an increasingly constructive model for identification, in the person of the analyst, that can be used for the patient's further maturation.

The psychotherapeutic techniques which the patient utilizes frequently include one or another form of catharsis and various forms of verbal, and much more often nonverbal, reassurance. The most important mechanisms are the primitive unconscious processes of introjection of the analyst's more ill components, and projection upon the analyst of areas of relative strength of the patient's ego (Searles, 1972b). By the introjection the patient attempts to take the analyst's illness into himself and treat the "ill analyst" so that a healthier analyst can eventually be born out of the patient. This takes place during the course of and as a result of the symbiotic phase of treatment.

It is obvious that the patient is relatively unequipped, either consciously or unconsciously, to carry out the primary and paramount goal of the *psychoanalytic* psychotherapist, namely, the analysis of the transference. I shall touch on this matter again in Part 3 of this discussion.

2. *Technique of Interpreting, or Otherwise Acknowledging the Presence of the Patient's Therapeutic Strivings:*   This is so complex a matter, so much a function of therapeutic intuition and timing, as to render unwise any attempt to generalize about the subject of when, and how, and to what extent the analyst interprets to the patient his striving to treat him. I rarely if ever acknowledge, in any explicit way, and surely not in any formal way, that I am receiving such help from the patient. The more I can comfortably accept these strivings as inherent to the treatment process, the more, I feel certain, does my whole demeanor convey an implicit acknowledgment that the therapeutic process involves both of us. Certainly, I make transference interpretations which implicitly convey my acknowledgment that the patient's endeavor to be therapeutically helpful (and in my interpretations I use no such stilted a word as "therapeutic") to the mother is at the same time an endeavor to be similarly helpful toward me as the personification of the mother.

The analyst is technically on relatively solid ground when any indications which he gives that he is finding what is transpiring to be personally helpful to him, are given in a relatively nonanxious, nonguilty and therefore nonconfessional way, but rather as data which are being shared with a collaborator.

Beside the hazard of failing to recognize and interpret the patient's therapeutic strivings, is the hazard of prematurely interpreting them. Generally, as long as patient remains oppressed by feelings of guilty responsibility, he will react with intensified guilt to any intimation from the analyst that he is finding the sessions personally helpful. The patient, in addition to all his other burdens of guilty responsibility, has now also become responsible for the analyst's life, or for that particular aspect of it which the analyst has just revealed.

I cannot say simply that interpretations of the patient's therapeutic strivings should be reserved for relatively late in the analysis, for as a generalization I think that is untrue. But I can say that, in most instances, it is only after some years of analysis that one detects a shift in the feeling tone with which the patient speaks of his family's psychopathology. The feeling tone, which in the earlier years of the analysis had portrayed etiologic family events or situations as burdens which were *imposed upon* him, gradually shifts in quality, as his more deeply repressed emotions of grief and loving devotion come to the fore, and conveys that he had also incorporated these burdens within himself in an active and lovingly devoted—what I am calling therapeutic—spirit. Transference interpretations of the patient's therapeutic strivings toward the analyst now are unlikely to intensify the patient's anxiety, confusion, or guilt. But I question whether this phase in the analysis can be reached, unless the analyst has engaged in interpretative activity at an earlier time, when it involves speaking with courage in the face of appreciable risk.

Relatively late in my preparation of this paper, a simple clinical vignette served to remind me how important is the timing of the analyst's interpretation of the patient's therapeutic strivings. A borderline schizophrenic woman from whom I have long been receiving therapeutic help of various kinds caused me to realize that it is not yet timely for me to begin interpreting this aspect of her ego functioning. She was reminiscing, as she often had before, of experiences with a previous therapist in which, seemingly at her initiative, he would soothingly hold her hand. This time she said, ". . . On other occasions he very much wanted to hold my hand, and I was very much aware that it wasn't what *I* needed; it got mixed up with what *he* needed . . .", and this was said with a tone of distinct regret.

She went on a moment later, "He seemed to believe in interaction; he wasn't like you at all. With you, nothing I do seems to matter; you're always the same way. I couldn't have *abided* someone like you [seizing her head in furious exasperation, as she had many times before in our sessions] you'd have driven me crazy! . . ." I felt convinced (particularly by her regretful reference to her previous therapist's need) that it was not yet timely for me to interpret her still largely unconscious therapeutic strivings toward me.

In general, to the degree that a patient is functioning in the treatment sessions in an autistic, infantile-omnipotent manner, he, like the woman just mentioned, is intolerant (despite all his complaints of the analyst's unresponsiveness) of the analyst's functioning in a tangibly alive and participative manner during the sessions—of the analyst's discernibly *contributing anything to* the analytic work, let alone *deriving anything from* it. The patient's infantile omnipotence would be greatly outraged. At a somewhat later phase of the patient's ego development, one finds instances in which the patient manifests a transference to the analytic *situation* as being a nursing mother, and to the analyst *himself* as being a rival sibling whom the patient is determined to keep barred out of this cherished situation of having mother all to oneself. But when this degree of object-relatedness has been achieved, the transference is more subject to interpretation. In any event I hope to have indicated here my cognizance of the fact that the patient's therapeutic strivings are not simply to be interpreted or otherwise acknowledged without considerable thought. The main theme of this chapter focuses upon the loss to both participants if the analyst, as the patient, remains unconscious of this dimension of the relationship and therefore fails to deal with it.

3. *Regression by the analyst, as it concerns his therapeutic strivings:*   In a previous paper which included some discussion of patients' therapeutic strivings in the course of my developing another theme (Searles, 1967), I wrote of these patients that

> "Their therapeutic techniques are outwardly so brutal that the therapeutic intent is seen only in the result. One apathetic, dilapidated hebephrenic patient of mine received considerable therapeutic benefit from a fellow patient, newly come to the ward, but, like him, a veteran of several years in mental hospitals, who repeatedly, throughout the day, gave my patient a vigorous and unexpected kick in the behind. From what I could see, this was the first time in years a fellow patient had shown any real interest in him, and my patient as a result emerged appreciably from his state of apathy and hopelessness."

During moments or even long phases of particularly intense anxiety in his work, the analyst undergoes regression such that his analytic orientation becomes primitivized (desublimated) to the level of relatively raw aggressive and sexual urges. This regression is a manifestation of the analyst's frustrated therapeutic strivings as well as those of the patient. In my work with the hebephrenic man just mentioned, it was only after some years of four hourly sessions per week, sessions filled with apathy and unrelatedness, punctuated only by moments of murderous rage, violent sexual urges, and acute fear, that I finally realized that it was possible for me to relate to him in some fashion other than the only two potential means heretofore available, those two means being, as I had thought of them, fucking him or killing him. To my enormous relief I realized that I could now be related to him without having either to kill him or fuck him.

It has long been my impression that a major reason for therapists' becoming actually sexually involved with patients is that the therapist's therapeutic striving has desublimated to the level at which it operated in childhood. He has succumbed to the illusion that a magically curative copulation will resolve the patient's illness which tenaciously had resisted all the more sophisticated psychotherapeutic techniques learned in his adult-life training and practice.

In my clinical experience, the temptation toward such activity is most intense in my work with patients whose childhood histories included the patient's having been involved in a relationship with a parent in which the child sensed the incestuous fulfillment would provide the parent with relief from neurotic or psychotic suffering. In such a childhood family situation, it is inordinately difficult for the child's therapeutic striving to become differentiated from, or sublimated beyond sexual strivings. All this becomes reexperienced in the transference relationship, with the analyst becoming the personification of the patient's child-self, feeling impelled to try to resolve the patient's neurotic or psychotic parental identification (introject) through actual sexual activity.

Unacceptable incestuous urges become acceptable to the therapist's superego by clothing themselves in the guise of healing.

In many instances the primitive healing strivings are no less powerful than are the sexual strivings, and the therapeutic strivings can be the most powerful of all in bringing about a tragic deforming of the therapeutic endeavor, predatory sexual behavior by the therapist under the guise of the emancipated healer. A need for therapeutic omnipotence can lead the therapist to seize upon any available, intentionally therapeutic measures, including actual sexual involvement with the patient.

I touched upon this problem of regression in an earlier paper (Searles, 1959b) concerning integration and differentiation in schizophrenia. In discussing the group symbiosis which develops in the ward life of the hospitalized patient, I stated that:

> "In the face of the increasingly intense conflictual feelings which permeate such a group symbiosis, regression deepens, not only in the patient's behavior but in that of the staff members as well. Not only do his demands become more infantile, but the personnel's mothering, good and bad, tends to assume more and more primitive forms. Just as he tends to become a suckling, demanding infant at the breast, they tend almost literally to offer him a breast, 'good' or 'bad' as the case may be, rather than provide more adult forms of mothering. . . ." (pp. 332-3 in Searles, 1965)

At that juncture I referred to one of Knight's (1953) articles on borderline psychosis, in which he described the treatment which a borderline-psychotic college girl had received from a woman dean and self-styled psychotherapist, prior to the girl's hospitalization. As the dean felt progressively cornered by the girl's demands, she allowed the sessions to go overtime; she allowed the girl to have sessions in the dean's home in the evenings and on weekends; she allowed the girl to use the dean's car; she allowed her to stay overnight in her home and, still later, to sleep in bed with her. Knight writes of the patient that

> ". . . At times she expressed irrational hatred of the dean and pounded her with her fists. At other times she wanted to be held on the dean's lap and fondled, and this wish was granted also. No real limits to her regressive behavior were set until she expressed a strong wish to suckle the dean's breasts. Here the dean drew the line. . . ."

Parenthetically, I now see in that material an element I did not see when I wrote that paper and which Knight also had not mentioned: The patient's own therapeutic striving to enable the dean to become strong and decisive enough, when sufficiently cornered by the patient's demands (and, more importantly of course, by the dean's own unconscious ambivalence) to draw a line. But to provide another clinical example of the point I am presently making, namely, the regression which becomes manifest in the nature of the doctor's own therapeutic strivings, I mentioned (Searles, 1970) in a paper concerning autism and therapeutic symbiosis that

> "I have been amused in retrospect—but only in retrospect—at something I would do from time to time when I would be feeling helpless in my work with one or another chronically paranoid patient who was sure I possessed the magic cure for his or her suffering, 'if you would only think nice thoughts about me,' or 'want me well.' I would have come, long since, to experience much fondness for the patient; but all my conventional analytic armamentarium had failed to help her resolve her psychotic symptoms. Now I would find myself smiling helplessly and pleadingly at the patient, with a feeling of wanting desperately to cure her, somehow, with my love. This, of course, like everything else I had found myself doing, did not work, and the intendedly magical love would be replaced by an equally omnipotence-based hatred, such that I would glare at the patient with, for example, a fantasy of burning out the inside of her skull."

To rephrase this point before going on to the next topic in this discussion, I am suggesting in essence that many instances of therapists' sexual acting-out with patients are motivated predominantly by the thwarting of the therapist's omnipotent healer strivings toward the patient. Surely this matter is related to a high percentage of negative therapeutic reactions: the resistive patient is holding out for the time when the therapist, out of his by now intolerable frustration and despair with the unceasingly futile results of his more conventional therapeutic efforts, will resort to throwing his sexuality onto the balance.

As it is with the therapist's sexual urges in his regressed omnipotent-healer state so, I suggest, it is with his aggressive urges also. At times my murderous urges toward a patient have taken the form of intended euthanasia—a rock-bottom urge to put him out of his misery. Since instances of therapists' bare-handed murdering of patients are surely rare, indeed, by contrast to the apparently not-rare instances of sexual involvement between the two, one can surmise that the sexual involvement gives unconscious release, as well, to the two participants' murderous urges toward one another. I have worked analytically with only one patient who had had an affair with a previous therapist, and I was not surprised to learn that powerful murderous urges evidently had been at work in both of them in the mutual omnipotent-healer strivings toward one another which had impelled them into that involvement with one another.

Turning to a less sensational area, in the course of our own work and in supervising the work of colleagues, we frequently see that a typical earmark of regression in the therapist, under the stress of his efforts to cope with his patient's intense ambivalence and his own responsive ambivalence, is that he, the therapist, has lost touch with the transference context of what is happening. His vision is narrowed by the anxiety and guilt aroused in him by his awareness that there are parts of himself which give immediate reality to the patient's transference to him. He cannot achieve sufficient emotional distance from the immediate interaction to view what is happening as a part of the patient's over-all life history. The realistic elements in the analyst may blind him to links between himself and earlier important figures in the patient's life, links between himself and the patient's childhood self, or evidence that the patient's present way of responding to him represents the activation of an important identification on the patient's part with some parent-image from the latter's childhood.

Here again, then, the therapist, in trying to carry through his therapeutic endeavor without, at this stressful time, the aid of his usual working knowledge and awareness of the dimension of transference, is himself very much like the typical patient in childhood who, in his or her efforts to bring therapeutic help to another family member has, of course, no awareness of the dimension of tranference—a dimension which Freud, among his other fundamental contributions to mankind, discovered and enabled us, in turn, to recognize.

4. *Additional Etiological Aspects of Childhood and Family Relationships:* Any full description of the warping by the family of the child's therapeutic strivings would require a book in itself. I shall add here only a few comments to what I have said about this subject earlier in this paper.

Typically, the more ill the adult patient, the more powerful have been the parent(s) transferences (largely unconscious, of course) to him as being the latter's parent(s). Therefore, whenever the child showed any therapeutic concern for the parent, the latter reacted to the child as though the child were the parent's parent. This role reversal threatened to undermine the parent's status as parent and threatened fulfillment of incestuous aims. For these reasons the child's therapeutic striving (inevitably, in this context, impelling the child toward fulfilling a *parental* role in the family) had to be subjected to, or remain under, severe repression and be acted out, within the family, in a manner largely unconscious to all the family members including the child himself.

During the hundreds of teaching interviews in which I have participated, at various hospitals, with adolescent or young adult patients who have become psychotic in the course of attempted emancipation from their families, through going away to college or making analogous attempts to become established as separate individuals, I have found evidence in a high percentage of these interviews that the patient had become overwhelmed with psychotic defenses against unconscious rage, guilt, anxiety, and grief at having proved unable simultaneously to (a) be a successful young college student (or whatever), and (b) be a mother who in this same process of going away to college has abandoned children (namely, the parents and other family members) back home. The young person's individuation needs have come into unbearable conflict, that is, with his therapeutic strivings toward his family members.

It has further seemed to me—although this, now, is somewhat more conjectural—that the same course of events has involved the parents (and other family members) at home in their response to the youth off at college (let us say) as being an unconsciously hated (as well as loved) parent figure, and a feared and hated *parental* (i.e., father or mother) oedipal rival, to such an extent that the parents have seized this very time, when the offspring is making tenuous and of course ambivalent efforts to become established as an individual, defiantly to cast him off as being a hated authority figure to them. Thus, partly in their unconscious rage and hurt at this mother or father who has abandoned them, the actual parents have severed him from the genuinely parental support which he needs, and which most young people evidently receive in sufficient measure. The more one comes to appreciate the familywide, overwhelming tragedy in these situations, the less one feels a sense of blaming any of the family members.

5. *Concerning Gratitude:* More and more during the past several years, I have come at last to see something of how frequently the analyst has cause to feel gratitude toward the patient. Any discussion of gratitude, in the psychoanalytic literature, usually is conducted in the implicit assumption that gratitude is inherently, predominantly if not exclusively, unidirectional in nature: the *patient*, over the course of successful treatment, has increasing reason to experience gratitude toward the *analyst*, and if the former does not manifest this, he remains to that degree neurotic or psychotic. Hill (1955), for example, in the final chapter of his book concerning the psychoanalytic therapy of schizophrenic patients, notes that ". . . one hears very little about gratitude from these patients. . . ." (p. 206). Surely one hears little, likewise, of an analyst's gratitdue toward his patient, and it has been only after decades of work in this field that I am becoming at all accustomed to such an emotion. I was still relatively rigorously defended, unconsciously, against experiencing gratitude toward patients when I discussed (Searles, 1966) the sense of identity as a perceptual organ:

"Following a single consultative interview (several years previously) with a schizophrenic man—one who had been making a thoroughgoing ass of himself with certain hebephrenic symptoms—I experienced myself, driving away from that hospital, as being an incredibly gifted and perceptive consultant. But then I caught myself and wondered what this was saying about the patient's dynamics. I was immediately struck with the likelihood that he tended to project onto other persons, including me, his own best ego capacities. This man, who had done such wonders, transitorily, for my self-esteem while abasing himself, committed suicide about two months later. We never know why about these things; but among the likely causes is the possibility that he came to find insupportable the burden which others placed upon him in their unconsciously exploiting him for the enhancement of their own subjective identities. . . ."

I am sure that I experienced, during that interview, no gratitude toward that man; one has no reason to feel gratitude toward someone who one perceives as being, whether consciously or unconsciously, victimized or exploited. It is only as I have come to sense and perceive the lovingly devoted, self-sacrificing, therapeutic-striving determinants of such behavior as he had manifested, that I have found reason to experience gratitude toward the patient. Nowadays, during and following sessions—whether with my own analytic patients or with patients seen in single consultative or teaching interviews such as that just mentioned—which have proved to be unusually fulfilling for me both personally and professionally, I find in myself feelings of heartfelt gratitude.

For example, during my teaching interview with a borderline schizophrenic young woman at a nearby hospital a year ago, I quickly began feeling that the interview was being not only of unusual therapeutic value for her, but was in the same vein, deeply fulfilling and confirming for me in my identity as someone wanting to be a useful psychoanalyst. I was sure that I was being of use to her and to the several psychiatric residents who were observing the interview. I felt that she and I both were being of rare growth value for one another. I have no doubt that my keen appreciating of her was evident in my demeanor. The group of staff members present fully shared, as was evident in the postinterview discussion, my appreciation of how much this patient had done for all of us. It struck me how illusory is any assumption that a therapist experiences such professional gratification as an expectable, everyday, mundane part of his work. I am trying here to suggest that the therapist has reason to feel as rare and memorable and intense a form of gratitude as has the patient whose therapist has effected, as we conventionally say, a remarkable cure.

On the very next day I had, at another nearby hospital, again in the presence of a group of staff members, an interview with a young man who was suffering from schizophrenia and drug addiction. This interview was in quality more like those to which I am accustomed, although this was one of the more extreme examples of its type. This interview gave me fantasies and feelings of giving up this profession entirely as a useless endeavor. The patient seemed to feel called upon chronically to justify his existence, and at the same time to feel unable to justify it. His impact upon me and upon the audience was as one not worth trying to save, and no one with the possible exception of myself—certainly not his therapist whose initial presentation of the case, prior to the patient's coming into the room, showed thoroughgoing disdain for the patient—seemed to feel at all interested in trying to save him. This interview served to enhance my gratitude toward the young woman I had interviewed on the previous day.

REVIEW OF RELEVANT LITERATURE

This review is not comprehensive. But the existing literature concerning the subject is scanty, indeed.

It is striking that this particular subject is so conspicuously absent from classical psychoanalytic papers concerning the analysis of nonpsychotic patients. For reasons of space I must resist quoting passages from such articles which would highlight their failure to acknowledge therapeutic strivings, conscious or unconscious, on the part of the patient.

Even in the literature concerning schizophrenia, in which illness the patient's therapeutic strivings are overwhelmingly significant and relatively easy to discern, most authors continue to view schizophrenic patients as basically parasitic. Typical of the abundant literature which views the patient as suffering from a crippling ego defect, as needful primarily of supplies from without, and as being oriented, therefore, toward receiving from, rather than giving to, his environment, is the volume by Burham, Gladstone and Gibson (1969), *Schizophrenia and the Need-Fear Dilemma:*

"... a key element of our theoretical system ... is the proposition that the schizophrenic person, because he lacks stable internal structure, is exceedingly dependent upon and vulnerable to the influence of external structure. . . ." (p. 13)

"We turn now to discuss the schizophrenic person's disordered object relations, particularly his intense need-fear dilemma. Because he is poorly differentiated and integrated, he lacks reliable internal structure and autonomous control systems. Accordingly he has an inordinate need for external structure and control. He requires others to provide the organization and regulation which he is unable to provide for himself. . . .

"The very excessiveness of his need for objects also makes them inordinately dangerous and fearsome since they can destroy him through abandonment. Hence he fears and distrusts them. He may attempt to alleviate the threat of abandonment by repeated pleas or damands for proof of the object's constancy. Such pleas are insatiable because much of the inconstancy of his percepts of objects stems from his inner instability. Another defensive tactic, also of limited value, is the attempt to deny his need and his fear of separation." (pp. 17-28)

The authors describe the patient as attempting to cope with his need-fear dilemma by object clinging, object avoidance, and object redefinition. Concerning object clinging, for example, they say that

"In this attempted solution . . . the patient, in effect, gives himself over to the need side of his conflict. He abandons efforts at differentiation and independence and attempts to fuse inseparably with others. A bewildering variety of terms has been employed to describe this type of relationship: symbiotic, narcissistic, orally fixated, object-addicted, anaclitic, self-centered, unilateral, possessive, overdependent, receptive, demanding, devouring, hunger-fulfilling, and others. These terms share common reference to the excessive need for supplies from the object, with little regard for the reciprocal needs of the object; in other words, a wish to receive but not give. . . . The schizophrenic person wishes the object to provide the inner balance and integration he has been unable to achieve for himself . . ." (p. 32).

Similarly Gibson (1966), in his paper, "The Ego Defect in Schizophrenia," while documenting a remarkably impressive degree of clinical improvement on the part of a chronically schizophrenic woman still in treatment with him, consistently portrays the patient as improving on the basis of strength borrowed from the therapist, portrayed as vastly more powerful than herself:

"This patient was struggling with a basic dilemma—the *need* for an object from which to borrow ego strength, and the *fear* of the same object because of its threat to ego organization. . . . The need-fear dilemma arises out of a deficit in ego functioning. I do not think of this defect as limited to a specific area of ego function; so perhaps it would be more accurate to speak of ego weakness rather than defect." (pp. 88-9)

Writing of the schizophrenic person in general, Gibson says that

". . . His vulnerability to disorganization of ego functions makes him desperately need objects to provide the support and structure which he lacks. His lack of ego autonomy leaves him unable to resist the influence of objects and thus makes them frightening to him. The poor reality testing of the schizophrenic makes all object relations extremely tenuous." (p. 89)

Concerning the particular patient upon the treatment of whom his paper is mainly based, he says,

"I believe, to recapitulate, that this schizophrenic patient had an inordinate need for objects to compensate for an ego defect. . . ." (p. 92)

". . . At times, her prevailing feeling was one of extreme gratitude to me, and she took pleasure in our relationship. But, quite regularly, she felt threatened by the thought that she might lose it. At other times, she resented the enormous power over her that this gave me. She also feared that she would have to satisfy my dependency needs just as she had those of her parents. . . ."

"The inevitable vicissitudes of object clinging are illustrated by this sequence of events. Object clinging occurs as a response to the need-fear dilemma in the schizophrenic when the need is dominant. An effort is made to compensate for the ego defect through fusion with an object. The object becomes an auxiliary ego that shares the responsibility for organizing behavior, managing and controlling drives, and testing reality. This device may work remarkably well. Superficially at least, patients may seem fully intact so long as this kind of a relationship to an object is maintained."

". . . The patient will see in the therapist an object to which he can cling to strengthen his weakened ego, but this can rouse all of the fears I have just described. In addition the therapist may be seen as a controlling agent that will threaten the patient's autonomy." (p. 94)

Gibson describes the mother as having been extremely dependent upon the patient during the latter's childhood:

"The patient and sister (younger by three years) grew up with the mother, who was extremely dependent on both of her children, especially Eileen [the patient], and did everything she could to keep them from becoming independent. . . ." (p. 90)

But, although he writes that "She . . . feared that she would have to satisfy my dependency needs just as she had those of her parents" (p. 94), his account includes no acknowledgment of any personal dependency feelings on his part toward her, of any anxiety lest he lose her, nor, by the same token, of any therapeutic strivings on her part toward him. It seems to me probable that such factors help to account for her maintenance of a predominantly positive tranference toward him, of which he takes note in his account:

"Eileen required a fair degree of selective inattention to maintain the idealized view of me as an entirely benevolent helper. . . . By always displacing negative transference feelings onto someone other than the therapist, she was able to avoid any feelings of hostility toward the therapist that might have led to thoughts of terminating treatment. Such thoughts were intolerable to Eileen when she had to rely completely on me to serve as an auxiliary ego. . . ." (p. 96)

It is only in the most general terms that Gibson alludes to a conjectured dependency on the part of the therapist toward the patient when, early in his paper, he comments that

"To some extent, this need-fear dilemma is a part of the experience of all human beings capable of relating to an object." (p. 88)

and when, in his closing sentence, he conjectures, concerning what the therapist offers which proves therapeutic in this regard, that

". . . Perhaps most of all, the psychotherapist shares in the need-fear dilemma, and in so doing establishes a new kind of relationship for the patient—a relationship that nurtures ego growth." (p. 97)

As a portrayal of an important part of the state of affairs which one finds in the schizophrenic patient, the above-quoted descriptions by Burnham, Gladstone, and Gibson seem accurate enough. But the basic psychodynamics of such schizophrenic phenomena warrant, in my clinical experience, an utterly contrasting emphasis as being the truer one, and this emphasis is crucial for any successful psychotherapy of the schizophrenic person. His impairment in whole-ego functioning, his inability to function as a whole individual, is due most fundamentally to a genuinely selfless devotion to a mother, or other parent figure, the maintenance of whose ego functioning requires that the child not become individuated from her (or him). In the course of our work with him now as a chronological adult in psychotherapy, we entirely miss the main point, in my opinion, if we regard him as suffering most fundamentally from a crippling ego defect, a result of early deprivation or other trauma, and as needful of receiving supplies of various sorts from our own whole and intact ego. Ironically, the crucial issue is, rather, whether *we* can become and remain conscious of the symbiotic (pre-individuation) dependency which *we* inevitably develop toward *him*, and which is necessary for the success of the treatment.

In this regard we personify in transference terms the parent whose relationship with him over the preceding years has been fixated at a symbiotic level; but, as I have emphasized repeatedly, it is not "only transference." The therapist comes to feel that he *really* is, to a significant degree, at one with the patient, and to experience as a *real* question whether he, the therapist, can bear the loss to his own ego functioning of the individuation toward which the therapeutic endeavor is directed. Thus in retrospect the schizophrenic patient's "ego-defect" toward which it is so easy to feel a kind of pitying condescension, becomes translated as "a frightening degree of personal importance to the therapist's very self" (with the patient being emotionally equivalent, for example, to the therapist's heart or mind). The more *conscious* the therapist becomes, and remains, of these processes, the less likely is any acted-out *folie à deux*. If we never become conscious of them, we remain relatively comfortable in our condescending view of the schizophrenic patient, and he retains his usual status of someone we perceive as a pathetic and needful cripple. I can confidently say that the great bulk of our psychoanalytic and psychiatric literature is such as to make our recognition of the patient's symbiotic-therapist striving orientation toward us more, rather than less, anxiety-arousing, embarrassing, humiliating, and otherwise difficult for us.

Many authors in the field of psychotherapeutic work of all kinds acknowledge patients' contributions to our understanding of psychodynamics and of increasingly effective techniques of psychotherapy, but stop far short of perceiving the patient as needing to help the therapist. It is not uncommon for authors to dedicate books gratefully to their patients, though few acknowledge the patients' help so explicitly as does Milner (1969) in the dedication of her book:

> "To all my teachers in psychoanalysis, especially my patients."

Jones (1953), in his biography of Freud, describes the following event as one of the landmarks of the Breuer period:

> "Freud was still given to urging, pressing, and questioning, which he felt to be hard but necessary work. On one historic occasion, however, the patient, Frl. Elisabeth, reproved him for interrupting her flow of thought by his questions. He took the hint, and thus made another step towards free association." (pp. 243-4)

Although Freud and his patient together achieved this fundamental technical refinement as long ago as 1892 or shortly thereafter, it is still common to find technical psychoanalytic discussions that do not acknowledge patients' therapeutic strivings, which latter seem to me a necessary aspect of any adequate treatise on the subject of analytic technique in a truly interpersonal context. For example, Olinick et al. (1972), in their paper, "The Psychoanalytic Work Ego: Process and Interpretation," state that

" . . . The timing of an interpretation is an acquired art that involved the synthesis of empathic and cognitive processes [and is in part, I suggest, the analyst's response to the patient's therapeutic strivings to enable the analyst to function, for example, as a successfully nursing mother or as a sexually potent father]. Partial and spontaneous interventions, of the kind described, are then further elaborated in the course of subsequent working through [which subsequent working through, I suggest, presumably consists in part in the consolidation of the analyst's therapeutic benefit at the hands of the patient]."

In the above-quoted passage, my rude intrusions of my own thoughts are attempts to depict how pervasively significant, to *any* of the much discussed psychoanalytic topics (such as interpretation and working through), is our cognizance of the patient's own therapeutic strivings toward the analyst. Similarly as regards the literature concerning the "therapeutic alliance" (for example, Zetzel 1956 and Greenson 1965 and 1967), where such writings imply that what is being discussed is alliance for therapy for the *patient*, I hold that what is actually at work is an alliance for therapy for *both* participants in the treatment situation.

The first writing, to my knowledge, which at all explicitly describes the patient's functioning as therapist to the doctor is Groddeck's (1923) *The Book of the It*. It is noteworthy that even this courageously pioneering statement portrays the therapeutic process at work as being, in essence, therapy *for the patient*, exclusively, in the long run; nonetheless, Groddeck is a pioneer of high courage in his reporting that

" . . . His childlike attitude towards me—indeed, as I understood later, it was that of a child of three—compelled me to assume the mother's role. Certain slumbering mother-virtues were awakened in me by the patient, and these directed my procedure. . . . And now I was confronted by the strange fact that I was not treating the patient, but that the patient was treating me; or to translate it into my own language, the It of this fellow being tried so to transform my It, did in fact so transform it, that it came to be useful for its purpose. . . . Even to get this amount of insight was difficult, for you will understand that it absolutely reversed my position in regard to a patient. It was no longer important to give *him* instructions, to prescribe for *him* what I considered right, but to change in such a way that *he* could use *me*." (pp. 262-3).

Whitaker and Malone (1953), in discussing the motivations of the therapist, suggest that

"The enthusiasm and elation felt when contemplating the possibility that schizophrenic patients may be amenable to psychotherapy may reflect a perception that some residual needs can perhaps be answered only in therapeutic experiences with the schizophrenic." (p. 101)

This statement does not explicitly attribute a therapeutic motive to the patient, but implies that certain therapists, presumably more ill than most, may somehow find therapy for their own aberrant needs in their work with schizophrenic patients. Therefore the above statement is much more at odds with, than consonant with, the theme of this paper. Later on, the authors go far beyond the statement quoted above. In an extremely interesting chapter entitled, "Patient-Vectors ["vectors" meaning, so I gather, forces] in the Therapist," which they consider a more meaningful concept than that of countertransference (a view which I do not feel moved to embrace) they make the following statements, clearly in reference to patients generally (rather than exclusively schizophrenic patients) and to healthy therapists:

" . . . the bilateral character of therapy constitutes its most effective dynamic basis. . . . In the best therapeutic relationship, the therapist recurrently brings his own patient-vectors to the patient. . . . Indeed, a therapeutic impasse can often be resolved only by the therapist's willingness to bring his patient-vectors to the patient quite overtly. This principle inplies that were the therapist free of all patient-vectors, he would be no therapist at all." (p. 165)

They do not give any details as to how the therapist may usefully "bring his patient-vectors to the patient quite overtly." If by this they mean to recommend that the therapist on occasion share with the patient information about the therapist's own personal life, I must part company from them, for in my own work I probably do little more of this than does any classical psychoanalyst.

In 1968, Marie Coleman Nelson et al. published their volume, *Roles and Paradigms in Psychotherapy,* describing a method of psychoanalytic psychotherapy which they had developed during the previous ten years, and which they call *paradigmatic* psychotherapy. A paradigm is defined as demonstration by example, and paradigmatic psychotherapy is the systematic setting forth of examples by the analyst to enable the patient to understand the significant intrapsychic processes or interpersonal situations of his life, past and present. The authors see this technique as most appropriate for borderline patients who are unable to utilize the verbal interpretations basic to the usual psychoanalytic approach; but it is a technique which the authors convincingly demonstrate to have implications for the treatment of virtually every patient.

One of their standard techniques they term "siding with the resistance" (p. 75), which they further define as

" . . . joining with the irrational aspects of a patient's responses and thus inducing him to oppose his own pathology, which the therapist has now taken over.

When this technique is followed persistently, it soon appears that the patient is much more reasonable and healthy than the therapist, who then appears as a paradigm of the patient's own presenting pathology" (p. 75).

At the end of one of the clinical examples of the use of this technique, the author (Strean) formulates that

"Joining the patient's resistance in the above instance was narcissistically enriching [for the patient] instead of depleting. The patient and therapist were colleagues, with the former helping the latter. As the therapist enacted the role of the passive, naive, ignorant child, Mr. B. was in no way threatened by potential attack [whereas he had so reacted to more conventional psychoanalytic responses]. On the contrary, he could teach the therapist psychological facts. The therapist's role (the naive, ignorant part of Mr. B.) stimulated the patient to educate the therapist. For Mr. B., educating the therapist was, in effect, educating that part of himself which needed enlightenment but resisted it" (p. 183).

Despite a recurrent note of superficial game-playing, which in my opinion does far less than justice to the patient's genuine importance as therapist to the therapist, these authors' work is of much significance and value for anyone who wishes to pursue further the theme of this present paper. On occasion their accounts of their work convey a genuine and moving portrayal of their patients' functioning as therapists in the treatment situation, which go beyond what I can capture in these necessarily brief excerpts. For example, Strean (pp. 233-7), in his account of his work with a very withdrawn fourteen-year-old boy who could not read and who had been involved unsuccessfully with several previous therapists, describes his approaching the patient as being a consultant, with the patient's being in a position of "self-dosing," that is, providing his own prescription in the treatment situation. This came to involve the patient's functioning as teacher to the therapist:

". . . in the first interview . . . The patient was asked by the therapist, 'What should I do?' . . . Possibly he could teach the therapist techniques of passive resistance? . . . Joe stated that he might try for a little while to teach the therapist to be silent. . . . However, the patient insisted, 'You have to promise to say nothing. I'll be the boss around here.' . . .

"Several interviews passed uneventfully. Joe, instead of talking and teaching, remained silent. The therapist and patient merely looked at each other with no exchange except, 'Hello' and 'Good-bye.'

". . . When the therapist wondered if Joe could teach him something about electricity [in which he knew the boy was interested], Joe got up, walked out of the interview and stated dryly, 'You've got a lot to learn. I'll think about coming back and showing you.'

"Joe did return for two silent sessions, but without encouragement soon delighted in showing the therapist several electrical plans. Electricity became the sole mode of communication for several months, with Joe as teacher and the therapist as pupil. . . .

". . . Eventually, Joe entered a vocational school and specialized in electricity. . . .

"As he learned how to read and attained other academic and social successes, Joe suggested that 'the case be closed.' He wrote in his own handwriting, 'A Closing Summary on Mr. Strean' in which he both criticized and praised the therapist, giving a colorful picture of the treatment process. . . .
"For the therapist, the relationship had enormous meaning. . . ." (pp. 235-6)

In 1969 Milner published her previously mentioned 412-page account of her psychoanalytic treatment, extending over nearly twenty years, of a schizophrenic woman. Milner's volume is richly creative, scholarly in its evaluation of the many psychoanalytic writings which she found relevant in the course of this long treatment endeavor, and inspiring in terms of the author's clinical devotion and the patient's clinical improvement. One of the many fascinating aspects of her book, to me, consists in Milner's very long-delayed, but eventually at least partial, recognition of the patient's therapeutic strivings toward her.

On page 107, for example, I noted that thus far one could find no evidence that Milner was yet aware of ths patient's therapeutic strivings toward her, though such strivings were implicit in much data which she had been presenting from the patient. On page 120, although she surmises that the patient had endeavored, during the latter's upbringing, to cheer up her depressed mother, Milner shows no evidence that she finds this to be a factor in the transference relationship. On page 130, I noted that throughout the abundant data concerning mother-infant transference relatedness thus far, Milner assumes consistently that she is in the transference role of mother, and the patient in that of infant, whereas the reverse is often implied in the data from the sessions.

On page 177, referring to a time near the end of the seventh year of the treatment, Milner says that

"During the eight weeks of my summer break Susan wrote frequent letters to me from the hospital, sometimes four posted by different posts all in one day, calling me by my first name and ending 'with love'. . . . In the letters she said she was feeling quite terrible and was angry with the psychiatrist in charge, who, she said, had been tough with her and done nothing to help. . . ."

Milner seems to continue, here, to perceive the patient as being equivalent to a needful infant or child in relation to her as a mother, and not to perceive the patient's implicit maternal concern for the therapist as abandoned child—the patient's anxiety lest the therapist not be able to endure this separation, and her striving to assuage the therapist's loneliness and to reassure the latter of her, Milner's, indispensability.

On page 289, concerning a session the fourteenth year, Milner makes a statement, for the first time in her account, which takes relatively full cognizance of the patient's therapist potentialities, and which is fully consonant with my own concepts about therapeutic symbiosis:

"What I seem to have said in the session was that she had difficulty in believing in a way of coming together with me that is psychical and not erotically physical, and which could lead to something new being created, her new self *and mine*. . . . [italics by HFS]"

On page 292 the author notes a theme, evident at that juncture (in the fourteenth year of the treatment), "of her attempt to avoid dependence on me by feeling she herself has all that she needs—and what I need as well." But the reader has no way of knowing, here, whether Milner conceptualizes "what I need as well" to be purely a distorted transference perception on the patient's part (if such were indeed possible), or whether there is a nucleus of reality in the patient's perception, here, of the analyst.

On pages 303 to 304, concerning a session a bit later in the fourteenth year, in which the patient did a drawing of a baby duck within a larger duck, Milner notes that

". . . there was not only the question of the part of herself, as the baby duck, being ready to come out from inside me, there was also the related task of her becoming able to let me out, let me be born out of her. . . ."

Still later in the fourteenth year, when the patient continued to be involved in a process lasting more than ten months of becoming ready to be born, Milner reports that

"On 27 July she says she remembers sitting on her mother's knee and feeling so depressed, and how her mother was always saying she [the mother] was going to die. Now she wonders if she was always trying to stop her from dying." (p. 322)

When, a few months later, the following material emerges, I would infer that the patient is concerned therapeutically to provide life to the analyst, a depressed mother not only in transference terms, but also, I would assume, to a degree *really* depressed. Mrs. Milner sees this *only* as a transference projection:

"On Thursday 25 November she brings a dream:
"She dreamed that I was telling her how my husband had left me his mummied heart in his will, and I was crying and so was she. But we were both quite separate from each other.
"Her own association to the dream . . . was that she could only give me a dead heart, which means that she will never get well. I said that in the dream she does seem to have a heart, because she is crying and feeling sorry. I said I thought the dream was more about artificially keeping a live heart dead than artificially preserving a dead one; that is, she has been trying to blot out the inner movement of feeling to do with love and sadness." (pp. 347-8)

In my own similarly prolonged work with Mrs. Douglas, some aspects of which I have described at length earlier in this paper, I found, by contrast, that my real feelings of depression in addition to (or, in my terms, as a nucleus of) the patient's long-familiar transference perceptions of me as being the personification of her depressed mother, or of her depressed self, helped greatly to account for the tenacity of her "crazy talk" (as it has been referred to for many years in the sanitarium where she lives) during the sessions.

Specifically, innumerable times during recent years, as she has become more able to face her tremendous and long-repressed feelings of grief, this has involved our having to face a very considerable risk of her suicide; that is, her feelings of healthy grieving are not yet well-differentiated from those of a psychotically depressive nature. Partly as a function of this phase of my work with her (as well as from various other sources in my current life), I have found myself experiencing, concomitantly, feelings of depression of a formidable degree during our sessions. In fact, during at least one of our sessions some two years ago, I experienced considerable fear lest *one or the other* of us commit suicide immediately following the session.

Hence it is to a degree understandable to me that the following sequence occurred innumerable times in recent years, during a phase which now seems largely behind us, as she has become better able to grieve. She used to come into the session and instead of starting to pour forth her usual appallingly fragmented, yet irresistibly fascinating and in a sense entertaining "crazy talk," she would sit silently, appearing to be filled with mute grief and despair. Consciously I welcomed this development, in each such session. But each time when, after a few or many minutes of silence, she then started verbalizing her usual "crazy talk," and her demeanor came within a few minutes later still to show little if any of the feelings of grief and despair, *against my will* (so it felt) I would find myself feeling relieved at her being her long-familiar, chronically crazy self. There were abundant data, in such sessions, indicating that she tended to feel that she was thus keeping her mother (= HFS) alive, or bringing her mother back to life, by this craziness. If I had thought of such perceptions on her part, of me, as being "just transference," the remarkable tenacity of her craziness would have been much less understandable to me.

For a great many years following her admission to Chestnut Lodge, it was clear that her social role at the Lodge was of one whose craziness seemed designed to relieve depression in others. It was typical of her that when, a few days before a certain Christmas, while the patients were reacting with an intensively depressive pall to efforts on the staff's part to encourage them to join in carol singing, Joan's caustically scornful voice came loud and clear and masterfully sure over the group's tragically depressed and nostalgic efforts at singing, "What's the *matter* with you *idiots,* singing *Christmas carols?* Don't you realize it's *March the tenth?*" This broke up the crowd, staff members and patients alike, with relieved laughter at her craziness.

In the course of my careful reading of Milner's book, I recall no mention by the author of her feeling any such despair as has been so familiar to me in the work with Joan. On page 366 Milner describes her realization, in retrospect, of how caught up she had been in a compulsion to be helpful to her patient (much as I had described in a paper in 1955 [Searles, 1955]). In such a state one is in no position to discern the patient's therapeutic strivings toward oneself:

"... my early tendency to do too much for her and to interpret too much in terms of the 'good object', not taking enough account of the 'good subject'. ... my overanxiety to be a 'good' analyst in those early years of my practice, overanxiety leading to giving too many interpretations . . . ." (p. 366).

The following passage, concerning a dream which the patient reported early in the 16th year of the analysis, shows how much more clearly the author has come to recognize the significance of the patient's own love—highly relevant, of course, to the theme of the present paper:

"... So now I see the . . . dream as expressing this basic conflict she has been battling with all these years, the issue of whether she can accept any limitations on her loving, both in how she gives or how she takes; whether she can give up her belief that she can make herself one with what she loves by eating it, accept the fact that the food she eats is not actually the same as the breast that she loved, that she wished to become one with by eating; and also whether she can accept limits in her giving, accept something less than an actual giving up her life; and find instead, by discrimination between inner and outer, a surrender that is not physical death." (p. 370)

Somewhat later in the sixteenth year of the analysis, Milner describes that

"A few months after Susan's getting a room of her own her mother died; it was the ending of a long illness during which Susan had been very good to her, in spite of the fact that her mother could never recognize her devotion or give her any thanks; for instance, in the last year of her mother's life Susan would often visit her, taking her a box of chocolates, and her mother would eat them without ever offering Susan one. And when the nurse looking after her mother said, in front of them both, 'You have a very good daughter,' her mother had said nothing." (p. 388)

In a footnote to the above, Milner comments:

"This inability on the part of her mother to acknowledge her daughter's reparative activities highlighted important aspects of Susan's account of her childhood . . . [and] certainly tended to confirm the psychoanalytic view that the lack of opportunity for and recognition of reparative activities can greatly encourage psychotic states of mind." (p. 388)

It can be seen that what Milner (following her usual Kleinian conceptualization) terms reparative activities I would term therapeutic strivings, regarding these strivings as being more a part of the infant's primary potentialities for giving love than secondary to the individual's hostile strivings (and therefore expressive, in Kleinian terms, of an attempt at reparation for the fantasied damage wrought upon the mother, in past experiences with her, by one's own hostility).

It is my impression that an analyst's rigid adherence to a classically psychoanalytic orientation, his remaining oblivious of and unacknowledging of the nuclei of reality in the patient's transference responses to him, fosters his being precisely as unacknowledging of the patient's therapeutic strivings toward him as Susan's mother was toward Susan in the above-described situation. One is left with a nagging sense of doubt as to whether, or to what extent, Milner regards her patient's transference reactions to her as being based in a nucleus of reality when, in the following passage in her closing pages, she implies that in order to become free of psychosis a psychotic patient needs to create the analyst—*really* needs to, to a very significant and crucial degree:

"... although I had myself been convinced through my own enquiries into painting [Milner, M., 1950] that the 'other' has to be created before it can be perceived, I had yet taken so long to realize the implications of this in clinical work, the full extent to which she had to be allowed to contribute from herself before she could feel that I was truly real for her. . . ." (p. 404).

The recent paper by Singer (1971), "The Patient Aids the Analyst: Some Clinical and Theoretical Observations," because of its high degree of consonance with the theme of this present paper, merits my quoting from it at length here. Singer begins,

"From their very beginnings most publications on psychoanalytic technique have stressed at least implicitly a dominant theme: that the analyst derives little personal satisfaction from his work other than the gratification the healer inevitably derives from the sense of a job well done and, of course, from the financial rewards attending his efforts. All other satisfactions arising in his working day have been suspect of countertransference tendencies rooted in the analyst's unresolved conflicts.

"Structuring the psychoanalytic relationship in these terms molded the process into a one-way street: the helping relationship was to be one in which the analyst aided the patient, in which he could not and should not expect any comparable aid from his client. . . .

"It is the purpose of this paper to explore . . . the potential power of the analyst's revealing his own life situation, thereby making it possible for the patient to be realistically helpful; and finally, as its main contribution, to support implications for a theory of personality development derived from these observations, implications at variance with those traditionally advanced in the psychoanalytic literature."

". . . unbending anonymity, while furthering the denouement of hidden destructive and other primitive tendencies, does not promote and activate reality-oriented and constructive qualities. . . ." (pp. 56-8)

Singer's paper resulted from the fact that his wife suddenly became seriously ill, which required him to cancel all his appointments until further notice, with a demeanor which he knew his patients had reason to detect as uncharacteristically anxious.

". . . My patients . . . sensed from my voice that this cancellation did not reflect a frivolous impulse and spontaneously inquired, 'What's up?' Too troubled to engage in lengthy conversations and hesitant about how much I wanted to say, I merely replied that I would explain when I saw them again. . . .

"With some trepidation I decided [in the interim] to tell them the truth. . . . I informed all patients about the reason for my absence.

"Their responses seemed to be astonishing, and that I was astonished reflected poorly on me. Concern, genuine sympathy, eagerness to be helpful with problems likely to arise, and, above all, efforts to be supportive and comforting—these reactions were eye-openers. As I listened, deeply moved and profoundly grateful, to the patients' efforts, it became apparent that each person expressed his desire to be helpful in his particular style, a manner which often, when occurring under different circumstances, had been identified as reflecting a pathological character orientation. I will give a few illustrations . . . . (pp. 58-9)

"I hope that these vignettes illustrate what I have learned: that the capacity to rise to the occasion when compassion and helpfulness are called for is part and parcel of the makeup of all human beings. Importantly, in no single instance did my disclosures have any ill effects; on the contrary, the insights, memories, and heightened awareness which followed my self-exposure proved remarkable, and I have the deep conviction that my frankness accelerated the therapeutic process in several instances.

". . . Strict psychoanalytic anonymity would have reduced my patients' opportunities to see their own strengths; and certainly it would have limited my knowledge of their caring and compassionate capacities. . . .

"My patients' efforts to search themselves much more seriously after my disclosures than ever before brought to light certain themes which up to now had never emerged or had at best been mentioned only fleetingly.

"Mrs. N., for instance, now genuinely attempted to grasp the truth of critical experiences and of the affect associated with certain of her present-day reactions to them. . . . With great pain Mrs. N. now began to reexperience instances of feeling totally unable to make any meaningful contributions to these all-knowing, all-successful, and seemingly 'need-less' people [i.e., her mother and her father] . . . . there is little doubt in my mind . . . that the admission of my pain made the vision of genuine usefulness a realistic possibility for her. . . . (pp. 62-3)

". . . much of the neurotic distress experienced by my patients seemed associated with their profound sense of personal uselessness and their sense of having failed as human beings because they knew that the only contributions they had made were embodied in nonconstructive reactions and behavior responding to equally nonconstructive demands. . . .

". . . those concerned with the origins of psychopathology and with efforts to rekindle emotional growth must give serious attention to the possibility that the most devastating of human experiences is the sense of uselessness. . . . (p. 65)

"This lack of authenticity in parent-child relations, the child's inadequate opportunities to express constructive relatedness, finds an analogue in the traditional analytic relationship. . . .

". . . For some patients the events described here accelerated a process of growth well underway. But others were reached emotionally for the first time in therapy by my disclosures and willingness to accept their help. . . ." (p. 67)

I have already indicated that I differ with one of Singer's main conclusions, namely that

". . . a marked reduction of the analyst's anonymity is essential to therapeutic progress. . . ." (p. 67)

In my own work, while I am relatively free about revealing feelings and fantasies which I experience during the analytic session itself, I tell patients very little of my life outside the office. But I feel sure that even the most critical reader of Singer's paper will find it difficult to write off his work as "wild analysis," for throughout the paper he manifests, recurrently, a commendably detailed, serious, and genuinely humble acknowledgment of the potential hazards of the departures from classical analysis which he is advocating. I myself regard the theme of this present paper as fraught with complexities; but it seems to me imperative that we enter this thicket and carve out of it some solid theoretical and technical area for our functioning as analysts, for in my opinion the classical analytic position contains an element of delusion to the effect that the analyst is not at all a real person to the patient, and therefore simply will not do. I find an analogy to this latter point in Lewin's (1958) charming little monograph, *Dreams and the Uses of Regression*. Lewin begins by saying that:

"Around the year 500 B.C., natural science began with a repudiation of the dream. . . ." (p. 11)

And then, toward the end of his essay, Lewin discloses the delightful irony that the view of the world as conceptualized by Descartes, the epitome of the natural scientists, is essentially dreamlike in nature:

"In short, I should like to hazard a hypothesis: when Descartes came to formulate his scientific picture of the world, he made it conform with the state of affairs in an ordinary successful dream. The picture of the dream world that succeeds best in preserving sleep . . . came to be the picture of the waking world that succeeded best in explaining it scientifically. . . ." (p. 50)

So, I feel, it is with classical psychoanalysis: to the degree that it is rigorously classical, it is essentially delusional.

Space does not allow for my trying to recapitulate all my own previous writings about the theme of this present paper; several of those have already been touched upon as I have gone along. The earliest published one is my paper (Searles, H., 1955) concerning dependency processes in the psychotherapy of schizophrenic patients, which includes a description of the role of the therapist's real dependency as it affects the patient.

SUMMARY

This paper advances the hypothesis that innate among the human being's emotional potentialities, present in the earliest months of postnatal life, is an essentially psychotherapeutic striving. The family-environmental warping of that striving is a major etiologic source of all psychopathology. The analyst's failure to recognize that long-repressed striving in the patient accounts, more than does any other interpersonal element in the treatment situation, for the patient's unconscious resistance to the analytic process. Despite the acknowledged complexities involved in our departing from classical psychoanalytic theory and technique in this regard, I believe that it is essential that we do so.

In this paper I place special emphasis upon the psychotic patient's therapeutic effort to enable the mother (and analogously in the analytic context, the analyst) to become a whole and effective mother (= analyst) to him.

A discussion of some of the relevant literature is included.

References

Burnham, D. L., Gladstone, A. I., and Gibson, R. W. *Schizophrenia and the Need-Fear Dilemma.* New York: International Universities Press, 1969.

Freud, S. (1922). "Some Neurotic Mechanisms in Jealousy, Paranoia, and Homosexuality." *Standard Edition*, 18, London: Hogarth Press, 1922.

Gibson, R. W., "The Ego Defect in Schizophrenia." In *Psychoneurosis and Schizophrenia,* Usdin, G. L., ed., 88-97. Philadelphia and Montreal: J. B. Lippincott, 1966.

Greenson, R. R., "The Working Alliance and the Transference Neurosis." *Psychoanal. Quart.* 34:155-181 (1965).

_____ . *The Technique and Practice of Psychoanalysis.* Vol. I. New York: International Universities Press, 1967.

Groddeck, G. (1923). *The Book of the It.* (English translation pub. in 1950 by Vision Press, London; the original, *Das buch vom es*, pub. in 1923 by Psychoanalytischer Verlag, Vienna).

Hill, L. B., *Psychotherapeutic Intervention in Schizophrenia.* Chicago: University of Chicago Press, 1955.

Jones, E., *The Life and Work of Sigmund Freud Vol. I*. New York: Basic Books, 1953.
Khan, M. M. R., "The Concept of Cumulative Trauma." *Psychoanal. Study Child* 18:286-306 (1963).
_____ . "Ego Distortion, Cumulative Trauma, and the Role of Reconstruction in the Analytic Situation. *Int. J. Psychoanal.*, 45:272-78 (1964).
Knight, R. P. (1953). "Management and Psychotherapy of the Borderline Schizophrenic Patient." *Bull. Menninger Clinic* 17:139-50. (1953).
Lewin, B. D., *Dreams and the Uses of Regression*. New York: International Universities Press, 1958.
Milner, M. (1950). *On Not Being Able to Paint*, 2nd edition. New York: International Universities Press; also London: Heinemann, 1957.
_____ . *The Hands of the Living God–an Account of a Psychoanalytic Treatment*. New York: International Universities Press, 1969.
Nelson, M. C., Nelson, B., Sherman, M. H., and Strean, H. S. *Roles and Paradigms in Psychotherapy*. New York and London: Grune & Stratton, 1969.
Olinick, S. L., Poland, W. S., Grigg, K. A., and Granatir, W. L. (1972). "The Psychoanalytic Work Ego: Process and Interpretation." Presented at meeting of Washington Psychoanalytic Society, Washington, D. C., March 17, 1972.
Searles, H. F. (1949). (I) "Two Suggested Revisions of the Concept of Transference" and (II) "Comments Regarding the Usefulness of Emotions Arising in the Analyst During the Analytic Hour." Unpublished.
_____ . (1951). "Data Concerning Certain Manifestations of Incorporation." *Psychiatry* 14:397-413. Reprinted on pp. 39-69 of *Collected papers* (see below).
_____ . (1955). "Dependency Processes in the Psychotherapy of Schizophrenia." *J. Amer. Psychoanal. Assoc.* 3:19-66 (1955). Also reprinted on pp. 114-156 of *Collected papers* (see below).
_____ . (1959a). "Integration and differentiation in schizophrenia." *J. Nerv. and Ment. Dis.* 129:542-550. Also reprinted on pp. 304-316 of *Collected papers* (see below).
_____ . (1959b). "Integration and Differentiation in Schizophrenia: An Over-all View." *Brit. J. Med. Psychol.* 32:261-281. Also reprinted on pp. 317-348 of *Collected papers* (see below).
_____ . (1961a). "The Evolution of the Mother Transference in Psychotherapy with the Schizophrenic Patient." pp. 256-284 in *Psychotherapy of the Psychoses*, ed. by Burton, A.; New York: Basic Books. Also reprinted on pp. 349-380 of *Collected papers* (see below).
_____ . (1961b). "Phases of Patient-Therapist Interaction in the Psychotherapy of Chronic Schizophrenia." *Brit. J. Med. Psychol.* 34:169-193. Also reprinted on pp. 521-559 of *Collected papers* (see below).
_____ . *Collected Papers on Schizophrenia and Related Subjects*. London: Hogarth Press, 1965; and New York: International Universities Press, 1965.
_____ . (1966). "Concerning the Development of an Identity." *Psychoanal. Rev.* 53:507-530, Winter 1966-67.
_____ . "The 'Dedicated Physician' in Psychotherapy and Psychoanalysis." pp. 128-143 in *Crosscurrents in Psychiatry and Psychoanalysis*, Gibson, R. W., ed., Philadelphia and Toronto: J. B. Lippincott, 1967.

————. "Autism and the Phase of Transition to Therapeutic Symbiosis." *Contemporary Psychoanalysis* 7:1-20, Fall, 1970.

————. (1971). "Pathologic Symbiosis and Autism." pp. 69-83 in *In the Name of Life—Essays in Honor of Erich Fromm,* ed. by Landis, B. and Tauber, E. S. New York, Chicago, and San Francisco: Holt, Rinehart and Winston.

————. "The Function of the Patient's Realistic Perceptions of the Analyst in Delusional Transference." *Brit. J. Med. Psychol.* 45:1-18 (1972a).

————. "Intensive Psychotherapy of Chronic Schizophrenia." *Int. J. Psychoanalytic Psychotherapy* 1:30-51 (1972b).

————. (1973). "Concerning Therapeutic Symbiosis: (a) the Patient as Symbiotic Therapist, (b) the Phase of Ambivalent Symbiosis, and (c) the Role of Jealousy in the Fragmented Ego." To be pub. in *The Annual of Psychoanalysis, Vol. I,* ed. by Pollock G. H. Chicago: Chicago Institute for Psychoanalysis, and New York: Quadrangle Books.

Singer, E. "The Patient Aids the Analyst: Some Clinical and Theoretical Observations." pp. 56-68 in *In the Name of Life—Essays in Honor of Erich Formm,* ed. by Landis, B. and Tauber, E. S. New York, Chicago and San Francisco: Holt, Rinehart and Winston, 1971.

Whitaker, C. A., and Malone, T. P. (1953). *The Roots of Psychotherapy.* New York: Blakiston, 1953.

Zetzel, E. R., "Current Concepts of Transference. *Int. J. Psychoanal.* 37:369-376 (1956).

Chapter III

Comment on H. F. Searles, "The Patient as Therapist"

Alfred Flarsheim, M.D.

In a letter Dr. Searles said that he considers this paper "Possibly the most important paper that I have ever written." It is supersaturated with insights that are of immediate help to any psychotherapist. This, however, is true of all of Searles's papers, and it is difficult to say that any paper could be more valuable to the clinician than are many of his previous papers. I believe that the fundamental point he makes in this paper is one which integrates and synthesizes insights which he has achieved in many previous papers.

The mother of an autistic child described her baby's birth and subsequent psychosis as a "Messianic hope that ended in a cross" (Tustin, F. 1972). Such observations confirm, if confirmation be needed, parents' need to be rescued by their children. But Searles carries this much further, and says that the child has an inherent need to rescue the parents, and that later the patient has an inherent need to rescue and heal the analyst. Searles gives us moving descriptions of ways in which the patients' need to construct and repair is manifested in the transference and countertransference. He works out in great detail the vicissitudes of the patient's "unconscious therapeutic strivings toward the analyst."

At first sight Dr. Searles's observation could be explained by the concept of reparation, as formulated by Klein (1935). Dr. Searles states that this concept is inadequate to account for the whole of the patient's "therapeutic" impulses toward the analyst. In contrast to reparation, in which it is the infant's and the child's, and later the patient's, destructiveness from which the parent and the analyst must be rescued, he is describing a different process.

When Searles refers to an innate therapeutic striving toward parents he does not rule out processes as sophisticated as reparation in reaction to destructive fantasies, but he stresses that the strivings which he calls therapeutic are more widespread and are found in patients whose ego organization is not sufficiently structured for the integration of sadism and reparation. One must look for more primitive, more generally applicable concepts than reparation to explain Dr. Searles's observations of the "therapeutic striving" in the transference reactions of all patients, which he says are especially important in the treatment of schizophrenics.

Discussing the work of Marion Milner (1969) in his chapter, Searles says,

"What Milner (following her usual Kleinian conceptualization) terms reparative activities, I would term therapeutic strivings, regarding these strivings as being more primarily a part of the infant's potentialities for giving love, than secondary to the individual's hostile strivings and therefore expressive in Kleinian terms of an attempt at reparation for the fantasied damage wrought upon the mother, in past experience with her, by one's own hostility." So Searles regards the infant's and the patient's therapeutic strivings as primary, and does not need to derive them from other intrapsychic sources.

In his summary, Searles begins: "Innate among the human being's emotional potentialities, present in the earliest months of postnatal life, is an essentially psychotherapeutic striving." He makes such striving innate, or at least an innate potentiality.

Many authors have pointed out that the mother and the infant influence one another reciprocally (Benedek, 1959). D. W. Winnicott (1965) said that a healthy baby creates a family, and this can be the link that we need between Searles's "psychotherapeutic striving," and the infant's innate disposition.

The healthy baby stimulates nurturing behavior in the healthy parent. Such a response on the part of the parent fosters integration of the parents' personality, and in turn fosters integration of the developing personality of the infant. If the parent fails to react in a nurturing way to the potentially object-directed impulses of the infant, or if the parent responds in ways that are inappropriate and maladaptive to the infant's need, the result is impairment of the developing ego integration of the infant. The normal, healthy infant stimulates protective and nurturing behavior, mature behavior, in the healthy adult. Insofar as nurturing and protective behavior are part of maturity, the infant's needs contribute toward the parent's achievement of maturity. Failure of the family to respond in a nurturing fashion to the needs of the newborn, which following Searles we can now regard as the family's failure to achieve a higher level of mature functioning in response to the needs of the neonate, results in failure of integration of various ego nuclei of the developing infant. This failure of integration is what we ordinarily consider the "basic fault" (Balint) in schizophrenic disorders. Searles emphasizes that failure of the family to acknowledge the "therapeutic strivings" of the infant and child are the *most* significant predisposing factors to psychotic disorder.

Defective infants have less capacity than do healthy infants to stimulate parenting behavior, and the capacity of adults to respond to infants in a mature parental way which can facilitate maturation and development is variable, and is a measure of their capacity for emotional health. These two factors, the capacity of the infant to stimulate mature parental behavior and the capacity of the adult to respond to the infant in ways that facilitate the infant's maturation and development, exist in a complementary series. Further, the supportive environment in which the parent lives helps to free the parent to nurture the infant, and this is another variable.

Similarly, the analytic orientation permits the analyst to be open to be *educated* by the patient as to how the analysand's mind works, rather than needing to oppose him and to enter into a power struggle aimed at suppressing the patient's behavior which is incompatible with the analyst's or society's values. In the process of being taught by the patient about how the patient's mind works the analyst provides a setting in which split-off and repudiated parts of the patient's personality can, at least ideally and potentially, be integrated into his general functioning rather than being separated off and consuming energy in defensive operations. Failure of the parent to respond to the infant's maturational pushes and failure of the analyst to respond to the patient's strivings toward mature development are conventionally considered traumatic. It is this failure of an appropriate response by the parent and the analyst to which Dr. Searles is referring. This is also what Khan (1960) described as "cumulative trauma."

I am reminded of one of the most famous case histories in all of psychoanalysis, the Wolf Man (Freud, 1918). A. J. Lubin (1967) states that forty years after the end of his treatment the Wolf Man believes that the most important thing about his treatment was his feeling that he had made a significant contribution to the developing science of psychoanalysis. Freud frequently stressed that he was constantly learning from his patients, learning from them eagerly, and it is my impression that this was perhaps the most important thing he offered to many of his patients, and that it remains quite frequently the most important thing we offer to our patients today.

References

Balint, M., *The Basic Fault,* Tavistock: London, 1968.

Benedek, T., "Parenthood as a Developmental Phase." *Journ. of Amer. Psychoanal. Assoc.,* 7:389-417 (1959).

Freud, S., (1918), "From the History of an Infantile Neurosis," *Standard Edition,* Vol. XVII, London: Hogarth Press, 1955.

Khan, M. M. R., "The Concept of Cumulative Trauma" in *Psychoanalytic Study of the Child,* New York: International Universities Press, 1960.

Klein, M., "A Contribution to the Psychogenesis of Manic-Depressive States." *Internat. Journ. of Psychoanal.,* 16:1935.

Lubin, A. J., (1967), "The Influence of the Russian Orthodox Church on Freud's Wolf Man: An Hypothesis." *Psychoanal. Forum,* Vol. 2, pp. 145-174 (1967).

Milner, M., *The Hands of the Living God.* London: Hogarth Press, 1969.

Tustin, F., *Autism and Childhood Psychosis,* p. 136, New York: Jason Aronson, Inc., 1972.

Winnicott, D. W., *The Family and Individual Development,* London: Tavistock, 1965.

Chapter IV

The Therapist's Collusion with the Patient's Wish for Suicide

Alfred Flarsheim, M.D.

Freud wrote extensively about transference but very little about counter-transference, and when he did write about the latter he was mainly concerned about the doctor's response to the patient's erotic feelings (Freud, 1915a). The term countertransference implies that the patient represents an archaic parental imago for the therapist, but it is sometimes used to refer to any reactions of a psychotherapist to a patient's transference and at other times it is used to refer only to primary process elements in the therapist's reaction to his patient's transference. Any reaction includes both primary and secondary process elements. Winnicott (1960) suggests that the term countertransference be used to refer to neurotic features in the therapist that spoil his professional attitude and disturb the course of the therapeutic process as determined by the patient. In the same paper, Winnicott says that the borderline psychotic patient breaks through the therapist's professional attitude and forces a primitive direct relationship, "even to the extent of merging." Winnicott agrees with Little (1957) that a therapist's reaction to such an event should be classified as a total response rather than as countertransference. Winnicott (1947) and Martin (this volume) have discussed the therapist's hostility toward his patient, not only hostility that is derived from the therapist's projection of archaic imagos onto the patient (the countertransference) but also hostility that is stimulated by realistically "obnoxious," behavior of the patient toward the therapist.

The patient's dependence on the therapist has been discussed more than the therapist's dependence on the patient, except in the writings of Harold Searles. He has developed the idea of the mutual dependence of the patient and the therapist (Searles, 1961, 1975). We are dependent on patients for our practice, and our practice becomes an important part of our identity. The therapist is concerned that patients should continue in treatment, beyond considerations of clinical responsibility and conscientiousness. This is not only a matter of economics, since we experience it not only in private practice but also in free clinics.

Out of the total problem of the mutual dependence of patient and therapist I want to select one aspect: the therapist's anxiety about a patient's suicide. I will present case material which illustrates a link between a patient's self-destructiveness and my hostility to the patient. The patient made me hate her and want to get rid of her, and I will pursue the significance of her stimulating hostility in me as a repetition of her infantile trauma and as a means of mastering the consequences of that trauma.

A twenty-two year old girl was referred because of anorexia nervosa with cachexia. She had isolated herself in her college dormitory room, not participating in any social or academic activities. When she first came for consultation she said she did not know of any reason to have psychotherapy, nor of any reason not to have it. Later this turned out to be a manifestation of a sense of futility about all relationships with the world of reality. At the start, though, I acknowledged that we did not yet know her treatment goals, and agreed to work with her to find them. She then mentioned feeling mildly depressed. Although this was true, she used it to justify coming for treatment before she could tell me of symptoms that were more disturbing. The patient was unusually frank and open about her sexual and masturbatory history. One reason for this was that her primary anxiety was elsewhere, related to food, eating, and vomiting. At the beginning she did not mention any of these oral preoccupations; it required two years of treatment before she could discuss them.

She was mostly mute, and the information that I have is derived from the occasional things she was able to tell me, notes that she wrote to me, my observation of her behavior, and from my own subjective reactions. However, she was able to tell me in the first month that she was not separate from me and that she had "known" this from the first moment she saw me. She was absolutely intolerant of any suggestion that we were two separate persons. This was not a gradual, developing transference, but rather she brought it into the treatment situation fully formed and she just fitted me into it; it was her initial reaction to starting her treatment. It was not a delusion, but at the same time she insisted upon it; she had two parallel realities. She knew she was a separate person and at the same time "knew" that we were "one." This coexistence of two parallel realities, with objective perception of the therapeutic relationship and at the same time a delusional transference reaction, is characteristic of borderline states, in contrast to frankly psychotic states in which delusion pervades all perception.

She had to "keep dead" her capacity to want anything from me, because if her wants were to "come to life" she would "want too much," that is, to be inseparable, to be "inside of" me in a state she called "oneness." The need for the fusion to "become real" was "wanting too much," and her fear of inevitable disappointment of this need had contributed to her inability to say why she had come in in the first place. In connection with "wanting too much," she remembered her father saying that when he would bring candy to her as a small child, she could not appreciate it but only was unhappy when the candy was gone; so he stopped bringing it to her. She felt that his reaction proved that she should not have wanted the candy in the first place.

The insistence upon "oneness" with me was expressed in letters which she wrote to me demanding that we interpenetrate one another, inseparably, as the only condition for her survival. The demands for fusion made the notes she gave me sound like love letters of the most erotic nature, but the important point about them was that they were not sexual demands; what she wanted was total fusion rather than genital union. She expressed despair about surviving without living in me so that I could "live for" her. There could be "no life" without interpenetration. The desperation about her demands that I relieve the "deadness" by becoming "one" with her suggested that she needed me to displace a dead image with a living one, and that, in contrast to sexual desires, this demand represented a primitive need that could not be satisfied by an adult in reality. The patient did not begin to experience sexual desires until much later in treatment.

Variety of experience characterizes health and is not found in severe disorders, whether they be emotional or physical. *In severe disorders the person's whole life is engulfed by one or a very few major symptoms or personality traits.* For example, the life of a paranoid patient is dominated by fear of persecution, while the life of a patient with left ventricular cardiac failure is dominated by dyspnea. I will refer repeatedly to this patient's states of "oneness" and "separateness" and to the eating and vomiting. This repetition is unavoidable, because they dominated her life and her treatment, which consisted of understanding their various meanings and their progressive modification. The process of working-through involves repeatedly experiencing the same conflict in different contexts and with emphasis on different aspects of the experience. In discussing working-through Freud (1914a) said, "The doctor has nothing else to do than to wait and let things take their course, a course which cannot be avoided nor always hastened. If he holds fast to this conviction he will often be spared the illusion of having failed when in fact he is conducting the treatment on the right lines." In this passage Freud was referring to the overcoming of resistances that maintain repression of instinctual impulses in neurotic patients, rather than to the slow development of psychic structure in patients with severe ego defects, but his words are nonetheless a valuable guide in the latter situation. The process of working-through is one reason that description of a treatment requires repeated reference to specific clinical phenomena. Another reason for such repetition in this paper is that in several instances I will use the same clinical data to illustrate different processes.

The form of the sessions during the first years of her treatment formed a consistent pattern. When the patient entered the office, she kept her eyes averted or closed and did not look at me. She lay quietly on the couch, and if I said anything she gave no indication that she was aware of my existence. I felt that she was in a massive withdrawal. At the beginning of a session I would be aware that I had a patient on the couch, but then gradually I would find myself withdrawing into my own thoughts, as though she did not exist. At the end of the sessions she would glance at me as she left, and her demeanor usually expressed dissatisfaction and displeasure.

Much later it turned out that from one point of view I was mistaken when I thought she had been withdrawing from me. She was eventually able to tell me, partly verbally and partly through notes, what actually happened in those early sessions. She had not been able to look at me because she could not tolerate the great distance between us, and when I thought she was withdrawn, she actually was "concentrating" on feeling that she and I were "one." The same was true with speech during the sessions. To talk to me was to acknowledge that she and I were separate persons, while silence meant that things were as they "should" be, namely that I knew her thoughts directly, without any need for speech. Early in her treatment, she said, "I feel things, but when I talk the words never are what I feel. If I were to get inside of you . . . I needed to get inside of mother when I was a child. It's the only way, then you would know what I feel and I would know what you feel; talking can't do that."

I interpreted that these needs were appropriate for the part of herself that was in touch with earliest infancy, and mentioned that it was unfortunate that the infantile needs could not be satisfied in her grown-up body. This interpretation had to be repeated frequently because she tended to feel that if only I wanted to do so I could "make the oneness real." As a separate person she could not allow me to exist. If she had let herself see me at the beginning of a session, or if she talked to me, she immediately would have had to be aware that we were separate persons and that the session would not last forever but that it would have an end, and it was this that she had tried to eliminate from her awareness. For a long time I thought that when she showed disappointment and displeasure at the end of each session, she was reproaching me about some shortcoming of mine during the session. Although this was also true, we found that a more important reason for the disappointment was simply the fact that the session had ended rather than being interminable.

After about two years she became able to recognize that she had two pictures of me—one loving her and one hating her. We then realized that another reason for closing her eyes during the sessions was to help her concentrate all her efforts on perceiving me as all-loving, and to eliminate awareness of the other, all-hating picture of me in her mind.

This patient suffered overwhelming pain, and the pain was diffuse, all-encompassing and unlocalized. She said: "The pain is not in me, I'm in it." Sophisticated symbolic processes certainly contributed to this experience. For example, the pain represented the mother into whom she remembered needing to return as a child, or the pain represented me enclosing her in a state of "oneness." Regardless of such meanings, pain of such an all-inclusive nature indicates a severe ego defect, characterized by incapacity to organize and localize stimuli in such a way that effective response would be possible. Such failure of ego organization constitutes a defective "barrier against stimuli." (Freud, 1920, Jones 1957) As we shall see, the symbolic meanings became relevant later when the patient reached a higher level of ego functioning and began to symbolize her relationships and localize her feelings. At the beginning, however, she felt the pain as all-pervasive, and said that as a result of the pain "suicide seems sensible, nothing else makes any sense."

PAST HISTORY

I did not take a formal history, and the following material emerged gradually during her treatment. One advantage of this way of working (by starting therapy immediately, without preliminary history-taking) is that historical material comes into the treatment when the patient is ready to assimilate it. In addition it permits the therapist to offer psychotherapy from the start, so that the patient can know what it is and can select or reject psychotherapy as a mode of treatment on the basis of his ability to utilize it rather than on the basis of authoritarian prescription by the therapist. In this way the patient's autonomy can be fostered from the start. I think this is a very important consideration and have developed it in a previous publication (Flarsheim, 1972).

The patient was the youngest of four siblings. She felt that the parents were disappointed with all the children, but the others had all been able to finish college and establish themselves as independent adults. She was the only one of the siblings with a severe crippling emotional disorder, and her development had suffered from earliest infancy.

The mother had tried to nurse the patient, but this was unsuccessful. She had adequate milk secretion, but her nipples were inverted. Very gentle sucking produced some milk flow, but because of the inverted nipples the result of vigorous sucking was a reduction rather than an increase of milk flow. The baby cried continually, and the mother suffered breast discomfort and pain. After about a week the effort at breast feeding was abandoned and a nurse was hired to care for the baby. Up to now the story was the same for this patient as for her three older siblings, but a different nurse was hired to care for the patient than the one who had cared for the siblings. This nurse "guaranteed" to make any baby quiet and undemanding, to "make any baby no trouble within three weeks."

The patient did not, of course, remember the events of her early infancy. She learned about them when her mother recommended the same treatment for the baby of a relative, boasting about how effective it had been in the patient's infancy.

The nurse's technique was very simple. She was intuitive and sensitive to the needs of infants and would decide what she thought the baby wanted, and then do something different. For example, if she thought the baby was hungry she would change her diaper; if she thought the baby was cold, she would feed her. She did not neglect or abandon the baby, but did something active when the baby showed signs of discomfort. There might be a difference in the result if a baby were treated with neglect and abandonment, in contrast to this girl, who was treated by something being done to her, something deliberately maladaptive and therefore actively assaultive (Giovacchini, 1972).

The nurse's objective was to make the baby stop crying and stop making demands, and the treatment worked: the patient became compliant and un-complaining. The patient could not remember any time before the global pain, and she believed that it started in infancy and had "always" been present. There could, however, have been some compensations, such as thumb-sucking. But an older sibling had sucked his thumb, and the parents vowed to stop it in the patient. They guarded her when she was in bed at night, and when she started to suck her thumb, they pulled it out of her mouth. Then they put metal covers over her hands so she could not suck her thumb.

My patient had been told that she changed her own diapers as a toddler, and she could not be certain whether she remembered doing it or whether she only remembered having been told about it. She did remember, however, that around age five she started masturbating, and, in contrast to the thumb-sucking, she managed to do it secretly. She masturbated with a bit of rolled-up Kleenex or her father's sock which she remembers as having represented a penis, or as she put it, the Kleenex or sock *were* her penis. She rubbed the Kleenex or the socks against her external genitalia, always wanting to insert something into her vagina but never doing so. An interesting attitude about her masturbation is that the anxiety-relieving and pleasurable feelings she attained from masturbating were experienced as being felt by the Kleenex or sock rather than by herself.

Such ego splitting would not be needed in order to defend against pleasura-ble feelings, and I assumed that all feelings must have been potentially threatening. This is consistent with a repetitive dream that started at the same time that ego splitting was manifest in masturbation. In the dream her mother tied her to a railroad track and a train ran over her and killed her. Another self remained alive, watching herself writhing in agony and being killed, while the observing self felt no pain. There were two parallel realities in the dream: she was on the track suffering and she was watching. Another example of parallel realities was in her sexual identity: she knew that she was a girl, but also, when she was masturbating, she "knew" that she "was a boy." Being a girl was "hopeless" because all good feelings were experienced by the penis and the capacity for pleasure belonged to the "boy self" and would be lost if she were to "become" a girl.

She thought of her mother's body as scarred, damaged, and frightening, without being able to account for this idea by any specific injury or scarring. She liked her father's body and in childhood she assumed that she would grow up to have a body like her father rather than like her mother. Masturbation was an intermittent activity, but it meant having a secret, idealized nurturing companion (the penis and the "boy self") with her all the time. In addition "the boy" could get angry and fight; especially "he" could fight against any child who insulted her mother. The patient's mother was an alcoholic and the patient remembers beating up another child who said her mother "looked sleepy."

Despite her alcoholism, the patient's mother was skillful and devoted in nursing the maternal grandmother, who was bedridden due to a stroke, lived in the home all during the patient's childhood, and died when the patient was 17. The grandmother required difficult nursing care; for example, she was heavy, and had to be lifted on and off a bedpan. The patient felt jealous when she saw her mother moving her grandmother and feeding the grandmother small pieces of toast by hand. She felt guilty about this jealousy, because she was able to walk to the toilet and to eat whole pieces of toast while her grandmother could do neither.

The relation between the way she experienced her infancy and the way she reacted to me is clarified by a memory that the patient recovered later, after about two and a half years of treatment: She remembered that, as far back as her memory went, she thought her parents were plotting to abandon or kill her when they put her to bed at night. Her defense was to "kill *them*" by retreating into a "secret inner world" in which there were at first no people, but rather there were part-objects, breasts and penises, and in which later there was a satisfied baby. Still later, around age ten, her fear changed from being killed while asleep to having her feet stolen. To this she associated that as a child she had assumed that her penis had been stolen and would eventually grow back. The change from being killed to having her feet stolen, a change from fantasies of total destruction to those of partial destruction, was associated with a conviction that by "being a boy" she could protect her "inner world." The manifest reproach against the parents, and then against me, was that she had not been given a penis, but more fundamentally it was that she did not feel loved and valued, for herself, by the parents as an infant and by me during the treatment. The total fantasy of sex change included "starting over" and being able to love herself and not needing the parents' love. The penis was needed primarily to provide the nurture and love that she had not received as an infant, and only secondarily for its sexual meaning, which included getting into her mother with a part of her body when she despaired of getting in with her whole self. Hope in childhood lay in "growing a real penis" as hope during treatment lay in becoming "one" with me. She was unable to conceive of living if she thought these aims might not be realized.

In her secret inner world she was loved; there "wanting and having were the same." The secret inner world became the most important thing in her life. It was "about as large as a marble," and was sharply differentiated both from the "outside surface self" and from the external world which saw only the "outside self" and to which the "outside self" reacted without involvement of the "secret inner self." She maintained the "secret inner world" by trying to be self-sufficient and by compliance with the external world, so that people would let her alone. For example, she looked forward to starting school, but did not do very well. Part of the trouble was that she had to wear dresses to school, and there people saw her as a girl. Even worse, at school she had to think of herself as a girl, while away from school she could wear boy's clothing and "be" a boy. The family did not think it pathological that she was a "tomboy," but her parents and teachers put pressure on her about schoolwork. Finally she decided that life was worthless and that she could never be happy anyway, so that the only thing left to do was to get people to let her alone. The best way to achieve this was to be a good student. From then on she was near the top of her class, through grammar school, high school, and into the university, a selective Eastern school with high academic admission requirements. She stressed that the only reason for her academic success was that since everything was worthless anyway, it was a way of getting the world to let her alone. I think the development of this kind of defense in later childhood is consistent with the interpretation of her earlier infantile experience as one which was experienced as assault rather than as neglect, and this interpretation is consistent with her infantile history as she heard it from her mother. Caretaking procedures deliberately unrelated to an infant's needs would be experienced as assaultive, and withdrawal is an appropriate response to such treatment. Conformity was a way of protecting the withdrawn state. Bettelheim (1967) has described similar events in the backgrounds of infants who become autistic children.

The patient masturbated, with the fantasy of being a boy needing nothing from anyone, through an uneventful menarche at age thirteen, and until about age sixteen, when she discovered that other girls and women masturbate. She had always thought that this was something she had created for herself and that no one else did it. If other people masturbated, girls as well as boys, then masturbation no longer proved that she had a penis. Masturbation lost its significance as a reassurance of continuous self-sufficiency through possession of a penis and was no longer worth doing because it was now only an intermittent act. After the discovery that other girls masturbated she stopped masturbating and never did it again. Cessation of her masturbation was accompanied by what the family regarded as the first manifest sign of mental illness. In the eyes of the school and of her family this was a withdrawal from her previous involvement with social life, although she maintained her academic work. From the psychiatric standpoint, however, it is important to note that although this was the first sign of mental illness recognized by the family, the previous adjustment had been based on a delusion (of being a boy), and therefore mental illness long antedated the outward withdrawal.

She linked the renunciation of masturbation with the discovery of "the most important thing in my life." The new discovery at age seventeen was "something much better than masturbating, much better than anything I had ever known before." It took her two years to tell me what it was, and she "had never been able to tell it to anyone before." It turned out that, despite being so thin that anorexia nervosa had been suspected, she ate a great deal, secretly. She ate knowing that her purpose in eating was to vomit the food back out. She could tell me for the first time, after two years, that the main reason that she had been unable to remain in college was that the dormitory offered no privacy for this eating and vomiting.

Eating and vomiting was not a source of pleasure, but rather was experienced as secret magic necessary for survival. When a patient suffers from severe anxiety about survival, everything in his life is subservient to the need for reassurance. Even an overt suicidal act can have the meaning of taking destructiveness into one's own hands rather than feeling vulnerable to uncontrolled destructiveness. Under such circumstances there is no room for seeking pleasure for its own sake. Pleasure and pain, as all other experiences, are pressed into the service of reassurance against overwhelming anxiety.

She had told me earlier that she stopped masturbating when she learned that other girls masturbated. Now she said that when the preoccupation with food replaced masturbation she was at a boarding school away from home, at around age sixteen to seventeen, and was extremely "homesick" for her mother. "From then on, food was not food, I was never hungry but I started eating all the time and gained weight." At age seventeen her invalid grandmother died and an older sister announced wedding plans; it was at this time that the cyclic eating and vomiting began. The eating and vomiting was associated in her mind with the memory of trying to get close to her mother as a child. She would hug her mother, "trying to get inside her," and when she realized that she could not do so, she would feel hopeless and try to feel "nothing." She said "the girl in me needed mother, but when I was a boy I didn't need anyone. As a boy I could live outside of mother, but as a girl I needed to get inside of her, and could not." She said that when eating and vomiting replaced "being a boy" as a "basis for surviving," concentration on eating and vomiting enabled her to be "neither boy nor girl" and to "feel nothing." It served, therefore, more to enable her to deny needs than to gratify needs. The oral function was not integrated into the total ego; the patient said "What to do with mouth" [not "*my* mouth"] "has never fit with the rest of me." As a child the patient remembers vomiting after large meals, as at Thanksgiving and Christmas. She was particularly afraid of vomiting, and noticed that other people regarded it as repugnant. Her mother was the only person who was not repelled by her vomiting as a child, and after vomiting she was allowed to sleep in her mother's bed while her father slept in another room. When she gained voluntary control of vomiting, she had mastered her earlier fear of it, but continued to consider it particularly repugnant to others, now including her mother, from whom it was particularly important that it be kept hidden. The main reason for this was that if mother were to know about the voluntary vomiting, she would know about the "full" state preceding the vomiting, and it was of mother's discovery of the "full" state that the patient was particularly frightened.

Compulsive eating and vomiting gradually replaced most other activities. Along with this came severe weight loss, constipation, and anemorrhea, which were still present when she started treatment. Despite being undernourished she was very active and athletic, taking long walks, swimming, bicycling, and engaging in other strenuous activities. Although emaciated, she was horrified of the idea of being fat, and exercise reassured her against fears of becoming fat, and even of *being* fat.

Eating and vomiting had many meanings, one of which was to feed herself from inside, so "wanting and having are the same." Although it was an intermittent activity, she thought of it as a continuous and uninterrupted cycle with no beginning and no end. Being "full" was more dangerous than being "empty" though, because once inside her the food became dangerous. In order to achieve a reassuring state of emptiness she had to eat and then vomit. Such reassurance did not last, however, and she therefore needed to eat and vomit repeatedly, and devoted whole days to this activity.

The change from masturbating to eating and vomiting can be looked upon as regressive. Regression unfortunately has at times been given a moralistic connotation in addition to its scientific meaning. The use of the term sometimes carries the implication that the patient has more mature adaptive capacities that he could use if he only "would" do so. Another way to look at regressive symptomatology is to ask ourselves the question: "How could this patient function if he did not have this symptom?" From this viewpoint the symptom is an adaptive achievement of the patient's ego. It was in this way that I viewed her eating and vomiting, and I assumed that it permitted her to get more nourishment than she would have obtained if she could not eat at all and that, since it "deadened" her feelings and stopped "the pain," it protected her against suicide (Bettelheim, 1972).

CHANGES DURING TREATMENT

When she first told me about eating and vomiting, which had been her chief activity and interest in life for five years, she said that one reason for vomiting was that as soon as the food got in it became dangerous and threatened to cause the all-encompassing pain and to destroy her. She had to vomit to protect herself against the poison. In the course of the treatment this changed, and the food came to represent me, or rather, as she expressed it, the food "was" me, and she became afraid *for* the food rather than *of* it. At this point, the pain was replaced by sadness and guilt about wasting good food by vomiting. Still later, she stopped this pattern of eating and vomiting altogether, and instead became extremely sensitive and vulnerable to feeling neglected, forgotten, abandoned, and hated by me, particularly during the intervals between appointments. She "knew" that at a certain time I had "forgotten" her or had started hating her, and she would begin to suffer global pain, and later, "great sadness." She was absolutely sure about the changes in my attitudes toward her. It seemed to me that our task became to investigate *her* thoughts in *my* mind, for she could not perceive that she had a mind separate from mine, in which changes in *her* attitudes *toward* me could occur during her sessions or while we were apart. She only knew that there was hatred in our relationship and that it existed in me and was totally beyond her control. She said that for her to hate me was inconceivable. "It would be the same as my hating the air I need to breathe or a fish hating the water he swims in." Also, love and hate were experienced entirely separately, as "all-love" or "all-hate." For this reason to hate me would have been to destroy our relationship altogether.

Her reaction to separation gradually changed. In the second year of treatment, I told the patient that I would be away on a two-week vacation, and she said she did not know whether she could survive it. I told her she could telephone me while I was away. But she said this would be of no use because at the moment when she would *need* to call me she could not *want* to, "there would be no you to call," and therefore it could only be helpful if I would call her. I believed that this meant that her needs were not sufficiently structured to be experienced as object-related desires, and to enable her to take action in relation to the outside world. I therefore did call her, daily, while I was away. A year later, the third year of our work together, I again took a two-week vacation. This time she was able to telephone me periodically and this was enough to sustain the relationship during the separation. This change is a small one from an economic standpoint, considering the enormous cost of a year's treatment. It illustrates the pace at which this treatment proceeded. It was my impression that the process was one of building, for the first time, of personality structure that never had a chance to get started because of the traumatic way in which this patient was introduced to life in her earliest infancy (Bettelheim, 1967).

Another symptom was what she called "explosive feeling," which was related to loss of the "oneness," and which, like the pain, was relieved only by the eating and vomiting. The "explosive feeling" occurred at times when I would have expected her to be angry; for example, when I accepted telephone calls during her sessions. However, she did not experience anger; she experienced only loss of "oneness," "explosive feelings," hopelessness, and pain.

Her use of the term "oneness" led me at one point to talk about "twoness," but I noticed that she did not accept this term. Finally she was able to tell me there was no such thing as "twoness," there were only "oneness" and separateness which was "broken oneness." She could not conceive of there being two people in a relationship. Separation, for example at the end of hours, or when during her hours or between hours she felt that I was not thinking about her, and that I had started hating her, led not to a feeling of two people separating, but to "the pain" or to "explosive feelings," both of which she relieved by eating and vomiting. All feelings were either the diffuse "pain," or "explosive feelings." She used the term "being dead" to refer to her way of relieving pain and explosive feelings by eating and vomiting. Since all feelings were explosively painful, a state of affective "deadness" was a necessary defense, and suicidal impulses were a logical outcome. She went to a restaurant to eat and then vomit immediately after each session. This symptom was clearly life-saving, serving, as she described it, to achieve "deadness" as a defense against painful awareness of separateness, which she said would require suicide. Later she was able to tell me that the reason it had taken two years for her to tell me about the eating and vomiting was that she had feared that any doctor would try to "cure" such a symptom; and she would perish.

Symbiosis I: Repetition of Traumatic Environment of Infancy in My Response to Patient

The patient was constantly searching for evidence that I was ill-disposed toward her, particularly that I wanted to "get rid of her." She said that during early childhood she felt that she should "get rid of herself," die, or at least stop existing, because in some way this would "make everything better." I believed that this suicidal impulse represented the patient's reaction to her mother's having wanted to "get rid of" her aliveness during the fateful first few weeks of life, before self-object differentiation, and therefore at a time when the mother's wish for her to not exist was equivalent to the infant's wishing for herself to not exist. When the patient felt that I wanted to "get rid of her," at times when the "oneness was broken," and she was feeling "separate" from me, she was reliving the trauma of infancy. However, she was now doing this in a way that enabled her to feel persecuted by me *separate* from herself, and *therefore* as someone against whom she could defend herself better than she could defend herself against the suicidal impulses that ensued when the object that wanted her to die was part of her self. This could be formulated in terms of complex mechanisms of introjection leading to superego formation, but in view of the early date of the trauma and in view of the continuity of psychopathology from infancy through childhood and into adulthood, it seems more economical to formulate it in terms of fixation at the level of primal undifferentiation between herself and her mother rather than in terms of incorporation of a discrete and separate object representation, for example, for control of it. This is consistent with her inability to structure a stable paranoid projection, but instead "becoming dead" was used as a defense. It is also consistent with the fact that eating and vomiting, prototypes of introjection and projection, were an unbroken never-ending cycle; predominance of neither could provide a stable defense. There was, however, one period, during later childhood, during which she was able to project in a structured way, and that was when she felt that adults were plotting to abandon her and to destroy her. I can interpret this preoccupation as representing not only a primary anxiety but also a defense against anxiety. By this I mean that in feeling that she was being persecuted by separate external persons, she was more able to defend herself than she was against suicidal impulses that derived from feeling that the persecution came from internal objects more or less identified with the self. The later fantasy of "killing the family by withdrawal" was a further defensive step. Defensive withdrawal; fantasied role reversal with identification with the aggressor in the form of "being a boy"; and projection of vulnerability onto others, were more effective when the destructive force was experienced as coming from the outside world, that is, from other people. The patient remembered a repetitive childhood dream in which her whole body was surrounded by pins and needles pointing at her but not touching her. Spitz (1965, pp. 63-64) describes the parasthesia of pins and needles pricking the skin as representing a derivative of the "perception of an overload of stimulation." It seemed to me that her dream of the pins and needles was comparable to the global, unlocalized pain, but that the dream represented successful projection and the pain indicated failure of projection.

A destructive impulse toward her, coming from outside of herself, became real in the treatment in my attitude toward her. After about two years of treatment, her pain and hoplessness were intense, and "being dead" was a continuous wish. I found myself feeling compelled to try to relieve her pain, and hunted for encouraging things that I might say in order to relieve it. The content of what I said was interpretive but I later saw that my intent was to make her change and stop complaining about pain, and stop wishing to be dead. *Anything hopeful that I tried to say made her worse.* She felt abandoned when on one occasion I used the phrase that she was "going through a painful time," because this implied that I did not realize her "pain was interminable." I felt guilty, and had fantasies of being reproached by her family and by my colleagues if she were to kill herself. I found myself wishing that she were not my patient. I began to realize that I was wanting her not to exist as she was, suffering and suicidal, and that, in effect, I wanted to get rid of her. Suddenly I recognized that this feeling of mine duplicated the feelings of her mother and nurse in her infancy, who needed her not to cry, not to make demands on them, not to exist as she was. In a similar fashion, I wished her not to exist as she was, suffering and suicidal. When I began to recognize this I interpreted it as completely as I could to the patient. I told her that my wish that she not suffer was not only a helpful impulse, but also was a rejection of her as she was. It was a corollary of her wish to not exist, to be dead, and was a repetition of the attitudes of her mother and nurse in earliest infancy, when she had not yet experienced herself as a person separate from her mother. My wishing to be rid of her represented her suicidal impulses and thus paradoxically corresponded to the "oneness" that she felt with me. This interpretation produced the first relief of her pain. She felt "for the first time" that we were "fighting the problem together," in a relationship, an alliance, rather than her having to fight alone.

I concluded that she had *needed* to create this situation between us. It was a faithful repetition of an infantile situation in which her mother and her nurse had needed her to not exist. *This situation had occurred in infancy before self-object differentiation and before development of sufficient ego structure to form memory traces that could be recalled without reliving them.* My wish to get rid of her was a reflection of her own suicidal wish. This in turn was in part derived from the mother's unconscious wish to destroy her, which had become part of herself. The patient could only begin to separate herself from her wish that she die *after* it had become mine in a state in which she was feeling merged with me in what she called "oneness." I concluded that *my anxiety lest she commit suicide had been in part a manifestation of my latent wish that she cease to be. Rather than to try to counteract her suicidal impulses directly, my task became to deal with my feelings, my wish that she not exist as she was, which I had at first experienced as anxiety lest she commit suicide.*

As one would expect, the relief following this one episode was only temporary. I had to go through a crisis of anxiety about her, that corresponded to her "explosive feeling," and to do something about my own reaction to her overwhelming urge for self-destruction, before she could advance from this destructive symbiosis, in fact, before we together could advance from it. This came about in the following way: She relapsed again into tortured silence.

There was no communication between us; suicide seemed to her "the only sensible thing," and I began feeling more and more uneasy about her. She was "only pain" to herself; she was only pain to me. I could call my reaction an "explosive feeling" in the countertransference. I found the situation intolerable. Another therapist might not have reacted as I did. It is a truism that applies to cases of every kind to say that the course of treatment of any given case would be different with different therapists. In every case the course of therapy is dictated not only by the patient's needs and the therapist's technical ability, but also by the idiosyncratic personal characteristics, needs, and tolerances of the therapist. This is particularly true in treatment of cases like this, who need to establish an undifferentiated state of unity with the therapist. When the patient's ego is in a fluid state, without clearly defined boundaries in the transference relationship, the personality of the therapist influences the patient more and is *at the same time* more influenced by the patient than is true with patients who have clearly defined ego boundaries.

Except in the instance of a *folie á deux,* with a fully developed countertransference psychosis, the state of "oneness" has more reality for the patient than for the therapist (Little, 1960). Still, in lesser degrees the problem is frequent. Both in my own practice and in discussion with colleagues I have often found that one patient in the therapist's case load is particularly disturbing to the therapist and forces the therapist to examine his own motivations more than do his other patients. It is often a patient with failure of differentiation of self from not-self who has such an effect, and the strain on the therapist derives from the extreme sensitivity of the patient with fluid ego boundaries to the therapist's behavior, with the resulting necessity that the therapist examine details of his own behavior to which other, more integrated, patients do not react (see Giovacchini, 1972a).

In this instance I finally could no longer tolerate the patient's mute suffering. I did of course realize that the anxiety it caused me was only a pale reflection of the patient's suffering. But it became intolerable to me, and I finally said: "I've got the explosive feeling and I'm feeling pain about all this, so I want you to go into the hospital. The reason for hospitalization is for me; I can't take it." I felt that it was important to tell the patient that *my* anxiety was the reason for recommending hospitalization. My reason was that I needed the help of the hospital and its staff to protect the patient in order to relieve me of my concern lest she commit suicide. We had found that she needed me to accept her as she was, suffering, rather than to try (and fail) to relieve her. To have recommended hospitalization because of her suffering would have implied rejection as well as an omnipotent promise that the hospital would relieve her suffering. If the hospital did relieve some of her suffering, so much the better, but this was not the main purpose. When psychiatric hospitalization is recommended in order to relieve the patient's suffering, the next step often is to take more forcible and potentially destructive means, such as drugging the patient or administering shock treatment, not only in an effort to enable the patient to function more constructively, but often simply to get the patient to stop complaining. Despite the way I expressed it, there certainly was some element of omnipotent promise in my recommendation, but there was also simply the overlapping of our needs for relief from a difficult situation, an overlapping that was particularly wide because she was in a state of "oneness," with diffuse ego boundaries.

Symbiosis II: Communication, Memory, and Ego Integration

In the hospital, the patient refused food and liquids. Eating threatened her with destruction, and this had more reality for her than did actual death from starvation. Cohler (1975) points out that the relation between eating and survival becomes subjectively reversed in anorexia nervosa. Starvation becomes equated with survival while eating becomes equated with destruction and death. This may be pathognomonic of the syndrome of anorexia nervosa. She did not eat her regular meals but ate only secretly, in order to vomit. She could not tell the hospital staff about the secret eating and vomiting, and therefore the hospital staff thought that she did not eat at all. Later she was able to use some of the hospital meals for her purpose, mainly in order to stop the nurses from nagging at her about not eating.

Reconstruction of this patient's infancy, from what she was able to tell me in the hospital about her withdrawal, enables us to link the two pathological states that Mahler (1952) called autistic and symbiotic psychoses. The autistic infant avoids object contact, while the infant with symbiotic psychosis clings to the object (mother). The patient's manifest behavior was characterized by avoidance of contact with others. She spent her days sitting alone and immobile in a darkened room, with her eyes closed. Her only sign of recognition when anyone entered the room was to turn her head away and frown. While avoiding contact in reality as did Mahler's autistic patients, in her inner world of fantasy she was joined inseparably in a symbiotic union. In her private fantasy world this patient was not actively clinging but was "being held and carried." While objectively withdrawn, she lived subjectively in a state of fusion with an idealized nurturing and always bountiful object, and she used her mental image of me as the raw material from which she created this idealized object. In her fantasy we lived together inseparably in her hospital room, having no relations with anyone else, nourishing one another and neither eating nor eliminating.

The world outside of her hospital room contained all pain and discomfort, and these were absent from our idealized fantasy relationship. She cared about relationships with no one but me, and did not let herself know that I cared about anyone but her. This was maintained for months in the hospital (as it had been before she entered the hospital) despite the fact that she saw my other patients and talked with members of my family when she telephoned me at home. One of the reasons for telephoning was fear of losing me inside of herself. Thus we began to see that the "oneness" for which she longed was also felt to be dangerous, when it meant that she had incorporated me in a dangerous way. Although she had said that an ideal state was one in which "wanting equals having," it turned out that this could not be maintained without anxiety. Eating meant destructive incorporation, and keeping herself in a state of frustrated wanting could be a defense against the fear of containing destroyed and dangerous objects. In addition, eating meant stealing, originally from mother and now from me, as external objects, and frustrated wanting reassured her against guilt and fear about this. She said "If you were inside of me I couldn't want to get you inside, so I telephoned to hear your voice outside. If oneness happened I couldn't think of wanting it to happen, so my mind would dissolve. *That's what's wrong with eating.* If I am full I can't want to eat, and so being empty is better."

It was in the hospital that she told me that when she appeared withdrawn, she was "concentrating," and that she was concentrating on trying to retain or to build up memory traces of me to use as the basis of the idealized fantasy. She kept her eyes closed because to look at me was to discover that I was a separate person sitting across the room from her. So the behavior that I had thought of as withdrawal was, from one point of view, the very opposite of withdrawal; it was an effort to achieve oneness, rather than merely the communication and closeness that can be achieved through speech or through vision or other sensory modalities. During this time she said that "separation is so painful that it's better if the memory of you is destroyed at the end of a session—then there is no separation. The only time we exist is when we are together. When I am alone life isn't, there is no you who is away, no you to feel angry at. If there were a you there would either be terrifying fullness of having eaten you, or hopeless emptiness." She said that "being in the hospital was good because it was me dissolving into you and that's safe, but when you dissolve in me that's not safe. It's taking something away and makes me feel guilty."

We discovered that when she found it possible to remember me between sessions, she was temporarily free of the inside-outside split, with a secret inner world protected by "outer deadness" and by conformity and compliance with the demands of the outside world that felt meaningless and unrelated to her inner world. I will give three examples of this. She told me the significance of the events after they occurred; I did not know their meaning when they happened.

I telephoned her one Monday to say that I would be away on Tuesday afternoon, and that I could see her next at her regular time on Wednesday. Something about the way in which she responded, the way she said, "Yes, all right," left me feeling uneasy. Her words were appropriate, but I felt that her tone expressed something different, perhaps the feeling that she had at times called "being dropped," associated with losing awareness of a memory of our relationship. I called her back and told her that her way of speaking made me uneasy and that after thinking about it I realized that I could make a change in my Tuesday morning schedule, and could see her on Tuesday morning, replacing rather than cancelling the Tuesday afternoon session. This turned out to be of enormous importance for her. She had succeeded in communicating something in a nonverbal way, *to herself as well as to me*, and from her point of view she had felt understood, *and had understood herself*, in a primitive, preverbal way. She said afterwards that she had felt the diffuse "pain" when I cancelled the appointment but *only realized that she wanted me to reschedule it rather than to cancel it after I had called back and done so*. She said that at the moment I did so "the pain disappeared" and "the secret inner world became [temporarily] not important." For a few days after the episode she could remember me, and during those few days she felt that the split between the inside self and the outside self disappeared.

After she had been in the hospital for several months, she referred to the hospital as something that I provided which fit a need she had had without knowing what she needed. She wrote in a note: "Just as you could not stand my not being in a hospital, I couldn't stand not being in the hospital either, but *I didn't know the hospital existed, so I just couldn't stand being*. In the hospital I began to feel it could be good to be."

A third episode: We had arranged that she come to my office on days when I could not go to the hospital, and on one occasion I noticed that as she lay down on the couch she closed her eyes very tightly. There was a light over the couch, and I asked her whether the light was bothering her. She did not respond at all; it was as though I were not there. I said, "It bothers me to see you lying there with your eyes like that; it looks as though the light is bothering you. I'm going to turn it off because it bothers *me* to see you doing that." I turned off the light, and this turned out to be another important episode of successful nonverbal *communication, not only to me but to herself*: she said *she had not been aware that the light had been hurting her eyes until after I turned it off*. Again, after this episode she "could remember" me, and experienced temporary relief of the diffuse pain. Remembering me was crucial to her at this time, and it was only much later in treatment that she became able to forget me comfortably.

In these episodes I felt that it was important to tell the patient that by her behavior she had communicated discomfort to me, and made me uncomfortable and made me want to do something about it. Otherwise, without the emphasis on the patient's communicating, it could seem to a patient that we were reading his mind and foster the delusion that we could adapt to his needs magically, as this patient had said she needed me to be able to do in the state of "oneness."

These episodes can be contrasted with the way in which she was treated in the early weeks of her life, when there was the opposite of successful communication and adaptive response; her expressive gestures were deliberately misinterpreted by the nursemaid. Ekstein (1966) talks about infant care as the prototype of the psychoanalytic interpretation. A baby experiences some kind of inchoate discomfort, but has *at first* no memory traces of what would satisfy, such as mother's arms and breasts, milk, bottles, dry diapers, blankets, etc., and therefore no object-directed impulses. The mother "interprets" the baby's crying and other signs of distress, and does something which is more or less appropriate to relieve the baby's discomfort. From that time on the baby has memory traces of satisfaction and of things that can satisfy, and can cry with a purpose, instead of going into a tantrum or other disorganized state in which he cannot seek anything from the outside world. With my patient, I am assuming that failure of infantile nurture led to a schizoid state in which her relations to the outside world were separated off from her own inner world which had no experiences with the environment.

Symbiosis III: Idealization and Omnipotence

In 1914 and 1915(e) Freud said that schizophrenic patients have withdrawn libido from people and things, do not form transferences, and are therefore "inaccessible—and cannot be cured by our efforts." But earlier, in 1912, Freud had pointed out that the transference reactions of one class of psychotic patients, paranoid patients, tends to be unambivalently negative, and that "in the curable forms of psychoneurosis [the negative transference] is found side by side with the affectionate transference, often directed toward the same person." Later in the same paper (1912) he says: "Where the capacity for transference has become essentially limited to a negative one. . . . there ceases to be any possibility of influence or cure." In 1915 (a) Freud referred to the positive erotic transference as a "resistance." An unambivalent positive transference is just as much a barrier to ego integration, or an indication of failure of integration, as is an unambivalent negative transference. This was illustrated in the present instance when the patient was preoccupied with the idealized relation between us and felt immune to suffering. One night, after having concentrated all day on this idealized relation, she dreamed of an aunt who withheld sweets, while I gave them to her. The next day she was able to retain milk and cookies and became outgoing and generous with the other patients. She felt, however, that such bountiful feelings were possible only within the hospital. Outside of the hospital people were seen as deprived and withholding.

A dream of mine showed me how much I was immersed in the splitting of her ego and our relationship. This is an example of the interpenetration of the ego of the patient and the therapist which I believe is inevitable in intensive work with a patient with diffuse ego boundaries. On the evening before my dream, the patient had expressed smug satisfaction with being in the hospital, which linked us continuously, so that she had been able to be comfortable during the preceding 48 hours when I had not seen her. That night I dreamed of a sculptor creating a perfect statue. As I awakened I thought it had to do with my patient having found something that she needed in life. I knew also that the dream represented the restoration of a loss for me, and this was confirmed when I made a slip in reporting the dream to a colleague and used the word "surgeon" instead of "sculptor." This referred to my feelings about a recent serious illness treated surgically in a member of my family. My reactions to this surgical procedure had included a feeling of having suffered an irretrievable loss and having sustained a severe injury to myself. I knew that restoration (the perfect statute) was impossible in my own situation, and through my dream I realized how much I wanted to share omnipotent delusional expectations with the patient, and to believe that both of our idealized fantasies could magically be realized, so that we would be spared the necessity of the difficult task of acceptance of reality.

Symbiosis IV: Differentiation from Symbiosis

My patient often complained that she could not feel my presence during the treatment hours, and for a long time my response was to feel reproached and guilty, as though I should somehow make her feel my presence despite her withdrawal. *She was enormously reproachful when she talked about my perfection* as a nurturing object, since, except for the occasional moments of successful nonverbal communication, the "perfection" with which she invested me was not available for her. Except for accusing me of being unavailable, she was usually withdrawn during the sessions. It was helpful to me when I realized that *accusing and reproaching were the only ways she could spontaneously relate to me as myself, a real and separate person.* To try to behave in ways that made me ineligible to be reproached meant cutting off *the only way she could communicate.*

Although the patient reproached me for not being close to her and tried desperately to view closeness as only idealized and perpetually pleasurable, there were frightening aspects to closeness. We found that "oneness," fusion, was sought partly because closeness between two separate persons was intolerable to her not only because closeness was temporary and implied separateness, but also because closeness stimulated frightening impulses.

Thoma (1967) finds the kleptomania is a frequent symptom in cases of anorexia nervosa, presumably the outcome of inhibition of oral intaking impulses with a concomitant asceticism. The only way in which such greediness was manifest in this case was in her demand for my total, undivided attention. She was most ascetic in her attitudes except for her demand for closeness to me.

In contrast to this demand, she withdrew whenever I introduced any thoughts of my own into our sessions. Telephone interruptions, for example, not only took my attention away from her, but also introduced aspects of my own life into our relationship. In other words, telephone interruptions led not only to distance between us, but also to closeness, which she said she wanted but which was intolerable to her.

At the same time that she was demanding and reproachful about needing my undivided attention, she treated me in an unusually gentle and considerate manner, often adapting to my needs better than I adapted to hers. For example, she made whatever changes in her schedule were required in order that I could see her at times that were convenient for me.

In her notes to me she began to describe fantasies of sexual union with me and stressed her need for closeness. I noticed that when she handed the notes to me she did it so gingerly that she almost dropped them before I could grasp them. It was as though she was afraid to touch my hand. When I commented on the contrast between the contents of the notes and the way in which she handed them to me, her first association was that she was afraid that I would be disgusted by contact with her. Then she remembered that as a child she had "horrible, disgusting" dermatitis of her feet and was certain that her mother, when rubbing lotion on them as ordered by the dermatologist, had hated doing so. I felt at first that being hated was better than being regarded as nonexistent, and that she could maintain some control over feeling hated as long as she believed that something "disgusting" about herself caused it (Seton, 1965). Touching was conflictual also because it was linked with my being separate rather than a part of herself.

She insisted that she only wanted me to move into her room and live in bliss with her. We would need neither to eat nor to excrete, but would be totally preoccupied with one another and totally self-sufficient. Then she had a nightmare in which spiders moved into her room and totally filled it. Her association was that she had seen a frightening spider in the basement of her parents' home when she retreated down there to get away from feeling forced to react to others at a family gathering. I interpeted that the spiders represented me and at the same time represented the anxieties against which she wanted me to protect her. She then thought of her previous nightmares that usually had consisted of believing that she was "full" and could not get "empty." Before treatment she had feared being defenseless against dangerous food inside. During treatment these nightmares had changed, and she began to feel guilty about the fate of the good food she had eaten. Then she had a new memory, of having felt nauseated whenever close to her mother, at some period of childhood. She remembered that before this she had felt only longing to be closer to her mother than was physically possible. I interpreted that our neither eating nor excreting in the fantasied state of idealized oneness showed that our mouths and excretions were dangerous to one another. She remembered a childhood nightmare in which someone was trying to kill her and she picked up the telephone to call for help. But it turned out that the person to whom she called for help was the same as the one who was trying to murder her. It seemed to me that remembering this nightmare was consistent with the interpretation that I represented not only a rescuer but also a persecutor, and that we were working at a level where object differentiation was a central problem. She then said that it was her mouth that was dangerous, not mine, and that *there were two kinds of "oneness," a good kind and a terrifying kind. "Good oneness" meant that she was inside of me, while frightening, "bad oneness" meant that I was inside of her.*

The patient's hospital room was near the elevator. Once when she was feeling very badly I waved goodby to her as I left the hospital floor. From then on this became a requirement and I habitually waved to her as I left the floor. One evening I waved goodby to her as usual as I left, but later that evening I returned to the floor. I knew that waving to her was important but the second time I left the floor I was tired and did not go to her door to do so. The next day she told me that she had seen me at the nurses' station the second time, and so knew I had returned to the floor, and became "enraged" after I left, closed her door and began attacking furniture and bed clothes, and banging her head against the wall. She kept repeating "I can't believe it." What she "could not believe" was first that I hated her so much as she decided I did. Then she realized that the state of being enraged contained potential anger at me, and she "could not believe" that she possessed such anger. She also "could not believe" that she was dependent on a separate person and "could not believe" that she was not a boy. *Until I pointed out the connection in the next session, she had not known that her rage and anger were precipitated by my failure to wave to her.* Before I linked her "rage" with my behavior, she knew only that she had decided that I hated her. I told her that I had known that it was important to her for me to say goodby to her but that it had felt too burdensome to me at that moment, so I left without doing so. She felt *relieved* when I told her this. She could accept my feeling tired and burdened, and such feelings were less threatening to her than the hatred she imagined I felt toward her. In the same way, open expression of my resentment of her combinations of demanding and rejecting behavior always brought relief to her. Only after we repeatedly went through periods during which I became aware of my own negative feelings toward her and toward continuing to work with her and interpreted them, did she begin to be able to sustain a nurturing memory that did not turn hateful between sessions.

The following episode illustrates integration of previously dissociated mental images and affects. On one occasion my schedule required that there be thirty-six hours between her appointments rather than the usual twenty-four hours. She telephoned me in the middle of the interval and said that she "just needed to call, and didn't know why." Over the telephone I commented that I understood her need to call as a reasonable consequence of the unusually long interval between appointments and that I was glad that calling was helpful to her. The patient heard my words but simultaneously felt, and believed with a sense of absolute reality, that I was thinking and feeling the opposite. She felt that I was thinking that it was unreasonable of her to call, and that I hated her for calling. This while I was saying that it was reasonable for her to call and that I was glad that it was helpful for her to call. She heard the words, but at the same time became aware of thoughts which she felt were in my mind, opposite from the words that she heard me say. Then during the night she had a nightmare in which her sister was saying critical things about her.

This was an important episode because during her next session the patient was able to recognize that she had created the image of my hating her. In contrast to her usual grimness the patient smiled when I pointed out that the criticizing sister and the criticizing me were both products of her own feelings. She was able to bring somewhat closer together the two pictures of me, one hating her and one loving her, which were so important to her. Previously, good experiences had failed to counteract her "nightmare expectations" because the nightmare expectations had been kept so widely separated from the good experiences that the two had not come into contact with one another. Along with realization of conflict about closeness, which she called "two feelings in myself," she became aware of two pictures of me. She had perceived me, as she had perceived her mother in childhood, as "all good," no matter how I treated her. She began to be able to be aware of me as having human failings, being unable to see her some days and seeing other patients, for example, rather than her having to go out of existence and not be aware of interruptions, or to deny them by means of delusional oneness.

At this point she recovered a memory of a mixed perceptual image that she had when she saw her mother's breasts in childhood. At the same time that she saw her mother's breasts as they actually were, she had a mental image of hallucinatory vividness, of bloody destruction. Here again, as in the initial transference reaction of simultaneous awareness of separateness and oneness, there were two parallel realities: the realistic external and the revised internal perception. Both felt real, although she recognized the need to keep secret the perception of bloody destruction. In her relationship with me, the patient needed to be able to deal with two perceptions that were both self-created, the nightmare and the beautiful dream. She externalized both onto me, and then needed to get me to deal with her nightmare by changing my behavior from a personification of a nightmare to a personification of a beautiful dream. The therapeutic problem was that I repeatedly felt as though I really and truly were her nightmare, and as though I should behave in "antinightmarish" ways, to impersonate an antidote to waking and sleeping nightmares. This correlates with the fact that she had felt, and believed with absolute sense of reality, that the hateful thoughts and feelings about her existed in my mind while she heard me say the opposite over the phone. This was a delusional transference, and I had constantly to deal with a delusional response to it within myself.

Symbolism and Continuity

In talking about intolerable separations from her mother in childhood she said "Mother went away into another part of her life, but I had no life except with mother, so I died whenever she left." Therefore "there was not a reunion when mother returned," but rather the patient had to "start life again" each time. As a result of this, time was discontinuous for her.

She repeated this exactly with me. Whenever I had to cancel an appointment, she got no comfort from the fact that we had another appointment the following day. "Time ceased to exist, and there was no tomorrow." Her defense was the "oneness," to which she withdrew during the sessions, and which she tried to maintain between the sessions, the alternative being pain and deadness.

An interpersonal relationship can be constant, but instinct-driven activity such as eating or sex is intermittent. The patient could only maintain a constant interpersonal relationship precariously, in idealized fantasy. There were a few occasions on which she could enjoy masturbation when she thought I wanted her to enjoy it, and much later she could enjoy it on the rare occasions when she became able to forget me. But both the feeling that I wanted her to enjoy it and the freedom to forget me without panic were difficult for her to sustain. Often she could not let herself enjoy anything, because of feeling that any enjoyment interfered with concentration on the positive relation between us. For example, she went to a concert, but could not let herself enjoy the music. She said that to have enjoyed it would have been a betrayal of our relationship and would have involved losing [her memory of] me. She said that even if she did not enjoy herself, just to survive when apart from me could be a betrayal of our relationship. "If I were true to you [during a separation] I would die, you and I would both die."

The way in which she began to move from discontinuity or defensive "oneness" between sessions toward a continuous relationship was by giving symbolic meaning to the physical surroundings. The hospital came to stand for an image of me as loved and loving and always with her. This she said was the main reason why it was better for me to see her at the hospital than for her to live at home and see me at the office. The important thing was, she said, that since I saw the room at the hospital that was *hers*, in contrast to my office, which was *mine*, the hospital environment came to have the meaning of bridging space and time between us, establishing continuity from one visit to the next. It became important for her that I be interested in her physical environment. Gradually she began to introduce her own possessions into her hospital room, and was pleased and relieved when we discussed her books and hobby materials. But I noticed that she rarely initiated discussion of them. At first I waited until she mentioned them. It took me a long time to realize that having them in view was a communication to me, and that she needed me to notice and acknowledge them and bring them into our discussion. Otherwise, "the risk of talking about them is too great. If I would start talking about them it might make you too far away, because there's a feeling of jumping into another part of my head when I talk about those things before you do, and it's scary if it's jumping away from you." I think that she was afraid to initiate discussion of the books and other objects because talking about them involved relating to me as a separate person, and she needed reassurance that I was with her when she "jumped into other parts of her life." The physical environment of the hospital acquired the significance of a "transitional area" to which we both contributed and in which our relationship could have continuity (Winnicott, 1953). In this area the patient could not only link one visit to the next, but also could link her subjective perception of herself, of me, and of our relationship, with objective external perceived reality. She was able to broaden the area in which she felt confident, and began taking courses in a local university, saying that she could do so because I had shown interest in her books.

The gradual but slow evolution of symbolism led toward a midposition between absolute union, "oneness," and absolute separateness, "broken oneness." The patient found that she liked to be awakened an hour or so before she had to get out of bed in order to have "drifting time." She said that always in the past she had gone to sleep and awakened quickly, and that now for the first time there was "a between," and that this "between" was very valuable to her. The "between" depended on trusting the hospital bed and the hospital room, trusting that she would not wake up to see an enormous threatening "presence." The main thing that made it important for there to be an "in between," a state in between sleeping and awakening in the morning, was that it enabled her to "remember dreams, rather than to have feelings from dreams carry over into waking life." She said that before she had the "in between" time she would dream of eating me during the night and then awaken suddenly in the morning and feel afraid and guilty all day about the consequences of having eaten me. When she was able to have the "in between," she remembered the dream and *remembered* the feeling in the dream but was free of this feeling during the day.

The patient was addicted to me except when she could use symbols of our relationship, and this depended on a change from ideal and persecutory images of me to an "ordinary" one, which included my shortcomings, such as my accepting phone calls during her sessions, and included her feelings of sadness about the loss of the idealized relationship.

This went along with her having let herself be aware, at about the same time, of the existence of my other patients. On days when I could not go to the hospital she came to my office, and it was then that she experienced jealousy "for the first time," in the waiting room at the office. She had of course been exposed to my other patients before, but "never saw them until now."

Understanding of her intense jealousy of other patients helped me to deal with it nondefensively. The patient was the youngest of four siblings, and for a long time I thought that her preoccupation with jealousy of other patients was based on fear of sharing a limited supply of nurture with real and imaginary siblings. However, her complaint was not just that she had to share me with others. It related more to the *reasons* for my seeing her. The way in which she experienced jealousy of other patients was related to her feeling that I came to the office or to the hospital not to see her but to see someone else, and only happened to see her just because I happened to be there. She stressed that she needed to see me in order to survive, and that she was dependent on seeing me but the dependence was on my whim or on my being available only because some other patient needed to see me and I was there to see the other patient, not to see her. Eventually I recognized that this experience, as almost everything else in her life, could be understood in terms of her traumatic infantile history and her dominant anxiety. It was not that the other patients were so much rivals for my attention, taking some of my attention away from her, as it was, more specifically, that she was making use of what I offered "for survival," without being able to feel good about it, because what I offered was not based only on her needs, but on other considerations. In this instance the other considerations were my obligations to other patients, which determined what I did, and if she happened to be able to utilize what I happened to do for her, she could "survive." I felt this related to the infantile situation. In infancy she received nurture which enabled her to survive, but which was not given in a way that enabled her to join up the nurture with her own inner needs. As a result she had never been able to connect appetite arising from inside, with food as something to satisfy her appetite. Instead, she ate compulsively and did so in relation to other feelings than appetite.

In infancy she had been given to on the basis of her mother's needs and by the nurse who demanded she be "no trouble to them." As a result of this she had survived, but had never been able to enjoy what she received. The scheduling of what was given to her as an infant was based on the needs of *other* people, and I think that this is the important element that was repeated or remembered in the complaint that I saw her on the basis of the needs of other people, at times that I arranged to fit the needs of other patients rather than to fit her needs. She was unable to see that she was one of the people whose needs determined when I came to the hospital. The idea of overlapping or mutuality of needs such that her needs, the needs of other patients, and my own needs all contributed to the time that I came to the hospital, was not meaningful to her. If I did things for any other reason than *exclusively* for her, she felt that what I did was done in order to shut her up, to make her stop wanting, stop existing, to destroy her. In a note the patient wrote: ". . . why can't I be satisfied seeing you instead of needing also to be the only reason behind it all? I am ashamed that I need to be the reason you come to the hospital tomorrow. Seeing you is not enough."

The meaning of her need to "be the reason" for my behavior was made clear by her reaction to my anger, as I gradually became more free to express it toward her: she found it particularly satisfying, and we found that this was because she felt that I became angry at her because of something she had done and this was a "link between us." This differed from usual masochism in that the patient was not *motivated* to provoke me to mistreat her or to be angry at her. She did, however, get relief and satisfaction when she could see that her behavior had provoked me to anger. She contrasted this with the way in which she had experienced her mother's anger: "Mother used to get angry at me but it never had anything to do with me." So just as with jealousy, the essential need was for me to react personally to her rather than to subject her to my behavior, loving *or* hating, based on motives derived from other aspects of my life, not related to her.

As her awareness expanded, she was increasingly disturbed by the limits of my attentiveness, interest, and dependability. For several reasons this was a problem for me. The patient almost never experienced anything good happening during the therapeutic hours. Just as with the compulsive eating and vomiting which the sessions replaced, she "needed them [the sessions] to survive," but anything which made her feel really positively good was something which occurred outside of the framework of the regular therapeutic routine. If someone had asked her what was good about her relationship with me she could only have mentioned events in "the other 23 hours," or things that were not part of the routine, formal, therapeutic interaction during her sessions. By this I refer to such things as the way I greeted her or said goodby to her, or the way I responded to her when she telephoned, or the episode of my turning out the light, things that were not part of the routine therapeutic interaction between us. I once got up and closed a window to reduce outside noise when the patient was talking very softly, and later she wrote me a note expressing gratitude that I had wanted to hear her. Listening to her for years did not convince her that I wanted to hear her—only a concrete action did.

Things that made her feel bad could of course happen both outside of the standard therapeutic situation and within it. Outside of the sessions there was always the chance that she would encounter another of my patients, or that I would make her feel bad by failing to respond in just the right way when she telephoned, or that I would cancel a session, or in some other way fail to meet her expectations. For example, she always hoped to see me outside of the office. When one day she actually did see me downstairs in the lobby of the building in which I have my office, she felt that this was "awful," because actually seeing me outside of the office threatened or destroyed her internalized image of me as part of herself rather than having a separate existence outside of her.

The routine interaction became something absolutely taken for granted as "necessary for survival." Its disruption could be felt to have negative value, but she did not experience its presence as having positive value. It was simply a basic condition necessary for existence. I found it to be a source of considerable strain on me in working with this patient, that she was aware only of my shortcomings, deficiencies, and unreliability, and was constantly hurt by them, while showing no appreciation of any positive elements in my work with her.

Here I want to expand on the nature of the strain which I felt in connection with this particular aspect of the patient's behavior and feelings. For the first two years of her treatment she was not disturbed by my other patients and was not disturbed by my accepting occasional telephone calls during her sessions, or my rustling papers during long silences. Later, when she began to be disturbed by these things, she said that heretofore she had been unaware of them. As she became aware of them she began to show continual reproachfulness toward me because of my unreliability. She had never cried in my presence, but now she began to have tears running down her cheeks, and to feel sadness rather than pain. She began to remember every instance in which I cancelled an appointment or accepted a telephone call during her session or in some other way failed her. On the other hand she had "no memory," she said, of times between these disturbing episodes, times when I was in fact reliable for her. The strain I felt resulted from a feeling that I expended great effort to be reliable for her, and yet she reacted only to instances of my unreliability. I needed to find some understanding of this in order to help myself not to become irritated and discouraged with her when over long periods of time the only thing that she expressed toward me was how hurt she was by my shorcomings. I was helped by realizing that she could not have been aware of the episodes of unreliability if it had not been for a surrounding framework of reliability with which the unreliability contrasted. From this point of view I could say that *she was implicitly recognizing reliability and showing appreciation in the only way that she could, by being hurt by my unreliability* (Winnicott, 1954).

The patient complained about being unaware of my presence during her sessions. While she said this, she was sitting with her eyes closed, immobile, looking altogether withdrawn. She seemed to be reproaching *me* because of *her* defenses, as though I should make the defenses unnecessary, perhaps by impersonating a loved and loving object that could be identified with the idealized "all good" picture of me with which she tried to establish "oneness" and from whom there would be no need to withdraw. We found that it was futile for me to try to accept her invitation to break into her isolation from me as a real, separate, external person. There were many opportunities for me to accede to her requests that I say or do something of an actively giving nature, which momentarily gratified her and reduced the withdrawn behavior. It had temporary comforting effect for her, but then the withdrawn state recurred, and when it recurred while I was still trying to reach out in active ways, it did so despite my efforts. At such times I became frustrated by the failure of my efforts, and became resentful of the patient. I would again find myself thinking of getting rid of her, wondering whether she should be treated by some other psychiatrist, perhaps with drugs or even with shock. This fantasy clearly expressed my hostility to the patient, and I told the patient how she made me feel. I found it necessary to interpret to the patient that I wanted not to try to violate her isolation. This interpretation was partly for her, but it was mainly necessary for me, to remind myself not to be drawn into trying the impossible. Gerald Adler (1972) reports very similar experiences. He describes patients who feel hopeless and helpless and stimulate hopelessness, helplessness, and hatred. In agreement with Freud's (1910, 1915a) stress on the patient was often re-creating an early infantile relationship with a parent, in which the patient and the parent had experienced mutual hopelessness, helplessness, and hatred. In agreement with Freud's (1910, 1915a) stress on the inevitable failure of efforts to gratify by concrete action the infantile impulses that arise in the transference, Adler warns of the dangers of trying to gratify the patient's expectations of magical rescue. He points out that such efforts can lead to mutual regression of patient and therapist with destructive consequences.

I interpreted to the patient that I had to inhibit my reaction to her withdrawal, which was characterized by my trying to reach out to her and then becoming resentful and wanting to get away from her when I failed. I interpreted that when I felt this way we were again and again repeating the infantile pattern, with me again and again becoming a mother who wanted her to not exist. For a long time the patient did not experience withdrawing as something which she did, but experienced it only as something coming from me. Her demeanor was accusing and made me feel as though I should be reacting to the accusation by some change in my behavior that would relieve her discomfort and make withdrawal unnecessary. It always helped when I talked about learning from her that it was inadvisable for me to make efforts to counteract the isolation which she imposed on our relationship, exploring as fully as possible my own reactions and interpreting the repetition of the infantile situation. She said, "You're like the penis and eating and vomiting, except you're a person instead of a thing." But she needed me to be as dependable as a "thing," totally under her control, and she became "terribly sad" when she had to recognize my failure to be reliable. At the same time, she said that she "would not want to go back to things," and was concerned about my being unable to stand the intensity of her needs. The absolute all-or-none quality of her needs was somewhat softened and some capacity for compromise and mutuality appeared at times, when I could express my feelings and when she could let herself be aware of my feelings. When I could acknowledge my shortcomings compared to a material possession and at the same time feel and express a wish to be reliable for her, this could at times be "as good as your actually being as controllable as a thing," but at other times she expressed only reproach for my failure to be a possession, a part of herself, or to make her a part of myself.

The following is a note that I wrote at this time. It illustrates my efforts to deal with her reproachfulness:

The only feeling that Miss X. is able to initiate toward me *as a separate person* is reproachfulness. Other than that, she is withdrawn into a relationship with an idealized figure, which she wants me to impersonate. To behave in a reassuring manner that involves an attempt to impersonate the idealized figure could be looked at in many ways. On the positive side there is the idea that I could perhaps hope to bring the idealized figure more into line with external reality by principal way of relating to the external world, and that without it she has little well as in the inside world. But on the other hand it seems to me that such impersonation cuts off awareness of the one relationship with external reality that she is able to initiate with me *from her end*, namely reproachfulness.

Her reproachfulness could be understood on a symbolic basis. Reproaching me for being too distant could provide reassurance that she has not incorporated me, while at the same time she is identified with a reproachful, damaged, incorporated image of me.

It is possible that one of the reasons that this patient is at times difficult for me is that I have a particular, personal, idiosyncratic hypersensitivity to the kind of mute, accusing reproachfulness that I have to absorb if I am to have any relationship with her at all. It is helpful to realize that reproachfulness is her principal way of relating to the external world, and that without it she has little or no relationship with that world.

If I behave in ways that block her from feeling reproachful to me, then in one sense I am rejecting her only way of achieving a relationship with an object that is truly external and real. It is not only by an angry reaction to her reproaches that I reject her way of relating to me as an external object, but also by being so intimidated by her reproachfulness that I try to change into an impersonation of an idealized, all-giving guardian angel.

The patient felt greatly *relieved* after I told her how her constant reproachful-ness made me angry at her and made me not want to see her. She said that when I expressed my anger she did not have to concentrate on trying to figure out what I might be feeling because she now knew, and it was better when anger was "really between us rather than growing wild in my head. It's not as frightening to know as to imagine. I had to think of mother as perfect. When your hating me is in my head it just grows and grows, but when you said you were angry at me that was good; it didn't keep growing. It was in between us rather than only in you or only in me. When I knew you hated me really, I knew you loved me too, but before, when it was only in you or only in my head, it turned into all hate."

At this point she had a few moments during which she recognized that exclusive love was not an answer either: "When I think you have only love for me I have to feel the same way, only loving, and if any other feelings come in they have to stop or to be turned against myself or against someone else."

Fantasies of doing things to one another, such as biting, swallowing, and sexual activities, and the need to call repeatedly between hours, when she felt hated, gave way temporarily to a feeling of dependable continuity of the relation-ship, with feelings of being loved, after I expressed my anger toward her (Winnicott, 1947). She said that while she was feeling that the relationship was dependable, she could forget about me without anxiety.

Memory and Time

One of her constant complaints was that she would always and eternally be unhappy. Some feeling of hope that she could lead a better life arrived at the time when she began to *remember* experiences such as depression and other unhappiness in the *past*, rather than experiencing them as always overwhelm-ingly present and immediate. *During periods when she could remember un-happiness in the past, she did not feel doomed to interminable unhappiness in the future.* The idea of eternity seemed to stem from the continuous experi-ence in the present of something which could not be experienced as a memory of the past. Rather than repression and the lifting of repression, I believe that what we saw was the development of mental structure so that, in certain areas of feeling, the function of memory could come into operation for the first time.

When the patient had used "deadness" as a defense, she had felt that time and the passage of days were meaningless because, she said, "This is not my life, my life has not started yet. It will start at some future time." I think that the division of her personality into a secret inner self surrounded and protected by an "outer self" was a determinant of this particular experience. The "secret inner self" did not have relationships with other persons, and had therefore accumulated no memories of experiences with the outside world. In addition, the "secret inner self" included the vulnerable infantile self, and remained an infant. This is an aspect of fixation. When the patient "started remembering" and was more hopeful, she called it "being alive." She valued this highly but considered it frightening. It made her feel vulnerable to intense feelings in ways that she never had been when she was what she had called "being dead." She was intolerant of any and all changes in her surroundings. For example, when the hospital administration moved her from one hospital room to another she felt desperate and distraught. She said that in her previous "world of eating and vomiting" she had been immune to the passage of time and to environmental changes.

Risk of Feeling Alive

As she began to feel more alive and more vulnerable she wondered whether she was wasting opportunities for experiencing life. This added to her sadness, which was associated with the beginning of integration and the experiencing of ambivalence in the transference. Earlier, her reaction to the threat of integration of a kind that would lead to the achievement of ambivalence had been to "go out of existence," subjectively. This is characteristic of schizoid reactions (Klein, 1948). It is possible to correlate this with the lesser suicidal potential of schizoid and schizophrenic patients compared with depressive patients. In the schizoid type of reaction, one part of the personality is put out of existence, destroyed, or, in the patient's words, "killed." The schizophrenic patient is protected against the dangers of actual suicide which the depressive patient experiences because in schizophrenia the destruction, the "death," has already occurred. When, however, the patient takes the risk of coming to life subjectively and affectively, he becomes vulnerable to depression and actual suicide. This patient said that in the past all she ever wanted to do was to die and to be dead and to stop feeling, and that eating and vomiting, "full and empty," was a way of stopping feelings. She now said that she was experiencing a different kind of sadness than any which she had previously experienced. Sadness now included there being "something to be sad about," a new development for her. She was sad about the memory of her relationship with me and my absence during intervals between sessions. With greater integration and continuity of experience, and "something to be sad about," she felt "human," rather than making herself into a "feelingless thing" which she said she had done in the past. Any disruption of the continuity of our relationship now led to the sadness but she *no longer had the global, all-encompassing pain.* As to causes of disruption, she showed *less* disturbance when I went away for a week than when I cancelled one session or accepted a telephone call or rustled papers during a session. The reason she gave for this difference was that when I went away for a week she became "numb and dead again, and did not know it; time stopped so I didn't really wait for you to return." When I cancelled one session, however, she remained "alive," and had to "stretch" her ability to wait for the next session, and suffered. It was this kind of experience that made her "question whether [she] ever should have come to life."

The following is a note that I wrote after a session at this time. It illustrates the fluid state of my ideas, and how I had continually to try to sort out my feelings from hers:

Wednesday:

"Miss X. has 'come to life,' and has memories of being "with" me. As a result she is thrown into deepest despair when she feels that she is not "with" me, while we are sitting in the same room. I suppose this is what is meant by statements that psychotherapy of schizoid patients is cruel when it leads to synthesis of the ego. She no longer has the compulsive eating and vomiting to resort to, to avoid needing continuity of relatedness with another person. Therefore when she remembers times when it felt as though she and I were "together," she feels infinitely sad about the loss of something, which previously she did not have to lose. Her need to try to avoid the experience of separation can still lead her to feel lack of contact. If we are not 'together' during the time that I am with her during the sessions, then there is no parting. This is a partial explanation only. I don't think that I fully understand the way in which she experiences lack of contact. There certainly is an implicit reproach which is of course of positive value in that it presupposes the possibility of self-object differentiation. When I empathize with her suffering, it makes real (realizes) a state of oneness between us. If suffering is shared, and if she suffers because of me, then suffering can help to bridge the time between one session and the next. On the other hand, she often is right when she complains about lack of contact; I do find myself drifting off into my own reverie during her long silences. I am wondering if I can somehow or other use this in connection with the previous formulation about the necessity for me to deal with my death wishes against her before she can deal with her own suicidal preoccupations. Certainly it is true that 'reassuring' comments have a negative effect on her. She seems to gain relief from my open expression of the way in which she affects me, although this is difficult to detect, since her principal characteristic is silent immobility. When she can see ways in which she affects me it affirms contact between us, and this may be of more importance than the question of whether she affects me in positive or negative ways."

In schizophrenic and schizoid states, defensive "deadness" has either occurred already or subjective aliveness has never been achieved. When this patient began to make tentative steps toward advancing from schizoid withdrawal, however, she was running the risks of being alive in relation to me. As a result of being alive she could cease to be alive or commit suicide. While becoming more "alive," "human," dependent and vulnerable, she lost the compulsive eating and vomiting as a universal comforter, a symbol of denial that she was a separate person who needed other persons.

Period of Symptomatic Improvement

The patient left the hospital and lived in her apartment. She resumed her college program at a university and worked part-time in a typical student's job in a restaurant. She did well in both her academic work and her job and enjoyed them. Part of the enjoyment was zest for the activities, part of it was still that studying and working distracted her, and part of it was that exercise reassured her against getting fat. She ate selectively, mainly salads and cereals, but gained weight so that she was only thin, not emaciated. She was no longer constipated, and menstruation returned.

She continued writing notes to me between sessions, but she became able to talk to me freely. Writing the notes remained an important activity linking one session with the next, but communication no longer depended upon the notes.

When she first substituted concentration on our relationship for compulsive eating and vomiting she could eat almost nothing because the food "was" me. The ability to eat and to retain food was not achieved until she began to be able to retain a memory of me and of our relationship during periods between sessions. This depended on her ability to use symbols for our relationship. When she could do this she became able to forget me at times, and to eat more freely. Even after she began to be able to eat and retain other foods, however, she could not eat meat. She had liked apples, and one day she was eating an apple as I left the hospital floor. Immediately the apple became poisonous, and from then on she could not eat apples. I assume that the apple came to represent me at the moment of separation and was introjected with destructiveness (Freud, 1917, 1923). Later she became able to eat one half of an apple, keeping the other half visible to reassure her that it was truly an apple and not me.

Impulses and anxiety about biting off my penis appeared in her dreams and fantasies, rather than anxiety only about consuming my whole body.

When she could use symbols for our relationship, such as the hospital room and its furnishings, she was able to keep the continuity of our relationship alive between sessions. Whereas eating and vomiting had served to deny a relationship or the need for one, these new symbols were those of a relationship rather than representing denial of separateness or denial of need for anyone separate. Later she became aware that I had other patients and a family life, and she began to have moments during which she could even forget me and concentrate on other things. She began to experience the wishes for "oneness" as sexual wishes, and then for a time she resumed a sexual relationship with a man with whom she had had a brief sexual relationship in high school. At that time it had been unsatisfying, but when she resumed it, it was somewhat satisfying. She did not feel emotionally intimate with this man, and she could not permit penetration. During sexual activity, as in masturbation in childhood, she "always wanted something to go inside but nothing could because if it did, then I couldn't want anymore. To have things destroys them. I have to keep everything far away so I can still want it." What satisfaction she experienced during sex play now depended on her feeling secure that the memory of me would not be displaced by the relationship, and this depended on her feeling that I wanted her to be happy, a belief that was difficult to achieve and sustain. When something occurred that to her meant the loss of the idealized relationship with me, such as my going away for a holiday or becoming too real to fit her fantasy of me, she withdrew from other interests and activities. Others had told her to become active, and to direct her interests outward. But the problem was that when she lost the relationship with me she lost her capacity to want anything, and therefore her attachment to me, which I am calling an addiction, was still a prerequisite to other interests. As a result, I was not replaceable. I use the term addiction to describe her dependence on me, because of her need to use the relationship to deny that we were two separate persons (Winnicott, 1960a).

The gains that the patient made during treatment are important for this paper not because they were particularly striking. They were repeatedly achieved and lost, and were modest considering the enormous investment of time and effort by the patient and the enormous cost of treatment to her family. Their importance lies in the understanding of ego processes we achieve from observing the relation between clinical changes and events in the psychotherapy. It is for this reason that we so often stress clinical improvement in case presentations. I think the rarity of reports of cases in which there is no clinical improvement is not only the result of hesitation on the part of therapists to reveal failures, or of a need to boast about successes. I think it is rather that when there is no change in the clinical state during treatment, it is very difficult to describe a therapeutic *process*. We can then describe a clinical condition, for example, in conventional psychiatric terms, and we can describe the events of the psychotherapy and the psychotherapeutic relationship. However, the relationship between these two sets of data, the clinical state and the psychotherapeutic procedure, constitutes the therapeutic process, and this eludes us unless we can correlate changes in the clinical state with our psychotherapeutic procedure. Focusing upon the therapeutic process leads to emphasis on change, *both* progressive and regressive. It often happens, as in this case, that while we observe progressive changes in the process of therapeutic interaction, and can learn much from them, changes in the gross, objective, clinical picture are relatively small. Changes that look small to an outsider can be of the highest importance to the individual patient. For example, the replacement of compulsive eating and vomiting by addiction to me enabled the patient to feel alive and hopeful, but her total life was still restricted. Her gains were precariously held, and few of them were sustained continuously. They were achieved repeatedly, but lost whenever something happened that interfered with the continuity of our relationship. Too much stress upon "the thread" of our relationship threw her back into the earlier state, but with one difference, which I think is crucial: "the pain" did not recur. She felt sadness now, rather than diffuse pain. Sadness was associated with remembering me as a separate person, and remembering our relationship, during times when she felt that I was failing her. One advantage of sadness was that, like any suffering, she experienced it as a constant reminder of me and therefore a help in bridging separations. When she was able to forget about me, to abandon the need to remind herself constantly of my existence, there were other changes. Along with replacement of pain on separation by sadness came two new experiences: (1) What the patient called "drifting time," or "cloud time," a time between waking and sleeping, "between dreams and reality." It permitted her to remember frightening dreams rather than to have them fill her waking time with fear. (2) Enjoyment of hobbies, friends, and just living. She contrasted enjoyment with the previous dichotomy; pain and relief of pain. "Enjoyment" was something different from pleasure, which was linked in her mind with denial of pain and sadness. She called enjoyment a "between state," between pain and pleasure.

The patient was able to get along without telephoning during a four-day interruption. She said that this was because she was able to believe I was keeping my memory of her alive in my mind, although she still did not believe that *she* had preserved *her* memory of me during the interruption.

Negative Therapeutic Reaction

The patient began seeing a young man whom she had met in the hospital. She felt that she had much in common with him, and was able to talk more openly with him than she ever remembered having done with anyone before him. They spent nights together and she felt great peace and comfort in his presence. They had mutual masturbation and mouth-genital contact. She especially enjoyed swallowing his semen, because "the penis wanted her to have it," and there was no question of her stealing it from a reluctant source. She also enjoyed his fondling her, but they had no actual intercourse.

Then within the same few days two things happened that completely upset her adjustment: she told the man about her greatest secret, the eating and vomiting, and they had sexual intercourse. The day after intercourse, food became a dire threat, and she vomited after breakfast for the first time in over a year. This was the beginning of a recurrence of all her symptoms.

She felt that the young man had become "too real," and as a consequence I, too, had become "too real." In addition, she said that before intercourse he had "been" me, and after it he became a separate person, separate both from me and herself. Her major preoccupation again became the fear of losing me. Improvement meant "being disloyal" to me, and that I would abandon her. Therefore, she welcomed the return of her symptoms.

I cannot evaluate just how important my reaction to her improvement was in precipitating her exacerbation, but in one sense she was correct in linking improvement with losing me. I had welcomed the increased intimacy she was having with the young man. When she told me of her trust in him and her happiness with him I viewed it as an indication that she would become less dependent on me, and I had assumed that it signalled a successful end to her treatment in the near future.

When discussing this patient after the exacerbation of her symptoms, Dr. Bruno Bettelheim said that he would have forbidden her to have sexual intercourse. He said that this prohibition might have reassured the patient that I was not pushing her away. He said she may never achieve the independence that will enable her to sustain a sexual relationship.

The regression not only brought up problems similar to those we had experienced earlier but new problems as well. She was terrified that I could not tolerate the hatred of me that emerged, and tried to "feel nothing" rather than to experience it. Again, vomiting became a way of "feeling nothing."

The patient lost ten pounds and became weak and dehydrated. She recognized that starving was a way to avoid hating me. At the same time that I recognized that she needed to behave as she did, I found it difficult to preserve my objectivity while also being responsible for her total management, medical as well as psychiatric. I arranged to have an internist take responsibility for medical management during this time (Flarsheim, 1967). Thoma (1967) reports that this division of therapeutic responsibility is often helpful because patients experience forcible feeding as punishment. In addition, he reports that tube feeding of anorexia nervosa patients is often followed by suicide. With this patient, intravenous fluid was used on several occasions when the vomiting led to dehydration and electrolyte imbalance, but tube feeding was not used.

One Thursday she was particularly angry and hopeless, and then I was away for the following Friday, Saturday and Sunday. On Monday she said that this had been "a test," and the "test" had failed. By going away I had shown that I could not tolerate her anger, and that she could not trust me; it was "not safe" for her to have feelings and she now felt "nothing," and had no desire to live. She had frankly paranoid fears and delusions. She felt suicidal, and could not sleep at night because of fear that I or someone else would creep into her room and kill her. She no longer wanted me to be her therapist.

I told her that she did not have to want me, or like me, or trust me in order to see me, and she found this reassuring. It meant that we both might be able to include hateful as well as loving feelings in our relationship. She was then able for a time to link the need to call me between sessions with fear that her anger at me had destroyed me or our relationship.

She began to be able to take nourishment again, and wanted someone to feed her, so that she would not have to feel guilty. When she fed herself she felt that she was stealing food.

She was still likely to behave in self-destructive ways when frustrated rather than to become aware of anger at me, but when she could sustain the anger she also began to sustain the idea that I wanted her to live, and this helped her avoid self-destructive behavior such as starvation.

As the clinical condition improved, she became able to use help from other people in addition to myself. First, she asked to be fed by certain members of the hospital staff, selecting for this purpose particularly intelligent, sensitive, and dedicated young male psychiatric aides. A few weeks later her mother was feeding her, at first very hesitantly, and then with great pleasure both to the patient *and* to the mother. The mother told the patient that she was giving her the kind of care that she had not been able to give when the patient was an actual infant.

At the time of writing this the patient is again beginning to enjoy various activities that she had given up at the time of her regression, which I have called the negative therapeutic reaction. She is using her parents' home as a "base," and says she feels closer to them, and is able to be more open with them than she ever remembers having felt before. For example, she has been able to tell them about the eating and vomiting, which she considered so "shameful," and feels comfortable since they now understand some of the reasons for what was to them incomprehensible behavior in the past.

Thoma (1967) stresses the necessity for removing the anorexia nervosa patient from her family as a precondition for successful treatment. The reunion with this patient's family was something which she and her family arrived at spontaneously, and was something which neither she, the family nor I had anticipated. It is my impression that the type of nursing care the patient received from her mother was something which she had needed as a way of maturing beyond the infantile needs that the mother satisfied for her. If this is true, this care would have had to be provided by someone else if her family were not available. There are certain advantages in having it provided by the family. In the first place, who but the family would be sufficiently motivated to provide such care over whatever period of time is needed, and to make the sacrifices of other interests and activities in order to make time available to give such care? Secondly, as both the patient and her mother realize, *their new relationship enables the mother to relieve some of the guilt she felt because of having been unable to give the care that the patient needed during her infancy.* This was important, both for the patient and the mother. Because of feeling less guilty toward the patient, the mother became able to be less critical of her, and thus a "benign circle" was established which I believe will provide the patient with a better basis for subsequent development toward independence than she would have had without this reunion.

I believe it is important to stress that the reunion between the patient and the family was not imposed, or even suggested, by me. It evolved spontaneously, at a time and in a form that the patient and the family selected.

SUMMARY AND CONCLUSIONS

I have presented a suicidal patient with anorexia nervosa. My anxiety lest she commit suicide was based in part on my wish that she cease to exist, my wish to get rid of her. The patient had stimulated such a wish in me, and the course of her treatment shows promise that we will be able to use my ambivalence toward her as a way of freeing her of her own suicidal impulses.

In early infancy, her mother had wanted the patient not to exist. Although the mother's destructive wish toward the patient was originally an external factor, it started to affect her before she could conceptualize an external world of separate persons. Partial development toward individuation occurred, but the mother's destructiveness remained part of the patient and led to suicidal impulses and to defenses against suicide—first the delusion of being a boy and then compulsive eating and vomiting. Both of these served to support a withdrawn state in which no object-directed needs were experienced.

In the treatment, self-destructiveness again became destructiveness external to her, in my destructive impulses toward her, and this occurred before she was able to conceptualize a relation to me as a separate person. She needed to preserve loving "oneness" with me, and she maintained this by continuously concentrating on a self-created, idealized image of me. This meant no relationship with me as a separate person, profound withdrawal from relationships with anyone, and lack of integration of various aspects of her personality. Diffuseness of ego boundaries characterized not only her transference but also my reaction to her.

A psychotic transference characterized by addiction to the delusional "oneness" with me replaced her other symptoms, and my reaction to the psychotic transference was a crucial problem in the treatment. I believe this is an inherent part of the treatment of patients with defective ego boundaries. Experience and increased understanding of ourselves and of our patients raises the threshold at which we react to patients in primitive ways. My thesis is, however, that intensive work with patients with defective ego boundaries momentarily (for shorter or longer moments) disrupts our capacity for understanding and for implementation and application of that understanding in our work with the patient. Our therapeutic task becomes the *restoration* of that capacity within ourselves, and we can help the patient by sharing with him our problem of disruption and restoration of our own capacity for objectivity *insofar* as he is responsible for the disruption.

In order to have a separate life, and to be able to forget me, this patient must first build up constant dependable memories of herself and of me as separate and whole persons, hating as well as loving, failing one another as well as meeting needs, and in order to do this she must develop a capacity to symbolize the relationship between us, thus achieving continuity in the relationship. She made steps toward this when I interpreted my ambivalence to her, and related this in detail to the many ways in which her behavior led me to feel rejecting of her just as her mother had. After this happened several times she was able to experience her own ambivalence, and she began to separate herself from me and to retain sufficient integration of her ego—an intrapsychic rather than interpersonal "oneness," to survive as a separate person. She included all of herself in relationships.

Improvement of her life adjustment, and particularly success in an intimate relationship with a man, led her to feel abruptly separated from me and threatened with abandonment. At this point her symptoms recurred, and we again had to work through problems of "oneness" and separateness and of eating others and being eaten by them, that we both thought she had overcome.

My reaction of welcoming her independence may have contributed to her fear of independence, and her regression. Again, interpretation of *my* ambivalence, when I realized it, was followed by increased awareness of her own ambivalence toward me, and by the ability to seek help from other people, including her parents.

References

Adler, G., Helplessness in the Helpers," *British Journ. of Med. Psychol.*, Part 4, 45:315-326 (1972).

Bettelheim, B., *The Empty Fortress*. New York: Macmillan, 1967.

Bettelheim, B., "Regression as Progress," in *Tactics and Techniques in Psychoanalytic Therapy*, Vol. I, ed. by P. Giovacchini, pp. 189-199. New York: Jason Aronson, 1972.

Cohler, B. (1975). "The Residential Treatment of Anorexia Nervosa," This volume.

Ekstein, R., "The Acquisition of Speech in the Autistic Child," in *Children of Time and Space, of Action and Impulse*. New York: Appleton-Century-Crofts, 1966.

Flarsheim, A., "The Separation of the Therapeutic Setting from the Management of a Paranoid Patient," *Intern. Journ. of Psychoanal.*, Vol. 48, Part 4, 559-572 (1967).

Flarsheim, A., "Treatability," in *Tactics and Techniques in Psychoanalytic Therapy*, Vol. I, ed. by P. Giovacchini, pp. 113-131. New York: Jason Aronson, 1972.

Freud, S. (1910). " 'Wild' Psychoanalysis," *Standard Edition*. Vol. II, pp. 219-227. London: Hogarth Press.

Freud, S. (1912). "The Dynamics of Transference," *Standard Edition*. Vol. 12, 97-108. London: Hogarth Press.

Freud, S. (1914a), "Remembering, Repeating, and Working-Through," *Standard Edition*, Vol. 12, 146-156. London: Hogarth Press.

Freud, S. (1914b), "On Narcissism, an Introduction," *Standard Edition*. Vol. 14, 67-102. London: Hogarth Press, 1957.

Freud, S. (1915a), "Observations on Transference Love," *Standard Edition*. Vol. 12, 157-171. London: Hogarth Press, 1958.

Freud, S. (1915e), "The Unconscious," *Standard Edition,* Vol. 14, 159-215. London: Hogarth Press, 1957.

Freud, S. (1917), "Mourning and Melancholia," *Standard Edition*. Vol. 14, 237-258. London: Hogarth Press, 1957.

Freud, S. (1920), "Beyond the Pleasure Principle," *Standard Edition*. Vol. 18, 3-64. London: Hogarth Press, 1955.

Freud, S. (1923), "The Ego and the Id," *Standard Edition*. Vol. 19, 2-66. London: Hogarth Press, 1961.

Giovacchini, P. L., "Transference, Incorporation and Synthesis," *Internat. Journ. of Psychoanal.,* 46:287-296 (1965).

Giovacchini, P. L., "Transference, Incorporation and Synthesis, *"Internat. Journ. of Psychoanalytic Therapy,* Vol. I. pp. 137-169, New York: Jason Aronson, 1972.

Jones, E., "Pain," *Internat. Journ. of Psychoanal.,* Vol. 38:255-256 (1957).

Klein, M. (1946), "Notes on Some Schizoid Mechanisms," in *Developments in Psychoanalysis,* pp. 292-320, London: Hogarth Press, 1952.

Little, M., " 'R', The Analyst's Total Response to his Patient's Needs," *Internat. Journ. of Psychoanal.,* 38:240-254 (1957).

————. "On Basic Unity" *Internat. Journ. of Psychoanal.* 41:377-384 (1960).

Mahler, M., "On Child Psychosis and Schizophrenia—Autistic and Symbiotic Infantile Psychosis," *Psychoanal. Study of the Child,* 7:286-305 (1952).

Martin, P. (1974), "The Obnoxious Patient." This volume.

Searles, H. F. (1961), "Phases of Patient-Therapist Interaction in the Psychotherapy of Chronic Schizophrenia," in *Collected Papers on Schizophrenia and Related Subjects,* pp. 521-559, New York: International University Press, 1965.

Seton, P. H., "Uses of Affect Observed in a Histrionic Patient," *Internat. Journ. of Psychoanal.,* 46:226-236 (1965).

Spitz, R., *The First Year of Life,* New York: International Universities Press, 1965.

Tabachnick, N., "Counter-transference Crisis in Suicidal Attempts," *Arch. of Gen. Psych.,* 4:64-70 (1961).

Thoma, H., *Anorexia Nervosa,* New York: International Universities Press, 1967.

Winnicott, D. W. (1947), "Hate in the Countertransference," in *Collected Papers, Through Pediatrics to Psychoanalysis,* pp. 194-203. New York: Basic Books, 1958.

Winnicott, D. W. (1951). "Transitional Objects and Transitional Phenomena," in *Collected Papers, Through Pediatrics to Psychoanalysis,* pp. 229-242. New York: Basic Books, 1958.

Winnicott, D. W. (1954), "Metapsychological and Clinical Aspects of Regression within the Psychoanalytic Setup," in *Collected Papers,* pp. 278-294. New York: Basic Books, 1958.

Winnicott, D. W. (1960), "Countertransference," in *The Maturational Processes and the Facilitating Environment,* pp. 158-165. London: Hogarth Press, 1965.

Winnicott, D. W. (1960a), "String: A Technique of Communication," in *The Maturational Processes and the Facilitating Environment,* pp. 153-157. London: Hogarth Press, 1965.

Chapter V

The Obnoxious Patient

Peter A. Martin, M.D.

INTRODUCTION

I have previously reported descriptively on obnoxiousness in psychiatric patients and others (Martin, 1971). The subject of obnoxiousness was then in an early stage of investigation and consideration. Further studies have allowed for the presentation in depth in this paper of the psychodynamic and meta-psychological aspects of obnoxiousness. Since starting these studies, I have found no references to the subject of obnoxiousness in psychiatric or psychoanalytic literature. This is in itself surprising since once one's attention is called to the subject, recognition of its frequency in psychiatric patients is unavoidable. In retrospect, it was like discovering the obvious. Not only was it brought to my attention through my own patients but also through supervision of psychotherapy by psychiatric residents. A telling comment of a colleague was that my surprise at its frequency was due to the fact that I had not practiced hospital psychiatry for several years. It is constantly seen in hospitalized patients.

I think the most important reason for the lack of references to obnoxiousness in the literature is that it is not a symptom experienced by the patient. It is not something the patient feels, such as a mood or an affect. As will be shown later, it is a by-product of a disorder in reality testing resulting from the excessive use of the mechanism of denial. The patient, in fact, is not only oblivious of its presence but vigorously denies it when it is pointed out to him. Obnoxiousness is a feeling experienced by someone other than the individual who is being obnoxious. The dictionary defines the adjective, "obnoxious," in current use as "something objectionable, offensive or odious as, *obnoxious* practices or laws," and quotes from Macaulay's *History of England,* "Persons *obnoxious* to the government were frequently imprisoned without any other authority than a royal order." An important understanding derives from the phrase "to the government."

My awareness of the problem resulted from a series of patients presented to me by residents in whom obnoxiousness was an outstanding complaint *of the* family, ward personnel, and therapists, without awareness of it in the patients. Some of the patients presented would not have been hospitalized and some would have been discharged earlier had the level of their obnoxiousness been of a lower order.

The word *obnoxious* is not found in any diagnostic manual or in the index of any textbook of psychiatry or psychoanalysis. However, as so often happens, once my curiosity and interest were aroused the subject continued to be brought to my attention from surprisingly diverse sources.

Philippe Pinel, the first psychiatrist in France, converted the institutions for the care of psychotic patients from prisons to hospitals. The story of Pinel unshackling the inmates at Salpêtrière contains an interesting facet. Many of the people who were freed from their chains by Pinel and released were not mentally ill. They were public nuisances, individuals who were obnoxious to the authorities and then conveniently removed from the streets by being placed with mentally ill patients who themselves in their own way had become obnoxious to their families or to their society. Many of those released were political prisoners, which also was true in England, as indicated in the dictionary definition of obnoxiousness quoted above. In this vein, current newspaper reports from Russia indicate that individuals who are critical of the government are declared mentally ill and hospitalized for years. In many communities in the United States laws have been in effect for many years that make it a punishable offense to be "undesirable, objectionable, or generally obnoxious." That these laws are enforced selectively has but recently led to controversy and to a Supreme Court decision that struck down a Cincinnati ordinance making it a misdemeanor for "three or more persons to assemble on any of the sidewalks and there conduct themselves in a manner annoying to persons passing by." The Court declared the ordinance unconstitutionally vague because the individuals could not know in advance when they might be committing a crime. If it is against the law to be obnoxious, how many are sure they will escape?

The same holds true with psychiatric patients. There are psychiatric patients who could not legally be declared insane who are committed on temporary restraining orders before the court hearing. Hospitalization takes place for many reasons—one of these is to get an "obnoxious" person out of the family.

CLINICAL MATERIAL

The quality of obnoxiousness can be observed in patients falling into various diagnostic categories:

A. *Manic-Depressive Personality*

A striking clinical example of this phenomenon is the manic-depressive personality. During the depression, the patient is sad, experiences inner pain, is uninterested in caring for himself, and is to a degree a burden on the family. The patient may even ask to go into a hospital but the family refuses, stating that the patient is no big burden. The depressed keep to themselves in their low periods and cause little irritation. Gradually, as the patient's depressed mood lifts, the family is delighted as the patient is now active, helpful, and a pleasure to be with. In a typical case, the patient, feeling good, cleaned the house, went shopping for new clothes, had her hair done, and prepared dinner for the family. But she continued on into hyperactivity in which she became loud, threatening, seductive, combative, angry, critical, and insomniac. The patient, expressing her pleasure with life, felt no need for treatment. The family stated that she was now obnoxious and wanted her committed. This is a common picture in manic-depressive histories. *Obnoxiousness is one of the characteristics of the manic state.* Other diagnostic categories also include this characteristic.

B. *Borderline Character*

One patient, diagnosed as borderline character, was hospitalized because of verbal and physical battles with his wife and remained hospitalized because of similar battles with attendants and nurses. He would repeatedly criticize others for not doing what he though they should do for him. It was clear that his reality testing was defective. His irritating approach did not cause others to give him the attention and love which he demanded. Indeed, it achieved just the opposite response.

C. *Paranoid Personality*

Paranoid personalities are another category of patients in whom the quality of obnoxiousness intrudes upon interpersonal relationships. Their suspiciousness, distrust, denial of reality, attributing of hostile qualities to the other person, and inability to comprehend evidence to the contrary contributes to their being experienced as obnoxious individuals.

D. *Sociopath*

Some sociopaths are an interesting paradox in terms of obnoxiousness. At times they are the opposite of obnoxious. They can be so charming and personable that they have little difficulty in using and abusing other people. They have an ability to locate the weaknesses in the other person's reality testing and subtly to distort reality. It may be only after long suffering that the victim sees through the deceptions and in self-defense becomes outraged and indignant. Many therapists have found themselves in such predicaments. When the erstwhile victim attempts to reestablish the reality which he holds valuable, strong feelings of negativism arise and the sociopath is experienced as obnoxious.

E. *Hypochondriacal Personalities*

Physicians have a common term for a type of patient who they find obnoxious. They call them "crocks" and attempt to get rid of them by referral to psychiatrists. These so-called crocks are hypochondriacal patients. Repeated examinations disclose no organic reasons for the chronic complaints of the patient, who is not swayed in his needed conviction that he has a physical ailment. This attack on and distortion of the physician's reality evokes strong countertransference reactions in the physician, causing him to abdicate his position as a physician and to rid himself of this irritating, hypochondriacal distorter of reality.

F. *Character Disorder, Obnoxious Type*

The above nonofficial diagnostic category is the only one which fits the following person's history. It is given in greater detail than in the preceding diagnostic categories to convey the flavor of the quality of obnoxiousness as experienced by other people.

This twenty-five-year-old believed that her difficulties began when she was dismissed from law school for personal reasons. She was succeeding quite well academically at the school; however, she had many personal conflicts with the faculty who subsequently dismissed her. According to the patient there were no definite reasons why she was being dismissed, but a multitude of "small occurrences." These included such things as giving poor presentations and having poor interpersonal relations. On many occasions, she would tell teachers that they were doing a very poor job. Her treatment of secretaries was often rude and arrogant and there were many complaints regarding this. Prior to her senior year she was forced to see a psychiatrist because of her poor interpersonal relationships. After being forced to leave law school the patient worked in a law office and was subsequently dismissed because, again, she was unable to get along with the lawyers and secretaries. The patient quotes the lawyer as saying that she was "arrogant, overbearing and domineering," very similar terms to those used at the law school from which she was dismissed.

She got a job at a prison where a similar pattern was set up in her relationship with fellow employees. She was called to task several times by her supervisors because of the way she conducted herself with the prisoners. These difficulties seemed to be primarily those of berating prisoners, calling them names and treating them very much like "animals." She had much difficulty in relating to the secretaries and was totally lost as to why they seemed to shun her and to avoid inviting her to most of their social gatherings.

The mental status examination was essentially within normal limits. Mechanisms of denial became very prominent throughout therapy and the patient denied having any difficulties. Other instances of this patient's difficulties with other people can best be exemplified by the following examples. While in law school the patient was severely criticized by a professor because while the latter was conducting a seminar with the students, the patient was reading various magazines. When this was called to her attention, the patient put the magazines down, but only to return to them shortly afterwards and in later sessions. When the patient thus failed the course, she could not understand how this could be since she thought she had done very well. She quoted the professor as calling her a "terrible person" and a very "sick person."

At another job, she again had similar encounters with her boss, such as keeping him waiting while she talked to a friend on the telephone. After this incident the boss made it very clear that he came first and that personal calls would have to wait. This did not change the patient's behavior whatsoever and, in fact, she was reprimanded several more times for reading a newspaper right in front of the boss when she should have been working.

During the course of treatment, the patient would constantly contradict her therapist, get up from her chair in the office and take pencils out of his pencil holder without asking, and fondle them during the interview. At the termination of treatment, which the patient did against advice, she left without paying the remainder of her bill, on which she stated she was paying regularly to the clinic but which was not true. The general feeling that her therapist was left with was one of marked frustration.

DYNAMIC AND METAPSYCHOLOGICAL CONSIDERATIONS
OF OBNOXIOUSNESS

Jacobson (1953) in describing the development of the concept of the self states: "with advancing psychosexual and ego development and the maturation of reality testing, a more stable, uniform, and realistic concept of the self and a lasting firm cathexis of the self representations will normally be established." Development of reality testing also contributes to the concurrent establishment of lasting, firm cathexis of object representations. An understanding of the disturbances in these processes during early childhood leads to a deeper understanding of the problem of obnoxiousness. As indicated in the clinical material, a disturbance in reality testing is present in such individuals. If the function of reality testing involves a comparison of internal psychic reality with external, objectively verifiable reality, followed by a correction of internal reality where it is in blatant conflict with the external one, the individual experienced as obnoxious is lacking in this capacity. Instead of having the internal reality readily available for comparison and correction in the light of external reality, this type of individual desperately needs to deny the validity of external reality and to *force* the objects in reality to accept his internal reality as being the true state of the external reality. When he attempts this often impossible task, he may be experienced as obnoxious by others. Like Don Quixote, he dreams the impossible dream and attempts to force it upon reality.

Strangely enough this maneuver sometimes succeeds. In the cases of a *folie à deux* the primary psychotic individual may be experienced as obnoxious by others including his mate. In order to prevent separation and to resolve the conflicts, the mate adopts the inner psychic reality of the partner as his or her own inner psychic reality. The result is *folie à deux*, harmony between them, but now the two of them may be experienced as obnoxious by others. When hospitalized and separated, the primary partner maintains the psychosis while it fades away in the mate. Such accommodations in reality testing take place in all intimate relations but are not as dramatic or obvious as in *folie à deux*.

Jacobson (1953) states: "By a realistic concept of the self we mean a concept that mirrors only or mainly the state and the characteristics of our ego: of our conscious and preconscious feelings and thoughts, wishes and impulses, attitudes, and actions." The unrealistic concept of the self demonstrated in the patients studied resulted from their self-representations assuming the coloring of infantile images which remained cathected in the unconscious. Reconstruction during therapy of their childhood traumatic experiences placed their conflict in the area of an inability to give up their infantile belief in their own omnipotence. Maintaining this belief by distortions of reality and excessive utilization of the mechanism of denial was more important to them than the normal developmental pathway of accepting a strong love object that gives security and accepting the perceptions of external reality as directed by this love object. Although an inner psychic reality is achieved in which the belief in his own omnipotence is maintained, it results in (1) disturbances of reality testing; (2) maintenance of the pleasure principle as the guiding principle; (3) unrealistic self and object representations within the ego system; (4) and defective superego formation resulting from early infantile images of the self and the love objects (which form the core of the superego add ego ideal) remaining predominantly infantile and not being covered over by reality-oriented later additions. It is this inadeqate operation of superego functions which contributes to the sociopathic aspects of the obnoxious personality noted above.

The successful imposition of inner reality upon outer reality eliminates the necessity for distinctions between truth and falseness, reason, and unreason and the rule of reality principle over pleasure principle.

A clinical vignette illustrates the struggle of this narcissistic phase of psychosexual development. The woman described above had what was for her a typical relationship with a man. Her libidinous overcathexis of self along with an aggressive overcathexis of the object led to narcissistic and sadistic attitudes to the object. She played with him as in Freud's illustration of the child playing with the spool of string (making it disappear and reappear at his will to overcome his feelings of helplessness at his mother's disappearance and reappearance at her will) (Freud, 1920). She would get him to love her and then tell him she did not want him. When he proposed marriage, she lost interest, felt she could do better, and went looking elsewhere. He reacted to her obnoxious treatment of him by proposing to and being accepted by another woman. The impact of this reality finally shattered her mechanisms of denial and her misperception of reality. She had been firmly convinced that he could never find anyone as great as she was and that he would always be at her beck and call. She panicked, broke into his apartment when he refused to see her and pleaded with him to take her back.

This material led to childhood memories whose dynamics had determined her character structure. Her mother had been a demanding, controlling, tyrannical figure whom her husband could not tolerate; he abandoned her for alcohol and other women. The patient fought her mother's tyranny by developing a fantasy world of her own. She had an imaginary cat as a friend in whose existence she firmly believed and acted accordingly. She did not accept this overpowering love object for the sake of security. She preferred pleasure in a world of her own to security from her mother and thus never accepted the reality principle over the pleasure principle. Her poor reality testing and her missionary-type efforts to impose her inner psychic reality upon others caused her to be experienced by others as obnoxious from childhood on through chronological adulthood. The destruction of her mechanism of denial by her boy friend's action towards marriage with another and her inability to sway his decision resulted in her experiencing overwhelming anxiety in the face of the forced recognition of her helplessness.

The distinctions between truth and falseness, correctness and incorrectness, reason and unreason are not made by these patients and the acceptance of what is realistic and reasonable is intolerable to them. When the denial mechanism fails, as noted above, the first reaction is to master the narcissistic injury and build up the self by disparaging the love object. This the patient had done by projection onto him of her own inability to love. She tried to repair the hurt by switching the whole aggressive cathexis to the object representation and the libidinous cathexis to the self-image. As Jacobson (1953) has shown, this is the same process utilized by individuals suffering from cyclothymic depressions. When successful, it prevents the onset of a depression.

OBNOXIOUSNESS AND NARCISSISM

It is clear from the above material that obnoxiousness is closely related to the problem of narcissism and that obnoxiousness occurs in narcissistic personalities. Kernberg (1970) states that patients with narcissistic personality structure may not present seriously disturbed behavior on the surface. Their main characteristics are grandiosity, self-centeredness, and lack of empathy for others in spite of eagerness to obtain admiration and approval from them. They experience intense envy of others, lack emotional depth, fail to understand complex emotions in others and their own feelings lack differentiation.

With those patients whom I have studied during the lengthy analyses needed for such disorders, their narcissistic problem stems from early failure to accept the clear-cut distinction of the "I" from the "not-I." The panic and threat of an autistic type of psychosis forced them into the symbiotic character structure so typical of this failure to differentiate. Their self- and object-representations are never firmly laid down and never cathected as distinct, separate, and different.

The greater the obnoxiousness, the more certain there is to be a narcissistic personality structure. Their maintenance of the narcissistic orientation of the early months of infancy accounts for the defective ego functioning in reality testing as noted throughout the above paragraphs. *The obnoxious quality emerges whenever the individual attempts to impose the reality which he values upon the other individual.* Of course, he (note the irritable paranoid) experiences the other individual, who does not accept his version of reality, as obnoxious.

In interpersonal relationships people tend to prefer a bit of uncertainty in others. A degree of not being sure, of being anxious, tends to evoke a positive response. In contrast, when someone is absolutely sure of and pleased with himself, and takes other people too lightly, he is often disliked and experienced as obnoxious by the other person. In addition, obnoxious people are characterized by oral stubborness and insist on imposing their own inner reality upon others.

This material raises the question—why, in contrast, the oft-used expression in psychiatry, the "lovable schizophrenic"? Certainly the schizophrenic has a serious defect in reality testing. He suffers from narcissistic problems. Why then "lovable" instead of the expected term "obnoxious"? Obviously the schizophrenic has a conflict between his ego and reality; but those schizophrenics to whom the term "lovable" is applied have withdrawn into their own world and are not trying to impose it upon others. They wish to be left alone. In contrast, the obnoxious individuals—whether nonlovable schizophrenic, manic, paranoid, phobic, obsessive-compulsive, or hysterical—tend to be bullies, exploiters, and manipulators of other people. When the "lovable" schizophrenic is shut out from the other person's responses, he goes away. When the obnoxious individual is shut out, he tries to break the door down and impose his reality upon the other person.

Marion Milner's (1969) account of a psychoanalytic treatment, *The Hands of the Living God,* and Peter Giovacchini's (1970) review of her book, help us to understand such periods of disturbed personal relations between patient and therapist. Milner and her patient, Susan, often experienced peace and contentment when the dominant transference theme was symbiotic fusion. Such conditions are often nonthreatening and do not disrupt the course of treatment. In contrast, Milner describes her discomfort when Susan behaved in an organized manner. When Susan's paranoia effectively made use of secondary process elements, the therapist experienced a wish to drop the treatment.

Giovacchini describes his own reaction of irritation to the well-developed paranoid system of one of his patients, a reaction to the rational arguments the patient presented to support his delusional system. The paranoid superstructure clothes psychotic mechanisms in secondary process elements. Giovacchini states, "The closeness of such a superstructure to external reality, and especially a reality the patient senses the therapist may be especially interested in, makes the maintenance of the analytic setting difficult as it provokes disruptive countertransference reactions."

References

Freud, S. (1920), "Beyond the Pleasure Principle," *Standard Edition*. Vol. 18, p. 3. London: Hogarth Press, 1950.

Giovacchini, P., "The Delicate Touch of Analytic Dedication," *Psychiatry and Social Sci. Rev.,* 5:22-28 (May 26, 1971).

Jacobson, E., "Metapsychology of Cyclothymic Depression," *Affective Disorders*. ed. Phyllis Greenacre, 49-83. New York: International Universities Press, 1953.

Kernberg, O. F., "Factors in Psychoanalytic Treatment of Narcissistic Personalities," *Journ. of the Amer. Psychoanal. Assoc.,* 18:51-85 (1970).

Martin, P. A., "Obnoxiousness in Psychiatric Patients and Others," *The Psychiatry Digest,* August: 9-16 (1971).

Martin, P. A., "Obnoxiousness in Psychiatric Patients and Others," *The Psychiatric Forum.* ed. Gene Usdin, 59-65. New York: Brunner-Mazel, 1972.

Milner, M., *The Hands of the Living God.* New York: International Universities Press, 1969.

Chapter VI

The Patient Who Is Difficult to Reach

Betty Joseph

In this chapter I intend to concentrate on some problems of technique, focusing around a particular group of patients, very diverse in their psychopathology, but presenting in analysis one main point in common. It is very difficult to reach them with interpretations and therefore to give them real emotional understanding. My aim is to discuss some manifestations of the problem and some technical issues that arise in handling this type of case. I shall not attempt to make a study of the psychopathology of these patients.

In the treatment of such cases I believe we can observe a splitting within the personality, so that one part of the ego is kept at a distance from the analyst and the analytic work. Sometimes this is difficult to see since the patient may appear to be working and cooperating with the analyst but the part of the personality that is available is actually keeping another more needy or potentially responsive and receptive part split off. Sometimes the split takes the form of one part of the ego standing aside as if observing all that is going on between the analyst and the other part of the patient and destructively preventing real contact being made, using various methods of avoidance and evasion. Sometimes large parts of the ego temporarily seem to disappear in the analysis with resultant apathy or extreme passivity—often associated with the powerful use of projective identification.

It follows from what I am discussing that for long periods in the treatment of these patients the main aim of the analysis is to find a way of getting into touch with the patient's needs and anxiety in such a way as to make more of the personality available and eventually to bring about a greater integration of the ego. I find that with these rather unreachable patients it is often more important to focus one's attention on the patient's method of communication, the actual way that he speaks and the way that he reacts to the analyst's interpretations rather than to concentrate primarily on the content of what he says. In other words, I am going to suggest that we have to recognize that these patients, even when they are quite verbal, are in fact doing a great deal of acting, sometimes in speech itself, and our technique has constantly to take account of this.

I want first to examine this problem of the unreachable patient by considering the nature of the splitting in those patients who seem apparently highly cooperative and adult—but in whom this cooperation is a pseudocooperation aimed at keeping the analyst away from the really unknown and more needy infantile parts of the self. In the literature this problem has been discussed by such people as Deutsch (1942), with the as-if personality, Winnicott (1960), with the false self, Meltzer (1966) with his work on pseudomaturity, and Rosenfeld (1964) with the splitting off of the dependent parts of the self in narcissistic patients.

In psychoanalytic discussions on technique stress has frequently been laid on the importance of a working or therapeutic alliance between analyst and patient. What impresses one early in the treatment of this group of unreachable patients is that what looks like a therapeutic alliance turns out to be inimical to a real alliance and that what is termed understanding is actually antiunderstanding. Many of these patients tend to respond quickly to interpretations or to discuss in a very sensible way previous interpretations, using such expressions as "do you mean," referring to previous dreams and the like and seeming eminently cooperative and helpful. One finds oneself in a situation that looks exactly like an on-going analysis with understanding, apparent contact, appreciation, and even reported improvement. And yet, one has a feeling of hollowness. If one considers one's countertransference it may seem all a bit too easy, pleasant, and unconflicted, or signs of conflict emerge but are somehow quickly dissipated.

One may find oneself presented with specific problems that a patient wishes to consider: Why did he respond in such and such a way to such and such a situation? The patient makes suggestions, but free associations are conspicuously absent. The analyst finds him or herself working very hard intellectually to understand what is being asked of him, and may begin to feel he is involved in some kind of analytic guessing game. Here we can see one of the types of splitting of the ego I am discussing. The patient talks in an adult way, but relates to the analyst only as an equal, or a near-equal disciple. Sometimes he relates more as a slightly superior ally who tries to help the analyst in his work, with suggestions or minor corrections or references to personal history. If one observes carefully one begins to feel that one is talking to this ally *about* a patient—but never talking *to* the patient. The "patient" part of the patient seems to remain split off and it is this part which seems more immediately to need help, to be more infantlike, more dependent and vulnerable. One can talk about this part but the problem is to reach it. I believe that in some of our analyses, which appear repetitive and interminable, we have to examine whether we are not being drawn into colluding with the pseudoadult or pseudocooperative part of the patient.

This type of split can be found in different kinds of patients and may be maintained for different reasons, connected, for example, with unconscious anxiety about infantile feelings, or feelings of dependence, intense, but usually warded off, rivalry and envy of parental figures, difficulties concerning separateness, and so on. As I have mentioned, I do not want to discuss this aspect of the work, since my principal aim is to look at the technical side.

I shall start with brief material from a patient with a rigid, controlled, and anxious personality, who consciously wants help, but unconsciously struggled against getting it by the use of the kind of splitting I am describing, and whose communications could, in part, be viewed as acting-out in the transference. It is, of course, extremely difficult in reporting fragments of case material to convey this acting-out, which after all one mainly intuits from the effect that the patient's words produce on oneself and the atmosphere that is created. This patient, whom I shall call A., was a young teacher. He came into analysis when he was in his early twenties. He was married and had a young baby. He had already read a certain amount of analytic literature. When he had been in analysis over three and a half years and when we had done considerable work on his manic controlling, he started a session saying that he wanted to talk about his problems about clearing out his cupboards. He was spending so much time on them. He described how he had got to clearing things out and how he did not seem to want to stop. This was put forward as if it were a problem with which he needed help. He added that, in fact, he really did not want to go to visit friends in the evening because he wanted to go on with his clearing out.

He paused as if he expected something from me. I had the strong impression that I was expected to say something about his clearing out his mind or something rather pat, so I waited. He added that, anyway, he did not really like going to these people in the evening, because the last time they went the husband was rude. He had turned to watch the TV while my patient and his wife were there and subsequently made dictatorial statements about children's school difficulties. I suggested to him that I got the impression that he had been waiting for me to make some pseudo-Kleinian interpretations about the clearing out of his mind and inner world and when I did not, I became the rude husband who watched my own TV and was somewhat dictatorial in my views as to what his difficulties were, that is to say, I did not refer to his preconceived remarks. In other words, I considered his preoccupation with cupboards a type of acting-out designed to keep our work sterile and to avoid new understanding. At first he was angry and upset, but later in the session he was able to gain some understanding about his touchiness. He also got further insight momentarily into his competitive controlling.

The following day he said that he felt much better and had had a dream. He dreamed that he and his wife were in a holiday cottage. They were about to leave and were packing things in the car but for some reason he was packing the car farther down the lane, as if he were too modest to bring it to the front door or the lane was too muddy and narrow. This was unclear. Then he was in a market getting food to take home, which was odd: Why should he take food if he were going home? He was choosing some carrots—either he could take Dutch ones which were twisted or some better French ones which were young and straight, possible slightly more expensive. He chose the Dutch twisted ones and his wife queried why he did so.

His associations led to plans for the holidays at a house they were thinking of taking, and to his preference for France over Holland. Carrots led to his memory of the advertisements during the war of carrots as good cheap food and a help against night blindness.

Briefly I suggested that his pseudomodesty about bringing the car to the door was really linked with the fact that he was not too keen that I should see what he packed inside, following the feeling of having been helped the day before. But now we could see that his attempts on the previous day to force me to interpret in a particular way, as well as the understanding he had gained about it, had becomed linked with attempts to pack my interpretations inside himself, not to use for himself but for other purposes, as, for example, to use for a lecture which he was actually giving that evening. This then becomes food which he himself buys to take home, not food he gets from home-analysis. He chooses carrots which should help his night blindness, which should give him insight, but what he actually selects are the twisted ones. This would suggest that part of him has insight into his tendency to twist and misuse material—the false interpretations he tried to get from me—and avoid the clear, direct contact with firm, straight, fresh, and new carrots, i.e., nontextbook interpretations. This insight is not yet felt but is projected into his wife who queries why he has to do things in this wrong way.

The patient tries to manipulate me into making false and useless interpretations which could then keep me away from contacting anything new and unknown and thus from contacting the part that wants real understanding. The pseudocooperative part of the patient therefore clearly works against real emotional understanding. When I did not collude, his anger is described in terms of the anger toward the man who watched TV. Then the dream shows partial insight into the work of the day before. It clarifies the way in which he packs the interpretations into himself secretly, the car up the lane, rather than uses them to help the needy part of himself. This needy part is kept at bay, and from the carrot material, we can see it needs feeding.

In this type of situation I like to be certain that each step is clarified with the patient in relation to the immediate material and not left at a symbolic or quasi-symbolic level. Here we clarified the nature of the twist, that is, the falsification of interpretations, the link between interpretations and insight—night blindness. The interpretations are clearly felt as potentially good food but food that can be used, taken in wrongly, and then emerge twisted. One might then postulate that the twisted carrots stand for the nipples taken in in a twisted way but I would not wish to take that step until the intermediary material has been worked through.

In considering this type of problem I am stressing how often the pseudocooperative part of the patient prevents the really needy part from getting into contact with the analyst and that if we are taken in by this we cannot effect a change in our patients because we do not make contact with the part that needs *the experience of being understood, as opposed to "getting" understanding*. The transference situation gives us the opportunity to see these different conflicting parts of the personality in action.

I have been stressing, with the unreachable patient, the importance of locating the splitting in the ego and clarifying the activities of the different parts. In many of these patients one part seems to stand aside from the rest of the personality, observing minutely what is going on between the analyst and the rest of the patient, listening to the tone of the voice of the analyst and sensitive to changes real or assumed. The patient is sensitive, for example, to any indication in the analyst of anxiety, pleasure at achievement, frustration at nonprogress, and so on.

Thus, it becomes very important to sort out and make contact with these listening and watching parts of the patient; they contain potentially important ego functions of observation, sensitivity and criticism but so long as they are being used to ward off the analyst and keep other parts of the self at bay they cannot be healthily available to the patient. The patient may have felt that he observed something in the analyst and may have, to some extent, exploited it. Thus a patient may think that he spotted anxiety in the analyst's voice, and may become excited and triumphant, using the resultant criticism of the analyst to avoid understanding interpretations. In such situations I find it imperative for the analyst to wait, work slowly, carry the patient's criticism and to avoid any interpretations suggesting that the trouble lies in projections of the patient's anxiety. It is important to show, primarily, the *use* the patient has made of what he believed to be going on in the analyst's mind. Sometimes we can see the listening or observing part of the patient emerging clearly as a perverse part, which uses interpretive work for purposes of perverse excitement. These patients provocatively "misunderstand" interpretations, take words out of context and attempt to disturb or arouse the analyst.

I think that in all these apparently perverse situations there is some degree of splitting going on and that we have both to be aware of the intense acting-out in the transference to which we are supposed to respond by acting out toward our patients, and to be aware that somewhere, split off, there is a part of the patient in need. This part may for a long time be beyond reach in the analysis, but if the analyst is aware that it exists, as well as being aware of the violent acting-out of the perverse part, his capacity for tolerating without acting out in response is likely to be very much increased. I now wish to discuss further this split-off, observing part and the nature of its activities by bringing material from an apparently different type of patient. But I want to show how here, too, one part of the patient acts as an observer, keeps an eye on the relationship between the rest of the patient and the analyst and uses evasive techniques. I have in mind a young woman, whom I shall call B., who was particularly impervious to interpretations. She was touchy, angry and miserable, constantly blamed the world, and felt hopeless about herself. Consciously, she felt very inferior. She seemed hardly able to take in anything I said and frequently became excessively sleepy after I had spoken.

If she retained what I said it seemed to consist of isolated words with little meaning to her. Often she seemed actually to misunderstand or to become confused. Usually she talked with a quiet shout in her voice. It became increasingly clear that it was futile for me to try to interpret the *content* of what she told me. I assumed that fragmentation occurred whenever anxiety was beginning to be felt. I also had the impression that a part of her was *actively* breaking up interpretations and preventing contact with a more sanely receptive part of herself.

Then I began to notice many references to her boyfriend and how she would watch him speaking with interest to another girl. Then she would become consumed with rage. This type of situation began to emerge in dreams. For example, she had dreams of having a row with her boyfriend because of his interest in another girl. I commented that the dream situation was being lived out in the analysis.

If something really got through in a session and she felt I was able in a lively and alert way to talk to a part of herself that was interested and in contact, another part of herself immediately felt left out, not really jealous but terribly envious that I did the talking and part of her had actually been listening. The onlooker part became wild and reacted with fury. I believe it was this latter part that enviously could not bear me to make contact with her. It defensively shouted and kept me at bay and then felt attacked. One day, she brought a dream in which she was watching her mother bathing a baby, but the mother could not cope. The baby kept slipping out of her hands like a slippery fish. Then it was lying face up under the water, almost drowning. My patient then tried to give the mother some help. It was difficult to convey exactly the way the dream was told—but it stressed mother's stupidity and ineptness and her need for my patient's help.

I interpreted her self-destructive slipperiness and how the infant in her kept, like a slippery fish, evading being firmly held and explosively shouted so as to make it impossible to hold an interpretation or a bit of understanding. I pointed out that she wanted to make me a poor, inferior, inadequate mother. As I interpreted her further slipperiness bit by bit she stressed that there was a part of herself that was perfectly capable of helping her mother-analyst to hold her and to hold interpretations in herself. This shift was very important, since the problem with the unreachable patient is that one ordinarily has no proper ally. It also interests me as a point of technique that as a patient gains understanding, aspects of a dream may emerge, a dream which seems to have become part of the current session. If this happens I believe it is an indication of movement within the session, that is to say, a readjustment between different parts of the personality in a more integrated and constructive way.

Although B. is in almost every respect different from the young teacher A., from the point of view of the difficulty of reaching him there are important similarities. Thus the observing part in B. which we could see in the dreams of jealousy of the boyfriend, becomes slippery and evasive. In A. there is a different type of evasiveness, pseudocooperation. However, the slippery fish is not so different than the twisted carrot. In both patients one can sometimes find a part capable of responsiveness and contact. In A. this contact can often be quickly established, whereas in B. the enviously watchful aspect of the personality prohibits meaningful communication. It is striking how this watchfulness can confuse and disrupt the patient so that B. almost seems dull and stupid, which I very much doubt. The watching part shows itself to be very quick and terribly destructive and self-destructive. It has a perverse quality.

I want now to consider another method of achieving unreachability, where again the part of the ego that we need to work with us gets split off, and in addition becomes particularly unavailable because of being projected into objects. This type of projective identification was, of course, described as long ago as 1946 by Melanie Klein in "Notes on Some Schizoid Mechanisms." In some cases, when real progress has been made, insight has been gained and, for example, omnipotence has lessened and more warmth and contact have been established, one finds all further progress blocked by a markedly increased, apparently intractable passivity. The patient seems to become apathetic, to lose contact, interest and any involvement in the work which we may believe to be going on. He does not appear to be actively uncooperative, just helplessly passive. One often gets the impression following an interpretation that everything has gone dead and flat and at the same time that nothing will happen unless one does say something. This is often true. The patient remains quiet or subsequently comes up with a very superficial remark. Then slowly one has the sensation of mounting tension, as if the analyst ought to do or say something, or nothing will ever be achieved. It then feels as though one ought to bring pressure to bear on the patient to talk or respond.

These situations I find extremely instructive. If one does talk because of this kind of silent pressure, without realizing what is going on, nearly always the session gets going but becomes superficial or repetitive or acquires a kind of superego flavor. If one then examines the experience one can often find that the patient appears to have *projected the active, interested or concerned part of the self into the analyst, who is then supposed to act out, feeling the pressure, the need to be active and the desire to get something achieved.* Technically I think that the first step is for the analyst to be aware of the projective identification taking place and to be willing to carry it long enough to experience the missing part of the patient. *Then it may become possible to interpret without a sense of pressure, about the process being acted out, rather than about the content of whatever may have been under discussion before.*

I have frequently watched this kind of process going on in a very passive patient with a rubber fetish, whom I shall call C. In him I began to see the continual retreat to a kind of balance that he established, in which a weakly pseudocooperative self talked to me, but the emotional part remained unavailable. Repeatedly we experienced a sequence in which within one session he made progress, became deeply involved and moved by what was going on, but the following day it was a mere flat memory. Then I would find him talking in a bland way, very superficially: "Yes, I remember the session, it is fully in my mind," then nothing, or perhaps a remark of a slightly provocative type, such as that despite the session things were not going too well with his wife. I then felt as though I really ought to spur him into activity and understanding, and that if I would do so he would be perfectly willing to think and remember and get going again. I believe that he had split off his capacity for activity, concern, and active distress about his condition and projected this into me. As a result of his projection, I felt that he would be able to move and to make contact and use his insight if only I would take the initiative.

However, this is exactly the major part of his problem, that is, his hatred of really making contact with the loving, concerned and very needy part of the self and bringing it into relation to anyone enough to move physically or emotionally toward them from inside himself. If I push him—however analytically discreetly—he has won, and lost. By my pushing I would confirm that no object is good or desirable enough to attract him sufficiently for him to seek it out and involve himself with it, and therefore that part of the self that can take initiative remains unreachable. Next, I want to look at another aspect of this patient's passivity, also based on splitting and projective identification, of a different type, which manifested itself unobtrusively in a type of acting-out in the transference and thus threw light on the way he kept part of himself out of contact.

C. was at this time feeling insecure about the progress of the treatment, being very much aware of its length and feeling rather hopeless and impotent. This type of depression and open anxiety was unusual. During a session he was able to understand a point that I had been making. Then he realized that although the understanding seemed helpful to him, he had become quiet. I commented on the feeling of his having made a sudden shift to passivity. C. then started to speak and explained that he felt "pulled inside" and as if I would now expect him to speak, to "perform," and he felt he could not. I was then able to show him that he had felt understood but this experience of being understood was concretely experienced as if he were being drawn into the understanding, as into my inside, and then frightened that I was going to expect him to pull outside and to talk, "to perform."

Subsequently he added that he felt as if he were in a box lying on his side looking outwards, but into the darkness. The box was closed round him. After a few minutes he started to talk about "something else." At a dinner party the other night he had met a woman colleague. She was wearing a very lovely dress; he had congratulated her on it; it had three, horizontal eye-shaped slits near the top—if only he had had three eyes and could have looked out of all three at once. It was almost the end of the session, and I commented that what he wanted now was to get completely inside me through the slits with his eyes, with his whole self, totally inside me and remain there, as in the box. I also added that from the way he spoke he was conveying a very urgent need to make me aware of the importance of his desire to be shut away inside.

When he arrived the following day he commented that the end of the previous session had touched him deeply, but afterwards he had felt as though I had caught him in some guilty secret. I suggested that he had experienced my interpretation of his intense desire to be inside via the slits in the dress, as actually encouraging him to project himself into my inside, and that "understanding" had then been experienced as my doing something exciting and illicit with him. He had therefore been unable to integrate this understanding. It had a concrete quality and had become comparable to his rubber fetish—he could get inside the fetish, nowadays in fantasy only, in such a way as to pull away from relating to me and from maintaining real understanding and communicating wth a real person. So one could follow the movement of the session from real understanding and direct contact between analyst and the more responsive parts of the patient to a flight into a concretely experienced inanimate object, which again rendered him passive and withdrawn and largely unable to be reached.

These examples from C. illustrate the living-out in the transference of some mechanisms which he uses to achieve unreachability. They have certain similarities with those used by the other patients I have discussed. They are based on a splitting off of the responsive part of the patient, but are more clearly associated with projective identification. In the first example, the actively alert, needy and contacting part is projected into me so that I should bring pressure on him; in the other the responsive part which came very much to the fore in the session was concretely projected into me or my "understanding" and there became unavailable. Then the situation became sexualized; this made real understanding unavailable.

As a final example of a similar but slightly different mechanism of achieving unreachability and nonunderstanding, I want to bring material to show a type of splitting and projective identification going on in the session which enabled the patient to get absorbed into, that is to say, project part of himself into, his own thought processes and fantasies, leaving me in contact with only a pseudounderstanding part of the self and therefore unable to give him real understanding. I want to illustrate the technical importance of looking not only at the content but also at the way the material emerges. The patient's behavior and the movement of the material in the session may reveal which parts of the ego have disappeared and where we might look for them.

This fragment of material comes from patient A., whom I described first in this chapter. He had always tended to become absorbed in daydreams. He came one Monday with a dream about people being stuck in quicksand in a cave. There was some urgency about rescuing them but while the patient was fussing around looking for long boards, another man came and quickly helped. A. then went on to talk about having been absorbed in sexual fantasies over the weekend, but nevertheless feeling more in contact with what had been going on in the analysis. I interpreted that the fantasies seemed to be quicksand in which he tended to get stuck. He told about a fantasy of his childhood, of which he had spoken before, of looking at a cow or horse from behind, watching the anus and thinking of getting inside with only his head sticking out. He also spoke about some excitement in watching animals defecate. I, probably mistakenly (I will come back to this), discussed how getting into his fantasies was like getting into the animal's body, and I linked this with his mother's body and with his putting his fingers up his own anus. He then had many fantasies about babies being born. I could show him that he was proliferating fantasies in this session and getting absorbed into them, and this became his stuck state, like quicksand, so that instead of trying to understand and examine what had happened he was getting more and more absorbed and trying to pull me in with him. This he understood.

Next, he talked about the summer holidays. He and his wife were exchanging houses with some people from abroad. The other people had sent photos, but he had no photos of his house taken from the outside. I interpreted that as he gets absorbed in his fantasies, like the quicksand, they enable him not to have to see the outside, not to recognize separateness from me or an actual relationship with me, not to have to visualize me as really existing as an analyst in the room or away over the weekend. As I discussed this he became increasingly uncomfortable, suggesting that interpretations which brought him into contact with the analyst and the outside world were disturbing.

I think that it is probable that I made a technical error in interpreting the cow fantasy too fully, or rather prematurely, in terms of the mother's body, and that this encouraged my patient unconsciously to feel that he was actually succeeding in pulling me into his exciting fantasy world and thus encouraged him to proliferate his fantasies about babies being born. It might have been better to have kept more on the preconscious level until he was really in contact with me and my understanding, and only later to have linked the fantasy about cows and the dream about caves with the pull toward the inside of the mother's body.

It is also interesting to compare this material of A. with the previous material quoted about C., since in both the projection of part of the self into an object can be seen: in C., the projection into "understanding" concretely experienced, and in B., the absorption into phantasies felt as quicksand. In both patients, contact with the external world or with internal reality, and the experience of separateness and relationship with an object are largely avoided and the patients become temporarily unavailable to interpretive work or real understanding. I have brought this material not only to show this aspect of unreachability but to highlight the importance of considering the way the material is presented as opposed to concentrating primarily on its content or symbolism.

Before concluding I should like to expand a few of the technical points that I have touched upon in this chapter. The first concerns the nature of the transference situation. I have been stressing the importance of the way the material comes into the session and how this enables us to understand the subtle nature of the patient's acting-out in the transference and thus to tease out different parts of the ego and their interaction. Throughout the history of psychoanalysis the need for an uncontaminated transference has been stressed. This is, I believe, of particular importance if we are trying to understand the rather unobtrusive type of acting out that I am describing. I have given examples of a patient unconsciously trying to manipulate me into pressing him into action, or a patient trying to convince me to join him in a pseudoanalytic discussion. *If we allow ourselves to be manipulated in this way, the transference situation becomes blurred and then we are cut off from parts of the ego with which we need to make contact.*

We also then make it extremely difficult to see the shifts and movements of the patient's defenses and parts of the personality as they emerge, alter or disappear in our consulting room. In a sense our ability to remain constant and unaltered in the face of these movements has been much emphasized recently, particularly following the work on projective identification of Melanie Klein (1946), and then of Bion (1962), Rosenfeld (1964), and others concerning the need of the analyst to be able to contain the patient's projections. The kind of acting-out and the projective identification of parts of the ego that I am discussing can very easily pass unnoticed and bring a very subtle type of *pressure on the analyst to live out a part of the patient's self instead of analyzing it.*

Associated with this type of acting-out in the transference another technical issue arises—that is, the need for the analyst to keep interpretations in constant contact with what is going on in the session, since we are trying, with these unreachable patients, to observe whether our interpretations are really able to make contact or whether they are being held up or in some way evaded. I think we shall only succeed if our interpretations are *immediate* and direct. Except very near a reasonably successful termination, if I find myself giving an interpretation based on events other than those occurring at the moment during the session, I usually assume that I am not in proper contact with the part of the patient that needs to be understood, or that I am talking more to myself than to the patient.

Useful understanding usually comes from an interpretation of events that are immediate. If it is too far from the actual experience going on in the room, it leads only to verbal understanding of theory. Patients capable of considerable ego integration and of good, whole object relationships may at times be able to integrate interpretations based on putting together previous material. But the kind of patients I am concerned with in this chapter are using much more schizoid mechanisms and are communicating much more concretely by acting out in the transference—even though with apparent verbal sophistication. We must pay constant attention to this in selecting our technique.

References

Bion, W. R., *Learning From Experience*. London: Heinemann, 1962.

Deutsch, H. (1942), "Some Forms of Emotional Disturbance and their Relationship to Schizophrenia," in *Neuroses and Character Types*. London: Hogarth Press, 1965.

Klein, M. (1946), "Notes on Some Schizoid Mechanisms," in *Developments in Psychoanalysis*. London: Hogarth Press, 1952.

Meltzer, D., "The Relation of Anal Masturbation to Projective Identification." *Intern. Journ. Psychoanal.*, 47 (1966).

Rosenfeld, H. (1964), "On the Psychopathology of Narcissism; a Clinical Approach," in *Psychotic States,* London: Hogarth Press, 1965.

Winnicott, D. W. (1960), "Ego Distortion and the True and False Self," in *The Maturational Process and the Facilitating Environment*. London: Hogarth Press, 1965.

Chapter VII

Negative Therapeutic Reaction

Herbert A. Rosenfeld, M.D., F.R.C. Psych.

The term "negative therapeutic reaction" was first defined by Freud (1923) in *The Ego and the Id*. According to Freud, "This reaction manifests itself when one speaks hopefully to the patient or expresses satisfaction with the progress of treatment. The patient reacts with discontent and the condition invariable becomes worse." Freud reaches the conclusion that these patients are not only unable to endure praise but are reacting adversely to the progress of treatment. "Any partial solution that ought to result in an improvement or a temporary suspension of symptoms produces in them for the time being an exacerbation of their illness: they get worse during the treatment instead of getting better, they exhibit what is known as a negative therapeutic reaction." Freud thinks that he has discovered the source of this reaction in an unconscious sense of guilt which is consciously experienced as illness. However, the patient cannot accept the interpretation of this motive but believes that treatment by analysis is not the right remedy for his case. Freud is of the opinion that if this sense of guilt is severe then it must be regarded as a limitation to the effectiveness of analysis. In his paper (Freud, 1924) on "The Economic Principle of Masochism" he returned to the discussion of the negative therapeutic reaction. He discusses here the difficulty in making patients aware of the unconscious sense of guilt and wonders whether it would not be better to speak instead of the need for punishment. He also points out that the sadism of the superego and the masochism of the ego supplement one another, resulting in a severe sense of guilt or conscience, both the sadism and masochism being derived from the destructive or death instinct. These views of Freud would imply that he regards the negative therapeutic reaction as related to the death instinct.

The only cases of negative therapeutic reaction which Freud regarded as prognostically good were those where a borrowed sense of guilt could be found which was relieved by the analysis of the underlying identification with an abandoned love object. There are only very few papers on the theory and the clinical approach to the negative therapeutic reaction and I shall concentrate on discussing the main contributions.

In 1936 there were two important papers on this subject by Karen Horney and by Joan Riviere. Horney in her paper on "The Problem of the Negative Therapeutic Reaction" made a number of important clinical observations and offered technical suggestions on how to handle this difficult problem. She observed that the negative therapeutic reaction occurs most frequently after a particularly good interpretation, which is experienced by the patient as a sign of the analyst's superiority and high intelligence, to which the patient reacts with resentment, disparagement, and belittlement leading to attempts to assert his own superiority over the analyst. As a second point she stresses the narcissism of the patient, his need to be perfect, flawless, and beyond reproach. As a good interpretation exposes some weakness in the patient, he experiences it as a severe narcissistic blow and feels humiliated. Horney thinks that it is the analyst's effectiveness which endangers the patient's belief in his absolute supremacy and he retaliates by trying to humiliate the analyst and make him feel insignificant and ineffectual. Thirdly, she stresses the patient's fear of improvement through the analyst's help since such success is always related in his mind to "crushing others and maliciously triumphing over the crushed adversaries," an attitude necessarily leading to a fear of retaliation and failure. The fear of success may be phrased in the following way. "If I attain success I shall incur the same sort of rage and envy that I feel toward the success of other persons." Horney sees similarities between Freud's view and her own. Freud, however, stresses the guilt feelings in this type of patient, while Horney emphasizes the role of anxiety about fear of retaliation, and does not relate it to the superego. Horney deliberately refrains from relating the problems connected with the negative therapeutic reaction to infancy but emphasizes that she "selects out of the material offered by the patient those parts which she can relate to his reaction to the analyst, and interprets those only."

Riviere, in her paper, "A Contribution to the Analysis of the Negative Therapeutic Reaction," is particularly concerned with investigating the question as to why the negative therapeutic reaction should be regarded as more unanalyzable than any other obstacle to treatment. She argues that Freud regarded psychotic and narcissistic patients as equally inaccessible to treatment. She implies that the negative therapeutic reaction may not be a reaction to a good interpretation but to an incorrect one which should lead the analyst to look for deeper causes of this problem. She then discusses in general the analysis of all particularly refractory cases and reports in detail on Abraham's paper on "The Neurotic Resistance Against Treatment," "which he virtually names narcissistic type of character resistance." This leads her to ask the question: "What is narcissism?" She compares the old view of any marked degree of narcissism as presupposing a withdrawal of libido from external objects into the ego, with the newer one, highlighted by Melanie Klein's work on internal objects, which shows that the distribution of ego libido can now be recognized to be extremely complex.

She proposes that in especially refractory cases of the narcissistic type, we should pay more attention to the analysis of the patient's inner world of object relations, which is an integral part of his narcissism, and that we should not be deceived by the positive aspects of narcissism but should look deeper for the depression which will be found to underlie it. She gives a detailed description of the manic defense against depression, the patient's omnipotent denial of psychic reality and the denial of affects, particularly regarding the ego's object relations and its dependency on them. She also stresses manic contempt and depreciation of objects and the control and mastery over them which, in her view, explains the narcissistic patient's denial of the value of everything the analyst says. Riviere emphasizes the narcissistic patient's need to maintain the status quo by his omnipotent control because the lessening of the manic omnipotent defense brings him face to face with his hopeless despair related to his depressive anxiety which he fears will become reality to him. She believes that what makes the negative therapeutic reaction so stubborn is the unconscious love and anxiety for the destroyed or dying internal objects, producing an unbearable sense of guilt and pain. The patient needs to sacrifice his own life for others who represent these internal objects, and therefore faces death or suicide. She states that this situation is not identical with Freud's unconscious sense of guilt. She relates the negative therapeutic reaction to the patient's feeling that he deserves no help from the analyst and is unworthy of it until he has helped to restore and cure his internal objects. She also suggests that omnipotent control is specifically related to the negative therapeutic reaction: If the patient's state begins to change he loses control and so he quickly has to reinstate the former situation, which has proved bearable. Her paper is full of technical and clinical details as to how to deal with this difficult clinical problem.

She specifically warns the analyst not to overdo the analysis of aggressive impulses because she feels that nothing will more surely lead to a negative therapeutic reaction than the analyst's failure to recognize anything but aggression. She says, for example, that not all negative reactions to treatment should be regarded as attempts of the patient to defeat the analysis. The patient's feeling of prior obligation to rescue damaged internal objects may take precedence over his freedom to accept help for himself. It is important to strive to understand the whole situation and to interpret details of the patient's defenses and anxieties, and this may gradually lead to a more positive response.

In evaluating Riviere's contribution it is important to understand that it was made before Klein's paper, "Notes on Some Schizoid Mechanisms" (1946), in which Klein described in detail the anxieties and defenses prevalent in the paranoid schizoid position—the phase preceding the depressive position and its manic defenses. She suggested that splitting, omnipotence, idealization, denial and control of internal and external objects are in the earliest position the main defenses of the ego against persecutory anxiety and the destructive or death instinct. It is only at a later date, when splitting diminishes and the ego is more integrated, that depressive anxieties can be experienced. Many of the earliest defenses such as omnipotence, idealization, and control of objects continue to be active and become part of the manic defenses against depression and depressive anxieties. Klein's later paper on "Envy and Gratitude" (1957) may be regarded as an examination of the deeper sources of the negative therapeutic reaction in the predepressive phase of development.

I shall now discuss briefly Abraham's paper (1919) on "A Particular Form of Neurotic Resistance against the Psychoanalytic Method." Here Abraham describes patients who show a chronic resistance to analysis by constantly controlling their free associations. Hidden underneath an outward eagerness to be analyzed there is an unusual degree of defiance against the analyst representing the father. In illustrating the patient's narcissism he says that he grudges the analyst the role of the father and takes over the role of analyst. He does not want to free-associate and allow the analyst to be the cleverer one. In fact, he wants to do the analysis by himself. He relates the patient's attitude to envy and anal erotism and stresses that the patient feels the analysis as an "attack on his narcissism which is an instinctual force upon which our therapeutic efforts are most easily wrecked." In this paper Abraham makes a very clear link between narcissism and envy. His description of the outwardly eager attitude of the patient to analysis would suggest that much of the envy remained hidden and was defended against in his case material, and that it was actually his analytic work which brought the hidden envy to the surface. Abraham regards envy, in this paper, mainly as an anal character trait but in the later paper on "The Influence of Oral Eroticism on Character Formation" (1924) he stresses the origin of envy in the oral sadistic phase.

Horney's discussion of her patient's superiority and sensitivity to narcissistic blows is similar to Abraham's much earlier views. Abraham's observations on the importance of the relation of narcissism and envy remained apparently unnoticed until much later.

In her book *Envy and Gratitude* (1957), Klein discusses how "envy and the defense against it play an important part in the negative therapeutic reaction in addition to the factors discovered by Freud and further developed by Joan Riviere." She states that "for some patients a helpful interpretation which brought them relief and produced more hope may soon become the object of destructive criticism. It is no longer felt to be something good which they have received and have experienced as an enrichment." She explains that the envious patient grudges the analyst the success of his work and the interpretation which she has given is spoilt and devalued by the patient's envious criticism. This interferes with the acceptance of interpretations. The envious patient may also, out of guilt about devaluing the analyst's help, feel that he is unworthy of benefit by psychoanalysis. (This sense of guilt is clearly related to Freud's view on the importance of the sense of guilt in the negative therapeutic reaction.) Melanie Klein's observations of envy being aroused by good interpretations is almost identical to Horney's description of the competitive patient who devalues the analyst and the interpretation. Horney relates it to the negative therapeutic reaction, however, only in terms of the patient's fear of envy of other people which prevents him from attaining success. Riviere discusses in detail the patient's disparaging contemptuous attitude but she regards this simply as part of the manic defense not as part of the manic attack.

Klein stresses the danger of success when envy is stimulated. The patient manically triumphs over the analyst, representing the good object, and devalues him. This leads to severe guilt feelings and depression. In this situation it is quite clear that the negative therapeutic reaction does not occur as a result of the breakdown of the manic defense, as Riviere observed, but is itself caused by the destructive element in mania represented by envy. The depression following an envious attack contains not only guilt feelings but severe persecutory anxieties. The persecutory fear relates both to fear of being enviously attacked by external objects as well as by internal objects, represented by an envious superego, which is experienced as devaluing and disparaging and which grudges the ego any goodness and success. When envy is located in the superego it becomes an important part of the negative therapeutic reaction. As the envious superego is particularly difficult to bear, it leads to denial and splitting (this would link up with Freud's comments on the sadistic superego and the difficulty in making it conscious). Horney gives the impression in her paper that competition, rivalry, or envy appear in the analysis of patients showing negative therapeutic reactions in a quite undisguised way. It is, however, apparent from the study of Klein's work that the most powerful negative therapeutic reactions ccur when the envy remains hidden or silent, due to the creation of powerful defenses against envy. Defenses against envy include splitting, idealization, confusion, flight from the original object leading to dispersal of feelings, devaluation of objects and self, violent possessiveness and reversal of the envious situation by stirring up envy in others through success and possessions. Some of these defenses, particularly idealization and splitting, are identical with those which Klein had previously described as the very earliest defenses of the ego belonging to the paranoid schizoid position which are directed mainly against the destructive or death instinct.

This is in line with her view that she regarded early oral envy as a derivative or expression of the death instinct and stressed its existence from the beginning of life. Klein gave a detailed description of the importance of split-off envy which she frequently observed clinically as an incapacity to accept with gratitude interpretations which in some part of the patient's mind were recognized as helpful. The splitting off and projecting of envy into the analyst is an important hindrance in the analytic situation because the analyst is constantly mistrusted since he is unconsciously again and again turned into a dangerous and retaliating figure. Melanie Klein writes, "When through the analysis of the split-off aspects of envy the ego is strengthened, and when the feeling of responsibility becomes stronger and guilt and depression are more fully experienced, the projection onto the analyst diminishes so that the analyst in turn finds it easier to help the patient toward further integration. That is to say, the negative therapeutic reaction is losing its strength." It is clear from this description that envy and the defenses against it prevent the integration of the ego which is necessary for reaching the depressive position. It is therefore often quite noticeable that patients showing long-drawn-out negative therapeutic reactions tend to be rather more schizoid than depressive and it is only when the envy has become conscious and has been worked through in the analysis that the depressive anxieties can be fully experienced and worked through. The negative therapeutic reactions which Riviere described, namely, the manic defense against depressions, are generally less severe and intractable but there are exceptions to this as when, for example, excessive envy has become part of the patient's manic system.

The point which I myself would like to examine in more detail is the relationship of narcissism, or the narcissistic organization, to the negative therapeutic reaction. As I have already indicated, the importance of narcissism in most negative reactions to analysis has been stressed by Freud and Horney, and linked with envy by Abraham. Riviere related this narcissism to Klein's description of internal objects and Freud's theory of secondary narcissism. Mrs. Klein herself did not go into the question of the relationship of the negative therapeutic reaction to narcissism.

In investigating the psychopathology of narcissism some years ago I stressed that narcissistic object relations are mainly part-object relations and are dominated by the ego's omnipotence. Identification of self and objects achieved either by introjection or projection plays a dominant part, and the desirable parts of the objects are incorporated into the ego which claims complete ownership, at the same time the undesirable parts of the self are projected into external objects. I have stressed that narcissistic object relations obviate feelings of aggression caused by frustration and any awareness of envy. It seems particularly related to the latter that the narcissistic patient either keeps up his feelings of superiority by devaluing the analyst, or when he benefits by the analysis gives himself the entire credit for it.

Similarly, he often takes over the analyst's capacities by omnipotent projective identification which implies a very concrete feeling of being inside the analyst and thus controlling him so that all the analyst's creativity and understanding can be attributed to the patient's ego. When the analysis succeeds in making some impact on these narcissistic omnipotent structures so that their controlling powers lessen, an infantile part of the patient appears in the analysis which is experienced as separate from the analyst. We are accustomed to describe this part as a dependent part of the patient who then forms an object relation to the analyst as the feeding mother.

It is after a session where some contact with the dependent part of the patient has been made that the negative therapeutic reaction is most likely to occur. Occasionally at such times conscious aggression expressing frustration or jealousy aroused through separation anxiety or envy of the analyst standing for the feeding mother appears. More frequently, however, the patient is quite unaware of any aggressive reactions. He seems to have forgotten the last sessions and seems entirely out of contact as if something has occurred which has completely wiped out the experience of the day before. But it is not only the good experience with the analyst which has disappeared but also the infantile self which received help which has been lost. I have observed that this negative therapeutic reaction is due to a powerful counterattack of the omnipotent narcissistic and often megalomanic part of the patient which was felt to have been dislodged from its dominant position through the progress of the analysis and which reasserts its power by attacking and overpowering the infantile dependent part to reestablish the status quo and to regain control over the ego. Often the patient is scarcely able to talk in such a situation, and complains of feeling cut off and imprisoned. Sometimes he describes a feeling of being completely overpowered, or he says that something has been killed or lost. Generally he is quite unable to give any information about the reasons for this attack which seem to him to come completely out of the blue.

During the analysis the patient gradually becomes able to report and observe the details of his reaction. He feels a great dislike of a part of himself which criticizes him, accuses him of being weak and inferior and despises him. It may tell him to be independent and not to be such a baby. One might be inclined at first to regard this violent attack as being related to the superego but clinically *it is extremely important to differentiate between the attacks of the narcissistic omnipotent self and those of the superego. In my experience interpretations referring to guilty feelings and superego reactions at such times may cause severe confusion.*

One of my psychotic patients described the omnipotent part of his personality as arrogant and superior. It often made speeches to him criticizing the analysis and throwing doubts on my interpretations. At times when his trust and cooperation in the analysis increased and he allowed himself to be helped by me, this omnipotent part criticized him for being weak and inferior, and belittled him so violently that he came to the next session feeling shocked and battered and almost smashed to pieces, fearing that he would break down completely or be driven to death since he could not stand up against these attacks. He complained: "What is the good of making any progress if I am torn to shreds afterwards?" He was particularly aware that his capacity to think clearly came under attack at such periods and that *everything* that he had gained from the analysis was endangered. The patient's life had been geared to having prostitutes once or twice a day for many years. The analysis had gradually helped him to understand the meaning of this addiction, which he had not only used for evacuating any anxiety or concern but which had prevented any loving dependent relationship. During the time when he began to resist going to prostitutes for several weeks the internal attacks became particularly any meaningful dependent relationship to the analyst, and would would be good for him to have a prostitute and that everything would be all right again, if he followed this suggestion. The relationship to prostitutes related to the patient's ruthless power and control over women with whom he felt he could do anything he wanted. He realized that he was being blackmailed by a part of himself to believe that if he gave up any progress, particularly any meaningful dependent relationship to the analyst, and would allow his omnipotent narcissistic part to regain control so that it could indulge in uncontrolled masturbatory pleasures without any care for his objects, he would be all right again.

When the analysis progressed in spite of the negative therapeutic reactions, murderous rages against people in the ouside world appeared which led to constant obsessional anxieties about having killed somebody inadvertently. When we were able to trace the origin of his murderous feelings he admitted that they always occurred when he started to compare himself with other people. It was particularly when he felt that somebody was superior to him that these murderous feelings came to the surface, in other words, *the murderous, omnipotent envy which was hidden behind this narcissistic omnipotent control had been able to emerge.*

I shall now report some case material of a patient whose narcissistic character structure represented a serious obstacle to the analysis over a period of several years. At a particular period in the analysis he began to cooperate more and a dependent relationship developed which was followed by a negative therapeutic reaction which could be clearly defined in a dream during that time.

The patient is a young, unmarried man of thirty of continental origin. He is an industrial consultant who also gives talks to groups in industry. For many years the patient's narcissistic omnipotence was mainly located in the feminine part of himself. This part was often presented in dreams as a dancer, an ambition and fantasy which had existed from early childhood. Once or twice in his dreams a marriage was arranged between himself and the girl representing this feminine part. When this feminine self was projected in the outside world onto narcissistic girls, often dancers, he felt very much attracted to and sometimes fell in love with them. It was very difficult to show the patient that his love for certain girls represented a self-idealization and self-love which excluded any real object relationships. In the analytic situation he wanted me to share his admiration for his feminine part. He had the greatest difficulty forming a dependent relationship to me and the infantile nature of the feminine part was always denied. The delusional conviction of a baby part, which believed that it was a mother by omnipotently taking over the mother's body and particularly the breasts and babies, was reinforced by a masculine part of himself which was completely taken in by this omnipotent assertion. This formed an almost unbreakable alliance which was only slightly shaken when the girl began to appear in dreams as mad and deluded.

The narcissistic love affair between feminine and masculine infantile parts of the personality who delude themselves about their adult status is a very important part of the narcissistic organization. Gradually this patient began to develop some insight and, following some disillusionment with an idealized girl friend, he began to be much more involved in analysis and to listen to me: This could be interpreted as the beginning of a feeding situation.

During this time the patient had a dream: He was in the analyst's house. The analyst was talking in the kitchen. The patient's father was doing acrobatics pulling himself up on the wardrobe in the bedroom and was doing very well. The patient knew in the dream that the father was dead (he had, in reality, died some time ago). He remembered his funeral and asked his mother whether she could see his father too. At that moment his father felt very upset and the patient woke up with a severe pain in his heart and was afraid of dying. The patient added that, in the dream, the analyst knew the father. In his associations he talked with admiration of how strong and acrobatic his father had been.

It seemed to me that the main importance of this dream was the appearance of the analyst in the dream representing the feeding mother who helped him get in contact with the infantile situation which revived his admiration and jealousy of the father in the oedipal situation. The father, not the patient, is made to feel small and left out. This triumph over the father causes the patient to wake up from the dream with a pain in his heart and the fear that he was going to die. This dream seems clearly a move forward from the narcissistic position to dependency, the oedipal situation, and the depressive position.

Two days later the patient was very disturbed with severe pains in his chest and reported a nightmare. In the nightmare he was living in a flat with his mother. A very paranoid, megalomanic Indian insisted that the flat belonged to him and tried to force his way in and take it over by threatening to shoot the patient in the chest with a bow and arrow. The patient wanted first to shoot him because he was so dangerous but then he felt afraid of the Indian who was much younger and so he gave in. He woke up again with an intense pain in his chest and fearing that he was going to die. He associated his latest girl friend with the Indian. He explained that while he had admired her greatly for a long time, recently he had become quite frightened of her as he realized how narcissistic she was. The patient could think of no other associations to the Indian and he stressed how paranoid and deluded he seemed to be. I had explained previously that his girl friend had stood for his feminine omnipotent self which recently had been more represented in dreams as mad and deluded. This feminine part is now simply represented as a paranoid, deluded man, an acknowledgement that the feminine delusion has diminished. In the dream this psychotic, mad part is making a takeover bid claiming possession of the flat which represents both his ego and his relationship to the mother-analyst. However, the attack is not directed against the mother but against the sane, dependent part of the patient, which when threatened with death gives in to the narcissistic part, allowing it to regain charge of his ego and the analysis. This dream was followed by a setback which lasted for several weeks and it illustrates the struggle involved in the negative therapeutic reaction. It is the narcissistic omnipotent delusional part of the patient which feels threatened by progression and insight. The progress of the analysis in making contact with the infantile part of the patient had mobilized envy on an infantile level, particularly envy of the feeding breast. This threatened to expose the emptiness and delusional quality of the narcissistic structure which actually may break down at such moments. The attack on the dependent self serves to reinforce the delusional possession of the breast which is basic to the narcissistic structure which denies any need and envy of the breast. Progress in the analysis of such patients can only be made when the narcissistic omnipotent structure finally breaks down and the underlying infantile parts of the patient with all his needs, feelings of frustration, and envy can be fully worked through in the transference situation.

SUMMARY AND CONCLUSIONS

In this chapter I have tried to outline the outstanding contributions to the psychopathology of the negative therapeutic reaction and to show how the different approaches are related. The negative therapeutic reaction has close links with all chronic negative reactions to the psychoanalytic process, as Riviere has stressed. This made it essential to include Abraham's important paper in this discussion.

Narcissism, as most contributors agree, seems to play a fundamental role in all negative therapeutic reactions, and therefore I reviewed some of the research on this subject. I described a particularly persistent form of the narcissistic organization which one may call "the delusional form of narcissism" which has its roots in earliest infancy and which relates to the omnipotent delusional taking over of the mother's body, particularly her breast and her creativity. This leads to a delusional form of pseudofemininity in later life which is reinforced by the masculine part of the self which colludes with it, thus strengthening this delusion. This structure can defend itself against any real object relationship and presents a severe obstacle to treatment. It is, I believe, of central importance in the negative therapeutic reaction because it attacks any saner dependent part of the self that tries to develop and that does not submit to the narcissistic collusive system. The analysis of envy, particularly to its earliest root in infancy, is an important element in breaking through the negative therapeutic reactions.

The importance of manic defenses in treating negative therapeutic reactions, which Riviere described, is still an important clinical consideration but must be related to the latest research which stresses aggressive elements, particularly envy and manic triumph. In this way mania is not only guarding against depression and the negative therapeutic reaction but seems often the cause of both the depression and the negative therapeutic reaction, which are closely allied.

The superego is an important factor in most negative therapeutic reactions. It is, however, important to differentiate the attack by the superego on the ego from the violent, apparently critical attacks derived from the narcissistic omnipotent organization which turns against the infantile dependent part of the self. The superego in the negative therapeutic reaction is not easily accessible to direct interpretations as Freud pointed out. It seems mainly to have a persecutory character and contains many envious components which give it this begrudging, delusional and spoiling character which tries to spoil any success or progress in treatment.

It is only through the detailed analysis of the aggression and envy in the analytic transference relationship and the related persecutory anxieties projected onto the analyst that the superego and the negative therapeutic reaction become more accessible to analysis.

Horney (1936) has stressed the need to work through competition and envy in the transference situation. It has, however, been found that most of the severe envious reactions have to be traced to their earliest sources, namely, to the relationship to the mother in the feeding situation, in order to make it possible for the patient to take in the interpretations and the help of the analyst. The capacity of the patient to take in and retain good interpretations instead of immediately spoiling them develops only gradually. This is the central therapeutic factor in our attempts to tackle the problem of the negative therapeutic reaction.

References

Abraham, K. (1919), "A Particular Form of Neurotic Resistance against the Psychoanalytic Method," in *Selected Papers of Karl Abraham*, pp. 303-312. London: Hogarth Press, 1942.

Abraham, K. (1924), "The Influence of Oral Erotism on Character Formation," in *Selected Papers*, pp. 393-407. London: Hogarth Press, 1942.

Freud, S. (1923), "The Ego and the Id," *Standard Edition*, Vol. 19. London: Hogarth Press, 1961.

Freud, S. (1924), "The Economic Problem of Masochism," *Standard Edition*, Vol. 19. London: Hogarth Press, 1961.

Freud, S. (1937), "Analysis Terminable and Interminable," *Standard Edition*, Vol. 23. London: Hogarth Press, 1964.

Horney, K., "The Problem of the Negative Therapeutic Reaction." *Psychoanal. Quart.*, 5 (1936).

Klein, M., "Notes on Some Schizoid Mechanisms." *Intern. Journ. Psychoanal*, 27:99-110 (1946).

Klein, M., *Envy and Gratitude*. London: Tavistock; New York: Basic Books, 1957.

Riviere, J., "A Contribution to the Analysis of the Negative Therapeutic Reaction," *Intern. Journ. Psychoanal.*, 17-304-320 (1936).

Rosenfeld, H. A. (1964). "On the Psychopathology of Narcissism. A Clinical Approach," in *Psychotic States*. London: Hogarth Press, 1965.

Chapter VIII

The Formative Activity of the Analyst

Richard F. Sterba, M.D.

Habent sua fata Libelli.*

During my 50 years of activity as a psychoanalytic writer I have published two papers which I consider contributions of some importance, one to the theory and the other to the practice of psychoanalytic therapy. The first one I presented at the International Psychoanalytic Congress in Wiesbaden in 1932. Its title was "Das Schicksal des Ichs im therapeutischen Verfahren." In English the paper appeared in 1934 in the *International Journal of Psycho-Analysis* under the title: "The Fate of the Ego in Psychoanalytic Therapy."

At the congress in Wiesbaden there were no discussions scheduled for the papers. However, many of the participants of the Congress privately expressed their disapproval of the concept of the "therapeutic ego split" (therapeutische Ichspaltung) which in my paper I had considered a regular and necessary occurrence during the analytic process. Particularly Paul Federn expressed rather forcefully his well-meaning negative criticism of my idea of an ego split in therapy since an ego split was supposed to take place only in schizophrenics.

At that time it was customary to devote one meeting of the Vienna Psychoanalytic Society to the presentation of the paper which any member had read at the International Congress so that there would be an opportunity to discuss them. When I reread my Congress paper in the fall of 1932 in this meeting of the Vienna Society, the reaction of the majority of the members was almost violent opposition to my proposition. The criticism was mainly directed against the concept of "therapeutische Ichspaltung," the therapeutic ego split, since an ego split was supposed to occur only in psychosis. Anna Freud was the only member who found the concept acceptable and appropriately applied to the dynamic factors of the therapeutic process. She said that she did not quite understand why the term "ego split" met with so much objection since it correctly designated a phenomenon in therapy which one has opportunity to observe constantly in one's analytic work. A few weeks later the new series of introductory lectures appeared in which Freud wrote: "The ego can take itself as object, it can treat itself like any other object, observe itself, criticize itself, and do heaven knows what besides with itself.

---

*Little books have their special fate.

In such a case one part of the ego stands over against the other. The ego can, then, be split; it splits when it performs many of its functions, at least for the time being. The parts can afterwards join up again.''

This settled the matter. The ''therapeutic ego split'' as well as the term ''therapeutic alliance'' which I established in the same paper were gradually acknowledged and are now indispensable concepts in the theory of psychoanalytic therapy.

Eleven years later (1943) I presented to the American Psychoanalytic Association at its annual meeting in Detroit another paper dealing with the therapeutic process. This paper was of a more practical, technical nature. The title of this paper was ''The Formative Activity of the Psychoanalyst.'' I presented this paper because I felt the need to express myself against the teaching and practice of the superorthodox, ''blank screen'' attitude of the analyst, which illusionary concept had then begun to be preached and practiced, particularly at psychoanalytic institutes. Neutrality, objectivity, aloofness, exclusively interpretative purity, and total avoidance of any ''contamination'' of the operational field in therapy were considered absolutely necessary for the optimal effectiveness of the so-called ''classical'' technique. What one could conclude concerning Freud's own therapeutic attitude from the printed presentation of his own cases was either ignored or shoved aside with a *Quod licet Iovi non licet bovi* (What is permitted to Jupiter is not permitted to an ordinary ox).

My paper was then written as a reaction to the impersonalization of the psychoanalytic therapist and therapy which dominated the field of therapy from the early forties until recently. Here it is reprinted as I presented it in Detroit in 1943:

Franz Alexander was the official discussant. He began with the somewhat belittling remark: ''Dr. Sterba's neatly written paper. . .'' But this was the only good thing he had to say about it, although from his own writings which I quoted in the paper one would have expected a more positive response on his part. However, it was a bad time for a presentation of this type of paper because the swelling current of the era demanding the (illusionary) impersonal purity of the analyst had already dominated the analytic scene. When I sent the paper to the *Psychoanalytic Quarterly* for publication it was rejected and Gregory Zilborg, at the time one of its editors, told me privately that although he agreed with most of what I said in the paper he found the time inopportune for its publication since there were so many deviations from the classical therapeutic technique coming in vogue then that a paper like mine would be used to legitimize such an ''aberration'' from the strict classical technique.

I then submitted the paper to the *International Journal of Psycho-Analysis* where it appeared in Volume XXV, 1944. That it had been accepted for publication in the *International Journal* only reluctantly is obvious from the footnote of the editors to page 148, where they object to my correcting the translation of Joan Riviere, citing quotations from Freud to demonstrate that Freud meant the mobilization only of the patient's own psychic forces that would lead him into a new decision. To this I can only requote the clear statement from Freud's paper on lay analysis written in 1926: "This personal influence is our most powerful dynamic weapon; it is the means by which we introduce something new into the situation and bring it into a state of flux. The intellectual content of our explanations cannot effect this."

The numerous places in Freud's writings in which he speaks of the "suggestive" influence of the physician necessary to bring about a change in the patient speak for themselves.

The period following the publication of the paper was one of greatest caution not to deviate from a fictionally ideal attitude of the analyst, consisting of his being completely neutral a-human and sterilized. Any personal remark or active suggestion, nay, any human communication of a noninterpretative kind on the part of the analyst, made him guilty of a "parameter." The parameter phobia which swept through the analytic community led to an anxious avoidance of reports of analysts on their own activity in the psychoanalytic situation, since for many analysts it was impossible not to react in a more than completely neutralized "uncontaminated" atmosphere which would have met with a violent condemnation by his colleagues. The ideal model of the analyst became the bloodless and colorless nonpersonality behind the couch whose only activity was neutral, impersonal, and unemotional interpretation. It is understandable that my paper, if it was ever mentioned, was reacted to negatively.

Approximately 10 years ago the scene began to change. The rigidity of the merely mirroring, silent, purely interpreting, otherwise nonparticipating psychoanalyst is, very gradually, yielding to the approach to the patient of a more human, less impersonal attitude. Analysts might have realized that their rigid, abstract approach was partly responsible for so many people seeking help where an abundance of abusive human contact—emotional and even physical—was offered by the numerous new types of nonanalytic, free-emotional-discharge psychotherapies from group therapies to encounters and interactional approaches. One could easily recognize from reading Freud's case histories or from asking some of Freud's former patients that his approach was in all situations human and natural, albeit with all the limitations that make a truly psychoanalytic therapeutic situation possible.

Everywhere we see psychotherapy done with a method based on an erroneous and misleading psychodynamic model which Freud had originally adopted but with further insight had abandoned more than seventy years ago. Forced abreaction is obviously not the cure of repressed dynamic quantities for it does not bring about structural changes, the only ones which are genetically curative. On the other hand, the nonhuman, and sometimes inhuman, completely inactive, non-Freudian attitude of the analyst, though certainly less harmful than the other extreme, is not the optimal one for the patient—not natural for the analyst and harmful to the reputation of psychoanalytic therapy. I hope very much that my opinion will gradually be the generally accepted one and that my paper then *habeat fatum meliorem* (will have a better fate).

It is neither by mere chance nor as a result of one-sided interest that so many of our papers on psychoanalytic therapy concern themselves with interpretation. Interpretation is and will always remain our paramount technical method in therapeutic procedure, as long as we do not work (Freud, 1904) *"per via di porre,"* that is, by strengthening the repressive forces, but *"per via di levare,"* by undoing repression and thus making the unconscious accessible to the ego so that it can integrate parts of the id and use its newly acquired energy for its manifold purposes. Our ultimate dynamic aim in interpretation is the strengthening of the ego through the addition of instinctual energy which has hitherto belonged to the unconscious. There can be no doubt that interpretation is our main pump in the therapeutic "draining of the Zuyder Zee" (Freud, 1933, p. 106).

The fact that the direct interpretation of recognized unconscious material is not usually the means of achieving our therapeutic purpose was a fairly early discovery. Very often the patient is unable to accept the interpretation or even to understand it. Preinterpretative measures must be taken so that he will be able to understand and accept our interpretations. Such measures consist mainly in the analysis of the ego-resistances or ego-defenses against the expression of unconscious material. Excellent papers by Sigmund and Anna Freud, by Wilhelm Reich, Otto Fenichel, M. N. Searl, Edward Glover, James Strachey, and others have been devoted to the preparatory steps of interpretation. In contrast to these, the postinterpretative states and procedures have been neglected in analytic literature. It is in my opinion a necessity that we should focus our attention upon the dynamic situation which exists after a correct and, if necessary, well-prepared interpretation has been given to the patient. For in my experience many analysts stop their therapeutic activity at the point where the interpretation has been supplied to the patient. For such analysts interpretation is the only work. Interpretation, and the preparation for it, is their contribution to the therapeutic procedure. The rest of the process has to go on within the patient. He is, so to speak, left alone with the interpretation. In my opinion this attitude on the part of the analyst is a continuation of the "take it or leave it" policy of the earliest lines of analysis, which is so well expressed in Freud's dream of Irma's injection (1900). The only difference is that owing to the analysis of the resistance the possibility of the patient's "taking it" has been enlarged in comparison with Freud's earlier therapeutic measures.

Even if the interpretation of a patient's behavior, or of his defense mechanisms, is repeated on different occasions, a merely interpretative attitude neglects the further tasks of the analyst, who must help the analysand to do something with the interpretation, that is, with the newly acquired knowledge about himself.

This merely interpretative attitude on the part of the analyst seems to me an expression of belief in interpretation as a kind of magic formula which works with miraculous efficacy immediately upon its pronouncement by the analyst. But in my opinion the analyst has the further duty of helping the patient to overcome mental inertia, of showing him how to use the newly acquired insight into himself, into his pathological repetitions, anxieties, and defenses constructively, so that a reorientation toward his inner as well as his outer world shall result. The achievement of this reorientation is our final therapeutic goal, in the light of which our interpretation of the patient's defense mechanisms and unconscious material can be considered only as a preliminary and preparatory procedure. It is true that in many cases the reorientation for which we are working takes place automatically as soon as the patient develops intellectual and emotional insight into his unconscious as well as into his pathological and inappropriate reactions. But it is far from true that after the patient has accepted our interpretation we can *always* leave it to him to do the remaining therapeutic work of reorganizing his personality. He simply would not do it. The reasons why he does not take advantage of his newly gained insight are many. In general, they represent the same forces which we find active against any change in our adaptations, and "mental inertia" is a term which summarizes them. It is needless to remark that infantile anxieties and unconscious instinctual gratifications may prevent the necessary changes, and that therefore further purely analytic interpretative measures must be taken. But the necessity for changing in itself, the need to give up old ways of restoring the mental equilibrium in favor of new adaptations, creates a type of resistance to which Freud gave the name "resistances of the id," although we can easily see that the ego, too, in most instances, refuses to undergo changes in its reaction patterns. To me it seems a therapeutic necessity to help the patient in effecting these changes by something more than the preliminary act of interpretation. This additional function of helping the patient, which may even amount to forcing him to establish a reorientation of his personality and readaptation to his outside world, I should like to describe as the "formative activity" of the analyst. It no doubt belongs to the "working through" part of our task.

It is difficult to describe in detail what this formative activity consists of. It is operative within a wide range, from energetic activity to a mere attitude hardly sensible to the patient. Its methods vary with the personalities of patients as well as with their analytic and emotional situations. I am inclined to describe formative activity in a general sense as a continual effort to exert pressure on the patient in order to force him from a state of unhealthy pathological reactions and fixations into better adaptation and a more satisfactory solution of both his inner and his outer problems.

Psychoanalytic treatment has often been compared to orthodontic procedures. Freud once used the term ''redressement,'' probably with reference to the forceful treatment in orthopedic therapy. Both comparisons imply the exertion of pressure from the ouside. The means which we use in order to force the patient to change are manifold. In many instances we show him what he did and what he had better have done in certain situations. We use the frustrating effect of interpretation in order to prevent him from repeating his pathological gratification and reactions. We use his respect for our own opinion in order to make him feel ashamed of his lapses into useless infantile behavior. If necessary we show him more or less drastically what his repetition of pathological reactions will bring him to, what dangers or frustrations will result from such repetitions. We have to use all these and other means of *personal influence* to mold our patients into a healthier personality formation.

Freud says in his *Introductory Lectures* (1917) that in our therapeutic work, particularly in those phases where infantile conflicts are renewed, we must use ''all our available mental forces in order to press the patient into a new decision.'' (See footnote at the end.) In my opinion these mental forces consist in persuasion and threat, promise of reward, encouragement and praise, as well as all the rest of the mental equipment we employ when we try to make somebody do a thing that he originally does not want to do. However, such means are exactly those which we use in *education* in order to effect the shift from pleasure principle to reality principle. In this respect psychoanalysis is true education. As I once pointed out (Sterba, 1932) education can be considered the extended psychological repetition of birth, that is, of the change from intrauterine existence. Analytical therapy is the last act of this psychological repetition of birth, and, like all the preceding psychological acts of birth in the form of education and like the physiological act of birth itself, it must be accomplished by pressure and force.

The dynamic basis of this energetic influence of the analyst on his patient is the transference. Infantile dependence, love, admiration, and confidence are the expressions of the positive transference which enables us to direct our patient mentally toward our therapeutic goal. The actual superiority of the analysts's personality to that of his patient is of considerable help in this process. But as in hypnosis, in our formative activity in analysis, we work mainly with borrowed energy.

There can be no doubt that formative activity requires certain personal qualifications which should not be missing in a good analyst. Formative activity is a part of our work which can hardly be learned, and for which we can give neither prescription nor technical advice. Such work is truly creative, like the work of good education, and the personal gift of handling other people is a requisite in an efficient analyst. Personal influence must be exerted in such a way as to be at the same time flexible and consistent. The comparison with a good fisherman, who knows how to play the fish after it is caught on the hook (of transference), is a ready one. Formative activity is at once the most difficult and the most satisfactory of our many therapeutic activities. If analytic intuition and insight into the patient's mental content can be compared to the inspiration of the creative artist, the formative activity in our therapy can be likened to the other power essential to the artist's creation: the ability to give his idea *form,* to body it forth into the final artistic product. Intuitive insight into the patient and the ability to use this insight constructively for the transformation of the patient's personality are the equivalent constituents of analytic therapy.

I am well aware of the many limitations we must impose upon our formative activity. We are not supposed to set ourselves for it, neither should we impose upon the patient our own *Weltanschauung,* or our opinions on various matters. Even our own personality pattern is not supposed to be a model for our molding the patient into a new orientation toward life. Much objectivity is needed. The process of temporary identification, which resembles the mechanisms described by Ludwig Jekels (1930) in his excellent paper on the psychology of pity, seems to be an important factor in gaining this objectivity. In formative activity more than in any other part of our work the personality of the analyst is a decisive factor.

I know very well that in all I have said I have stepped on ground in the realm of therapy which to some analysts seems as dangerous as a minefield. Such an attitude contradicts their analytic thinking. Their idea of the analyst is of a very neutral, colorless, and impersonal image, invisible to the patient and without influence upon his decisions, whose only function is to offer the patient material for better judgment. But I may remind those who think in this way that human beings are very little influenced by their intellectual insight, that they need strong emotional support in order to use it for their own benefit, and that the neurotic in particular is a weak person in this respect.

I have mentioned already that I have found very little on this subject in psychoanalytic literature. Our technical papers show a rather rigid attitude in cautiously avoiding discussions of any activity on the part of the analyst that is not merely interpretative. There are some exceptions, however. Franz Alexander (1935), for example, emphasizes the fact that the analyst has the task of assisting the patient's ego in his synthetic endeavors. He states that, "what we call 'working through' has the function of aiding the integrating process,'' and speaks of the active influence of the analyst upon the assimilating process going on within the patient. "The standard technique," he says, "as it is used since Freud's technical recommendations, consisting in interpretations centering around the transference situation, really involves an active participation of the analyst in the integrating process."

Melitta Schmideberg (1939) recognizes how often steps and activities which are not merely interpretative are applied in therapeutic analysis and how they contribute to the therapeutic result. Searl and Glover give some indication that they recognize noninterpretative influence on the part of the analyst. Edward Bibring (1937) recognizes that pedagogic measures have their place in analytic therapy.

And last, but certainly not least, Sigmund Freud has much to say about the influence of the analyst on his patients. In this connection Freud uses a term which for us nowadays has a flavor that we do not like to connect with psychoanalytic therapy. This is the term "suggestion." For us the term "suggestion" used in connection with psychotherapy has the connotation of making the patient believe things that are not so, and keeping him from recognizing others which really exist. But this is not Freud's understanding of the term when he speaks of suggestion in connection with psychoanalytic treatment. He, and this he makes quite clear in his *Group Psychology* (1921), uses the term to mean *any personal influence* on the patient. Having this in mind, that in the following quotations, chosen from among many similar ones, Freud uses "suggestion" to mean *"personal influence,"* it will be found that in his writings we can discover many clear expressions of what I call the formative activity of the analyst. Again, Freud (1922) speaks of "the suggestive influence which is inevitably exercised by the physician." In his twenty-eighth lecture (1917, p. 377) he says, comparing hypnosis with psychoanalytic therapy: "Analytic therapy takes hold deeper down nearer the roots of the disease, among the conflicts from which the symptoms proceed; it employs suggestion to change the outcome of these conflicts. . . .The labor of overcoming the resistance is the essential achievement of the analytic treatment; the patient has to accomplish it and the physician makes it possible for him to do this by suggestions which are in the nature of an *education*. It has been truly said therefore, that psychoanalytic treatment is a kind of re-education." Further on in the same lecture (*ibid*, p. 381) he says again: "The change that is decisive for a successful outcome . . . is made possible by changes in the ego ensuing as a consequence of the analyst's suggestions," that is, under the personal influence of the physician. I quote finally from Freud's *Laienanalyse* (1926): "This personal influence is our most powerful dynamic weapon; it is the means by which we introduce something new into the situation and bring it into a state of flux. The intellectual content of our explanations cannot effect this." In the sentences following this he speaks of the great "suggestive" influence in psychoanalytic therapy. Many other quotations from Freud's writings could be added, in which he expresses his opinion about the significance of *personal influence* in psychoanalytic therapy which has to be used *over and above* interpretation.

Goethe once declared that man's most important study is man. No other psychologist has contributed so much to that study as Sigmund Freud. But through the analytic method of psychotherapy he did more: he gave us the possibility of remodelling individual personality structures of an unfavorable and neurotic kind. His study and insight into the human mind enable us to form and mold distorted minds and personalities into a better shape. And so we who are psychoanalytic therapists can, by using the vital tool of our formative activity, take into our hands the useless structures and neurotic mazes of distorted personalities, can work, shape, and form the valuable energies that have been wasted in them into the living pattern of an efficient human being, and in so doing we go beyond the *study* of man to the active and most important *work* of man, namely the work of building man.

Note:

Translated by the author. The English translation by Joan Riviere does not give the right meaning of Freud's words: "*Das entscheidende Stueck der Arbeit wird geleistet, indem man im Verhaeltnis zum Arzt, in der 'Uebertragung,' Neuauflagen jener alten Konflikte schafft, in denen sich der Kranke benehmen moechte, wie er sich seinerzeit benommen hat, waehrend man ihn durch das Aufgebot aller verfuegbaren seelischen Kraefte zu einer anderen Entscheidung noetigt.*" (*Gesammelte Schriften,* VII, 472)

Editorial Note: Dr. Sterba's criticism of Mrs. Riviere's translation seems unjustified. Her version of the passage is as follows (*Introductory Lectures,* Revised Edition, 1929, 380): "The decisive part of the work is carried through by creating—in the relationship to the physician, in "the transference"—new editions of those early conflicts, in which the patient strives to behave as he originally behaved, while one calls upon all the available forces in his soul to bring him to another decision." Thus the difference of opinion between the two translations is as to whether the forces that are to be evoked are the patient's or the analyst's own. The actual words seem capable of either interpretation and the question is best settled by an examination of the context as well as of any other passages from Freud that deal with the same point. Two sentences earlier, Freud writes: "In order to dissolve the symptoms it is necessary to go back to the point at which they originated, to renew the conflict from which they proceeded, and with the help of propelling forces which at that time were not available (*mit Hilfe solcher Triebkraefte die seinerzeit nicht verfuegbar waren*) to guide it towards a new solution." Similarly, in the *New Introductory Lectures,* 1933, 198 (*Gesammelte Schriften,* XII, 314), where Freud continues the same discussion, he writes: "Only too often one seems to see that the therapeutic process is merely lacking in the necessary motive force to enable it to bring about the alteration. Some specific tendency, some particular instinctual component, is too strong in comparison with the counterforces that we can mobilize against it (*eine gewisse Triebkomponents ist zu stark im Vergleich mit den Gegenraeften, die wir mobil machen koennen*)." It seems hardly possible to doubt that in all of these passages Freud is concerned with the economic balance of forces within the patient, with the possibility of the analyst evoking one set of forces in the patient to operate against another, rather than with the notion of the analyst bringing forces of his own to bear upon the patient. Further consideration will perhaps convince Dr. Sterba of the correctness of Mrs. Riviere's version.

References

Alexander, F., "The Problem of Psychoanalytic Technique." *Psychoanal. Quar.,* 4:608 (1935).

Bibring, E., "The Theory of the Therapeutic Results of Psychoanalysis." *Internat. Journ. Psychoanal.,* 18:188 (1937).

Freud, S. (Revised Trans. 1932). *The Interpretation of Dreams.* 114ff. London: Allen and Unwin, 1900.

Freud, S. (Trans. 1924). "On Psychotherapy." *Collected Papers,* Vol. 1, p. 253. London: Hogarth Press, 1904.

Freud, S. (Revised Trans. 1929). *Introductory Lectures on Psychoanalysis.* London: Allen and Unwin, 1917.

Freud, S. (1921) (Trans. 1922). *Group Psychology and the Analysis of the Ego.* Vol. 18, London: Hogarth Press, 1955.

Freud, S. (Trans. 1942). "Two Encyclopedia Articles." *Internat. Journ. Psychoanal.,* 23:104 (1922).

Freud, S. (1926). "Die Frage der Laienanalyse." *Gesammelte Schriften,* Vol. XI, 353.

Freud, S. (1933) (Trans. 1933). *New Introductory Lectures on Psychoanalysis.* 21 London: Hogarth Press, 1964.

Jekels, L. "Zur Psychologie des Mitleids." *Imago,* 16:5 (1930).

Schmideberg, M., "The Role of Suggestion in Psychoanalytic Therapy." *Psychoanal. Rev,* 26: 219 (1939).

Sterba, R., "Zur Theorie der Erziehungsmittel." *Z. psychoanal. Paedag.* 6:422 (1932).

Chapter IX

The Patient's Unconscious Perception of the Therapist's Errors

Robert J. Langs, M.D.

INTRODUCTION

There is currently a growing interest in the psychoanalytic literature regarding the role of the therapist's errors in technique and his human failings in the psychoanalytic and psychotherapeutic situations (Greenson, 1965, 1967, 1971; Langs, 1973). It is the purpose of this presentation to contribute to our understanding of this subject, especially as it relates to errors of which the therapist is unaware. I will approach the subject in the following way:

1. By presenting clinical material which will demonstrate some of the most common manifestations of the patient's conscious, and far more frequently, unconscious, perception of the therapist's errors.

2. By utilizing these clinical observations as a means of cataloging indicators in the associations from patients that the therapist has made a mistake, thereby facilitating their recognition by him.

3. By discussing the technique of handling such errors with the patient, including the consequences of the therapist's failure to detect his mistakes and correct them.

Briefly, this study is primarily the outcome of my work as a supervisor of insight-oriented psychoanalytic psychotherapy. Material from twice-weekly therapy of patients suffering from character disorders and borderline pathology was presented in weekly supervision. At various points in such presentation, I identified specific, major errors in technique and predicted their consequences based on the nature of the error and the patient's character structure and psychopathology (Arlow, 1963, and Langs, 1973). Among the responses to such errors, one group included derivatives of the patient's unconscious awareness of the therapist's mistake, including the patient's fantasies about why the therapist had erred.

This study is based in part upon many fine papers on countertransference in the psychoanalytic literatures. (See Cohen, 1952; Orr, 1954; Greenson, 1967; and Langs, 1973.) Errors in technique may be based on inadequate training, faulty conceptualization of the material from the patient, an incorrect theoretical framework, the utilization of unsound technical measures, and unresolved personality difficulties within the therapist—countertransference problems (Greenson, 1967, and Langs, 1973). They may manifest themselves as acute traumatic interventions, or failures to intervene, or they may be expressed as chronic and recurrent disturbances in the therapist's stance. Elsewhere (Langs, 1973), I have investigated this matter in some detail and have termed the patient's responses to the therapist's errors "iatrogenic syndromes," a label which emphasizes the therapist's role in evoking the patient's response, while acknowledging the patient's responsibility as well.

These errors by the therapist may be detected by him through his subjective awareness (Cohen, 1952, and Langs, 1973), and by the patient's immediate association following the therapist's error (Langs, 1973). While patients occasionally are able to express their awareness of these mistakes directly to the therapist, in almost all of the several hundred clinical situations I have observed in which such errors were made, the patient's response was essentially unconscious and expressed through disguised derivatives and displacements.

In all, this paper will focus on one source of detecting mistakes made by therapists, namely the patient's immediate associations following the error. It will be limited further to one specific type of response—associations which centered around the patient's unconscious awareness that the error has been made and his unconscious concept of the error. Some other types of responses to the therapist's mistakes have been presented elsewhere (Langs, 1973). These include such reactions as ruptures in the therapeutic alliance; various forms of acting-in against the therapist; premature termination of treatment; erotic responses to the therapist; acute symptoms and symptomatic regression of all kinds; and major and minor episodes of acting-out. In general, a patient's responses to errors in technique will include a mixture of these reactions in various sequences.

CLINICAL MATERIAL

While I have not formerly collated my findings from the more than 800 clinical vignettes that I have documented from my supervisory work, some general impressions will be helpful as an orientation for the vignettes which are to be presented (Langs, 1973). By and large, the identification of major errors in technique proves to be consistently feasible so that well over 90% of those behaviors and interventions of the therapist identified in supervision as clearly incorrect were followed by ample validation in the subsequent material from the patient. Since most of the therapists were relatively inexperienced, errors in technique were rather frequent and averaged at least one per pair of sessions presented to me. In response to these errors, at least 90% of the time the patient did not express any direct conscious awareness or belief that the therapist had made a mistake, but instead responded strongly and unconsciously, and expressed his reaction through derivatives. The main exceptions to this were those situations where the patient directly disagreed with the therapist's intervention and went on to present material that supported his disagreement, and then eventually offered derivatives related to the correct area in which the therapist should have intervened.

The exact nature of the patient's response to these errors in technique depends on a number of factors. These include the nature of the error, the rapidity or slowness with which the therapist detects it, his ability to modify and correct it, and the extent to which he is able to explore the patient's conscious and unconscious reactions. On the patient's part, contributions are made mainly from his past and present relationship, his character structure and psychopathology, his on-going relationship with the therapist, and his current life situation. To illustrate some of these points I present the following vignettes:

Mr. A was a young man who was divorced and living alone. He came into therapy because he was depressed and had not been able to mobilize himself to find employment, to develop new relationships with women, or to visit his children, who lived with his remarried wife. He tended to withdraw from others and to smoke a good deal of marihuana; at times, he took other drugs as well. He was diagnosed as a narcissistic personality and was being seen in twice-weekly psychotherapy.

He had been in treatment for about two months when he began to think about seeing his children again. With this in mind, he contacted his wife and in their conversation, she mentioned the possibility of her present husband's adopting their children so that they could take his name. The patient was noncommittal, and in his sessions after the call, he ruminated about whether he really wanted to see his children at all, and how being detached from them was fine with him. To see them again would just be a hassle. Yet, he spoke of receiving a call from his parents and missing them, a unique feeling for the patient. Associations went to his search for relief by taking drugs and his fears of "cracking up." The therapist remained relatively silent, saying only that the patient seemed to want something from him.

In the following two sessions, the patient requested psychotrophic medication and spoke about leaving the area. He thought of writing notes to the therapist and retreated into marihuana smoking. He had suicidal fantasies, and an intense sense of depression and despair. The therapist pointed out the patient's wish for immediate relief, and Mr. A. spoke of his mounting sense of anxiety and of a boss he once had whom he hated and blamed for his suffering on the job. He felt terribly misunderstood by him, and was eventually fired. When the patient ruminated further about blaming others for his suffering, the therapist pointed out how he dumps things onto others and assumes it is their problem, rather than his. The patient demanded medication and began to fall silent during his hours, stating that he had nothing to say. The therapist pointed out his anger over not being given enough in treatment, and the patient went on to talk about his rage at his insensitive wife who had never returned his last call; it made him feel like "crap." He then went on to speak at length of his guilt for ruining his children's lives, of his wish to not be a "once-a-week father," and of his rage at his wife for her affair with her husband while married to the patient.

The patient was late for the next session and felt very depressed. He talked about how uncomfortable he felt when things came up in treatment, but could not specify what it was about. He was feeling frightened of people and felt that it was hardly worthwhile getting up that morning for his session. The therapist said that his lateness seemed related to his doubts about therapy.

He began the following hour by asking about a picture of the therapist's children which was on his desk. He thought about his brother and sister, and the ways in which he had failed them, of a vague sense of guilt, and of how he could not look at a picture of his parents in his own apartment. Once again, he thought of running away. The therapist picked up the reference to the picture of his children and to the theme of guilt, and said that he wondered if the patient wasn't feeling guilty about his children. The interruption surprised Mr. A., who then spoke of his concern about seeing them again and messing up their lives. He reviewed in some detail the ways in which he had failed them and how terrified he was to start up with them again, fearing that he would explode. He was furious with his wife and her present husband for their contribution to the situation. The therapist intervened again and spoke of the patient's rage and of the manner in which the patient blamed others for his troubles, pointing out that he seems to be doing this with his wife and her husband, rather than facing how he, himself, had been paralyzed into inaction. In response, the patient said that he was confused and that treatment was a very painful journey that was hurting him a great deal.

He had been on a bus the other day, when a man got on and was putting money into the coin box. It dropped to the floor several times. The patient laughed loudly, causing everyone on the bus to look at him. The patient then noticed that the man had a cane and he felt like "crap." Nevertheless, he continued to laugh to himself.

He fell silent and remembered a time in his childhood when he sat with his grandfather and put chalk into rags that he then used to beat up children he didn't like. During those years, he would have nightmares that there was a gorilla in his closet and he would never go into a dark room. He remembered a time from his early twenties when he roomed with a fellow who was a criminal. They would have relations with women together and he remembered that once this friend nearly killed his girl friend. The friend had held up a medical supply house, looking for drugs, and had been shot in the process. He had been in psychotherapy with a doctor who had a beautiful office; the patient had once gone there with him. The doctor would stare at his friend and they both thought that the psychiatrist was crazy. Because of that experience, the patient had hesitated a long time before seeking therapy himself.

Mr. A. began the next session by talking about how he had idealized his father and now was disillusioned. He spoke about putting walls around himself and again alluded to his feeling disappointed. He had been under the influence of drugs since the last session and he had refused to share his apartment with a friend who was leaving his wife and children. He had little else to talk about. The therapist commented that something he had done in the previous session seemed to have turned him off, suggesting that this was reflected in his reference to the blind man, perhaps he had missed something and this had frightened the patient. Mr. A. responded that he would like things to be good for himself, and he began to speak again about his children and the times that he had felt close to and happy with them. He was afraid that they might not know him or might hurt him if he reached out to them again. He went on in considerable detail about the painful conflicts that he was feeling over whether to see them again and whether to maintain his position as their legal father.

In discussing this vignette, one must identify the therapist's errors, since they form the fulcrum for the patient's responses. These errors fall into two groups, one set related to the patient's problems with his children and the other pertaining to his relationship with the therapist. As to the first of these, I believe there were two main mistakes which stemmed from difficulties the therapist had in being empathic and in recognizing the patient's great suffering regarding his children. As soon as the patient began to talk about the possibility of losing his children, I suggested in supervision that this was a very important problem and adaptive task (Langs, 1972, p. 73) for this patient, and that it would evoke significant realistic and intrapsychic conflicts. The patient's main defenses of denial and withdrawal into drugged states were also quickly identified. The balance of the material then centered around various feelings of guilt, depression, and rage, and the accompanying conscious and unconscious fantasies related to the patient's struggles regarding the possible loss of his children. This included strong expressions of longings to be with them and to undo his own destructiveness toward them.

In this context, the therapist's early interventions regarding the patient's tendency to blame others were not only insensitive to his plight, but were also accusatory and hostile. In response, the patient's depression intensified and he began to question his therapy and to demand medication. His recollection of a boss who did not understand him is an early expression of the patient's unconscious perception of the therapist's failure to recognize his suffering; the reference to being fired is probably a derivative of the patient's thoughts of leaving treatment.

It is rather typical in response to errors of this kind for patients to express

*some rage, to regress and question treatment, to indicate some of the uncon-
scious fantasies about the therapist's insensitivity, and to then return to
important intrapsychic conflicts.* Mr. A. did just this by getting back to the
problem he was having with his wife and children, and doing so with considerably more affect and pain. His wishes to be a good father may also be
viewed, in addition to realistic aspects, as a fantasy expressing some longing
to have an understanding therapist-father. When the latter did not respond
either with an empathic statement or with some effort to explore the patient's
conflicts, the patient spoke about his wife's present husband who had cuck-
olded him; this reflects some of the patient's mistrust of the therapist who
remained out of touch with him. The therapist, despite supervisory discussions, was having difficulty referring specifically to the patient's conflicts
about his children, and the patient seemed to feel confused.

Then, in the most dramatic session of this series, the patient once more
brought up the subject of his children by alluding to the therapist's picture of
his own children. Again, the patient spoke at length about his children and his
guilt over being a poor father. The therapist correctly intervened by referring
to this guilt. It is interesting that the patient expected the therapist to ignore
these communications, and then went on to add some new material about the
intensity of his desires to see his children again. It was at this point, after the
patient had spoken about his rage at his wife and her present husband, that the
therapist made his most dramatic error. It consisted of an incorrect intervention in which he once more criticized the patient for blaming others and
directly faulted the patient for the difficulties which he currently found himself facing. The therapist seems here to have been insensitive again, and to
have a strong unconscious need to deter the patient from talking about his
children and his longings to be close to them.

The nature of this disturbing intervention was discussed with the therapist,
and the prediction was made that the patient would react with derivatives
expressing considerable rage and mistrust. This was borne out by the reference to the blind man and to the patient's own inconsiderate blindness as well.
As an unconscious perception of the therapist's own difficulties in seeing and
understanding, it is a poignant communication.

The patient went on to speak of his latent destructiveness. In my previous
work (Langs, 1973), I found that it is extremely common for patients to
become self-accusatory when they are furious with their therapist. The reference to the patient's senseless attacks seems admirably suited to communicate
his perception of the therapist's inappropriate, senseless criticisms. Mr. A's
other associations suggest a terrifying image of his relationship with the
therapist.

During the last session presented here, the therapist attempted to correct his
error. The patient was talking about his disillusionment in therapist-

displacement figures, this time referring to his father. When the therapist finally acknowledged his error of the previous session, he did so without specifically referring to his failure to understand the patient's grief about the situation with his children. The therapist was vague, but he discussed in some detail the patient's reactions and fantasies to his insensitivity and failure to perceive the patient's distress. He admitted that his attitude had been unjustifiably critical. In response, the patient spontaneously began to talk again about his children and the conflicts that were plaguing him. In a manner not described until now, the patient described fears that he would explode, and said that he felt much as he had as a child, when he had been sick in bed and his doctor had laughed at him for having such a small penis. His father, he went on, had been a destructive man who would do anything for the patient, even cut his arm off, and had begged the patient not to be like him. Yet his father laughed at the doctor's remark and the patient had been deeply mortified. After these comments, the patient returned to the exploration of his problems with his children and to some of the intrapsychic difficulties that had prevented him from being an adequate father.

It is noteworthy that even this incomplete effort at acknowledging and correcting a series of errors in technique was successful in reestablishing a positive therapeutic atmosphere and alliance. It enabled the patient to express one last unconscious fantasy regarding his perception of the therapist's recent behavior, namely that of his deep sense of inadequacy and humiliation. Following this, the patient was able to return to the exploration of inner conflicts.

I will not similarly trace out this therapist's failure to respond adequately to Mr. A's search for care and gratification of dependency needs in his relationship with the therapist. This was an on-going difficulty in this therapy, and the many self-accusations regarding poor fathering refer, on this level, to the frustrations with the therapist; fantasies of rage in this connection are the counterpart of the patient's guilt with his children. The blindness, then, is not only the therapist's failure to interpret properly to the patient, but also a deeper failure to recognize his needs and demands for help and care.

Let us now consider the following vignette:

Mrs. B was in psychotherapy for multiple phobic symptoms and depressions; she had been seen twice weekly for about six months. Prior to the last session before the therapist's vacation, the patient, who had been informed of the temporary cessation of treatment, had wandered from the waiting room. The therapist searched and found her outside the hospital talking to other patients; she returned with him.

The patient began the hour by saying that she had been thinking that she should not come to her sessions because she would get too upset. She reported a dream in which a little child fell from a window in her apartment. Her associations were to a cousin who had had premonitory dreams of something happening to a child, after which a serious accident or injury had occurred. Other associations, which touched upon themes of separation, suggested that the dream was related to the therapist's pending vacation. They were not interpreted. The therapist's extension of the boundaries of the relationship between himself and the patient, as reflected in his going outside to find her, was also not alluded to.

The patient began the first session after the therapist's vacation by stating that she had been thinking about her treatment, but had reached no conclusions. She dreamed that afternoon while napping that the therapist was screaming at her that she is always late and keeps missing her appointments. She associated her dislike of tardiness and added that in the dream the therapist was actually standing in front of the clinic yelling across the street at her. She then discussed moving because of her husband's business commitments, and spoke of her mother's destructiveness—she had not watched her children carefully.

The patient's unconscious perception of the therapist's lack of reference to his finding her for the previous hour (in my opinion, an error) is conveyed in the dream. In the dream, the patient returned to the therapist's seemingly innocuous deviation in the ground rules of therapy and boundaries of their relationship (Langs, 1973). Unconsciously, the patient felt that the therapist was angry over her lateness and therefore came to get her. Most likely the dream reflects the patient's own anger regarding the therapist's seductiveness.

During the two following sessions her associations focused upon derivatives of erotic feelings toward the therapist. He had been provocative prior to the reported session so her eroticized responses could not be attributed specifically to his error in pursuing the patient.

Thus, Mrs. B alluded to the therapist's deviation in technique in an almost undisguised fashion, but dissociated it from the precipitating incident and the context to which it referred. As a result, she was able to maintain repression of the incident and the fantasies that it had evoked in her, and because the therapist similarly repressed the incident, its consequences were not explored or resolved.

The next patient was in twice-weekly psychotherapy for about five months when her therapist took a three-week vacation. The material before and immediately after this vacation, which later proved to be linked in her mind to the pending forced termination of her therapy, indicated that the patient had had a very intense reaction to the separation, which she denied directly but expressed through acting-out and other derivatives. For example, the patient returned to her home for the first time in years and took a number of articles from her parent's mementos, even though they did not belong to her. She also got involved in a long battle with her present boyfriend, a divorced man, over the possibility of his leaving her, and expressed tremendous need for him.

Expressions of rage regarding a number of people who had deserted her earlier in life appeared. She also had a severe depression with suicidal feelings. The therapist had not connected any of these feelings to his vacation; instead, he focused upon her difficulties with her boyfriend. The pervasiveness of derivatives related to the therapist's vacation, however, indicated that this was technically incorrect.

Soon after the therapist returned, the patient spoke about how well the therapist looked. She also expressed a strong need for his help. She described an argument with her boyfriend; she had become completely disorganized when they had attempted to discuss the issues involved. She went to a party with him on the night of the quarrel and attempted to make him angry by completely ignoring him. At the party, she met a nice man who was friendly but who had no idea of what was going on. She thought of leaving the party with him, but left alone; her boyfriend stayed on with another girl. She later went to his apartment, only to find him with the girl from the party. She created a terrible scene. The man she had become involved with on the night of the party had seen a psychiatrist, and had told her that some of them were pretty crazy. She felt that her therapist was helping her, but wanted him to tell her how she could keep her boyfriend.

Here, the themes of remaining in the darkness, and of being nice but not knowing what was going on, were very apt descriptions of this warm and concerned therapist, who did not recognize the need to interpret the patient's maladaptive separation reactions to his vacation. Once again, the direct reference to a psychiatrist, and especially to psychiatrists who have problems of their own, confirmed the prediction made in supervision that the patient was indeed talking about her awareness of the therapist.

DISCUSSION

Technical errors and the patient's adverse reactions to them often cause the therapist to feel anxious and guilty. Errors in technique and even failures to respond humanely will occasionally occur during any treatment. The goal is to minimize their frequency and to develop means by which the therapist can recognize his mistakes and correct them with the patient, resolving within himself those difficulties which prompt him to make repetitive errors (Greenson, 1972, and Langs, 1973). While it is clear that there is no substitute for adequate training in psychoanalysis and psychotherapy, and for a personal psychoanalysis, it is useful to attempt to develop systematic ways of recognizing such errors. The primary vehicle for such recognition has always been the therapist's subjective awareness of these mistakes, for which his own analysis sensitizes him considerably (Cohen, 1952 and Langs, 1973).

A second means of detecting technical errors is to recognize the patient's unconscious communication of his reactions to the therapist's error. I have described the indicators of such mistakes in some detail in my previous work (Langs, 1973) and have attempted here to isolate one specific form that such material takes.

It is generally known that the patient is unconsciously exquisitely sensitive to the therapist's conscious and unconscious communications, including his mistakes. As a result, it behooves every therapist to be sensitive to all of the patient's communications which refer to conscious and unconscious fantasies about the therapist, the therapeutic alliance, and the therapeutic atmosphere. While I am not suggesting that psychotherapy should focus on such communications or make them the primary area for the work of treatment, I believe it is essential to the maintenance of a sound therapeutic alliance to remain in touch with this level of the patient's communications. By maintaining such observations, it becomes easier for the therapist to search out his own technique when he detects disturbances from the patient that suggest some technical error.

I will now list and briefly discuss the main implications of the findings presented here:

1. Among the general indicators of technical errors are ruptures and disturbances in the therapeutic alliance; acting-in, such as lateness, absence, and premature termination; the appearance of regressive symptoms, acting-out, and somatic and psychological symptoms (Langs, 1973).

2. There are some recurrent themes in the patient's manifest and latent associations which should alert the therapist to the possibility that he has made an error in technique. Such themes often reflect a sensitive, unconscious awareness of the nature of the therapist's error:

(a) Included here are themes of blindness, failure to be helpful, sensitive or understanding, and of being mistreated, frightened, seduced, or attacked.

(b) Among the displacements and disguises commonly used by patients to express such feelings and fantasies, parental figures and persons who are in the healing professions are commonly used, as are teachers and other authority figures.

(c) It is also extremely common for patients to become self-critical and self-attacking over failings and disturbances which they have discovered in the therapist.

3. When the material from the patient directs the therapist to review his technique, and he becomes aware of a technical error, the following general principles may be used in dealing with it:

(a) The therapist should review the patient's material subsequent to the error and formulate it as a manifest and latent response to the error.

(b) The therapist should recognize that *the analysis of the patient's reac-*

tion to the error must take precedence over all other therapeutic work, since it is essential to the restoration of a proper therapeutic alliance (Langs, 1973). Should there be another crucial problem in the session, he must deal with both his error and the patient's pressing difficulty. If there is no urgent outside conflict, he should then focus on his error and its consequences until the patient has analyzed and worked through his responses.

(c) As the patient's subsequent associations permit, the therapist should eventually acknowledge his error in simple words, as the starting point for his intervention. This is best done as the material from the patient fosters a discussion of the error, and, as it generally will, relates to it on a latent level.

In acknowledging the error, the therapist should not go beyond a simple recognition of it to the patient and, at times, a comment to the effect that the patient can be assured that he is endeavoring to understand its basis within himself. It is inappropriate for the therapist to discuss the inner sources of his mistake.

(d) Having acknowledged the error as the starting point for interventions, the therapist should then go on to detail the patient's conscious and unconscious fantasies and conflicts which it evoked. It is often helpful if the material recalls childhood situations and relationships. References to acting-out and to other behavior prompted by the therapist's error should also be discussed.

Although acknowledging his error, the therapist neither blames or condemns himself or the patient for what has happened. He acknowledges that he is human and will inevitably make mistakes. The patient will respond and much can be learned from the interaction.

Finally, the therapist wants to be in tune with the patient's reaction to his acknowledgment of the error.

4. I want to note certain pitfalls. It is important to be specific regarding both the error and the patient's reactions in fantasy and behavior. It is also crucial that the therapist not overemphasize his mistakes, nor refer to them more than the patient's response requires. Each patient needs an intact therapist, and repetitive errors damage the image of the therapist and the patient's basic trust in him. Should these incidents occur too often, it may prove necessary to refer the patient to a colleague—a matter I will not pursue here (see Greenson, 1969 and Langs, 1973).

5. I have been impressed with the fact that the frank acknowledgment of an error in technique, and the exploration and working-through of the patient's reaction to it, can provide a unique and growth-promoting, insight-producing experience for both the patient and therapist. In addition, these errors, when correctly understood and resolved, can lead to some of the most human and

moving experiences possible between patient and therapist. Thus, an error should not be seen as a terrible faux pas, or as dreaded failure, but as a human inevitability which can be turned into a productive, therapeutic experience.

SUMMARY

In this paper I have presented material related to one of the many indicators in associations from the patient of errors in technique by the therapist. I have presented evidence that patients are almost always unconsciously in tune with the therapist's error, which will be reflected in their associations. The means through which such associations can be understood and utilized have been detailed. On this basis, the technique for handling such mistakes and the patient's responses to them have been presented. Errors in technique are an inevitable part of psychotherapy—and psychoanalysis—and while they should be kept to a minimum and within certain limits, their proper exploration and analysis can provide both therapist and patient with some of the most moving and insightful experiences possible in treatment.

References

Arlow, J., "The Supervisory Situation." *Journ. of the Amer. Psychoanal. Assoc.,* 11:576-594 (1963).

Cohen, M. B., "Countertransference and Anxiety." *Psychiatry,* 15:231 - 243 (1952).

Greenson, R., "The working Alliance and the Transference neurosis." *Psychoanalytic Quarterly,* 34:155-181 (1965).

———, *The Technique and Practice of Psychoanalysis.* New York: International Universities Press, 1967.

———, "The 'Real' Relationship Between the Patient and the Psychoanalyst." In *The Unconscious Today,* ed. Mark Kanzer, New York: International Universities Press, 1971.

———, "Beyond Transference and Interpretation." *Internat. Journ. of Psychoanal.* 53:213-218 (1972).

——— and Wexler, M., "The Nontransference Relationships in the Psychoanalytic Situation." *Internat. Journ. of Psychoanal.* 50:27-40 (1969).

———, "Discussion of the Nontransference Relationships in the Psychoanalytic Situation." *Internat. Journ. of Psychoanal.,* 51:143-150 (1970).

Langs, R., *The Technique of Psychoanalytic Psychotherapy,* New York: Jason Aronson, Inc., 1973.

Orr, D. W., "Transference and Countertransference: a Historical Survey," *Journ. of the Amer. Psychoanal. Assoc.,* 12:621 - 670 (1954).

Chapter X

The Love That Is Enough: Countertransference and the Ego Processes of Staff Members in a Therapeutic Milieu

Bruno Bettelheim, Ph.D.

Simultaneously with working through and mastering of past psychological traumas, therapy must permit development to proceed as it would have but for the original trauma. Were it not for the innate developmental drive toward growth and normal functioning, no amount of tender, loving care from the environment could bring about the vast changes we have observed in our patients.

In what follows I shall try to set forth those factors which motivate members of a therapeutic milieu not only to achieve the intellectual and personal skills which they need for serving patients well and for becoming contributing partners in a common enterprise, but also what motivates them to engage in the much more difficult venture of changing themselves enough so that they not only can do this demanding work but can find it more rewarding than anything else they could do at this moment in their lives, because it helps them to become more what they wish to be.

Senior staff members have already achieved maturity, and since only a few deep alterations are necessary, they change much more slowly than do beginners. As persons, they have gained that mature personality integration which Erikson (1959) describes as generativity, Goldstein (1939) and Maslow (1972) as self-actualization, and others in still different terms. As therapists they have reached that familiarity with their own unconscious which permits ready empathy with the unconscious of the patients, while their grip on reality is so firm that they no longer fear what even the closest relation to a patient may evoke in them.

We found that some staff members* attained the qualities necessary for being considered senior, which includes suitability to serve as models to be emulated by younger staff members and by patients, after some three years of having been part of the therapeutic milieu, though more often it took four or

Adapted by Marjorie Flarsheim from *A Home for the Heart* by Bruno Bettelheim, Ph.D.
*At the Sonia Shankman Orthogenic School of the University of Chicago, Chicago, Illinois.

five years to reach this level of maturity. We usually knew, if not by the end of the first year then surely by the end of the second, whether the worker really wanted to become part of the therapeutic milieu.

Prior to joining us, most new staff members for one reason or another were confused as to what they wanted to do with their lives, and who they wanted to be. It may be that this is why working with psychiatric patients was attractive to them, since they dimly felt that if they should prove to be able to help the patients to find answers to such questions—as they must if they were to succeed in their work—they then would be able to do the same for themselves. Helping others in order to help oneself, if one is sincere about helping oneself, is, after all, not such a bad motive.

Most of them were considerably younger than was the author of *The Divine Comedy,* Dante (Alighieri) (1951), when he found himself seeking the right way out of temporary darkness. Most of them were roughly in their early twenties to early thirties. But like Dante, circling with understanding and compassion among those condemned to live in their private hells was also what they needed to find their way to a higher realm of clarity. Perhaps the conviction of their own importance to others, and the realization of how much they could do for them, was what they most needed in order to find themselves and their rightful place in the order of things, including in their chosen profession.

This seems to have been true for a psychiatrist who, when he was nearing thirty-five years ôf age, became a member of our staff and began his perilous journey to discover the deeper meaning of life. I select for an example here the tribulations of a psychiatrist to illustrate that even the best of professional training in a closely related field is not enough for becoming a meaningful participant in a therapeutic milieu. In his psychiatric practice, he had become disillusioned with what he was doing. Neither treating patients nor directing the work of others had been satisfactory personal experiences for him. He took the advice of one of his mentors who suggested that he try working as a counselor at the Orthogenic School.

Before he became part of the therapeutic milieu this psychiatrist had found treating patients unrewarding. This changed only as he slowly relinquished his view of psychotherapy as merely a complex intellectual task, and began to recognize to what degree it is also a direct emotional and personal encounter. He then learned that formerly he had tried to understand his patients intellectually without taking them seriously enough as persons, nor had he brought enough of himself to their treatment. As with so many others, his "conversion" began with recognition of the deep emotions that underlay his intellectual attitudes, which he had been convinced were nothing more than correct perceptions of what went on in others. For instance, he viewed a patient's deep concern with elimination as the consequence of anal fixations, which he correctly traced to parental attitudes of disgust. He tried to convince the patient how wrong his parents had been in this respect, and how little reason there was now for him to feel the same way. He encouraged him to deal with the problem in various ways, such as smearing with fingerpaint, and messing with water and sand in the sandbox. All this was done according to what he had been taught, and was in line with how he understood the patient's problems. But when in the course of such efforts the patient began soiling his pants, then somebody else—anybody, the therapist did not care who—was expected to clean him up. This is how he had handled such situations in the past. It did not occur to him that by doing so he may have impressed the patient that he, too, did not want to have anything to do with such messy affairs. Eventually he became aware of the deep inner revulsion he felt about what up to then he had always viewed as simply an "anal fixation" that needed analysis. This disgust, which was quite severe, was kept from awareness by regarding anal problems as something patients suffered from, and which were of no personal concern to him. This understanding was his first step toward the larger realization that deep down he had always felt that his patients were inferior human beings, and that he was untouched by what were problems for them.

He had yet to learn that if we judge something another person does as of no importance, then by implication we make the same judgment about the person himself. And if we do so in regard to an interaction of another person with us, we also prejudge ourselves as of little significance to this person. To accept this idea was even harder for this man because in regard to anality he had accepted its importance in theory, and had only denied its personal meaning to him. To take seriously what he was convinced was a triviality required a much more far-reaching change in his value system. One of the many experiences he had to undergo to change himself may illustrate how this came about.

While he was working as a counselor with a group of teenagers at the school, a heated discussion arose between them about the best way to start a car engine on a very cold day. He gave them factual information, but to little avail because they continued to disagree violently. In discussing the incident—which he saw no point in doing, "it was just the boys' usual jealousy of each other which made any issue good enough to fight about"—it emerged that he had been annoyed at their pettiness and cantankerousness, and also at their inability to use what he had so patiently explained to them. All of which was just another demonstration of how useless it was to try to teach them anything, even something they seemed so wrought up about.

In examining the incident with him, I began by suggesting that the issue of how to start a car could not possibly, in itself, be so important to these particular boys that they would argue with such violence; that behind it must be hidden some very personal issue. Since they had fought about it in front of him, their behavior must somehow be connected with him. This he found hard to believe. Not being sufficiently convinced of his importance to them, he could see no connection. On further questioning he recalled that the last time that he, the boys and a car were in some relation to each other was on a previous, very cold day. He lived close by, and the boys, while out for a walk, had seen him get into his car in front of his home and drive off. It then emerged that the argument initially began around quite another difference of opinion. One boy had insisted that the psychiatrist got into the car to drive to the school to take better care of him. But the other boys were worried by the fact that he, the father of two small children, should desert them for any reason; fathers should stay home to take care of their own children. It was only because the psychiatrist did not accept his importance to the boys that their fight seemed to have nothing to do with their personal involvement with him. Instead he believed it had only to do with how to start a car, and he had viewed the argument as caused by the boys' nastiness to each other.

Thus it turned out to be something other than an unimportant fight. Essentially it was a statement of the boys' deep emotional involvement with him. Only by taking them and what they had done very seriously, only through unraveling and understanding what lay behind the argument about how a person operates an automobile, did annoying behavior become meaningful to him. Certainly such understanding added to his sense of being important to the boys, and it did this much more effectively than anything I, or anyone else, could have told him. It is possible that one reason he had not recognized his importance was that it is not only flattering but also a great responsibility to be so important in someone's life. Such understanding helped him accept what up to then he had so strongly disapproved of in himself that he had had to repress it, such as his disgust with elimination. Intellectual teaching, convincing as it may be, fails to help the therapist change himself. Recognizing the repressed would have been a severe blow to his self-esteem, therefore he had to keep it in repression. But once his ego had been powerfully strengthened by the narcissistic supplies gained from recognizing how important he as a person, and all his doings, were to others, his thus buttressed ego could afford to accept some blows, such as the realization that he was by no means beyond suffering from problems akin to those of the patients.

It is the emotional supplies which one directly or indirectly derives from working with patients within a therapeutic milieu which permit the staff member to restructure his personality. Not only because the work requires it, though this is part of it, and not only because it presents so many challenges, though these help, too, but also because *the work strengthens the ego while it threatens it*. That the worker's reactions, as in this example his unwillingness to attach any seriousness to the boys' behavior, and his annoyance at them, are viewed as worthy of the most serious considerations and that others felt that he and what he did were important enough to make sustained efforts to help him understand himself better; this, in itself, independent of any understanding he gained, was also ego-strengthening. Had not Virgil, as the poem suggests, taken Dante seriously enough to explain everything to him that they encountered together, he could not on his own have undertaken his journey.

In the preceding example the psychiatrist could not recognize the importance of his own person, and hence of the particular action (leaving his home and children) as it appeared to those in his care. Having to recognize their behavior as due to their positive involvement with him was not easy, but neither was it painful.

Often it *is* painful. Patients often behave annoyingly just because we are important to them. They continuously ask themselves: Is he willing and able to take care of me? Is he able to help me with my problems?

Let us now return to the psychiatrist. All his life he had found it difficult to conform. At the school he found himself extremely annoyed with a schizophrenic boy who, on walks, could never keep up with him or the others. It was this boy's way of repeatedly stating his feeling that he was far behind everyone in life, and could never catch up or keep up with the rest of the world. But it was also an assertion of his wish for independence and autonomy. Up to now the psychiatrist had never considered the hostile element in his own struggle for independence which had enabled a poor farm boy to become a psychiatrist; he had only been aware of its positive value for him. Unconsciously the schizophrenic boy had recognized this and acted as if to ask: "You, who so vigorously assert your independence, are you ready also to grant it to me, a helpless schizophrenic?"

With his behavior the patient questioned not only the psychiatrist's dominant method of mastery but, which was more painful, whether he could retain it if he wished also to become a therapist of schizophrenics. This threatened and hence annoyed him. His irritation was deepened by an even greater, and much more consciously experienced threat: the danger to his self-image as a person who was able and willing to accept schizophrenic behavior. In this experience, it took considerably more effort to show that it was the psychiatrist's importance to the boy that had motivated the probing into his defensive system. That which had seemed mere annoying behavior had been a crucial testing question: "Are you, who are so far ahead of me, ready to slow down to a snail's pace for my benefit?" Or even more deeply probing: "Are you ready to relinquish some of your striving for independence so that I can safely become dependent on you?" In any case, to recognize that such a seemingly simple thing as being laggard on walks was deeply connected with the psychiatrist's importance to the boy helped this therapist toward becoming a fully participating member of the therapeutic milieu.

This time, the strength the psychiatrist's ego derived from understanding that lingering signified his importance to the patient made it possible to modify what up to then had been one of the most rigid features of his character: his hostile stance of independence, which had prevented him from truly learning from others, and worse, had prevented him from permitting himself to become intimate with even those close to him, because of his fear that this would infringe upon his autonomy. It was this inability to permit his patients to have an emotional impact on him, because of the defensive and protective nature of his independence, that had made the work of a psychiatrist so unrewarding to him, and had robbed him of success with his patients though he had tried his best to help them. It had also made it impossible for those whom he directed to work closely with him. After a few years at the school, having overcome his anxiety that he would lose his own strength if he did not at all times protect his independence against the emotional impact of others, he was so changed as a person that he could successfully return to the profession which earlier had been a burden to him.

Most of the residential staff of the Orthogenic School were in their twenties when they began their training there. Though many were working for an M.A. or Ph.D. degree, what was most important to them was to experience as participants the common enterprise of milieu therapy and to reach the level of personal development required for "senior" staff. When they started their work they were dissatisfied with themselves and some aspects of their lives. They felt a need for change, for intellectual and emotional growth. They believed, or at least wished to believe, that change was possible, and that there were no limitations either to their potentialities or to their ability to achieve self-realization. The intensive training program, which included many hours of regular staff meetings, in addition to individual conversations with senior staff and daily "bull sessions" among the workers, tried to meet these needs.

Nevertheless the outcome was not always favorable. For each worker who was able to restructure his personality through work experiences, two others failed and left the school. Those who failed felt repelled by the demands made of them, or beset by terrifying anxiety. They would simply leave, giving a variety of reasons which served as rationalizations for not recognizing that their inner integration had been threatened. Among such rationalizations were the difficulties of the work, the inconvenient hours, offers of better pay elsewhere, and so on. Actually, these claims served the purpose of preventing the individual from realizing that, contrary to his conscious desire to get close to such patients, he was disgusted or upset by their behavior, or afraid of them.

A characteristic example is that of a young woman who, because of her unusual abilities, had been given a special fellowship for training in the education of blind children. For more than a year she had lived in an institution for blind children, working very successfully with the most emotionally disturbed of them.

She later joined our staff, because we treated the type of children she felt she particularly wished to work with. When she started, we pointed out the difficulties involved in working with these unintegrated children, but she said with much conviction that she could accept all of them. She was a well-educated and well-brought-up young woman, successful in her adjustment to life and in her profession. At first the children did not respond badly to her, and her beginning work showed promise.

About six weeks after she began working at the school, an autistic girl bit her. She took this with a certain Spartan attitude and resisted efforts to help uncover her feelings about the injury. When offered the opportunity to rest for a day or two, she insisted she wished to continue working despite the localized pain. The next time she was with this autistic child the patient suddenly ran away to escape the anger she felt in the worker because of the injury she had inflicted. Our explanations of the cause of the child's fear were of no avail. The next time worker and child were together the patient began to hurt herself severely, biting herself worse than she had bitten the worker a few days before. Clearly, for the safety of the child, we could not permit the situation to continue. The new worker now seemed to become dimly aware that, contrary to her self-image as a person who loved emotionally disturbed children and was not afraid of their hostility, she had been repelled by the child's unintegrated behavior all along, a repulsion that may very well have led to the child's biting her. Since the injury, she had been very much afraid of the child. She could not accept at all what seemed obvious to those who were observing her—namely, that she had also begun to hate the child. *This hostility was probably caused much less by the injury than by the fact that her inner response to the child's action was one which threatened her self-image.* She now became emotionally frozen and another group of children who had tentatively accepted her before these events now began to reject her because she could no longer respond spontaneously to them.

Obviously, to continue her work with us, the worker would have had to realize at this point that her self-image of accepting emotionally disturbed children, no matter what their behavior, did not stand up under stress. She would have had to recognize that on occasion she rejected children and, in reaction to their attacks, was afraid of them—perhaps even hated them. Such realizations probably would have led her to become conscious of her own hostility, which until then had been so well controlled that she could remain unaware of it. Such recognition would have presented her with the immediate task of achieving better integration in many respects. Later, starting with this or other experiences, efforts at integration would also have had to extend to other aspects of her personality as yet not fully integrated.

But the worker, either unwilling or unable to accept the help other staff members offered, suddenly decided that her salary was not adequate. In an attempt to show her that she was denying her true motives for wanting to leave, an offer was made to increase her salary. She did not accept it and instead left the school, and gave up working with emotionally disturbed children. Being a person with a healthy, normal personality, excellent training and abilities, and realizing that her present level of integration was perfectly adequate for average life activities, she immediately secured a teaching position in a school for normal children. In doing so she protected herself against the further disintegration of her personality that might have resulted from working with psychotic patients.

This worker's reactions were responses to the impact of the primary process behavior of the patients, and to the requirement inherent in the therapeutic milieu not to meet it defensively but acceptingly and with therapeutic intent and action. Once such workers, whose personality integration is certainly quite adequate to meet the ordinary demands of life among ordinary people, have left the institution, they succeed in reestablishing their old personalities. Their ego disorganization is not a pathological process that continues, but is a temporary and inevitable response to the pressure for that higher integration needed not only for meeting special work tasks but for living up to the ethos of the milieu. They are not able to use the temporary disorganization as a step toward reorganization at a higher level.

Other beginning workers, with stronger motivation for devoting themselves to these patients, try harder. While better able to accept primary process behavior in patients, they still may not be ready to face what it activates in themselves. The patients' physical, verbal, and sexual assaults awaken deep anxieties and self-doubts in these hitherto secure and adjusted young adults, and their personal integration is threatened. They experience the reactivation of the primary process in themselves as they watch it in others. They may then resort to defensive efforts to suppress the patients' expression of uncontrolled instinctual behavior, trying to force them to conform to more acceptable standards of conduct. If their personalities or therapeutic convictions—the latter strongly supported by the mores of the institution and by supervision— do not permit them to suppress the patient's behavior, then they will try to reinforce their inner defenses against the primary process within themselves. They become, for a while, quite rigid.

These relatively well-functioning individuals, who had sufficient ego strength to enter and do well in graduate school and who have a background of success in working with people, sooner or later, but usually soon after they begin living and working intimately with these unintegrated patients, appear to develop quite serious neurotic behavior. Some become hostile or even punitive to patients, and hostile and unmannerly to other members of the staff.

They are very uncomfortable, and resent the institution and its mores and the other staff members who expect them to be able to accept the patients' threatening behavior without undesirable counterreactions. Other new workers defend themselves by feeling nothing, or by other forms of emotional withdrawal. Still others try to erect new and (they hope) better defenses, such as intellectualization, against the new violently activated inner pressures.

For a worker to succeed in the task of restructuring his personality, all other members of the therapeutic milieu must understand and accept that such developments, though often unpleasant and seemingly quite neurotic, are normal reactions to particular stress situations. These are emergency reactions. They spring from the realization that a system of defenses and a level of inner integration which until now were considered fully adequate, are suddenly insufficient. Matters are made even more difficult because what has broken down this level of integration and system of defenses are professional activities chosen freely by the worker as his preferred vocation. It has become obvious that to work successfully with these patients, an infinitely higher level of personal integration is necessary. This must include a familiarity with and much greater acceptance of one's own and other persons' unconscious and primitive mental life than is required for almost any other activity in society. Disillusionment with oneself, if not open despair, is one of the reactions to having to realize that one's defensive system and level of integration, once apparently so adequate, have suddenly, under the very special conditions of working with psychotics, turned out to be inadequate.

This is a critical moment in the development of a staff member. It takes varying periods of time for different persons to reach it, usually between six months and, rarely, as much as two years. Once this point is reached, the successful staff member begins the process of slowly giving up both old defenses and newly erected ones. He begins to gain greater tolerance of the existence of primitive impulses within himself. Then, he begins to be able to accept and deal constructively with the patients' expression or acting out of the same impulses.

By realizing that the experiences which therapeutic work provides will be a continuous challenge to higher integration, the worker will consider the discomfort inflicted by patients to be a relatively small price to pay for the very considerable benefits.

Many have remarked on the "dedication" of these young members of the therapeutic milieu. Dedicated they undoubtedly are, but not merely to the patients under their care. They are dedicated also to achieving their own integration. No longer needing or wishing to put a barrier of emotional distance between themselves and the problems the patients' behavior poses for them, as well as being prevented from doing so by the ethos of the milieu, they have to find ways to integrate the emotions aroused by their experiences.

The following case description is an example of how the unresolved residues of childhood problems of a worker significantly aided the formation of interpersonal relations with patients and also led to some resolution of the after-effects of the old problems. In infancy this staff member had not received the maternal care she needed. Because the ethos of the therapeutic milieu approves the gratification of infantile desires, and because this young woman needed to participate in a relationship in which such needs were gratified, she was able to respond enthusiastically to the few infantile satisfactions that a very frightened child could permit herself. The patient, Jane, was thus able to regress, and accept and enjoy infantile gratifications, and became cheerful through this satisfaction. In psychoanalytic treatment before Jane came to the school, an experienced psychoanalyst had not been able to help Jane to move out of her defiant and depressive pseudo-stupidity or to give up her destructive acting out.

In her early life this staff member had been prevented from gaining true independence by an overstrong and extremely ambivalent attachment to her mother. She felt that giving and receiving infantile satisfactions, free from all ambivalence, was the most wonderful thing in the world, and this was exactly what she could offer Jane. Since she had projected her negative feelings onto her mother, she concentrated only positive feelings on Jane, whom she experienced, reacted to and spoke of as "such a wonderful baby." To her, Jane's angry defiance and often wild acting out, far from detracting from the counselor's positive feelings, actually added to them. She let Jane do to her what she had wished to do to her mother when she was a child and had not dared to do; what unconsciously she still wished she had done. Had she been able to behave toward her mother as Jane did toward her, the counselor felt, she would have had a wonderful life.

As a child, Jane had had to repress totally her intense hostility toward her mother. Therefore, it was extremely meaningful to be confronted with a mother figure who had fullest empathy with and approved of hostility toward a mother. This became the unconscious basis for a close relation between worker and child. Because of it, and also because the worker could recognize and respond emotionally to the positive aspects of Jane's desire for babying, Jane for the first time was able to relax her defenses against permitting herself the satisfactions she craved so much.

There were other bonds between the child and her worker. Jane, more than the counselor, suffered from guilt about her destructive wishes against her mother which prevented her from accepting herself and accepting gratification. The worker, since she saw mothers as frustrating, felt that hostile wishes against them were justified, and her conviction reassured Jane and alleviated her guilt. Although the worker's inability at this stage to see either Jane's or her own contribution to the bad relations between child and mother was unrealistic, it was also helpful. In order to maintain the image of her mother as all bad, the worker had to prove that it was possible to give to others un-limitedly, despite Jane's sullen resistance and defiance. By getting Jane to accept infant care the counselor vicariously could enjoy gratifications she had missed in childhood. But this was of little importance compared to the vital significance of proving that an all-giving mother could exist and that her anger at her own mother therefore was justified. At no moment could she allow herself to become a disinterested, disappointing, rejecting mother, as she felt her mother had been. Thus she was strongly motivated to accept and even thoroughly enjoy Jane's regression to infancy, as well as her hostility and destructiveness.

If the situation had not worked out as it did, it probably would have become necessary through supervision to have the worker recognize, accept and limit Jane's hostility and eventually to help her integrate it. However, as is often the case, this was not necessary because the patient forced such insight on the worker. The following episode helped the worker understand some of her exaggerated feelings.

Jane and another girl got into a scuffle and the worker had to separate them by force. She was apprehensive that she might have acted too severely toward Jane. To her astonishment, Jane, to quote the worker's report, ''seemed rather relieved that I stopped her when I did in the way that I did, rather than hating me for it. Actually it puzzled me that her reaction was one of relief instead of anger.'' In terms of the therapist's need to separate herself from her mother, she had to see all interventions by mother figures as hateful and as justifying anger. She was still loath to recognize that some interventions she experi-enced as a child might have been justified and for her benefit, and might even have caused her to feel relief. Jane's reaction to her active interference was the needed challenge, since it suggested that the worker's evaluation of her mother might not have been valid. It started a process that led her to see her mother, and herself and Jane as well, not only in black and white, as either angels or devils, but as wholly human persons.

In milieu therapy, much stress is given to the consideration not only of the positive, but also of the negative transference. A patient from time to time would spit at a counselor, and there were many staff discussions regarding it. Redl (1966) writes: ''I have run into people who really love 'crazy youngsters' and are quite willing to sacrifice a lot. Only they simply cannot stand more than half a pound of spittle in their faces a day, professional attitude or no.'' Unfortunately, he does not tell us what they do until the amount of insult which is their limit has been reached. Do they at first pretend it doesn't matter, and then suddenly act as if it matters a great deal? Or does it really not matter to them at first but only later, and if so, why? Is the message the patient is trying to convey in barely disguised symbolic form any different after the half pound of spittle has accumulated?

Would not the worker's reaction be different, if instead of believing that the patient's behavior expressed hatred and depreciation, he thought that since he is so important to the patient, the patient had needed to find out whether he is acceptable to the counselor even when abusive? Perhaps at this moment the worker had come to be identified with early experiences with a mother who never permitted the patient to spit out his food, and even forced it back down his throat when he tried to spit it out. If the worker has been helped by the rest of the staff to react to the patient simultaneously as a person and as a therapist—rather than just trying to accept or control the patient's behavior, *neither of which is therapeutic*—then he will make some judgment about the meaning of the patient's behavior, and respond on that basis. Even though he may be wrong in his initial evaluation of what it all signifies, his personal response (as opposed to an institutionalized one) will usually provoke the patient to react in a way which will permit making a more correct assessment.

The staff in most psychiatric institutions does not know how to react to a patient who arouses deep emotions. Rather they retire into "professionalism," which inhibits, and hence protects against, an emotional response. It is not so much the patient's actions or feelings against which the staff seeks protection, but mainly their own. If, for example, I believe that things have to be done at a certain moment and in unalterable ways, then this conviction—irrespective of whether anything else in reality justifies it— protects me against being devastated by what I inflict on others when I force them to submit to these routines. If I view some persons as subhuman, then when I do what I believe is necessary, I cannot be shaken by their discomfort.

The therapeutic milieu must support the worker so that he does not need to withdraw behind the protective wall of insensitivity; at the same time it must help him to reintegrate his own personality, not just at the preworking level but at a higher one. There are many ways for the staff member to do this. One is to open himself to the patients, and thereby give them a chance to act on him as much as he acts on them. This may be illustrated by a sequence of recollections from a former staff member who, looking back and understanding what had happened, wrote:

> I had entered into the work full of the usual ideas about being understanding of, and nice to patients. I wanted to see myself as a good fellow doing an admirable job on behalf of those poor lost souls. Instead I found myself exasperated, ineffective, and losing my temper. . . . I explained (this) as the result of the patients being basically different from me. I was sane, an adult, taking care of them. The gist of these efforts was to protect myself by maintaining a gap between me and them . . . it was their fault for being different. (Wright, 1957).

It made this worker angry that the patients' behavior and his reaction to it prevented him from seeing himself the way he wanted to be: understanding, helpful, in short, some kind of saviour. The frustration of his wish and consequent anger explain his making himself insensitive to patients. These feelings can be neither understood nor positively dealt with unless they are recognized as the worker's desperate effort to maintain his integration—which is indeed threatened by the feelings patients evoke in him.

Just because the intentions of the new staff member are good and still do not achieve anything for patients (or do not seem to, which is a possibility a beginner may not be aware of), the worker reasons it must be the fault of the "difference" of the patient and so hardly deserves further effort. Most workers in psychiatric insitutions do, indeed, begin with good intentions, having long forgotten where the path thus paved leads.

At this point, the staff must be helped not to give up. There is no universal way of assisting staff members with the problems of badly damaged narcissism and self-esteem, which stem from lack of success in their early efforts. But in many instances, it was sufficient to ask the staff member to project himself into somebody else who for years had all his hopes disappointed, and was unable to believe in anybody's good intentions. After reminding him of some of his patient's specific traumatic experiences, we asked him how *he* would react to having to contend with such a past, even if somebody approached him with the best of motives. The beginner's answer often was that he would be delighted, because it would give him desired and hoped-for relief. The worker was surprised when we pointed that neither he nor the patient seemed to have learned anything from past experiences—since the worker stated that despite all, he would still approach any new experience with such naiveté. This led to the realization that indeed it would take months or maybe years of experiencing an entirely different approach before the patient could believe in its sincerity.

Another quite effective way to evoke empathy is to remind a worker how much time it takes and how much a mother must do for her infant before he can feel sure of her love and does not respond to any frustration with a fit of screaming. This happens even in instances where the infant has not yet had any bad experiences; and it happens in one of the best, least ambivalent relations known to man.

If none of this convinces the staff member that the patient's negative response to his positive efforts, far from proving him ineffective, is just what should be expected—then it may be effective to ask him how many positive things he has done, and for how long, to counteract all the bad experiences the patient has had. In his imagination, the worker should try to put the patient's unending series of bad experiences on one side of the scale, and the good experiences he has tried to provide on the other, and decide what the balance or imbalance is likely to be.

Such homespun appeals to common sense are much more constructive in developing empathy for the patient's predicament than the elaborate theoretical explications the beginner craves, pertinent as these may be from a scientific point of view. There are several reasons why the beginner seeks technical explanations about the nature of a particular patient's psychiatric disturbance, its origins, the psychoanalytic meaning of his symptoms, and similar information he thinks will help him "understand" the patient. One reason is that practically everyone genuinely interested in this type of work wants to learn about human beings, but in the abstract; that is, in ways that will not hit home. Whether or not they are aware of it or can admit it, they fear knowledge that does not apply exclusively to the patient; because such knowledge may have unfathomable consequences for themselves and thus is best avoided. Yet unconsciously, they do want to find out about themselves: They may even wish to find themselves through working with psychiatric patients; at the same time they consciously feel that this is a bad, selfish motive which would invalidate their belief that they want to help these unfortunate people. There is also an unconscious fear that what one might discover about oneself might be unbearably upsetting or unacceptable. It was only after one or more episodes of such conflictual, repressed emotions were brought to consciousness, with the increased inner ease, comfort, and integration which accompanied the new awareness, that the new counselors could appreciate the strength of their repressive faculties and the positive value of relaxing their restraints.

However, the senior staff could not permit themselves or others to hide behind the professional language of psychopathology. No patient actually engaged in "primary process behavior," or acted "insane." He did concrete things: He spat or threw up, he struck something or somebody, he gorged himself, he cowered unmoving in a corner with his back to the world. Our reaction to particular types of behavior could bring to awareness some of our specific problems. Why was it so upsetting and degrading to be spat upon, for example, given the fact that we all as infants spat up on those who fed us? Why, we could begin to wonder, has spitting—once probably an expression either of affection, of feeling well fed, or of feeling that something disagreed with us—become one of the worse offenses in our society? Why should we react with such strong emotion? It is easy to believe that a patient's "primary process behavior" does not affect us; it is impossible to believe that one has no reaction to his spitting on us, his screaming out his anger or distress, or to his utter lack of response when we try to reach him.

There is a seeming contradiction in the fact that it usually was easier for the new staff members to recognize (acknowledge) and try to understand their *negative* feelings and the effects of these upon the patients they worked with rather than become aware of their great importance to their patient, and the beneficial effect of their efforts. This apparent inversion can be explained by understanding the enormity of the responsibility the staff member felt for the patient. He might think, "If my acceptance and warmth toward this patient is helping him to get better, I will have to remain strong and giving because he has come to need me so much, and I'm not sure I can continue to do it so well." In my experience every new staff member defended himself against recognizing how terribly important he could be to a patient. Each felt it much easier to admit having made a mistake (convinced that he would not repeat it) than to accept such a great commitment. We all can live quite easily knowing we have made an error, or that we have been lazy or inattentive; but it is not as easy to realize that we are able to break, or have broken, another person's heart.

The following example is illustrative. A staff member had been working very hard for several months with a most difficult patient who, largely because of her efforts, had begun to make considerable progress. Another staff member joined her for a day, interested in learning how she managed to survive the onslaught of this patient's violent outbursts. The patient had been told that this staff member was only visiting. Suddenly he reverted to his original behavior, becoming totally unreachable. Distraught, his worker asked a senior staff member for help. Being less involved, he immediately understood the patient's behavior. It seemed that despite what he had been told, the patient feared that the visiting staff member might take the place of his worker. When the senior staff member explained that they understood his fears, unwarranted though they were, the patient immediately reestablished contact.

Devoted though this worker was to the patient, later discussions revealed that she had some reservations about exposing herself at all times to difficult behavior. Unconsciously, she did not want to feel deeply obliged to continue working with him indefinitely; to prevent this, she had not permitted herself to recognize how terribly important she had become to him. This incident gave her confidence in how much she meant to the patient, how desperate was his anxiety about losing her. Because of a better understanding of what she already had achieved with him, she no longer worried about whether she would have the emotional strength to continue to work with him.

In every staff meeting all suggestions, whether from the senior psychiatrist or the newest staff members, had to be viewed as equally important. How the worker *feels* about what he has learned has a much greater impact on his work with the patient than what he now *knows* should be done. The patient understandably often reacts more to the tone in which something is said, than to the overt content.

For example, no intellectual understanding of how important it is to give a patient a long and pleasant bath, to play with him in the tub, even to encourage him to defecate into the tub (which in the case of a psychotic boy broke the lifelong inability to move his bowels without the help of enemas) will be enough if the staff member has not really examined his own feelings about the body and its excretions. The patient knows how the staff members feel about him and about his body by the way in which he is approached in innumerable daily encounters: how they wake him up and put him to bed, feed him, hold his hand when he tries to hurt himself, or others. But these underlying feelings are most clearly revealed in the behavior of a staff member who is physically or psychologically attacked, slapped or kicked, held up to ridicule, lied to, spit upon; by how he reacts when the patient smears his stools on himself, the furniture, or the staff member.

It is impossible to teach empathetic sensitivity. Staff members acquire it only by experiencing their own feelings; if one is vomited upon it is "natural" that one is disgusted, but rather than viewing this reaction in terms of "right" or "wrong," it has to be understood and respected as an important indicator of one's deeper feelings.

A staff member must understand how terrorized a patient would have to be to hold onto his stools for weeks on end. He must realize how this would force him to think continuously about avoiding defecation, to the point that it becomes an all-consuming preoccupation. Then when he holds the patient's hand for hours while the patient is sitting on the toilet, empathy with the patient's panic about letting go or dirtying himself becomes the staff member's dominant emotion. There is no place left for disgust. A counselor's direct empathy with the panic about letting go finally enabled one patient to eliminate freely, first in the bathtub, and later in the toilet.

Unresolved remnants of one's past can either be the most serious impediments to working with psychiatric patients or the greatest of assets. They are impediments when they are *acted out*; assets when they are judiciously *acted upon*. Those who work with psychiatric patients are often expected to refrain from acting on the basis of their own emotional preoccupations. Since we all have emotional problems, this is impossible. Without these emotional preoccupations, the therapist could not do the work; they are the main incentive for him to help psychiatric patients on their incredibly difficult road to recovery. *Without this source of empathy with the patient, psychotherapeutic work could never succeed.* Everybody who wants to work with psychiatric patients must have some ability to develop empathy. One of the main reasons for a prospective worker's trial visit to the school is to ascertain whether he has this ability.

Unfortunately, in English there is very little literature on empathy. Were there greater understanding and appreciation of the important role of empathy in all good human relations, behavior modification could not enjoy such favor among psychologists as it does at the moment. Anybody who could have empathy with the recipient of behavioral manipulations—including the inner experience of how degrading it is to permit oneself to be bought off by candies or tokens by somebody who claims to "know" how one should behave— would feel a revulsion when thus manipulating another person. The dominant traits of our culture and its pragmatic and behavioristic temper are mirrored in the tendency to manipulate not only things but also persons as if they were objects, as opposed to understanding them and aiding them to work matters out in their own way.

Empathy is not anything that can be done "in order to" that is, for a purpose; as a matter of fact, nothing interferes more with empathy than a person's being goal-directed in any way. Freud does not specifically discuss empathy, but relies instead on his explanation of what is going on when it occurs. He speaks of what he calls, "the sympathy of one unconscious to another," thus making it clear that this can never be a rational process. On the contrary, he warns that conscious rationality interferes with it (Freud, 1924).

Projection is entirely different from empathy. *Projection is essentially self-centered, while empathy, though drawing on one's inner experiences, is centered on the other.* In projection, one sees oneself in the other; in empathy, one feels the other in oneself, not as a totality as in introjection, but only as the other is feeling at this very moment, and without going beyond the boundaries of the self, which remain intact.

While compassion motivates one to do something for the patient, believing that it will be good for him, it can still lead one severely astray. Approaching the work scientifically, and understanding exactly what the patient's psychological problems are, results in decisions which are based on what he may need in the long run, rather than what he needs at the moment.

For example, in an incident in which a relatively new staff member encouraged patients to throw water around, the worker thought it would be a relief for the patient to relax his self-control; he even thought that patients in general might benefit if they could unleash their frustration and act out violent feelings. But he had not really considered his relationship with them at the moment. Thinking that the worker had relinquished his ego-supporting role and had temporarily suspended his ability to control expressions of anger, they became carried away by their anxieties. Because the worker acted out of sympathy, and projected his own feelings onto them, he was not able to move freely with them as the situation developed. He was carried away by his own desire to act out of anger. But, had he felt empathy, he would have been able to see at just what point the patients became frightened by lack of control and needed help in reestablishing control over their aggressions; he would have "felt into" their fear of being swept away by their feelings.

In a way, empathy is a back-and-forth, oscillating process; in the "back" swing, one goes back into one's own primary process thinking and feeling; in the "forth" one returns to one's adult integration of these same processes and uses them to come closer to the core of the other's experience of the moment. Since these primary processes all go back to the time before our personality was fully formed and became controlled by the ego, empathy requires that "the adult (be able to) allow himself to live with the sufferings of his childhood and reach a degree of reconciliation with them" (Blos, 1962).

The problem is how the therapeutic milieu can help staff members reconcile their childhood sufferings and thus enable them to feel empathy, to feel into those primitive, basic emotional experiences which characterized our world when we were children—and which, if we have not integrated them into our personality, continue to interfere with our ability to cope in the present. Only the staff's ability to achieve such an inner reconciliation can form the basis from which they can help the patients do the same.

Insofar as possible our policy was to let the patient and worker select each other. The patient found something in a particular worker that he felt would enable him to work out his problems better than with any other available person. The worker found something in the patient especially interesting and appealing. Then as the work progressed, unconscious pressure from crucial but as yet unresolved childhood conflicts of the worker would resonate with complementary ones in the patient. This may be illustrated by the case of Dana and her worker.

In order to save her life, Dana, a girl suffering from anorexia nervosa, had spent three prolonged periods in the psychiatric ward of a university hospital. During the first two hospitalizations the friendly and accepting attitudes of a nurse—the opposite of the extreme rejection she had experienced with her mother—had soon permitted her to gain weight and be out of danger. But within months after each return home she was again dangerously anorexic, leading to the next hospitalization. The third time nothing seemed to help, nothing could induce her to eat, and artificial feedings failed to improve the situation. In addition, she became openly schizophrenic. She would stand at the window catatonically still, unable to move and looking at the sky.

After her transfer to the Orthogenic School she soon began to eat, within a few months becoming obese, but without change in her catatonic rigidity. One way we induced her to eat was to place her bed by the window so she could look out, watching the sky as much as she wished. Otherwise we were as "stuck with her" as she was with herself, despite all we tried. Then a new worker took to her, and Dana in turn seemed ready to be approached by this particular worker. Toward others Dana's behavior did not change, but, as became known much later, she viciously assaulted this worker, in secret, beating her up each time the two were alone.

The worker, by now deeply devoted to Dana, but as yet unsure of her position within the staff, and of what was expected of her in such a situation, kept Dana's attacks on her hidden, as did Dana. As she revealed later, she had kept Dana's attacks a secret partly because she felt she did not merit any better since she did not know how to help this wretched girl, but mostly because she had feared that if she admitted her incompetence she would no longer be considered suitable to remain on the staff and to work with Dana. The relation had become so vitally important to her that she was ready to protect it at all cost, even that of enduring almost daily beatings, severe pinchings, kickings, and other mistreatment. She had asked to work closely with Dana, and look what happened: Dana had recognized that she was not able to be of help, and with justice, punished her for it. Interestingly enough, as later came to light, Dana always managed to hit or kick her when nobody could see it, and to hurt her at places on her body which the worker could hide, so that others did not become aware of what went on. Eventually after more than a year Dana became obviously less rigid in other situations, though not any less schizophrenic. The rest of the staff believed that things were progressing with Dana and the worker, however slowly. But the bruises could no longer always be hidden, and the worker's explanations that they were due to her clumsiness and other chance circumstances began to wear thin. The staff, concerned with the worker's well-being, refused to accept her excuses, and some guessed the truth. Eventually the worker admitted that because she felt inadequate to help Dana she had accepted being punished by her. Why should she stop it, when she deserved it? By letting herself be pummelled she was at least of some use to Dana, if she could be of no other.

Her "confession" of deserving punishment permitted others to argue that her failure to do better with Dana was not a sufficient explanation, particularly in view of the obvious fact that she had done better with her than anybody else, small though Dana's progress had been. Though the worker was not yet able to accept this, her belief was a bit shaken when the others, whose devotion to their patients she knew, told her they would not accept such abuse, because to do so would be demeaning to both the patient and themselves. Yet for quite some time she insisted there were no other reasons but her deep involvement with Dana. Finally when we asked whether Dana, or her relation to Dana, resembled or reminded her of any other person she had known, or any relationship she had experienced in her past, she came to the startling realization that her relation to Dana reminded her of that to her next younger sister, though she could not understand why because this sister had never attacked her, but on the contrary had always been very dependent on her.

To summarize what took hard work and considerable time to unravel, only a little of which need be noted here, the worker, the eldest of several sisters, from an early age had had to play the "mother" role with her younger siblings. Their mother claimed to be incapacitated by illness, something the worker, though consciously accepting it, unconsciously had never believed and hence had resented. One afternoon, seemingly without reason, she had run after this sister with a kitchen knife, an event she had entirely "forgotten" for all these years, remembering only how much she had loved her sister. She recalled that during this episode she was so "out of it" that she did not know what might have happened had the sister not been able to elude her, which gave her a chance to get hold of herself. Ever since, though the entire event had been repressed, she had felt like a murderess who deserved severe punishment.

Dana, before she met the worker, could not give up her catatonic immobility since any move—given the inner rage that consumed her—would have meant attack. She had somehow guessed that against this person she might be violent without being destroyed in retaliation. It had begun by her kicking the worker under the table, as if by chance. When the worker accepted it—consciously pleased because Dana had begun to move her body, but unconsciously encouraging Dana to continue to mistreat her in order to relieve her guilt—Dana became more violent in her attacks. Full of murderous anger against her mother, she had found in her worker a mother-figure who was ready to accept her fury.

Thus, each had sensed in the other a strong constellation of motives that would permit each to derive satisfaction of an unconscious need. The worker sought unconsciously to be punished for what she had wanted to do to her sister and hence atone for it, while Dana sought to express her rage so that she would no longer need to repress it catatonically. The attraction each had for the other was thus based on complementary needs. This is true in most cases in which patient and worker spontaneously select each other, as distinguished from situations where only the worker prefers a particular patient.

Young people need to identify with suitable adults. But, *in order to mature emotionally they must identify with characteristics they do not as yet possess but wish to acquire.* It is a different situation when the adult who should provide leadership identifies with the immature parts of the patient. This leads to a stalemate since the immature person cannot relinquish those parts which are the essence of the adult person's attachment. Thus, such identification represents an immature object-choice on the part of adults, narcissistically pleasing but not suitable for a constructive relation because instead of promoting growth it retards or prevents it. In education the best teacher is the one who, while he behaves so that the students can identify with him, does not himself identify with the student's immaturity. Rather, the mature educator sees his function as developing in the student what is still lacking in him. This is even more true in therapy, and counselors at the school never succeeded if they could not master a need to identify with immature aspects of the patients' personalities. Only those workers whose commitment was to supply the patient with something that was missing succeeded in helping him achieve autonomy. Sometimes the worker would discover something similar missing in himself, and hence had to develop this aspect of his personality so as to be able to provide it for the patient. This often was the challenge our young staff members needed to become more mature themselves.

The patient, on the other hand, may benefit greatly from identifying with a staff member's emotional maturity. Thus while the spontaneous self-selection of worker and patient often had for its basis unmet childhood residues which were complementary, and while this could be a good, and sometimes as in

Dana's case, a necessary starting point for the relationship, if it is permitted to remain pegged at this level it will result only in a *folie á deux*. They are narcissistic choices, because if one wishes to relate to what is most strongly developed in oneself, one tries mainly to relate to one's own image, as did Narcissus, and not to the other person. Relations based on complementing each other in respect to what is most mature in one but less well-developed in the other, are not merely the best but the only bases for mature relationships.

The danger in relations based on complementing one another's childhood residues, or each others's neurotic needs, or the neurotic needs in one (the worker) and the psychotic in the other (Dana) is that both participants may become fixated at this level. While it offers relief from pressure, it does not lead to higher integration. It is cathartic, as Dana's beating up her worker was cathartic for both, but not therapeutic.

An object choice based on complementary, immature needs permits some relief of pressures and with it some satisfactions of needs which otherwise would remain unmet. It makes regressions and fixations and all their defensive counterparts such as reaction formation, denial and projection, less necessary. Such complementary choices when well handled may permit the partners to move on to higher levels of integration, not directly, but by opening up the potential for it through the relief thus provided, which in turn frees energy for other endeavors. Everything then depends on how this energy is invested. It is the ethos of growth (which is the opposite of continuance of sameness), which in the therapeutic milieu militates against fixation at the level of object choices based on neurotic identifications; it promotes relationships that can start only if based on complementary needs, without permitting them to remain there.

The worker's self-examination began in earnest when she was asked why she had kept Dana's attacks secret from the staff, especially since she believed it was good for the patient to unload her rage against her mother by beating the worker. Was it not expected of a worker to report such an important move in a patient to the rest of the staff? She replied that she was convinced that Dana's behavior was fully justified because she had been rejected by her mother, and that her not discussing it, as certain as she was that Dana's behavior was good for her, was due to the fact that she did not know where to go from there. But if the worker were only insecure about how she was progressing with Dana—a feeling which she correctly stated—would this not be even more reason to report that with her Dana could unfreeze and cathartically attack a mother figure?

Eventually the worker realized that she had kept the violence hidden because to her it was something very precious that only the two of them had together and which would lose much of its meaning if others were to know about it. From there it was an easy step to realize she was also afraid that if it became known, the senior staff would in some way stop her from being beaten up. She really had not wanted it to stop. Was she then so much of a masochist? And if so, did she misuse a patient to satisfy her own masochistic need? I do not have to describe the righteous indignation with which the worker responded to such an accusation, which indeed was exaggerated inasmuch as she had not just used Dana to meet some of her own unconscious needs but had also offered Dana the same opportunity. Still, being the conscientious person she was, it remained very troublesome to her that she might have taken advantage of Dana to satisfy her own needs, and with this she began asking for help in understanding what was taking place. She was not masochistic, she asserted; she had truly been joyous that with her Dana had come to life, though Dana also hurt her; and for some time she remained convinced that she did not mind the suffering, because Dana with her was now active also in other, constructive ways. But perhaps, certain as she was that Dana had excellent reasons to beat up a mother figure, was there not also something in her own past which suggested that she deserved such punishment? (This question was motivated by the idea that she might be seeking punishment for some oedipal guilt, perhaps for having wished to beat up her own mother.) It was this line of inquiry that led to the entirely unexpected recall of the incident of going after her sister with a knife.

Such scrutiny of staff members' attitudes and behavior toward patients often produces positive results. It is almost impossible to know the inner motivations of another person. However, one can make shrewd guesses. If those doing the guessing come close enough—that is, if they are correct in assessing what the psychological constellation and emotional pressures may have been, though in error about the specifics—such hitting close to the emotional truth permits the person to recall what *did* happen.

Even with this new knowledge available to the worker, it became necessary to refer back to why she had wished the injuries to remain unrecognized. As long as she was not aware that she accepted them as deserved punishment for what she had intended to do to her sister, there may have been reason for her to keep them a secret, but why did she persist in making light of them? She answered in the usual fashion: she accepted the punishment because since this was all she could do for Dana, she deserved it. But if this were so, then she must have believed there were better ways to help Dana; what were they? She replied that she was just too inexperienced to know them; the senior staff should tell her what to do.

So we then tried a different approach, one we have found most useful. How had she felt about herself when she tried to harm her sister? What a stupid question, she said, had we not already found out that she still felt so miserable about herself that she welcomed being punished for it? Good and fine, so how did Dana feel about hurting her? Obviously, she replied, as she had already pointed out, it felt good to Dana finally to be able to do to a mother, at least a substitute mother, what she always had wanted to do. Well, if it was good to be able to express anger in attack, how was it that she felt she deserved to be punished for having attempted the same thing? "Would not any moral person feel this way?" was her answer. Then she obviously must feel that Dana, so important to her, was not a moral person, because otherwise she would expect Dana to feel miserable for venting violently what basically was justified anger, as her anger had been at having to take over the care of her sisters.

What is here compressed into a few questions and answers took months to achieve. For after each such question, the purpose of which was to have the worker find out more about herself, she had to be given ample time and opportunity to work on what it aroused in her. Sometimes a week, sometimes a month, had to elapse before the next step could be taken. In the meantime, in the daily meetings of the staff other problems were ventilated, discussions with other workers in regard to this patient and others took place, all of which now took on a different meaning to the worker because of what she had come to understand about herself. She participated in, or at least was present, during many discussions which while dealing with complex psychological problems did not directly refer to the one she was struggling with. This led her to recognize that now that she understood more about herself she also comprehended much better what went on in others. This, in turn, made it much more difficult for her to repress what was coming to awareness.

For Dana's worker, the biggest step was made when she finally understood that the basic flaw in her relation to Dana had been in viewing Dana as somehow less human than herself. She had felt terrible about herself because of her destructive wishes toward her sister; but Dana, she had been convinced, felt just fine about violent, destructive behavior. It comes as the greatest shock to a worker who is deeply involved emotionally with a patient to recognize that, contrary to his conscious convictions, he actually had unconsciously held the patient in very low esteem. Dana's counselor had been convinced that it was good for Dana to beat a mother-figure, and that all that was needed was to accept it. While she knew she was supposed to help Dana understand herself, and thus often had asked Dana why she did it, she had accepted Dana's reply that she was just so angry she would explode or return to catatonic immobility if she could not get rid of some of her inner violence. Up to this point she had never asked Dana how she felt about herself when she abused the person closest to her, who tried so hard to be of service to her.

The worker had to learn that she had done Dana a great injustice by believing that, although she felt terribly guilty about her own aggressive wishes, Dana could unambivalently enjoy and profit from open acts of violence. She was then able to approach Dana with the thought that she too would feel guilty if she hurt somebody of great importance to her, regardless of how much anger she might feel toward that person. Now Dana really exploded. More viciously than ever before she attacked the worker, screaming: "Your letting me beat you up made me think that you, too, saw me as a savage animal, which I believed of myself anyway;" and then she broke down, sobbing for the first time in her life that she could recall.

While the worker was accepting Dana's attacks, both the worker and Dana were functioning at a similar sado-masochistic level. After the worker began to understand the sources in her own childhood that contributed to her attitude toward Dana, she no longer accepted the attacks, began to have more self-respect, and offered Dana a more mature focus of identification.

We cannot be certain whether Dana would have moved out of her catatonic rigidity had things begun differently. The counselor's acceptance of Dana's violence and her approval of the only move toward the world that Dana could then make were probably crucial for Dana's being able to unfreeze a bit. It had proved how important she was to the worker, despite the implications of the worker's low opinion of her. By keeping it a secret, the worker had proved herself utterly trustworthy. She had accepted the savage in Dana, and perhaps this had been necessary before Dana could believe anybody could accept her also as a moral person with guilt feelings about her misbehavior.

A direct consequence of the worker's having convinced Dana that she did not see her as an inferior human being and did not believe she had attitudes different from her own permitted Dana to become aware of and to let her in on her deepest secret: the reason she had stood motionless by the window in the hospital was because of her need to see the sky to watch the changes in the weather. Why this had been and still was so important, she could not tell. But around the matter of weather she began to overcome her intellectual blocking, and even became physically agile, running out of doors innumerable times to get a better view of the sky and the weather than she could gain from her window. During the next two years she accumulated an incredible amount of knowledge about the weather. While she was seemingly engrossed in other activities, without our noticing that she had even looked up, she would tell how the wind had shifted and how its velocity had altered. At times, although seeming to be fully occupied with something else, she would suddenly rush to study the cloud formations because they had changed. From the variations in temperature, in humidity, all of which she "knew" as soon as they occurred, from the constellation of the clouds, the direction of the wind and what not, she was much better able to predict the weather than the Chicago Weather Bureau.

It is feats such as this which have led some to think that schizophrenics experience an expansion of their minds. They are extraordinary abilities, but far from having experienced an expansion of his mind, the schizophrenic has concentrated on the most minute focus, as the solution of the riddle of Dana's startling weather predictions will show.

For the next two years we explored Dana's past and her reactions to it, and helped her to understand herself and to build up her ability to meet the world and people. Repeatedly the counselor and Dana had to go over what had happened in the early days of their relationship, how it had started to go wrong at first, because the worker had been so caught up in her own needs. One day the old anger and violence emerged again, but this time only in words as Dana savagely told the worker, "How stupid you are, you still don't know what weather means to me." The worker, admitting once more her old, and probably still present, stupidity, asked to be enlightened. At which Dana went to a blackboard and wrote in large letters, "We eat her," saying, "That's all there is to weather." Weather symbolized her infantile relationship with her mother, in which there had been intense fears of eating and being eaten. She felt that she could not predict her own or her mother's oral aggressive impulses, but she could predict the weather, which symbolized these impulses.

Dana's anorexia had been due to her anxiety that she, another Gretel, would be devoured by the witch, as she saw her mother. One way to forestall this danger, and not an unusual dynamic of anorexia, was to have as little body as possible, so that it would not be attractive enough to be eaten up in childhood or to be used sexually in adolescence. Of this possibility we had been cognizant all along, as well as that her obesity had been her response to her security when she felt that at the school no such danger existed. But we had been in error in believing that the anxiety which had caused anorexia was no longer with her in its most primitive form. Somehow we failed to connect the two symptoms, the old one of anorexia, and the newer one of monomanic preoccupation with weather. She could let us in on her secret when she finally believed that the worker did not just devote herself to her because she was a patient; that the worker not only liked her, but also respected her as a person.

After this admission she was through with the fixation on weather. All her good intelligence, which had gone into being a weather expert, now became freed for other interests; her rage against the world had subsided because she felt she could have a good life. Within a year she could have left the school, but she preferred to remain to give her newly won mental health a chance to become better established and secure, wishing to take advantage for a while longer of what the therapeutic milieu had to offer until a year later, when she left to enter college. She decided to become a teacher because she liked the idea that, on the basis of her experience, she would be able to teach children how important words are, and to know what they really mean. In summing it up she said, "Not the crazy way I thought what weather meant."

One might think from this brief case history that the unraveling of the intricacies and complexities of the schizophrenic mind require consummate psychoanalytic skill and knowledge. These are needed; but as this story shows, and as every staff member must learn, even they are easier to come by than common sense. As in Dana's preoccupation with weather, what seems totally incomprehensible is due to the patient's inability—because of his anxiety, the depth of his repressions, and the disorganization of his higher mental functions—to recognize the usually simple and primitive derivation of symptoms. The constructs he has woven around their origins hide their very nature from himself and others, transforming simple fears into elaborate and confusing symptoms and behavior patterns. To be able to see through all the screens behind screens takes considerable knowledge of oneself, and acceptance of how simple one's own psychology really is, behind the elaborate constructions we erect to hide this fact from ourselves. To recognize the extremely simple needs, hopes, anxieties, and exasperations behind psychotic constructs, to assess their true nature from overt behavior and fantasy productions, to understand how elaborate symptoms can hide very different and much more primitive preoccupations, all this demands training, knowledge, insight, experience, and most of all application. But underlying this skill are experiences common to us all. In order to succeed in therapeutic work, every worker has to struggle through to this realization, though for some it is easier than for others.

SUMMARY

A therapy that relies on the impact of human relations must consider most carefully all those who engage in it. Even in classical psychoanalysis we recognize the tremendous importance of the countertransference for success or failure of treatment. If this applies to the psychoanalytic setting where interaction is quite restricted, it is even more relevant when therapist and patient encounter together all the vagaries of life. If the experience between therapist and patient is to become a meaningful one—and unless and until it is, nothing good will come from it—those who enter into it together form a human relation. To be sure, the contribution of the two will be quite different. We, the therapists, will have to nurture the relationship patiently and understandingly for a long time before the patient may be able to consider, at first tentatively and with many reservations, the possibility of his relating. But even though therapists have a definite goal in mind and go about it in a deliberate, purposeful way, this relationship, like all other true human relationshps, must be very meaningful to both partners, to each in his own way; the partners must become very important to each other.

The mental patient lives as if he is in a deep, dark hole without exit, imprisoned there both by his anxieties and by the insensitivities of others. We have to invent and construct a way out for him—let us say, a ladder. We have to build this from our own past, our knowledge, our personality, and our understanding of the patient, but most of all through our empathy that tells us which unique, and uniquely human ladder will be suitable for this particular patient. Contrary to his old convictions that there is no exit, the patient must first discover that he can climb out of his prison on this ladder, and then eventually try to do so. To bring this about, it must be possible for him to watch us work long and hard putting this ladder together, which must be very different from all others that have ever existed before. The patient will try to destroy the ladder, convinced for a long time that we do not fashion it to help him climb to liberty, but only to induce him to move into a worse prison (which we wish him to enter for some unfathomable reason that will benefit us more than him, and which will only project him into more dangers). After all, the patient knows his old prison, as terrible as it is, and somehow has learned to protect himself against its most painful features through his symptoms. These symptoms—his protective devices—he knows we want him to relinquish. How can he trust us who have such evil designs? He also will try to dismantle the ladder in much the same way as the child destroys the toy whose workings he wishes to understand.

We will have to climb down on this ladder of empathic understanding, into the hole where the patient vegetates, while the patient tries to destroy it, if for no other reason than to test our determination.

If a patient decides that he does not wish to use this avenue of escape offered to him, we must accept and respect such a decision—without stopping our efforts to be with the patient in his now no longer inescapable, but self-chosen abode, so that at least he will not dwell alone in his misery. Any slight suggestion that our way of life is superior to his is arrogant—another rejection of the patient, another demonstration that we do not understand him. His mode of life, whatever it is, is indeed superior to ours as far as the patient is concerned, because it offers him much-needed protection, which he did not find in our world.

Our hope is that our taking care of him as well as possible, where he desires to be, will eventually convince him of our good intentions. This then may induce him to change his mind about wishing to remain permanently in his dark hole. Any impatience on our part, any insistence that he should change the miserable conditions of his life (apart from our improving them for him as much as we can without interfering with his autonomy) is nothing but pushing a person around who has already given up functioning because he was so overpowered in his past. Again and again it has been our experience that only after our willingness to join the patient where he dwells emotionally has been recognized by him as genuine, will he consider also joining us—for a long time only very tentatively, perhaps only for moments—where and how we wish to live. Actually, what happens is that because of the services we render him, he becomes interested in us and wishes to find our more about us, including why we prefer our way of life.

Even more important than professional training for a therapist is a person's ability to use therapeutically not only his particular talents and idiosyncrasies but his life experiences. Among these he must be able to distinguish between that which has been meaningful and supportive, and that which has been actually or potentially destructive, so he can make full use of the first and prevent himself from letting the second enter into the therapeutic relation.

Over the years, we found that every person who was truly successful in helping those suffering from the most severe psychiatric disturbances had undergone experiences which, for one reason or another, made this type of work so attractive that he could accept the severe hardships it imposed, and therefore succeed in helping patients recuperate where others might have failed.

In this chapter I have described our effort to translate into effective action the therapist's wish to help the patient, so that it may indeed become a love that is enough.

References

Alighieri, D. (Dante), *La Divina Commedia,* Rome: Albrighi Segati & Company, 1951.

Blos, P., *On Adolescence,* New York: The Free Press, 1962.

Erikson, E., *Identity and the Life Cycle,* New York: International Universities Press, 1959.

Freud, S. (1924), "The Loss of Reality in Neurosis and Psychosis," *Standard Edition,* Vol. 19, London: Hogarth Press, 1961.

Goldstein, K., *The Organism,* New York: American Book Company, 1939.

Maslow, A., *The Farther Reaches of Human Nature,* New York: Viking Press, 1971.

Redl, F., *When We Deal With Children,* New York: The Free Press, 1966.

Wright, B., "Attitudes Toward Emotional Involvement and Professinal Development in Residential Child Care," Chicago, University of Chicago, Doctoral Dissertation, 1957.

Part 2

EGO STRUCTURE
AND EVALUATION

Introduction

Peter L. Giovacchini, M.D.

Both of the chapters in this section are concerned with evaluation, but they approach the situations they are investigating from what might be considered opposite ends of the spectrum. David Roth and Sidney Blatt use academic techniques, relying on Rorschach analyses and fragments of material, mainly manifest dream content. Their approach is nonanalytic but their conclusions have far-reaching implications for the clinician. Arnold Modell, by contrast, makes evaluations concerning patients by scrutinizing the transference and noting his own reactions. From the latter, he can make cogent inferences about the patient's character structure and degree of narcissistic fixation. Each approach gives us considerable information about the form of the patient's psychopathology.

These chapters demonstrate the relevance of knowledge about the developmental factors involved in psychopathology. This type of understanding enhances our functioning within the therapeutic context. Roth's assessments of ego states, by examining spatial configurations, enables him to make predictions about the patient's mood and to anticipate disruptive behavior such as suicide. Perhaps, as analysts, we may not be able immediately to use such information for analytic purposes, but it seems to me such information must find some use somewhere.

I placed Modell's chapter in this section rather than the previous one where the main focus is on countertransference. True, his chapter would have fit well with those in Section I. But he uses his reactions specifically to make diagnostic assessments. Other authors writing on this subject also make diagnostic assumptions, but they do so ultimately and not as their chief endeavor; they were primarily interested in other facets of the transference-countertransference interaction such as therapeutic impasses and disruptive feelings within the analyst.

The value of diagnosis as a factor involved in determining psychoanalytic treatability has been questioned by some analysts. Modell does not address himself to phenomenology. Rather, he focuses upon the interaction between himself and the patient and uses his feelings as a barometer for making judgments about certain facets of the patient's character, primarily related to narcissistic fixations and defenses. Naturally, such assessments will have some relevance to therapeutic response.

The type of research discussed in these chapters provides us with further information that is needed for expanding our vistas of the therapeutic process. Knowledge about the spatial configurations of the ego provide us with an architecture, so to speak, of the psychic apparatus which must be characteristic of specific types of psychopathology. The analytic interaction adds to such assessments by providing us with insights regarding where the patient is on the progression-regression scale.

The specific effects insights about psychic structure and additional methods for gaining such insights will have on psychoanalytic technique are not directly discussed here. For the clinician this must be the crucial question. This section provides us with another dimension thtat will help us deal with patients by sharpening our recognition of the structural aspect of specific types of psychopathology.

Chapter XI

Ego Structure, Psychopathology, and Spatial Representations

David Roth, M.D.

Sidney J. Blatt, Ph.D.

On the basis of extensive clinical data, we have noted a close parallel between levels of psychological organization and the mental representation of space. Integration of our observations with conceptualizations from Piaget (Flavell, 1965), Schilder (1935), and Werner (1957) led to a model of the sequential development of spatial constructs. Consistent correlations were observed between the level of spatial organization in object representations and clinical dimensions such as defenses, symptom formation, transference phenomena, and basic ego organization.

Different types of character structure were found correlated with differing modes of organizing space in the description of fantasies, dreams, and Rorschach responses. The psychological inference is that such spatial representations exist in the "mind" and have some constancy over time. Our focus here will be on the ego state rather than the relation these spatial configurations have to abstract mental operations and the vicissitudes of instinctual development, subjects which have been treated in other studies (Roth, 1972; Roth and Berger, 1973).

Representations which contain an emphasis on polarities (juxtaposition of opposites or dissimilarities) have been found associated with schizophrenia. Representations of verticality (stratification of objects or attributes as above and below in layers) have been observed in paranoid patients and in regressed homosexuals. Emphasis on symmetry and regular sequences of lines or planes occurs primarily in obsessionals. Three-dimensional representations such as preoccupation with volume occur primarily in depression. Transparent boundaries between areas have been observed in patients who were preoccupied with suicidal impulses. Hysterical features appear to be associated with the representation of three-dimensional objects traversing a three-dimensional field (Roth and Blatt, 1971).

POLAR ALTERNATION

The retention of internal object representations depends upon the level of self-object differentiation achieved and therefore parallels libidinal and aggressive development and the elaboration of object relations. The psyche has to be able to organize the object's representation with a certain degree of structure and differentiation before it can be "registered" or "retained." This itself becomes an index to the structure of the psyche and where it can be placed in the hierarchy of differentiation and object relations. In our studies it became apparent that certain features of spatial organization might point toward clinical states otherwise not easily observed or inferred. Thus, in a study of adolescents (Roth and Blatt, 1961) whose aggression had been unleashed in a severe fashion against their mothers or maternal surrogates, we inferred from various spatial configurations that this assault may have constituted a restitutive attempt at maintaining ego boundaries and avoiding schizophrenic disintegration.

An earlier study (Roth, 1961) noted the alternation of male and female references in the subject's associations as primitive attempts in a schizophrenic adolescent to maintain boundary awareness. This was accompanied by preoccupation with mouth or mouthlike apertures and male and female part-objects. While object and part-object representations were still undifferentiated here, in the adolescents of the later study part-object and object representations were seen as distinct, but self and object representations were still perilously fused.

This suggests that the latter adolescents had not yet integrated symmetry, which we believe to be a spatial feature of obsessionality, into their psychic structure, and that they regressed to the representation of space in terms of polarities which seemed to indicate that the fear of fusion of the self and object representations overwhelmed them.

Several hypotheses about specific spatial configurations were extrapolated in this way to characterize unstable clinical states of pathological regression or fixation.

The establishment of early developmental levels is initially based upon the experience of alternation of polar qualities, such as light-dark and pleasure-pain. The temporal juxtaposition of polar qualities establishes the first differentiation of reality and the perception of ego boundaries. The spectrum of sensation such as pleasure and pain, or light and dark, is not perceived as having continuity. Earlier research (Roth, 1961; Roth and Blatt, 1961), indicated that a preoccupation with polar alternation and boundary distinction is characteristic of the more severe forms of psychopathology. Male-female, human-animal, animate-inanimate, living-dead or the alternation of vivid colors are some of the more frequent themes that are used to alternate polar properties in the struggle to establish boundaries.

In the initial stages of the movement toward organization, there is a sequence of various polar experiences: hot and cold, discomfort and comfort, pain and pleasure, "mother absent," "mother here." Most probably, these sensations are initially recognized as representations only when their opposite is evoked. In other words, there may not even be an acute awareness that warm is warm and no awareness that cool is cool other than when the infant experiences the alternate property in sequence.

To maintain this sense of differentiation, constant alternation has to occur. Anyone who has seen the number of people in state hospitals who rock for rocking's sake, or the head-banging of children might sense their need for these movements to gain awareness of their own body or their body boundaries as a beginning delineation of internal from external awareness. An alternation of kinesthetic experience such as pressure and no pressure or an alternation of proprioceptive experience somehow establishes an awareness of the body as a separate and distinct entity. According to Schilder (1950) the body surface becomes perceptible as the boundary between inner and outer space as the skin receptors are activated by the alternate pressure and lack of pressure from an external object.

Alternations between animate-inanimate, human-animal, male-female and love-hate also seem to be attempts to establish differentiation and separation between various perceptions as well as between oneself and others. Such alternations as human-animal and male-female are less extreme than animate-inanimate and therefore probably represent less of a need for polarities to establish and maintain differentiation and integration.

VERTICAL STRATIFICATION

We have observed preoccupation with vertical stratification (e.g., images of one thing on top of another—figures in an acrobatic act, a rainbow, or a Jello parfait) primarily in homosexual and paranoid patients whose relationships are often focused on hierarchical issues such as power-weakness, superior-inferior, good-evil.

Many homosexual and paranoid patients have presented themes of stratification in dreams reported in analysis and psychotherapy, and in their Rorschach protocols. Stratification can occur with diametrically (polar) opposite attributes or it can occur without polarities.

To the extent that any spatial representation requires the use of an earlier or more primitive level to sustain it, the less stable we believe it to be, because clinically these combinations correspond to more severely fixated states. The following two examples illustrate this distinction. When stratification occurs without resort to polar alternation, the regression to the homosexual paranoid position is mild and defensive in nature. When stratification requires polarities to sustain it, the paranoid homosexual transference is highly regressed and indicates severe early fixation as illustrated in the second case.

Numerous examples of stratification in paranoid and homosexual patients could be presented but probably a most noteworthy example was presented by Freud (1900) in his ingenious interpretation of the "Lovely Dream." This dream, also referred to as the "Sappho Dream," was presented to Freud by a man being treated for claustrophobia, and represents stratification with homogeneous rather than polar elements in what can be surmised to have been a regressive homosexual transference. The patient reported:

"He was driving with a large party to X Street in which there was an unpretenti-ous inn. (This not the case.) There was a play being acted inside it. At one moment he was audience, at another actor. When it was over, they had to change their clothes so as to get back to town. Some of the company were shown into rooms on the ground floor and others into rooms on the first floor. Then a dispute broke out. The ones up above were angry because the ones down below were not ready, and they could not come downstairs. His brother was up above and he was down below and he was angry with his brother because they were so much pressed. (This part was obscure.) Moreover, it had been decided and arranged even when they first arrived who was to be up above and who was to be down below. Then he was walking by himself up the rise made by X Street in the direction of town. He walked with such difficulty and so laboriously that he seemed glued to the spot. An elderly gentleman came up to him and began abusing the King of Italy. At the top of the rise he was able to walk much more easily" (p. 285).

Freud's interpretation of this dream is based on a literary source.

"The piece of the dream-content which described how the climb began by being difficult and became easy at the end of the rise reminded me, when I heard it, of the masterly introduction to Alphonse Daudet's *Sappho*. That well-known pas-sage describes how a young man carries his mistress upstairs in his arms; at first she is as light as a feather, but the higher he climbs the heavier grows her weight. The whole scene foreshadows the course of their love affair, which was intended by Daudet as a warning to young men not to allow their affections to be seriously engaged by girls of humble origin and of dubious past.

"Though I knew that my patient had been involved in a love affair which he had recently broken off with a lady on the stage, I did not expect to find my guess at an interpretation justified. Moreover the situation in *Sappho* was the *reverse* of what it had been in the dream. In the dream the climbing had been difficult to begin with and had afterwards become easy, whereas the symbolism in the novel only made sense if something that had been begun lightly ended by becoming a heavy burden. But to my astonishment my patient replied that my interpretation fitted in very well with a piece he had seen at the theatre the evening before. It was called *Rund um Wien* (Round Vienna) and gave a picture of the career of a girl who began by being respectable, who then became a *demimondaine* and had liaisons with men in high positions and so 'went up in the world,' but who ended by 'coming down in the world,' (pp. 285-286)."

After elaborate interpretations of a heterosexual nature, Freud turns finally to some other associations.

"The patient's (elder) brother also appeared in the content of the dream, this brother being *up above* and the patient himself, down below. This was once again the *reverse* of the actual situation; for, as I know, the brother had lost his social position while the patient had maintained his. In repeating the content of the dream to me, the dreamer had avoided saying that his brother was up above and he himself 'on the ground floor.' That would have put the position too clearly, since here in Vienna if we say someone is *'on the ground floor'* we mean that he had lost his money and his position—in other words, that he has *'come down in the world'*. Now there must have been a reason for some part of the dream being represented by its *reverse*. Further, the reversal must hold good of some other relation between dream thoughts and dream content as well (cf. below, p. 326 f.); and we have a hint of where to look for this reversal. It must evidently be at the end of the dream, where once again there was a *reversal* of the difficulty in going upstairs as described in *Sappho*. We can then easily see what reversal is intended. In *Sappho* the man carried a woman who was in a sexual relation to him; in the dream thoughts the position was reversed, and a woman was carrying a man. And since this can only happen in childhood, the reference was once more to the wet nurse bearing the weight of the infant in her arms. Thus the end of the dream made a simultaneous reference to *Sappho* and to the wet nurse (pp. 287-288)."

Up to this point, Freud considers the various parts of the dream work as manifestations of regressive defensive maneuvers; his final conclusion that the homosexual regression is used as a defense could have been reached directly had Freud observed the spatial representation of stratification.

Freud parenthetically alludes to the role of homosexuality in the patient's neurosis, presumably based on involvement with the brother, and the infant-mother relationship is also alluded to as a regressive defense. In further reference to this and other dreams, Freud writes:

"I think, moreover, that all these dreams of turning things round the other way include a reference to the contemptuous implications of the idea of 'turning one's back on something' (e.g., the dreamer's turning round in relation to his brother in the *Sappho* dream, p. 287 f.). It is remarkable to observe, moreover, how frequently reversal is employed precisely in dreams arising from repressed homosexual impulses (p. 327)."

In his interpretation of this dream, Freud clarifies the concept of reversal and relates it to repressed homosexuality, thus preparing the groundwork for his later discussion of paranoia. But this dream is so replete with examples of stratification that Freud also referred to it as the "Up and Down Dream."

Another example of stratification, but with polar alternation, occurred in the course of analysis with a male engineer in his mid-thirties who had shown a rather intellectual approach to his analysis, conveying much of what was affect-laden through ideas he attributed to his wife. He had begun to talk about some of his sexual attitudes or experiences and then related the following dream (there had been no prior suggestion of intense homosexuality or erotic attachment). Historical material suggested that he had hungered for a closer relationship to his father who had held himself aloof. He said:

"I woke up from my dream frequently, running to the Frigidaire to get some milk (as my stomach was hurting me). In the dream I was driving along in a truck all by myself down a highway. It looked like an ordinary street, and then I saw a huge giraffe moving down the road alongside of me. Riding on the giraffe was a man standing up. The man and the giraffe had a trained act and they were about to perform. And then suddenly I saw a woman standing in front of the giraffe and the man. The giraffe picked the woman up with his neck, threw her up, and she was now standing on top of the man on top of the giraffe. As this occurred the giraffe's speed began to pick up and I suddenly noted that he was going faster than I was. After the woman was picked up, a man was picked up and the same thing happened. The giraffe picked this man up and threw him on top of this woman and there they were—all three of them standing on top of the giraffe. Then, the act, which became a circus act, became quite frightening, because they were going to try to get themselves down without falling. It seemed to be that it would be quite frightening because they were going at great speed. And I was quite frightened by it all. Suddenly the dream shifts and there is a crash. This time it seemed to be that of an automobile. I see nothing more of the people or the giraffe—just pieces of the automobile strewn around. All that is left of the automobile are two wheels and an axle. It is then I come to a fork in the road with my car and I become confused. I don't know whether to turn to the right or to the left."

The patient's associations referred to his fear about the outcome of analysis; as he continued, his associations focussed upon his wanting to know the analyst as a person, and he expressed curiosity about the personal life of the analyst more directly. He also became preoccupied with whether he had the analyst's approval. The patient arose from the couch a few minutes before the end of the hour, ending his associations by expressing a desire toward a woman, saying he really never had discussed his sexual feelings openly in treatment and that he would like to continue the discussion during the next hour.

The spatial stratification and polar alternation in the dream suggested, however, repressed homosexual impulses and fears of fusion. Based on the spatial parameters, a prediction was made that severe homosexual panic and a fear of the dissolution of ego and possibly even body boundaries would probably occur.

The analyst summarized the following hour:

"The patient said that his heart was pounding but denied any fear. He wanted a very long session because he had so much to say and he noted he had a feeling of happiness this morning but it overflowed and he burst into tears and some sobbing with some anxiety followed. He expressed gratitude to the analyst for teaching him how to deal with people better, feeling that he is learning something directly from him. He indicated some forgetfulness about whether or not he had been here the previous day as if he had amnesia. He then began speaking about the dream as having been an indication that he had passed a certain danger point in the analysis. He was crossing a road where he was almost hit, but not quite. He went on to talk about some drawings he had seen whose perfect symmetry appealed to him. He spoke with affection of his son and then spoke about never having received much from his father. At this point in the interview, he spoke about feeling that his tongue had enlarged and filled his whole mouth. This reminded him of what he had said in the previous hour—that he must remind himself to talk about sex to the analyst. At this point he revealed a desire to caress other men in high school and in college, and an impulse to perform fellatio. He described this as being terrible, but felt good that he had 'gotten the poison out.' Then he began breathing deeply and rapidly and said that he felt paralyzed. He kept saying, 'Oh God, oh God, how terrible it is.' He began crying and his legs lay stiff and straight and his hands were both held with fingers hyperextended and thumbs drawn up in almost spastic form. He said he felt like his whole body was paralyzed though he moved his arms occasionally. This went on for six minutes. The patient could not describe what had happened to him, just that he felt he had been paralyzed, and some time after, he became almost amnesic for the episode. The analyst described him during this brief period as showing rigidity and, on being directed to move his limbs, a kind of waxy flexibility that suggested catatonia. The analyst considered the episode a massive conversion reaction. The patient expressed the fear he would have lost the use of his arms and legs if it had gone on much longer.

"Throughout the rest of the hour he alternated from a sitting to a lying position, occasionally looking at the analyst. At the end of the hour, he said that he may possibly have had a homosexual attachment or experience with highly ambivalent feelings with an older brother. In parting, some of the defensive reversal and projection came into play; he indicated that he would like to be finished with the analysis or far enough along so that he might be able to call the analyst a bastard."

It became apparent that the patient was struggling with the issue of intimacy, but that his own differentiation was too tenuous to allow for much closeness. His disintegration and paranoid maneuvers and preoccupations led to a reconsideration of the patient's level of organization, and the analyst eventually considered him borderline. After several hundred hours, the patient interrupted the analysis.

DEPRESSION: DEPTH AND VOLUME IMAGERY

The awareness of depth or volume imagery in dreams, fantasies, and Rorschach responses is associated with depression.

In a detailed study of dreams of analytic patients, a correlation between several forms of degenerating volume percepts and various negative therapeutic reactions was found, suicide or self-destructive tendencies being but one special example (Roth, 1972). Depth representations or volume imagery often appear in regressions of depressed patients.

Manifest dream material consisting of an interface, a box opening on one side, for example, is usually associated with regression from higher levels of drive-defense conflict. Dream elements characterized by translucency, such as transparent walls, however, usually indicate fixation with suicidal tendencies.[1] The suicidal state may lead to the patient's acting-out or counterphobic behavior, his defense against unbearable transference feelings, and suicidal preoccupations may be hidden behind a "flight into health" (Roth and Blatt, 1972).

The relationship between transparency and suicidal intent is illustrated in the following analytic experiences.

A young lady who was initially diagnosed as "belated adolescent state" had experienced difficulties in separating from and competing with women. She felt intense anger toward her analyst because of frustrated fantasies of fusion with him, and this was accompanied by a mild or moderate depression.

She reported a dream of looking through a glass, holding it up to the light, and sometimes seeing "mother," and sometimes a particular date scratched on the glass.

She revealed in the same hour that she had been gathering a cache of drugs, and had been contemplating suicide for several days. A week later she called her analyst after ingesting these pills and required emergency treatment and hospitalization to survive. Subsequently, she reported more dreams of transparency just prior to her suicide attempts, in some of which the glass broke. The date in her dream seemed to relate to the time of her brother's birth when the mother abandoned her for him.

The next patient is a middle-aged man whose birth was the result of an accidental pregnancy and whose mother became toxemic during the last weeks of pregnancy. Because of her illness, his father hated him from the very outset of his life and blamed the patient for his mother's postpartum depression. He experienced this direct antagonism from his father and marked

---

[1]A further investigation of this hypothesis indicates a significantly great number of translucent and transparent responses in the Rorschach protocols of patients who committed suicide than in a closely matched control sample of patients. (Blatt and Ritzler, unpublished manuscript, 1972, [2])

ambivalence from his mother who would alternatively overprotect him and reject him.

The patient revealed homosexual conflict and depression which were intensified by the analyst's absence on vacation, and volume and depth imagery were prominent in his dreams.

Upon the analyst's return, the patient reported having had feelings of urgency, headaches, stomach upset, jitteriness, and smoking "like a fiend" while the analyst was absent. He described time as going too fast; he experienced "instantaneous time." He denied resentment about the analyst's absence but described explosive anger during the analyst's vacation, consisting of self-destructive impulses and competitive destructive feelings toward men. The boss became closer to one of his co-workers, and he felt shut out. He became involved with Machiavellian schemes for unseating his boss, presumably because he wished to prove his adequacy in a self-righteous manner. He reported a recurrence of an old symptom of kleptomania for bolts, screws, and guns.

The following dream, characterized by volume degenerating into translucency, occurred during the period of self-destructive impulses.

> He was walking through his factory and showing men the various aspects of the chemical processing. He was the leader of the group and felt quite aggressive and powerful in this stance. He led them all to a large water tank and descended down the ladder into the tank while demonstrating the phenomenon to be observed.
>
> A large cylinder of phosphorus was lowered into the water and could be seen beneath the water's surface, through the transparent body of water. It was put in the water to contain its explosive force and to prevent interaction with oxygen which would cause severe fire and hazard.

Apparently the patient equated the phosphorus bomb with his self-destruction and with his inability to alter what appeared to him to be an inevitable pattern he followed on every job. If he were fired, his analysis would be terminated in the absence of financial support. In the dream work, the patient reflects depressive constellation and its suicidal implications.

DISCUSSION

Schilder (1955) and Piaget (Flavell, 1965) provide a theoretical framework which is elaborated when combined with the findings of this study on spatio-temporal representations. In separate ways these authors suggest that the psychological origins of the distinction of near and far may be related to the sensory difference of perceiving near space by sight, i.e., the tactile and visual modes of development. The field of vision is instantaneously and simultaneously both near and far, whereas that of grasping defines only the area near the body. When these become perceptible as separate portions, space can be organized in sequences. Schilder sees the world of the psychotic as one where all objects come within immediate range of aggression, perhaps because of the absence of a graspable near object and an uncoordinate love drive remains fused with an uncoordinated aggression. The objects of aggressiveness or the whole world of the not-me are brought from optic space into the space of grasping. It would appear, then, that when aggression against the not-self is limited to near space, there is also a beginning of the perception of self as having limited extent in space. Thus, differentiation of near and far occurs and signifies progress beyond the primitive perception of space based upon simultaneity or instantaneity of action.

The last patient described reported that awareness of "instantaneous time" and the kleptomanic impulse (near-space, grasping) occurred at the time of the analyst's departure, which stimulated self-destructive feelings in the patient. Volume degeneration and translucency followed, which suggests that the active physical presence of the analyst was required to maintain both near space and the volume binding of differentiated self and object representations. When such binding could no longer be maintained, internal and external volumes became exchangeable, opaque boundaries no longer prevailed, optic and grasping space were fused, and surfaces were collapsible by implosion or explosion as well as penetrable by the aggression of looking. Three-dimensional volume imagery was lost, and external and internal aggression were unbuffered in the confusion of external and internal space. A series of transparent planes, that is, a sequence of two-dimensional space, is used to maintain a faltering sense of depth. The appearance of this type of representation is an indicator of the instability of the spatial representation of volume.

The early histories of the patients we have studied reveal that the first two years of life were marked by maternal absence, withdrawal, or depression. The absence of the "volume binding" of a responsive maternal presence in the "near space" of the child during early crucial developmental phases is associated with failure of integration of libidinal and aggressive drives.

This progression from translucency to a sense of volume accompanied by a gradual perception of a seeing and touching mother is beautifully described in the parable about the maturation of the legendary monster Grendel by John Gardner.

Other writers have made similar allusions as in De Maupassant's short story, "The Horla," and a less apparent reference is to be found in Nabokov's novel, *The Defense*. The following quote from "Grendel" is the most persuasive in its imagery and conclusion:

> "I lived those years, as do all young things, in a spell. Like a puppy nipping,
> playfully growling, preparing for battle with wolves. At times the spell would
> be broken suddenly: on shelves or in hallways of my mother's cave, large, old

shapes with smouldering eyes sat watching me. A continuous grumble came out of their mouths; their backs were humped. Then little by little it dawned on me that the eyes that seemed to bore into my body were in fact gazing through it, wearily indifferent to my slight obstruction of the darkness. Of all the creatures I knew, in those days, only my mother really looked at me, stared at me as if to consume me, like a troll. She loved me, in some mysterious sense I understood without speaking it. I was her creation. We were one thing, like the wall and the rock growing out from it. Or so I ardently, desperately affirmed. When her strange eyes burned into me, it did not seem quite sure. I was intensely aware of where I sat, the volume of darkness I displaced, the shiny-smooth span of packed dirt between us, and the shocking separateness from me in my mama's eyes. I would feel, all at once, alone and ugly, almost—as if I'd dirtied myself—obscene. The cavern river rumbled far below us. Being young, unable to face these things, I would bawl and hurl myself at my mother and she would reach out her claws and seize me, though I could see I alarmed her (I had teeth like a saw), and she would smash me to her fat, limp breast as if to make me a part of her flesh again. After that, comforted, I would gradually ease back out into my games. Crafty-eyed, wicked as an elderly wolf, I would scheme with or stalk my imaginary friends, projecting the self I meant to become into every dark corner of the cave and the woods above.''

SUMMARY

We have found correlations between the types of spatial imagery that predominate in dreams, fantasies, and Rorschach protocols, and specific clinical syndromes.

Hierarchical vertical stratification is frequent in paranoid and homosexual patients, and volume representations characterize depressed patients. Clinical evidence indicates that the instability of these representations leads to the use of developmentally earlier spatial representations which, in turn, support these later acquired states.

To the extent that the stratification is of opposite rather than similar or homologous elements, the paranoid homosexual position is probably severely regressed and a sign of early fixation rather than mild or defensive.

The degeneration of volume representation and its use of sequential planes to help sustain the awareness of depth, that is, transparency or translucency, indicate a suicidal potential and the probability of self-destructive ideation or behavior.

References

Blatt, S. J., Quinlan, D. M., and D'Affliti, J., "Magnification and Diminishing of Image Size and its Effects on Psychological States." *Journ. of Abnorm. Psychol.*, 80: No. 2, 168-175 (1972).

Blatt, S. J., and Ritzler, B. A. (1973). "Suicide and the Representation of Transparency in Rorschachs." (Unpublished manuscript.)

Flavell, J., *The Developmental Psychology of Jean Piaget*. New York: Van Nostrand Reinhold, 1965.

Freud, S. (1900). "The Interpretation of Dreams," *Standard Edition* 4, pp. 285-289, 305, 326-327. London: Hogarth Press, 1953.

Gardner, John, *Grendel*. pp. 15-17, New York: Alfred A. Knopf, 1972.

Roth, D., "Unit Transfer: An Exploratory Study." *Arch. of Gen. Psych.* 4: 85-95 (1961).

_____ (1970). "Volume Degeneration and the Negative Therapeutic Reaction." (Unpublished manuscript.)

_____ (1972). "Spatial Configurations and Abstracted Operations." (Unpublished manuscript.)

_____, and Berger, M. (1973). "Spatio-Temporal Representations and the Instincts." (An in-process tsudy of vicissitudes of transference.) (Unpublished manuscript.)

Roth, D., and Blatt, S. J., "Psychopathology of adolescence: Spatio-Temporal parameters." *Arch. of Gen. Psych.* 4:95-104 (1961).

_____ (1971). "Spatio-Temporal Parameters and Psychopathology." Scientific Paper. Winter Meetings, American Psychoanalytic Association. New York, 1972.

_____ (1972). "Spatial Representations of Transparency and the Suicidal Potential." Presented to the Summer Meetings, International Psychoanalytic Association, Paris, 1973.

Schilder, P. (1950). *The Image and Appearance of the Human Body*. pp. 85-87, New York: New York University Press.

_____ . "Psychoanalysis of space." *Internat. Journ. of Psychoanal.* 274-295 (1935).

Werner, M., *Comparative Psychology of Mental Development*. New York: International Universities Press, 1957.

Chapter XII

Comments About Ego Structure, Psychopathology, and Spatial Representation

Peter L. Giovacchini, M.D.

I believe Roth and Blatt have presented a perspective that many psychoanalysts would consider controversial. I wish to outline briefly some general features (not so much about the actual content of the chapter but about their choice of subject and their methodology). Later I will concentrate on content.

First, concerning choice of subject. Of course, any investigator has the freedom to choose whatever area he wishes for exploration. The question then follows: How is one to classify this area, under what rubric does it fall? Can it still be considered within the domain of psychoanalysis? Freud's concentration was initially and understandably upon the id, which led to a succession of hypotheses, finally culminating in a dual instinct theory. Freud also dealt with the anatomy of the psychic apparatus—one which he developed as a consequence of his increasing sophistication about instincts and their vicissitudes. Roth does not deal with drives, infantile sexuality, and so on—in other words, his focus is not upon development from an instinctual viewpoint.

Still, he is dealing with a hierarchal theory of development that is concerned with psychic structure rather than with drives, and then he discusses the relevance of his concepts to psychopathology. If his conclusions can be applied in a clinical context, then I believe we are justified in considering his subject as belonging to one aspect of psychoanalysis which is receiving increased emphasis, ego psychology centering around perceptual and cognitive factors.

Next, I expect many would criticize his methodology. He presents data derived from the Rorschach as well as incompletely presented clinical vignettes and dreams which have been examined primarily in terms of morphological features of manifest content rather than by exhaustive associations within a transference context. Here again we may come up with an easily made, glib criticism that the data do not justify the conclusions.

I believe one has to be moderate and cautious before expressing such a judgment. True, in some cases there is no apparent connection between the observable and the conceptual. On the other hand, Roth's reference to formal qualities and relating them to various ego states and types of object relationships is plausible. One may not be convinced. One may object to a too casual approach, one that has not been subjected to rigorous data analysis, and so on. Still, I cannot help but be struck by the plausibility of the connection he makes even if he avoids the tedious manipulation of more "objective" scientific approaches. Freud often reached conclusions from abbreviated presentations whose scientific work and clinical usefulness is indisputable. Roth's conclusions will gain stature only if they can be used by clinicians and from a theoretical viewpoint become more firmly established when the intervening links between the data of observation and hypothesis can be established so we can think in terms of psychic processes.

For example (and now I am turning away from general issues and will be focusing upon content), what is the significance of the form in which a dream is related or external objects perceived for our understanding of the self-representation? Alternation of animate and inanimate, male and female, verticality, sequences, and dimensionality are, according to Roth, significant manifestations of various types of self-representations. As I have stated, I believe these are plausible correlations but there are many intermediary explanatory concepts required to establish these connections more solidly.

In essence, we are dealing with a hierarchy of self-representations and corresponding methods of relating to objects. Specific self-representations view mental representations, the endopsychic registration of external objects, in a characteristic fashion. Naturally the patient's psychopathology is reflected in these relationships.

The treatment of patients suffering from characterological disorders highlights the importance of a thorough understanding of these ego systems and shift our emphasis to modalities and styles rather than on exclusive preoccupation with psychosexual content.

Psychoanalysis still has some reluctance to make this shift and this was evident as early as the *Interpretation of Dreams*. I am referring to Freud's ambivalent acceptance of Silberer's functional phenomenon. Freud agreed that the operations of the mind as well as its concrete depictions were demonstrated in Silberer's dreams but he found himself more pressingly occupied with other problems.

Today, clinical necessity justifies our further pursuit of such operations. So one can again emphasize such questions as the significance of space to the formation of the self-representation. I wish to make a few brief points concerning the hierarchal elaboration of spatial constellations as they are intrinsic to the developing sense of self which reaches culmination in the establishment of a coherently organized, flexible identity.

The prementational neonate supposedly operates on a visceral level and presumably mentational (psychological) elaboration does not occur. However, very soon some type of mentational activity takes place and we are accustomed to view early narcissistic phases as recognizing, in a vague unde-termined fashion, an object—at least in the sense of an extension of the self. The reconstructed ego state of patients in deep transference regressions indi-cates that space is experienced in an amorphous incomplete fashion. The patient feels himself, as one of my patients described, as being all over and at the same time of being nowhere at all. He is not in his own body but diffused into his surroundings. He does not exist as a spatially oriented entity. He does not function within his enclosure because his symbiotic fixation is charac-terized by blending and a lack of a discrete frame of reference.

With consolidation of the self-representation as separation from the mater-nal universe is achieved, the person creates his *umwelt*. A certain amount of space has to be constructed without blending with another person's space. He is within his own body and operates within an area that is distinct and truly his own. In ego psychological terms one can conceptualize a shrinkage of a global but amorphous self-representation, one occupying the whole ego, to a discrete identity system with space between it and other structured ego subsys-tems. From this point, one can investigate how that space undergoes further development and modification, that is how it progresses from linearity to multidimensionality.

Structural pathology as seen in cases suffering from ego defects, ranging from character neuroses to psychoses, would of necessity create difficulties in the development of a spatial hierarchy. The schizophrenic, for example, depending upon his ego defect, may not have achieved a shrinkage of a fused state to a self-representation, or he may have a tenuous self-representation with a frightening surrounding space that threatens to suck him into anonymi-ty. The space he has to allot to object representations is perceived as usurping his own. Many of the schizophrenic's defensive maneuvers can also be under-stood as feeble, unsuccessful attempts to remain in their own body and to stay in their *umwelt*. Their attempts at psychic survival and adaptations will be reflected by specific configurations which Roth is attempting to identify.

How one perceives what we might refer to as *intrapsychic space* will also determine how one perceives the space surrounding him on the couch. In other words, a person's structural composition will be manifested in the analytic interaction as well. In addition to determining the form of his associa-tions and the content and sequence of manifest dream elements, he will also create what might be referred to as a characteristic analytic ambience.

For example, a young woman vacillated between adopting a bizarre and peculiar posture on the couch and lying absolutely still. The former is difficult to describe but she seemed to be all over the place. At times her position was almost ludicrous; the way she twisted her neck and legs and bent her torso could create a comic effect. She would seem to envelop the couch and I often had the impression that only she was there, the couch being superseded by her. In contrast, on other occasions she would compress herself into a tiny ball and would almost seem to vanish into the leather covering of the couch. Of course, she could be seen but I often had the impression that she simply disappeared. In both instances she never turned her head so that she could see me.

One is immediately reminded of Balint's (1955) classification of oncophils and philobats, spaces being either friendly or destructive. My patient reacted in both fashions. She had to fill her surrounding space in order to reassure herself that she existed or she had to, in a sense, defensively deny her existence. However, both her need to affirm herself and her defensive denial can be understood in terms of developmental vicissitudes.

This patient's preoccupations centered around the fear of being abandoned or of being crushed if she asserted herself. Commanding attention was dangerous, but passive relaxation could lead to desertion. Reaching out toward someone would cause a person to dissolve.

The patient brought many fantasies to her sessions as well as dreams but her position was important, that is, whether she were above or below a certain point. The content of this material usually related to her being attacked or murdered. Often, she would envision herself on a strange planet surrounded by inanimate objects such as empty castles. She would then find God who would dissolve into an ectoplasmic void if she tried to touch him. She sometimes dreamed that she was deeply imbedded in a high wall in a two-dimensional fashion, and as long as she remained in this inanimate, rigid posture others would pass by and admire her.

The tenuousness of this patient's sense of identity is highlighted in this material. Intrapsychic conflicts caused her to construct defenses which are reflected in her dreams and fantasies. However, her problems are mainly characterological and were manifested by the vulnerability of the self-image and the quality of its surrounding space.

To summarize, our increased focus upon psychic structure, demanded by the type of psychopathology frequently confronting the clinician, causes us to highlight certain aspects of the patient's perceptions and responses to various segments of the external world. As Winnicott (1967) has emphasized, the structuring of space is an important factor in both psychic development and the attainment of higher levels of psychic integration as manifested in play and creativity. The psychoanalyst in his attempts to make assessments concerning fluctuations in the patient's ego state during regressive and progressive movements in analysis has to be sensitive to various nuances that hitherto have received comparatively little attention. The examination of spatial configurations of manifest dream content as well as the patient's construction and reaction to the psychoanalytic ambience are meaningful extensions of our methods of access to understanding the structure and operations of the patient's mind.

References

Balint, M., "Friendly Expanses—Horrid Empty Spaces." *Internat. Journ. of Psychoanal.* 36:225-241 (1955).

Winnicott, D. W., "The Location of the Cultural Experience." *Internat. Journ. of Psychoanal.* 48:368-372 (1967).

Chapter XIII

Affects and Therapeutic Alliance in Narcissistic Disorders: A Structural Evaluation

Arnold H. Modell, M.D.

Ever since Freud's distinction between narcissistic and transference neuroses, it has been assumed that the quality of the observed transference relationship has nosological implications. Freud (1924) defined the narcissistic disorders in terms of their relative incapacity to form a transference. We know now that Freud was not correct in this assessment and that a transference is formed in the narcissistic disorders, but one which is qualitatively different from that of a transference neurosis. Freud originally intended the term "narcissistic neurosis" to include the schizophrenias, but if we leave the problem of the schizophrenias to one side, there are two broad nosological groups comprising the narcissistic disorders, groups which can be held in contrast to the transference neurosis—narcissistic character disorders and the borderline conditions. If the transference can be utilized as a means of determining nosology, it should then be possible, by means of the transference, to differentiate these two conditions.

The starting point of my own interest in the borderline syndrome was a similar attempt to differentiate the transference of borderline patients from that of the schizophrenias. I soon found the transference manifestations in the borderline groups could be more easily studied as they evidenced a certain stability of defenses so that they were able to maintain lengthy therapeutic relationships. This was in contrast to the instability of defenses in the schizophrenias, leading to massive regressive states that disrupt therapy and require hospitalization. I came to believe that it was this stability of defenses itself that provided the basis for a clear nosological separation of the schizophrenias from the borderline states (Modell, 1963, 1968). Correspondingly, the differential diagnosis between the borderline state and a transference neurosis is not always evident and in many cases needs to be postponed until the characteristic transference manifestations evidence themselves as the therapy develops.[1] Let me review this description of the transference in the borderline

---

[1]Without intending to minimize the differences between psychoanalysis and psychotherapy, I have noted that similar transference elements appear in the psychotherapy of borderline patients, albeit in a truncated and fragmented form.

patient. Characteristically, the borderline patient acknowledges the person of the therapist as the nonself, but only partially so. For, by means of the process of projection and introjection, the therapist is endowed with qualities of the primitive self. In the earliest phases of treatment he is endowed with omnipotently powerful beneficial attributes. Later, when the transference becomes negative, as it inevitably does, the therapist is perceived as malignantly destructive. In both instances, in the states of positive and later negative omnipotence, the actual qualities of the person of the therapist as a separate person are perceived but disavowed by means of massive denial.

I have followed Winnicott's suggestion that the therapist becomes, in a very literal sense, a maternal environment. When the transference is in the positive stage, the patient acts as if the person of the therapist is interposed between himself and the dangerous environment. As long as the contact with the therapist can be maintained, and this may mean as long as he is in the physical presence of the therapist, he is safe from the dangers of the external world. In the negative phase the therapist is again equated with the environment, only in this instance the demands of the therapist are equated with the demands of a hated reality, and accordingly, the therapist becomes the target of unwelcomed and unprovoked hatred. Unlike the more circumscribed negative transference of the neurotic where the hatred may be displaced from a parental imago, here hatred is a reflection of the patient's hatred of the frustrating reality for which he holds the therapist responsible.

I have used Winnicott's transitional object concept (Winnicott, 1953) as a paradigm to describe the nature of this primitive object relationship. As is true with the child's first possession, the person of the therapist is placed between the self and the dangers of the external world. The therapist is perceived as the nonself, but only imperfectly so, as this only partly external object has given life by processes that occur within the self.

When we refer to the transference as a diagnostic instrument we also include the countertransference. Here, I mean not the analyst's neurotic responses to the patient but his awareness of the affects that are evoked within him as a result of the patient's transference. It is these affects, I believe, that form a fundamental source of psychoanalytic data. It is in this area that we find the sharpest distinction between the transference manifestations of borderline states and those patients suffering from narcissistic character disorders. The transference of a borderline patient is usually one of great intensity, and correspondingly, the countertransference is also one of great intensity; whereas in the narcissistic disorders there is a characteristic quality to the countertransference, that is, one of defensive boredom and sleepiness. This defensive boredom and sleepiness is not necessarily a neurotic response but a human reaction to the patient's state of nonrelatedness. It is indeed an injury to our narcissism to be continuously in the presence of someone who does not seem to be interested in us.

While diagnostic categories do not permit absolute differentiation between neighboring syndromes, I believe that it would be accurate to state that the condition of affective nonrelatedness is a characterological trait of the narcissistic personality disorder. The borderline patient is, at times, capable of adopting this position but he cannot maintain it for his object hunger is too great.[1] Affects thus are the leading edge of this diagnostic differentiation. The intensity of affects in the borderline state and the nonrelatedness of the narcissistic character disorder reflect differences in ego structure, and it is this question that we must now attempt to clarify.

This structural differentiation can be illustrated by reference to Gitelson's (1962) distinction of the "open" and "closed" system, as observed in the opening phase of psychoanalysis. Gitelson quotes Anna Freud as follows: "The infant and child do not present us with a 'closed system,' and therefore it is necessary to pay more regard to the environment and less to the biological reasonableness and synthetic functions of the ego. The aim with children is to lift them to a secondary level of development through the use of the analyst as a new object." Gitelson observes that "we may say that this 'secondary level of development' is an intrapsychic structure which in the end, is, effectively, a 'closed system' leading to relatively greater autonomy vis-à-vis the environment."

The structural difference between the narcissistic character disorder and the borderline states is a consequence of the fact that the former has achieved some degree of this secondary level of development and presents us with a closed system, while the borderline patient remains in this more regressive open system. We believe, with Winnicott, that the borderline state may result from a failure of the maternal environment in the first and second years of life, that is, a relative failure in "good enough mothering" (Winnicott, 1960). This relative failure of an object relationship results in a miscarriage of the normal process of identification, a failure to take something in which is specifically a failure to identify with the preoedipal mother. As a result, a relative autonomy from the human environment has not been achieved and consequently there is persistent object hunger with the illusion that an object stands between the person and the dangers of the environment. This is analogous to a young child who makes executant use of its mother before identification has been achieved.

With the narcissistic character disorder there is not this massive failure of the environment as seen in the borderline case. The problem is more subtle. Object constancy does not seem to be at issue, but the problem is more in the area of maternal reliability. The human child, as is true of all young primates, is

---

[1] In my book *Object Love and Reality*, I have described this condition of nonrelatedness as "being in a plastic bubble." At that time I had not sufficiently differentiated the narcissistic character disorders from the borderline states.

absolutely dependent on the mother to protect it from the dangers of the environment. The mother stands, as it were, as a protective buffer. I have the impression that for the analysis of narcissistic disorders, the patient as a young child, perhaps at the age of two or three, directly perceives that there is something wrong with his mother's judgment of the world and that she does not adequately serve this protective buffering function. One patient who was intellectually precocious perceived that his mother was, in fact, crazy, although the extent of her craziness was to a large extent hidden as she was able to maintain certain social functions. This particular mother did not neglect or abandon the child. She was a constant object, but her judgment was off and the child sensed it. In another patient, the mother was not psychotic but seemed to be flighty, childish, and fatuous, and this also was perceived at an early age. This mechanism was also observed by Masud Khan (1971) who suggested that the "ego of the child has prematurely and precociously brought the traumata of early childhood under its omnipotence and created an intra-psychic structure in the nature of an infantile neurosis which is a false self-organization."

There is here a need to establish a precocious autonomy from the environment by means of a total identification with the preoedipal mother. It is as if the child states, "I cannot trust my own mother; therefore, I'll become a better mother to myself." This internalization, however, is imperfect and does not aid in structuralization, nor does it lead to a true autonomy from the maternal environment but only an apparent one. For such people are inevitably extremely dependent although their dependency may be minimized and denied. They feel as if they reside within a self-sufficient cocoon and minimize the fact that a cocoon needs to be attached to something. The illusion of self-sufficiency can only be maintained in the presence of another object, and this is repeated in the early phase of analysis where the state of nonrelatedness is maintained alongside a deep dependency upon the analyst. One has the impression of a child playing by itself happily as long as the mother is nearby. (See Giovacchini, 1974, p. 153). As Khan has observed, this state of nonrelatedness is betrayed by the nature of the affective response. There may be the absence of genuine affects or there may be the expression of "false affects"—affects that serve the function of compliance, whereas the true affects remain hidden and secret and effectively cut off from the self. It will be noted that we are referring to a phenomenon that was first observed by Helene Deutsch, who described this falseness of affects as a characteristic of the "as if" personality (Deutsch, 1942). The narcissistic character learns to hide, that is, to deny his true feeling for fear of losing the object and develops what Winnicott has described as a false self, a self based upon compliance. All of this is repeated in the psychoanalytic situation so that the analyst may learn that the transference affects are false, in fact, motivated by the need to comply and to manipulate.

Again, to contrast the structural difference between borderline states and narcissistic character disorders, in the borderline state there is a failure of identification with the maternal object whereas in the narcissistic character disorders there is a precocious, imperfect identification with the maternal object. This structural differentiation may account for the differences in reality testing in the borderline patient and those with narcissistic disorders, for in a technical sense I believe the borderline patient to be psychotic while this is not true of the narcissistic character disorder. That is to say, in the borderline case the transference that develops becomes a psychotic transference and the patient is unable to distinguish that which arises from within as a fantasy from that which is given from without as external reality. In my book *Object Love and Reality,* I have discussed the importance of the sense of identity and the capacity to differentiate inner from outer reality. The patient with a narcissistic character disorder does not experience the same loss of the sense of self that borderline patients experience. Consequently, the disturbance of reality testing occurs in the latter and not in the former. The loss of a sense of reality and reality testing is no greater in the narcissistic character disorders as in the transference neuroses.

THE OPENING PHASE OF PSYCHOANALYSIS AND THE
THERAPEUTIC ALLIANCE

It has been suggested by Gitelson and Winnicott that psychoanalysis, especially in its opening phase, may provide a specific gratification, a gratification that is dyadic and maternal. Winnicott (1963) has described the analytic setting itself as a maternal ''holding'' environment; at the deepest unconscious level the analytic relationship is experienced as dyadic. I wish to propose that the importance of this dyadic experience is in direct proportion to the degree of actual privation that has been suffered during the patient's earlier development. It is generally agreed that for the normal development of object relations there is required a fitting in of specific responses from the human, that is, the parental environment; a failure in this fitting can be described as an actual deprivation. Where the privation has been greatest, as in the case of the borderline patient, the entire analytic experience may be that of a maternal holding environment. For the narcissistic character disorder where privations are less severe, the gratification afforded by the maternal holding environment may occupy the first and possibly the second year of the analysis. For the ideally chosen transference neurosis this type of maternal gratification may be only marginally significant. I am suggesting further that this issue of actual privation and the gratification afforded by the analytic setting itself is related to the capacity to establish a therapeutic alliance. Before the therapeutic alliance itself can be achieved, the analytic setting must first function as a kind of replacement therapy. Lest I be misunderstood, I am not suggesting the introduction o special parameters of active therapy, of giving love in Ferenczi's sense, but I am suggesting that in the usual, well-conducted analysis there is gratification implicit in the analyst's constancy and reliability. And further there is gratification implicit in the analyst's capacity to perceive the patient's unique identity. The analyst is able to maintain the patient's identity in focus over time. This is the mirroring function that Spitz (1965) observed in the mother's response to the child's smile. This is the capacity to perceive the patient as a "thou" (in Buber's terms). A person with an impaired sense of identity experiences himself as something evanescent and relies on the continued perception of the self by others over time, a perception that he can perceive in the analyst's response to him.

During this period of consolidation there are not two people in the consulting room. This is a phase prior to the therapeutic alliance in which it can be said that the patient is "not yet working in the analysis." In order for work to be done there has to be the acceptance of separateness, that is, the acceptance of two people in collaboration.

The analyst has the experience, during this phase, that nothing seems to be happening. (See also Winnicott, 1969; Khan, 1969; and Giovacchini, 1972.) I would suggest that during this period the patient may be experiencing a silent structural growth. It is a period in which the analyst accepts what unfolds and is not so demanding as he will be later. The length of this early phase may be determined by internal and environmental factors. Internal factors relate to the narcissistic wish to be unique in the analyst's affection, to be constantly admired, etc. When these wishes remain ungratified, covert anger begins to accumulate. The environmental factors refer to the analyst's increasing demands that the patient accept the reality of the analytic situation. When this opening stage is interrupted depends on the analyst's sense of timing. The experienced analyst will probably respond intuitively. When he senses that this has gone on long enough, he will be more demanding. Here again, I believe that the length of time of this opening phase is determined by the degree of structural development in the patient, that is, the degree to which the patient requires the analytic setting itself to function as a maternal holding environment. When the interruption of this phase begins, it is invariably met with the development of a negative transference. Winnicott (1969) has suggested that the aggression may not simply be the response to the patient's encounter with the reality principle, but that "the destructive drive creates the quality of externality." He suggests that it is a necessary accompaniment of this process of individuation.

Expression of rage will differ in the narcissistic as compared with the borderline patient. In the narcissistic patient the rage tends to be more muted, and the resulting sadistic response may be projected onto the analyst, whereas in the borderline patient the rage is more open. The analyst's continued acceptance of this rage remains one of the more difficult aspects of the treatment. The capacity to accept the patient's negative response without retaliation also has its analogy in the early mother-child relationship. For it is similar to the mother holding a child in a temper tantrum or accepting the child's soiling. This does not mean that the analyst does not define the limits of the patient's aggression, but that he does not respond to it with retaliation.

What we are describing are processes that occur before the development of the therapeutic alliance. This fact in itself poses problems for the theory of the therapeutic effects of psychoanalysis. This has been a controversial area of psychoanalysis for at least several decades. (See Zetzel, 1956.) One school of thought would maintain that effective analysis depends on a sound therapeutic alliance, a prerequisite for which is the integration before analysis of certain mature ego functions. A contrary point of view would hold that therapeutic progess is indicated by changes in ego function which result from changes in object relationships through the interpretation of the transference. It can be seen that my own position is closer to this second point of view. The function of interpretation in this opening phase of psychoanalysis is far from clear. If we assume that the ego consolidation which takes place is related to the unconscious maternal aspects of the psychoanalytic relationships, there is an implicit depreciation of interpretation. Yet one wonders if the same ego consolidation would occur if the analyst did not in some way communicate his understanding of what is taking place.

There is a further complication—the effects of interpretation will be different depending on the presence or absence of a therapeutic alliance. A narcissistic patient, for example, who still maintains a grandiose, self-sufficient view of himself repudiates what others have to give and tends to dismiss or forget the analyst's interpretations. This is in contrast to a patient with a classical transference neurosis in a good therapeutic alliance where the analyst's communications are received with suspended, independent judgment to be worked over and either accepted or rejected.

In the narcissistic character disorder I have the impression that we are observing a consolidation of the ego itself, a building up of psychic structure. This consolidation may be a consequence of the healing influence of the object relationship implicit in the analytic setting, and not simply the consequence of specific analytic interpretations. The presumption of structural change is suggested by the fact that in successful cases, after this initial period, there will be the emergence of a transference neurosis at least in embryonic form.

Some narcissistic patients do not develop a transference neurosis and it is a question whether the analytic results in such instances will be as effective as in those patients where a transference neurosis has been developed and has been analyzed.

Anna Freud has expressed skepticism regarding the therapeutic results of psychoanalysis in such patients (A. Freud, 1969). For she believes that in those patients where there is poor differentiation of psychic structure, such as in the narcissistic character disorder, the analysis goes beyond the area of intrapsychic conflict which has always been the legitimate target for psychoanalysis and "into the darker area of interaction between innate endowment and environmental influence." She remains skeptical as to what extent psychoanalysis can alter the bedrock upon which the personality formation rests.

The transference in the narcissistic character disorder is peculiarly uniform. The fact that there is a uniform content to these transference manifestations is further evidence that we are witnessing the externalization of certain structural qualities of the ego itself. This is in contrast to the very specific historically idiosyncratic content of a transference neurosis—the familiar imagos of the infantile neurosis.

The relationship between the transference neurosis and the therapeutic alliance requires further comment. In the classical transference neurosis, the transference resistance must be interpreted in order to establish a therapeutic alliance. For example, a male patient with an intense oedipal rivalry with the analyst may perceive the analysis itself as part of the analyst's equipment and attack the work of the analysis in order to belittle the analyst. This is all quite familiar. We know that interpretation of this facet of the infantile neurosis will (hopefully) lead to a reduction of this form of the resistance and the establishment of a better therapeutic alliance. However, in the narcissistic neuroses, there is not always a capacity to form a therapeutic alliance, that is, the therapeutic alliance will not necessarily be established when the resistances have been interpreted. For the therapeutic alliance itself requires a further consolidation of the ego. One might say that in the transference neurosis there is always a latent capacity to form a therapeutic alliance, whereas in the narcissistic disorders this capacity may require a further consolidation of the ego for its emergence. In some instances it may never emerge.

SUMMARY

1. The quality of the transference and countertransference can be used as a means of distinguishing the narcissistic character disorders from borderline states.

2. The condition of affective nonrelatedness which leads to a countertransference response of boredom distinguishes the narcissistic personality disorders from the borderline conditions. In contrast, the borderline patient demonstrates affect hunger and an intensity of affects. Affects are, therefore, the leading edge of this differential diagnosis.

3. The narcissistic patient has achieved a greater degree of structural differentiation as compared to the borderline case. In the narcissistic patient there may be a precocious maternal identification, whereas in the borderline case there may be a failure of a maternal identification. In this sense the narcissistic

patient may have achieved a precocious closure from the environment, whereas the borderline patient remains, as does a young child, an "open system" in relation to the environment.

4. The psychoanalytic setting itself may be unconsciously experienced as a maternal environment, especially in the opening phase. The importance of this dyadic experience may be in direct proportion to the degree of actual privation experienced in the patient's earlier development.

5. The gratification implicit in the analytic setting experienced as an object relationship may be the mutative factor that leads to a consolidation of the ego in borderline patients and those with narcissistic character disorders.

6. These processes occur before the development of a therapeutic alliance and are usually characterized by the absence of a transference neurosis. With the consolidation of the ego a therapeutic alliance and an embryonic transference neurosis can be achieved in some but not all patients with narcissistic character disorders.

7. The effect of interpretation in the absence of a therapeutic alliance and the limitations of the therapeutic results of psychoanalysis are discussed.

References

Deutsch, H. (1942), "Some Forms of Emotional Disturbance and their Relationship to Schizophrenia." In *Neuroses and Character Types*. New York: International Universities Press, 1965.

Freud, A., *Difficulties in the Path of Psychoanalysis*. New York: International Universities Press, 1969.

Freud, S. (1924), "A Short Account of Psychoanalysis." *Standard Edition*, 19:191-209. London: Hogarth Press, 1957.

Giovacchini, P., "The Treatment of Characterological Disorders." In *Tactics and Techniques in Psychoanalytic Therapy*. New York: Jason Aronson, 1972.

_____. (1975) "Various Aspects of the Psychoanalytic Process." *This volume*.

Gitelson, M., The Curative Factors in Psycho-Analysis. *Internat. J. Psychoanal.*, 43:194-205 (1962).

Khan, M., "On Symbiotic Omnipotence." In *The Psychoanalytic Forum*. New York: Jason Aronson, Inc., 1969.

_____. "Infantile Neuroses as a False-Self Organization." *Psychoanal. Quart.*, 40:245-263 (1971).

Modell, A., "Primitive Object Relationships and the Predisposition to Schizophrenia." *Internat. J. Psychoanal.*, 44:282-292 (1963).

_____, *Object Love and Reality*. New York: International Universities Press, 1968.

Spitz, R., *The First Year of Life*. New York: International Universities Press, 1965.

Winnicott, D. (1951), "Transitional Objects and Transitional Phenomena." In *Collected Papers*. New York: Basic Books, 1958.

————, "The Theory of the Parent-Infant Relationship." In *The Maturational Processes and the FAcilitating Environment*. New York: International Universities Press, 1965.

————, "Psychiatric Disorder in Terms of Infantile Maturational Processes." In *The Maturational Processes and the Facilitating Environment*. New York: International Universities Press, 1965.

————, "Psychiatric Disorder in Termos of Infantile Maturational Prcoess." In *The Maturational Processes and the Facilitating Environment*. New York: International Universities Press, 1965.

————, "The Use of an Object and Relating through Identifications." In *Playing and Reality*. New York: Basic Books, 1971.

Zetzel, E., "The Concept of Transference." In *The Capacity for Emotional Growth*. New York: International Universities Press, 1970.

Part 3

SEXUALITY AND
CHARACTER

Introduction

Peter L. Giovacchini, M.D.

Psychoanalysis and sexuality have sometimes been considered synonymous. Certainly sex has played an important role in psychoanalytic theory and has had a significant influence in determining our concepts concerning emotional development. Historically, one of the strongest resistances to the acceptance of psychoanalysis was the refusal to accept and often to understand Freud's sexual theories.

In the early days of psychoanalysis, patients reflected the public aversion to discussing sex. Frequently, they would find it difficult to reveal their attitudes about sex or to discuss the intimate details of their sexual life; yet their material was often replete with childhood seductions, preoccupation with masturbation, bizarre perversions, and varied forms of sexual behavior. Sex was definitely related to psychopathology and conflicts concerning the expression of sexual needs were found regularly in the psychoneuroses.

Consequently, one of the fundamental aims of psychoanalytic treatment was to overcome resistances which prevented the patient from functioning adequately. This usually meant sexually adequate, a tangible result of successful psychoanalytic resolution.

Theories regarding sex have changed since Freud's time and its importance for the production of psychopathology has been viewed from another perspective. Freud's concepts about penis envy and the inferior psychosexual position of women have been vigorously attacked and recent biological concepts lend support to such arguments. The feminine position may be primary in both sexes with maleness being a specialized differentiation of the original female matrix. Still, these are complex matters and require much further exploration.

For the psychoanalyst, several factors are important. Do sexual conflicts play the same determining role in our patients as they did in Freud's patients? Again, one returns to the question as to whether psychopathology or simply the manifestations of psychopathology are different in our culture from those of a mid-Victorian culture. When one deals with structural defects and problems, sexual material may not be particularly prominent.

Over the course of two decades, I have seen striking changes in patients' attitudes about sex. My first patients were similar to Freud's, that is, in their shame, embarrassment, and reluctance to talk about the intimate details of their sexual lives. Frequently, their expectation that they should discuss their sexual attitudes and feelings (often toward the analyst) led to intense anxiety, even panic. This would be a rare situation today. Most patients can speak of their sexual lives candidly and calmly.

Cultural attitudes are, of course, important in determining this relaxation about erotic material. Probably, reluctance and prudishness to discuss money matters have replaced sexual inhibitions. Still, one cannot help wondering whether sexual expression and conflict are not, in some ways, less dependent upon cultural changes and more related to attitudes that are the outcome of character synthesis or lack of synthesis. Perhaps sex, per se, is not the main issue. Other more fundamental impulses and feelings may be involved which in Freud's day expressed themselves in erotic terms and today tend to be expressed more directly in feelings and behavior.

For example, Robert J. Stoller, who has written considerably about many facets of sex and sexual identity, discusses perversions as being the expression of hostile impulses. In fact, if the perverse act is not a reification of a destructive fantasy, then, according to Stoller, it is not a perversion. This has many implications for both psychopathology and treatment since many forms of sexual behavior may simply be rare variations and not necessarily representative of inner conflict.

Alfred Flarsheim carries the exploration of sexuality further into clinical areas and includes attitudes about motherhood. He presents a patient who had had a very active sexual life before entering analysis. She seemed to have no inhibition in this area and rather blithely indulged in various affairs. The effects of treatment were, on the surface, paradoxical. After analysis she became inhibited; she even became frigid, except in particular circumstances, whereas previously she claimed to have been able to reach orgasm indiscriminately. Apparently relationships with others had become meaningful to her and painful feelings were involved. Before treatment, she was not really relating in a mature genital fashion. Men were used for defensive sadomasochistic purposes.

Both these chapters demonstrate that overt behavior and even changes in behavior during treatment have to be viewed from a multifaceted perspective. These authors focus upon character structure and are then able to assess how the patient may handle sexual feelings. Patients suffering from ego defects, such as those discussed in this section, often act out in a sexual fashion while, in actuality, they are deling with much more primitive aspects of themselves.

Chapter XIV

Perversion and Hostility

Robert J. Stoller, M.D.

INTRODUCTION

Although it may seem quaint in these sophisticated times, I believe perversions—not just variants in sexual practice—really exist. Almost no other researcher on sexual behavior says this. More and more these days, decent people—scientists—are concerned at the price their fellows, even more, whole societies, pay in the effort to suppress victimless, aberrant sexual behavior. And so, in the name of decency, it has become the style, using the trappings of science, to try to get rid of the concept of perversion. This is done not only by changing the term to ones with less severe connotations, such as "deviation" or "variant," but by trying to show that there are no (or very few) states that actually fit the nasty connotations of "perversion." These workers reach their conclusion by objective means they feel avoid the dangers of introspective material, such as by studying brain mechanisms in animals and man, which reveal capacities for aberrant behavior inherited and laid down in CNS-hormonal organizations; by statistics that unmask how wide-spread are these alleged rare and heinous acts; by anthropological studies that reveal aberrant sexual behavior to have been the usual—not the strange—throughout history and across cultures; and by observation of or experimentation on intact animals. In all these cases, data have been gathered disclosing that aberrant sexual practices are found throughout animal species and are ubiquitous in human behavior. It is easy then to conclude that the widespread aberrance in man does not signify willed behavior—that is, sinfulness, a disobedience of accepted morality—but rather a natural tendency of the sexual impulse in the animal kingdom.

Conversely, others—philosophers and essayists rather than formal researchers—who serve a different but also admirable decency try to call us back from the abyss of licentiousness, pointing up the dehumanized, unloving aspects of sexual behavior that emphasizes anatomical more than interpersonal gratification. To reduce another person to a breast or a penis before one can succeed in concentrating his lust, or to be able to manage only when one's sexual object is not even human, is very sad—and dangerous; such severe failure of potency and degradation of lovingness only augment the other processes that today disintegrate one's humanity.

The first group of workers wants to be rid of the concept of perversion because it has moral connotations that have no place in the scientific study of behavior and because the term can be used by the repressive forces in society. The other group wants "perversion" retained because we need a sin-laden word to preserve the old morality, which, tested for so long, gives society structure.

There is some truth in each posture. But both are also wrong. What follows is an attempt to establish a position that any careful observer can find but a bit different from what others have done heretofore. Let me say what I think an aberration, a variation, and a perversion are and then review the data and concepts that led to the definitions. I shall state that perversion does exist; that its harsh connotations reflect a dim awareness that in the core of the perverse act is desire to harm others; and that the concept be retained, not because it is a useful propaganda weapon for preserving society but because the condition is demonstrable.

DEFINITIONS

By *aberration* here I mean an erotic technique or constellation of techniques one uses as his complete sex act that differs from his culture's traditional, avowed definition of normalcy. Sexual aberrations can be divided into two classes: variants (deviations) and perversions. By *variant* I mean an aberration not primarily the staging of forbidden fantasies, especially fantasies of harming others. Examples would be behavior set off only by abnormal brain activity, as with a tumor, experimental drug, or electrical impulse from implanted electrode; or an aberrant act one is driven to, *faute de mieux;* or sexual experiments done from curiosity and found not exciting enough to repeat. A *perversion* is a fantasy, usually acted out but occasionally restricted to a daydream—either self-produced or packaged by others, i.e. pornography. It is a habitual, preferred aberration necessary for one's full satisfaction, primarily motivated by hostility; the hostility takes form in a fantasy of revenge hidden in the actions that make up the perversion and serves to convert childhood trauma to adult triumph. To create greatest excitement, the perversion must also portray itself as an act of risk-taking.

While these definitions remove former incongruities, they add the new burden of requiring us to learn from a person what motivates him. But we are freed from a process of designation that did not take the subject's personality and motivation into account. We no longer need to define a perversion according to the anatomy used, the object chosen, the society's stated morality, or the number of people who do it. All we need know is what it means to the person doing it; while this may be difficult for us to uncover, that is still no reason to reject this technique for defining.

Case Material

Let us concentrate on clinical data from which we can distill theory. What we shall see are four common themes. First, the perversion depicts the running of risks that, as the sex act unfolds, are experienced as being surmounted. Second, inside the sexual excitement are desires, usually conscious, occasionally unconscious, to harm others in order to get revenge for past traumas and frustrations. Third, the perverse sex act serves to transform childhood trauma to adult triumph. And fourth, trauma, risk, and revenge establish a mood of excitement that is intensified when they are packaged as mystery.

The report of each following case is arranged to emphasize one or another of these aspects of the dynamics of hostility in perversion. In each is found, grossly or hidden but essential in the act, hostility, triumph, and—an element that especially concerns us in our search for perversion—a dehumanized object. While each case could represent all the dynamics, for clarity each will be used mainly to spotlight only one of the above themes. Note also that an element of revenge is hidden in the fantasy in each case.

Case 1: This material primarily underlines that dynamic of hostility in which risk-taking is predominant. We shall see how the perverse act, in this case, exhibitionism, seeks the right sort of risk to create excitement. For most people, sexual excitement is not the spontaneous lust of animals; full arousal occurs only when cautionary measures have been taken. The sex, behavior, appearance, social class, religion, species—almost any attribute of one's object—may raise or lower anxiety (excitement). Only after years of trial and error, from infancy on, does one arrive at a rendering that works smoothly (and some never even manage that). One marks his failure in construction on one side by lack of sexual interest—boredom—and on the other by anxiety. Both are manifested by disturbed potency. If the excitement is to work, there must not be too much anxiety, which in unadulterated form is the enemy of pleasure. But one can reduce anxiety, without also ending excitement. This is done by introducing a sense of risk into the act. A *sense* of risk; in reality, the risk cannot be great or the anxiety will rise. One can only have the impression of risk.

This requires a few words now and in the case material that follows. There are sexual acts in which gross risk-taking is essential for orgasm, for instance, hanging oneself to achieve orgasm. What we must distinguish, however, is that the risk buried among the sexual act's fantasies is not the same as the one that threatens in the real world; the risk from the noose is not the risk that the scenario of the act must avoid.

"Exhibitionism" here refers only to those whose preferred or necessary form of genital pleasure is exhibiting their genitals. Why are exhibitionists caught so often? Of competent intelligence, not psychotic, aware of the possibility of arrest, and in many instances having already suffered severe social consequences, why do they persist in their dangerous behavior? The explanations come when one looks at the structure of the perversion.

This man, married, overtly heterosexual throughout his life, unremarkably masculine in demeanor, with a masculine profession, has been thrice convicted for exhibitionism. Although he has been imprisioned before and is now on parole, he risks his marriage, profession, and reputation by still performing his perverse act once or twice a fortnight. This usually occurs following a humiliation, most often at work or from his wife. He is then driven into the street by a tension he does not sense as erotic, to search an unfamiliar neighborhood for a woman or girl to whom he displays his penis. He chooses strangers; he has never done this with a familiar woman. In fact, he is shy about being seen nude by his wife, who takes him and his penis for granted. (He says she does not respect him; she agrees.) He expects to shock the stranger and does not show his penis as a precursor to intercourse; he does not know why he does so, only that he is compelled to. On occasions when women are not upset but joke with him, pretending they are interested, he flees. But when the woman is angry and calls the police—when he seems to be running the great risk— he finds himself reluctant to get away fast. Although his fear mounts, it becomes mixed with a sense of confusion that slides into immobility. And when this excited lethargy persists too long, he is caught. caught.

The nonexhibitionist, unable to comprehend, thinks this man is stupid. How much more odd then, must seem the arrested man's mood while he is being booked: at the center of his feelings of disaster is a crazy, peaceful, pleasant quietness. I think we can understand this: risk has been run and surmounted; trauma has been converted to triumph.

Our mistake would be to think the police were the risk; they are not. They are, rather, agents of the triumph. The real risk, from the viewpoint of the perversion, arises from the trauma of the humiliation earlier in the day, which is, for this vulnerable man, a repeat of childhood humiliation that has left in him a fracture line, a fear that he is not a free-standing, potent, formidable male.

And so the risk, the lifelong risk, is not that he will be arrested but rather that the humiliation will persist. Displaying his penis, he shows in the most concrete way that he has not been humiliated, that he is not unmanly, that he is not castrated, that he has not been defeated by women; and it is his way of protesting, insisting, that he still is a man. Therefore, the woman who is shocked, who becomes angry, who creates a fuss, and who brings on the police is complying with a necessary part of his perversion; now she is the attacked one and he the attacker. Even if he is arrested, he is peculiarly tranquil because the arrest indicates that in fact he does have a fine penis, powerful enough to create such disturbance in society. We are not surprised to learn, then, that the rate of the combination of arrest, imprisonment, and recidivism in exhibitionism is higher than in any other perversion.

Case 2: This condition, transvestism (cross-dressing that causes sexual excitement), is a bit more subtle than the last in that the dynamics of hostility are not manifest grossly; one needs to descend into the fantasy underlying perversion, in fact, that underlies all sexual excitement, and to the historical past to find how the trauma of childhood becomes the triumph that preserves the adult's potency.

This biologically normal little boy developed in a masculine way in his first 3 years, when his mother suffered a chronic physical illness that hospitalized her permanently. He was put in the care of an aunt who hated males. She immediately made, with her own hands, clothes for him of a style considered effeminate in the community where they lived and disparaged all signs of developing masculinity. When he was 4, his mother returned home on his birthday for a visit, shortly before dying; to celebrate the occasion, this aunt dressed the boy in girls' clothes, introduced him to his mother as a neighborhood girl, and photographed the occasion of this joke.

He has no memory of this; he dates the origin of his fetishistic cross-dressing from age 6, when as a punishment he was forced by another woman to put on her clothes. On that occasion, he became strongly sexually excited and has done so invariably to the present with women's clothes. Despite this need to cross-dress, the sense of maleness that was created in the first months of his life persists, as does his masculinity. He is a forceful man, in a business that requires an intense use of masculine qualities and in his bearing and appearance is unquestionably masculine. His overt sexual life has been exclusively heterosexual. He is married and has children. His sexual capacity, not surprisingly, is invaded by his fetishism, so that he has problems in potency unless dressed as a woman. He finds it of greatest importance that his wife dresses him as a woman and pretends for the moment that he is a woman—with a penis.

How, if the trauma is recapitulated in the perversion, does pleasure replace anguish? By reversing the action. The victim becomes victor. The little boy was humbled, but there, now, presides the adult pervert, dressed in the women's clothes. These garments, formerly the agent of trauma, now delight him—strong, full of anticipation, powerfully potent, intact, penis and self gathered up in full strength, competent for orgasm. How better to prove he is triumphant than to be potent in the presence of the original trauma. He has his revenge. The women, so mysteriously powerful in childhood, while not reduced in strength, are not able to overpower him; he proves it every time he puts on their clothes. Each occasion demonstrates that they failed.

But unfortunately, he has to repeat endlessly, for somehow he knows the perversion is only a construction, a fantasy; it can never truly prove that he has won. It does so only for the moment, and each time in his life that circumstances arise to echo the original traumatic situation, he can placate his anxiety only in repeating the perverse act whose function is to tell him again that he is intact and a victor.

This description leaves out much that is important, such as the transvestite's belief in phallic women, both the powerful sorts who originally attacked him and the kind that he represents with his erect penis beneath the women's clothes; or the symbolic meanings the clothes have for him; or the fact that in the natural course of the perversion, as time passes and sexual power wanes with age, fetishistic behavior may become less commanding than the desire to pass in the world as a woman. These issues, however, shall be set aside lest they draw us away from the simpler goal of defining the concept of perversion.

If these hypotheses are correct, they should be borne out in the transvestite's pornography, for in his responding to it he says, "Only this pornography really excites me; the rest, which excites someone else, is not for me." And we see, when we look at the pornography our patient has used, that all these historical elements, the events that happened to him in the real world and the defense he created with his fantasy, are recapitulated. (Pornography is an instantaneous, accurate test of psychodynamics; whoever gets excited by such a picture has had a childhood like this patient's.) The story in the illustrated booklet tells how a masculine young man, with masculine name, appearance and interests, is captured by beautiful but dangerous women, forced against his will into women's clothes and reduced to humiliation. The high point of the story occurs when, following the awful experience, he discovers that the fashions are delightful, the textures sensual, and the women warm and friendly, so long as he succumbs to their clothes. And, outside of the story, holding the book in his hands, is our patient, wearing women's clothes but now the victor, his potency successfully expressed in masturbation. He needs this performance only intermittently, the rest of the time living unremarkably as a man. Remember that he was a masculine boy, and that, despite the feminine disguise in his perversion, he preserves maleness and masculinity. He does this even and especially when it most seems reversed, that is, when he puts on women's clothes.

In this effort to show that the concept of perversion is meaningful, I said that perversions are aberrations in which fantasy is used to convert trauma to triumph. Now let us confirm the other thesis, that perversions can be contrasted to variants, in which this dynamic is not present; our example, the transvestite, illustrates the difference. Now let us contemplate another male who also cross-dresses, the transsexual. Here we have someone who has never been masculine in childhood and has had no masculinity later in life. As soon as any gender behavior appears, usually around the first year of life, it is feminine. Such a male never gets excited by women's clothes (any more than women do); while not denying he is a male, he hates that state and early in childhood already talks of growing up to be an anatomically normal female. In time, he will demand that society convert him to female, and as early as his teens, he will pass, unrecognized, as if a normal female. He has (as I define transsexualism) no history of masculine appearance, masculine behavior, heterosexuality, fetishism or other perversions, fluctuation between masculine and feminine behavior, employment in masculine professions, capacity to have intercourse with women, or a need and pleasure in preserving male genitals. There is no hostility directed toward women and no fantasy, conscious or unconscious, of revenge against them; he has no need for that, since they did not traumatize or frustrate him in childhood. Quite the reverse. So there is no sense of victimization and no need to transform catastrophe into triumph.

The transvestite and the transsexual have in common a sexual aberrance: they both wish to put on women's clothes. But when one examines what goes on in their minds, when one troubles himself to find their motivation, not to say the details of their past history, the two no longer look the same.

Case 3: The above propositions are most vigorously tested in the least perverse circumstances; the major perversions do not give them much of a challenge, for there the dynamics are too visible. So let us now look at one of the most normative sexual behaviors of our society in which, despite its frequency, these dynamics of hostility may nonetheless be present: sexual looking. (I prefer to use that term, rather than "voyeurism," which clearly connotes perversion.) Can one say that the ubiquitous sexual looking of men in our society contains in it risk-running, the desire to harm others, a need for revenge, the dehumanization of one's sexual object, and, what this example will be used to underline, mystery used to heighten excitement? If all that were so, we would be faced with the possibility that perversion, to some degree, is ubiquitous. I shall take a chance anyway and see if these concepts apply.

Let this case be the men of modern society. An obvious fact starts us off. No one is keenly interested, in societies where there is unlimited nudity, in looking at the freely available anatomy. On the other hand, in one such as ours, in which certain anatomy is proscribed, sexual curiosity is aroused for just those parts. The subtleties and shifts in degree and parts proscribed create fashions in dress, carriage, fantasy, and pornography. In our time and culture, looking is far more intricate and stylized for males, and for females, being looked at.

Our topic, now, is mystery, a quality so important to sexual excitement that the two are almost synonymous. Such mystery derives from childhood and the convoluted way our society obscures the discovery of the anatomical differences between the sexes. Our knowledge that anxiety is an essential element of mystery is confirmed, as Freud showed long ago, in oedipal development and those of its anxieties deriving from the anatomical differences.

It is no news that mystery is exciting, and most analysts are probably aware that it is an element in all perversion, and, I would add, in most sexual excitement. How does it work?

1. In the first year or so of life one begins to believe he is a member of one sex or the other.

2. Then the anatomical differences between the sexes are discovered; attitudes expressed within the family and in society inform the boy and girl differentially that this is a subject of keenest importance.

3. The desire to satisfy oneself as to the nature, especially the appearance, of these differences is great because of the implications of danger to one's sense of maleness or femaleness inherent in these differences. The genitals are the only way anatomy communicates the crucial differences of sex assignment in childhood. (Length of hair might, and to the extent it does, cutting it is seen as castration threat. Breasts do also, though for different beings: adults.) But the need to explore so as to find out (i.e. to end the fear that the sex differences exist and/or are dangerous) is, in our society, frustrated more in boys than in girls; so the desire to look and the promise it would be worthwhile is heightened just by the styles used to thwart it. The more hindrance, the greater the overvaluation and distortion. One becomes very curious. (To be more precise, both boys and girls may be told it is naughty to look at the genitals of the opposite sex or to show one's genitals thus. The messages are subtly different, however. The boy learns that no one is surprised he does so; he is expected to be a bad, cocky little aggressor. The girl, on the other hand, anticipates the boy's trying, while she is supposed to resist. These attitudes, inculcated in each sex, are reflected in such automatisms as proper leg crossing or the skirt-pulling "habit" of cultured women.)

4. At this stage, phallic importance due both to a physiological increase in penile and clitoral erotic sensation and simultaneous oedipal desires and dangers make this curiosity even more exciting and frustrating. From such fertile ground grows the fantasy of the female phallus, a child's attempt at explaining mystery that only heightens it.

5. Chronic, intense frustration, an essence of mystery, with the built-in threats if one tries to gratify himself, functions as a cumulative trauma. But to reduce the tension of the "instinctual" desire by sexual looking is risky. So the mystery increases: yet, thus far, no gratification. Excitement comes in two parts: danger and gratification. The problem facing the child is how to avoid danger (punishment) and how to get pleasure (reward)—which arises from three activities: by decreasing frustration, by successfully doing what was forbidden, and by one's body being erotically stimulated.

The explanation for excitement in sexual looking goes like this so far: When the inevitable curiosity about the differences in the sexes arises in the small child, the desire to look becomes intense, insatiable, and permanent to the extent that the body parts to be looked at are forbidden and at the same time considered desirable by the parents; in their forbidding, parents let their child know there is dangerous pleasure possible. Therefore, in our society where the female anatomy is the more forbidden, but enticingly so, males will tend to overvalue and be excited by looking and females by being looked at. If we say that excitement is made up of danger, with its painful affects, plus pleasure, components of which are relief and erotic sensation, a piece of explanation is, however, still missing. When one is anxious about the mystery and frustrated and angry in attempts to fathom and end it, what converts these painful affects to pleasure?

6. Somehow the danger must be undone. Fear cannot in itself yield pleasure, nor will rage. Something new must be added to release one's body for erotic response. The psychophysiology of fear and rage must be shifted into new channels if excitement is to change its quality and its course from muscles and gut to genitals. For the looking to be sexually exciting—if the thesis is correct—a man must believe he is acting forcefully, sadistically, upon an unwilling woman: he is doing what, so goes his fantasy, she decidedly does not want. If he can do so, he defeats her; he gets revenge for past frustration. Finally it is woman's turn to suffer; the excitement in pornography requires a depicted victim, though the more normative the perversion, the less obvious the depiction (e.g., a picture of a quietly nude female hides the dynamic more than a picture of a woman being tortured). Inherent in sexual looking is a desire to degrade females. (The envy buried in this will not be discussed in this paper.)

Sexual looking, found especially in the use of pornography, employs dehumanization, fetishization, and reinvention. The story line is easily controlled; any detail one does not like can be remedied by buying a book or photograph that removes an unwanted or adds a wanted quality, as one can do even more easily when constructing his own daydreams. Aspects of sexuality are chosen in which are focused the essentials of the perverse dynamics, even in the mildest of the heterosexual male pornographies, photographs of nudes. These reduce the actual woman to a two-dimensional, frozen creature helplessly impaled on the page, so that she cannot defend herself or strike back, as she might in the real world. Even if she has a dangerous look about her, that implied risk is negated by her imprisonment on the paper. She can be insulted, dirtied, forced to act according to the viewer's will, and remain uncomplaining, smiling, or even phallic, but immobile. And she is not only displayed, available for any fantasied sexual hostility, she is also idealized. She does no harm, she brings satisfaction, she is aesthetic perfection (if not, another picture is chosen), she is retouched, she infinitely repairs herself, she demands no revenge, she is absolutely cooperative, she keeps secrets, she costs almost nothing in money or time, she need not be understood, she has no wants of her own: ideal. While it is more difficult to get the same submission when actually performing a perversion rather than just imagining it in pornography or daydreams, the properly planned perversion still permits one to choose objects in the real world that can be dealt with in this way. Thus, for instance, fetishism (the use of inanimate objects), or the use of prostitutes (humans hired to act like puppets), or the choice of people, like the transvestite's compliant wife, whose own neuroses complement—that is, find use for—the perverse act.

We can stay with the trivial; we need not use such obvious perversions as rape, exhibitionism, sadism, or homosexuality for confirmation of hostility's presence. A woman in a drawing room treasures (or acts to others and perhaps herself as if she treasures) the privacy of every inch of thigh that might be displayed beyond her permissible level. (It used to be ankles.) But on the beach, the formerly contested vision is just skin, simply because the man knows she does not care there. Likewise, a strange woman is exciting, while for too many men, the familiar is a bore.

A pseudoexplanation for boredom is "familiarity," but that does little more than give a name. It does not explain why familiarity, in most arenas of erotic behavior, reduces excitement; without understanding the dynamics of hostility or without having lived in the world, one might as well have expected familiarity to produce greater pleasure; it sometimes does with happy couples.

Sexual boredom is in good part the result of the loss of sense of mystery and risk. So, even if the rest of the elements are present in the fantasy/pornography, it does not work well unless one pretends to be just a bit fearful, uncertain of a successful outcome. (The same dynamic of risk applies elsewhere. It is vividly present in jokes; with second telling, little or no tension or big laugh. And it is probably also at the bottom of art appreciation and the rapid dating of art styles; committed art critics, like connoisseurs of pornography, are honestly and deeply unable to respond to a different set of expressed dynamics.)

DISCUSSION

Just as every human group has its myth, perhaps for every person there is *the* sexual fantasy. In it is summarized one's sexual life history—the development of his or her erotism and of masculinity and femininity. In the manifest content of the fantasy are imbedded clues to the traumas and frustrations placed upon the sexual desires in childhood by the outside world, the mechanisms created to assuage the resultant tension, and the character structure used to get satisfaction from one's body and the outside world (one's objects). The analyst has the opportunity to study this sexual fantasy and uncover these origins. And the findings of the single analysis may be confirmed en masse: by pornography. Pornography is the communicated sexual fantasy of a dynamically related group of people. That is why there are many pornographies and why what is exciting for one person bores another.

In its opposite, sexual boredom,* we can find clues about excitement. Aside from heightened excitement that is the result of changed physiology (such as prolonged abstinence, puberty, or other causes of shifts in hormone levels and CNS function), it may be that for most people heightened sexual excitement occurs when the circumstances approximate *the* sexual fantasy. Is this equation possible: increased excitement equals increased impact of (one's own) perverse elements: i.e. cruelty? Modest excitement (barring physiological shifts) would mean, then, fewer perverse elements, and minimal excitement or boredom would mean few or no conscious perverse elements (they being absent or inhibited).

And so, if we want to understand perversion, we shall have to study *fantasy,* that vehicle of hope, healer of trauma, protector from reality, concealer of truth, fixer of identity, restorer of tranquility, enemy of fear and sadness, cleanser of the soul. And creator of perversion. I believe that in humans, fantasy is as much part of the etiology, not just a concomitant, of perversion as are the physiological and environmental factors the researchers are helping us understand. The details of a sex act, the story line, is incomprehensible in its origin and meaning if one ignores the process and function of fantasy. You can study every cell of the brain and every animal in the kingdom and not know why a man gets excited by wearing a woman's shoe, or by a dead body, or by an amputee, or by a child, or by being defecated on, or by talking dirty on the phone to a strange woman, or by the nudeness of an unknown woman, or by his neighbor's wife but no longer by his own.

I do not see how fantasy can be left out of one's calculations about human sexual behavior; it is no secret that fantasy, in the form of daydreams, is present consciously in much of sexual activity. In fact, on hearing of a person without sexual fantasy, we suspect that an inhibition is in force. But run through the names of the great researchers on sexuality of the past generation or more. You will note that, no matter what area they study, or what techniques used, or what findings reported, they have generated data of sexual excitement not motivated by fantasy, that is, not motivated by story-telling that fashions a new, better "reality." Most research on sexuality emphasizes the noninvented, nonconflictual, extrapsychic origins of sexual excitement,

---

*I use "boredom" here to mean a state in which something is "monotonous, wearisome, and tediously devoid of interest" (*Webster's Third New International Dictionary*). This implies an actively dynamic state, not merely that excitement has been emptied out to leave a quiet state of reduced energy or interest.

whether perverse or not. It is as if intrapsychic manifestations are not there. Example: a handful of cases have been found in the whole immense universe of man, in which aberrant sexual behavior was set off by a CNS seizure; conclusion: perversion is the result of epilepsy. Example: free-ranging animals occasionally use a component of the reproductive behavior of the opposite sex, such as when a cow mounts another cow momentarily; conclusion: homosexuality is part of animal activity, and man, being part of the animal world, is only expressing his natural inheritance when he is a homosexual. Example: a male chimpanzee in New Orleans masturbates while fondling a boot; conclusion: fetishism is the result of simple conditioning. Example: certain societies consider as nonperverse, sexual activity we define as perversion; conclusion: the act, performed in our society with the same anatomy, will have the same meaning to the individual and spring from the same psychic sources as in the alien culture.

If you are familiar with such studies, you know that they unite in ignoring psychic motivation, substituting primeval forces like evolution, chromosomal and genetic inheritance, neurophysiology, culture, and conditioning and imprinting that act on a defenseless psychobiology, or by proclaiming that normative is normal. They seem to show, have been designed to show, that wilful, motivated desire to hurt or diminish others, i.e. perversion, does not exist. I disagree, but in this disagreement I believe these above factors are (or in some cases yet unproven, may be) essential inputs to human sexuality. I ask, as do you, only that the modern sex researchers also include the intrapsychic effects of a person's past, especially as expressed in the subtleties of interpersonal relationships. Its complexity at present puts this factor beyond the grasp of experimental techniques; research methods of the scientific establishment are not yet competent to reveal or probe fantasy. But the researchers should not be so impatient; if fantasy exists, it can be studied. And while we wait for science to catch up, perhaps we should continue to search with that uncertain and yet powerful technique of discovery, the psychoanalytic method and its bemused offspring, analytic theory.

Only in studying the sexual fantasy that underlies the sex act can we make sense of that act, for only then can we discover the nature of the hostility that energizes the excitement. Often hatred is a central feature of the manifest contents and marks, even for the untrained observer, the bizarreness of the excitement. In fact, usually, the more bizarre we consider the act, the more rage we will find in it. Murder that sexually excites, mutilation for excitement, rape, sadism with precise physical punishments such as whipping or cutting, enchaining and binding games, defecating or urinating on one's object—all are on a lessening scale of hostility toward one's sex object, in which an essential purpose is for one to be superior to, harmful to, triumphant over another. And so it is also in the nonphysical sadisms like exhibitionism, voyeurism, dirty phone calls or letters, use of prostitutes, and most forms of promiscuity. Look closely at cryptoperversions such as rape, or a preference for prostitutes, or compulsive promiscuity (Don Juanism or nymphomania), which the naive observer may see only as heterosexual enthusiasms. You will discern that the object is a person with a personality, while the perverse person sees a creature without humanity—just an anatomy or clichéd fragments of personality (e.g., "all women are bitches," "all men are brutes"). Statistics, watching animals, and manipulating the brain put us nowhere in understanding why and how these excitements work, but getting into another's mind and searching out the nature and origin of the need to harm one's partner is possible and tells so much.

As a first line of defense, children fantasy situations that reverse trauma and frustration. In time, with modifications and disguises, they put into behavior the action formerly only fantasied. This is done progressively with toys, in games with peers, and finally in real situations with people who do not consider themselves simply actors in one's script. (Perverse people, however, deal with their partners as if the others were not real people but rather figures in a script to be manipulated on the stage where the perversion is played.) In the perverse act, one endlessly relives the traumatic or frustrating situation that started the process, but now the outcome is not awful but marvelous. And not only does one escape the threat, but now immense sensual gratification is attached to the consummation. The whole story, precisely constructed by each person to fit exactly his own painful experiences, lies hidden but available for study in the sexual fantasy of the perversion.

There are two hypotheses amenable to future testing, for which I do not yet have confirming data, that round out this part of the explanation. First, the trauma or frustration of childhood was aimed precisely at the anatomical sexual apparatus and its functions and/or at one's masculinity and femininity. If the target was other, nonsexual parts or functions of the body or psyche, the result is one of the nonsexual neuroses (e.g. the compulsive personality when control especially excretory, is forced on the child too early, too hard, or too long).

The second is that sexual excitement is most likely to be set off at the moment when adult reality resembles the childhood trauma or frustration. This implies there is more anxiety felt during the perverse sex act than is present in less perverse sexuality. This anxiety—anticipation of danger—I believe, is experienced as excitement, a word used not to describe libidinous sensations so much as a rapid vibration between fear of trauma and hope of triumph.

Prevalence of Perversion in Males versus Females

An odd fact needs explanation: perversions are far more frequent in males than in females. (I think of only two exceptions to this. First, perverse, and especially masochistic sexual fantasies, though not practices, are common in women. Second is homosexuality, a subject so complicated that I dare not approach it now; I would only say that it seems a whole different category of aberration than the other conditions we list as perversions, the main difference in homosexuality being that it is made up of a number of different aberrations, in many of which warm interpersonal relations are maintained.) Simply to remind you with examples, recall that necrophilia, sadistic sexual assault as necessary for generating excitement do not exist in women, and even fetishism, common enough among men, is very rare with women. My explanatory hunch derives from the above dyamics regarding trauma, frustration, and hostility. Boys are vulnerable to a form of trauma and frustration aimed at their genitals and gender identity that girls are usually spared: the boy, if he is to become masculine, must succeed in breaking free from the tempting intimacy of his mother's body and psyche. While children of both sexes must learn to separate from their mothers, and while disturbances in that process produce pathology in girls as well as boys, the aspect of the separation that has to do with the boy learning the maleness of his body as different from the femaleness of his mother's is not usually a problem for little girls. In fact, intimacy with her mother makes it easier for the girl to absorb, identify with, appreciate, her mother's femaleness and femininity. This is not purely conjecture; it is known that those boys who from birth on have too intimate and blissful an experience with their mothers, extended over too long a time, do not separate from their mothers' femaleness; they never develop masculinity. These are the transsexual males noted above. And there is also reason to believe that the most masculine females, the female transsexuals, were separated from their mothers too soon and too severely and were encouraged not to identify with their mother's femininity but with their fathers' masculinity.

Perhaps, then, this additional task of separation that boys must perform to become masculine makes their masculinity more at risk than is typical of the femininity of girls. So I wonder whether perversion is not often, in males, the result of this increased vulnerability to the threat of not being masculine enough?

CONCLUSIONS

I believe, then, that the concept of perversion is still useful. First, it allows us to detect two different classes of aberration even when the behaviors seem similar to an observer. This could lead to more precise selection of treatment methods.

Second, we have a new perspective when doing research on the causes and structure of perversions, if we can confirm that these different classes of aberrations exist.

Third, we have clues for constructing a new diagnostic system that may help us communicate better about our patients.

Fourth, this view of perversion from inside the psyche—from the viewpoint of a person's motivation and fantasy life—restores our focus on human sexual behavior as a richly complex experience, a position closer to reality than one that explains all in terms of neurophysiology or normative statistics. How enervating it is that analysts must still remind others of the obvious, that while we humans are members of the animal kingdom, we also have unique psychological features. And prime among these is the capacity to fantasy and to use fantasy consciously and unconsciously to undo traumas and frustrations inflicted upon us when, especially as children, we could not adequately defend ourselves. It is marvelous that no one has to be taught how to create a perversion; century after century the myriad perversions are invented anew.

Obviously, much has been left out, especially those contributions of psychoanalysts from Freud's earliest work on. These findings can be omitted safely, I believe, because they are familiar and well-established in fact and theory. The ideas in this presentation serve only to complement those origins of perversion we know from the conflicts arising out of the earliest stages of infantile and childhood development, arranged conceptually as oral, anal, phallic, and oedipal. The ruthless possessiveness and destructive urges of early life, more or less encapsulated by those psychic functions we call the superego, provide data and a framework essential for understanding perversion. All that is present, if unheard, in the ideas I presented.

The overt goal of this presentation was to describe how hostility plays a central role in perversion; and so I focused on the anger and cruelty that arises in the early frustrations and traumas and traced how these feelings and their accompanying sense of victimization are converted to sexual pleasure; with full gratification, trauma becomes triumph. But in doing so, and especially in turning to ubiquitous behavior like sexual looking, I had a larger goal in mind: a search for psychodynamics not only of perversion but of all sexual excitement. Sexual excitement condenses into an instant one's emotional life history, its problems, and its solutions. The manifest form of this life history is *the* sexual fantasy, which is present in—more, is necessary for intensifying—excitement. And so, it is suggested, if we want to understand everyone's sexual life, we must learn his sexual fantasy; when we know it well, we shall find in it the direct connection between permutations of hostility and sharpness of excitement and gratification. Then we shall see that the mechanisms used in perversion contribute to all human sexual excitement.

Chapter XV

The Influence of Psychoanalytic Treatment Upon a Woman's Attitudes Toward Sex and Motherhood

Alfred Flarsheim, M.D.

The psychoanalytic treatment of women always includes consideration of feminine identity. Therefore, I will start with a brief comment on feminine identity. In reading panel discussions on the development of sexual identity, we find that clinical observations can be interpreted in various ways. Modern studies tend to trace adult character traits to the vicissitudes of the very early mother-child unit. The older literature tended to stress oedipal triangular conflict with retreat from adult heterosexuality and responsibility, and the traumatic effect of the discovery of the anatomical difference between the sexes. Some modern writers still consider these factors to be of primary importance in disorders of gender identity and sexual role.

I would like to refer to an early paper to illustrate a change in the way of viewing feminine gender identity and sexual role. In the 1934 *International Journal of Psychoanalysis*, Joan Riviere reviewed Freud's *New Introductory Lectures on Psychoanalysis*. She pointed out that according to Freud the girl baby starts off with a phallic orientation, and turns to femininity entirely as a result of an external experience, the "accidental trauma of discovering that she has no penis." There is "no recognition by Freud of innate feminine characteristics in the small child." Joan Riviere goes on to say that "when a woman's oral libido, later carried over to her genital zone, has developed free from undue anxiety she has a freedom and satisfaction in acquiring, possessing, and ultimately in cherishing 'good' objects within her. . . . and, here surely is the foundation and ultimate pattern of development of a woman's psychology, interwoven though it may be with masochism and the additional complications of her castration complex and rivalry with her father and brothers."

In Freud's later papers, e.g., in "Analysis Terminable and Interminable" (1937), he shows that he retained his views that all infants start out with a phallic disposition and a need to "repudiate femininity."

In 1923, in *The Ego and the Id*, translated by Joan Riviere before she reviewed the *New Introductory Lectures*, Freud stated that at the beginning object relationship and identification are indistinguishable. In this statement he anticipated modern thinking about ego development from primary narcissism. From this standpoint the need for "repudiation of femininity" is a need to repudiate the primary identification with the mother, and (in both sexes) can be considered a defense against regression to the undifferentiation and dependency of infancy.

Going further back, we find that at least as early as 1914, Freud anticipated modern views on feminine sexual and maternal function. His comments on male and female love in his "On Narcissism," (1914), have been at times regarded as those of a man depreciating women. But we can see here, as so often, the profundity of Freud's insight. He said that men love women and women love themselves, and need to be loved rather than to love a separate person. The woman achieves complete object love in her relation to her child, "a part of her own body." In order to love her child a mother must be able to value herself and to accept being loved. This leads directly to a modern ego psychological viewpoint in which maternal functioning is described not so much in terms of actively feeding a baby, or passively permitting the baby to use the mother as the object of the baby's object-related instinctual impulses, but rather in terms of the mother's capacity to participate in the primary and undifferentiated union, mother-infant, before self-object differentiation (Winnicott, 1956, 1972; Little, 1960).

Next, I want to present some clinical material to illustrate changes in a woman's feeling about herself during treatment, and to illustrate how these changes were reflected in two closely interrelated areas: (1) her sexual adjustment, (2) her attitude toward motherhood.

CLINICAL ILLUSTRATION

A twenty-eight-year-old, recently divorced woman sought psychotherapy for insomnia, diffuse anxiety, and fear that she would repeat her unsatisfactory marriage in the future. Before marriage she and her husband had been "intellectual companions" and she had wanted the relationship to continue that way. He had wanted marriage but after marrying her started drinking excessively and totally ignoring her. She was a successful business woman, and when she first saw me she stated firmly that her career was of first importance to her and she wanted to be certain I understood that I must never expect her to interrupt her career to have children. She was interested in the Women's Liberation Movement, and had much feeling about discrimination against women in business.

Soon after high school the patient had refused any financial assistance from her parents. She had scholarships and jobs during college and postgraduate work. During her marriage she had remained totally independent of her husband financially.

SEXUAL ADJUSTMENT

Any contact with a man might include a sexual relationship without other involvement. She achieved orgasm relatively independently of the quality of the object relationship with her sexual partner, and she felt that there is little difference between the experience of orgasm, regardless of the circumstances. The only important condition was that the man not be sexually aggressive. She withdrew phobically if a man pursued her with any intensity. The men she chose for sexual partners tended to be relatively impotent and uninterested in sexual activity. She had orgasm quickly and regularly with intercourse, without foreplay or other stimulation aside from intercourse. The superiority of her own sexual performance to that of the man was always prominent in her descriptions. Not only were her sexual partners relatively impotent, but they treated her quite regularly in a neglectful way. She objected to this when it was extreme, but it was preferable to what she called having her whole life "swallowed up" by the insistent attentions of aggressive men. For example, she would not agree to spend a whole weekend with a man or agree to a standing date each week, even when she did not have other plans, and even when a man was attractive to her.

The patient was convinced that she would be abandoned by any man on whom she let herself become dependent, and she chose men who did, in fact, neglect and abandon her, but upon whom she did not depend. The men tended to become dependent upon her, and she took care of them in their helplessness, while resenting it. It was part of the defensive pattern of this patient that she established relationships with men she could not depend upon. In this way, as we will see, she avoided her own conflict about being cared for.

ATTITUDE TO BABIES AND MOTHERHOOD

Although without apparent physical defect, the patient felt that she had a "defective body" and, therefore, only a defective child could be created by her. She felt that no man could love her, considered this another reason why any child of hers would necessarily be defective and why she would not be able to function as a mother.

The patient considered herself adaptable and able to adjust to the needs of other people in crucial situations. One might expect this to correlate with a high degree of wish and capacity for adapting to the needs of an infant. This turned out not to be the case. She had a defensive identification with those who were providing care and protection and an incapacity to identify with anyone needing such care. She had "no interest in babies and no understanding of them" and only talked about them either as a lot of trouble or no trouble to their parents.

She had been told that in her infancy she was nursed for only a few days and then transferred to bottle feeding because her mother had too little milk.

She fed poorly and at three months became ill with an undiagnosed febrile illness which lasted intermittently until she was nine years old. During this entire period from three months to nine years she was in and out of hospitals, first in France, where she was born, and then in the United States, to which the family came when she was six. The illness was characterized by lymphadenitis, fever, and also by occasional attacks of bronchial asthma. Leukemia was suspected, but no specific diagnosis other than that of bronchial asthma was made.

Her descriptions of her childhood illnesses at the beginning of treatment were interesting in that they were entirely from the viewpoint of her parents and absolutely not at all from the viewpoint of having been an ill infant. For example, she talked about the great cost in money of her repeated hospitalizations and the enormous amount of trouble and strain to which her parents had been subjected because of having a sick child. This involved a denial of her suffering as a child, and only gradually and piecemeal did she become able to remember some of the actual suffering. She also had another defense. She decathected her whole body so that she was in a depersonalized state in which she could not be hurt by doctors doing things to her body. She remembers using this defense as a child also when her mother screamed at her because of disobedience. She retained this mechanism into adult life, for example, when she had gynecological examinations.

The patient's mother told her that "when God gave out bodies you were near the end of the line and just happened to get a bad one." She accepted this literally, and always felt that she had something bad within her so that if she were ever to have a baby it would necessarily be deformed and defective. Despite, this, she grew up to have an attractive female personality. It turned out, though, that her winning feminine demeanor was primarily designed to disarm men because of her anxiety about phallic competitiveness and assault.

In her early twenties she developed a toxic goiter which required surgery. Her reaction to this illness was the same as her reaction to her childhood illnesses, namely that she thought of it primarily in terms of the worry that *other* people felt about possible malignancy. She also thought of the difficulties of other patients in the hospital, which she tried to alleviate, rather than feeling as though she were a patient herself.

Later, while in treatment with me, her gynecologist discovered an ovarian cyst and observed it for several months until it disappeared. After he decided it was not serious the patient expressed her sorrow for having imposed worry about her on me.

TREATMENT

In treatment, the patient traced a change in her attitude toward her body to an event in therapy which I would not have expected to have had such an influence. She had been given phenobarbital during her childhood illnesses "to help her not to bother people." When she first came to see me she was taking sedatives at bedtime each night. I suggested that in the interest of her treatment it would be desirable if she could get along without sedatives, even if it meant not sleeping, and calling me if necessary. She was able to stop taking medication, substituting imaginary conversations, of hallucinatory vividness, with me. These were fairly realistic anticipations of her next therapeutic session, characterized by her telling me in her imagination about the anxiety (e.g., fear of helplessness and dependence) which otherwise would have kept her awake. She also counted the hours until the next session. She never called me at night, but a few times called for extra appointments when she could not sustain the comforting fantasy image of me from one session to the next. Thus she was able to use me for what she called "a sleeping pill." This we traced back to a similar use of her pediatrician in her childhood. When she was actually with him as a child there was always the danger that he would administer some painful treatment procedure, or that he would abandon her. But alone in her bed, when she used the idealized mental picture of him as a "sedative," he picked her up and held her on his lap and stroked her, and did not administer injections. We found that the mental image of the pediatrician as a comforter and sedative at bedtime was superior to his actual presence.

When she was actually with me there was always the danger that I might say something surprising or even "shocking." When she thought of me, I was silent, doing nothing unexpected, listening to her and not speaking at all, and she found this idealized fantasy of our relationship very comforting.

While in the office she was always careful to avoid making any demands of me. For example, she would carry her shoes to the waiting room before putting them on in order not to take any extra time at the end of the hour. Later, she managed to slip her shoes on in the consulting room, but she still went into the waiting room to tie them. She also tended to keep close watch on the time by looking at her wrist watch, not only to avoid being surprised by the end of the session, but also in order to be ready to leave immediately. In addition, she was always hesitant about saying anything she thought might upset me and when she managed to say something she expected to be upsetting to me she was very apologetic. Actually, she used considerable energy and ingenuity in protecting me from her anger, thinking I must have good reasons for saying and doing anything she did not like, such as changing or canceling an appointment.

The patient often spoke in a soft, almost inaudible manner. She had spoken softly since early childhood, and remembered doing so when her mother screamed at her in anger. Her inaudibility served different functions at different stages of her development, as it has also served different functions at different stages of her treatment. At the deepest level, audible speech is not necessary if one is communicating with a part of one's self, and it is fruitless if one is totally isolated. Her inaudible speech was certainly an unconscious demand that I pay special attention to her, and that I speak softly to her, rather than to scream at her as her mother did. More superficially, such speech had a defensive function. She said that if I did not hear her I would be prevented from making "shocking" intrusive interpretations, and that even if I were to make an interpretation when she had been speaking softly she could have some confidence that since I had not heard most of what she said, "the interpretation could not be painfully accurate."

At the same time I had another patient, a man, who spoke so softly that I could hardly hear him, and at one point I had my hearing tested to be certain that it was not deafness that had made it impossible for me to understand them. When the hearing test proved to be normal and I still could not hear her, I began to realize how helpless she was making me feel. Her associations to *my* feeling of helplessness led from efforts to control mother's angry screaming, to more threatening and anxiety-provoking memories. We found that as a child she had felt panic and helplessness while going under anaesthesia, hearing the doctors and nurses talking softly and being unable to understand them. She had felt they were plotting and planning to torture and kill her. I assumed that stimulating a feeling of helplessness in me was a way of controlling and distancing herself from her own feeling of being helpless and threatened. The consulting room had become the operating room of childhood, and she saw me as herself, a helpless child, while she became the frightening doctors and nurses. At first, when I mentioned how helpless her inaudible speech made me feel, she felt reprimanded, as her parents and others reprimanded and still reprimand her for it. This situation uncovered a worse feeling than being reprimanded: later in the hour she began to experience a return of the childhood feeling of panic and helplessness. It was no longer just a memory, but had become living reality in the present. I had first felt the helplessness, and interpretation had the effect that the patient began to feel it herself (Bettelheim, B., 1967; Borowitz, G., 1970).

Another defense against feeling threatened by me was that she had to know exactly what evidence led me to make an interpretation. I found myself making efforts to reconstruct the steps by which I had reached any interpretation. This became irksome and constricting to me, and I attempted to free myself from the necessity of doing so. I told the patient I did not want to feel obliged to make such reconstructions, but this response was ineffective, and her requests for me to justify my interpretations continued. Later, as we shall see, we found that this need stemmed from conflict about a particular kind of closeness, that includes understanding and being understood empathically, with longing for this understanding combined with fear of it. Only after we found this meaning did she lose her need for me to document interpretations.

After two years of treatment she became aware of a fear that she might become exceedingly "demanding." In her imagination, when she was using the mental picture of our sessions as a "sedative," this problem was not prominent. It is not so much that she was free to imagine making demands on me or saying things which would be putting me under a strain, as that when alone she imagined me as an idealized internal object, a possession or a part of herself. At such times she was not aware of needing anything from a separate person. As she became aware of this, her dawning awareness of her needs enabled us to understand some of her anxiety. The demands of men that she had been unable to tolerate certainly can be considered, at least in part, a projection of demands of her own of which she was unaware. Her excessive independence, her phallic competitiveness, and her fear of the sexual needs of men, turned out to be based on fear of the aggressive components of her own infantile needs for nurture, which had been both repressed and projected.

Changes in Attitude Toward Sex

I want to relate this patient's experience to the observations of Masters and Johnson (1970). This patient would not have consulted Masters and Johnson, because she was not initially aware of any sexual problem. I notice that Masters and Johnson (1970) provide therapeutic sexual partner surrogates for men and not for women. This is because they have observed that object relatedness tends to be associated with sexual satisfaction in women more than in men. This was not true with this patient when she first came, but became true during treatment. With the change she also came to have sexual problems, as we shall see.

The change came about as follows: There were repeated abreactions of intense anxiety associated with the feeling that her parents had wanted her to die when they left her in the hospital during her childhood illnesses, and that she was rescued by the pediatrician then, and was being rescued by me now. At night in bed she imagined telling me about this, and usually she managed to stave off the anxiety until she got into the office. After about a year, however, she began to be afraid of my interpretations, and it was *at this time* that she regained memories of the pediatrician as someone who gave her painful treatments, or went away, rather than being always present as a rescuer. She began to regard both me and the pediatrician with ambivalence rather than as idealized figures. She also remembered some positive feelings toward her parents, regarding them ambivalently also, rather than only as persecutors wanting her death to free them from burdens.

At this time the patient established a new relationship with a man. This man was more affectionate and more interested in her sexually than were any previous ones. He took up more of her time than did any others, but still this relationship was characterized by definite limits, both of his concern for her as she perceived it, and of the degree of his involvement with her.

This was illustrated by the patient's reaction to my disturbance when my wife was ill, soon after the patient began the new relationship. She felt that her lover could not care enough for a woman to become as distressed about her illness as I was about my wife's. She also felt, however, that she could not tolerate having her life so dominated as she thought it would necessarily be in a relationship with a man who could and would be so concerned about her. Despite these limits, this relationship was vastly different from any previous one. The differences were in the areas of increased mutual involvement, and in *something new for the patient, that she called a "sexual problem."* She had "difficulty in becoming sexually aroused." Orgasm used to be an invariable accompaniment of every intercourse. Now the patient reached, *as an achievement,* a state that shared elements with what Masters and Johnson (1970) call "situational orgasmic dysfunction." Looked at purely phenomenologically, that is from the outside only, one could regard this change as the development of a relative frigidity, compared with her previous state. But the patient felt that she had made great progress. It was characterized by a new need, to be "cuddled" and held in order to become sexually stimulated and satisfied. There was also a new link between her sexual response and the way in which she and her lover were getting along in the hours and days before intercourse. This was not always positive. For instance, she sometimes responded sexually with more ease following a painful experience, or an argument with a reconciliation, than after a peaceful friendly evening. In the past with previous partners there had been no apparent relationship between her sexual response and the way in which she was getting along with the man, and now there was.

Another difference was what the patient called a much deeper and more meaningful subjective experience of the total love-making. In order to enjoy sex, she now needed her partner to want her to enjoy it, and to enjoy it himself, and she began to include various pregenital foreplay activities that earlier were meaningless, offensive, or even frightening to her. For example, she let her lover bite her shoulder during intercourse, first fearing, then sharing, his passion. *Orgasm was no longer achieved automatically, regularly, and reliably, but when achieved it was a more deeply meaningful experience than it had been previously. Along with this, her sexual enjoyment became vulnerable to disturbances of the object relationship,* but had become deeper and more satisfying when the relationship was intact.

This patient made it clear that orgasm is not simply a response to stimulation of the clitoris or the vagina, but is a reaction of the total personality, the total self, in a complex, interpersonal environment (G.A.P., 1966, Leavy, 1966).

Changes in Attitude Toward Motherhood

The patient has become interested in the techniques of mothering as she observes them in her friends who have infants and children, and she is particularly interested in the provision of the kind of setting for a child which facilitates natural development rather than one which forces a child to be prematurely independent, or alternatively ill. She says that "it is important for a mother not to be competing with anyone for anything." Changes are illustrated by a "game" which she recently thought of, and which she considers to be particularly intimate, a game which utilizes soft speech. In the game two persons, either two adults, an adult and a child, or especially a mother and a baby, whisper to each other wordlessly. She had an associated fantasy that this "would not be an appropriate game if an infant were to be born already capable of adult speech, crawling and walking, and feeding himself." Under those circumstances, she said (typically viewing the matter from the standpoint of a mother rather than that of a baby), a mother would not identify with her infant. The game, in other words, is one that belongs to the preverbal state in which the baby is as yet undifferentiated psychically from the mother, and the mother is identified with the baby. I believe that this "game" illustrates a new integration of primitive ego functions, and a new capacity for identification. It was after this patient became able to depend upon certain aspects of the therapeutic relationship that she began to need and to accept the adaptive efforts of partners in the sexual situation. Along with this came a capacity to identify with infants.

One of the patient's recent experiences illustrates this new capacity for identification. She saw a mother send a two-year-old child out to play. The child was afraid to go, and the patient empathized with his fear. The mother, annoyed by his anxiety, insisted that the child go out because "she wanted to get him out of her hair." When the little boy went out, compliantly, "trying to be independent," the patient commented: "It was all I could do to keep myself from going over and picking him up, because I could not stand seeing him so afraid." *She described this from the standpoint of the child, distressed and anxious, rather than from the standpoint of the mother.*

At the same time that she started to identify with children she began to enjoy, rather than to fear, being understood by me, as she called it, "like mind-reading." This consisted essentially of searching for wider application within herself for my interpretations, rather than needing me to provide intellectual explanations for them. For example, rather than demanding that I justify every interpretation, she could allow herself not to know exactly how I had reached a conclusion: She then felt that I had understood her empathically, "like mind-reading," because she could remember experiences that were relevant to the interpretation. Previously her attention had been so consumed by the need to understand the basis of any interpretation that she had been unable to consider its relevance.

Defenses against her own "demandingness" and anxiety about being assaulted gave way to some degree to a capacity for identification. Certainly it seems sensible to classify this capacity as a quality fundamental to feminine development, since maternal care in early infancy is based upon the mother's empathic "interpretation" of the infant's nonverbal (preverbal) behavior. This, in turn, depends upon the mother's integration of her own infantile memories into her adult personality. By her appropriate response, based on empathy, the mother enables the infant's behavior to become a modality of communication, a signal. This includes both interpersonal and intrapsychic communication. This means that communication is fundamental to the integration of the ego and to continuity of development that enables the child, when grown up, to facilitate the maturation of the next generation.

The term "regression in the service of the ego" has been used to describe this expansion or extension of the integrative capacity of the ego to include, in the personality of the adult, mechanisms and processes characteristic of childhood and infancy. The ego retains adult structure, while also including a capacity for the freedom of undifferentiation. This ego expansion, when it occurs in the therapeutic setting, includes dependence on the therapist and the therapy as representatives of the supportive environment of infancy, and ultimately (in favorable cases) introjection of significant aspects of the therapeutic experience. This is not the same as being rescued, as this patient felt rescued by me at the beginning of her treatment. *Being rescued is similar to being persecuted in that they both involve using the therapist as an unassimilated part-object. Dependability of the therapeutic setting is introjected and is utilized by the patient for the integration and assimilation of the patient's vulnerable infantile self, previously defended against by splitting-off, projection, denial, or repression.* In this way the therapeutic introject becomes an extension of the ego of the patient (Giovacchini, 1965).

As a result of this process, the patient's ability to accept care for herself, including her infantile self, developed. At the same time she became able, *without resentment,* to care for others, including actual infants and the infantile elements in adults.

Along with these changes there came about in this case a change in the concept of the role of women generally. The Women's Liberation Movement had been important to her earlier, and she was preoccupied with the obstacles that women face in their business careers. She did not change so much in her attitudes toward the rights of women as she decathected this particular area as she became more interested in infant care and potential motherhood.

In the past the patient had refused to accept any financial help. Now, she planned on marriage and looked forward to having a child. She said that although she would easily be able to support herself and a child by her own earnings, she wanted her husband to provide completely for her and for the child she hoped to have.

I think it is clear from this material that the patient was able to experience anxieties and needs of an infantile nature in the transference relationship, and that when she was able to accept these she became ready to accept mutually dependent relationships with men on the outside which previously had been unacceptable to her. At the same time she changed in her attitude toward mothering, although up to the time this paper was written this new attitude had not yet been put to the test of actual motherhood.

SUMMARY

A "liberated" woman achieved orgasm regularly with every intercourse regardless of the quality of the relationship with her sexual partners. She had no desire for children and "no understanding of them." During treatment, her attitudes toward sex and motherhood changed radically. She developed a need for a continuing, reassuring relationship with her sexual partner as a necessary condition for orgasm, and at the same time developed the capacity to identify with infants and a wish for motherhood.

In health a mother has the flexibility to relinquish other interests and to permit herself to be cared for so she can devote herself 100% to the care of herself, and of the neonate who is so much a part of herself. It is pathological when a mother cannot accept being cared for and relinquish other interests to devote herself to infant care. This pathology contributes to the protest that women are asked to give up their own lives to care for infants. In health a woman also has the flexibility to relinquish preoccupation with the infant as the infant matures. It is pathological if a woman cannot relinquish this preoccupation as her child matures. This pathology contributes to the specter of the empty life of mothers of grown children (Komisar, 1970).

We need to reevaluate the relation between orgastic capacity and maturity in women. In order to devote herself to the care of her infant, a mother must be free from external pressures. This requires someone else to care for her, and requires also that she be able to accept such care.

A sexual relationship in which a woman requires a man to make special adaptations to her needs sets a pattern for him to make provision later, when she is a mother needing to be cared for, so she can adapt to the needs of her infant.

The principle thesis of this chapter can be clarified by speculation about possible application to evolution. A woman's need for special adaptation as a necessary condition for sexual gratification contributes to her selection of a mate who will care for her, and therefore helps to assure the survival of her offspring.

References

Bettelheim, B., *The Empty Fortress*. New York: The Free Press, 1967.

Borowitz, G., "The Therapeutic Utilization of Emotions and Attitudes Evoked in the Caretakers of Disturbed Childen," *British Journ. of Med. Pscyhol.*, 43:129-139 (1970).

Freud, S. (1914), "On Narcissism, An Introduction," *Standard Edition*, Vol. 14. London: Hogarth Press, 1957.

Freud, S. (1923), "The Ego and the Id," *Standard Edition*, Vol. 19. London: Hogarth Press, 1961.

Freud, S. (1937), "Analysis Terminable and Interminable," *Standard Edition*, Vol. 23. London: Hogarth Press, 1964.

Giovacchini, P., "Transference, Incorporation and Synthesis," *Internat. Journ. of Psychoanal.*, 46:287-296 (1965).

Group for the Advancement of Psychiatry, *Sex and the College Student*, 1966.

Komisar, L. "The New Feminism," *The Saturday Review*, 27-38 (1970).

Leavy, S. A., "Psychoanalysis and Moral Change," *Psychiatric Opinion*, 33-38 (1966).

Little, M., "On Basic Unity," *Internat. Journ. of Pscyhoanal.*, 41:377-384 (1960).

Masters W. H., and Johnson, V. E., *Human Sexual Inadequacy*, Boston: Little, Brown and Co., 1970.

Riviere, J. Review of Freud's *New Introductory Lectures on Psychoanalysis*, *Internat. Journ. of Psychoanal.*, 15:323-339 (1934).

Winnicott, D. W., "Primary Maternal Preoccupation," *Collected Papers*, 300-305 *New York Basic Books, 1957.*

Winnicott, D. W., (1972) "The Split-Off Male and Female Elements in Men and Women—Theoretical Inferences," *Psychoanalytic Forum*, 4:360-398 J. A. Lindon, ed., New York: International Universities Press.

Part 4

SPECIFIC CLINICAL SITUATIONS

Introduction

Peter L. Giovacchini, M.D.

The previous sections dealt with broad issues such as the psychoanalytic process which gradually narrowed down to the discussion of specific character attributes such as the significance of sexual feelings. In the following chapters there is further narrowing as specific clinical issues are focused upon.

Just by perusing the titles of these chapters, one can get an idea of the varied clinical situations that are to be discussed. The patients are unusual insofar as these types of patients are not usually considered in a psychoanalytic context and particularly in terms of psychoanalysis as a treatment modality.

For example, L. Bryce Boyer refers to treatment issues with schizophrenic and delusional patients. Perhaps, as this book and the collection of chapters in the first volume of this series illustrate, this is no longer unusual.

Daniel Offer, however, gives us a fairly detailed analysis of a woman suffering from what can be considered psychosomatic symptoms. Of course, psychosomatic conditions have received considerable attention from psychoanalysts. Offer differs from most others in one important respect. He does not deal with the symptom directly, either technically as a treatment issue, or theoretically. He analyzes the patient and does not give any special weight to the symptom. It is considered from an intrapsychic viewpoint as are other aspects of the patient's material.

Bertram Cohler presents a very disturbed young lady whose somatic symptoms threaten her life. She suffers from anorexia nervosa and was, at times, on the brink of starving herself to death. The maintenance of the psychoanalytic viewpoint during such a trying and dangerous situation is exciting to observe and, indeed, such an orientation seemed to be truly life-saving. As one becomes more involved with very disturbed patients, one's respect for the psychoanalytic method continues to grow. The preservation of the analytic setting seems vital.

Stanley Conrad and Vamik Volkan contribute further clinical material focussing upon specific factors found in the characters of patients who act out by being impostors (Conrad) and upon the psychic mechanisms and reactions of a patient whose ego used many primitive adaptations, such as splitting (Volkan).

Such focused clinical orientations implicitly answer many questions by providing us with empirical data. They also demonstrate how one can learn from the patient and enrich our conceptual understanding which, in turn, helps us treat him. Thus, our therapeutic armamentarium broadens. One begins with what has been considered an untreatable case or a dangerous situation. The patient, in turn, reveals certain elements of his character to the analyst who may react by being confused and even frightened. In time, however, the analyst learns and converts what had been previously inchoate and overwhelming anxiety into insights about how the patient's mind works. The specific patients discussed here show us how dedicated analysts are willing to wait for the patient to teach them, to let the patient reveal himself in an unhurried and unpressured fashion, that is, to let the patient maintain the maximum autonomy possible.

Chapter XVI

Treatment of Characterological and Schizophrenic Disorders

L. Bryce Boyer, M.D.

In this chapter a case fragment will serve to delineate a technique used in the treatment of certain characterological and schizophrenic disorders. It has evolved as a result of almost twenty years' use of psychoanalysis within the framework of the structural theory in the treatment of such conditions, without essentially modifying the procedures customarily employed with neurotics. I have avoided role-playing and consistently resisted patients' attempts to make me change my analytic stance. I have interpreted the psychotic and neurotic transference in their positive and negative aspects without using reassurance or formal educative techniques, and without attempting to foster the so-called positive transference.

The case study that is abstracted here was chosen for two reasons. First, its course was smooth and the technique used demonstrates the most recent of a series of modifications. In a sense, this study is misleading because the progress of the patient was unusually even and the apparently successful result transpired unusually quickly, that is, after just less than three years of psychoanalysis. No cure can be claimed yet because the analysis was terminated just three years ago. Second, the patient presented an uncommon symptom complex, a variant of the one described by Greenacre (1947) under the rubric: vision, headache, and the halo, which served the same defensive and adaptive purposes, and for which analysis was crucial to the therapeutic outcome.

This chapter will be divided into two sections: an abstract of the case history, in which I shall interpolate the rationale for the various technical procedures used, and a discussion.

CASE REPORT

The principal, although not initial complaint of an attractive, highly intelligent, twenty-five-year-old-woman was terrifying black sensations in her head, which had begun during puberty. She had kept the symptom secret, fearing that if it were discovered she would be hospitalized as mad. The sensations did not make her dizzy, but she always lay down while experiencing them, since she was apprehensive that she might become light-headed, or that she might fall down, scream, babble, lose excretory control, and reach a state of helplessness that would require permanent care as if she were an infant. Although she did not mention them during the first months of her analysis, she also had a number of phobias, some of which will be noted below.

General Information

This woman had gone through life smitten with guilt for infractions of an exceedingly high internal moral code and aspiring to be angelic in thought and deed. She had placed various people on pedestals, inevitably choosing those who disappointed her by being morally less than perfect; from her earliest memory, she had felt that she was unwanted and unloved, and she despised her parents, ostensibly because they argued, drank, and lacked respect for one another.

During her high school years, she had thought of herself as fat and ugly and thus had avoided opportunities for dates. She left her parents' home for the first time at the age of 19 to attend a university. While there, she could not concentrate on her studies. During her first term she became progressively withdrawn; she made no friends and felt that the world was unreal. She attended a few classes but became inexplicably frightened and soon found herself spending her days in women's rest rooms. There, she would lie on the sofa in a thoughtless, trancelike state until other girls entered; then she would sit on a toilet seat cover until she was alone again. She was afraid that if she were seen lying on a sofa, she would be reported and hospitalized as insane.

This woman failed a term and was placed on probation. During the next semester, a man who strongly resembled her father physically asked her out for an automobile ride. She passively submitted to a kiss but was frightened when he tried to be more intimate. He became angry and excited and masturbated in front of her. She experienced the black sensation in her head and felt guilty because she had not permitted intercourse. She readily accepted a second date on which she refused intercourse but performed fellatio, being careful to remove her mouth before ejaculation. She experienced disgust and gagged. Soon thereafter she permitted intercourse and became pregnant. The gestation was greeted ambivalently. Her mother had expected her to become a schoolteacher, a career toward which she had sharply mixed feelings. Now she had an excuse to marry and avoid further pursuit of that profession. At the same time, she feared her mother's wrath and abandonment. Once married, she studied subjects she enjoyed and was able to complete her college work with excellent grades, despite many hardships.

She found all sexual contact repugnant. Although before marriage she found fellatio less disgusting than intercourse, afterward she could not tolerate oral-genital activities and usually refused intercourse. She was grossly but unwittingly exhibitionistic and seductive; however, when her husband sought sexual relations, she taunted him until he either raped or slapped her. Usually he responded to her provocation by masturbating before her; observing his manipulations produced the horrifying blackness in her head. She gradually slept less with her husband; although she was tall and their bathtub was short, she chose to sleep in the tub, holding her arms about her while curled up in a near-fetal position. When she held herself so, she entered a trancelike, thoughtless state and drifted to sleep.

Later it was learned that her provocation of a fight before sexual relations imitated what she either assumed or observed in the relationship between her parents when she was four to 13 years of age. During that period, her father often came home late at night, intoxicated. Her mother responded by instigating a fight, which the patient believed was followed by sexual relations during which her mother complained that she was disgusted.

When the patient's son was born, she transiently believed his birth was the result of parthenogenesis. Although the marriage pattern did not change, she felt that she could not divorce "for religious reasons." Two years later, three events coincided. Her father died after a long illness, and she experienced no feeling about it. During the course of her analysis, she maintained that, as far as she was concerned, he had died years before; she consistently denied grieving when he actually died. A daughter was born and the patient once again briefly believed that the birth was parthenogenetic. Soon, thereafter, their marital life became so miserable that her husband left home and went to another state to continue his education. Although she was relieved, she soon became depressed and, in spite of the fact that she was a devoted mother, felt that she was neglecting her children. At about that time she started having nightmares in which she was beaten or raped by her husband, a Negro, or some middle-aged white man; these nightmares were followed by the black sensations. Progressively she came into conflict with her mother-in-law, out of fear that the mother-surrogate would take her children away from her. Afraid that she might go insane and harm her children psychologically, she sought treatment. Although her mother-in-law was paying for the analysis, she thought it was a gift to her children. The patient believed she was schizophrenic and had heard, that during treatment for that disorder, patients sometimes regressed. She reasoned that her mother-in-law thought she would become hopelessly insane during her treatment and thus would be able to take the children away from her.

Course of Treatment

The patient was referred for analysis by a colleague who had diagnosed her to be schizophrenic. She had seen him for marital counseling, complaining that her husband was brutal and preferred masturbation to intercourse. When that analyst suggested that she might have provoked some of her husband's behavior, she responded with righteous indignation because she needed to believe that she had been the innocent victim of his psychopathology. Yet, when she left that therapist's care in an apparent rage, she requested analysis by me, since she had heard from a former patient that I treated schizophrenics and that I was "tough." I inferred from this information that she was afraid she was insane, and might act unwisely or impulsively and therefore craved a strong superego and ego-surrogate who would care enough for her to insist that she behave.

In the first interview, she spoke under pressure; her sentences were so disconnected that I understood much of what she meant only because of my knowledge of the products of primary-process thinking. She complained that she had been wronged by her husband and former therapist. Before I discuss my response, I want to present some of my ideas about what must be accomplished in the initial stages of dealing with such patients and the techniques I have developed to accomplish this.

In earlier papers, I have suggested that the primary task in treatment is to restore and/or develop within the patient a reasonable ego and superego, and that this can be accomplished by modifying or replacing cold, unloving, and archaic introjects (Boyer, 1961, 1965, 1966a, 1966b; Boyer and Giovacchini, 1967). I have expressed the opinion that therapy must be directed toward the growth of intrapsychic and interpersonal communication techniques. I have come to believe that the most important initial step is to present to the analysand a calm, patient, objective, implicitly optimistic attitude with which to identify; to present a person who does not respond with anxiety to reactions of panic or attempts at manipulation, but who treats each production of the patient—verbal or otherwise—as though it is important, and who does not believe that the immediate satisfaction of urges is necessary. Although I feel that the most important contribution psychoanalytic treatment can make in the treatment of these conditions is to interpret the structuralizing of the ego, I do not think that interpretation can be optimally effective until the cathexis of maladaptive introjects has lessened and healthier ones have begun to replace them.

Loewenstein (1956) has differentiated three functions of speech: the cognitive, the expressive, and the appeal functions. In the psychotic, the last two predominate; it is the task of the analyst to respond to the appeal function only by interpretation, and to transform it to the expressive function by demonstrating to the patient that he expresses something about himself when he speaks of other persons or things. The analyst attempts to exclude both the expressive and appeal functions from his own speech. I believe that the analyst should begin this effort immediately; by using the cognitive mode, which appeals to the patient's ego rather than his id, the analyst will immediately reduce the tenuousness of contact between himself and the analysand. Technically, therefore, I make contact through interpretation and direct my interpretive efforts to the surface, stressing the defensive nature of the patient's productions. Let us now return to the case history.

Since I believed that the patient craved control and feared herself to be insane, I appealed to her rationality by responding in the cognitive mode.[1] Having understood her complaint about being wronged by her husband and previous analyst to mean that she was afraid she had provoked their behavior, I told her that it seemed to me she was worried that she had a problem related to provocativeness for which she thought she should feel guilty. She was indignant at this and threatened not to return. I ignored this irrationality and again appealed to her ego, saying that we could begin regular interviews the next day.

In the second interview, she was obviously calmer and reassured. She said she should talk about her sexual problem (which had not been mentioned before), but she could not do so, and therefore she decided to tell me about her past. During the next five interviews, she recounted many dreams and events from her early childhood and complained bitterly that she had never been loved. Her sentences were fragmented and frequently contained a series of loosely related subjects. She had a tendency to make clang associations. The material was laden with massive denials and contradictions. When I gently confronted her with obvious contradictions, she acknowledged them briefly and then proceeded as if I had not intervened. She made numerous highly cathected black-and-white oversimplifications. Her dreams all dealt with the theme of falling or flying, and her associations were regularly of being abandoned. At the same time she said that she had hated her parents. She complained that she had never been held, even as an infant, and simultaneously said that she could never tolerate being touched by either parent. She claimed that her mother and father had always drunk immoderately, but also said that her father had been a successful businessman (except for a short time) and that her mother was puritanical. She asserted that her parents had always argued loudly but remembered with scorn that her mother enjoyed doing things for her father. She said that she had been afraid that one parent would murder the other; although her parents did not have physical fights, she had hoped for the

---

[1]Concerning her treatment, I said that I would expect her to make a sincere effort to tell me whatever came to her mind and to keep me informed about her emotional and physical experiences during the interviews. I said that I did not send statements but that I expected to be paid accurately during a specific interview of the month. I told her that she would be charged for any cancellations unless her time were filled by another patient, and that I was generally absent several times a year for short periods and once for an extended period. I have found with such patients that specific conditions offer needed ego and superego support.

death of one or the other to spare her the terror she felt in hearing their arguments. She maintained that her parents had no love for each other or for any of their six children. She was the second child and had a brother two years older; her sister was one year younger, and she had brothers three, five, and seven years her junior. She complained that her sister and youngest brother had been parental favorites. Early memories also included scenes in which her older brother was beaten by the father for disobedience and one in which her mother whipped her when she was about five years old because of exhibitionistic and voyeuristic play with her older brother.

In the sixth interview, she said that she would never lie on the couch, although the subject had not been brought up before. Since she had presented so much material negatively, I inferred that she meant she now felt sufficiently secure to be able to lie on the couch. During her earlier interviews, I had generally been passive. Sometimes when she became very tense and was silent for some minutes, I suggested that she might be feeling embarrassment because of her awareness that some of her denials and gross contradictions were logically inconsistent. On three occasions, after I had made some simple, clear remarks, she asked me to repeat what she had said. I understood this to mean in part that she was testing to see whether I would humiliate her by responding as though she were truly incompetent; I said that she seemed to feel the need to view me as someone who did not believe she could remember and make use of her memory (Hoedemaker, 1967). Each time she was obviously relieved, indicating that she knew very well what I had said, and temporarily stopped speaking in a confused manner.

In the seventh interview, she lay on the couch. She blushed, alternately pressed her thighs tightly together and spread her legs slightly, and manipulated the buttons and zippers on her modest dress. She was frightened and complained for the first time of the black sensations in her head. It was obvious that she was having fantasies—conscious or unconscious—of sexual attack; it seemed probable that the black sensations were associated with fantasies of seeing an erection. However, I chose to ignore the phallic or genital fantasies, and I merely asked her to elaborate her experience of the black sensations so that I could obtain some factual historical data about them.

I have eventually come to the conclusion that to deal with genital sexual material in the early psychoanalysis of schizophrenic patients is contraindicated. As with Rosenfeld (1966), I do not then interpret apparently oedipal material on a libidinal level. Such a procedure is often interpreted by the patient as a seductive invitation from the analyst, and it may cause acute psychotic excitement. The patient's anxiety increases regularly, and it frequently results in defensive regressive maneuvers if he believes he has forced the therapist out of his analytic role. If I refer to such material I do so from the standpoint of its aggressive and manipulative aspects; or I interpret upward, using a technique I learned from Loewenstein in a seminar he conducted for candidates of the San Francisco Psychoanalytic Institute some 20 years ago. Thus, for example, if a patient relates that he has open fantasies of intercourse with his mother, I respond that he must love her very much. I believe that the patient who suffers from a severe characterological or schizophrenic disorder has massive fears of the vicissitudes of his aggressive impulses, and that treatment will proceed most smoothly if his attention is directed gently but consistently toward the analysis of the protective maneuvers he employs to defend against his fear that his hostility will result in the analyst's death or his own.

Thus, after the patient lay down and manifested fears of sexual involvement with the analyst as a parent-surrogate, I did not comment on it. When she remained silent for long periods and challenged me to prove that my silence did not mean I hated her, my remarks focused on the projective aspects of her own hostility as manifested by her self-devaluation.

After the first few weeks, she stopped speaking about her past. Long periods of shivering silence were broken by highly emotional accounts of her present interpersonal difficulties, all of which she attributed to the ill will of those around her. She assumed that their alleged hostile treatment was due to her physical ugliness. She admitted no positive feelings toward anyone but her children, and she was convinced that they preferred their paternal grandmother to her. At the same time, anticipating a possible divorce in the future, she quickly learned the necessary skills and found a fine job as a private secretary; it appeared to the analyst that in her office she was treated with deference and trust, but she felt she was slighted and scorned. It was impossible to obtain coherent information from her about any current event, because of a combination of causes. She was apparently unaware of her provocativeness; she interpreted others' gestures and expressions to mean that they held adverse opinions about her; and she was terrified to report fantasies directly. Of course, she was also convinced that the analyst read her mind and that his silence indicated disgust with her; yet she consciously withheld information. It became apparent that she generally believed she was reporting events accurately but that her perceptions of external events were grossly distorted because she projected unconscious sadomasochistic, voyeuristic, and exhibitionistic wishes onto others. Before discussing the technical procedure I used at this time, I shall synopsize its rationale.

By this time, although she was still frightened, the patient had begun to introject to some degree the analyst's attitude of calm and patient optimism and to feel that she might be worth saving. Whereas previously the patient had spoken only despairingly of her future, now she uttered occasional words of hope. Earlier she had felt panicked by frustration either within or outside the consultation room, but now she asked herself the analyst's question: "What do you fear might happen if you do not get immediately what you want?'' Thus, she was able to avoid a temper tantrum or withdrawal into a state of apparently thoughtless inactivity. Yet, she still wanted the analyst to do all of her thinking for her, and it was obvious she ascribed omniscience and omnipotence to him. It seemed that the major problem in her analysis was the need to form a therapeutic alliance. Such an alliance requires the patient to develop some distance from his problems and emotions so that he can both think about and experience them. This woman was engaged in three principal kinds of behavior which she did not understand. She massively projected parts of her own identity into others; she grossly misperceived external as well as intrapsychic events; and she provoked hostility on the part of others, which she then used to rationalize her own anger. It was obvious that she was reenacting her childhood behavior, both living-out and acting-out. I use the words *living-out* to mean repeating earlier behavior that is not connected directly with the analytic situation and *acting-out* to mean behavior that attempts to solve problems by action transference. Rosenfeld (1966b) has recently discussed the relationship between acting-out and the aggressive drive.

As stated above, I concluded that in dealing with such patients, interpretations should be directed toward aggressive drive derivatives during the early stages of treatment, and that oedipal libidinal interpretations are generally useless, if not actually damaging, to treatment. I have also learned that confronting the patient gently and consistently with his inconsistencies and misperceptions arouses his curiosity about the meaning of his behavior and thinking. On reviewing the case histories of my recent patients, I find that I have been confronting them more and more with their misperceptions, inconsistencies, and distortions of events in the consultation room and less and less with external events (Boyer, 1967a). Where the events are known to the analyst, who can then remind the patient of what actually transpired, it is more difficult for the analysand to maintain the validity of his altered presentations. Simultaneously, the patient is usually eager to use the psychoanalyst as an ego and superego model. However, in this case, a special situation made it seem preferable to direct the analysis toward the patient's understanding of her defenses against aggressive impulses, without focusing on her hostility toward the analyst.

From the outset, there had been a split transference of grand proportions. The patient had almost no awareness of hostility toward me; the principal focus of her anger was her mother-in-law, so clearly a substitute for her mother. Lesser and more diffuse aggression was directed at other relatives and colleagues at work. As stated earlier, I generally believe that interpretations are most effective when they are directed toward the surface, that is, toward what is closest to the patient's consciousness; this view is the exact opposite of that held by many members of the Kleinian school (Avenburg, 1962; Segal

1967). Ordinarily in treating such cases, I focus from the beginning on the defensive aspects of aggressive drive behavior (which manifest themselves in the transference situation) by directing attention primarily to what transpires in the consultation room. In the present case, as well, I did that. However, my remarks were met with little more than ridicule, while the patient focused on the hostility of her mother-in-law. The bulk of her hostility, as I understand the situation, was projected from the patient, although some was due to her provocative behavior toward that unusually kind woman. I decided to follow her lead and exploit the split transference.

To have a therapeutic alliance, the patient must develop curiosity about himself, but this woman seemed to have very little. She maintained that she had been mistreated by others in part because of their innate hostility, their greed, and their desire to use her, and in part because of her imagined physical ugliness. I decided to focus our attention simultaneously in two directions. I mentioned her slips of the tongue, gestures, habit of leaving the door ajar, periodic muscular tensions, and manipulations of her clothes. Initially she was furious that I called attention to such apparent trivia, but then she became interested in the possible meanings of such phenomena and was pleased with herself when she could analyze them. Yet she did not extrapolate from her experience inside the consultation room to events outside. Thus, I began to reconstruct aloud what I guessed might actually have occurred and then been misperceived by her in encounters with relatives, colleagues at work, and especially her mother-in-law. At first she was outraged and panicked when I suggested that these events had taken place in a different way than the one she had reported. Eventually, however, she checked my guesses and was amazed to find that they were generally accurate. At the same time, she was relieved to discover that I could make errors. Thus, she began to view me as fallible and to realize that her active cooperation was required in order to develop self-understanding. I also used another technical maneuver that I have found to be of value.

One task in treating such cases is to help the patient improve his intrapsychic and interpersonal communication. In any psychoanalysis, improving intrapsychic communication is implicit. However, it often happens with these patients that better understanding of interpersonal messages lags. When a patient presents data in a manner that is heavily influenced by the primary process, I generally understand a large part of his message. Nevertheless, even when I think I comprehend everything he has told me, I tell him that, although I think I understand what he has said, I want him to tell me more about it in different words. Thus, the patient is both reassured that I have gleaned some of his meaning and yet frightened by my implication that his message is obscure. He will then present his material in a somewhat more logical manner. After some time, he will begin to test his new manner of communication with people outside the office and will be pleased to observe that he is better understood and has fewer interpersonal difficulties.

Returning to the present case, during the course of a few months, I reconstructed the past events in this patient's life from her actions in the consultation room as well as from her current interactions with others. Then she began to consider the possiblity that her past perceptions had also been awry and began to admit that she might not have been treated as badly as she had remembered. Subsequently her provocative livings-out and actings-out diminished and a solid working alliance was established. From the end of the first year, she actively conducted her own treatment.

The following example shows how she corrected an ongoing interaction. As was noted earlier, she had been convinced that her mother-in-law was trying to take her children away from her and that they preferred their paternal grandmother to her. When I guessed that she had been unwittingly provocative and then had misinterpreted the mother-in-law's contributions to their strife, she gradually validated my notions positively. As she did so, she remembered how, as a child of seven or eight, she had secretly played with her youngest brother, trying to nurse him on her body and investigating his genitals. With her typical use of denial reversal, she recalled that she had believed one of her brothers was her own child and that her mother had stolen him. After recalling these memories, she gradually changed her attitude toward her mother-in-law; they became friendly and cooperative. Simultaneously her fear that her children preferred their grandmother disappeared. As she renounced her earlier attitude toward the older woman, she repressed again the memories of her activities with her youngest brother. As the hostile components of her relationship with her mother-in-law were analyzed, she was gradually able to focus on some of the hateful aspects of her behavior toward me and the split transference disappeared (both positive and negative aspects had been centered on me).

Let us turn to the problem of the black sensations in her head. When she first lay down on the couch, she behaved like a frightened girl who expected to be attacked sexually. Although the temperature of the consultation room remained fairly constant, she often became cold all of a sudden and complained bitterly that the analyst was secretly manipulating the heater and the air conditioner in such a way that she experienced physical sensations. There was a blanket on the couch but she wouldn't touch it. I always worked in my shirt sleeves. She was incredulous that I was not uncomfortable when she thought the room was insufferably cold. When she entered the office, she only looked at my face but it became obvious that, while she knew in detail the contents of the room that she could see while lying down, she was also consciously aware of items in what she termed my "half of the office." Her dreams indicated that she had unconsciously observed the details of my dress and all of the office furnishings. On various occasions, when she suddenly felt cold, she also experienced the black sensations. Interpretations indicating that she had romantic thoughts about the analyst were dismissed with indignation. Then the black sensations and experiences of sudden temperature stopped. Because her symptoms ended without having been understood, I assumed that she was engaging in some unreported acting-out. So I asked whether she was withholding information about her behavior outside the office, and she reported that she was having an affair but she couldn't bring herself to say much about it. She vigorously denied that she was attempting to protect herself from disturbing thoughts about the analyst, but she terminated the affair and had no further social engagements with men. Then she became consciously aware of the contents of my half of the office. For some months there was no recurrence of the black sensations or of perceived temperature changes. During this period she rarely mentioned her husband except to complain when he was tardy in sending money for child support. After she renounced her affair, she said she had decided on divorce but then she didn't say any more about relations with her husband or whether she was doing anything about a legal separation or divorce. Just before the black sensations stopped, she described them visually, saying that they were "like a ball of collected black strings, with the ends sticking out everywhere." (Later on she said that each of the strings was the surface manifestation of a fantasy that had to be unraveled.) From this time forward, she made the black sensations and their visualization a conscious focus of her analysis, attempting to relate most major associations to them.

During the first half of the second year of analysis, the patient developed a routine before going to sleep. She would lie on her side, knees drawn up, and hug herself. Then she would rock herself, while visualizing that she was being held and rocked in the analyst's arms, like a baby. She felt blissful at such times and denied awareness of any sexual sensations or thoughts. She was reliving the trancelike state that she had formerly experienced without conscious thought or feeling in the bathtub during her marriage; now however, she experienced satisfying thought content and intense physical sensations of warmth and comfort in the upper half of her body. Gradually she began to have fantasies of nursing on the analyst's penis, and she savored the sensations of fullness in her mouth and the milk she drank from his penis. With no suggestion from the analyst, she consciously equated the penis with her mother's breast. She said that she should have been jealous of her younger brothers and sister, but she couldn't recall them as nursing babies nor could she remember having seen her mother's breasts except when she was much older and they were flat and sagging. The patient said she thought she should also be experiencing some sexual feelings while visualizing herself sucking on the analyst's penis, but she said that she did not and she steadfastly denied having any sexual desires for her father, mother, or analyst. She was happy and contented; her earlier feelings of having been discriminated against at work and elsewhere, although conscious at times, were superficially cathected. She often withheld information; although she recognized that her behavior was illogical, she said she intended to prolong the analysis as long as she could because she was happy for the first time in her life. She voluntarily equated the money she received from her mother-in-law to pay for analysis with mother's milk and permission to be held by father, but she said she needed the experience of being loved and prized, even though she was aware that the fantasies and actions were entirely unreal in terms of actual expectations from the analyst or anyone else in her adult life. During approximately a six-month period, the analyst waited and was almost totally silent, except for responding to her greetings at the beginning and end of each hour. Then came a change. However, before discussing that, I shall explain my rationale for remaining quiet for the six-month period.

Hartmann (1939a) stressed the need for the presence of an average, expectable environment for the unfolding of innate maturational tendencies and the differentiation of id and ego. We are accustomed to think of the serial development of the oral, anal, phallic, and genital phases of psychosexual and psychosocial development.

I have analyzed or am now analyzing 30 patients who suffer from severe characterological or schizophrenic disorders. All had undergone obvious regressions, usually phenomenologically psychotic, at puberty or later when unresolved oedipal conflicts were reawakened. Thus they had experienced environments that were favorable enough to permit the unfolding of innate maturational phases. The predominant symptomatology reflected strong oral fixations, perhaps combined with developmental failure. In the analytic situation, the identificatory processes and the structuralizing effects of interpretations had resulted in the replacement of unhealthy introjects by more mature ones in most of these patients. When their pregenital problems had been more or less satisfactorily resolved, they were able to analyze phallic and genital conflicts with at least moderate success. These data suggest the optimistic but unproved supposition that in the therapeutic situation such patients may achieve a controlled and adaptive regression (Hartman, 1939b; Lindon, 1967; Winnicott, 1955) to a period with a more optimal mother-infant relationship than the one that actually existed when the patient was an infant. When such a relationship has developed, innate maturational tendencies can continue to unfold (together with changes in the far-reaching effects of early learning), provided there are no ill-timed actions on the part of the psychoanalyst. I hesitate to suggest that the same may be true for patients who have remained autistic from infancy or who have had childhood psychoses that are traceable to the failure of separation-individuation (Mahler, 1963; Mahler and Furer, 1960, 1963; Mahler and Settledge, 1959; Mahler and Le Perrier, 1965). I have no clinical material from which to draw conclusions.

My patient eventually seemed to establish a therapeutic alliance. She had the capacity to regress and to observe simultaneously, and she was curious to learn about herself. Her regressive behavior was limited largely to her pre-sleep routine and the analytic room. Her interpersonal relationships were steadily improving and she was handling family problems more realistically. She was promoted rapidly in her work and soon achieved a responsible position. I was comfortable with her period of regression and thought she should have time to experience the sense of well-being she seemed to need, inasmuch as there was continuous evidence of improvement.

Let us return to the case presentation. Although earlier in the analysis the patient wouldn't touch the blanket that lay on the couch at her side, now she began to contemplate covering herself in order to experience in the office the presleep experiences she had so repetitiously described. As she did so, the black sensations returned, but with diminished intensity and scant fright; they were viewed as interesting and worth investigating. She finally ventured to cover herself with the blanket, and for a time she relished the comfort of lying on the couch, visualizing that she was being held by the analyst and was sucking on his penis; for the first time she pictured it clearly as erect and circumcised as had been her brothers' and her husband's. She recognized the absurdity of her fantasy since it involved lying on the analyst's lap and she was only a little shorter than he. Then she began to feel sensations of bladder fullness, whether covered with the blanket or not, and this confused her. She had always urinated at home just before coming to the office, but now she also began to use the toilet provided for patients. Soon there were episodes of watery diarrhea (for which no medical explanation was found). She had always been mildly curious about the analyst's other female patients, but now she became moderately interested in both male and female sibling-surrogates. Later she became aware that when she had sensations of either urinary or fecal urgency while lying on the couch she was also sexually excited.

It will be recalled that when the patient had had the presleep experiences in her home, she had felt warmth only in the upper half of her body; there were no genital sensations. Apparently the experiencing and analysis of her period of regression had helped to remove repression and to structuralize certain needs. Whereas previously her bladder, anal, and vaginal sensations had remained at least partly fused, now she was able to separate them.

There had been no conscious sexual excitation for many months. Now she revealed that she had never knowingly touched herself between her legs since she was five or six years of age except to cleanse herself or care for menstrual discharge. Before analysis she had suffered from dysmenorrhea and profuse flow, but while she was living out the fantasy of being held and nursed, she had felt no menstrual discomfort and excessive flow had been rare. But now the menstrual symptoms reappeared. She found herself tempted to explore her genitals with her hands. In contrast to her previous blissful serenity while in the analyst's presence, the patient became fearful that he disliked her and would abandon her if she touched her genitals. For months she had not reported any dreams; then she had nightmares in which she was violently attacked by men, resulting in mutilation and bleeding. The manifest content gradually changed so that at first genital mutilation was caused by knives and then by inserting huge instruments. She thought that as a child she must have feared sexual assault by her oldest brother, but she could only remember that they had handled each other and exhibited themselves. Eventually she decided that she should explore her genitals. She said, "The ends of the strings are sticking out and I want to see whether I can unravel them."

She began to explore her genitals and rectum with her fingers. She put all of the fingers of both hands into each orifice and stretched it. She remembered in detail much sexual play during her third and sixth years, principally actions that took place while she was alone in the bathtub. She was convinced that at that time she had stretched both the vagina and rectum and inserted various objects, including the nursing bottle of her younger brother, a cream bottle, a lipstick, and a tube of toothpaste, the contents of which she either squeezed into her vagina (or rectum) or ate. Always aware of her hatred for and envy of her younger sister (whom she felt was favored by both parents), and now with highly cathected fantasies of the analyst's sexual involvement with his other female patients, she remembered her intense childhood jealousy and an attempt to murder her rival.

One of the phobias with which she had entered analysis was that of going into dark places either alone or with a man. During the early weeks of analysis she had recalled that at the age of six, her father had been angry with her because she was afraid to go to the basement to get food for her mother; he had dragged her into the cellar over her screaming protests, presumably to show her that there was nothing to fear. In the version she presented at that time, her father had been drunk and her mother had stood by while he struck the child. This memory now returned but in a different light. She recalled that before that episode she had eagerly gone to the basement and had enjoyed sitting on the washing machine while it was hot and vibrating. On one occasion she had taken a lipstick with her and had painted her genital area; then her mother had spanked her. In her reconstruction she supposed that she had used the lipstick to make her genitals more attractive to her father, equating the mouth and the vagina, and that the red coloring had also been a substitute for blood which she had assumed was the result of some activity between her parents. After presenting these data (which preceded the episode in which her father took her to the basement), she remembered that her father had been listening to a romantic opera, one of his favorites, and that she had disturbed him to ask him to help her look for a toy she thought she'd left in the basement. He had reluctantly agreed, whereupon she became panicky that he would beat or attack her sexually. Because he was angry that she had interrupted him, he insisted that she go with him.

She could not recall ever having seen her mother naked or pregnant, or having seen any evidence of menstruation. During her early years her father had been a successful businessman, who was apparently respected by her mother. However, when the patient was four or five, her father became an inveterate drinker for some years. At that time her mother had been the efficient member of the household. The patient hypothesized, but did not remember, that she had equated her mother's efficiency with the acquisition of her father's penis and had thought babies were transformations of the stolen penis that could emerge in the form of either fecal sticks or infants. Finally she wondered whether she had ever seen either of her parents naked.

During the next few interviews, black sensations recurred frequently but were accompanied by little anxiety. At times she visualized the black strings as the heads of snakes that could bite and swallow. Then she recalled with embarrassment that at three or four years of age she had tried to nurse on a bitch, shoving the puppies aside, and got black hair in her mouth. For the first time she spoke of her lifelong fears of snakes and spiders in terms of oral-genital fantasies in which she equated them with pubic hair and penises that could bite. She said that those fears were gone and I never heard of them again. Then, while she was visualizing the black mass in her head, the mass began to jump up and down and assumed the form of a huge black phallus.

On occasion she mentioned that there had been a Negro maid in the family all during her childhood. Now she said she had wondered if that woman were her true mother and said she remembered having seen the maid's pubic hair while she was urinating and had been awestruck. She also remembered that at various times throughout her analysis when she was not in the office, she had visualized an erection and experienced the black sensations. She had meant to inform me but had forgotten. Finally she said she thought she recalled walking into her parents' bedroom and seeing her father alone, in profile and naked. She had been four years old at the time, and her mother was pregnant with her second youngest brother.

A week later, the following detailed interview took place. The patient entered the office looking amused and said she thought she now understood the meaning of the black sensations in her head. She remembered a dream which had surpised her because she had not thought of her husband for several weeks. Their divorce had become final several months before. She said:

"My husband had a baby, probably literally had a baby. He carried it around as a little girl would a doll she liked. I talked to him or to you as I stood before a mirror. I squeezed blackheads out of my face and each time one came out I'd say, 'This is to show you that I'm not afraid of such and such.' He carted the baby around. I was somehow in the picture. He also had an enormous penis, at least twice as big as his erection, that is, twice as long."

At this point in the interview she wrapped a facial tissue around her index finger like a bandage.

"There were about twenty of me and I remember having intercourse over and over again. No. I just remember the feeling of his penis outside of me while he held me. His penis was white and shining and there were no hairs. It was like Jesus' would be if He had one. I was as surprised and awestruck as those three little girls must have been in Portugal when they saw the Virgin Mary. It was a miracle. I can't remember actually seeing the erection so much as seeing it glow. I was really astonished the first time I saw and felt my husband's erection; it was so long and hard."

Now she was tearing the tissue to shreds and continued:

"I feel like an animal in a cage. I wish the hour would end so I wouldn't have to use another piece of tissue and make a bandage of it and tear it up, too. I think I'm playing with it instead of masturbating. Now I have to go to the bathroom. I couldn't masturbate here and I dislike even wanting to. Now I want to put my hands in my mouth. It would feel good to make my mouth bigger and take all of that huge penis inside. Now I want to spit. When he shoved his penis in my mouth I gagged and gagged. I was trying to get all of it inside me and swallow it. Maybe I wanted to have a penis after my brother was born and then believed I'd had my brother all by myself. I'm not confused about my father and his penis anymore. I'm confused about my mother. How did I graduate from wanting to suck on a breast to wanting to suck on a penis? My mother was so capable that I thought she must have a penis, too, and that both men and women could have babies all by themselves. I'm glad I no longer believe I *am* a penis and I want to lose the idea I have a penis somewhere. I've always feared my clitoris would grow into a real penis. I was afraid my mother would catch me in the bathtub when I'd rub on it and make it hard. Maybe she'd see it and take it away and then I couldn't have babies all alone."

During the interviews of the next two weeks, her productions were largely limited to attempts to understand the dream. She saw the blackheads as representing the black ends that stuck out from the ball of tangled strings. She recalled vividly and with much abreaction her invasion of her parents' bedroom. Her father had been alone, standing in the lighted closet of an otherwise darkened room. She was convinced she had seen his erection in profile and had been awestruck. As she spoke of the experience, she had urinary urgency and saw light in her head. She was sure she had experienced the sensation of a great light in her head when she had viewed her father, had felt dazed, and had an intense urge to urinate. She had groped her way to the toilet and "almost blacked out." When she was somewhat older, she had seen a brother masturbating. She thought that when she saw her father naked, unconsciously she had decided that he had been masturbating; she thought that subsequently she had tried to provoke men to masturbate before her, hoping that they, as father surrogates, would rape her. When the son with whom her mother was pregnant was born, the patient believed that the child was her own. She thought, but did not clearly remember, that when her mother was quite large she herself had become seriously constipated, and that she finally had a large bowel movement when her mother went to the hospital to have the baby. When her own son was born, her experience had been that of having a large bowel movement. She had believed that a girl was born with a penis but that some injury cut it off, leaving only an internal stub that might grow into a large penis once again. An alternate hypothesis had been that a woman could obtain the penis during intercourse by biting it off either with her mouth or her vagina.

During this period the patient did not mention certain ideas she had presented as theoretical during earlier interviews. However, she spoke of all her recollections from childhood with vividness and conviction. Other data were offered, but perhaps only one item should be emphasized. At the time when she had the fantasy of nursing on my penis, there were a number of interviews during which she lay quite rigidly on the couch. Then she had several dreams in which she was a little girl sitting on her father's lap and then gradually stood up erect and stiff. She had offered the interpretation, with no hesitation or even wonderment, that she must have imagined that she was her father's penis. She thought she recalled that while she lay on one or another sofa at college, she must have been trying to allay her fears that she was displeasing her father because of her failure at school by imagining that she was his erection and therefore his prized possession.

During adolescence she had grown very fast and become quite tall. She had also suffered from acne and was especially ashamed of blackheads. From her early teens she had been convinced that one reason why she was disliked and mistreated was that she was fat and her skin was ugly. After the acne disappeared, her skin remained a bit oily. While she was analyzing the dream, she admitted that she had never been overweight. She decided that she had equated being tall with her father's erection and had displaced her concern about her height onto being fat, equating obesity and pregnancy. The blackheads were equated with snake-penises and also served as evidence that she was pregnant. After this bit of analysis, she was no longer unduly concerned about her physical appearance.[2]

The recovery of the visual trauma of seeing her father's erection was the last major step in this woman's analysis, which lasted only a few months

[2]This fantasy of childbirth through the skin in the form of blackheads resembles that of a former patient, who believed his mother bore children through blisters induced by applying suction cups used in the treatment of pneumonia (Boyer, 1959), and that of an author who wrote of a character who believed babies came from carbuncles (White, 1949).

more. She had very few and barely cathected recurrences of the black sensations, her self-depreciation disappeared, she increased her capacity to perceive correctly various events in her life and she became a happy and confident woman. One last fear was recognized and resolved. As noted earlier, when she began analysis she would only look at the analyst's face when she entered the consultation room, and would not consciously notice the office furnishings in his "half of the room." Although gradually she began to be able to see those objects, before the recovery of the visual trauma she could only look at the analyst's face. During the analysis there had been interruptions from time to time during her interviews requiring the analyst to walk past the patient; on each occasion she had sat up as he arose to go to the door. When asked why she had sat up, she had responded vaguely. Now there was another interruption and she remained supine. She became consciously aware that she had tried to avoid looking at the front of his trousers and that she had generally been afraid to satisfy a wish to look for evidence that a man had an erection.

As mentioned before, during one period of her analysis she had had a brief affair with a man who was her father's age at his death and, she believed, my age. Thereafter, she had accepted no dates although she had various opportunities. After recovery of the memory of having viewed her father naked, she continued to work through her tranference neurosis in oedipal terms. Then she established a highly pleasing relationship with a man who was eminently suitable to be her children's stepfather. Their sexual relations pleased her very much.

Throughout her treatment, there had been frequent (although usually brief) interruptions because of the analyst's absence. In the first two years, the patient's anxiety was analyzed in terms of oral-sadistic fears and impulses. Her relationship with her new partner began two months before another planned absence of the analyst, of two months' duration. Just before the separation, she tried to provoke her lover to leave her, using what seemed to me to have been largely voluntary misperceptions of his communications to her. During the separation, she got along well with her lover. On my return, we analyzed further the meaning of her behavior. Her use of regression was understood as a defense against separation and an attempt to deny that some aspects of her love for the analyst were based principally on transference elements.

During the analysis of the tranference neurosis in oedipal terms, it became clear that the visual trauma at the age of four had resulted in an attempt to master the psychic injury by the simultaneous use of a number of maneuvers. She had used regression, denial, repression, and reversal to defend against hostility pertaining to genital sensations and desires. Simultaneously she had discharged erotized aggression unsatisfactorily and guiltily by repetitious reenactments of the original trauma with her oldest brother, who became her father-surrogate. There had been an uneven and precocious development of a sadistic surperego. By engaging in voyeuristic and exhibitionistic behavior, she had provoked punishment from her mother. At the same time she had identified with both the phallus of the father and the pregnancy of the mother. Her fear that her mother had stolen her baby could be understood as a denial and reversal of her own wish to steal her mother's babies and to supplant her mother as the wife of her father. During the analysis little material emerged which could strongly support a theme that was implicit in much of the data: the patient's wish to supplant her father in his relations with her mother.

During the last months of her analysis there was another vicissitude regarding the black sensations in her head. While resolving the oedipal aspects of her tranference neurosis, she had fantasies of having intercourse with the analyst while, in fact, she was having sexual relations with her fiancé. Before that she had been preoccupied with the analyst's penis as a substitute breast. Now, while visualizing the analyst as a genital father-surrogate, the black sensations recurred, but with little emotional involvement. During the course of several weeks she repeatedly saw the skein of black threads; as she divested herself of unwanted ego and superego traits she had introjected from various family members, she saw herself pulling out individual black threads and discarding them. Thus, the black threads were seen as introjects.

Her relationship with her fiancé seemed to be solid. She felt secure and had little incentive to continue her analysis. Wedding plans were made, and she wanted to enter a new marriage without interference from a continued relationship with her analyst. It seemed fruitless to continue the analysis, although there had probably not been enough actual recall of primal scene and toilet training experiences, or of her implied, prolonged fantasy that she had been the analyst's penis. I felt that she would return for further analysis if later difficulties turned out to be particularly troublesome. I was optimistic about one phenomenon. The patient had given evidence that she had an unusual capacity either to analyze consciously without reporting the steps of her analytic activity, or to analyze preconsciously; as mentioned earlier, she had reported certain fears or phobias only after they had disappeared.

DISCUSSION

This material could be discussed from many viewpoints, but my principal aim is to illustrate a technique for certain patients who suffer from characterological schizophrenic, and schizoaffective disorders. In this section I will state my theoretical orientation (since a technical approach requires this), and I will also present two subjects which do not pertain directly to these matters but have interested audiences who have heard this material presented.[3]

[3]Versions of this paper have been presented before four psychoanalytic associations in the United States and eight in South America.

Theoretical Orientation

The structure of the ego and superego is determined in large part by introjects and is the product of the interaction of inborn and socialization factors. These introjects are potentially subject to modification. The roots of severe characterological and functional psychotic disorders can be traced to qualities of the symbiotic and separation-individuation phases described by Mahler and her co-workers. Infantile deprivation and overstimulation (Bergman and Escalona, 1949; Boyer, 1956) in infancy, whether due predominantly to consitutional defects within the baby or psychological defects within the mothering figures, do not produce all of the pathological attributes of patients who suffer from such disorders. Those patients have traversed to some degree all phases of psychosexual and psychosocial development; have manifold areas of developmental failure and fixations; and uneven levels of ego and superego development; and the various ego functions are affected differently from patient to patient. In borderline and schizophrenic patients, defensive regression is the typical response to adolescent or postadolescent stresses which reawaken unresolved oedipal conflicts (Arlow and Brenner, 1964; Glover, 1955).

I shall discuss the data obtained from certain investigations into the genesis of schizophrenia and assume that their implications hold as well for patients with characterological disorders. Investigations into the environmental influences on the development of schizophrenia have led to many studies of schizophrenic patients and their families (Boyer and Giovacchini, 1967). It has been shown that schizophrenic behavior serves various functions in particular kinds of family organizations and cultural groups and that serious impairment of ego functioning may be related to the failure of parents to transmit properly the usual communicational tools of the larger society. The families of schizophrenic patients have discouraged them from learning methods of communication based predominantly on secondary-process logic, including generally understood (rather than idiosyncratic) symbolic connotations. Individuals who have been reared in such unfavorable milieus do not learn to exchange information well in extrafamilial or cross-cultural situations. It seems probable that they regress defensively when their difficulties in sending and receiving messages are superimposed upon already existent intrapsychic conflicts.

Consistent with this theoretical view in the belief that the primary therapeutic task is to restore and/or develop a reasonable ego and superego. Theoretically this can be accomplished by modifying or replacing unloving and archaic introjects. A reasonable ego and superego can be developed by decreasing primary-process attributes and influences and by increasing those of the secondary process. In psychoanalysis, the effects of two phenomena are crucial to such id-ego differentiation: identification and the educative and structuralizing effects of interpretation. It is inherent in id-ego differentiation that intrapsychic and interpersonal communication will be improved, but sometimes technical maneuvers can be employed to speed up the development of the latter.

It is generally believed that it is especially difficult to treat disorders that lie near the psychotic end of a continuum of conditions that extend from the transference to the narcissistic neuroses because of two principal problems: The nature of the transference relationships and the patient's intense fear of the vicissitudes of his aggresssive impulses (Boyer 1965b, 1966c, 1967b).

Technique

The following is a brief and oversimplified statement of the technique for treating certain characterological and schizophrenic disorders; most of its elements were demonstrated in the case presentation. The first task of treatment is to encourage id-ego differentiation and reduction of the archaic and sadistic qualities of the superego. Such differentiation can be brought about by the incorporation of new introjects and the structuralizing effects of interpretation within the framework of the transference relationships.

Presenting the patient with a calm, accepting, objective, incorruptible, and intrinsically optimistic analyst offers him an attitudinal model with which to identify. The patient's two main fears constitute a severe hindrance to treatment: his fear of the magical powers of his aggressive drive derivatives and his fear of the loss of ego controls. The analyst's communications to the patient during the period when his transference manifestations are predominantly the result of his projection of part-objects should be directed toward his ego strengths and his aggressive drive derivatives. The analysis of pregenital drive derivatives should have two phases. In the first, analysis will be directed toward understanding the part-object projections and later, coincident with the development of a stable transference neurosis, the whole-object projections. Analysis of oedipal conflicts should follow that of pregenital conflicts.

Interpretations will be made from the side of the ego whenever possible, and the defensive nature of the patient's productions will be stressed, more from the side of object relations than from that of content. They will be directed toward this surface, although with such patients, the surface is sometimes more difficult to determine than with neurotics (Giovacchini, 1969). Verbalization of all communications will be encouraged. It should be demonstrated to the patient that awareness of unconscious fantasies strengthens rather than weakens ego boundaries. Psychoanalysts generally agree that interpretations that include genetic aspects are more convincing and structuralizing. Therefore, the recovery of actual memories is consistently encouraged. Such memories are more easily recovered when the patient is kept aware of what he is experiencing in the analytic situation and when his attention is directed to prior situations when he felt similar emotional and physical sensations. With most patients, analysis of posture, gestures, and physical tensions facilitates such memory recovery.

The analyst should not be overtly reassuring or formally educative, but should use reconstructions appropriately. One function of this step is to demonstrate to the patient the need for him to be participant-observer by revealing the analyst's fallibility. The development of a therapeutic alliance is mandatory. One aspect of that alliance is the patient's curiosity about the dynamic and genetic reasons for his special uses of defensive maneuvers. His controlled regression should be encouraged; and he should have sufficient time for development from earlier levels of integration and for working through.

Superego support will be given indirectly. The analytic framework should be of such a nature that the patient will know from the beginning what is expected of and permitted to him (Boyer, 1961). Special attention will be directed to the defensive purposes of regression and acting-out. When the patient consistently omits relevant material, the analyst will try to motivate him to fill in the obvious gaps.

The analyst will try to retain his anonymity and encourage the patient to reveal his fantasies. I doubt that an analyst who takes public positions on social and moral issues can successfully analyze such patients. When therapetuic plateaus are reached, the analyst will turn to self-analysis to try to determine if his own unconscious problems or attitudes may have contributed to his lack of understanding of what the patient has presented and to the lack of therapeutic progress (Marcondes, 1968). If such problems exist and if self-analysis does not alleviate the therapeutic block, the analyst will seek further personal analysis.

The analysis of superego introjects is as important as that of ego introjects. While the understanding of paranoid elements and their uses is mandatory, depressive elements must not be overlooked. Treatment can perhaps be speeded up if the analysis of depressive elements receives greater emphasis than paranoid elements whenever possible.

The patient's capacity to think, remember, and analyze for himself should be encouraged. His defensive uses of confusion, forgetfulness, and dependency on the therapist to analyze for him should be interpreted consistently. The analyst should be somewhat passive and make a minimum of interpretations, depending upon the patient's anxiety. I have the impression that certain of the interpretations given to such patients do more to alleviate the anxiety of the analyst than of the patient; others seem to be said *pro forma*. Unnecessary interpretations increase the patient's dependency and interfere with his self-growth.

Diagnosis

The difficulties encountered in trying to diagnose patients whose disturbances lie somewhere between the transference and the narcissistic neuroses is well-known (Boyer and Giovacchini, 1967). Some of them are exemplified by the present patient, whom I am inclined to classify as a "borderline psychotic," a term I find less ambiguous than the more popular "borderline case."[4] I am using the term "borderline psychosis" to mean that the patient has a serious characterological disorder and has undergone one or more transient states of regression, during which there were overt manifestations of psychosis that occurred in the apparent absence of severe external stress. I include those patients who experienced their first overt psychotic episode in psychoanalysis.

The nature of the transference relationships provides data that can be used to make a diagnosis (Little, 1966; Modell, 1963). I assume that borderline psychotics will develop transference relationships that for some time will reveal dominant psychotic characterisitics. My hesitation about classifying the present patient as a borderline psychotic is due to the fact that she did not experience an unmistakable psychotic episode at any time and did not clearly manifest a psychotic transference relationship.

In my psychoanalytic experience with 30 patients who have suffered from severe characterological, schizophrenic, and schizoaffective disorders, the transference has almost always been divided into two overlapping phases (Boyer, 1961, 1965a, 1966a, 1966b; Boyer and Giovacchini, 1967). In the first, the tranference is marked by the presence of psychotic features. During its analysis, the patient achieves a higher degree of id-ego and id-superego differentiation than he had before. In 25 of these patients who have had or appear that they will have a favorable outcome of treatment, there has been a second phase in which a stable neurotic transference has developed. In perhaps a dozen of those cases, the analysis of the transference neurosis seems to have led to the resolution of both pregenital and genital problems.

The seven patients who began analysis while floridly psychotic or just after they had been unsuccessfully treated with shock or drug therapies developed reactions of the type called "transference psychosis" by Rosenfeld (1954) and "delusional transference" by Little (1958). In such a transference the patient projects onto the analyst mainly introjects of part-objects. When there is an elaborate psychotic transference, the analyst may be reacted to as though

---

[4]The status of the concepts "borderline state" and "borderline case" has been the subject of many articles, symposia, and reviews; for example, Schmideberg (1959), Rangell (1955), Grinker, Werble, and Drye (1968), and Paz (1963). The consensus has been that in order to diagnose the individual case, one must assess the libidinal orientation and make an inventory of ego functions. Recent reports of studies of such an inventory include: Bellak and Hurvich (1969), Grinker, Werble, and Drye (1968), and Kernberg (1967).

he were an actualization of a mental representation of a part of one person and then another. Such projections may be evanescent and the patient may experience the analyst as representing parts of many important people from his past during the course of a single interview. It is difficult to understand what is transpiring. Cathexes are now and then easily displaced so that an intense, brief reaction may be misjudged by the therapist to indicate a more serious involvement with the introjected (and usually distorted) aspect of the person represented than will be shown by later analysis. Fromm-Reichman (1939, 1950), Pichon Rivière (1951), and many others have written of the transference relations of the schizophrenic. Searles (1963) has described the transference psychosis manifestations of the chronic schizophrenic. Such a person has regressed to a state of ego functioning that is marked by severe impairment of his capacity to differentiate among and to integrate his experiences. He tends to believe that the therapist is an important person from his past or that at different times he *is* different significant people; the therapist does not merely remind the patient of these people. I have not done psychoanalytic work in a hospital setting nor have I had the opportunity to try to treat chronic, severely regressed pshychotics who have been hospitalized for a number of years. Such phenomena also characterize the transference psychoses of patients who have had recurrent episodes of acute psychoses, but the duration of these phenomena is usually brief, lasting from only a few days to a few months.

The 23 patients I have analyzed or am analyzing who were not acutely psychotic when treatment began have demonstrated severe disturbances characterized by varying proportions of the symptoms of the hysteric, the obsessive-compulsive, and the impulse neurotic. Six of them had been hospitalized at least once and treated with shock or drug therapies for schizophrenia or schizoaffective psychosis. A dozen had experienced brief psychotic episodes during which they were not immured, or else (as in the case of the present patient) they had suffered dubious psychotic reactions. After varying periods of analysis, 20 of these patients developed a transference state in which for some time the projection of part objects predominated over that of whole objects and the primary process was dominant in influencing production. One patient who began treatment while acutely psychotic with schizomanic symptoms and one who was not acutely psychotic but had been treated in a hospital for many months for a paranoid psychosis with depressive features committed suicide while in analysis. The treatment of three cases who had never experienced an unquestionable psychotic reaction prior to analysis failed; in two of these cases, the failure was probably due to unanalyzed problems of the analyst.

Let us now discuss the diagnosis of the present case. During the patient's first four years, there were no feeding problems. She was completely toilet-trained before she was two years old and was never incontinent after that.

When she was three she tried to kill her younger sister, of whom she remained inordinately jealous until her analysis. She also tried to nurse from a bitch at the age of three. As far back as she could remember, she had avoided physical contact with her parents but was less reluctant to be touched by a Negro maid. She reported that she had learned to speak clearly and to read at a "very early age." There was no personal myth (Kris, 1956) in which she believed she had parents other than her own, but she wondered whether the maid were her true mother.

Following a visual trauma at four when she saw her father's erection, she experienced a "great light in her head" and had an urge to urinate. There was much exhibitionism, voyeurism, and sexual play (including an unusual degree of polymorphous perversity) up to a rather late age. She expressed identification with her pregnant mother through somatic compliance. She was severely constipated toward the end of her mother's pregnancy and had a large bowel movement after her mother delivered. She believed the baby was hers and had been stolen from her by her mother. Early in analysis she claimed that from the age of four to 13, she had heard continuous, loud, angry arguments between her parents at night. Later she revised this information, saying that arguments were rare; usually there were quiet discussions which she associated with her parents' lovemaking. We do not know whether she consciously felt sexual excitement, but her rage from lack of gratification was experienced as terror that one of her parents might be killed; apparently she identified with the excitement of both parents. She believed she had a small penis that could be made to grow larger and that she would be able to have children parthenogenetically. She believed that at least one of her mother's babies had been stolen from her. It also seems probable that some of her anger was turned against herself. She claimed that as a small girl she had put large objects into her vagina and rectum and during analysis she had inserted all of the fingers of both hands into both orifices. Such activities must have hurt her. She appears to have identified with her pregnant mother and also perhaps with her father's phallus.

At five or six the patient was reprimanded by her mother for sexual play, and her brother was punished physically for his participation. Believing that she had a small penis that could be made to grow larger, she was very much afraid of castration. This terror led to a latency period that was marked by an abrupt cessation of sexual activity and intensified desire to be good. It is not known whether she had nightmares about falling before the latency period, but she definitely had them at that time. During latency she was well-behaved and highly moralistic. She took care of her youngest brother voluntarily and tried to nurse him from her nipples. So far as is known, there were no obsessional thinking patterns or compulsions. She did not become a tomboy in the sense of amusing herself primarily in athletic activities or dressing like a member of the opposite sex. However, she very much enjoyed wrestling with her older brother and did not develop confidential relationships with girls. She idolized certain schoolteachers and church figures, but her fantasies about her relations with these people were vague, and she always found moral fault with them after a time. It would seem that she turned her anger against them because she was unable to maintain favorite-child relations with them.

Besides her earlier defense mechanisms, during latency she had a strong tendency to repress and to use reaction-formations of goodness. If any diagnosis could be made up to this point, it would have to be in the direction of hysteria.

With the onset of puberty, she began to have terrifying sensations of blackness in the head. As was learned during her analysis, such experiences were associated with unconscious fantasies about erections. There was a tendency to schizoid behavior. She was ashamed of her changing physical appearance and did not manipulate her breasts or genitals. The modesty of her latency period became intensified. Her body image was distorted; although she was pretty, she perceived herself as fat and ugly. She was very much concerned about her physical appearance and thought that other people inferred from her acne that she had reprehensible sexual thoughts and desires. Gradually she became a social recluse and accepted no dates with boys. She spent her time doing excellent schoolwork and participating in religious activities; however, she did not ruminate about religion or philosophy.

When she left home and started college, she underwent episodes that had hysterical qualities but also suggested nascent catatonia. She spent long periods in lavatories (which she called bathrooms) where she would enter a trancelike state and have no awareness of sexual fantasies. She was repeating symbolically and thoughtlessly her prelatency sexual activities. She had her first date at the age of 19 and then behaved unusually, performing fellatio on her second date. After she was married, there was a more obvious return of the repressed. She was unwittingly exhibitionistic and voyeuristic. She provoked her husband to display himself and to masturbate before her. She experienced the black sensations and then retired to the bathtub, where she entered thoughtless, trancelike states and engaged in unconscious sexual fantasizing. During the oedipal period, she had denied her wish to replace her mother and to have her mother's child, claiming secretly that her mother had stolen her baby. After marriage, she was convinced that her mother-in-law wanted to steal her children—an obviously false idea.

Before she began analysis, then, the data would indicate a probable diagnosis of a hysterical personality disorder with schizoid tendencies. There were episodes suggesting incipient catatonia, but the effects of powerful repression make this classification questionable.

In psychoanalysis, no obvious transference psychosis developed. I believe the reason for this was that from the beginning there was a definite split transference. This was my only patient who presented such a constellation. To be sure, her productions for the first few months were heavily influenced by the primary process; her associations were loose and sometimes had a clang quality. Her principal defense mechanisms were denial, projections, reversal, living-out, acting-out, and repression. So far as I could tell, there were no massive projections of fragmented introjects onto the analyst. During the prolonged period in which she rocked herself to sleep and visualized herself sucking on my penis as a breast substitute, she did not seem to lose sight of the fact that the experience was the product of her own mind, and she did not consciously confuse me with anyone else. In addition, there was no evidence of a problem typically experienced by schizophrenics in analysis: their conviction that either the analyst will destroy them or vice versa. This was my only patient who had a relatively undisturbing need to try to reexperience and detraumatize early nursing experiences while replacing undesirable introjects with warmer, healthier ones. I cannot satisfactorily explain this phenomenon. We have become accustomed to thinking of patients with such disorders as having had unhealthy early childhood experiences with their mothering figures. However, this patient may have had consistently warm experiences with a Negro maid, although she said little about her during the analysis. All of the patient's siblings had obvious psychological difficulties, but none was ever hospitalized for psychiatric reasons. Two of her brothers had obsessive-compulsive personalities; her sister was grossly exhibitionistic and impulsive; and her other two brothers remained excessively dependent. The fact that none was more seriously afflicted may be due to the fact that the maid exercised a normalizing influence in the household. Possibly the patient had a smooth course of treatment because of healthy introjects taken from the Negro maid. It could be accounted for by my increasing skill or by the split transference that was exploited in therapy. The split transference seems to have simplified the working through of aggressive phenomena. After she had partly analyzed her uses of me as the giving maternal figure, she was able to bring about a reconciliation with her actual mother and mother-in-law and to develop affectonate relationships with them. Then she used me as a father-surrogate and worked through genital aspirations and rivalries to an extent that may prove to be satisfactory. A transference neurosis had been established by the end of the first year, in which I served first as a remodeled mother and later as a genital father figure.

The borderline syndrome is being increasingly studied from the standpoint of ego functions (Grinker, Werble, and Drye, 1968). The present case revealed symptomatology and ego deficiencies that coinside with the average common denominators found in these authors' résumé of the writings of representative observers, which curiously, say nothing of Bellak's contributions. Among the psychoanalysts who have heard and discussed this paper, those who have been significantly influcenced by Kleinian psychology almost uniformly believed the patient was schizophrenic, whereas those who are more oriented to structural theory tended to believe that she suffered from the borderline syndrome. A few preferred the designation "psychotic character" (Frosch, 1964).

Vision, Headache, and the Halo

Let us turn now to a brief dicussion of this case in terms of Greenacre's (1947) syndrome: vision, headache, and the halo. While studying reactions to stress in the course of superego formation, Greenacre found patients that presented material showing a relationship among visual shock, headache, and the development of a halo. She wrote:

> Schematically the sequence is as follows. The child receives a stunning psychic blow, usually an overwhelming visual experience which has the effect of dazing and bewildering it. There is generally the sensation of lights, flashes of lightning, bright colors or some sort of aurora. This may seem to invest the object or objects seen, or it may be felt as occurring in the subject's own head experienced literally as seeing stars. The initial experience always produces the most intense emotions, whether of fear, rage, or horror. There is at first a feeling of unreality, or of confusion. The shocking stimulus arouses an erotized aggression which demands subsequent mastery. Sometimes the little voyeur feels impelled to repeat the experience as though to test its reality. Peeping or fantasies of peeping are accompanied by sensations of tension and strain in the eyes or across the frontal region. Headaches occur later when new situations reactivate the original trauma. Mastery is attempted by successive repetition in fantasy (reality testing), partial regression, or by the development of severely binding superego reaction-formations of goodness which are supplemented by or converted into lofty ideals. As the tense goodness relaxes a little, the headache improves and the ideals are loftier but less exigent. Figuratively, the child develops a halo to which, if it remains too burdensome, he reacts by throwing it defiantly away . . . or by endowing someone else with it. Such children and adults seem to overvalue enormously those whom they love, projecting onto them the extreme ideals and demands they first required of themselves. Quite often the loved one is seen as a saint on the pedestal, worshiped rather than loved, and kept almost inviolate in an overestimation which is in actuality a devaluation. . . . Such strong visual stimulation adds very much to the stress of superego formation at whatever time it occurs, although its effects are much abated during the latency period.

Greenacre found the sight of the genitalia of an adult of the opposite sex to be most likely to produce visual overstimulation. However, sight of the female genitals was never invested with the shining light. The symptom complex occurred particularly in patients with strong obsessive and compulsive trends, and the symptomatology was strikingly clear in schizophrenic patients.

The similarities between the symptom complex and its gensis in my patient and that of Greenacre's vision, headache, and the halo are striking, as are the defensive and reliving purposes and their effects upon superego development which she described. It is unnecessary to detail every area of agreement and the minor variations. There are two obvious differences: my patient's symptom complex was vision, black sensations in the head, and the halo; and she did not reveal a strong anal fixation, resulting in obsessions, compulsions, and the use of displacement as a cardinal defense maneuver. This woman's character structure was more like the hysterical personality disorder.

Neither I nor the many discussants of this material were able to explain the reasons for the variant symptomatology. Garma (1968) made an interesting observation: he said that the patient gradually visualized the blackness in her head more and more concretely; what she originally perceived as a black mass later became a tangled skein of strings that appeared to be phalluses with oral-sadistic characteristics. Long (1968) and Simmonds (1968) suggested calling this patient "The Medusa Lady." In a study of headaches, Garma (1958) demonstrated that they sometimes represent negative hallucinations. Schechtmann (1968) has supported this finding. Greenacre (1967) believed that the second difference was perhaps more apparent than real. She noted that the patient had an unusual amount of polymorphous perversity in her psychosexual development and that one manifestation of her erotized aggression was her anal and genital manipulations using the fingers of both hands. Greenacre thought that further anaysis of the patient's toilet training and its effects on her personality development would reveal more obvious characteristics of the obsessive-compulsive neurotic. Similar views were expressed independently by Aray (1968) and Teruel (1968).

The symptom complex—vision, blackness in the head, and the halo—appears to be unique in the psychoanalytic literature. Abraham (1913) was the first to discuss blackness before the eyes as a symptom expressing an inhibition of scopohilic tendencies. He wrote of a man who had a pronounced fear of looking at his mother and sister, even when they were fully clothed. The patient suffered from anxiety that he might unintentionally impregnate one of them. The libidinal wishes directed toward his mother were transferred to other (mainly older) women, but did not truly reveal themselves; they were expressed as a dread of looking at such women. When he looked at mature women, there was a blackness before his eyes.

In this way the patient was prevented from seeing women who were attractive to him. That he should have found a substitute along hallucinatory paths for this imposed privation is in complete agreement with the psychology of dementia praecox. He would, for instance, see lying naked before him a middle-aged woman who, according to his own account, bore a great resemblance to his mother. He furthermore admitted in a way which carried conviction that his avoidance of the sight of female persons was in effect an avoidance of the female, or more correctly, of the maternal genitals.

There are obvious similarities between Abraham's case and my patient; both experienced black sensations when confronted with visual stimuli that reactivated forbidden incestuous wishes. However, Abraham's patient saw the blackness before his eyes while my patient saw it within her head; the man had to avoid looking at women who reminded him of his mother, whereas the woman could not look at men's lower halves lest she see a bulge that would remind her of her father's erection; each hallucinated the object that the black sensations were intended to obliterate.[5]

SUMMARY

A technique for the treatment of certain characterological, schizophrenic, and schizoaffective disorders within the framework of the structural theory has been presented by setting forth a fragment of analysis with interpolated explanatory remarks. Problems pertaining to diagnosis have been discussed.

The analysand had a symptom complex: a visual trauma followed by sensations of blackness in the head and the development of a figurative halo, strongly reminiscent of the syndrome described by Greenacre—vision, headache, and the halo. This patient's symptom complex was similar in origin and psychological uses to that of Greenacre's patients. Its analysis was crucial to the apparently satisfactory result that was achieved in an unusually short time.

References

Abraham, K. (1913), "Restrictions and transformations of scoptophilia in psycho-neurotics; with remarks on analogous phenomena in folk psychology." In Selected Papers on Psychoanalysis. London: Hogarth Press, 1948.

Aray, J., Discussion of the Present Paper at a Meeting of the Grupo Venezelano de Estudios Psicoanaliticos, Caracas, May, 1968.

Arlow, J. A. and Brenner, C., Psychoanalytic Concepts and the Structural Theory. New York: International Universities Press, 1964.

Avenburg, R., "Modificaciones estructurales en un paciente esquizofrénico a traves del primer mes de análisis. "Revista de psicoanálisis 19:351-365 (1962).

[5]Clinically, patients often complain of a triad of symptoms, each of which is the neurophysiological result of a change in peripheral blood flow: headaches, sensations of blackness, and dizziness. For elucidation of the meanings of the dizziness symptom, see Giovacchini (1958).

Bellak, L. and Hurvich, M., "A systematic study of ego functions." *J. Nerv. Ment. Dis.*, 148:569-585 (1969).

Bergman, P. and Escalona, S. J., "Unusual sensitivities in very young children." *Psychoanal. Study Child*, 3-4:333-352 (1949).

Boyer, L. B., "On maternal overstimulation and ego defects." *Psychoanal. Study Child*, 11:236-256 (1956).

———. "An unusual childhood theory of pregnancy." *J. Hillside Hosp.*, 8:279-283 (1959).

———. "Provisional evaluation of psychoanalysis with few parameters employed in the treatment of schizophrenia." *Int. J. Psychoanal.*, 42:389-403 (1961).

———. "Tratamiento ambulatorio de pacientes esquizofrénicos." *Acta Psiquiátrica y Psicológica de América Latina*, 11:147-154 (1965a).

———. "Desarrolo histórico en la psicoterapia psicoanalitica de las esquizofranias: contribuciones de Freud." *Cuadernos de Psicoanalisis*, 1:355-381 (1965b).

———. "Office treatment of schizophrenic patients by psychoanalysis. "*Psychoanal. Forum*, 1:337-356 (1966a).

———. "Tratamientos de pacientes esquizofrénicos en el consultorio: el uso de la terapia psicoanalitica con escasos parámetros." *Revista de Psicoanálisis*, 23:287-317 (1966b).

———. "Desarrollo histórico de la terapia de la esquizofrenia: contribuciones de los discipulos de Freud." *Revista de Psicoanlisis*, 23:91-148 (1966c).

———. "La terapia psicoanalitica della schizofrenia." *Rivista di Psicoanalisis*, 12:3-22 (1966d).

———. Author's reply. *Psychoanal. Forum*, 2:190-195 (1967a).

———. "Freuds Beitrag zur Psychotherapie der Schizophrenia." *Psyche*, 31:869-894 (1967b).

———. and Giovacchini, P. L., *Psychoanalytic Treatment of Schizophrenic and Characterological Disorders*. New York: Jason Aronson, 1967.

Fromm-Reichmann, F., "Transference problems in schizophrenics." *Psychoanal. Quart.*, 8:412-426 (1939).

———. *Principles of Intensive Psychotherapy*. Chicago: University of Chicago Press, 1950.

Frosch, J., "The psychotic character: clinical psychiatric consideration." *Psychiat. Quart.*, 38:81-96 (1964).

Garma A., *El Dolor de Cabeza*. Buenos Aires: Editorial Nova, 1958.

———. Discussion of the present paper. Asociación Psicoanalitica Argentina, Buenos Aires, April, 1968.

Giovacchini, P. L., "Some affective meanings of dizziness." *Psychoanal. Quart.*, 27:217-225 (1958).

———. "The influence of interpretation upon schizophrenic patients." *Internat. Journ. of Psychoanal.* 50:179-197 (1969).

Glover, E., *The Technique of Psychoanalysis*. New York: International Universities Press, 1955.

Greenacre, P. (1947), "Vision, headache and the halo." In *Trauma, Growth and Personality*. New York: Norton, 1952.

———. Discussion of the present paper, then entitled "Vision, Headache and the Halo:

Further Considerations'' at the Fall Meeting of the American Psychoanalytic Association, New York, December, 1967.

Grinker, R. R.; Werble, B.; and Drye, R. C., *The Borderline Syndrome: a Behavioral Study of Ego-Functions*. New York: Basic Books, 1968.

Hartmann, H. (1939a), *Ego Psychology and the Problem of Adaptation*. New York: International Universities Press, 1958.

_____. (1939b), "Psychoanalysis and the concept of health." In *Essays on Ego Psychology: Selected Papers in Psychoanalytic Theory*. New York: International Universities Press, 1964.

Hoedemaker, E. D., "Intensive psychotherapy of schizophrenia: an initial interview." *Canadian Psychiat. Assoc. J.*, 12:253-261 (1967).

Kernberg, O., "Borderline personality organization." *J. Amer. Psychoanal. Assoc.*, 15:641-685 (1967).

Kris, E., "The personal myth: a problem in psychoanalytic technique." *J. Amer. Psychoanal. Assoc.*, 4:653-681 (1956).

Lindon, J. A., ed., "On regression: a workshop." *Psychoanal. Forum*, 2:293-316 (1967).

Little, M., "On delusional transference (transference psychosis)." *Intern. Journ. of Psychoanal.* 39:134-138 (1958).

_____. "Transference in borderline states." *Intern. Journ. of Psychoanal.*, 47:476-485 (1966).

Loewenstein, R. M., "Some remarks on the role of speech in psychoanalytic technique." *Intern. Journ. of Psychoanal.*, 37:460-468 (1956).

Long, R. T., Discussion of the present paper at meeting of the Psychoanalysts of the Southwest, San Antonio, June, 1968.

Mahler, M. S., "Thoughts about development and individuation." *Psychoanal. Study Child*, 18:307-324 (1963).

_____, and Furer, M., "Observations on research regarding the "Symbiotic syndrome." *Psychoanal. Quart.*, 29:317-327 (1960).

_____, Furer, M., "Certain aspects of the separation-individuation phase." *Psychoanal. Quart.*, 32:1-14 (1963).

_____, and Le Perrier, K., "Mother-child interaction during separation-individuation." *Psychoanal. Quart.*, 34:483-498 (1965).

_____, and Settledge, C., "Severe emotional disturbances in childhood: psychosis."In *American Handbook of Psychiatry*, S. Arieti, ed. New York: Basic Books, 1959.

Modell, A. H., "Primitive object relationships and the predispostion to schizophrenia." *Intern. Journ. Psychoanal.*, 44:282-293 (1963).

Paz, C. A., "Ansiedades psicóticas. Complejo de édipo y elaboración de la posición depresiva en un borderline." Paper read before the Asociación Psicoanalítica Argentina, Buenos Aires, March, 1963.

Pichon Rivière, A., "Algunas observaciones sobre la trasferencia en los pacientes psicóticos." *Revista de Psicoanálisis* 18:131-138. (1957).

Rangell, L. (reporter), "Panel report on the borderline case." *Journ. of the Amer. Psychoanal. Assoc.*, 3:285-298 (1955).

Rosenfeld, H. A., "Considerations regarding the psychoanalytic approach to acute and chronic schizophrenia." *Intern. Journ. Psychoanal.*, 35:135-160 (1954).

———— . Discussion of paper by L. Bryce Boyer. *Psychoanal. Forum,* 1:351-353 (1966a).

———— . "Una investigación sobre la necesidad de "acting out" enlos pacientes neuróticos y psicóticos durante el análisis." *Revista de Psicoanálisis*, 23:424-437 (1966b).

Schechtmann, J., Discussion of the present paper at meeting of the Asociacion Psicoanalitica Argentina, Buenos Aires, April, 1968.

Schmideberg, M., "The borderline patient." In *American Handbook of Psychiatry*, S. Arieti, ed. New York: Basic Books, 1959.

Searles, H. F. (1963). *Transference Psychosis in the Psychotherapy of Chronic Schizophrenia.* New York: International Universities Press, 1965.

Segal, H., "Melanie Klein's technique." *Psychoanal. Forum,* 2:198-227 (1967).

Simmonds, C., Discussion of the present paper at meeting of the Psychoanalysts of the Southwest, San Antonio, June, 1968.

Teruel, G., Discussion of the present paper at meeting of the Grupo Venozelano de Estudios Psicoanaliticos, Caracas, May, 1968.

White, E. L., "Lukundoo." In *The Pocket Week-End Book*, P.v. S. Stern, ed., New York: Pocket Books, 1949.

Winnicott, D. W., "Metapsychological and clinical aspects of regression within the psychoanalytical set up." *Intern. Journ. of Psychoanal.,* 36:16-26 (1955).

Chapter XVII

Somatic Elements: A Case of Psychogenic Anosmia

Daniel Offer, M.D.

INTRODUCTION

The case of Miss F. is presented in order to shed further light on the importance of the sense of smell in the course of human development. Miss F. had the symptom of anosmia for 18 years before entering psychoanalytic treatment; it was cleared up during the psychoanalysis. This case is of particular interest because with one exception (Breuer and Freud, 1895). "The Case of Miss Lucy R," it stands alone in the psychoanalytic literature. There is no other clinical description of anosmia. The psychoanalytic literature that will be summarized below deals exclusively with hyperosmia.

This paper will present psychoanalytic data on the development of the symptom as well as on its disappearance. Theoretical statements about the evolutionary meaning of the sense of smell will be presented and anosmia will be related to two crucial factors in the development of an individual: affect and sexuality. This paper will be divided into three major sections: review of the literature, case report, and discussion.

REVIEW OF THE LITERATURE

In discussing psychoanalytic and psychiatric writings on the sense of smell, it seems appropriate to divide the literature into clinical observations and evolutionary aspects of the sense of smell.

CLINICAL OBSERVATIONS

The first clinical observations on the importance of olfaction in psychiatric illness was documented by Freud in his description of Miss Lucy R. in *Studies on Hysteria* (1895). Freud stated that Miss Lucy R. had hysterical symptoms of analgesia that affected the nose too, so that the latter lost its function as a sense organ. She did, however, have a subjective sense of smell that bothered her constantly, namely, that of "burnt pudding." After Freud elicited the

The author wishes to thank Drs. C. Kligerman and P. Giovacchini for their helpful suggestions. Presented at the Fifty-Sixth Annual Meeting of the American Psychoanalytic Association, Miami Beach, Florida, May 2, 1969.

origins of the patient's psychic trauma, that her wish to marry the father of the children she was caring for had been rebuffed, the smell of "burnt pudding" disappeared. It was replaced by a "smell resembling cigar smoke." When Freud analyzed the later symptom he was able to help the patient overcome her difficulties. He was happy with the treatment results and stated: "I then examined her nose and found that its sensitivity to pain and reflex excitability had been almost completely restored." Freud discussed the symptom in relation to hysteria in general: He saw the trauma as a psychological one whose main problem was conversion of psychological excitation into somatic innervations in order to *repress* the disturbing idea. Once the repression was lifted, the idea returned to consciousness and there was no further "need" for the symptom.

As stated above, prior to Miss F., Freud's case was the only one of anosmia in the psychoanalytic literature. Analytic writers have generally described cases of hyperosmia. (See for example, Abraham, 1927; Ferenczi, 1950; Jones, 1914; Brill, 1932; Fenichel, 1945; Friedman, 1959; Bieber, 1959; and Rosenbaum, 1961). Some of these authors describe the emergence of strong olfactory sensations under a variety of circumstances. For example, Abraham relates the exaggerated sense of smell with obsessional reactions. Brill describes a patient whose sexual potency was entirely dependent on the sense of smell. If a woman had any odor that the patient associated with his mother, he would become impotent. Even pouring perfume on the woman did not help. Friedman describes a case that manifested deep regression to anal-oral eroticism. This woman's entire psychic life seemed to be imbued with and governed by the sense of smell. Bieber has examined the dreams of patients in psychoanalytic treatment where olfaction was present during their dreams or appeared during their associations to them. He notes that the olfactory productions almost always refer to incestuous objects. Kalogerakis (1963) reports that the son of one of his patients had a remarkably well-developed sense of smell between the ages of two and five. Astonishingly the boy was able to detect by smell when his parents had had sexual intercourse the night before and so he would step back in obvious displeasure. Later he admitted that what he was reacting to was the parents' odor and he was invariably correct. A similar, but less extreme, observation was reported by Freud (1909) about the "Rat Man" who, as a child, recognized everyone by smell.

To summarize the above clinical observations, we can agree with Brill (1932) that the sense of smell is much more active and important in children than in adults. What happens to the sense of smell? According to Freud (1895), "to put it crudely, the current memory stinks just as an actual object may stink; and just as we turn away our sense organ (the head and the nose) in disgust, so do the preconscious and our conscious apprehension turn away from the memory. This is repression."

EVOLUTIONARY ASPECTS OF SENSE OF SMELL

In *Civilization and Its Discontents*, Freud (1930) discusses what he feels were the important changes that took place when man changed his posture from a four-legged animal to an erect animal. He postulates that the sense of smell was no longer as important for the sexual excitement of the male and that visual excitation became central in man. The genitals became visible when man assumed the erect posture and consequently required protection; according to Freud, they provoked the feeling of shame.

The incitement to cleanliness originates in an urge to get rid of the excreta, which have become disagreeable to the sense perceptions. We know that in the nursery things are different. The excreta arouse no disgust in children. They seem valuable to them as being a part of their own body, which has come away from it. Here upbringing insists with special energy on hastening the course of development which lies ahead, and which should make the excreta worthless, disgusting, abhorrent, and abominable. Such a reversal of values would scarcely be possible if the substances that are expelled from the body were not doomed by their strong smells to share the fate which overtook olfactory stimuli after man adopted the erect posture. Anal erotism, therefore, succumbs in the first instance to the "organic repression" which paved the way to civilization. The existence of the social factor which is responsible for the further transformation of anal erotism is attested by the circumstances that in spite of all man's developmental advances, he scarcely finds the smell of his own excreta repulsive, but only that of other people's. Thus a person who is not clean, who does not hide his excreta, is offending other people; he is showing no consideration for them. And this is confirmed by our strongest and commonest terms of abuse. It would be incomprehensible, too, that man should use the name of his most faithful friend in the animal world, the dog, as a term of abuse if that creature had not incurred his contempt through two characteristics: This is an animal whose dominant sense is that of smell and one which has no horror of excrement and is not ashamed of its sexual functions.

In the same year, C. D. Daly and R. S. White (1930), English psychoanalysts, agreed with Freud's basic postulates but added that from their own studies of mythology they concluded that the primary taboo was an incest taboo and not one on menstruation. They stated:

"There is evidence of odors of a subtle nature operating directly in the service of the functions of reproduction which are to be differentiated from the coprophilic odors. The interesting problem is why the conscious recognition of them is so repressed in man. I believe the solution is that of the inhibition of the sexual impulse from causes which were the inevitable result of the severity of the primary law of incest and taboos."

Thus, in an attempt to explain the apparently diminished significance of smell in human life as compared to animals, Daly substituted for Freud's concept of "organic" repression (the consequence of raising the nose from the ground), a psychological one, which relates repression of the sense of smell to the taboo against incest. Daly added: "The hypnotic sex-attractive odor given off by the female in 'heat' must have been one of man's greatest temptations to violate the incest taboo. Whilst the menstrual period, because of the flow of blood (which coincided with the strongest emanation of these odors) came to represent a terrible reminder of the consequences of violating this taboo."

The changes described above by Freud have been attributed to evolutionary developments. What is the present functional significance of the relatively large area in the central nervous system that once belonged entirely to the olfactory system? In addition to Freud's and Daly's postulations about the relationship between the sense or smell and sexuality, Grinker (1953) hypothesized that:

"The refinement of anxiety as a signal developed as the distant receptors evolved, especially that of olfaction, for this enabled the organism to project itself in future time and anticipate far ahead the satisfaction of needs or the presence of danger. The great forces by which sensory systems activate the cerebral cortex particularly affect the rhinencephalon or visceral brain which Herrick long ago stated exerts a tonic effect or learning pressure on the cerebral cortex. It is this primarily olfactory and secondarily visceral brain which, standing between inner signs of need or pressure (the 'I') and outer social symbols of safety and satisfaction (the 'not-I'), seems most vitally concerned in the development of the anxiety signal."

Grinker saw the sense of smell as originally helping the animal project itself into the distance to literally "smell out danger." As such, the sense of smell was the most sensitive sensory apparatus that could alert the animal to be prepared for danger. The infant, then, recognizes the mother by her smell. However, with growth and development the infant represses most of this ability to differentiate people on the basis of their smell. But we may still have the remnants of smell that Freud (1930) referred to. Smell has a primitive, phylogenetic meaning. For the infant, smell can warn of danger and also represent object-seeking. Later, when "organic repression" takes place, smell loses its function. When the repression is not successful, there is a clinical manifestation of hyperosmia, which has often been described in the literature.

The Case of Miss F.

Background

Miss F., a thirty-year-old secretary, sought psychoanalytic treatment for the first time because: "I am going to be thirty years old and I want to be married; but I only talk and never follow through with my relationships with men. I appear self-assured and cool, but inside I am very anxious. I just am not comfortable with myself.'' Her affect liability was striking and evidenced by her tendency to cry whenever discussing her feelings. She was dating a professional man who seemed stronger to her than other men who she had previously dated. She was worried, though, that he, like the others, would leave her.

The patient was the oldest of three children; she had a sister one and a half years younger and a brother three and a half years younger. The sister was described as outgoing, charming and a social butterfly; she was married and had two daughters. The brother was unmarried. The parents had immigrated to the United States from Europe when they were children. The father was retired but had a successful business career. He was a college graduate and was described as a man of the old world, authoritarian but warm and quite interested in his children. When the patient was seven, the father had a brief ''nervous breakdown.'' It manifested itself with a depression and phobias. The patient felt that when her father recovered, he was a much nicer person; therefore she had wanted her mother also to have a nervous breakdown. The mother was described as an outgoing, active, and efficient housewife, but she was nervous and often acted like a martyr. She was pretty, petite, and very feminine, very much like the patient's sister. The patient felt that her mother did not accept her and always wanted her to be like her sister. Physically, the patient strongly resembled her father.

During adolescence, the patient did not date much. She preferred to read or to play the piano. She did, however, have many girl friends. She often fantasied that ''a knight'' would come along and marry her. She was beginning to doubt whether that would indeed be the case. The patient denied having had any early sexual experiences. She claimed that she never thought of sex in adolescence and that she did not know about masturbation either. Her first sexual intercourse was at the age of 25.

The patient has had a long and involved history of allergic illnesses, which included severe hay fever and mild asthmatic attacks, but her last asthmatic attack was at the age of 19. She had a tonsillectomy at the age of nine. She was often examined by allergists and was always told that her problems were basically somatic. At the age of 12, the patient started to menstruate; at that time she also developed the symptom of anosmia, which had been complete until she entered treatment. At the age of 12 she also developed the habit of crying easily, especially when she felt sorry for herself.

Treatment

I will enumerate only those aspects of Miss F.'s psychoanalytic therapy that were relevant to the anosmia. As the relationship deepened, the patient began to react more strongly to separations. Before the analyst's first summer vacation, the patient has "accidentally" burned the front of her hairline while lighting the oven. She was not seriously hurt, although she was quite frightened. Later it became apparent that she had reacted to her fantasy that the analyst would die in an airplane crash during his vacation and therefore had turned the aggression onto herself. For a short time during her fifth and sixth month of analysis, the patient's resistance became more manifest. Any interpretation I would make, she "had already thought about prior to his mentioning it." She also became irritated each time I interrupted her flow of "free association." She was intensely competitive with all patients, with a strong wish (and need) to be considered the favorite. She was also intensely curious about my wife's personality and talents. It was all part of a generalized form of resistance that the patient had manifested. She used the relationship with her boyfriend to avoid deeper involvement in the analysis. This resistance defended against a masochistic position and had strong phallic components. She did not want to become vulnerable, "like other women," and so she strove to compete with men. Therefore, she defended herself against the basic identification with her mother, who was seen as a depreciated housewife. She could only allow herself to become committed to her analysis after her boyfriend had left Chicago for another city without marrying her.

Her main conflicts centered around: 1. Defense against identification with her mother which led to a preference for weak male friends who were "below her"; 2. Strong sibling rivalry which forced her to regress to an earlier (pregenital) psychic organization; her problem with separation anxiety was reexperienced and worked through during the analysis; 3. Oedipal guilt, which manifested itself in masculine protest type behavior.

To summarize, the patient developed a transference neurosis that was eventually resolved during the analysis. The analysis lasted 457 hours and the patient had a successful termination. There were no unusual technical variations or parameters used in this analysis. The symptom of anosmia was of special interest and so the rest of the paper will focus on this.

Anosmia

After hour 112 the erotic transference intensified; for the first time the patient was able to talk openly about her sexual feelings in general, and specifically to mention the fact that she could not reach orgasm. She expressed anger at that time, mainly toward her sister. Shortly afterward, the patient went home for Christmas, the first time since beginning analysis. The first night at her sister's house she had the following dream: "I came to a room where I was supposed to be. The corridor leading to the room was decorated in a fancy way like Versailles. The air in the room was smoky and I tried to open the door but could not. I thought that someone might come and help me, if not, I would die. Then, I said, 'Ray, I love you.' And I woke up.''

On awakening something dramatic happened to the patient: for the first time in 18 years she was able to smell. The return of the sense of smell has improved consistently throughout the analysis. The patient believed that the precipitating event for the dream was first, a phone call from Ray, her boyfriend, who promised to visit her on Christmas, and second, the fact that she felt angry at her sister that evening and later felt guilty about it. The smoke in the dream reminded her first of her father smoking cigars. It also reminded her of her brother's baby powder (the brother had suffered from severe eczema during his first year of life and therefore had special ointments and powders; his room always had a special odor that the patient could still recall). Since I was smoking a cigar while she was telling me her dream, I commented on the similarity between her father's and my smoking. The patient was absolutely amazed. She turned around to look at me and said, "I had never noticed it." Then she added laughingly, "But, then, of course, I could never smell before." The patient's associations to the corridor that resembled the one at Versailles led to the fact that my office was at the end of a long corridor.

I perceived the disappearance of the symptom as a transference manifestation signaling the onset of the "transference cure." The data presented above can be summarized psychodynamically in the following way: Anosmia is due to repression of sexuality and oedipal rivalry with special environment factors contributing to formation of the symptom (such as the father's smoking or the brother's "smelly" medications).

The patient then began to develop a more intense transference neurosis. Soon thereafter she realized that there was a connection between her sexual feelings and the sense of smell. She thought the smell might mean menstruation and womanhood (bearing children) to her. She felt that women were vulnerable and easily attacked; consequently they had to be extremely careful. She also mentioned in passing the wish to exhibit herself.

In hour 290, shortly before the second Christmas vacation, the patient recalled that her mother always liked to use perfume; she had many bottles of it on her dressing table. The patient remembered that she had a strong impulse to do either or both of the following: to use her mother's perfume on herself in order to smell as good as she, or to smash all of her mother's perfume bottles with one stroke.

A few months later, the patient developed an intense fantasy about being pregnant; she wanted to have a baby by the analyst. For one week during that period she felt bloated, nauseated, and dizzy, with the underlying fantasy that she was pregnant. A short time later the patient was able to experience orgasm for the first time (hour 359). After that experience she began to show the first signs of entering the termination stage.

I would like to examine in more detail the meaning of the sense of smell and its subsequent loss to this patient. But first, let us turn to the relevant psychoanalytic literature.

DISCUSSION

Smell as a percept is so closely related to affect that we will focus on the meaning of smell from the affective point of view. We will attempt to trace the development of Miss F.'s anosmia in light of her major childhood traumata. Although we can never fully answer the question of why a patient chooses a particular neurosis or symptom, we believe that by illustrating the factors that contributed to the formation of the symptom of anosmia in Miss F., we should be able to understand more about smell and its relationship to other experiences in the developing child.

The symptom of anosmia in our patient can be traced developmentally in the following way:

1. The sense of smell was an important affect for Miss F. in her first year of life as part of her normal development. It allowed her to feel close to her mother (that is, secure, trusting, and confident). Whenever she smelled her mother's body she recathected the image of her mother. This early object relationship helped Miss F. in the separation process and to begin developing her own sense of self. Therefore, it served partly as an anxiety-controlling mechanism.

. The patient probably began to feel rejected by the mother at the age of one and a half when her sister was born. At the age of three and a half, when the brother was born, the patient was even more neglected by the mother; as a result, her feelings of rejection intensified. She probably had the fantasy of giving birth to a child herself, anally, in competition with her mother. The smelly medication used to treat the brother's eczema increased her fantasy of the brother as an "anal production." It also helped the patient connect the sense of smell with the brother's presence, that is, with the absence of the mother. The patient tied the percept of smell with her mother and thus perceived it as an external trauma; in order to heal the narcissistic injury of being rejected by her mother, she developed a conflict regarding the sense of smell that laid the foundation for the later regression (Freud, 1936; Basch, 1968).

3. During the oedipal period, the father's smoking cigars intensified the patient's interest in smell. The partial identification with the father in the form of masculine protest helped to erotize the sense of smell. The numerous problems with the nose (due to allergies) during early latency helped to erotize the nose, and hence the olfactory mucosa, even further.

4. At the onset of puberty, the increase in instinctual energy brought about a new stress. The possibility that the patient would become a woman threatened her. Unconsciously, to her it meant that she would be able to bear

children like her mother, which symbolized extreme rejection. To her it also represented castration and mutilation, in short, the masochistic position. The possibility of becoming a mother reminded her of the threat of new siblings, an experience she could not tolerate. The patient associated her emerging sexuality (that is, menstruation) with feelings of shame and disgust; she associated smell with sexuality. Sexual feelings and impulses were intolerable to her. We postulated earlier that the sense of smell had been drawn into conflict. Under the new crisis of puberty her defenses had a hard time checking her anxiety. She had never developed good affect control since she began to cry often and "for no reason" (Fenichel, 1954; Peto, 1967).

5. Smell also symbolized her father's masculinity and her oedipal feelings toward him. It seems reasonable to postulate that at this point in the patient's life she used the defense of massive repression; its function was as follows: "If I cannot smell that I am menstruating, then I am not menstruating." At this point the conversion symptom of anosmia appeared; its development was overdetermined. By that time the patient's upper respiratory system in general and her nose in particular had become hypercathected. It is entirely possible that the nose as an organ was also the site of displaced sexual feelings. Miss F. was often preoccupied with her severe allergy and undoubtedly also obtained certain sexual gratifications from the many sensations in her nose (for example, the frequent manipulations of her nose by doctors, and adenoidectomies). The sense of smell was, therefore, repressed when the patient became overwhelmed with her newly emerging sexual feelings, which she connected with the sense of smell. Olfactory sensations were insufficiently integrated into her ego because of her childhood experiences. These two considerations, together with the fact that the nose was a hypercathected organ, made it possible for Miss F. to choose the symptom of anosmia.

This symptom had certain obvious conversion qualities. It is interesting that such a phylogenetically primitive sensory modality became involved. Part of the answer lies in the specific environmental circumstances that combined traumatic experiences for this patient with smell. The patient's difficulties with separation might refer her to an ego that had difficulties coping with separation and individuation (that is, the patient felt trapped by her murderous rage and had to institute an archaic defense against the emerging feelings). Hence, it is possible to speculate that the repression of smell was instituted because of its anal, destructive connotations. This utilization of a primitive modality must be seen in the context of a relatively well-functioning ego. In other words, we have here one of those rare patients who has a broad spectrum between primary and secondary processes and can utilize a large variety of defenses. The symptom was overdetermined and persisted for 18 years. The patient was unable to achieve orgasm during that time; although she functioned relatively well, she could not accept her identification and function as a woman. She was terrified of marriage and childbirth, although she often stated that she wanted nothing better than to settle down and have a family.

When the patient began analysis much affect was mobilized. She alternated between father, mother, and sibling transferences, but most affect was elicited during the phases when the threat of separation (for example, vacation of the analyst) was imminent. Her rage at her siblings and her mother that had been repressed slowly returned. As the patient experienced these feelings as well as sexual feelings toward the analyst, she no longer needed to deny her various childhood experiences. As her repression lifted she no longer needed to disavow her sense of smell. It is our impression that the patient needed both the positive transference toward the analyst and the working through of the sexual transference in order to regain her sense of smell. Once she had regained the sense of smell, she spent many months delighting in the new experience, trying new aromas, and in general reegotizing the sense of smell. She often felt like smearing and dirtying the analyst's office. She also discovered that the odor from his cigar stank (now that she could smell it)! As she began to work through these conflicts she was able to enjoy sexual relations on a mature level. They no longer threatened her existence. She could tolerate anxiety well within the ego and had no need to externalize, that is, to disavow her affect, her rage, or her sexuality; hence, the repression could be lifted and so the symptom disappeared.

Many questions remain unanwered at this juncture. Why did Miss F. develop the very rare symptom of anosmia at the onset of puberty? Why did she not develop bouts of it at an earlier period? And, finally, why is this symptom so rarely encountered by psychoanalysts in their practice, in comparison with hyperosmia, for example? These questions remain to be answered in the future.

Epilogue

Four years after Miss F. terminated, the author met her in a restaurant by chance. She seemed pleased to meet the therapist. She told him that two years after she terminated she got married to her boyfriend. She has one daughter. During the pregnancy she almost called the therapist. She had developed a hysterical blindness in one eye which lasted for two days. Soon after she decided to consult her former analyst for consultation, the blindness disappeared!

It seems that the patient once again developed a conversion reaction, when under stressful conditions (pregnancy) her regression was not as far back as when the symptom of anosmia appeared. With the working through of her original neurotic conflict she was able to cope with the stress and work it through herself. The fantasy of seeing her therapist was enough to reinstate her defenses and ward off the impulses and the regressive pull.

SUMMARY AND CONCLUSION

A case of psychogenic anosmia was presented and the pertinent psychoanalytic literature reviewed, in order to explore the following: 1. The role of smell in early object relationships and its relationship to affect; 2. The relationship between smell and sexuality; 3. The possible developmental linkage between organic repression and the later development of the conversion symptom of anosmia; and 4. The resolution of the symptom of anosmia in the course of psychoanalytic treatment and its relationship to the development of a therapeutic alliance.

References

Abraham, K., *Selected papers*. London: Hogarth Press, 1927.

Basch, M., *"External Reality and Disavowal."* Unpublished manuscript, 1968.

Bieber, I., "Olfaction in sexual development and adult sexual organization." *Amer. J. Psych.*, 8:851-868 (1959).

Breuer, J., and Freud, S. (1895). "Studies on hysteria." *Standard Edition*, Vol. 2. London: Hogarth Press, 1955.

Brill, A. A., "The sense of smell in the neurosis and the psychosis." *Psychoanal. Quart.* 1:7-16 (1932).

Daly, D. D., and White, R. S., "Psychic reactions to olfactory stimuli." *Brit. Journ. Med. Psychol.*, 10:70-84 (1930).

Fenichel O., *The Psychoanalytic Theory of Neurosis*. New York: Norton, 1954.

_____. "The ego and the affects." In *The Collected Papers of Otto Fenichel*. 2nd series. New York: Norton, 1945.

Ferenczi, S., "The ontogenesis of the interest in money." In *Sex in Psychoanalysis*. New York: Basic Books, 1950.

Freud, S. (1896), *The Origins of Psychoanalysis*, M. Bonaparte, A. Freud and E. Kris, eds. New York, Basic Books, 1954.

____ (1909), "Notes upon a case of obsessional neurosis." *Standard Edition*, Vol. 10, London: Hogarth Press, 1955.

____ (1930), *Civilization and its Discontents, Standard Edition*, Vol. 21, London: Hogarth Press, 1961.

____ (1936), "A disturbance of memory on the Acropolis." *Standard Edition*, Vol. 22, London: Hogarth Press, 1964.

Friedman, P., "Some observations on the sense of small." *Psychoanal. Quart.*, 28:307-329 (1959).

Grinker, R. R., *Psychosomatic Research*. New York: W. W. Norton, 1953.

Jones, E. (1914), The Madonna's conception through the ear." In *Essays in Applied Psychoanalysis*. London: Hogarth Press, 1951.

Kalogerakis, M.D., "The role of olfaction in sexual development." *Psychosom. Med.*, 25:420-432 (1963).

Peto, A., "On affect control." *Psychoanal. Study Child*, 22:36-51 (1967).

Rosenbaum, J.R., "The significance of the sense of smell in the transference." *J. Amer. Psychoanal. Assoc.*, 98:312-325 (1961).

Chapter XVIII

The Residential Treatment of Anorexia Nervosa

Bertram J. Cohler, Ph.D.

Anorexia nervosa refers to a syndrome characterized by a psychologically determined refusal of food. Not a specific nosological entity, and associated with a variety of both psychotic and nonpsychotic disorders, this disturbance occurs primarily in young women between the ages of about twelve and thirty. While loss of weight and emaciation are the most significant clinical symptoms, most female patients experience both amenorrhea and constipation, probably as a result of the nutritional deficit which accompanies loss of weight.

Recent reviews of the extensive literature in this area arrive at several common conclusions (Nemiah, 1958; Bliss and Branch, 1960; Thomas, 1961; Kaufman and Heiman, 1964; Bruch, 1965, 1966, 1970a, 1970b; Rowland, 1970; Gifford, Murawski, and Pilot, 1970; and Thander, 1970): (1) Quite often, symptoms are directly connected with present interpersonal and intrapsychic conflicts; (2) anorexia nervosa symbolizes both the basic issues of feeding, orality, and nurturing care of the original mother-child relationship, and the expectation of care which is repeated anew in the transference; (3) about ten percent of all anorexic patients die during treatment, a fatality rate which is relatively high for psychiatric illnesses. The possibility of fatal outcome presents a particularly difficult problem for the therapist, who feels both personally and professionally threatened by the failure of his patient to thrive and to respond to psychotherapy. The treatment of anorexia highlights issues both of transference and countertransference in ways which can provide greater understanding of these issues in psychiatric treatment.

The present paper is concerned with certain problems in the psychotherapeutic treatment of anorexic patients, as illustrated by the detailed case presentation of a late-adolescent girl who, for the past five years, has been in a residential treatment center for children and adolescents. Through the discussion of this case, we shall attempt to show that the treatment of anorexia nervosa is so difficult because of the fact that, as a result both of the patient's transference and her therapist's reaction to this transference, it is difficult for the therapist to maintain perspective on the adaptive significance of the patient's symptoms (Eissler, 1943; Berlin, Boatman, Sheimo, and Szurek, 1951; Palazzoli, 1971). However, before discussing this case, we should consider briefly the problems involved in the treatment of this syndrome.

COUNTERTRANSFERENCE IN THE TREATMENT OF ANOREXIA NERVOSA

Typically, the therapist is only consulted when the patient's physical condition has seriously deteriorated, increasing the risk of a fatal outcome. The patient's disturbance continues to be reflected in her emaciation, and weight gained is frequently lost during periods of crisis in psychotherapy, leading to increased criticism of the treatment from both the patient's family and from fellow mental health professionals. Such criticisms tend to make the therapist feel inadequate to provide good treatment, a feeling which is intensified by his patient's challenge that he cannot be of help and that she will never get well. In addition, the therapist is often faced with the prospect of treating a patient who does not believe that she is ill and who is terrified of the possibility that her therapist might attempt to control her food intake and attempt to control her life.

Considering the intense feelings of anger and despair evoked by the therapist by prolonged psychotherapeutic contact with anorexic patients, it is little wonder that those who find themselves in the position of having to treat such patients often have recourse to behavioral manipulation and modification. Although such behavioral approaches do not yield sustained favorable results superior to those obtained with the best intensive psychotherapy, even psychodynamically oriented reports attempt to resolve the problems resulting from the therapist's feelings of frustration by recommending manipulative procedures in the treatment of anorexic patients (Eissler, 1943; Groen and Feldman-Toledano, 1966; Bachrach, Erwin, and Mohr, 1965; Lang, 1965; Hallsten, 1965; Leitenberg, Agras, and Thomoson, 1968; Blinder, Freedman, and Stunkard, 1970).

Psychotherapy with anorexic patients leads to intense emotional reactions in the therapist; perhaps the most intense one encounters in a therapeutic relationship. However, the capacity of the therapist to bear these feelings of anger, hopelessness, manipulation, and powerlessness is of the greatest importance for the treatment process. It is precisely when the patient can attribute these feelings to a therapist who can accept and endure these feelings himself, that the patient is first able to achieve personality change and to experience a greater sense of intrapsychic integration.

Having attributed her distress to her therapist, the patient has successfully been able to split off the hating and bad internal object from the loving and good internal object and, having kept out and kept in check the bad object, she is able to perceive herself as a worthy person who can be in control of her own life. She is then able to relax her need for inner control which first motivated the development of anorexic symptoms (Sours, 1969; Palazzoli, 1970, 1971). The problem in psychotherapy with anorexic patients is not that of fostering such splitting of the ego, for the defense of splitting already exists as a characteristic of the patient's arrested emotional development (Freud, 1939;

Klein, 1952; Winnicott, 1950-55). The problem is that of fostering the therapist's capacity to bear and sustain these painful feelings, and to accept the discomfort which develops as an inevitable concomitant to feeling so intensely the patient's pain and despair.

We believe that the therapist's feelings of anger and hopelessness in the treatment of anorexic patients is a genuine and intrinsic part of the treatment process and not, as is often believed, an element of countertransference. The latter is typically regarded as the therapist's reactions to the patient which are based on his earliest childhood experiences and which prevent him from being able to react to the patient as a separate person. The concept of counter-transference assumes that affective reactions to the patient interfere with the therapist's objectivity and, therefore, are harmful to treatment. Indeed, Freud recommends that the analyst adopt an attitude of emotional distance modeled after that of the surgeon (1912, p. 114). This recommendation must be inte-grated with Freud's advice (1912) that the analyst use his unconscious as an instrument in the analysis.

Two separate aspects of the psychotherapeutic process are often confused when defining the concept of countertransference: (1) feelings which are based on the therapist's own prior life history and relationships with signifi-cant figures in his own parental family and (2) feelings which arise from the therapist's sensitivity to the patient's self and to the patient's characteristic relations with others.

Feelings toward the patient which are based on the therapist's own prior life history and from the therapist's own unresolved intrapsychic conflicts, as determined by his entire life history, are those which are typically classified as countertransference. Typical of such countertransference reactions is that of the therapist who forgets an appointment with a patient who is, at the point in treatment, dealing with inner conflicts, the content of which are relevant to the therapist's own unresolved conflicts.

These countertransference feelings must be differentiated from another as-pect of what is often viewed as a component of countertransference—the therapist's affective response to the patient's feelings which stem from the patient's transference and which, when detected by the therapist's sensitivity, is of positive therapeutic value. Typical of such feelings are those of a therapist treating a desperate, suicidal patient who feels overwhelmed by a desperate need to help the patient. The therapist's feelings of being over-whelmed are his empathic response to his patient's inner distress.

If the therapist can accept and contain these painful feelings, then the patient may be able to free himself from them, and experience symptom relief. In the case of the suicidal patient, if the therapist becomes the bad, evil, or unacceptable part of the self, while the patient adopts the benign or positive aspect of the self, the fact that the therapist can feel overwhelmed and desperate may make it possible for the patient to feel some hope. In order for this process to have a therapeutic effect, the therapist must maintain his own objective and self-observing function at the same time that he is experiencing the patient's feeling of being desperate and overwhelmed. If he is *only* detached and objective, or if he is *only* feeling desperate and overwhelmed, he cannot be helpful to the patient.

EARLY CHILDHOOD: DEVELOPMENT OF SYMBIOSIS AND CONFLICT REGARDING CONTROL

Two themes emerge in the review of the literature regarding the etiology of anorexia nervosa: (1) conflict regarding the patient's capacity for individuation and for resolution of the mother-infant symbiosis (Mahler, 1968, 1972a, 1972b), and (2) feelings of loss of control of her capacity to determine her own life (Sours, 1969). All published reports which consider the importance of family relationships in the development of this syndrome stress the significance of the mother's personality, life experiences, and relationship with her daughter from birth through adolescence as the most critical factor determining the daughter's development of anorexia (Cohler, 1972b). To summarize features observed repeatedly in these studies, we can describe a hypothetical paradigm: The mother of the typical anorexic patient is an emotionally immature woman who feels that she received poor maternal care. She was, and continues to be, dependent upon her own mother, a controlling woman who provides criticism but little support, and who feels an obligation to direct her daughter's life. This issue of control reaches a climax with the prospective patient's birth. At this time, the mother's mother attempts to run the family and to care for her daughter during her confinement and the immediate postpartum period while, at the same time, remaining aloof and critical of her daughter's child-care attitudes and practices.

The daughter feels unprepared to become a mother and resents having to care for another when she, herself, still wants to be cared for as an infant. She is uncertain of the meaning of the baby's cry or of the relationship between signs of the baby's distress, and inner needs such as hunger. Feeling unfulfilled herself, she cannot understand her infant's needs as different from her own unmet needs. Since she could not understand the manner in which she might get her own inner needs cared for, she feels unprepared to care for her infant daughter. In addition, because the infant is a girl, self-object differentiation is even more difficult for the mother.

During childhood, the mother of the prospective patient controls her daughter's life just as her own mother had controlled her life. Unable to "let go" or to foster individuation, she remains tied to her daughter in special ways that are not true for other children in the family. At the same time, her daughter is willing to be compliant and is an especially helpful girl who enjoys emulating her own mother's life, particularly that part of her mother's life which focuses on food preparation. She also emulates her mother's concerns regarding eating, weight loss, and inner control, adopting her mother's regulatory mechanisms of control, and becoming domineering over herself.

During adolescence, experiencing renewed conflict regarding self-control, the prospective patient relies even more on the mechanism of strict self-control which she had learned from her own mother who was both controlling of her and controlled by the mother's mother. At the same time, the prospective patient experiences the demands of adolescence that she achieve greater psychological distance between herself and her own mother as a threat to this impulse-control system which was founded upon emulation of her mother. Unable to accept the extent to which she was dependent upon her own mother for the maintenance of inner controls, and fearing both this dependence upon her mother, as well as the possible loss of this dependence, she begins to attack her mother's domineering and controlling behavior. Feeling defeated and controlled by her mother and, without recourse, she attempts to demonstrate inner control in terms of limiting her intake of food.

There are several reasons why food so often becomes the focus of this conflict regarding control. In the first place, eating represents a highly cathected area of the patient's life, in which conflict over control had already been experienced earlier in life, both intrapersonally and interpersonally. This concern is heightened by the emphasis in contemporary culture upon slimness in women, in which renouncing food becomes a sign of "will-power" and of control over one's impulse to eat and realize immediate gratification. Control of food intake has fairly immediate and direct consequences, for changes in body proportions and loss of weight can be observed fairly clearly and directly, and can be clearly measured by such evidence as being able to wear smaller-size clothes. The ability to observe so directly this tangible evidence of inner control, as evidenced by the ability to refuse what is desired, becomes an important source of reassurance that other disturbing impulses may also be controlled, and that such control can come from within, rather than from without, in the person of the punishing and controlling mother.

Finally, it should be noted that dieting serves as a proof that the patient can control her own desire to swallow up other persons. As long as she is able to refuse food, and sees that she is becoming slimmer, she can be certain that she has not realized her own wish to perpetuate her symbiosis with her mother by having her mother live inside of her where she is always and immediately available.

What starts as an attempt to demonstrate the capacity for control of dangerous impulses becomes a process of emaciation which goes beyond what even the patient had expected to take place. Since hunger signals have been confused since earliest infancy and since it has always been difficult for the prospective patient to be certain when she was hungry, failure to eat at the usual times leads gradually to a loss of hunger signals and, over time, diminution of the desire to eat. The patient is unaware of the extent to which her control of her eating threatens her very life, and cannot understand why it should be that her parents and others should become concerned about her weight loss. Of course, the daughter's refusal to eat and subsequent loss of interest in food lead her mother to become increasingly anxious about the quality of her own nurturant care; and the ensuing guilt increases the mother's determination that her daughter should eat, and, in turn, this determination intensifies the daughter's determination not to eat and surrender her control and yield to her mother's wishes by eating.

The conflict regarding control now becomes a real conflict in the mother-daughter relationship, and as long as the daughter can resist her mother's demands, she can assure herself that she has the necessary control to avoid impending inner chaos. As her mother becomes ever more anxious and controlling in the attempt to make her daughter eat, her daughter becomes even more determined not to eat for she must be able to prove to herself her continuing capacity for control: As long as she does not give in to her mother she can both test and prove her capacity for inner control. For the daughter, although clearly not for her mother, the issue is primarily one of control rather than of survival. Of course, the longer the conflict between mother and daughter continues, the more important it is to the daughter to refuse food. Feeling dominated by her mother, food refusal becomes her only means for obtaining control of her own life. It is usually at the time when the patient has lost more than a quarter of her original weight that the family first seeks psychiatric assistance.

SYNDROME AND TREATMENT: THE CASE OF ROSE

At the time of her enrollment in residential treatment, our patient, whom we shall call Rose, was fifteen years old and had been cachectic for more than two years. A frail, beautiful girl, with long, dark brown hair, and intense, sad brown eyes, her emaciation only accentuated the delicacy of her appearance which, according to her mother, had been evident even in earliest infancy. Rose had always been a sad and frail child. Indeed, her mother notes that the first thing that she observed after Rose was born was how delicate she appeared to be.

Rose's intensity was keenly felt by other family members who regarded her as a distant, brooding, and somewhat menacing person. Her constant criticism of the apparent superficiality of other family members was particularly unusual in her family and neighborhood. Primarily Italian in ethnic background, most members of this lower-class neighborhood in a large Midwestern city share a common outlook on the world which is cautious, conservative, and prosaic. Rose's devotion to the church was also unusual in its fervor, even in a culture in which women, in particular, are devout and dependent upon the church (Parsons, 1969).

Catholicism has particular significance for Rose. As early in the morning as her father, a plumber, might arise in order to be at work by seven, Rose, his third child and eldest daughter, was always awake before him. At the age of thirteen, Rose regularly attended early morning Mass. She said that she enjoyed awakening early in the morning. At any rate, she had great difficulty sleeping, and she would arise frequently in the middle of the night to pace the floor. Often, she would encourage her mother to sleep while she fixed breakfast for her father, a task which she particularly enjoyed.

Nowhere in the daily routine was Rose's personality so strongly felt as at mealtimes. Cooking was regarded as an important skill for a woman to have, and both Rose's mother and grandmother were superb cooks. Even Rose's grandmother, who criticized almost every other aspect of Mrs. M.'s life, admitted that she was a good cook.

After the onset of her illness, Rose continued to help her mother in the kitchen. She displayed grace as she served her parents, two older brothers, and younger brother. There was only one incongruous element: after serving her family, she did not eat what she had helped to cook, but retired to the kitchen where she nibbled at rare roast beef and red Jello, which she insisted upon preparing by herself. Furthermore, she refused to sit with the rest of the family, explaining that "it made her sick" to watch other family members "stuff" themselves.

Everyone in her family and all her classmates in school knew that something profound was troubling Rose. When Rose walked into the room the girls in her classroom at the parochial school would cease their conversation in much the same way as when Sister came into the room. It was clear that she exercised the same influence over classmates that she exercised over her family. Her best friend at school, with whom she had grown up, said she was "mystified" about how best to help her. This capacity to mystify others is one of the most striking aspects of Rose's personality. She is both pleased and terrified of her capacity to baffle others, and even to baffle herself. In residential treatment, her continual question, which she poses to all who work with her, is whether they think they really understand what is "bothering" her and can help her to get well. She claims to feel a strange and powerful force within her, completely alien, which she cannot control, and which pushes her to be frantic.

FAMILY BACKGROUND AND EARLY CHILDHOOD

Rose was born into a family in which there was considerable tension. The entire extended family was living together in one building, and Mrs. M. felt under great pressure to please her mother, a domineering and critical woman, who in Mrs. M.'s own words, "can hurt an awful lot by what she says and what she does." Mrs. M. notes that her stomach begins to seethe whenever her mother is around. Mrs. M.'s father was a man of special importance for her, and thirty-five years after his death she still mourns for him. Whenever she feels in need or hopes for a miracle, she prays to her father and, while she was still a young woman, whenever something particularly fortunate happened to the family, she would attribute this good fortune to the fact that her father was looking out for them from Heaven. This belief infuriated her mother, who deprecated her deceased father and teased Mrs. M. about her love for him. It is interesting to note that Rose almost always lights a candle for her deceased grandfather at morning Mass, as if she has joined her mother in mourning her grandfather (whom she never knew).

Mrs. M. and her mother have been involved in a complex and symbiotic relationship throughout their life and which became even more intense after Mr. M.'s marriage. Whereas earlier in their marriage, the M.s had lived by themselves, shortly after the second child was born they decided to move back into an apartment which had become vacant in the building in which Mrs. M.'s mother lived. With two boys to care for, and with her husband's erratic work schedule which was further complicated by the outbreak of the Korean war and his return to active military service, it seemed best to move back into her mother's building where Mrs. M. could receive help in caring for the boys. Mrs. M's brother and his family had also moved back into the building, some months prior to the M.'s decision to move, and this was also a factor in their own decision.

The three-generation extended family can provide support for members of each generation. However, it is more likely that such close living arrangements intensify conflicts previously existing in the family (Cohler, 1972). This proved to be the case with the M.s. Mrs. M. notes that much of her time was spent settling disputes between various relatives. As a result, her own children often wondered where she was and what was happening. At the same time, serving as peacemaker was a difficult task for Mrs. M., particularly in view of her own conflicts with her mother.

Mrs. M's mother has been critical of almost every aspect of her life including her marriage. Mrs. M.'s husband comes from the same cultural and religious background, to such an extent that Mr. and Mrs. M.'s mothers now share an apartment together and serve as co-leaders for the senior citizen group at their church. Despite this, Mr. M.'s mother was initially very critical of Mr. M.'s background and his family, and particularly of the fact that Mr. M.'s father had been hospitalized many times for chronic mental illness. Later, Mrs. M.'s mother was critical of the couple's decision to have several children and with each miscarriage or birth her criticisms of her daughter grew more strident. Finally, just after Mrs. M. told her mother she was pregnant with Rose, her mother complained to her that: "All you do in bed at night is to make love. Don't you ever sleep? Don't you ever do anything else?"

Mrs. M. had considerable difficulty carrying pregnancies to term, and preceding each birth, she had several miscarriages. Indeed, over an eight-year period, from 1949 to 1957, Mrs. M. was almost continually pregnant. Her mother had paid little attention to her when the boys were born but, when she heard that her daughter had had a girl, she showed real interest in her grandchildren for the first time. At the same time, as was so characteristic in her relationship with her daughter, she was very critical of the way in which Mrs. M. was caring for the new baby. As Mrs. M. says, in recalling this time just after Rose was born:

> "It was like my mother was having a baby all over again. I know she meant well, but she kept telling me what I should do with the baby. She was particularly concerned about how I was feeding Rose, and I *was* having trouble feeding her. With the boys I had plenty of milk, but, with Rose, my milk dried up and I couldn't continue breast feeding."

For Mrs. M., having a daughter must have been particularly difficult. Her difficulty in carrying to term had already led her to feel defective as a woman. As a child she had been envious of what she saw as her brother's relatively greater freedom, and the birth of her first daughter evoked conflicts regarding her own femininity that were not evoked by the birth of her two sons, who could provide her with the masculinity she envied.

The conflict between Mrs. M. and her mother, and the impact of this conflict on her capacity to care for her baby, are consistent with the literature on the personality of mothers of anorexic patients. In the first place, as Rowland (1970) and Gifford, Murawski, and Pilot (1970) have observed, the mother of the anorexic patient is, herself, involved in a complex and symbiotic fashion with her own mother, and one in which the mother's mother intrudes into the mother's relationship with her infant. Mrs. M.'s mother is quite obviously intrusive and controlling, and while Mrs. M. resents her mother's involvement, she also seeks it. She depends upon her mother's criticisms and advice and frequently calls or visits her several times a day. Unfortunately, these calls and visits provide little comfort or satisfaction. Mrs. M. reports that she is quite tense all the time, but that on days when she has visited her mother, she feels especially upset. In view of the fact that her daughter developed an eating disorder, it is particularly significant to note that Mrs. M. feels this tension particularly in her abdomen. Finally, just about the same time that Rose became anorexic, Mrs. M. developed a peptic ulcer for which she was hospitalized for several weeks. Following her doctor's suggestions, Mrs. M. no longer eats with her mother, nor does she spend long periods of time with her.

From the outset, Rose was a difficult baby to care for. Jaundiced following birth, she was frail and her pediatrician became concerned that she might die if she became ill. Indeed, she developed a febrile respiratory illness and was hospitalized for several days. Rose's feeding difficulty may have been due to her inability to suck very hard. Mrs. M. complained that because Rose was so listless and difficult to care for, she was never certain when Rose was hungry. Rose would fuss, but the fuss did not seem related to food and eating. As she observes:

> "From the beginning, Rose was never a good eater. She was slow and you had to coax her. Sometimes she would go to sleep over the bottle, while she was obviously hungry, and then one of her brothers would steal the bottle and finish what was left."

Mrs. M. notes that while she often held the bottle, there was so much to do around the house that sometimes she propped up the bottle while she did something for the other children or tended to some problem with her mother or brother.

Once more, we see a striking parallel between the literature on anorexia nervosa and Rose's early development. Bruch (1970d, 1971a) noted that the future anorexic patient is not taught in infancy that inner needs are related to satisfaction. Rose's mother could not read the cues which Rose provided of her needs, so consequently Rose never learned to connect inner hunger signals with food and with the satisfaction of hunger needs. Indeed, given the tendency of her brothers to take away her bottles, it is probable that Rose often went hungry. Of course, Rose's own constitution played a significant role in the development of this confusion about body signals. Her listlessness and lack of a strong drive to suck made it additionally difficult for her mother to determine whether Rose was hungry or full. In addition, her difficulties in learning to suck, her early hospitalization, and her mother's own inner tension all conspired to insure that Rose would not be able to feed from her mother's breast.

Mrs. M. reports that, as a young child, Rose showed relatively little feeling. Her mother remembers few times when she was either very happy or very sad. However, developmental milestones during early childhood were reached at the appropriate times, and Rose was able to sit up alone at five months, walked at about a year, and began talking in partial sentences by about the time she was a year and a half old. There was little difficulty in toilet training. Mrs. M. resolved, at about twenty months, that her daughter should be toilet-trained and, within about a week, she had "gotten hold" of Rose's urine and bowel movements; one she had established this control, Rose's control never again failed. In Mrs. M.'s description of how she toilet-trained her daughter, we see the beginning of her determined control of her daughter's behavior which continued to the time of Rose's admission to residential treatment and which, together with the mother-daughter symbiosis, contributed so significantly to the development of Rose's later disturbance.

Illness in Mother and Daughter: Dieting as an Expression of the Symbiosis

Beginning with the sixth grade, Rose began to show violent rage when there was even the most minimal disturbance of order in the home. At about this same time, Mrs. M. had become increasingly preoccupied with her relationship with her own mother. It was during this time that Mrs. M. first complained of the pain in her abdomen which was to be diagnosed within the next months as an ulcer. At the same time, Mrs. M.'s doctor told her that she must begin to lose weight in order to control hypertension, which was diagnosed at about the same time as her ulcer. As Mrs. M. commented:

"Everyone was yelling at me that I was too fat. At that time, I weighed 179 pounds and the doctors said I had to lose at least fifty pounds."

In addition, at about the same time Mrs. M. began to experience menopause. This change, together with her illness and a subsequent hospitalization where she nearly died from internal bleeding associated with the recurrence of her ulcer, could not have come at a worse time for Rose. Just as she was beginning to notice changes in her own body, her mother became seriously ill; and just as she was beginning to menstruate, her mother was experiencing menopause. At a time when Rose's temper was becoming more difficult to control than before, as, indeed, was true for other aspects of her impulse life, her mother was hospitalized with a life-threatening illness.

Rose felt that she was responsible for her mother's illness and feared that growing up would mean that she would suffer the same fate as her mother. Rose's guilt and feeling of responsibility for her mother's illness were increased by her father's admonition to the family, just prior to her mother's return from the hospital, that any conflict within the family, any expression of anger or any discussion which might lead to tension within the family, would cause a repetition of Mrs. M.'s illness.

At this time, Rose felt abandoned by her mother, angry at her, guilty about the supposed effects of her anger, and unable to express this guilt or anger, except toward herself. It was at this time that Rose first began going to Mass each morning, hoping in some way to receive forgiveness for the sin which she felt she had committed against her mother.

After her illness, Mrs. M. had to be extremely careful about her diet. Rose was especially sensitive to this issue of dieting and becoming fat and ill like her mother. Becoming an adult meant becoming like her mother, a possibility which was particularly frightening to her since Rose was little able to differentiate between her mother and herself. In addition, she felt that her mother was envious of the fact that she had reached womanhood at a time when her mother had just reached the menopause. To grow up was to provoke her mother's jealousy, a theme which has been repeated throughout Rose's psychotherapy, but is nowhere as explicitly stated as in her story to a card in the Phillipson (1955) picture thematic series:

> It seems like this mother, or whatever she is, looks very frustrated after having one of these fights with her daughter who of course doesn't want her to go out, because she thinks that it's too early and she does not feel like doing anything. Because she was out really late the night before. And this mother was really jealous whenever her daughter does go out with some boyfriend or whatever. She just wants to beat her up in any way she can. And she wants to try to make her daughter very ugly by working her down to the bone. The daughter just lies there cursing her mother, not really giving a damn whatever she does or what she says. The daughter feels like if it takes killing her mother to go out, then she'll do it.

This somewhat confused story tells the story of a mother-daughter conflict of such intensity that one or the other must be destroyed. At the beginning of the story, it is not clear whether it is the daughter who does not want the mother to go out or the mother who does not want the daughter to go out. In view of Rose's difficulties in separating from her mother, it is consistent with her conflict regarding this issue of separation and closeness that she should resent her mother's own life and interests. At the same time, the mother in the story jealously resents her daughter's adolescence and her attractiveness to boys, in just the manner described by Anthony (1970). The mother will retaliate in the manner of Cinderella's mother, by working her daughter "to the *bone*" (surely, an important metaphor in an anorexic adolescent) and the alternative which the daughter sees to being killed by the mother is to kill her mother. The only means for avoiding a situation of either killing or being killed is not to grow up and become a woman, and one sure way of not growing up is not to eat.

Each of the issues of dieting, eating, fatness and slimness, pregnancy and impulse control were involved in Rose's decision, shortly after her mother's return from the hospital, to go on a strict diet in which she ate one sparse meal each day. Since one is not supposed to eat before attending Mass, obviously Rose could not eat at breakfast. Lunch was a hurried time, between classes, so there was little time in which to eat. This left supper, which was always the same: thin slices of lean, rare roast beef, and red Jello. Even the choice of these foods for a diet is interesting. Rose insisted upon lean beef in order to insure that she would not become "fat." Fatness meant both becoming like her mother and, ultimately, requiring hospitalization for hypertension and ulcers, together with the fatness of pregnancy which she had seen over and over throughout her childhood. Issues of eating, control, and pregnancy became confused in Rose's mind, as the following picture thematic story demonstrates:

To me, this looks like someone's getting scared. This one looks like he or she is in despair or is going to *eat this person or control it, or have a baby,* or something. This picture here looks like someone who is just kind of helpless. I also think it's an ugly picture. (Examiner: What's going to happen, what's the outcome?) The person will eventually fall apart . . . the helpless person.

Rose's view of her mother's care was parallel with the Hansel and Gretel fairy tale: her mother provided her with food in order to fatten her up to eat her. For Rose, childhood is a process of slow torture in which the child is fattened up by the mother, and, as the victim, the child is slowly driven crazy by the mother's care. The way in which to prevent the catastrophe of being eaten is to turn passivity into activity and to diet, becoming nothing but unappetizing skin and bones. However, there is another component to this fear of being eaten: projection of Rose's wish to eat others (Klein, 1937, 1952; Kernberg, 1966). From this perspective, dieting serves as reassurance that the wish is not being translated into action. However, Rose was able to find a compromise with this wish to eat others in the form of both sacred and profane diet rituals. For Rose, communion was the most important part of the religious ceremony, and she seldom missed an opportunity to receive communion, and the wine and the wafer which are said to represent the blood and the body of Jesus. Her diet of red Jello and rare roast beef may be viewed as the profane parallel to the sacred communion diet.

This fear of loss of control and of cannibalism is enacted repeatedly in Rose's response to the Rorschach blots. Typical of these responses is her response to card II:

(II., 2.) This part of it here (top red) reminds me of two parts staring into each other. Like one part, but it is split, being cut into half, I guess.

(Inquiry). The two faces you can tell, these are two faces, I'm sure of that, these are mouths and it looks like they are going at each other and they look more evil than happy . . .

For Rose, control is necessary both as a protection against eating her mother, and as a protection against being eaten by her mother, and either outcome is equally possible since, in her mind, images of mother and daughter are fused. Since she interpreted her mother's continual pregnancies and miscarriages during her childhood as fatness, they provided confirming evidence for her belief that her mother swallowed people, for first her mother became fat and then she went to the hospital and came home with a new person who had been cut out of her. A strict diet serves as protection against swallowing up another, although the content of the diet provides a compromise with the impulse to swallow another and to have the other inside of her. At the same time, if she is emaciated, she will not be a palatable object, and she can forestall the possibility of being eaten herself. *Dieting represents one means of defending against the symbiosis, for the concept of eating and being eaten is, in itself, a respresentation of a destructive symbiosis in which one no longer exists, except as a part of another.*

In Rose's life there was certainly evidence of a problem of separating from her mother. She began life prevented from being her own person and separate from her mother. Rose was born on the anniversary of Mrs. M.'s own father's death. From the outset, Rose already stood for another person of critical significance in her mother's own life. Then, to make matters even more difficult, Mrs. M.'s own mother first became involved with Mrs. M.'s children only at the time of Rose's birth, forcing Mrs. M. to struggle for her own autonomy with her mother, which further deprived Rose of her mother's attention. It is especially important, in view of Rose's problems in establishing transference relationships in treatment, to note that she has never forgiven her mother for being so able to control her life, that, as she believed, her mother could even arrange for the date of her birth.

In view of these psychological issues, it is not difficult to understand why it was that Rose's overt disturbance began at the time or in the manner that it did. Immediate precipitants included her mother's illness, her impending graduation from grammar school, which is a "rite of passage" marking entrance into the world of adolescence, her own physical development and beginning of menses, and her mother's almost simultaneous menopause. The fact of her mother's diet provided a means for Rose to emulate her mother's behavior and to use aspects of her identification with her mother as a means for fostering her own adaptation to both intrapsychic and intrafamilial conflict. Since dieting provided Rose with a means for dealing with her own conflict, it represented a truly significant achievement of the ego. Without the control provided by the dieting and later by her anorexia, Rose believes she would have been flooded with anxiety, would have experienced complete psychic disorganization, and, ultimately, would have been devoured. Dieting represented an active solution where passivity would have led to inner chaos.

The alternative to chaos is the active struggle to prevent such disorganization which dieting, with its emphasis on active inner control, provides. Consistent with the observations of Waller, Kaufman, and Deutsch (1940), DuBois (1949), and Rowland (1970), Rose's fastidiousness and her ritualized activites, along with her diet, represented aspects of an obsessional defense against this anxiety about psychic disorganization.

Exacerbation of the Disturbance and First Experiences With Psychiatric Treatment

Mrs. M. returned home from the hospital late in the spring, when Rose was in the seventh grade. According to her mother's memory of events at this time, Rose began her diet within a few weeks of her mother's return home, and began rapidly to lose weight. Rose's frantic activity, which began at this time, represented a further attempt to lose weight, and during the summer months, Rose spent nearly all her waking hours furiously peddling her bicycle, returning home only for supper. Mrs. M. was aware of this weight loss, and became increasingly concerned about it. However, her pediatrician assured her that there was no problem and told her not to worry.

By the following fall, Rose had begun to look seriously emaciated and, at this time, her pediatrician referred her to medical tests, believing that Rose was suffering from a serious physical illness. Only when all diagnostic tests came back negative was the physician willing to recognize the seriousness of Rose's emotional disturbance. Her weight now down to sixty pounds, Rose was hospitalized in the psychiatric ward of the same community hospital where, the previous winter, her mother had been a patient. Tube feeding was begun at once, and during the first days it took three strong orderlies to hold down the frail girl in order that the procedure could be instituted.

Rose was terrified of tube feeding. *Since gaining weight meant losing control and being consumed, Rose viewed being forced to eat, rather than starvation, as life-threatening.* Confused about the meaning of body signals, she did not understand that she needed to eat in order to stay alive. As became increasingly obvious later during her residential treatment, *Rose equated eating with death and starvation with life.*

The hospital staff forced enough nourishment into her that Rose gained fifteen pounds. Since the staff did not realize how afraid she was of growing up and of becoming increasingly like her mother, which meant being part of mother, the staff believed that Rose would like to return home and graduate from eighth grade with the rest of her class. In their community, graduation from grammar school is celebrated with the same significance as is graduation from high school in many other communities. The grammar school graduates wore dignified robes, marched in solemn ceremony, and received engraved diplomas. Even though some of the parents thought this much ceremony to be inappropriate, there was strong pressure for such an elegant graduation ceremony. Rose managed to march in the procession, but after the ceremony was completed, became terrified, presumably of the transition to adolescence which this ceremony signified. In desperation, feeling overwhelmed and terrified, she fled into the girls' washroom where she broke a window and slashed her wrist. She was discovered almost immediately and rushed back to the hospital by ambulance.

This event was terribly painful for Rose's parents. In the first place, they were afraid that she would never recover since she had already been hospitalized for several months and had exhausted Mr. M.'s remaining hospitalization insurance; and yet there appeared to be little improvement in her condition. Not only did the M.s feel depressed by their daughter's lack of progress, but, in addition, they felt completely humiliated. There, before the entire parish, their daughter had been taken away in an ambulance as a result of self-inflicted wound, a mortification increased by the fact that suicide is regarded as a sin in their religion. Mrs. M.'s mother had also witnessed this event and now berated Mrs. M. for having raised a mentally ill daughter who had shamed the entire family.

Mrs. M. recalls that, after her daughter's attempted suicide, she kept thinking that "if it's God's wish to take her, I only wish that he would take her soon." For Mrs. M., her daughter's death would have solved several problems. She believed that life was merely a preparation for an afterlife of reunion and comfort. Mrs. M. felt that her daughter had already suffered enough, and she wished that Rose could have the benefits of this better eternity as soon as possible. In this way, Rose could attain the status of the grieved, lost, ideal figure into which Mrs. M. had already made her father. Rose sensed her mother's wish for her death and both wished for and feared death. To some extent, Rose's desire to die also represented a response to her mother's wish for her death, a wish determined both by her mother's desire to join her own deceased father for whom she still mourned and also by her frustration and anger at trying to deal with Rose. In response to this wish on her mother's part, Rose adopted an attitude of scorn and defiance which was expressed by the desire to be rid of her destructive and consuming mother by dying and finally achieving separation.

Given her mother's very mixed feelings, hospital visiting hours became a nightmare for the hospital staff, Rose, and the family. Rose would rush at her mother, accusing her mother of wanting her dead, and of trying to control her life and her body. She also accused her mother of being humiliated by her illness and of caring more for what the community thought than for her recovery. Rose was particularly sensitive to her mother's feelings, and these accusations were very painful for Mrs. M., who became visibly upset and developed additional gastrointestinal symptoms. As a result of such encounters, the administrative psychiatrist felt that it was essential for mother and daughter to be separated and recommended residential treatment where the family's visiting privileges could be controlled. In making this recommendation, the administrator echoed Charcot's (1889) admonition in treating anorexia nervosa in which he says:

> I have held firmly to this doctrine for nearly fifteen years, and all that I have seen during that time—everything that I have observed day-by-day—tends only to confirm me in that opinion. Yes, it is necessary to separate both children and adults from their father and mother, whose influence, as experience teaches, is particularly pernicious.
>
> Experience shows repeatedly, though it is not always easy to understand the reason, that it is the mothers whose influence is so deleterious, who will hear no argument, and will only yield in general to the last extremity (1964, p. 163).

Of course, in Charcot's time, there was little understanding of the concept of mother-daughter symbiosis and of the powerful role that this symbiosis can play in intensifying the daughter's disturbance. Residential treatment is one powerful means for interrupting such an intense symbiosis, and it is for such reasons that the administrator of Rose's case had so strongly urged enrollment in residential treatment.

For a patient like Rose, feeling controlled by a world too complex for her to master, residential treatment is especially suitable, because, ideally, residential treatment can provide an environment in which there is only minimal pressure and in which the daily routine is sufficiently simplified that the patient can feel comfortable and safe (Bettelheim, 1949, 1950, 1955, 1956, 1960; Bettelheim and Sylvester, 1948; Noshpitz, 1962). Separating the patient from his family and minimizing demands for socializing are often sufficient to lead symptoms to begin to disappear as the patient begins to feel that his life is no longer in imminent danger, and begins to feel control over the environment. As Bettelheim comments, in discussing residential treatment:

> . . . to begin life anew, the total extreme situation which destroyed autonomy must be replaced with a total living situation over which he can exercise control. As he was overwhelmed by his environment, he must now be able to control it . . . This means that it must be simple; it must not offer complex challenges nor make complicated demands. . . . When living under such conditions, even a very weak ego can begin to function more adequately (Kaufman and Heinman, 1964, pp. 516-517).

The Psychotherapeutic Relationship in an Inpatient Setting: Transference and Empathy

Rose strongly resisted the recommendation that she attend a residential school for young people with serious emotional conflicts. Denying that she had any problems, Rose refused the scheduled appointment to meet with the staff, and only agreed to cooperate when her mother promised that Rose's stay would be a short one and that she would be able to return home by summer. Once she had been accepted into residential treatment, Rose became upset at the possibility that she would have to be separated from her mother. In part, she worried about the possibility that her mother would once more become pregnant and in her absence replace her with another child. This concern was expressed primarily in terms of Rose's younger sister who, during Rose's hospitalization, had also developed an ulcer and now shared a symptom in common with her mother. Rose became convinced that her mother would have a boy to replace her and said that if she had been born as a boy, she would never have been rejected.

Given these fears that she might be replaced in her mother's life by her sister or by another brother and, given the fact that her sister was already developing symptoms which would intensify the sister's relationship with her mother, Rose's strongest reaction to enrollment in residential treatment was that she would have to live in a dormitory with six other adolescent girls and would have to *share* a counselor-therapist with them. For Rose, having to share her counselor-therapist with other young people was like having to share her mother with her sister and brothers.

In observing the way in which she formed a relationship with her new therapist, it was possible to gain new appreciation both of the manner in which she had preserved her symbiosis with her mother and of her mother's reaction to this symbiosis. From the outset, Rose was an important presence in the dormitory. In the afternoon, when the girls returned from school, they would gather around the group table, having snacks, and discussing the day. The following observation is typical of Rose's reaction to life in the group setting:

> The group was sitting around the table discussing what they might do during the afternoon. Rose, as usual, was pacing back and forth around the dormitory. Occasionally, she would punctuate the conversation with a remark like "I really hate my body; it really sucks." These remarks were made with considerable feeling, and were addressed directly to her counselor. Her counselor was unprepared to deal with such feelings at a time when the group was trying to decide upon its afternoon activity, and yet Rose's remark was offered with such emphasis that all other conversation stopped and the attention of both children and staff was focused on Rose. Her counselor attempted to console Rose and suggested that she come and sit by her and have some juice and cookies. Rose then said, spitefully, "Don't feed me any of that shit. I know you hate my body, you hate your body, and you are trying to make me fat like you are."
>
> With this remark, tossed out in a tone of intimidation, Rose proceeded once more to pace back and forth across the dormitory. The silence continued as the attention of everyone in the group remained on Rose and her challenge to her counselor-therapist. "Look," she said, "you've got to realize you're trying to fuck up my body with that crap." Then, as a final challenge, she announced that her counselor-therapist couldn't help her get well. "You don't even know how to help me get well, do you?" Her counselor arose from the table, walked over to Rose, led her by the hand to the group table where she sat down beside her and continued the discussion with the group about feelings of helplessness, as expressed by Rose.

In this vignette, we can see how Rose succeeded in getting her therapist to leave the rest of the group and tend to her, and then managed to refocus the discussion from the afternoon's activity to a discussion of the problem of helplessness. This behavior in the group setting is similar to Rose's behavior at home. Her mother noted, for example, that the whole family might plan a

Sunday outing, and just as they were almost ready to leave, Rose would announce that she was not going along. On the other hand, the family might decide on a trip to the forest preserve for a picnic, and just as they arrived at their destination and had settled down for the day, Rose would announce that she had to go home. Mrs. M. complained that by such behavior Rose could throw the family into complete confusion.

In discussing Rose's behavior in the group, her counselor-therapist also noted how intense Rose was, and how she often felt that Rose was boring a hole into her with her gaze. The therapist's feelings paralleled those of Rose's mother, who felt that Rose was so unlike the rest of the family in her serious, questioning approach to the world. Where other family members were concerned with prosaic, commonplace events, Rose asked serious life-and-death questions which disturbed and annoyed the rest of the family. Indeed, other family members expressed relief after Rose was first hospitalized and they no longer had to undergo her intent and questioning gaze as they went about their daily business.

For Rose, this intensity had an adaptive significance. In a large family, her intensity made it possible for her to be differentiated from other family members—not an easy task for a daughter involved in a symbiotic relationship with her mother—and made it possible for her to be noticed by her mother, a woman who was especially insensitive to subtle emotional nuances, and who had a difficult time distinguishing between her own needs and those of her daughter. Rose was sufficiently intense that even her own mother had to recognize her separate feelings and pay attention to her needs.

Rose's counselors spoke frequently of their reaction to this intense demand for recognition. One of her former therapists at the residential treatment center notes that, although she would begin the session feeling that Rose's problems were different from her own, during the hour she would begin to question this. Rose would accuse her of being fat and of trying to make her fat. Having learned about the concept of projection, Rose would accuse her therapist of attributing her own troubles to Rose and would shout defiantly, "Why don't you get your own therapist? Why should I have to straighten out your head?"

Through the transference, Rose was repeating once more the conflict between her mother and herself in which her mother, unable to differentiate between her own needs and those of her daughter, had been unable to help Rose to see her own needs and her own personality as separate and had involved Rose in her own conflicts. Rose needed to try to make her own problems into her therapist's problems and to bind her therapist to her by not differentiating between their personalities. Most significant in this regard is her therapist's reactions to this effort to erase the differences between them. She reported feeling confused and completely smothered and overwhelmed by Rose. Although she had always had a robust appetite, as she sat with Rose and tried to drink some of the milk which she brought to the session room, she felt uncertain whether or not she was thirsty and, indeed, began to question whether she could interpret her own body sensations.

Terrified by feelings of merging with her patient, she had begun quite consciously to tell herself before starting the hour that she really was a different person from Rose and that it was she who was the therapist. Rose had succeeded so well in her attempt to merge with her therapist that her therapist, who had always had a regular menstrual cycle, now stopped menstruating, and reported the fantasy that she was pregnant with Rose who would live forever inside her body. As her therapist became increasingly afraid that she was losing her own self and merging with her patient, Rose became increasingly disturbed, for she not only needed to be able to establish such a symbiosis as the only way she knew of being sure that she would be cared for, but also was afraid of it. As long as she was a part of the therapist and a significant aspect of her therapist's own personality, her therapist would have to take care of her, for Rose would be little more than a part of her therapist's self. At the same time she was afraid of being controlled and dominated, "swallowed up." Despite this fear, there was an adaptive aspect to the way Rose made her therapist feel, and this could become operative when her therapist was able to bear the feelings of being smothered and of losing her own identity as a separate person. As long as her therapist could accept these feelings, Rose could begin to feel that it was her therapist who lacked a sense of self and who needed to get her head "straight," while Rose could feel strong and in control of a relationship rather than, as with her mother, being controlled by it. If she could deposit her feelings with her therapist, Rose could begin to feel safe enough to examine these feelings, first about the therapist, then about her mother, and finally about herself.

It is only as a result of sharing in the patient's feelings and perceptions that the therapist is able to understand the significance of the patient's particular perceptions of self and others for the patient's adaptation and survival. Nowhere is this more important than in the treatment of anorexia nervosa where feelings of loss of a sense of separateness and loss of control are so important in understanding symptom formation.

One of the advantages of residential treatment is that the issue of food and eating and the transference and countertransference issues which it represents may be studied directly, and conflict and symptom formation observed by both patient and therapist as it actually takes place. Observation of the patient's behavior at mealtime over the course of many months enables the patient's therapist to begin to understand the complex meanings which the patient attaches to food and eating. This understanding, while not in itself sufficient to lead to major changes in the patient's behavior, is important in terms of the patient-therapist relationship, for it conveys to the patient her therapist's interest in getting to know her as a person with her own feelings and beliefs. Our observations of these anorexic patients do not agree with Bruch's (1965, 1966) earlier observations that, in contrast to schizophrenic patients, anorexic patients develop few symbolic interpretations of food.

Our anorexic patients, of whom Rose is characteristic, all attributed a variety of complex meanings to food. One patient, the daughter of parents who were active in the antiwar movement, refused to eat all food manufactured or processed by companies having any association, no matter how remote, with the Vietnam conflict. She would only eat food processed by neutral countries, and would refuse lobster, steak, roast beef, or chocolate sundaes in favor of imported foods such as kidney pie. Rose, herself, refused to eat hot dogs or sausages, which reminded her of penises; all forms of casseroles, which reminded her of vomit; eggs, which reminded her of fetuses; and potatoes, which reminded her of brains. On the other hand, as we have already observed, she was willing to eat rare roast beef and Jello, which she understood as profane parallels to the sacred Host of the Mass. Her therapist's interest in Rose's unique understanding of these foods and in knowing why she accepted or refused particular foods was a first sign for this patient that her therapist cared about her, and wanted to understand her.

One of the central issues in the literature on the treatment of anorexia nervosa concerns the advisability of forcing the patient to eat, particularly when her life is in danger. Bliss and Branch (1969), in their thorough review, note that two contrasting positions have been adopted by those who have treated anorexia nervosa on an inpatient basis. Some authors insist that the therapist should be authoritarian and should demand that the patient eat. Others believe that such aggressive treatment is disastrous. Bliss and Branch put this debate into a useful perspective when they note that:

> Unfortunately, these are dialectical exercises rather than scientific conclusions. They do point to the need to view the situations as an interaction between the physician and the patient, in which both parties, their needs, attitudes, and tolerances play a part. One can not simply study the patient who is receiving therapy since the treatment cannot be understood unless it is seen as related to the therapist and the setting in which the treatment is given . . . (1960, pp.112-113).

Typically, the desire to see the patient eat arises as much from the therapist's concern about his professional reputation as from his concern for the patient herself. Since the patient knows that the desire for her to eat arises as much from institutional concerns as from the desire to help her gain greater autonomy, it is not surprising that she should have little desire to fit in with institutional requirements. After all, the symptom of not eating arises from the fear of loss of control and the need to maintain some autonomous control.

To the extent that the patient is not certain that she has such control, the symptom of not eating has adaptive significance. When the staff can acknowledge that their need for the patient to eat arises at least in part from their anxiety about their professional reputations they may achieve greater success in their goal of helping the patient gain weight, for in such a circumstance, the patient may not so directly perceive the issue of eating as a power struggle (Sours, 1969).

We have already seen that in Rose's life, the refusal to eat had adaptive significance. It was the one area of her life where she could demonstrate both to herself and to others that she retained control and mastery. Attempts to force Rose to eat were met by the determined refusal of one in a situation of desperate fear for survival. In Rose's conception of the world, survival was equivalent to not eating, and destruction was equivalent to eating.

Largely as a result of her own anxiety, acknowledged to Rose as such, Rose's counselor-therapist applied continual pressure to get her to eat. The following observation in the dormitory, just prior to supper, provides a good illustration of this pressure:

> Rose's counselor-therapist walked out into the hall, looked at the clock, and came back into the dormitory, informing the group in general that it was five-forty, and that in five minutes it would be suppertime. (All dormitory groups eat in common dining room where supper is served at five forty-five each evening.) Rose, who had been frantically wringing out her favorite sweater in the sink, came out of the bathroom at that moment to announce that she was not eating any of the school's ''shitty supper.'' Her counselor replied that she wanted Rose to eat and that she (the counselor) knew that supper—fried chicken—was among Rose's favorite foods. Rose denied this and said that she had no favorite foods and, indeed, never intended to eat again.
>
> She began screaming that she hated her counselor-therapist, that her counselor didn't understand her and was trying to kill her by forcing her to eat, and that she refused to eat. Her counselor was frustrated by a difficult afternoon in which Rose had spent most of the time in the bathroom washing her sweater, pacing back and forth in the dormitory, and cursing everyone in the group and saying that she wanted to die. The cumulative effect of this on the counselor led her to scream back that she wanted Rose to live, and that Rose must eat. Rose flew at her counselor in a rage, and almost attacked her physically, before regaining self-control. By now, it was past suppertime, and the group started downstairs. Rose sat next to her counselor and ate two helpings of fried chicken, as well as dumplings and ice cream for dessert.

After the day was over and all the girls were in bed, the staff sat down to talk about the quarrel between Rose and her counselor. Several staff members observed that Rose ate better after she had had a quarrel about eating than at any other times. Some staff felt that this pattern of quarreling and eating showed that Rose should be forced to eat since, when she was forced, she was able to eat. However, such a position was clearly at odds with Rose's terror of losing control and of being required to eat. It was suggested that the fact that her therapist had become upset by Rose's refusal to eat proved to the patient that her therapist really cared about her and wanted her to live, a concern which was of obvious importance to a girl whose own mother had expressed the feeling that, if it were God's wish that she should die, then she should die as quickly as possible.

However, of at least equal importance was the fact that, in becoming involved with Rose in an argument just before each meal, as so often was the case, *Rose was freed from being passive and controlled and now could be active and controlling.* As long as her counselor-therapist could realize the importance of bearing these feelings (and she did indeed feel very much controlled and ovewhelmed by her patient), Rose was able to let herself eat.

In time, as Rose began to experience being full, she could begin to feel the difference between this fullness and her previous feeling of emptiness. She could then begin to feel, for herself, the importance of eating for her survival. By providing an environment and persons whom she could control, rather than one in which she felt controlled, residential treatment made it possible for Rose to begin to give up her refusal to eat. At the same time, she could demonstrate her growing feelings of inner control in ways other than those related to eating. As the issue of eating and food refusal became somewhat less important, Rose's symbiosis with her mother emerged as the most critical therapeutic issue. Rose began to understand the basis of this symbiosis and, having been able to experience the symbiosis in the transference, was able to achieve a greater degree of individuation.

A significant breakthrough in the struggle to free herself from the symbiosis occurred in the context of Rose's attempt to emulate her mother's preoccupation with weight as a means of mastering internal conflicts. Rose had been preoccupied with the fear of becoming like her mother. Not only was her mother controlled by *her* mother but, in addition, she was domineering and burdened everyone in the family, especially Rose, with her problems. According to the patient, it was her mother's insistence upon telling Rose her problems that was the most difficult part of their relationship. Through her refusal to eat, Rose emulated one aspect of her mother's behavior; and while this in itself was frightening, she was particularly preoccupied with anxiety lest her fear (which was also her wish) would come true, and that she would become fat like her mother. A part of this fear of becoming like her mother was that her father would then find her sexually attractive in the same way he found her mother sexually attractive and that, out of jealousy, her mother would destroy Rose. This was yet one more reason for not becoming like her mother and becoming fat, and one more reason for maintaining strict control. Any sign that she was becoming in any way like her mother terrified her. If her mother sent her a picture of the family, Rose anxiously asked her counselor-therapist whether she now looked more like her mother than before. This issue of becoming like her mother was finally put in perspective but, as the following incident shows, not before it had become a major crisis:

> One morning, on arising, Rose inspected her body, as was her custom each morning, and asked her therapist if she thought that Rose looked any different that day. Her therapist assured her that she was still the same girl. She then went about the business of helping girls to get dressed and prepared for the school day ahead. Rose's therapist gave no more thought to this apparently off-hand question as the group had breakfast and went off to school. Rose had not eaten much that morning.
>
> Throughout the day, she was obviously downcast and upset. That afternoon, the group's other counselor was on duty, and Rose's counselor-therapist was out for the day. Rose was unwilling to form a relationship with anyone but her counselor-therapist (another manifestation of the development of a symbiosis in treatment), and therefore her other counselor tried to make her comfortable, but made little attempt to talk to her. That night, in her bath, she was seen crying. No one knew what to do, because when Rose's counselor-therapist was not on duty, the other counselor and the children in the group felt completely at a loss as to how to help her.
>
> When the group was ready for bed and the counselor had turned out the lights, Rose refused to get into bed. At first, she was only stubborn, but soon she became verbally abusive, and began accusing and threatening the counselor. By the time the director came through on his evening rounds, Rose and her counselor were screaming at each other; her counselor had tried to drag Rose over to her bed, and Rose had retaliated by hitting her quite hard in the stomach. The director took Rose outside in the hall. From the pallor on her face, it was apparent that she was in sheer terror. First she looked frozen in fear and the began to scream in desperation and flung herself upon the director, already an important person in her life, screaming that she was going to die or be killed, and she knew it to be so; she would not survive the night.
>
> After a long time consoling and quieting Rose, the following story emerged. That morning upon awakening, she had noticed a slight corn on one of her toes. In fact, the corn was in exactly the same spot, and appeared to be identical in shape, with a corn on her mother's foot. Rose became convinced that, during the previous night, she had suffered a metamorphosis in which she had assumed a physical appearance which was identical with that of her mother's. Her counselor's blithe reassurance had hardly sufficed to help her with this terror, nor had she been reassured by frequent visits to the bathroom where she studied herself in the mirror in order to be sure that she was still herself. She suffered a moment of pain during which she looked in the mirror and believed that the image was that of her mother: When she went to get into the tub for her bath, and inspected herself once more, she believed that she had become fat like her mother and, in fact, resembled her mother in each and every aspect of her appearance.

Terrified that the worst had happened, Rose was certain that her mother would murder her during the night out of revenge for her fantasies about her father. This concern, when expressed, provided considerable relief, and her awareness of the underlying wishes that contributed to her fear of becoming like her mother represented a first tentative step in her psychotherapy; Rose began to be able to decide for herself in what ways she did not want to be like her mother.

While Rose still had some difficulty in being able to eat freely, her weight stabilized at about 98 pounds, well within the normal limits for a girl of her height. With the anorexic crisis past, Rose and her therapist have started work on the many other conflicts which were inaccessible so long as this life and death crisis of the refusal to eat was uppermost in Rose's mind and in the minds of the staff members who worked with her.

While many factors contributed to Rose's first hesitant attempt at self-understanding after the most critical phase of her disturbance, perhaps the most important of these was her therapist's intuitive and empathic understanding of Rose's unique interpretation of her personal and interpersonal world. Her therapist needed to allow herself to feel controlled by Rose and to recognize this feeling of being controlled as the complement to the way in which her patient felt. This recognition made it possible to react not by attempting to put these feelings back on Rose, in order to avoid having to bear these feelings herself, but rather by allowing herself to be and to feel controlled by Rose, to serve as a depository for theses feelings of being controlled. As a result, Rose felt free to yield some of her own insistence upon strict inner control and, no longer needing protection from the world beyond her control, she gradually was able to give up her symptoms.

Summary

Anorexia nervosa is a symbolic expression of a patient's desperate need to maintain control over an interpersonal and intrapsychic world which is felt to be beyond her control. Because it provides a defense against feelings of being annihilated and destroyed, the refusal to eat of the anorexia nervosa patient represents an achievement of the ego, which is not likely to be helped by manipulation aimed at making this symptom disappear while anxiety about loss of control remains. The anorexic patient becomes disturbed as a result of a life in which, almost from birth, body signals have been distorted and denied. The ordinary sensations of hunger and satisfaction are not correctly perceived and provide no means of signalling physiological distress. At the same time, like the proverbial Jonah in the Whale, the anorexic patient feels swallowed up by her controlling mother who incorporates her daughter into her psyche and uses her for her own ends. Seldom does the future patient exist as a person in her own right; she exists only as a means for satisfying her mother's needs (who in turn feels controlled by her own mother). Not having been able to achieve differentiation or individuation from her mother, the anorexic patient develops the feeling that she is only one aspect of her mother's personality, and like the patient in this paper, that she will someday be transformed into her mother, a metamorphosis which she both fears and wishes.

The technical literature suggests that it is important to allow the patient to reexperience the original mother-daughter symbiosis in the transference. In the resolution of this symbiosis, the therapist must be prepared to be placed in the helpless position of being controlled by the patient. The therapist's acceptance of this development helps the patient achieve individuation and a sense of autonomy and to consolidate her identity.

References

Anthony, E. J., "The reaction of parents to adolescents and to their behavior." In E. Anthony and T. Benedek, eds., *Parenthood: Its Psychology ad Psychopathology,* pp. 309-324, Boston: Little, Brown, 1970.

Bachrach, A., Erwin W., Mohr, J., "The control of eating behavior in an anorexic by operant conditioning techniques." In Ullman, L., Krasner, L., eds., *Case Studies in Behavior Modification.,* pp. 153-163. New York: Holt, Rinehart, and Winston, 1965.

Berlin, I. N., Boatman, M. J., Sheimo, S., Szurek, S. "Adolescent alternation of anorexia and obseity: Workshop, 1950." *Amer. Journ. of Orthopsych.,* 21:387-419 (1951).

Bettelheim, B., "A psychiatric school." *The Quarterly Journ. of Child Behavior,* 1:86-95 (1949).

_____. *Love Is not Enough.* New York: The Free Press and Macmillan, 1950.

_____. *Truants from Life.* New York: The Free Press and Macmillan, 1955.

_____. "Schizophrenia as a reaction to extreme situations." *Amer. Journ. of Orthopsych.,* 26:507-518 (1956).

_____. *The Informed Heart.* New York: The Free Press and Macmillan, 1960.

Bettelheim, B., Sylvester, E., "A therapeutic milieu." *Amer. Journ. of Orthopsych.,* 18:191-206 (1948).

Blinder, B., Freedman, D., Stunkard, A., "Behavior therapy of anorexia nervosa: Effectiveness of activity as a reinforcer of weight gain." *Amer. Journ. of Psych.,* 126:1093-1098 (1970).

Bliss, E., Branch, C. H., *Anorexia Nervosa: Its History, Psychology, and Biology.* New York: Hoeber-Harper, 1960.

Bruch, H., "The psychiatric differential diagnosis of anorexia nervosa." In Meyer, J. E., Feldman, H., eds., *Anorexia Nervosa,* pp. 70-86. Stuttgart: George Thieme, 1965.

_____ . "Eating disorders and schizophrenic development." In Usedin, G. ed., *Psychoneurosis and Schizophrenia,* pp. 113-124, Philadelphia: Lippincott, 1966.

———— . "Family background in eating disorders." In Anthony, E. J., Koupernik, C., eds., *The Child in His Family*, pp. 285-309. New York: Wiley, 1970a.

———— . "Changing approaches to anorexia nervosa." In Rowland, C., ed., *Anorexia and Obesity*. p. 335-354. Boston: Little, Brown, 1970c.

———— . "Death in anorexia nervosa." *Psychosom. Med.*, 33:135-144 (1971a).

———— . "Family transactions in eating disorders," *Comprehensive Psychiatry*, 12:238-248, (1917b).

Charcot, J. M., Diseases of the nervous system, III. London: The New Sydenham Society, 1889, reprinted as some excerpts. In Kaufman, M. R., Heiman, M., eds., *Evaluation of Psychosomatic Concepts: Anorexia Nervosa–A Paradigm*. New York: International Universities Press, 1964.

Cohler, B., "Individuation and the Issue of Control in the Etiology of Anorexia Nervosa." Unpublished manuscript. Committee on Human Development, The University of Chicago, 1972b.

Cohler, B., Grunebaum, H., "Mothers and Grandmothers: Personality and Child Care in Three-generation families." Unpublished manuscript. Committee on Human Development, The University of Chicago, 1972a.

DuBois, E., "Compulsion neurosis with cachexia (anorexia nervosa)." *Amer. Journ. of Psych.*, 106:107-115 (1949).

Eissler, K., "Some psychiatric aspects of anorexia nervosa, demonstrated by a case report," *Psychoanal. Rev.*, 30:121-145 (1943).

Freud, S., Addendum to Notes upon a case of obsessional neurosis (1909). In *Standard Edition*. Vol. X. London: Hogarth Press, 1955, 251-318.

————. "Recommendations to physicians practising psychoanalysis (1912)." In *Standard Edition*, Vol. IXX. 109-120, London: Hogarth Press, 1958.

————. "Observations on transference love (further recommendations on the technique of psychoanalysis, III), (1915). In *Standard Edition*. Vol. XII. 157-171, London: Hogarth Press, 1958.

———— . "Analysis terminable and interminable (1937)." In *Standard Edition*. Vol. XXIII. 209-254, London: Hogarth Press, 1964.

————. "Splitting of the ego in the process of defense (1938)." In *Standard Edition*. Vol. XIII. 271-278, London: Hogarth Press, 1964.

Gifford, S., Murawaski, B., Pilot, M., "Anorexia nervosa in one of identical twins." In Rowland, C., ed., *Anorexia and Obsesity*, pp. 139-230. Boston: Little, Brown, 1970.

Groen, J. J., Feldman-Toledano, Z., "Educative treatment of patients and parents in anorexia nervosa," *Brit. Journ. of Psych.*, 112:671-681 (1966).

Hallsten, A., Jr., "Adolescent anorexia nervosa treated by desensitization," *Behavioral Research Therapy*, 3:87-91 (1965).

Kaufman, M. R., Heiman, M., *Evolution of Psychosomatic Concepts: Anorexia Nervosa—A Paradigm*." New York: International Universities Press, 1964.

Kernberg, O., "Structural derivatives of object relations," *Internat. Journ. of Psychoanal.*, 47:236-253 (1966).

Klein, M., *The Psychoanalysis of Children* (1932). New York: Grove Press, 1960.

————. "Notes on some schizoid mechanisms." In Klein, M., Heimann, P., Isaacs, S., Riviere, J., eds., *Developments in Psychoanalysis*, pp. 292-320. London: Hogarth Press, 1952.

Lang, P., "Behavior therapy with a case of nervosa anorexia." In Ullman, L., Krasner, L., eds., *Case Studies in Behavior Modification*, pp. 217-221, New York: Holt, Rinehart and Winston, 1965.

Leitenberg, H., Agras, W., Thomoson, I., "A sequential analysis of the effect of selective positive reinforcement in modifying anorexia nervosa," *Behavioral Research Therapy*, 6:211-218 (1978).

Mahler, M. S., *On Human Symbiosis and the Vicissitudes of Individuation*, Vol. I. *Infantile Psychosis*. New York: International Universities Press, 1968.

_____. "On the first three subphases of the separation-individuation process," *Internat. Journ. of Psychoanal.*, 53:333-338 (1972).

Murray, H., and associates, *Explorations in Personality*. New York: Oxford University Press, 1938.

Nemiah, J., "Anorexia nervosa: fact and theory." *Amer. Journ. of Digest. Dis.*, 249-274 (1958).

Noshpitz, J., "Notes on the theory of residential treatment," *Journ. of the Amer. Acad. of Child Psych.*, 1:284-296, 1962.

Palazzoli, M. S., "The families of patients with anorexia nervosa." In Anthony, E. J., Koupernic, C., *The Child in His Family*, pp. 319-332. New York: John Wiley, 1970.

_____. "Anorexia nervosa." In Arieti, S. *World Biennial of Psychiatry*, I. pp. 197-218, New York: Basic Books, 1971.

Parsons, A., *Belief, Magic, and Anomic Essays in Psychosocial Anthropology*. New York: Free Press, 1969.

Phillipson, H., *The Object Relations Technique*. London: Tavistock Press, 1955.

Rowland, C., "Anorexia nervosa—A survey of the literature and review of 30 cases." In Rowland, C. ed., *Anorexia and Obesity*, pp. 37-138. Boston: Little, Brown, 1970.

Sours, J. A., "Anorexia nervosa: nosology, diagnosis, developmental patterns and power-control dynamics." In Caplan, G., Lebovici, S., eds., *Adolescence: Psychosocial Perspectives*, pp. 185-212. New York: Basic Books, 1969.

Theander, S., "Anorexia nervosa: A psychiatric investigation of 94 female patients," *Acta Psychiatrica Scandanavia*, Supplementum 214, 170, 194.

Thoma, H. *Anorexia Nervosa* (1961, trans. by G. Brydone). New York: International Universities Press, 1967.

Waller, J., Kaufman, M. R., Deutsch, F., "Anorexia nervosa: A psychosomatic entity," *Psychosomatic Med.*, 2:3-16 (1940).

Winnicott, D. W., "Aggression in relation to emotional development" (1950-55). In Winnicott, D. W., ed., *Collected Papers*. pp. 204-218, New York: Basic Books, 1958.

Chapter XIX

Imposture as a Defense

Stanley W. Conrad, M.D.

Patients in psychoanalysis often express the feeling that they are impostors. This feeling is often conveyed early in treatment; in fact, one patient who was asked in his initial interview why he wanted to be analyzed replied: "I feel like an impostor." Actually, he was a bona fide physician with a good reputation in his specialty. His impostrous feeling resulted from the discrepancy between the status he had achieved in life and the way he really felt about himself, namely, that he was a young boy in a world of grown-ups.

The feeling of being an impostor can be expressed indirectly in many ways. For example, an attorney, in practice for 25 years, admitted that every time he appeared in court he was troubled by the following thoughts: "What am I doing here? I feel like a boy, and the others in the courtroom are all men." A Ph.D. in psychology, age thirty-five and the father of two children, experienced this same feeling whenever he was with his peers or even when he was driving his car on a busy highway: "I don't belong in this line of traffic; all the other drivers are adults and I am not." A successful physician wondered during an analytic session: "Why do intelligent people come to my office and even pay me? I'm not a real doctor; I'm a play doctor." Fenichel (1945) described a patient, a successful physician of many years' practice, who felt amazed whenever a pharmacist filled a prescription he had written because "The pharmacist, a grown-up man, actually does this work for no other reason than that I, a child, have written a prescription!"

This impostrous feeling is more common among males, although it is also found in females. A woman patient of forty, mother of two teenaged boys, was always amazed whenever she was asked to head or even join various committees. "Why do they ask me?" she would muse. "Can't they see how inadequate and incompetent I really am?" Actually she was a very capable individual and invariably did outstanding work; however, she always felt like a child, unequal to her peers. All her successful accomplishments failed to change her opinion of herself. She felt that she was a "phony," that she was constantly deceiving people, and that someday she would be exposed.

In general, the impostrous feeling exists whenever there is a discrepancy between one's appearance before the world and one's self-evaluation; this feeling is rather widespread. As Helene Deutsch (1955) observed: "The world is crowded with 'as-if' personalities, and even more with impostors and pretenders. Ever since I became interested in the impostor, he pursues me everywhere. I find him among my friends and acquaintances, as well as in myself.'' However, the feeling of being an impostor is only troublesome and perhaps a presenting symptom when there is a wide discrepancy between the disguise an individual believes he wears and his self-evaluation.

I believe that in most cases the subjective complaint of being an impostor derives from the castration complex and that this applies to both males and females. In the male, analysis will usually reveal a small-penis complex; he is convinced that his penis is smaller than that of most men and that, therefore, he is less masculine. The man with the small-penis complex continually compares himself (his wife, his car, his home, or his attainments) with other men and usually rates himself second-best. Behind his compulsion to compare is his wish to assure himself of his masculinity. But his wish is never fulfilled, for there is a strong underlying conviction that his penis is undersized. The small-penis complex, which, of course, is multidetermined (with id, ego, and superego determinants), usually underlies the feeling of masculine inadequacy. By imposture he pretends that he has a big penis. But all the external, material embellishments such as marriage, home, children, status, and financial success cannot neutralize this feeling of masculine inadequacy. Beneath the veneer of maturity and masculinity is the feeling of immaturity and lack of masculinity.

Among women the feeling of being an impostor is usually not consciously felt; it only becomes conscious during analysis, especially in the treatment of women who have excessive masculine strivings. Just as the male denies his ''small penis'' by imposture, the female denies her castrated state by fostering the illusion of a penis; thus, she tries to compensate for her feelings of feminine inadequacy. This illusion is maintained by anything associated with status; for example, vocation, possessions, achievements, or even children.[1] Failing this, she may achieve vicarious status by identification with a virile husband. The illusory penis is her defense against anxieties associated with femininity. Yet, although she may appear to be competent and capable, she is aware that her penis is just illusory, that she is still a female and she views herself as a castrate.

Some women feel like impostors because they consciously want to be feminine and they act as though they were feminine despite a strong masculine orientaion and identification. Sometimes they indulge in feminine acting-out, such as promiscuity, in order to reassure themselves of their femininity. A young woman patient constantly fought against identifying with

---

[1] A middle-aged spinster had the recurrent fantasy of being a mother of many children, but a husband was either vague or nonexistent. To her, marriage and motherhood were mainly status symbols rather than gratification of sexual and maternal drives.

her mother because she had uncouth manners, objected to makeup, and was in fact more of a masculine than a feminine model. Whenever this patient behaved in a refined (feminine) way she felt that she was not genuine. For a short time, especially when she was experiencing serious doubts about her femininity, she became promiscuous. On the surface this type of impostrous feeling appears to be different, the exact opposite of that which was described above. But analysis usually reveals that the core of the problem is the same in both, for the wish to be feminine is actually a defense against masculine wishes. When this defense is analyzed, the problem of the illusory penis is bared as is the woman's resultant impostrous feeling that she is denying her castration.

This chapter deals primarily with the "neurotic impostor," that is, the one who complains of the distressing symptom: "I feel like an impostor." It is not about the notorious, bona fide ("delinquent") impostors that one reads about from time to time in the newspapers, for example, men who are caught masquerading as physicians, college professors, or army officers.[2] The latter rarely come for treatment. There are several distinguishing features between the two types. The neurotic impostor is an individual who has earned the right to his achievement or status. In contrast, the delinquent impostor usually has not achieved any status on his own; instead, he borrows, steals, or adopts the higher status of another. In a moment he catapults himself from his inferior, lowly self to a highly respected member of his community and society. Whereas the neurotic impostor retains his own identity, the true or delinquent impostor assumes the identity, including the name, of another. The neurotic impostor has not set out to be an impostor; he just finds himself in this unpleasant situation. The delinquent, on the other hand, actively perpetrates his imposture. The neurotic impostor is troubled by his role-playing and his sham; the delinquent delights in his ability to deceive people. The neurotic feels guilty about any acclaim he may receive; the delinquent thrives on it. The neurotic fears exposure; the delinquent may secretly wish for it and even unconsciously arrange for it, either because of guilt or in order to receive recognition for his brilliant deception. In addition, I suspect that the delinquent impostor suffers from a pathologic superego defect and that he also derives some sadomasochistic gratification from his imposture. Yet, despite

---

[2] "Delinquent" impostors are almost always males, and some of them have made their mark in history. As far as I know, there has only been one important female impostor—Pope Joan, the woman who allegedly masqueraded as Pope John VIII. In a delightful story Royidis (1961) records from his research the story of Joanna, a ninth-century young nun who was persuaded by a monk to don a monk's cassock and join his monastery. Thus began Joanna's metamorphosis into Brother John. Later Brother John abandoned her lover, sailed to Rome, and became the secretary of Pope Leo IV, whom she succeeded as Pope John VIII. Two years later she died—in the travail of childbirth.

all of these differences, I believe the underlying problem is essentially the same for both types of impostors, namely, a feeling of genital inadequacy.

REVIEW OF THE LITERATURE

There is very little in the literature about the impostor and imposture. The first paper on this subject was written by Abraham in 1925: "The History of an Impostor in the Light of Psychoanalytical Knowledge." In this paper he describes an impostor whom he briefly examined during World War I. From a very early age this man showed an "uncontrollable desire for aggrandizement." "He had barely started school when he noticed with envy that some boys had *possessions superior to his own*, such as for instance, a lacquered pencil box or a pencil of a special color [italics added]." Because of his ingratiating manner and his ability to pose as a man of wealth, he gained access to exclusive society. However, his fraudulent acts and nonpayment of bills led to one prison term after another. Abraham was very pessimistic in his prognosis. About five years later, when he had the opportunity to examine this impostor again, he was surprised by a "great transformation." This man had become a trustworthy, reliable, and respected member of the community and had been so for several years. Abraham attributes this transformation to the fact that the man, who had felt unloved as a child, now had a living mother substitute and thus could direct his libido, which had been narcissistically fixated, onto a love object. Abraham concluded that the tendency to imposture was a result of narcissistic fixation and that imposture is diminished when the libido is transferred to an object.

The next important paper on the impostor was written by Helene Deutsch in 1955. Her paper is also based on the treatment of one psychopathic patient—a fourteen-year-old boy, who was sent to her because he was insolent, rebellious, and unable to submit to discipline at school. He tried to impress his friends with his financial expenditures. It is interesting that he complained that his teachers "pretended to be something they were not."[3] Her first contact with this patient was only for a short time; eight years later the patient returned.

The incident that precipitated his return to treatment should be mentioned because of its bearing on the thesis of this paper. The patient, having volunteered for military service during World War II, reported for duty on his new, shiny motorcycle, and soon he was able to impress his comrades with his grandiose spending and his alleged military connections. However, one day the news came that a commanding officer noted for his severity was to inspect the unit. The patient, realizing that he could not fool this officer, developed an

---

[3]By the mechanism of projection, impostors are keenly aware of and sensitive to imposture in others. They resent the "phoniness" in others just as they resent it in themselves.

anxiety attack, was hospitalized, and then discharged from the service. Undoubtedly his anxiety attack was due to his dread that he would be unmasked and exposed as a fake.

Deutsch compared her patient's imposture with two fairly recent, notorious impostors: Ferdinand Demara and Marvin Hewitt. Both had adopted the names and titles of certain men in order to secure prestige and fulfill their narcissistic conception of themselves. Demara, for example, without any formal training, impersonated a Ph.D. in psychology, a monk, a deputy sheriff, and even a surgeon—to name just a few in his history of imposture. (See Crichton, 1959.) Hewitt, under an assumed name, began teaching theoretical physics, mathematics, and electrical engineering in numerous universities with great success, although he had never finished high school. Deutsch noted that both her patient and Hewitt regarded themselves as geniuses and courted situations in which they would be exposed as impostors.

> "I believe that all impostors have this in common: they assume the identities of other men not because they themselves lack the ability for achievement, but because they have to hide under a strange name to materialize a . . . fantasy. It seems to me that the ego of the impostor, as expressed in his own name, is devaluated, guilt-laden. Hence he must usurp the name of any individual who fulfills the requirements of his own magnificent ego ideal. . . . He desperately tries—through pretending and under cover of someone else's name—to maintain his ego ideal, to force it upon the world, so to speak."

Greenacre (1958a), in her study of impostors, stated: "The impostor seems to be repeatedly seeking confirmation of his assumed identity to overcome his sense of helplessness or incompleteness. . . . The unconscious motivation [of the impostor] is to rob the overthrown father of his penis, which, it is imagined, furnishes a better equipment than the inferior, infantile one which the impostor feels himself to have." She deduced that certain notorious impostors of history were plagued by feelings of sexual inadequacy. For example, Titus Oates, a seventeenth-century impostor, had one leg shorter than the other and was noted for his extraordinary physical ugliness. He was a known homosexual with a predilection for sodomy. James Macpherson (1736-1796), a discredited poet who was essentially regarded as an impostor, was very sensitive about the thickness of his legs. William Bedloe, a confirmed impostor, was a transvestite. George Psalmanazar (died 1736) was a narcotics addict who lived beyond eighty years of age, yet never married. The Tichborne Claimant had a genital malformation that made him doubt whether he could have children. According to Greenacre, these notorious impostors had a "polymorphous perverse sexual organization with almost no object relationship." In her four analytic cases in which imposture was a symptom, all were men with considerable impairment of sexual potency; three had a small-penis complex, while the fourth showed this in reverse with the idea that his penis was oversized. Passive homosexual trends were marked in all four. Although Greenacre's observations apply specifically to delinquent impostors, they are indeed similar to my observations of neurotic impostors.

In another paper (1958b), Greenacre compared the impostor with the artist. She reiterated that the impostor suffers from a defective ego development so that he is unable to form object relationships; he also has a special disturbance in the sense of identity and reality. She felt that each imposture is a reenactment of the oedipal conflict in which the more powerful father is overthrown and his power is assumed.

Fear of Exposure

Illustrations of psychoanalytic concepts can often be found in ancient myths. Deception and the fear of exposure are nicely illustrated in the myth of the Phrygian King Midas: Apollo and Pan were once engaged in a musical contest. Apollo was judged the winner by Timolus, the appointed judge. Midas, a follower of Pan, attended the contest; he disagreed and imprudently argued that Pan should have been the winner. This case of frank hubris infuriated Apollo, who punished Midas in the following manner, according to Ovid:

> Such stupid ears
> Apollo thought, were surely less than human,
> And so he made them longer, stuffed them full
> Of gray and shaggy hair, and made their base
> Unstable, giving them the power of motion.
> The rest of him was human; this one feature
> Alone was punished, and he wore the ears
> Of the slow-going jackass. So, disfigured,
> Ashamed, he tried to hide them with a turban,
> But when he had a hair cut, then his barber
> Saw, dared not tell, and wanted to, and could not
> Keep matters to himself, no more than barbers
> Today can do, and so he dug a hole
> Deep in the ground, and went and whispered in it
> What kind of ears King Midas had. He buried
> The evidence of his voice, filled up the hole,
> Sneaked silently away. But a thick growth
> Of whispering reeds began to grow there; these,
> At the year's end full-grown, betrayed the sower,
> For when a light breeze stirred them, they would whisper
> Midas has asses' ears! You can still hear them.
> *Metamorphoses*, Book 11, lines 173-193.

Thus ends the account of Ovid. Other writers report that when Midas learned that his disgrace was common knowledge, he ordered his barber killed and then committed suicide by drinking bull's blood (Strabo, Vol. 1).

Midas was embarrassed by his newly acquired asses' ears and attempted to hide them under his turban. Once the secret was out, once he was exposed, he killed his barber and himself. This seems to be an overreaction, unless, of course, the asses' ears represent and symbolize something more significant. An ass, generally considered (even in ancient times) to be a stupid animal, has ears that would befit Midas, the possessor of "such stupid ears." Furthermore, the asses' ears represent the general stupidity of Midas, who dared to oppose an important deity.[4] The equation, mind or intellect=phallus, also holds true for its obverse: stupidity=castration. Thus, the asses' ears symbolize castration, and Midas feared exposure of his castrated state.[5]

Like Midas, the impostor also fears exposure. He is afraid that his castrated state (the small penis in the male and complete castration in the female) will be exposed. Just as Midas hid his defect under his turban, the impostor tries to hide his castration.

The male impostor pretends he is masculine as he assumes the role of a male. Sometimes this pretense may be carried to an extreme. For example, the bulging muscles of an athlete may be a coverup for sexual inadequacy; in essence he is saying "look at my big penis" in his attempt to hide his "small penis." Weissman (1963) described a patient who, suffering from feelings of sexual inadequacy, "did not have intercourse until after he entered analysis; when he did, he undertook it in grand style. He invited his girl to his apartment for dinner, served with Italian wine in a candle-lit atmosphere. He approached her in the character of a sophisticated, strong-willed lover with much élan and experience. Subsequently his sexual interest dwindled, and he returned to his former non-sexual relationship with the girl, alternately being consoled by her for his inadequacies and playing towards her the role of a father."

The female impostor pretends she has a penis, which unconsciously she believes she possesses, because she fears exposure of her castrated state. In discussing penis envy, Hayward (1943) wrote: "In identifying with the father the woman has achieved a penis . . . When with this illusory penis she seeks to compete with father's real one she is at a disadvantage. She risks being unmasked as an impostor, of having the penis proven to be merely illusory, of actually being castrated." Fenichel (1945) stated: "Exhibitionistic women always behave as if they were pretending and are afraid that the truth might come out. The idea of being exposed in their 'castrated' state is the main unconscious content of many a female anxiety hysteria." So long as the female impostor can maintain the illusory penis, then she feels adequate,

---

[4]His reputation for stupidity had already been established in an earlier myth, in which he made an unwise request to Bacchus: "Grant that whatever I touch may turn to gold!"

[5]Midas may have already had some doubt about his adequacy. In addition to the anal implication of the earlier gold myth, one might suspect that his obsession to acquire wealth was an overcompensation for feelings of inferiority.

self-confident, and capable; without it, she feels inadequate and insecure. With the illusory penis she can engage in and even enjoy sexuality; without it, she may become frigid. One sees this happen sometimes during psychoanalysis: Before treatment the female patient can participate in heterosexuality, but as treatment progresses, the illusion of the penis can no longer be maintained and frigidity may become a troublesome symptom.

Mrs. S., an attractive, thirty-eight-year-old woman, came for treatment because of depression, lack of interest in sex, and recurrent colitis. She appeared to be a very capable woman both in her home and in the various organizations in which she participated. However, she often referred to herself as an impostor because beneath this capable appearance, she felt very inadequate. Although she was usually not interested in intercourse, she would submit in order to please her husband. Two types of fantasies could arouse her: one in which she would identify herself with a phallic female, such as Mae West; the other in which a young woman would be dominated by an older, powerful male. Mrs. S. could only achieve orgasm by recourse to the following fantasy: A young, attractive girl would arouse an older man by displaying some of her physical assets; he would then present her with an expensive fur coat, and just at the moment of presentation the patient would have her orgasm. Analysis revealed that this was an oedipal fantasy and that the fur coat represented the penis.

This patient had an illusory penis. She would often see herself with a penis or with an enema nozzle protruding from her vagina, which she envisioned in other women also. Once she slipped and said, "I know I'm a male." Occasionally she would have the fantasy that she actually had a penis and was having intercourse with other women. These homosexual fantasies resulted in a great deal of anxiety and even a mild phobic avoidance of certain women. In addition, she was preoccupied a great deal with her looks, her attractiveness to men, and was, indeed, quite vain about her appearance. In fact, she would not wear her glasses in my office until after two years of analysis. She was very distressed at the idea of growing older and thus possibly becoming less attractive; she equated her body and face with the penis.

So long as Mrs. S. was able to maintain the illusion of possessing a penis, she was able to function fairly well. She did her household chores, fulfilled her social obligations, and was able to submit to her husband's sexual wishes. However, as she grew older and felt less attractive, it became more difficult for her to maintain this illusion. When treatment finally brought the illusion to consciousness, analyzed its significance, and, finally, demolished it, her faulty foundation crumbled. She became depressed and lost interest in her home and in her social obligations. She lost her desire for sex, and the act became repugnant and frightening to her; she could no longer use her former fantasies for arousal and orgasm. Regression became pronounced. She felt incapable of performing even simple household chores. She preferred to sleep and stay in her bedroom all day long, becoming almost completely dependent on her husband. Although she had felt like an impostor with her illusory penis, it at least sustained her; without it, she felt weak, inadequate, helpless, and frightened.

Fear of exposure, then, is the fear of exposure of the castrated state. But why should the impostor dread this? Let us examine what exposure of castration means to both the male and the female. The male fears exposure of his "small penis;" exposed, he feels defenseless and vulnerable to attack from an environment that he considers to be adult and hostile. Once more he feels like a boy who expects and fears castration from the potent father for his incestuous and hostile wishes. Furthermore, this exposure, which nullifies his pseudomasculine defense, may restimulate repressed homosexual and masochistic wishes. Thus, he fears not only the castrating father but also homosexual and masochistic submission to him. Furthermore, he fears that he may experience shame and embarrassment (narcissistic mortification) from exposure of his genital inadequacy.

In the case of the female, castration, with associated feelings of inadequacy, inferiority, and vulnerability to attack, may bring about anxiety. But I believe that the "castrated female's" main cause of anxiety is feminine masochism and that the illusion of having a penis is a defense that must be maintained to prevent the ego from being overwhelmed by this pathologic feminine masochism. Rado (1933) said: "The illusory penis is not a simple product of penis envy but a narcissistic reaction formation of the ego, its bulwark against repressed genital impulses, and it must be strong enough to resist these forces." Mrs. S. developed masochistic fears at the same time that she lost her illusory penis. She became frightened of men, particularly if they made mildly suggestive remarks or indicated some interest in her. Even her husband's erect penis frightened her, especially upon penetration; penetration also affirmed her castration. She began to have a fear of being raped; this fear was a defense against her masochistic wishes, which were often expressed in her fantasies and dreams. On the couch she would invariably become aroused (and anxious) whenever she had the masochistic thought or fantasy that the analyst was belittling her or was going to attack her sexually. In short, her illusory penis (and the resultant homosexual fantasies) had served as a defense against her feminine masochistic wishes.

Even though the feeling is unpleasant, the neurotic impostor maintains his impostrous façade at all costs. He cannot reveal his true self, for to expose his castration would produce overwhelming anxiety. Imposture, the lesser of two evils, is therefore the impostor's defense against this anxiety. In order to avoid exposure the impostor resorts to various defensive maneuvers. For example, he may avoid all situations and people where his deficiencies might be revealed. His interpersonal relations are, at best, superficial; he is afraid of getting close to people, for fear that they will find out about him. A latent homosexual patient would start to withdraw from people—men or women—as soon as they began to show some interest in him. He feared that they would discover his lack of masculinity. Another male patient resisted undergoing a routine physical examination. He had mild hypertension and tachycardia, which he had been told were caused by nervousness. Because he equated nervousness with lack of masculinity, he feared that the examining physician would also make this association. Fenichel (1945) described a patient who, whenever he went to a movie, would crouch behind the person in front of him and hide his face behind his turned-up coat collar. He did not want people to see him there without a girl, for fear that they would know he was impotent and laugh at him.

To avoid exposure, the impostor may attempt to introject or identify himself with a potent male figure (group, movement, or profession). So long as this relationship continues, he is imbued with vicarious strength; once it ends, however, he feels unprotected and vulnerable—like an Ajax without the skin of the Nemean lion. Occasionally, an impotent male will identify with a strong phallic woman; without her, he feels weak and threatened (Shevin, 1963).

Many inhibitions—such as work and learning—may result from this fear of exposure. Any productive attempt is fraught with anxiety, for fear that it may be imperfect, thereby revealing the individual as inadequate and vulnerable. A social worker, although very competent, had considerable difficulty writing up a case for presentation. He spent substantial effort on the report, writing and rewriting it. But since he could not achieve the perfection he desired, he feared that his supervisor and colleagues would find fault with it, thus recognizing his inadequacy. A female physician with a learning inhibition was extremely reluctant to study for her specialty boards. She felt that since she could never completely master her subject (that is, be a man) her imposture would eventually be exposed. She feared the exposure and loss of her illusory penis. From her point of view, taking the exam was like a man "putting his penis on a board and it would be cut off." An architect with a work-inhibition symptom finally submitted a drawing for a contest, but under an assumed name. He was afraid of embarrassment if he lost; he was also afraid to win, however, for he might not be able to maintain the high standards that would then be expected of him. A young man with an outstanding ability to write always did very well when he began a new job. But as soon as his superior would criticize him, no matter how trivial it was, he would find that he could not write and would then be fired. Criticism meant exposure of his inadequacy; he became vulnerable to castration.

A troublesome neurotic symptom found in many impostors is the difficulty—often the impossibility—of urinating in a public lavatory, especially if other men are present. Standing up to urinate is a situation par excellence where the impostor's "small penis" is actually exposed. Being thus exposed and vulnerable, he fears an attack—usually castration from other men in the lavatory, whom he automatically considers more powerful and aggressive. However, the feared attack may also stem from masochistic and homosexual wishes. The resultant anxiety causes a spasm of the urethral sphincter, and the individual, thus afflicted, cannot begin to urinate. After a while he sneaks out of the lavatory, embarrassed, hoping that no one has noticed that he had not urinated.

These men are able to urinate if there is no danger of exposure. For example, they can urinate in a public lavatory if they are alone. Although they may be anxious about someone entering, once they have begun to urinate, they can usually continue despite the presence of others. These men can also urinate standing up in an enclosed stall or sitting down on a toilet, whether open or enclosed. In these situations there is usually less difficulty because the penis is not exposed.[6] Furthermore, they can urinate in the presence of little boys, who have even smaller penises and therefore are not a threat.

Treatment

Neurotic impostors may hesitate to come for treatment because they are afraid others will find out about them. This concern may continue for some time after they have started analysis or psychotherapy. When questioned about their fear, they usually reply that others will think less of them or that going to a psychiatrist will stigmatize them. However, analysis usually reveals that they equate going to a psychiatrist with genital inadequacy and that this is the secret they do not want others to know about.[7]

Because the difficulty is usually deep-rooted, the treatment of choice for the neurotic impostor is psychoanalysis. In treatment there are problems of resistance and transference, as in other patients, but there are often quantitative and qualitative differences. Generally, these patients are afraid to expose themselves on the analytic couch, just as they have been afraid to expose themselves elsewhere. It is difficult, even after a reasonable period of treatment, to elicit their anxiety about castration. Any attempt to explore this problem may be met with various defenses such as isolation, denial, and rationalization; sometimes they may become hostilely defensive.

[6]Sitting down to urinate (like a woman) may also represent self-castration in order to avoid castration.

[7]Since insurance plans now pay a substantial part of the fee, patients sometimes face a dilemma. Recently, a young woman wrestled with this problem: should she keep her psychotherapy a secret by paying for it herself, or should she take advantage of her firm's major medical policy—which would pay 50% of the fee, but require her to fill out papers, thereby informing the personnel department that she was in psychotherapy?

In analysis the male patient fears exposure of his small-penis complex because the analyst, an adult, may castrate him; if the analyst is a male, the patient may also fear a homosexual attack. Thus, it is difficult for him to develop a satisfactory transference relationship with all its regressive, positive, and negative aspects. He must maintain his defenses, for fear that exposure will render him vulnerable to the analyst. A young engineer who began analysis for many months spoke in a loud, gruff voice, with much obscenity and profanity. He would often come for his session dressed in dirty work clothes, even though he had had sufficient time to change. He was afraid that if people saw him dressed in a suit and clean shirt during the day they might consider him a sissy. His great need to appear masculine was, of course, a cover-up for his unmasculine feelings, including strong latent homosexuality. Whenever I attempted an interpretation of this character defense—suggesting that perhaps he did not feel so masculine under his façade—he would become very defensive, accusing me of being sadistic, of wanting to stigmatize patients, and of drawing wrong conclusions. He had such a strong need to resist exposure of his inadequacy that it seemed to be an insurmountable resistance. After repeated attempts at this interpretation, which was always followed by hostile rebuffs, I finally stopped. After a long period of time, with much confirmatory evidence from his daily life experiences, fantasies, and dreams, he finally became aware of and was able to accept his passive homosexual desires. With this acceptance his pretension stopped.

The female patient fears that treatment will expose her illusory penis and that she will then have to relinquish it. This fear may be expressed early in treatment, even in the first dream. A twenty-eight-year-old, unmarried woman in her eighth hour related her first dream in analysis: "There was a little box, like a cottage-cheese container, with a snake in it. I was afraid the snake would get out." As the symbolism indicated (and was later confirmed by associations and history), this patient feared that she would lose her illusory penis. She needed this penis not only because it gave her a feeling of status (making her equal to her prominent father), but also because it was her defense against intense feminine masochism. Because of her natural ability and drive, she achieved recognition in her field and became an executive in her organization. At the weekly meetings where she was the only female present, she always felt like an impostor. She felt that she really did not belong there and feared that her inadequacy would be discovered (that is, that she was a woman, a castrate). The fear of exposing herself carried over into her analysis, creating an obdurate resistance, which finally resulted in her discontinuing analysis after 18 months.

As one might expect, the main difficulty in analyzing the neurotic impostor is his resistance to exposure, namely, of the "small penis" in the male and of the illusory penis in the female. Sometimes this resistance can be overcome, as in the case of the engineer; at other times, this resistance is insurmountable, as in the case of the female executive. This resistance will tax the analyst's patience and skill. If a good working relationship can be established—where the patient considers the analyst to be his therapist and not someone who will harm or take advantage of him—there is a fair chance he will give up his impostrous defense and present himself unmasked. At such a time, shorn of his defense, the patient may show a severe reaction such as anxiety, depression, or regression, as in the case of Mrs. S. If this occurs, handling the patient and the analytic situation will require the utmost skill of the analyst.

Summary

"I feel like an impostor" is frequently expressed by patients, especially in analysis. Superficially, this subjective complaint occurs when there is a discrepancy between one's outward appearance and one's self-evaluation. The individual appears grown-up and adequate; inwardly, he feels immature and inadequate. On a deeper level this complaint derives from the castration complex and applies to both males and females. The male adopts a veneer of masculinity to hide his small-penis complex; the female hides her castration behind her illusory penis.

This chapter deals primarily with the neurotic impostor, that is, the individual who complains of feeling like an impostor; it is not about the notorious, delinquent impostor. The two types are compared; although there are numerous differences, the underlying dynamics are essentially the same, namely, a feeling of genital inadequacy.

The neurotic impostor fears exposure. The male fears that his pretense at masculinity will be recognized and that his "small penis" will then be exposed. The female fears exposure of her castrated state behind her illusory penis façade. Exposure of the castrated state results in castration anxiety in the male and masochistic anxiety in the female. *Being an impostor is an attempt to avoid exposure; it is a defense against the overwhelming anxiety that would result if the castrated state were exposed.*

Fear of exposure carries over into treatment and may produce serious resistances. Severe reactions may result once the impostrous defense has been removed. The utmost skill is required to treat the neurotic impostor.

References

Abraham, K. (1925). "The History of an Impostor in the Light of Psychoanalytical Knowledge." In *Clinical Papers and Essays on Psychoanalysis*. New York: Basic Books, 1955.

Crichton, R., *The Great Impostor*. New York: Random House, 1959.

Deutsch, H., "The Impostor: Contribution to Ego Psychology of a Type of Psychopath." *Psychoanal. Quart.* 24:483-505 (1955).

Fenichel, O., *The Psychoanalytic Theory of Neurosis.* New York: Norton, 1945.

Greenacre, P., "The Impostor." *Psychoanal. Quart.* 27:359-382 (1958a).

———. "The Relation of the Impostor to the Artist." *Psychoanal. Study of the Child* 13:521-540 (1958b).

Hayward, E. P., "Type of Female Castration Reaction." *Psychoanal. Quart.* 12:45-66 (1943).

Ovid, *Metamorphoses.* Trans. by R. Humphries. Bloomington: Indiana University Press, 1957.

Rado, S., "Fear of Castration in Women." *Psychoanal. Quart.* 2:425-475 (1933).

Royidis, E., *Pope Joan.* Trans. by L. Durrell. New York: Dutton, 1961.

Shevin, F. F., "Countertransference and Identity Phenomena Manifested in the Analysis of a Case of 'Phallus Girl' Identity." *Journ. Amer. Psychoanal. Assoc.* 11:331-344 (1963).

Strabo., *Geography.* Trans. by H. L. Jones. Cambridge, Mass.: Harvard University Press, 1949.

Weissman, P., "The Effects of Paternal Attitudes on Development." *Inter. Journ. of Psychoanal.* 44:121-131, (1963).

Chapter XX

Cosmic Laughter: A Study of Primitive Splitting

Vamik D. Volkan, M.D.

There was a little girl
  And she had a little curl,
Right in the middle of her forehead,
  And when she was good
  She was very, very good;
But when she was bad she was horrid!
       (Jane's favorite nursery rhyme)

During early development the child creates integrated object and self-concepts in a piecemeal fashion, and only after repeated trials accomplishes the mending of the split between "good" and "bad" object and self-images. Although they disagreed on many fundamental points, both Klein (1932) and Jacobson (1964), in studying the earliest stages of psychic development, showed how these trials continue until the tolerance of ambivalence is at least attained.

The term *splitting* is used here in the restricted sense in which Kernberg (1966, 1968, 1971) employed it to refer to the process of active separation of introjects and identifications of opposite quality. The patient's self- and object images built up under the influence of libidinal drive derivatives are not integrated with the corresponding self- and object images built up under the influence of aggressive drive derivatives. This division, occurring at first because of the lack of integrative capacity in the early ego, later becomes defensive . . .

> . . . to prevent the generalization of anxiety and to protect the ego core built
> around positive introjections (introjections and identifications established under
> the influence of libidinal drive derivatives). (Kernberg, 1966)

The child's attempts to develop an integrated concept of self and relatedness to the simultaneously "good" and "bad" objects are not exactly like those of the adult patient who possesses aspects of an ego sufficiently differentiated to be used for observation or defensive functioning even when he

A preliminary version of this paper was first read at the annual meeting of the American Psychoanalytic Association in Washington, D.C., on May 2, 1971.

is pregenitally fixated or regressed to an earlier level. The clinical picture can be confusing; but the dominant clinical manifestation of the adult who uses primitive splitting is, nevertheless, that external objects are either "all good" or "all bad" ones "with the concomitant possibility of complete, abrupt shifts of an object from one extreme compartment to the other; that is, sudden and complete reversal of all feelings and conceptuatlizations about a particular person" (Kernberg, 1966).

The analyst treating a patient given to excessive use of primitive splitting observes that whenever the patient's "good" object becomes "bad" he will reverse the qualities of another object to maintain a balance. Moreover, with splitting the patient oscillates between extreme and contradictory self-concepts. In this paper I will describe a patient who made extensive use of primitive splitting, as well as introjective-projective relatedness. In the thirty-third month of her treatment she had a unique experience on the couch that she called "cosmic laughter." I believe that an examination of the genetic roots of this experience discloses its origin in recollections of experience at the breast—the sudden change of a gratifying breast into a bad one that no longer gratified. Thus "cosmic laughter" will be seen in the light of the Isakower phenomenon (1938) and Lewin's dream screen (1946, 1948, 1953). It presented itself as a turning point of her analysis since it was reflected in her ability to tolerate, with the help of identification with the analyst's analytic attitude and interpretive work, primitive feelings from which she had previously protected herself by primitive splitting.

On the surface cosmic laughter seemed to be a disorganization. Nevertheless, the beginnings of new organization were evident behind it.

CLINICAL ILLUSTRATION

The patient, whom I shall call Jane, showed a repeated pattern of making wide cathectic swings between libidinally investing an object, and then investing it with aggression.

She was a twenty-one-year-old art student attending a college within a hundred miles of her house when I first saw her. The college psychiatrist had made the diagnosis of acute schizophrenic reaction and sent her to us for hospitalization. He felt that her anxiety had increased as her college graduation approached; she reported seeing bizarre alterations in his office such as undulations in the walls and in the ceiling, and changes in colors.

Jane's father managed an estate whose present and long-time owner had inherited it, along with substantial holdings elsewhere, from her husband, whom she had met when as a young self-supporting woman she had nursed him through an illness. She occupied the main house little more than three months a year, and Jane's family had all the resources of a lavishly equipped farm at their disposal much as though Jane's father were himself the owner. The arrangement was one of long standing, since Jane's grandfather had been the manager before his death, and his son had lived on the estate since he was five years old. Jane felt a sense of unreality, however, as she noted the class and role differentials that came into focus when the real owner was in residence and Jane's mother lapsed from being the "queen" into being perforce a "lady-in-waiting" at the beck and call of the owner.

At the time of their marriage Jane's father was in his late twenties, her mother only seventeen. The couple's first child, a year and a half older than Jane, had a congenital heart-lung deformity and died in her mother's arms on the way to the hospital when Jane was a year and a half. The mother had experienced great anxiety over the frailty of the first child, and was unable to grieve over its death and unable to mother Jane adequately. (She later had two sons, three and seven years younger than Jane, respectively.) Moreover, while she was nursing Jane she had a breast infection. The first dream Jane reported in her treatment was one of being fed a huge bowl of oatmeal, falling into it, and starting to choke before her anxiety awakened her. She had had temper tantrums during the anal phase of her development; her mother had *laughed* helplessly at them, unable to harness the little girl's aggression. As Jane grew, her more differentiated parts related to external objects as other than self-representations, but the core of relationship to objects on the "symbiotic" or "early separation-individuation" levels (Mahler, 1968) remained unchanged.

When she was five, her father began to play sexual games with her. He would show her his erect penis, make her touch and fondle it, and he would kiss her genital area; there was no actual intercourse. Their "secret" at the oedipal level resulted in Jane's regression and aided the preservation of the earlier symbiotic core and kept alive the primitive object relationships. The incestuous relationship continued until the patient had her first menstrual period at which time Jane's father approached her in her bedroom and kissed her breast so hard that she screamed; her father never touched her sexually again.

As a teenager she aspired to a marriage that would bring her wealth and social position; in this goal she was an extension of her mother, and reflected the example of the estate's owner who had married so successfully. Her mother encouraged her to shine socially, but social climbing was hard for her. She was sent to a college traditionally acceptable to wealthy Southern girls, but had to wait on tables to meet her expenses; she raged silently over this necessity. Her acute psychosis appeared a few months before she was to have graduated.

THE TREATMENT

Jane's treatment lasted for six years and a month, during which time she was seen four times a week, except for a six-month period at the end of the first year when she was out of town finishing her requirements for graduation and could come to therapy only twice a week. Throughout the first 16 months she was admitted to the hospital from time to time for brief stays. However, I saw her in my office except for one or two occasions when she was too violent to leave the ward and I saw her there.

After she graduated from school and we had completed a year and a half of face-to-face work she switched to the couch; we were able to establish a psychoanalytic relationship and in due course to arrive at termination.

At first she declared that she was "empty," and complained of losing her identity. She reminded me of a silent kitten who would become a bloody tiger at times, physically harming herself or others. For a year she talked endlessly about dreams and fantasies of detached nipples, penises, and breasts. Bulls, horses, wolves, and cats appeared in her fantasies and dreams as devouring and bloody creatures, to be followed suddenly by objects that were soothing. She described all objects, animate or inanimate, as either "benign" or "aggressive."

While she was returning to her school during the six-month period she kept making "mental snapshots" of me during our sessions in order to "keep in touch" with me while she was away, and to be able to tolerate her life at school and to study.

After graduating she lived in the home of her parents and began going about with a psychotic young man with transsexual tendencies whom she had met in the hospital. On one level he represented her own split-off and degraded self-image; on another, she saw herself as his "savior."

After initially reacting to the couch with increased helplessness, she gave evidence that her thought processes were becoming better organized and her primitive splitting more crystallized. The head nurse of the hospital ward on which she had spent so much time became an "all-good" mother, and I was perceived as the "all-bad" mother, at times being condensed with "the devil"—the all-bad father. At the same time, after the transsexual left town, she tried to carry out her mother's unspoken command by dating a young man with "credentials," who took her from one humiliating event to another. She was able to deny her humiliations in order to be ready to go out with him again. Her past experiences with him were not integrated with present activities and expectations. Two years after her treatment began she found employment as a secretary to a surgeon.

In her repeating dreams her father's sexual attacks on her continued while the "noncaring," almost paralyzed mother watched without interfering. Then the nature of her dreams underwent subtle alterations, and Jane made attempts in them to protect herself from being attacked. Shortly after this an event in the external world had a significant influence on me and my patient. One of my small children was in an automobile accident and had to be hospitalized for some months because of a leg injury. As luck would have it, he was seen in the Emergency Room by the surgeon who employed Jane, so she learned of the event in the course of her work. She regressed, and in the transference I became the grieving mother who was concerned and waiting for the death of her first child as she withdrew her "breast" from Jane herself. In a gesture of saving the early mother-analyst she brought peaches for me to eat. She attempted to put them in my parked car at the hospital, and, finding it locked, temporarily broke with reality, connecting a widely publicized recent disastrous earthquake in Turkey with a view of me as an undependable, shaky, Turkish analyst-mother. I was now a "bad object" and the "boy with credentials" an "all-good object." She denied the reality aspects of the young man until he unexpectedly married another girl. This event had a shock effect. She had to keep me as "all bad"; her family, which could not give her emotional support at this time, was "all bad," also. She was unprepared to find an "all-good" object to soothe her. It was then she experienced her cosmic laughter episode, in which laughter burst from an oyster-colored cloud that represented the breast. Analysis indicated that she was also responding to the genetic aspect of her experiences at her mother's breast—its presumably sudden withdrawal from the nursing infant because of the pain of infection. With the help of interpretation she tolerated the generalized primitive emotions that stemmed from this experience. The ego was strengthened because primitive emotions were faced, and the need for splitting lessened. Energy previously used for the mechanism of primitive splitting was thus freed.

The next step was Jane's physical separation from her parental home, a few months after the experience of cosmic laughter. Her move to an apartment of her own represented intrapsychic separation from the symbiotic mother. The symbiotic tie to her mother was represented by the family cat, to which Jane referred as "my root into my mother." She submitted it to veterinary treatment she suspected would prove fatal, and went into genuine grief reaction when it died.

She began to exhibit "adult interest," speaking of current community affairs and public issues such as the war in Vietnam. Her father's sexual attacks upon her in her dreams came to an end when in one of the dreams she said "No!" to her attacker instead of waiting for her mother to come to her rescue. She befriended one of her brother's friends, and they fell in love "like two teenagers." I became again "an intruder." The remnants of primitive splitting continued, but now she could relate with ambivalence to me, to her boyfriend, and to others.

In the fourth year of her treatment much of the work focused on her ownership of a penis and the anxiety of giving it up to become "a perfect woman." She dreamed that she was lost in a forest with her boyfriend when they came upon a turbulent river which she could cross to reach a peaceful shore, but he could not. She separated from him in reality and went into a stormy grief. She was now ready to look for a man instead of a "boy" like the companion she had left behind.

When she gave up her "penis" she wanted to be the analyst's mate, to bear his children. A tolerance of affectionate feelings, particularly toward men, slowly appeared. She perceived me as an ideal and perfect man; this perception was punctured by the interpretations I made. She left her secretarial job and became an elementary schoolteacher after taking further qualifying studies. This behavior evidenced her identification with her analyst, a teacher in a medical school. She became a very good teacher.

A generalized grief over the termination of analysis anticipated it. In the termination phase she briefly "visited" her primitive splitting to mend it once again. In one of her dreams she faced a dangerous convict who represented her previously untamed aggression, and "tamed" him. In the last hour of therapy she spontaneously recalled her experience of cosmic laughter. She spoke of the Cheshire Cat in *Alice in Wonderland,* and how its grin had faded away. It was this way with her cosmic laughter, she explained.

Follow-up

I saw Jane briefly six months after the termination of her analysis. She unexpectedly appeared in my doorway, explaining that she had come to say goodbye before leaving town to begin life anew in a distant city where she had secured an excellent position. During the next two years I had a few letters that spoke of her doing well, and two years and a half after ending analysis she married a very suitable young man.

Cosmic Laughter

Preoccupation with Laughter

During the first two years of her treatment, especially during her disorganized moments, Jane expected to hear my laughter. This expectation, as her treatment progressed, was understood in relation to her mother's laughter as it appeared in one series of Jane's repeating dreams. In these dreams she sat in the middle of a circle of chairs, all of which were empty except for one occupied by her mother, who laughed helplessly while her child made convulsive gestures. In her analysis I came to understand these dreams as Jane's attempt to convulse out of the symbiotic core. The laughter was the grieving mother's discharge of tension brought about by her helplessness. Grotjahn's (1972) formulation concerning laughter may be usefully applied to Jane's preoccupation with *laughter* in the early mother-child relationship. Grotjahn stated that:

> The customary Freudian interpretation about the sudden release of dammed-up hostility, combined with some form of infantile pleasure, the saving of repressive energy, symbolic disguises and social acceptance, the release of no longer repressed hostility and the final liberation of this repressive effort in laughter remains valid.

He adds, however, that, "the symbolism of introjection and extrojection can help to interpret the specific unconscious symbolic significance of the act of laughter." Laughter, especially the explosive kind Jane expected to hear, might be in the service of releasing the bad introjects; in Grotjahn's words— one lets the cat out of the bag.

Events Prior to the Cosmic Laughter Experience

Four months before Jane underwent the experience of cosmic laughter, my small son was hospitalized for some months following the automobile accident previously mentioned. Jane sensed my distress although I did not convey it verbally; she vacillated between temporarily identifying with my son and trying to assuage my concern, feeling frustration in both positions. In the transference I became her mother who was anxious with the fatally ill older sibling as she fed and cared for Jane, and who suffered from a breast infection during much of the time Jane was at the breast.

Jane became fascinated with the pictures of cancerous breasts she found in medical books. The sight of them made her feel disorganized and gave her headaches. The introjective-projective relatedness to me was dominant. A primitive splitting of self and object representations was reflected in this type of relatedness.

The events of several hours during the 1½ months before the cosmic laughter experience will illustrate the cathectic shifts and changes reflected in the mechanism of introjection and projection. Such shifts and changes must occur until it becomes possible to tolerate ambivalence (Jacobson, 1964), and their excessive appearance prior to the cosmic laughter experience indicates Jane's inability to relate to objects with love and hate simultaneously, and her reliance on primitive splitting.

Without conscious awareness that November 22 was the anniversary of John F. Kennedy's assassination, Jane announced, at the beginning of that month, that her death would come about on that date.

November 3: She reported that "bad air" was trapped in her body. She wanted someone to stab her with an ice pick so that the raging evil could escape. She heard my voice saying, "Shall we start?" as an inner hallucination. I understood that she had taken me in as a soothing object to combat the evil.

November 4: Jane reported a deadness within herself after the previous session. I understood this as being possibly an autistic defense against the war raging within her. She spoke of wanting to become a surgeon, in a demonstration of her desire to excise the raging introjects and primitive self representations. Then she wanted to murder me; this wish I understood as a possibility that a sadistic image was projected on me, and that my annihilation was necessary for her protection. Lastly, she talked about having written a letter to a local radio station requesting ''good music.'' This seemed to indicate a wish for auditory introjection of good object representations to combat the evil within.

November 7: Jane talked about having rearranged her furniture. I felt that the items of furniture represented her self and object representations and that their rearrangement was indicative of an effort to control the eruption of primitive affect states.

November 8: I was ''all bad'' and she was panic-stricken. She spoke of wanting to be fat. This I understood as a symbol of protection against internalizing the ''bad'' image. She talked about a visit to the zoo and about snakes, alligators, monkeys, etc. (animalized, fragmented, and projected self and object representations. The inner world described by Kleinians also includes wild beasts perceived as very violent.)

November 9: Her muscles were filled with evil. She begged to be taken out of her body.

November 10: I became a vulture. Jane saw ''little people'' on the floor.

November 14: I was again all bad. She reported dreams of people being killed.

November 21: She expressed fear of being robbed by her mother.

November 22: She expressed surprise that she had not died, and acknowledged that this was the anniversary of the President's death.

At the beginning of the next month I went away for a week, according to my announced plan. On my return I found her denying aspects of my absence. The young man who was so ''socially eligible'' and had the right ''credentials'' was invested with primitive idealization. She hoped and believed that they would marry, and was shocked to hear from her mother in the middle of the same month that he had maried someone else. It later appeared that it was at that moment that she heard the cosmic laughter as an inner hallucination. She managed to withdraw from the experience, only to have it develop fully as she lay on the couch next day. I found it significant that Jane did not become fully disorganized at the moment of hearing the news of the wedding and that she waited until the next day on the couch to respond to it. It was evident that she brought the incident into the transference and the analytic working through, so the experience she had was in the service of observing, tolerating, and mastering this disappointment.

Description of the Cosmic Laughter

Jane began to stutter when she tried to tell me about the marriage of the "boy with credentials." She shook her head in violent negation as though she were using the first symbolic assertion (Spitz, 1957, 1965) to arrest her overwhelming emotionality. She clenched her fists as an infant does and tried to stop the shaking of her head by pressing it between her hands. Her body seemed in torment; she made crying sounds like an animal's and seemed no longer to be human.

When she finally mobilized her early ferocious introjects she put a stop to what she was doing by slapping her face and crying, "Shut up! Shut up!" Interestingly enough, she reported that part of her had been able to observe the experience. However, what she observed was not the logical connection between her emotional storm and her young man's rejection, or the rejection I had exemplified by my short leave from my office. Through defensive regression she was expecting a nursing experience in the transference, and I believe that what she observed was the symbolic representation of the earliest frustration at the breast, the sudden transformation of a "good" breast into a "bad" one, and that this was the earliest genetic root of her cosmic laughter experience.

FIGURE 1

Her explanation of what she observed was hard to follow. She offered to make a drawing to explain it more clearly. In the accompanying drawing (Figure 1), *A* represents Jane as seen through a *higher* level splitting. Because of this she was able to observe and report her unique experience. *B* is also Jane, represented as a circle. *C* is the "cosmic plateau," which she perceived as a puffy, oyster-colored cloud in which a window (*E*) appears. Over this window knelt an "omnipotent person" (*D*), mischievous and teasing, with whom at times Jane merged and became interchangeable. During the experience Jane felt that this omnipotent person's relationship with her self (the circle *B*) ceased *abruptly*, and that when it ceased the omnipotent person broke into cosmic laughter that echoed in Jane's mind long after it had stopped. The past, the present, and the future converged in what was happening. The omnipotent person seemed to Jane to speak or laugh through other people at times—through her analyst, for example.

Associations

In telling about cosmic laughter she recalled: (a) having had similar experiences in the first grade when the class had rhythmic singing and she would swing abruptly from a happy mood into one of distress; (b) having been at church with her family during the previous week, and being upset to learn from her father that she was sitting where communion would be offered, since she had decided never to take it again; (c) at the end of the hour she referred to certain Indian tribes where children are allowed to go hungry, given the breast briefly, and then deprived again in order to frustrate them and make it certain that they will develop into fierce warriors in adult life.

The Understanding of the Experience

Since the appearance of Isakower's (1938) widely known report on patients who recapture perceptually the experience of nursing at the breast, many other analysts have observed this phenomenon in their own patients. In a recent paper (Volkan, 1973) I described the appearance of the Isakower phenomenon during the analysis of a narcissistic patient who felt colored balloons filling his mouth as he lay on the couch. This was described as a regressive defense, recalling Fink's (1967) report on the Isakower phenomenon as a regressive defense against other disturbing recollections.

Related versions of the Isakower phenomenon are found in the dream screen (Lewin, 1946, 1948, 1953), blank dreams (Rycroft, 1951), blank hallucinations (Stern, 1961), and blank silences (Van der Heide, 1961). Garma (1955) and Sperling (1957) reported the appearance in their patients of experiences at the breast, condensed with other memories from a higher developmental level. Easson (1973) recognized the Isakower phenomenon in patients under the influence of LSD or other drugs.

In Jane's experience the cosmic plateau (*C*) may represent the mother's breast. The concepts of the Isakower phenomenon and the dream screen are related to Freud's assumption that the first object in life is the breast. Direct observation of infants shows that . . .

> . . . up to three months of life (and longer), a nursing baby will not look at the breast but at the mother's face. This is an observational fact. He does not look at the breast when the mother approaches him, he looks at her face; he continues looking at her face while he has her nipple in his mouth and is manipulating her breast. From the moment the mother comes into the room to the end of nursing, he stares at his mother's face. (Spitz, 1965)

Boyer (1956, 1960) observed that psychotics as well as babies watch their mother's faces and reactions as they feed. Elkisch (1957) and Greenacre (1958) wrote about the significance of the face in the developing object relations. Searles (1963) suggested that the therapist's face has a central role in the symbiotic interaction. Such observations made it necessary to modify the propositions of Isakower and Lewin; the Isakower phenomenon and Lewin's dream screen are not representations of the breast, but rather those of the visually perceived human face. Spitz (1965) offered the following modification . . .

> . . .While the Isakower phenomenon is a reactivation of the record of early infant contact perception. . . Lewin's concept of "breast" actually is a code symbol for the totality of the oral experience . . .

Almansi (1960) worked further on this modification, stating:

> . . . on a primitive perceptual level the face may be equated with the breasts, and . . . there is a particularly strong correlation between the nipples and the eyes . . .

Spitz refers to Stern's (1961) finding it improbable that the Isakower phenomenon—and, by implication, Lewin's dream screen as well—might be a regression to a blissful memory of a state of tension reduction and quiescence. Spitz continues:

> On the contrary, he (Stern) advances the proposition that it is a regression to mnemonic traces of deprivation in the same situation. This is a plausible idea even if for no other reason than that experiences cathected with unpleasure are more likely to leave memory traces than those cathected with the affect of pleasure . . . I see no objection to such an interpretation either . . . what seems essential to me is the regression to the nursing situation. (1965)

In Jane's drawing of the cosmic laughter experience the window (*E*) may represent the nipple/eye above her, the circle (*B*) represent her mouth-self. Jane made other drawings at a time when she said she was experiencing her "plugging stage." This occurred at a later time in her analysis when I had surgery and became for a short time an unavailable mother. She felt empty then and in need of "having her batteries recharged." These drawings added to my understanding of the cosmic laughter experience. They show the orifices of the body as electric outlets. Nipples are plugged into the body to supply needed energy. Breasts are seen from the inside. There is anger and frustration on the face of the infant recipient, who has secondary sexual characteristics. Her experience of nursing was certainly not a blissful one for Jane as she recalled it symbolically in these pictures. It is a matter of record that her mother had had infected breasts while nursing her, and it is highly possible that she may have jerked her nipple away from the baby because of pain, as I have indicated before.

The omnipotent person (D) in all likelihood represents the omnipotent mother with whom the child sometimes fused. Although the drawing shows a stick figure, it may represent the total mother as well as a part object. The cosmic plateau appears to be the nipple, the breast, and the mother, or at least the mother's reaction to nursing as her facial expression reveals it. The laughter comes whenever the omnipotent person abruptly terminates the relationship, and the affective response to it is "total humiliation."

In 1905 Freud stated that "the conditions for laughter are such that a sum of psychic energy hitherto employed in the cathexis of some paths may experience free discharge," and Kris (1952) suggested that the word *suddenly* should be added to this formulation, explaining that "the word is essential since it is precisely the 'shock nature' and suddenness of the discharge which is the specific precondition of laughter." Jane used the word *abruptly* in telling about her cosmic laughter experience and again in her associations.

It is quite possible that the mother may have laughed in an attempt to provide a symbolic and socially acceptable disguise for the sudden release of hostility. I am certain that aspects of Jane's experience that derived from the oral level were condensed with aspects from higher levels. The mother's laughter has been mentioned before in connection with the "circle of chairs" dreams; it represented the discharge of the helplessness that led her to leave her child to deal with her temper tantrums as best she could by herself during the anal and phallic stages.

In the last year of her analysis while talking about her fear of not finding a husband. Jane had a feeling that cosmic laughter experience would return. This was accompanied by dreams in which she felt "something" was dangling" before her. Her associations indicated that the "something" was her father's penis. He had "dangled" it before her, but she, in actuality, never possessed it. In spite of her fears of her father's penis, she was disillusioned by not having it. Briefly, the phallic aspect of cosmic laughter involved her perceiving her father's penis being "jerked away" from her; her primitive relatedness to the breast was condensed into the relatedness to the penis. The interpretation of this stopped her fear that cosmic laughter experience would return.

Clinical Improvement

In examining the similarities between the dream screen phenomenon and Jane's experience of cosmic laughter, and in viewing the latter as a turning point for the patient, I quote from Rycroft's (1951) report that in analysis . . .

> . . . the occurrence of a blank dream marks . . . a turning point, namely, from a narcissistic state toward a recathexis of the external world and a thrust in ego development.

Prior to the dream, Rycroft's patient had related to him largely on the basis of narcissistic identification. The dream indicated a shift of importance in the transference relationship. Van der Heide (1961) indicated a similar opinion when he held that the borderline patient's blank silences not only are defensive in nature but lead to clinical improvement. Boyer (1960), after observing the visual dream screen phenomena presented by seven schizophrenic or borderline analysands, offered the tentative hypothesis that dream screen experiences appear in therapy (a) when the patient reaches a stage of development in which narcissistic identification is giving way to true object relationships by means of transference; (b) when there is a threat of losing the new object; and (c) when an event in the external world reminds the analysand strongly of a severe childhood trauma that he interpreted as desertion by the mothering figure.

The end result of the cosmic laughter experience resembles the kind of thinking involved in the end results of what Wetmore (1963) called *effective grief*. He described effective grief in the unique ambiance of the psychoanalytical situation as different from the working through of ordinary day-to-day grief described by Freud (1917). He hypothesized that . . .

> . . . the child cannot grieve effectively, and therefore cannot relinquish the earliest essential object-relationships. This means that the repetition compulsion must continue in full command of the personality until the time when the ego discovers that it can tolerate the postponed separation anxiety, and, so strengthened, can face the work of grieving. . . . Effective grief-work results not only in giving up the object, but in a deintensification of the drive which determined the person's neurotic attachment to the object. The libido is not just transferred, but the inherent quality of the attachment is changed.

As already described, the events in the external world—the loss of the loved boyfriend at the time the analyst was representing an "all-bad" object—defensively resulted in regression to the experience at the mother's breast. However, because of the mother's grief and her infected breast, Jane's experience of nursing at her breast had been traumatic for her. Nevertheless, as Rycroft (1951) suggested concerning the appearance of the dream screen in analysis, the cosmic laughter experience represented for her a reestablishment of object relationship with the nursing mother in the course of her transference. Furthermore, cosmic laughter represents the eruption of primal feelings connected with libidinal and aggressive drives, occasioned by the sudden changing of the mother's breast (the analyst) from a gratifying object to a nongratifying one.

Because the analyst remained calm and maintained an analytic attitude, Jane's nursing experience on the couch was not a mere repetition of something from the past. Through her identification with the analytical attitude her ego could now *tolerate* the tensions and emotions from which her primitive splitting had previously protected her. The reestablishment of relationship to the nursing mother in the transference thus had a corrective influence and enabled her to start essential changes in her relatedness to objects. The tolerance of the primitive feelings in analysis accounted for the reduction of need for primitive splitting and Jane's progress toward ambivalent relatedness to objects, as well as her increasing ability to mend contradictory ego states instead of regressing to an autistic position. Kleinians may refer to this process as moving from a paranoid to a depressive position and reaching a "crucial juncture" (Klein, 1952) for the choice of neurosis or psychosis.

In the usual course of treatment the reach toward the "crucial juncture" is gradual. In Jane's case the dramatic and sudden experience of cosmic laughter, precipitated by external events, was quickly followed by actions on her part that represented an energetic attempt to break off symbiotic ties with her mother. Thus Jane's experience of cosmic laughter is consistent with the remarks of Rycroft (1951), Boyer (1960), and Van der Heide (1961) suggesting that the appearance of the dream screen of blank silence leads to clinical improvement.

SUMMARY

It has been suggested in the psychoanalytic literature that the appearance in analysis of the Isakower phenomenon and/or the dream screen phenomenon may be an indication of clinical improvement besides serving a defensive function. This paper describes a patient's unique experience, which she called "cosmic laughter," that occurred in her defensive regression, and relates how it led to the reestablishment, in the transference, of her nursing relatedness. It is demonstrated that during her cosmic laughter experience the patient felt and tolerated primitive feelings from which her primitive splitting had previously protected her. Thus the need for her to use primitive splitting was reduced, and her progress toward the capacity for ambivalent relatedness promoted.

References

Almansi, R. H., "The Face-Breast Equation." *J. Amer. Psychoanal. Assoc.* 8:43-70 (1960).

Boyer, L. B., "On Maternal Overstimulation and Ego Defects." *Psychoanalytic Study of the Child* 11:236-256 (1956).

————. "A Hypothesis Regarding the Time of Appearance of the Dream Screen." *Intern. Journ. of Psychoanal.* 41:114-122 (1960).

Easson, W. M., "The Earliest Ego Development, Primitive Memory Traces, and Isakower Phenomenon." *Psychoanal. Quart.* 42:60-72 (1973).

Elkisch, P., "The Psychological Significance of the Mirror." *J. Amer. Psychoanal. Assoc.* 5:235-244 (1957).

Fink, G., "Analysis of the Isakower Phenomenon." *J. Amer. Psychoanal. Assoc.* 15:281-293 (1967).

Freud, S., "Jokes and Their Relation to the Unconscious." *Standard Edition,* Vol. 8. London: Hogarth Press, 1905.

————. "Mourning and Melancholia." *Standard Edition,* Vol. 14. London: Hogarth Press, 1917.

Garma, A., "Vicissitudes of the Dream Screen and the Isakower Phenomenon." *Psychoanal. Quart.* 24:174-199 (1955).

Greenacre, P., "Early Physical Determinants in the Development of the Sense of Identity." *J. Amer. Psychoanal. Assoc.* 6:612-627 (1958).

Grotjahn, M., "Smoking, Coughing, Laughing, and Applause: A Comparative Study of the Respiratory Symbolism." *Intern. Journ. of Psychoanal.* 53:345-349 (1972).

Isakower, O., "A Contribution to the Pathopsychology of Phenomena Associated with Falling Asleep." *Intern. Journ. of Psychoanal.* 19:331-345 (1938).

Jacobson, E., *The Self and the Object World.* New York: International Universities Press, 1964.

Kernberg, O., "Borderline Personality Organization." *J. Amer Psychoanal. Assoc.* 15:641-685 (1966).

————. "The Treatment of Patients with Borderline Personality Organization." *Int. J. Psychoanal.* 49:600-619 (1968).

————. "Prognostic Considerations Regarding Borderline Personality Organization." *J. Amer. Psychoanal. Assoc.* 19:595-635 (1971).

Klein, M., *The Psychoanalysis of Children.* London: Hogarth Press, 1932.

————. *Developments in Psychoanalysis,* Joan Riviere, ed. London: Hogarth Press, 1952.

Kris, E., *Psychoanalytic Exploration in Art.* New York: International Universities Press (1952).

Lewin, B. D., "Sleep, the Mouth, and the Dream Screen." *Psychoanal. Quart.* 15:419-434 (1946).

————. "Inferences From the Dream Screen." *Intern. Journ. of Psychoanal.* 29:224-231 (1948).

————. "Reconsideration of the Dream Screen." *Psychoanal. Quart.* 22:174-199 (1953).

Mahler, M. S., *On Human Symbiosis and the Vicissitudes of Individuation: Infantile Psychosis.* Vol. 1. New York: International Universities Press, 1968.

Rycroft, C., "A Contribution to the Study of the Dream Screen." *Intern. Journ. of Psychoanal.* 32:178-185 (1951).

Searles, H. F., "The Place of Neutral Therapist Responses in Psychotherapy with the Schizophrenic Patient." *Intern. Journ. of Psychoanal.* 44:42-56 (1963).

Sperling, O. E., "A Psychoanalytic Study of Hypnagogic Hallucinations." *J. Amer. Psychoanal. Assoc.* 5:115-123 (1957).

Spitz, R., *No and Yes: On the Beginning of Human Communication*. New York: International Universities Press, 1957.

_____ . *The First Year of Life*. New York: International Universities Press, 1965.

Stern, M. M., "Blank Hallucinations: Remarks about Trauma and Perceptual Disturbances." *Intern. Journ. of Psychoanal.* 42:205-215 (1961).

Van der Heide, C., "Blank Silence and Dream Screen." *J. Amer. Psychoanal. Assoc.* 9:85-90 (1961).

Volkan, V. D., "Transitional Fantasies in the Analysis of a Narcissistic Personality. *J. Amer. Psychoanal. Assoc.* (In press) (1973).

Wetmore, R., "The Role of Grief in Psychoanalysis." *Intern. Journ. of Psychoanal.* 44:97-103.

Part 5

SUMMING UP

Chapter XXI

The Psychoanalytic Process: Concluding Perspectives

Peter L. Giovacchini, M.D.

Fruitful discussions of the psychoanalytic process often have a particular form and specific direction. Here, one can detect a pattern; first, the psychoanalytic process is considered in general terms which emphasize the patient-analyst relationship and concentrate on countertransference factors. In a sense, these are global issues which have a bearing on all aspects of the therapeutic interaction.

Next, diagnostic factors are considered, but not in the traditional fashion. The structure of the ego and specific narcissistic fixations are emphasized and different methods are used to make such evaluations. How such information can be relevant will be discussed later.

The consideration of sexual factors follows. Insofar as concepts about sex are historically and currently important, and, at one time, were considered synonymous with psychoanalysis, it seems appropriate to continue our structural explorations by focusing upon them. As the chapters devoted to this subject demonstrate, such studies have important implications for assessments of treatment.

The ultimate interest of the clinician is the therapeutic interaction, its theoretical and technical aspects, as it unfolds with a specific patient illustrative of a commonly encountered type of psychopathology. If the patient is representative of a group that has been considered difficult, if not impossible to treat, then all the better. One can profit from the experiences of psychoanalysts who either successfully or unsuccessfully have chosen to psychoanalyze patients who have been considered untreatable. The types of patients discussed in the final section of this book are eminent examples of the class of inaccessible patients.

As one continues to explore the treatment of patients suffering from characterological disorders, including the psychoses, one becomes increasingly aware that traditional diagnostic factors recede into the background.

As a digression, I wish to point out that when I have made this point in the past, I emphasized characterological disorders and if I mentioned the psychoses, I did so only gingerly. Now, as others have done before me, I can be more bold and forthright and include psychotic reactions in the discussion. I also recognize that when one concentrates on ego structure through the observational axis of the transference-countertransference relationship, there are so many regressive fluctuations with varying degrees of decompensation that it is difficult to view psychosis as a fixed entity.

I realize that here I am echoing the ideas of Klein and Fairbairn, who viewed the personality as containing a schizoid core which is fundamental to all psychopathology. My view, however, is somewhat different in that I do not find it necessary as Klein did to view schizoid constellations and mechanisms as part of a ubiquitous developmental sequence nor do I believe that the schizoid core *if it is universal to psychopathology* need play the same significant role in all patients. In any case, I believe that we will learn more about these issues from studying the analyst-patient interaction rather than by directly examining the content of the patient's psychopathology.

Freud once wrote of the mirroring function of the analyst and the importance of remaining an objective, neutral observer. Although this position has received much criticism, I believe that if one gives the mirror an active component, there is much merit to what Freud proposed.

Many analysts, especially those who wrote the chapters in this book, believe that the essence of analytic treatment is the spontaneous unfolding of the transference aimed at the enhancement of the ego's autonomy. To achieve this, the analyst has to keep his intrusiveness at a minimum. He remains neutral, reflects the patient back to himself and thereby both patient and therapist achieve understanding of unconscious processes. This is how Freud saw it.

I have heard variations of the above. Rather than being just a mirror, the analyst has been considered the servant of a process. He is a mirror but a *reacting* mirror; his reactions may determine the shape of the mirroring surface which then will reflect an image with a particular form. The content will be the patient's but it is the analyst's task to construct a surface where distortions will be minimal. Some of the chapters discuss situations where the analyst bends the surface in such a position that it leads to grotesque and confusing distortions.

Being a servant, especially to such a complex process, can at times be demanding and painful. On occasion, the image the patient projects may become mixed with some qualities that belong to the substance of the mirror itself rather than just its curvature. This would involve something more deeply personal in the analyst rather than simply altering the curvature, something which may occur because of inexperience or lack of knowledge per se. Now, the analogy may be dropped, because it must be clear that when one speaks of mixing the content of the patient's psychic productions with those of the analyst, one is dealing with countertransference and here is where difficulties and advantages may occur.

Many analysts, as the first section of the book amply illustrates, are eager to examine and share their countertransference experiences. This adds an important dimension to our concepts of what is treatable as well as pointing the way to many technical maneuvers which will make it easier for the analyst to remain a helpful but nonintrusive servant, as a good servant should be. Absolute pronouncements regarding analyzability are no longer relevant; the specific interaction between patient and analyst becomes the central focus and analyzability can be considered in terms of a relationship rather than unilaterally.

We can now see that not only characteristics of the patient but also *the assets or limitations of the analyst are important factors in deciding whether he can treat the patient and whether the patient is treatable.*

In some ways, I believe this approach makes our task easier. I have always found it difficult to apply fixed criteria (fixed but vague) to make judgments about patients. To me, this always signified an inherent, even if covert, moral judgment. As an overcompensation, many of us, as frequently occurred in diagnostic seminars at the Chicago Institute for Psychoanalysis, tended to stress the positive aspects of the patient's emotional makeup, his so-called ego strengths. We emphasized hysterical rather than schizoid features. By contrast, in continuous case seminars, the schizoid core of the patient received the most attention.

Similar, fixed, unilateral criteria of clinical judgment are also taught about conducting treatment. Some analysts and a few textbooks state what the correct response to specific material should be. If one responds differently or not at all, one is left with the impression that one has committed an error. This usually makes the beginner feel guilty and even more inept. Such edicts disregard entirely the therapist's personality and his individual style. The therapeutic atmosphere is stripped of an important element, the therapist. Only the writer's orientation is presented without recognizing that the situation might not be the same if one of the variables, that is, the therapist, were different.

The various elements of the analytic setting—therapist, patient, various adaptations and defenses on both their parts—have to be evaluated relative to each other. This allows for a certain amount of variation, but there are limits. It definitely does not mean that analysis is simply a matter of personal style and that the analyst has to be sensitive and mature enough to work out his problems in regard to the patient and then everything will proceed smoothly. As there is some homogeneity to the psychopathology of patients, there are also many similarities among analysts that enable us to concentrate on countertransference relations that are fairly characteristic of analysts and not simply idiosyncratic responses. Furthermore, within the context of these commonly evoked responses, certain technical maneuvers can be elucidated which are appropriate therapeutic techniques to resolve whatever difficulties resulted from countertransference. Here, one is emphasizing the personal factor, but it is not outside of or independent of one's training. Personal reactions have to be recognized and their contribution to our diagnostic judgments and therapeutic activity made part of our professional orientation. Technical factors, training and experience continue to be important and many of the chapters in this book stress that today they have gained even greater significance.

Patients' material sometimes becomes difficult to listen to because it may seem dull and monotonous. Rather than denying that patients can be tedious at times, it is much more fruitful to try and specify why the patient bothers us rather than simply pass it off as something inherent in the patient's style. It is inherent in his style, but we should be able to probe deeper and learn more about our relationship with the patient. This is especially true for patients suffering from characterological problems, patients who tend to be especially tedious. The uninteresting aspects of the patient thereby become an interesting problem that requires investigation. This book stress such a viewpoint.

Therapists have singled out delusions as particularly difficult orientations to analyze insofar as the patient, by having lost his ability to test reality, cannot become involved in a process where self-observation and the recognition of intrapsychic sources of behavior are the predominant elements. Experience does not confirm the viewpoint that all delusional patients are unable to make self-observations and to look within their psyches. Many such patients are very psychological minded, but they still provoke reactions in the analyst that make the continuation of analysis difficult.

Some patients attempt to fill, so to speak, the consultation room with their delusion. One of my patients went into endless details about every element of his delusional system, a very complex system that explained every event in the universe, past, present, and future. It was an omnipotent system, of course; it had a logic of its own and was very intricate. He could leave his body by "soul travel," communicate telepathically, predict the future and perform all types of magic. The sessions consisted only of this material. As the months went by, I began experiencing a feeling of heavy oppression.

One of his "masters" had made several predictions which were to be fulfilled by the end of the year. I feared some would materialize, such as his moving to a different city and stopping analysis, which could easily become a self-fulfilling prophecy. However, none of them came to pass.

I must admit that it was not without a sense of smugness that I asked him something to the effect of what he thought of the master now. I do not recall how I phrased it but my question was aimed at determining whether his belief had not, at least to a small extent, been shaken. I should have known better. Of course, it had not been shaken. It merely indicated that the master had negative vibrations against him, and if anything, this was further proof of the validity of his system. I was deflated. My smugness suddenly changed to indignation. I challenged him by stating that he had to revise his reasoning retroactively in order to cling to omnipotence.

My indignation was compounded by the fact that this patient is a scientist and quite capable of brilliant reasoning. He knows logic and scientific methodology well and is intimately acquainted with the tenet that a meaningful hypothesis must be capable of disproof.

The patient responded calmly and stated that, of course he had to cling to omnipotence, that he had to attach himself to something strong and invincible. He could not allow himself to expose his helplessness and vulnerability. I felt a little ashamed. The patient was reminding me that he was a patient and by implication that I should be an analyst and not someone who felt irritated by his symptoms. His reply helped me and I was able to listen to his delusional materal with a different mood.

I felt the impact of his delusion and, in a sense, I reacted with a delusion of impact. I had felt completely swallowed by his material and my analytic identity was submerged. I realize that to call my reactions delusional is dramatic exaggeration, but to have completely lost sight of my analyzing function must indicate that the deeper recesses of my personality had been affected. In any case, the patient helped me regain my analytic perspective and I will not be surprised if sometime in the future he will have to help me again.

This delusion of impact must be fairly common and the unconscious anticipation of its occurrence may deter some analysts from undertaking the analytic treatment of such patients. Inherent in the patient's psychopathology is a force which threatens to inundate one's analytic identity. The patient's delusion is all-pervasive and completely dominates the analytic setting. Fortunately, if one listens, some patients help us regain our analytic stance and possibly may have to "refuel" us from time to time so we can continue functioning within the analytic context.

Such delusions may create an impact in a different fashion. Rather than bringing the delusional world into the analysis some patients attempt the reverse, that is, to bring the analysis into the external world.

A paranoid patient frequently provoked people so that they sought legal retaliation against him. For example, he would make harassing telephone calls. Finally, the recipients of such calls would become sufficiently exasperated so that they would call or threaten to call the police. Since he harassed professional persons, the patient would appeal to me to intercede and to extricate him from a possible jail sentence. Since the first person he wanted me to contact was a colleague and a personal friend, I did as he asked. When he continued making such calls I refused to participate further.

The patient was then able to manipulate the people he was harassing to call me. Next, he wanted me to contact his former homosexual partner in order to persuade him to consider a reconciliation.

Apart from the therapeutic infeasibility of such interventions, I simply did not want to become involved. I felt the analysis slipping away from me as he was trying to drag me into his delusional world. To regain my analytic stance, I had to demand that the patient again become a patient. He had to stop getting me involved in his outside world. He could make demands but only in the consultation room. I forbade him to call me to make such requests or to manipulate others to call me. He tested my edict once. I hung up and that was the end of it for the time being. He had to reassure me that he was willing to be an analytic patient—at least, for a sufficient period of time so I could regain my analytic equilibrium.

Analysts have to have certain conditions in order to be able to conduct analysis. Some psychotic patients require that we set explicit conditions so we can survive as analysts, whereas other patients may not be so fundamentally threatening. What disturbs one analyst may not perturb another. The two patients just described, I believe, would affect most analysts in the fashion I have described. Being aware of what is occurring may save the analytic situation. In my examples, the first patient helped the analyst reinstate himself as an analyst, and in the second case the analyst had to insist upon the patient being a patient.

The reactions and manipulations of patients suffering from characterological problems can best be understood in terms of characterological, that is, structural concepts. This is achieved by studying the ego and its subsystems. Eventually such studies will lead us to evaluations of the self-representation, the integrative mechanisms of the ego, and developmental factors. Roth demonstrates how knowledge of the patient's methods of spatial representation tells us something about the integration of the self-representation as well as delineate specific aspects of psychopathology. Modell demonstrates further how such knowledge and the assessment of the amount of narcissistic fixation can be used for therapeutic purposes. Once again, the clinician returns to an examination of his feelings, that is, to countertransference, to make judgments about the intensity of patients' narcissistic fixations.

The majority of patients that analysts see today suffer from disturbances in the self-representation which are manifested by an incoherent identity sense. Here, one need not stress the conceptual nuances of concepts of the self or their clinical manifestations. I simply wish to emphasize that our viewing the psychic apparatus in such structural terms has been useful for understanding our interactions with patients. The self-representation and the evaluation of narcissistic fixation have gained in clinical importance.

To be fair to our predecessors it must be stressed that such evaluations in no way represent innovations. Freud himself made the first and in many ways still the most important contributions to ego psychology. His followers applied many of his formulations to help them treat patients. Consequently, it surprises many of us when we hear that *now* we understand the concept of narcissism and therefore are *now* enabled to treat patients who were previously considered inaccessible.

I do not wish to belabor this point. It is sufficient to point out that modern formulations of narcissism that have in some quarters been considered to be momentous contributions, if carefully examined, turn out to be nothing more than clumsy restatements of what Freud had stated laconically. The same is true of many other concepts which include developmental factors and various mechanisms involved in the clinical setting.

These opinions should not be construed as a fixation on Freud and a denial that psychoanalysis has progressed beyond him. Quite the contrary, I believe there has been much progress and one way to strengthen such a point is by being able to recognize real progress. Much of what has been recently stressed regarding narcissism is a reflection of the insights that many analysts, who for decades have been treating patients suffering from character problems and psychoses, have laboriously acquired. Recognizing our scientific heritage will enable us to see what has been done, where our confusion is located and what the progressive road really is. Otherwise, if something that has already been established is simply worked over and to no advantage, then one is imprisoned in a cul-de-sac.

The chapters in this book focusing upon the evaluation of the ego represent methods to gain further information about already accepted clinical structures and mechanisms. The latter may perhaps be replaced—that is, new paradigms may be established, but I doubt that we will then be dealing with psychoanalysis as we know it. It may be possible that creativity in psychoanalysis does not require a complete abandonment of basic concepts in favor of other systems, which some may speciously consider to be a scientific revolution. Working with patients would be difficult for many of us if we were to use other modes, which for the most part, are mechanistically oriented. I believe that psychoanalytic theory can be sufficiently modified, and has in fact, been undergoing such modifications in an imperceptible but continuous fashion so that it can be compatible with discoveries in other areas such as chemistry, genetics (particularly recent studies about seex), and biology.

Freud was severely criticized during the beginning days of psychoanalysis because of his emphasis on sex, particularly infantile sexuality. Later, he was attacked because of his particular formulations about masculinity, femininity, and sexual development. Most recently, his male-centered sexual theory has again been challenged, since apparently it cannot be reconciled with relatively new findings in genetics and physiology. This is an instance where psychoanalytic theory can undergo modifications which will cause us to reconsider certain clinical situations as well as to revise some of our notions regarding emotional development. I believe, however, that rather than threatening or weakening the psychoanalytic perspective, these modifications serve to pull various elements together and give the theory and practice of psychoanalysis a firmer and more logically consistent basis.

Stoller emphasizes the pregenital elements, primarily the hostile elements, behind perverse sexual activity whereas Flarsheim reevaluates the significance of overt sexual behavior for psychic equilibrium. In patients suffering from characterological problems, he conncludes that, in some instances, the inability to attain orgasm may represent progression in treatment, rather than what one might expect, fixation and regression. These contributions enhance our clinical understanding.

Insights gained from the study of patients will cause us to revise some of our ideas concerning psychic development, which in turn, will have further effects upon our evaluation of psychopathology. For example, the increased emphasis on the pregenital elements of behavior causes us to look at early developmental phases, and, as stated, some recent concepts have done little more than to restate what he formulated. Still, insofar as we are emphasizing these early phases in the production of psychopathology and in determining the nature of the therapist-patient interaction much more than Freud did, a further examination of the early stages of psychic life seems germane. Many of the clinical contributions in this book supply us both directly and indirectly with modified viewpoints regarding the infant's mental operations.

Briefly, Freud postulated a progression from autoerotism to primary and secondary narcissism and finally to whole object relationships. Somewhere in the narcissistic phase, one could think in terms of an infant who felt himself to be omnipotent, a stage Freud referred to as hallucinatory wish-fulfillment. Later in life the child might try to regain his lost omnipotence and Freud, in his exposition of the Schreber ccase, gave brilliant descriptions of the megalomanic manifestations of psychopathology. He also demonstrated such features in the obsessional patient.

As one focuses upon hierarchal sequences of structuralization, one can raise similar objections to these formulations as have been levied against Melanie Klein. Many clinicians today accept the usefulness of Klein's paranoid-schizoid and depressive positions for the understanding of psychopathology. One of the reasons that her ideas have had a belated and reluctant acceptance in some quarters, mainly the United States, is that Klein insisted that these positions represented sequences of normal, or at least ordinary, development. Many clinicians, if they give Klein's ideas any attention, prefer to view these constellations as psychopathological variants.

One can object in a similar fashion to Freud's ideas about the infantile stages of omnipotence. It is difficult to believe that the neonate's mind could feel and conceptualize such a sophisticated orientation as omnipotence. During the early weeks of life, it seems as if the infant is capable of only minimal mentational activity. He reacts primarily in physiological terms and his still rudimentary nervous system and undeveloped ego are not yet able to sustain complex feelings and affects. One could surmise that, at best, the neonate responds in terms of vague discomfort or quiet tranquility. Consequently, the stage of infantile omnipotence as a normal developmental phase does not seem consistent with a theory that emphasizes hierarchal structuralization. If such a phase is part of development, it would have to be placed substantially higher on the scale.

The clinical studies in this book would support considering megalomanic and magical orientations and expectations as defensive adaptations in the same way Klein's paranoid-schizoid and depressive positions may be viewed as consequences of the defective development of object relationships.

Many patients suffering from severe psychopathology view objects as either ideally omnipotent or destructively bad. Patients who have been severely traumatized during the neonatal period develop intense feelings of helplessness and vulnerability and objects are viewed as part objects that can magically rescue or destructively devour. Patients who feel so helplessly vulnerable make use of dissociative (splitting) and projective defenses. Splitting and projection, however, are the outcome of defective development and later become the predominant defensive modalities the ego of such patients adopt.

Thus, our formulations of psychopathology emphasize defective development rather than regression or fixation to a stage that is fairly representative of a stage that is found in ordinary, relatively nonimpeded emotional development. Regression and developmental fixations occur in our patients too, but the fixation usually occurs very early on the developmental scale. Furthermore, the fixated stage has very little resemblance to its normal counterpart. This is to be expected since it seems evident that the earlier the trauma the more effect it will have on structure and on determining the future course of development.

The effects of early trauma manifest themselves in specific ways which determine the course and the content of transference projections. Often the patient projects aspects of the self rather than instinctual impulses. Frequently the hateful aspects of the self-representation are projected into the analyst and the patient relates to the therapist in a characteristic fashion.

For example, patients often project what they consider to be garbage into the analyst and this may take various forms. Some patients, and I have noted this much more frequently recently, may shout and scream and punctuate their speech with vulgarities. Practically every word is a monosyllabic, four-letter obscenity, usually anal. Surprisingly, these are well-educated, well-bred patients who ordinarily speak in a cultured, dignified fashion. The analysis serves as an explosive outlet for the vileness the patient feels characterizes his self-representation. Such outpourings in analysis are in some ways similar to the abreaction of the traumatic neuroses and the patient usually obtains some relief after such a session, a relief that is manifested by the patient feeling better about himself. I recall a particular patient whose speech would be particularly obscene and violent on Monday and then its violence would gradually dwindle throughout the week. Apparently, on the weekend, his self-hatred built up and he brought it with full force to the analysis on the first session of the week. The analysis served to dissipate it.

For many such patients, analysis provides a setting where tension can be drained. This is not the essence of analysis; however, it helps create a situation where transference interpretations can be effective.

Some therapists have gone so far as to recommend that active measures be taken, such as prescribing drugs, in order to produce a manageable affective state. Calming the patient supposedly enables the disturbed patient to be reached by the analyst. What I have just described is different and in no way represents such a parameter.

The analyst has not actively tried to change the manifestations of the patient's psychopathology by extraneous methods. The patient spontaneously relieves himself of his inner tension by projecting it. The analyst has merely made himself available for such projections, but he has not engaged in any maneuvers to manipulate the patient. The patient's behavior, in fact, is representative of the patient's psychopathology, an aspect which in the past, had no or little opportunity for spontaneous expression. The analysis has simply made it possible to bring to light what the external world demands remain hidden. Such outpourings, besides being similar to abreaction, are also related to both the return of the repressed and acting-out.

The patient is able to release material that previously had no outlet. Indeed, the external world would have resisted any such explosions. The analyst, by contrast, makes himself a container, a *contenido,* as our Latin colleagues would say, for what the patient often considers "garbage." Consequently, the analytic setting promotes the expression of material that the external world would not allow. The external world often takes over the function of the patient's ego by instituting repression.

The patient is not usually aware of what he is doing. The vigor and vehemence he often displays gives his behavior a motoric quality which resembles acting-out. He is using words, invectives, as equivalent to muscular activity. This resembles repetition, or the wish to put into action, more than remembering. Sometimes, however, the patient feels his reactions as internal disruptions manifested by the urge to vomit.

I am emphasizing this aspect of the patient's behavior because I believe it is a fairly common manifestation of the behavior in treatment of many patients who seek analysis. At times, it seems so chaotic and confusing that the analyst may lose sight of its adaptive significance and its value for analysis. This type of "craziness" often achieves equilibrium for the patient so that the acquisition of insight becomes possible, provided the analyst does not lose his equilibrium by absorbing the craziness.

Of course, not all patients react in the just-described fashion, but many have similar underlying difficulties, in that they are burdened by vulnerable and hateful self-representations. The defenses used to maintain some adaptive equilibrium are fairly homogeneous even though the behavioral manifestations of such defenses may vary. The authors of this volume refer primarily to splitting, denial, and projective defenses.

The discussion of such defenses in the final section of this volume occurs in the frame of reference of clinical interactions with a specific type of patient. Such descriptions highlight the difficulties involved in treating patients suffering from particular forms of psychopathology by actively demonstrating them as they occur.

All of the chapters in this book are, more or less, concerned with the question of the obstacles therapists face when analyzing patients. Each section approaches such problems from different vantages, theoretical, diagnostic and clinical, and emphasizes the therapist's role as well as the patient's in producing therapeutic impasses. If one reviews the author's conclusions carefully, one common factor seems to emerge from most of the discussions. *The patient's defenses attempt to create a situation in treatment designed to force the analyst to abandon the analytic role.*

It is perhaps this quality above all others of the patient's defenses that has made us consider the treatment of patients suffering from ego defects arduous, if not impossible. Some patients are impossible. *The analyst may find it unbearable to have his analytic identity, that is his professional self-representation, threatened by a patient whose self-representation has been threatened and traumatized since early infancy. Or, the analyst's discomfort may be an attenuated version of the patient's misery as he tries to project it into us.* The patient has suffered all of his life. Is it surprising, then, that he wants us to suffer for him? Gradually we learn to absorb the patient's suffering without feeling too uncomfortable, a discomfort which is mitigated by our witnessing the release of the patient's developmental potential and the gradual emergence of his autonomy.

INDEX